Civil War Road Trip
Volume 1

A Guide to Northern Virginia,
Maryland & Pennsylvania, 1861–1863

First Manassas to Gettysburg

Civil War Road Trip
Volume 1

A Guide to Northern Virginia,
Maryland & Pennsylvania, 1861–1863

First Manassas to Gettysburg

MICHAEL WEEKS

The Countryman Press
Woodstock, Vermont

Frontispiece: View of Henry House from the crest of Matthews Hill, Manassas National Battlefield Park.

Interior photographs by the author unless otherwise specified; all others courtesy of the National Archives.

Maps by Aaron Porter © The Countryman Press

Book design and composition by Faith Hague

The Civil War Road Trip, Volume 1: A Guide to Northern Virginia, Maryland & Pennsylvania

978-0-88150-953-3

Published by The Countryman Press, P.O. Box 748, Woodstock, VT 05091

Distributed by W. W. Norton & Company, Inc., 500 Fifth Avenue, New York, NY 10110

Printed in the United States of America

10 9 8 7 6 5 4 3 2 1

To my wife, Charlotte, for her unending love and support,

and to all those fighting to preserve America's history.

CONTENTS

THE TOURS

The sites presented in this book encompass all of the major campaigns of the eastern theater during the first two years of the Civil War. Certainly, there was a lot more action in this area around the capitals than could possibly fit into one book in detail. But if you were to follow each of the tours laid out here, you would see the sites of all of the area's significant action from the fledgling armies' first meeting at Manassas to the Confederacy's high-water mark at Gettysburg.

Not all of these sites are preserved or in pristine condition. As cities and towns grow, some of them are gradually being lost to progress. Thankfully, because the sites in this part of the country are so well recognized, there is almost always something to experience. Some of the sites are large, some important, and others less so. You will find enough information in the book for you to determine for yourself whether making the journey from one site to another is worth your time.

BREAKING IT ALL DOWN

Each tour in the book will take you along one of the Civil War's major campaigns, culminating in one or more major battles of the war. The trips are designed to be taken over a weekend or long weekend road trip. Of course, some tourists will take longer, while others can do it in half the time.

Road trips can (and should) be a very personal experience, and everyone does them differently. Some people might throw the map out the window and go where the road takes them, eventually winding up at their destination. Others plan every detail, forming an itinerary that prescribes every point of the schedule. Most people fall somewhere in the middle. Although some of the areas are a bit off the beaten path, for the most part you'll almost always be very close to food and lodging. There's also a lot of natural beauty in the places you'll be visiting, so even camping will be an option. In short, don't be afraid to wing it.

No matter how you take your trip, please remember one very important thing. Getting out there and walking the fields where this history happened is essential—for you, for the local economies, and for preserving our country's history. However, the best thing you can do to not only learn about the Civil War but also create lasting memories is to stop and talk to people. Civil War history runs deep here, and being home to so much hallowed ground is a source of great pride. If you seek out conversations with the people who live and work here—from park rangers to the folks down at the local coffee shop—you'll learn things that simply can't be put into a book. These experiences are guaranteed to give you a whole new perspective on the Civil War, American culture, and other things that can't possibly be predicted. You'll have to go out there and discover for yourself what treasures await.

GETTING TO THE SITES

The classic gas station road map is a thing of the past. The modern road tripper, if relying on anything at all, is most likely to refer to a heads-up global positioning system (GPS), directions from MapQuest or Google, or their smart phones. The general driving directions to each site are within the chapters, but you will also find addresses and GPS coordinates (along with phone numbers and Internet sites, if available) for each site in Appendix A. (The Internet links are available at my website, www.civilwarroadtrip.com.)

LEARNING ABOUT THE CIVIL WAR

There is enough history in this book and at the sites themselves to ensure that you will learn a great deal during your tours. Still, you might want to read up a little before hitting the road. Because there have been so many books written on so many different aspects of the American Civil War, picking a good place to start can be a daunting task. There are books on individual campaigns, regiments, commanders, politics, technology, economics . . . the list goes on and on.

If you don't know much about the Civil War (which puts you in the majority), you have a few different ways to approach learning about the war as a whole. If you'd like to tackle a lot of material in one fell swoop, you can't do much better than Shelby Foote's three-volume set, *The Civil War*. While Foote's work has its critics, it has established itself as one of the best and most popular narratives on the war. If a single volume will do for you, James M. McPherson's Pulitzer Prize–winning *Battle Cry of Freedom: The Civil War Era* is the standard. Finally, if those are both still a bit too much for you, don't hesitate to get a copy of *The Civil War for Dummies* by Keith D. Dickson. Hey, we all had to start somewhere, and the *Dummies* book series has proven to be a great first step for many.

If you're a more visual person, head to the library and check out the videos of Ken Burns's nine-part documentary, *The Civil War*. Covering the war thoroughly in nine episodes is simply not possible, but this riveting series has inspired millions to further their knowledge of both the war and American history in general. Filled with great stories from great storytellers, Burns's film was an instant classic and is still worth watching today.

After visiting these places, you might come away with questions and will want to explore further. In each chapter you will find reading recommendations for each campaign from the staff of the Abraham Lincoln Book Shop in Chicago. Established in 1938, the shop is perhaps the most respected bookstore in the country focusing on Lincoln and the Civil War, and its original owner was one of the founding members of the first Civil War Round Table. (There are now more than 300 Round Tables, and members from around the globe still visit the shop and sit at the original "round table.") These guys are the experts, and you can be sure their recommendations will send you down the right path. You can find out more about the shop at www. alincolnbookshop.com.

COMMANDS AND COMMANDERS IN THE CIVIL WAR

SCRATCHING BELOW THE SURFACE of Civil War history can land you in a morass of names and terms that can quickly become confusing. The Union army promoted 583 men to the rank of general during the war, while the Confederacy had 425. That's a lot of names to remember, and when you begin to throw in brigades, divisions, and corps—none of which had a clear definition in this war—and further begin to attach numbers to them, it's easy to lose track of what went on.

Once you get the hang of military structure, however, remembering who, where, and when for the different battles (as well as the politics behind the scenes) becomes much simpler. Soon you may even find yourself following a certain general through various campaigns, and maybe even picking a few favorites.

Here are a few things to remember about the military during the war, along with the most prominent leaders who were part of the eastern theater of the Civil War from 1861–1863. These are only a handful of the names that will appear over and over in your travels.

MILITARY STRUCTURE

» ORDERS OF BATTLE

Occasionally in your history reading, you will see the term "order of battle," followed by a long list of various units and their commanders. At first glance, an order of battle can be overwhelming. After you've used them a few times, however, you will find them to be valuable references.

An order of battle is a representation of the command structure of an army and all its subsets. In some cases, it can be done all the way down to the tiniest unit, while in others it is kept very general.

In Appendix B, you will find abbreviated orders of battle for each of the armies discussed on your tours. They will help you keep track of who is in command of whom, as well as where each unit lies in the army's organization.

» MILITARY UNITS

The various units an army uses are not always consistently defined. In fact, during the Civil War, it was the exception, not the norm, to stray widely from these standard definitions and to change them often. Just as the sizes of each army varied, so too did the sizes of smaller units, such as divisions and brigades.

Here is a very general breakdown of the various military units, in order from smallest to largest:

Regiment—Regiments are the building blocks of an army. When you hear the name "15th Alabama" or "2nd Wisconsin," these are almost always regiments. The size of a regiment usually numbered in the hundreds, and could have been anywhere from 400 to 1,000 men. Regiments were usually broken down further into companies. If you walked up to the soldier on the field and asked what unit he belonged to, he would almost always refer to his regiment.

Brigade—Put two to four regiments together and you have a brigade. While brigades, like regiments, usually have a numerical designation, they are often referred to by the commander or by some other nickname, particularly on the Confederate side. For instance, the First Virginia Brigade is much better known as the Stonewall Brigade; during the Peninsula Campaign, the Union's Second Brigade of the Second Division of the III Corps was more commonly called "(Daniel) Sickles's brigade of (Joseph) Hooker's division." Brigade numbers hovered around 3,000 to 4,000 men, but could trickle to as low as 500 or even fewer as the war went on.

Division—Divisions were usually made up of two to four brigades. Just like the brigades, they are usually referred to by their commander and the next level up (e.g., Hooker's division of Heintzelman's corps). Divisions varied widely in strength, but were often somewhere around 10,000 to 12,000 men.

Corps—The corps structure is a little different than that of the other units. The idea of corps making up an army was a remnant of Napoleonic warfare, and neither army adopted it until the Civil War was well under way. A handful of corps generally makes up an army, but not every army used the corps structure; in those cases, the division would be the largest unit. Corps were usually made up of two to four divisions. Although still sometimes referred to by their commander, they are more commonly referred to by their number, designated by Roman numerals (e.g., Heintzelman's III Corps).

Army—You probably think that this is the easy one. Well, not all armies are alike. Some armies used corps, some did not. Some generals having less than 1,000 men in their command would designate their force an army. In addition, one side in a battle may have several armies on the field. For example, during the Second Manassas Campaign, the Union army tried desperately to unite the Army of the Potomac with the Army of Virginia, and corps from both armies fought side by side during the battle.

GENERALS: UNITED STATES OF AMERICA

Nathaniel Prentiss Banks

Born: January 30, 1816, Waltham, Massachusetts
Died: September 1, 1894, Waltham, Massachusetts
West Point Graduation: N/A

Although he received little formal education, Nathaniel Banks, nicknamed "the Bobbin Boy of Massachusetts" because of early work in his father's cotton mill, was admitted to the bar at the age of 23. Politics was an early and lifelong passion. Banks spent many years in the Massachusetts Legislature before entering the federal arena in 1853, when he was elected to the first of his 10 nonconsecutive terms in Congress, which included a stint as speaker of the House of Representatives. When President Abraham Lincoln appointed him a major general of volunteers in 1861, Banks left his position as governor of Massachusetts.

Over time, Banks has been used as a consummate example of the politically appointed general. Often ridiculed for his generalship, Banks actually held his own fairly well on the field, but his legacy is one of failure. It was his army that was the primary target during Stonewall Jackson's famous Shenandoah Valley Campaign of 1862, and he later lost to Jackson again at the Battle of Cedar Mountain. He was in command during the successful siege of Port Hudson in 1863, but Banks sealed his fate with his ill-planned and poorly executed Red River Campaign of 1864 in Louisiana. After the war, Banks returned to his life of public service, serving in several more offices, including U.S. marshal, before his death at age 78.

NATIONAL ARCHIVES

Nathaniel Banks

Ambrose Everett Burnside

Born: May 23, 1824, Liberty, Indiana

Died: September 13, 1881, Providence, Rhode Island

West Point Graduation: 1847

Ambrose Burnside, a major general who would briefly serve as commander of the Army of the Potomac, was almost universally liked. However, before the Civil War was over, his name would be associated with a number of disasters (along with, of course, the distinctive facial hair he kept, now familiarly known as "sideburns").

His father secured him an appointment to West Point, after which he served mostly in garrison duty through the Mexican War and on the frontier, finally resigning

Ambrose Burnside

in 1853 and moving to Rhode Island. After holding several positions (including one with the Illinois Central Railroad under George McClellan), Burnside was quickly in the heat of the action at the outbreak of the Civil War, commanding a brigade at First Manassas. He soon led a successful campaign to gain a toehold on the Carolina coast in early 1862, one of the Union's few successes in the eastern theater to that point.

In September 1862, he was leading the IX Corps of the Army of the Potomac at Antietam when his command had trouble overtaking a Confederate position on the opposite side of Antietam Creek. The crossing his men labored over for so long has since been known as "Burnside Bridge." Still, less than two months later, Burnside was given command of the entire Army of the Potomac, accepting the assignment only after refusing twice and finally being ordered to do so. Only one month later, the army would suffer a bloody and disastrous defeat at the Battle of Fredericksburg, for which Burnside would unfairly take most of the blame. Relieved of this command the following March, he was assigned to the west and successfully conducted the defense of Knoxville, Tennessee. Eventually called back to lead the IX Corps, Burnside conducted himself admirably until the embarrassing episode of the Battle of the Crater in Petersburg, another incident for which he unfairly shouldered a disproportionate amount of blame. Burnside resigned almost immediately after the Confederate surrender at Appomattox and went into politics, serving three terms as

WHERE'S GRANT?

When many people think of the Civil War, one of their first thoughts is often of Ulysses S. Grant and Robert E. Lee fighting on the fields of Virginia. However, Grant established his skill as a commander in the western theater, and it was there that he spent most of the war. Grant and Lee would first meet at the Battle of the Wilderness in May 1864—less than a year before Lee's surrender at Appomattox.

governor of Rhode Island and then in the U.S. Senate, dying shortly into his second term at age 57.

Joseph Hooker

> *Born: November 13, 1814, Hadley, Massachusetts*
> *Died: October 31, 1879, Garden City, New York*
> *West Point Graduation: 1837*

Major General Joseph Hooker has long been a discussion of debate and curiosity. Hooker achieved an unsurpassed record for gallant and meritorious conduct as a lieutenant colonel in the Mexican War, but beginning in 1848 he became something of a mystery. He briefly continued his service in the Pacific Division, some of which remains undisclosed, but resigned in 1853 to become a farmer in California. Several years later he asked for reappointment, but his requests were ignored until the outbreak of the Civil War.

Hooker was given a brigade during McClellan's Peninsula Campaign and led with distinction, and continued to do so through the rest of 1862, eventually commanding his own corps. After Burnside's defeat at Fredericksburg, Hooker was given command of the Army of the Potomac, mostly through political appointments. Hooker's first and only real test was in May 1863, when he faced the Confederate army at Chancellorsville. Although by all accounts his plan of attack was sound, the plan of his opponent, Robert E. Lee, was bold and brilliant, and he suffered a decisive defeat.

Joseph Hooker

After Chancellorsville, Hooker tried desperately to convince Washington that the Confederates were heading north and that he needed more troops; when they were refused, he resigned, officially handing over command three days before the Battle of Gettysburg. Hooker would go on to command in the western theater, where he also fought well, and eventually regained corps command, but resigned his position again, this time after a slighted promotion. "Fighting" Joe Hooker (a nickname which he despised) remained in the army until his retirement in 1868, dying at age 64 in 1879.

George Brinton McClellan

Born: December 3, 1826, Philadelphia, Pennsylvania
Died: October 29, 1885, Orange, New Jersey
West Point Graduation: 1846

The meteoric rise and precipitous fall of George B. McClellan is known to most casual students of the Civil War. From the time of his West Point graduation, second in his class, through the beginning of his Peninsula Campaign in April 1862, it seemed that nothing could stand in the way of the young general establishing himself as one of history's greatest military leaders. Soon, however, McClellan's legacy would be paralyzing cautiousness and even paranoia; or, as Lincoln famously put it, he had "the slows."

Early in his career, McClellan served on the staff of Mexican War hero Winfield Scott and distinguished himself with virtually every commander he had the chance to work with. His military career afterward was varied—instructor at West Point, engineer, explorer of the West—but it was his opportunity to study military affairs abroad that would form much of McClellan's outlook. He became a railroad man in 1857, first as chief engineer with the Illinois Central Railroad, then as president of the Ohio & Mississippi Railroad. When the Civil War came, McClellan was soon back in the army and led several successful campaigns in the western part of Virginia (now West Virginia), making quite sure that his spectacular victories (which they were not) distinguished him as one of the war's most successful commanders. After the

George McClellan

disaster at First Manassas, McClellan was a shoo-in to be the next leader of the army at Washington, and he soon replaced the great but aging Winfield Scott (whom McClellan took an active part in pushing out) as general-in-chief, commander of all Union armies.

It was only after he was given control of the Army of the Potomac that McClellan's deficiencies began to show—and for a man leading the largest army ever assembled on the continent, those deficiencies were severe. He quickly chalked up one great accomplishment by restoring the morale and confidence of the army, preparing them for any challenge and instilling a fondness for their commander that would not easily be broken. But McClellan took an inordinate amount of time planning a grandiose and unorthodox campaign to capture the Confederate capital at Richmond, and when the campaign was finally launched, he found every possible excuse not to move, mostly citing the overwhelming superiority of the Confederate forces, which he almost always outnumbered at least 2-to-1. McClellan also spent most of his time far from the battlefield, preferring to leave tactical decisions to his lieutenants. After the massive failure of that campaign, McClellan's popularity with his troops earned him another shot at command after a second demoralizing Union defeat at Manassas, but his similarly sluggish behavior following the battle at Antietam soon led to his dismissal. McClellan was sent home to New Jersey to await orders, but they never came. In 1864, he unsuccessfully ran for president against Lincoln, and served as governor of New Jersey for a short time, but his post-war career was otherwise unremarkable. McClellan died at age 58 after leading an exceptional but forever puzzling life, one that will continue to fuel debate for decades to come.

Irvin McDowell

Born: October 15, 1818, Columbus, Ohio
Died: May 4, 1885, San Francisco, California
West Point Graduation: 1838

Irvin McDowell will likely forever be remembered for the Union defeat at First Manassas, which happened under his command. He would also be associated closely with the Union defeat at Second Manassas, in which he took a conspicuous role. However, in all other aspects, McDowell was a competent and able general whose military career was cut short by his own political allegiances.

Spending much of his early life in France, McDowell graduated from West Point and was soon an instructor in tactics there, ironically teaching many whom he would later face on the battlefield. Although he did serve in the Mexican War, McDowell spent most of his military career behind a desk in Washington, D.C. McDowell was given a generalship when the Civil War came, mostly due to his relationship with

Irvin McDowell

Secretary of the Treasury Salmon P. Chase. Although he had not once held any field command during his long military career, he soon found himself in command of all Union troops in Washington.

By July 1861, with Confederate troops massing just south of the capital, political forces in Washington demanded that the Rebels be attacked immediately, scattered, and this small conflict that would become the Civil War brought to a speedy end. Against his better and much-expressed judgment, McDowell led his green troops to Manassas and conceived what was regarded on both sides of the battle line as a brilliant strategy. Unfortunately for the Union, this brilliant strategy was far too much to ask of inexperienced soldiers, and the result was a disastrous defeat. Although McDowell became a scapegoat for this and several other Union failures over the next few years, he retained corps command and performed well until the second battle at Manassas, where his questionable decisions and advice to Union commander John Pope brought further scrutiny. McDowell was eventually shipped out to the Department of the Pacific to serve out the war, and would later command that same department until his retirement. He died at the age of 66.

George Gordon Meade

Born: December 31, 1815, Cadiz, Spain
Died: November 6, 1872, Philadelphia, Pennsylvania
West Point Graduation: 1835

Although his name is usually only associated with one great Union victory—Gettysburg—George Meade led the Army of the Potomac longer than anyone else, seeing it through its ultimate victory at Appomattox. Unfortunately, odd circumstances put Meade in the shadows through virtually his entire command, and this is likely where he will stay.

Born in Spain to a wealthy American family, Meade was out of the army barely a year after his graduation from West Point, preferring to pursue an engineering career. He changed his mind again in 1842, rejoining the army's Corps of Topographical

Engineers. Here he stayed, with the exception of some service in the Mexican War, until the Civil War broke out. Meade made good use of his engineering skills by strengthening the defenses of Washington over the winter, but was given a field command at the opening of the spring campaigns. He joined McClellan outside Richmond just in time for the Seven Days battles, demonstrating his command capabilities on the field until he was wounded twice at the Battle of Glendale. He was back commanding his brigade by Second Manassas in August 1862, was awarded division command by the time the Antietam Campaign began in September, and was

George Meade

given the V Corps shortly after the Battle of Fredericksburg in December.

In June 1863, Joseph Hooker vacated his position commanding the Army of the Potomac. It seemed that nobody wanted the job—Meade was fifth in line for the position—but finally, on June 28, he accepted. Had command remained vacant any longer, the army may have found itself in quite a quandary, as the Battle of Gettysburg opened only two days later. Both sides took a beating, but Meade commanded ably and emerged the victor with Lee's withdrawal. After this, the army remained mostly inactive until the arrival of Ulysses S. Grant in 1864. In an odd arrangement, Meade remained in command of the Army of the Potomac. Grant, by now commanding all Federal armies, felt he needed to remain in the field and set his headquarters with the army, essentially looking over Meade's shoulder through the end of the war. Naturally, Grant earned all the accolades. Still, Meade retained several commands after the war, staying with the army until his death of pneumonia at age 56.

John Pope

Born: March 16, 1822, Louisville, Kentucky
Died: September 23, 1892, Sandusky, Ohio
West Point Graduation: 1842

If you read any biographical sketch of John Pope, you are almost guaranteed to find the word "bombastic" in one form or another. Pope certainly was that, but lost in this assessment is the fact that he was, in many cases, an able field commander. One loss, though—a significant one—and the boasts that preceded it would forever label him as—well, bombastic.

Pope grew up within the Kentucky aristocracy, and his family and neighbors were all of distinguished position. This eventually also included a link, by marriage, to the family of Mary Todd Lincoln, which certainly couldn't hurt his career. Pope served in the Mexican War and earned recognition for his gallantry. He remained in the army, working as an engineer, and was promoted to brigadier general in June 1861. Serving first in the western theater, Pope distinguished himself with important victories at

John Pope

New Madrid/Island No. 10 on the Mississippi River and at the critical rail junction at Corinth.

Following these victories, Pope was brought east to command the forces surrounding Washington that were not part of McClellan's Peninsula Campaign. The combination of two armies, two sets of leaders, and Pope's need to establish his command soon created jealousy and rivalry in the east, and he made few friends. One of his first acts was to issue a proclamation to his troops, boasting of his victories while slighting the soldiers he was now commanding, who had not met much success. He also issued a series of orders that put great hardship on the people of Virginia, orders that were seen as barbaric at the time, but which presaged the philosophy of total warfare that the Union adopted by war's end. Soon after all his big talk, Pope's army was almost destroyed at Second Manassas, mostly due to tunnel vision, as he ignored fully one half of the Confederate army. Soon afterward, he was reassigned to Minnesota to deal with an ongoing crisis with the Lakota Indians. Pope spent much of the rest of his career defending his record while serving at various posts into the 1880s. He lived to the age of 70.

GENERALS: CONFEDERATE STATES OF AMERICA

Pierre Gustave Toutant Beauregard

> *Born: May 28, 1818, St. Bernard Parish, Louisiana*
> *Died: February 20, 1893, New Orleans, Louisiana*
> *West Point Graduation: 1838*

The first Confederate hero of the Civil War, P. G. T. Beauregard seemed to be made for the part. Handsome, an able general, and gaining early victories, Beauregard quickly became a household name in the south, but by war's end his work was limited severely, partly due to his own pomposity.

Beauregard graduated second in his class at West Point, then distinguished himself as part of General Winfield Scott's staff during the Mexican War. Beauregard remained in the army, and was assigned to the position of superintendent at West Point. A remarkable honor, the assignment came in January 1861, before the war but after some of the Southern states had already seceded. Remarkably, Beauregard accepted, but held the position for only a matter of days before he was relieved due to his Southern sympathies.

After he resigned his U.S. Army commission the next month, he went to serve the Confederacy and presided over the opening shots of the war at Fort Sumter. As if this were not enough to earn Beauregard instant fame, three months later he was second in command at the great Confederate victory at First Manassas. He later went on to serve in the western theater, taking command at Shiloh after the death of Albert Sidney Johnston, but due to a combination of pretentiousness and a poor relationship with Confederate president Jefferson Davis, was bounced around the South. He eventually went back to successfully defend Charleston, and was instrumental in saving Petersburg from being overrun in the last moments of Ulysses S. Grant's Overland

P.G.T. Beauregard

Campaign in 1864. After the war, Beauregard went back to his native Louisiana, running the state lottery with fellow general Jubal Early until his death at age 74.

Ambrose Powell Hill

Born: November 9, 1825, Culpeper, Virginia
Died: April 2, 1865, Petersburg, Virginia
West Point Graduation: 1847

During a short but brilliant military career, A. P. Hill distinguished himself on the field and rose quickly through the ranks. Although his performance near the end of his career is questionable (due to some still-debated severe illness that frequently kept him out of action and affected his judgment), Hill's importance to the Confederate cause may be best indicated by the fact that both Robert E. Lee and Stonewall Jackson invoked his name on their deathbeds.

Hill served in Mexico and also in the Seminole Wars in Florida, remaining in the U.S. Army until just before the outbreak of the war. He entered the Confederate forces as colonel of the 13th Virginia Infantry Regiment. Before too long, Hill had advanced to the rank of brigadier general, and by the time the Peninsula Campaign was over, he had been promoted to major general and commanded his own division. It was Hill's "Light Division" that did much of the heaviest fighting during the Seven Days Battles.

Although by many accounts, Hill tended to rub people the wrong way (neither James Longstreet nor Jackson were particularly fond of him), everyone knew that he and his division could always be counted on. This eventually led to Hill's promotion to lieutenant general, but after the death of Jackson, it was inevitable that his performance would continually be compared to the late general's. It didn't help that Hill increasingly became unreliable—not for his performance, which remained stellar, but for his lack of presence on the battlefield. Hill was killed in action on the outskirts of Petersburg, Virginia, as Union troops finally ended their 10-month siege. Only 39 at the time of his death, Hill was, and remains today, one of the Confederacy's best and most underappreciated commanders.

NATIONAL ARCHIVES

A.P. Hill

Thomas Jonathan "Stonewall" Jackson

Born: January 21, 1824, Clarksburg, Virginia
Died: May 10, 1863, Guinea Station, Virginia
West Point Graduation: 1846

Few personalities of the Civil War, if any, have had the star power of Stonewall Jackson. Both during and after the war, the praise and respect given to Jackson both North and South have accorded him almost mythical status. Although in recent years historians have portrayed him as much more human than legend, Jackson will always be among the most celebrated figures of the war.

Thomas J. Jackson

Thomas Jonathan Jackson had quite a few nicknames before he earned the immortal "Stonewall" moniker. After service in the Mexican War, Jackson resigned from the army in 1852 to teach at the Virginia Military Institute in Lexington. There, his habits—such as his strict piety, rejection of alcohol, and distinctive fondness for lemons—earned him names like "Tom Fool" and "Old Fool Jack." However, the rigorous discipline that Jackson demanded of his Confederate soldiers—the same discipline he had demanded of his students—made both him and the brigade he commanded conspicuous for their skill and bravery. At First Manassas, the immortal name of Stonewall was given, and it has stuck with him through the ages.

During his short service in the war, Jackson became a household name. His Shenandoah Valley Campaign of 1862 is still studied for its brilliance, and his performance at both battles of Manassas made him a larger-than-life Confederate hero. That is not to say that Jackson did not have weaknesses. His actions during the Seven Days Battles and the later days of the Battle of Second Manassas have long been pointed to as instances where Jackson fell well short of his legendary status, and he was notorious for keeping his plans to himself, leaving his generals, staff, and entire army in the dark. However, the performances he was able to get out of his men when he had independent command were spectacular, and several of the marches Jackson took—in the

Shenandoah, before Second Manassas, and his famous flank march at Chancellorsville—were so well-executed and taken at such a blistering pace that his soldiers were sometimes referred to as "foot cavalry." Indeed, few generals prepared their men so well for the hardships they endured, and few were so loved by them. Ironically, it was a group of Confederate soldiers that brought him down in the end, mistaking Jackson's scouting party for a Union patrol in the darkness at Chancellorsville and shooting him twice. Jackson seemed to be recovering from his wounds, but developed pneumonia and died several days later at age 39. It was a devastating loss to the Confederacy, and the entire South mourned the passing of their beloved leader.

Joseph Eggleston Johnston

Born: February 3, 1807, Farmville, Virginia
Died: March 21, 1891, Washington, D.C.
West Point Graduation: 1829

There are many opinions about Joe Johnston. Some think he was a brilliant general, one of the best at defensive maneuver. Others think he showed too little aggressiveness in the field. It seems the only two things that people universally accept about him are that his relationship with President Jefferson Davis did him much damage and that he had an uncanny tendency for getting wounded.

Johnston fought in the Seminole War (where he was wounded) and in the Mexican War (where he was wounded twice). Along with those battle scars, he also earned high respect from his fellow officers. In April 1861 he joined the Confederate army and played a conspicuous role in the victory at First Manassas, quietly transporting reinforcements from the Shenandoah Valley by rail. Johnston kept command of the armies of Virginia through the Peninsula Campaign until he was severely wounded at the Battle of Seven Pines. Lee took his place and kept it through the end of the war.

Six months later, Johnston was fighting in the west, and received some criticism for not bringing his troops to battle during the Vicksburg Campaign. Johnston later took command of the Army of Tennessee, taking over the task of

Joseph E. Johnston

protecting Atlanta from Union general William Tecumseh Sherman. For three months, Johnston moved constantly and took strong defensive positions to block Sherman's advance. However, Davis, who had never been on good terms with Johnston, removed him from command for his lack of aggressiveness. The aggressiveness of his replacement, John Bell Hood, would cost the Confederacy 18,000 casualties in the next two weeks, compared to Johnston's 10,000 over three months. At Lee's insistence, Davis later gave Johnston another command in the Carolinas, again to stop Sherman, and although he nearly scored a stunning victory at Bentonville, it was not enough. Johnston surrendered to Sherman, and the two developed a strong mutual respect. After the war, Johnston served in the U.S. House of Representatives and held other government positions until his death at age 84. It is said that Johnston, a pallbearer at Sherman's funeral, died of a cold brought on when he refused to wear his hat out of respect, saying that Sherman would have done the same in his place.

Robert Edward Lee

Born: January 19, 1807, Westmoreland County, Virginia
Died: October 12, 1870, Lexington, Virginia
West Point Graduation: 1829

It's difficult to find a bad word against Robert E. Lee. While criticisms of many of his military decisions certainly exist, his overall skill as a commander is rarely questioned, and you usually won't find any disparaging comments about his character or his honor. It is this combination that has made Lee a hero of the South and a symbol of the Confederacy itself.

Lee's lineage practically guaranteed that he would hold some important station in life. His father was Henry "Light Horse Harry" Lee, hero of the American Revolution and part of a family that included two signers of the Declaration of Independence. Although his father would eventually incur serious debt that would harm the family's well-being, youngest son Robert still earned a commission to

Robert E. Lee

West Point, graduating second in his class and having no demerits on his record. For the next 17 years, Lee spent his time in the army as an engineer, overseeing much of the work on the mighty system of fortresses being constructed on the Atlantic Coast. It was also during this time that he married Mary Custis, a direct descendant of Martha Washington. In the Mexican War he served under Winfield Scott, and the two became very close. He was named superintendent of West Point in 1852, then served on the frontier in Texas. In 1857, his family moved into Arlington House overlooking Washington, D.C., and it was here that he made his decision to serve the state of Virginia. On April 18, 1861, Lee refused an offer by Scott to command the Federal armies, and only days later accepted command of all military forces in Virginia.

After spending some time in the field and as an adviser to President Jefferson Davis early in the war, Lee became commander of the Army of Northern Virginia on June 1, 1862, after Joe Johnston was wounded at the Battle of Seven Pines. Lee's impact upon taking command was immediate. Over the next three years, Lee would continually defeat larger Union armies, frustrating the Union efforts until 1864, when Grant arrived from the west. Grant was the first general to truly put Lee on the defensive, forcing him to move south and eventually into the earthworks surrounding Petersburg and Richmond. After a long siege, Lee attempted to lead his army to safety, but finally surrendered at Appomattox on April 9, 1865. Although the Civil War would continue for another two months, virtually everyone knew that Lee's surrender meant the end of the Confederacy. Lee went on to become president of Washington University, later renamed Washington and Lee University in his honor, and he remained in this position until his death at age 63. His legendary status is cemented in the South, and to this day his birthday is celebrated as a state holiday in parts of the old Confederacy.

James Longstreet

Born: January 8, 1821, Edgefield District, South Carolina
Died: January 2, 1904, Gainesville, Georgia
West Point Graduation: 1842

During his lifetime, particularly after the Civil War, James Longstreet was a very controversial figure. While he clearly distinguished himself as one of the Confederacy's best generals on the battlefield, his comments and actions after the war earned him much grief in the South. In hindsight, though, the qualities of the general that Lee referred to as "my old war horse" have brought him back into the limelight along with other more recognized Confederate leaders.

Longstreet remained with the U.S. Army after his West Point graduation until the Civil War broke out in 1861. During those 19 years before the war, he served with distinction in Mexico and in several of the Indian wars. Performing well at First Manassas and then particularly through the Peninsula Campaign, Longstreet quickly became known as a reliable general. When given his own independent command, the results were not so praiseworthy; his performance in North Carolina was mediocre, and he failed to lift the siege of Knoxville, Tennessee, after the Battle of Chattanooga. However, while under Lee's guidance with the Army of Northern Virginia (and at the Battle of Chickamauga, where his corps moved by rail to reinforce Braxton Bragg), Longstreet proved himself to be a bold and aggressive general.

James Longstreet

At the Battle of the Wilderness in 1864, Longstreet was severely wounded by friendly fire, under circumstances eerily similar to those that killed Stonewall Jackson a year before. Longstreet was able to return during the siege of Petersburg, and remained until the surrender at Appomattox. After the war, Longstreet did the unthinkable by serving in the Grant administration and becoming a Republican. These acts, along with criticisms he made of both Lee and Jackson that came to light, kept him from being celebrated as a hero of the war during his lifetime. He remained in public service, and was serving as a railroad commissioner in the Theodore Roosevelt administration when he died shortly before his 80th birthday.

James Ewell Brown Stuart

Born: February 6, 1833, Patrick County, Virginia
Died: May 12, 1864, Yellow Tavern, Virginia
West Point Graduation: 1854

Known for his daring exploits, J. E. B. Stuart's flair for the dramatic has made him one of the most entertaining characters of the Civil War. Although this daring would occasionally put himself (and, on occasion, the Confederate army) in grave danger, it also made him a legend in his own time. Stuart's accomplishments with the Virginia cavalry would earn him a place in the pantheon of the great Confederate generals.

Stuart spent most of his time in the U.S. Army on the frontier. When he resigned and pledged himself to the cause of the Confederacy, Stuart almost instantly distinguished himself, serving in the actions that sent the Union army to flight at First Manassas. When it came to collecting intelligence—one of the essential functions of cavalry—Stuart may have been without equal. During the Peninsula Campaign, while conducting a reconnaissance, he led his troopers on a famous "Ride Around McClellan," completely encircling the Army of the Potomac while gathering critical

J.E.B. Stuart

information for Lee. He made a similar ride during the Second Manassas Campaign, raiding General John Pope's headquarters wagon and collecting valuable documents and information. (He also took Pope's jacket. Since Union troops had captured Stuart's signature plumed hat during a raid, Stuart wrote Pope a letter suggesting "an exchange of prisoners." Pope did not respond.)

In June 1863, Stuart overextended his mission and became separated from the Army of Northern Virginia for days. Usually serving as Lee's eyes and ears, he was not able to provide Lee the critical information needed as the Confederates moved north into Pennsylvania. Stuart was not heard from until late on the second day of the Battle of Gettysburg, which may have turned out quite differently had Stuart been able to at least stay in contact. He would receive much criticism for this, but otherwise, Stuart served gallantly. Later in the war, when the Union cavalry was finally able to show some initiative, it raided the northern outskirts of Richmond, clashing with the Confederates at Yellow Tavern on May 11, 1864. Stuart was mortally wounded there, dying the next day at the young age of 31.

VISITING A CIVIL WAR BATTLEFIELD

IF YOU'RE LUCKY, when you visit a Civil War battlefield, all of the important features of the landscape, the movements of the armies, and the story of the battle will be laid out for you. In most cases, though, even the best-interpreted historic sites can't tell you the whole story. Not all battlefields are the same, and the variables are endless. They may be as basic as who held the high ground or as complex as understanding the personal tendencies of a particular commander and how he saw the field at the time of the battle.

Fortunately, viewing a battlefield today and understanding what happened there 150 years ago can be relatively easy if you go in armed with a few tips. In addition, smartphones and other gadgets are continually being developed that can help you better understand what you're looking at when you're looking at it.

Here are some helpful hints to keep in mind as you view these historic sites:

» PREPARING FOR THE VISIT

Obviously, the more you know about the battlefield before you go, the better off you will be in understanding what you're looking at. This could range from reading endless volumes on the battle and its context within a campaign to simply remembering to take a map with you.

Some key things to consider finding out before you set out:

What time of year did the battle take place?

Generally, but not always, the Civil War's major campaigns occurred in good weather, between April and October. So when you are looking at the field, consider not only when the battle was fought, but also the time of year when you yourself are looking at the battlefield. If you're visiting during the summer, when all of the leaves are still on the trees, you probably won't have the same view that the soldiers did if the battle was fought in October. In fact, you may want to plan your trips for later in the year, when the lack of foliage might enable you to see any battlefield more clearly.

How much has the battlefield changed?

For a variety of reasons, battlefield preservation has not always been a high priority, and many battlefields have changed over the years. Sometimes these changes are man-made, as towns and cities expand in size and population. Other changes occur naturally; tree lines move and rivers take a different direction. Knowing the differences between the past and present conditions going in will prevent you from misinterpreting a battlefield because either Mother Nature, a landscaper, or a housing developer made a change.

The Landscape

There are some principles of combat that are almost as old as warfare itself. One of the most well-known and well-established is that, generally, holding the high ground puts you in a better position. This was as true in the Civil War as it was in ancient times and as it is today. So when you take your first scan of the field, keep your eyes peeled for where the high ground might be. Don't limit yourself to looking only for a prominent hilltop; sometimes the slightest rises and ridges gave one army a tremendous advantage. Not only does more of the battlefield become visible from these places, but the placement of artillery on high ground meant domination of a greater expanse of the area and sometimes greater range.

The slight ridges you find may be important for other reasons, too. In some cases, slight changes in elevation were enough to conceal units of an army. At Antietam, for example, Union troops approaching the Sunken Road were not able to see what was really before them until they were only yards away from the Confederate lines, and they paid a heavy price for it. A good set of field glasses can help you spot these features from a distance (after all, that's what the generals used).

These ridges, as well as other natural and man-made features, often made excellent cover for an army as it defended its ground. Lying flat behind a small rise in the ground makes a very small target for an enemy marksman. Tree lines and forests also provided cover and concealment for a unit. (By the same token, trying to advance an army through a stand of trees is difficult, and how well this was done sometimes determined whether the enemy fought the entire force at once or in pieces as they emerged from the woods.) Of course, fences and walls—particularly those made of stone—have made enormous and infamous differences in Civil War battles, not only providing cover from which to fire, but also serving as obstacles to an advancing army.

Finally, rivers, creeks, wetlands, and even the smallest bodies of water made enormous differences in campaigns and how battles were fought. The Union army's inadequate maps of the Virginia Peninsula, which did not show the tiny Warwick River, held George McClellan's army up for a month. Just as important as these creeks are where and how the armies crossed them, either with or without supply wagons or artillery. During battles and campaigns, bridges and fords were key, as they could bottleneck an attacking force (such as at Burnside Bridge during the Battle of Antietam) or trap an army (as the Confederates almost were during their retreat from Gettysburg).

The best way to get the lay of a landscape, of course, is to walk it. The driving tours created for many parks are great, but there is nothing like walking across terrain to give you the feel of it. Walking the fields also will give you different views of the ground, and may reveal features that were not easily discernible before. In some cases, just the experience of a hike is enough to give you a good perspective on a battle. Walking where the Confederates advanced across the field at Gettysburg during Pickett's charge or, for the more extreme, hiking Stonewall Jackson's flank march at Chancellorsville will provide moments you will not soon forget.

» USING TECHNOLOGY

As you visit these sites, particularly the national parks, make use of every available resource they provide. Among the best features of the parks are the guided ranger programs, and within an hour or two you can learn things about the battlefield that most people would not even conceive of, either through the ranger's knowledge (which is always considerable) or the questions that other visitors ask.

Of course, most of the time, you will not be able to get a personally guided tour of a battlefield. However, with the emergence of smartphones, you may have a guide at your fingertips. Several groups have developed podcast tours of the better-known battlefields that will wait until you're in exactly the right spot before they tell you what happened there. Apps (applications), the seemingly can't-live-without features that can be found for your smartphone, are also being developed to guide you through battlefields, providing information, photographs, and maps along the way.

Your best sources for these tools:

National Park Service (www.nps.gov)—Podcasts are now appearing for many of the parks, and the orders of battle that are usually provided are extremely valuable when you're on the field.

Civil War Trust (www.civilwar.org)—The trust's mission of preservation is stretching to interpretation as a necessity, and you can find both podcasts and apps on its site. In addition, the trust's collection of maps, both modern (including animated) and historic, will soon become indispensable to you as you make your tours.

Civil War Traveler (www.civilwartraveler.com)—The organization behind the wonderful network of Civil War Trails signs that you will repeatedly run across on your tours now has podcasts available on its website.

Civil War Road Trip (www.civilwarroadtrip.com)—The Internet site for this book, which has links to all of the available Internet sites for the locations you'll be visiting.

A WORD ABOUT HISTORIC PRESERVATION

As you travel through Virginia and visit these sites, you will find instances in which landscapes and objects have remained virtually unchanged or pristine over decades or even hundreds of years. You will also come across some cases where historic sites are so unabashedly commercialized, disregarded, or destroyed that it may trigger embarrassment or even shame.

Historic preservation is more complicated than we'd sometimes like to admit. In a perfect world, we would be able to save it all, and it's doubtful that anyone would object to that if it were possible. Unfortunately, it's not, and compromises have to be made. The United States of America has grown a lot since 1861. In addition, the reason that battles were fought where they were was often because of the resources and cities nearby, and those cities have continued to grow over the past century and a half. When the armies moved on after the battle and left their terrible aftermath to the local townsfolk, people didn't always want to remember what happened. Pieces of battlefield were quietly covered and often quickly forgotten.

Today, the awareness and appreciation of historically significant sites is greater than it has ever been. In sensitive areas, federal, state, and local laws, along with national and local organizations, protect important sites as best they can. However, not every inch can or will be saved. As has been the case throughout human history, economics are often the first consideration. If money is to be made by building a shopping center on a battlefield, whether it is important or not, someone is likely to try it. The result is often something similar to the picture here, where the site is "memorialized" by some reference to its history. Subdivisions on battlegrounds are proudly named for the battlefield they destroyed, with streets named after the heroes who fought and died there. These developments happen on both large and small scales.

There have been wonderful success stories over the years. Gettysburg has fought off casino development adjacent to the battlefield several times (although the threat still looms), and parts of the battlefield now virtually replicate the 1863 landscape. For a time, a monstrous theme park threatened Manassas National Battlefield, but was stopped largely through grassroots efforts. Unfortunately, the defeats outweigh the victories, and the outcome is final.

Pelham's Corner, where Civil War history is most definitely history.

When a battlefield is lost, it is gone for good. These pieces of hallowed ground, as Lincoln so eloquently described them at Gettysburg, don't always seem as important today because the Civil War is history, not part of any of our collective memories. But the argument that a piece of ground on which Americans shed their blood for cause and country is merely historical is incorrect. These places, all of them, are no less hallowed than the beaches of Normandy, the deserts of Iraq and Afghanistan, or Lower Manhattan.

By visiting these sites, you contribute enormously to their preservation. Historic sites attract out-of-town money to local economies, leading those locals to protect and improve their history. This attracts more visitors, and a cycle of growth is formed that is not only a permanent generator of cash, but preserves these places, and the memory of those who fought there, forever.

Besides visiting the sites, you can also look to some of the various groups dedicated to preserving them. The Civil War Trust, a nonprofit organization dedicated to battlefield preservation, has been one of the most significant contributors to these efforts. You will come across many sites saved by the trust in your travels; some are still in their care, while others have been passed to the National Park Service and other organizations. Because of the trust's reputation for wisely managing its finances, it is often able to provide matching funding to aid preservation efforts. Finally, Charity Navigator and Guidestar, two independent and trusted groups that evaluate organizations for how well they spend donation money, have given the trust their highest ratings. You can find out more about the Civil War Trust at www.civilwar.org, where you will also find a wealth of resources on the war itself.

IMPORTANT THINGS TO REMEMBER

SOME OF THESE BATTLE SITES are on private property. If this is the case and contact information is available, be sure to ask before you trespass on someone's land. If you don't know, stay out or take pictures from the roadside.

Some of the sites in this book are only seasonally staffed, and either reduce their hours in the off-season or close entirely. Other smaller sites (for example, town and county museums) may only be open one day a week or month throughout the year. If there's any chance that a site may not be accessible, be sure to call ahead and find out.

All of these sites, including those overseen by the National Park Service, are desperately short of funding. Not only are the overseers trying to keep the site open, but they also want to heighten the experience for the visitor and, with some luck, acquire and restore surrounding battlefield land. In addition, many sites are staffed by volunteers. When you visit, add a little to the donation box and sign the guestbook so that when the time comes to ask for funding, they can demonstrate that the site is bringing people in to support the local economy.

Make sure that your vehicle is in tip-top shape. You don't want to get stuck with a broken-down automobile in a place where your cellular phone doesn't get any reception. Always plan for the worst—keep an emergency road kit with you, and make sure it includes first aid supplies.

As you make your journey, you will experience areas with their own unique flavors, customs, and cultures. You may even come to some areas where you feel a little out of place, as if you don't belong. Although you should always follow your better judgment, don't be afraid to approach locals and ask for directions, about the town, or where a good place to eat might be. They are just as friendly as you are, and will almost always be eager to help. In fact, you'll find that most people are proud of the history that surrounds them and will share what they know with you. These conversations will be the highlights of your trip.

Good shoes, water, sunscreen, and insect repellant: Keep these items with you and you'll be able to enjoy every site.

CHAPTER 1

Opening Shots: First Manassas and the Defense of Washington

ON THE MORNING OF APRIL 12, 1861, the Confederate States of America consisted of seven Southern states which had seceded from the Union in the wake of the election of President Abraham Lincoln. South Carolina led the way, followed in quick succession by Mississippi, Florida, Alabama, Georgia, Louisiana, and Texas. A number of other states, including Virginia, had considered the matter, but cooler heads had prevailed up to this point. Then came Fort Sumter.

Fort Sumter had been under siege in Charleston Harbor for months, and the garrison there was short on food and other necessary supplies. In a clever political stroke, Lincoln notified South Carolina that he intended to resupply the fort with necessities but no weaponry, and no soldiers would be added to the garrison. In doing this, he put the burden of starting a war squarely on the shoulders of the South—they could either allow the starving soldiers to be resupplied without incident, or they could fire on a supply ship that bore no ill intention. A furious Jefferson Davis, president of the Confederate States of America, concluded that the only acceptable action would be to reduce the fort before the supply ship could arrive. And so, very early on that morning of April 12, Fort Sumter was fired upon. Despite a heavy bombardment, neither the Union nor the Confederates suffered any casualties during the battle, and the fort surrendered the next day.

A monument to Stonewall Jackson stands atop Henry Hill at Manassas National Battlefield Park.

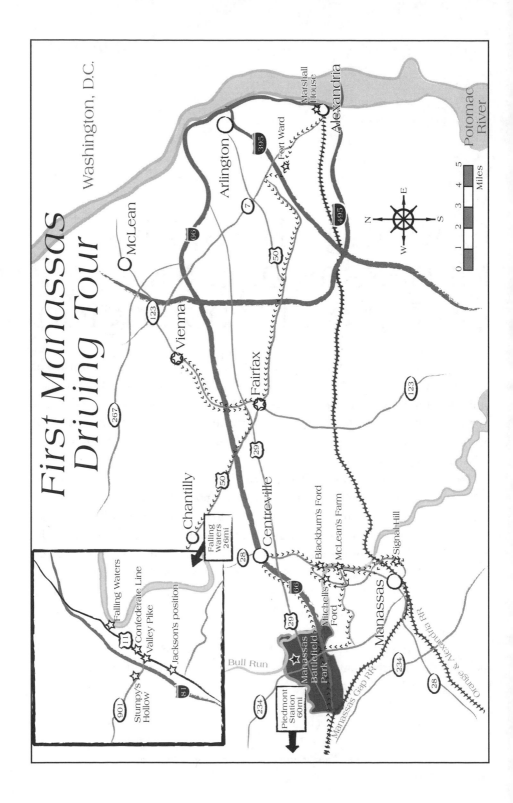

First Manassas Driving Tour

Washington, D.C.

Potomac River

Marshall House

Alexandria

Fort Ward

Arlington

39.5

495

McLean

66

7

50

N
W — E
S

0 1 2 3 4 5
Miles

123

Vienna

Fairfax

267

29

Chantilly

50

Falling Waters 26mi

Centreville

28

66

Blackburn's Ford

McLean's Farm

Signal Hill

29

234

Manassas

Mitchell's Ford

Bull Run

Manassas Battlefield Park

Manassas Gap RR

234

28

123

Orange & Alexandria RR

Piedmont Station 60mi

Falling Waters

Confederate Line

Valley Pike

Jackson's position

111

901

Stumpy's Hollow

81

The news spread across the South like lightning. Many Southern citizens who had been arguing—some successfully—for union were suddenly squarely on the side of secession. As a result of the battle at Fort Sumter and Lincoln's call for soldiers to suppress the rebellion, four more states quickly joined the Confederacy. The first of these, on April 17, was Virginia.

Just across the Potomac River from the capitol at Washington, D.C., Virginia presented quite a unique problem for the Union. It held some of the most important military assets the United States possessed, including the Gosport Navy Yard, the massive Fort Monroe, and Harpers Ferry, one of only two Federal armories in the country. Harpers Ferry was evacuated and burned the day after Virginia's secession, and would-be soldiers started to flock there almost immediately, hoping to fight for the cause of their state and the Confederacy. Men from the other Southern states also came to Virginia, and before long they were being concentrated near the critical railroad junction at the town of Manassas. Washington suddenly found itself with a hostile army just outside its gates.

Most people, North and South, thought that this "war" would be a short and relatively bloodless affair. Many flocked to the cause just to be part of something important, to say they were there, and possibly experience the so-called glory of battle. However, the events of the next three months, culminating in the First Battle of Manassas, would show that this was an illusion, or perhaps wishful thinking. The Manassas Campaign would prove a severe wake-up call for all.

BEFORE YOU GO

» PLANNING YOUR TRIP

While most of the action happened between Manassas and Alexandria, Virginia, just across the Potomac River from Washington, a critical part of the Manassas Campaign lies well west of this area in the northern part of the Shenandoah Valley. The soldiers who gathered and trained in and around Harpers Ferry played a critical role in this battle, one that can't be ignored. If you choose to see those sites at another time, they can neatly be tied in with the tour of Stonewall Jackson's Valley Campaign in the next chapter.

The tour starts and ends in Alexandria. There isn't a lot of ground to cover, even if you do head west to the valley. You will probably want to spend the majority of your time at Manassas National Battlefield, but be sure to take some time at the other sites as well, particularly

---

FIRST MANASSAS CAMPAIGN

Number of sites: 9

Total miles (short tour): 61

Total miles (long tour): 228

Estimated time: 1–2 days

IN DEPTH

William C. Davis—*Battle at Bull Run: A History of the First Major Campaign of the Civil War*

Ethan S. Rafuse—*A Single Grand Victory: The First Campaign and Battle of Manassas*

"Rafuse's study of First Manassas is a very good account of the campaign. Davis's book, although older, is still regarded as probably the best."

—Tom Trescott, Abraham Lincoln Book Shop, Chicago

in Alexandria. The area is rich in history dating back to the colonial era, and there is plenty to see and do.

One thing you won't have to worry about is food and lodging. The northern Virginia/Washington, D.C., metro area is full of hotels, motels, inns, and resorts of every size and variety, and you will never be far from a plethora of food choices. This includes the area in the northern Shenandoah Valley, particularly around Winchester.

» RECOMMENDATIONS

One thing that you *will* have to contend with is traffic. The entire area, including Manassas, is extremely congested, and it is often slow going getting from place to place. By contrast, the roads that pass through Manassas National Battlefield are some of the few open highways in the area, and commuters coming home from their workdays tend to fly down them after sitting in all that traffic. It can't be stressed enough: When touring the Manassas battlefield, use extreme caution every time you cross an intersection, slow down, or pull off.

Since there's not much you can do to avoid the traffic, you might want to make sure that you're staying in a nice, comfortable place at night. If you plan on exploring the Manassas battlefield over a few days, Manassas provides several options for bed & breakfasts. If you plan on exploring other sites, however, or want to spend some time in the capital, Alexandria is a great option. Not only does it have a wonderful history to explore, but there are plenty of historic homes to stay in, as well as easy access to Washington, D.C., using the Washington Metro.

Finally, before you go, check out the website for Manassas National Battlefield. Not only can you see if any special events are going on, but you can also look at the tour schedule. Ranger-guided tours are frequent during the summer, but taper off in the other seasons. It may also be worth your while to plan your trip around the anniversary events of one of the two great battles here, both of which happen during the summer.

THE CAMPAIGN TOUR

ALEXANDRIA

❯ *Begin your tour at the southeast corner of the intersection of King Street and South Pitt Street in Alexandria. Now the Hotel Monaco, this is the former site of the Marshall House.*

After Virginia's declaration of secession, the Federal government moved quickly to gain a foothold on Virginia soil. Although a small Confederate garrison was temporarily stationed in Alexandria, it was evacuated on May 5, 1861. On May 24, Union troops crossed the Potomac and occupied the town.

Although the Confederate soldiers had left, there was one casualty during the Union occupation. Colonel Elmer Ellsworth, commander of the flamboyant 11th New York Fire Zouaves, spotted a Confederate flag still flying over the Marshall House, which once stood at this site. Enraged, Ellsworth burst into the inn and climbed to the roof to take down the flag. On his way down, he encountered the home's owner, who promptly brandished a shotgun and killed him, only to be quickly killed himself by one of Ellsworth's men. Thus, Ellsworth became the first Union officer killed in the Civil War.

Though the home was torn down in the 1950s, a historic plaque was placed at the site by the Sons and Daughters of Confederate Veterans. However, it does not mention Ellsworth at all. Instead, it is a memorial to the innkeeper who shot the colonel, James W. Jackson, hailed as "the first martyr to the cause of Southern Independence."

A plaque marks the former location of the Marshall House in Alexandria.

❯ *Drive west on King Street (VA 7) 2.8 miles until reaching West Braddock Road.*
Turn left on West Braddock and travel 0.9 mile to the Fort Ward Museum and
Historic Site.

Before the first battle at Manassas, only six earthen forts had been built to defend Washington, D.C. After the battle, however, a flurry of shovels and pickaxes created a formidable network of 68 forts and miles of earthworks that encircled the entire city. The Fort Ward Museum and Historic Site not only contains a great collection related to Civil War Alexandria, but also offers one of the best-preserved examples of the earthworks that remain. The earthworks themselves are in a public park and are readily accessible; however, be sure to visit the museum (closed Monday). Inside you will find not only a great description of Washington's defenses, but also a wonderful exhibit on the occupation of Alexandria that includes Ellsworth's kepi, part of the Confederate flag that he took down, pieces of the Marshall House, and newspaper clippings and other objects that memorialize the incident.

Although losing Alexandria was a disappointment to the Confederacy, it was not unexpected and certainly not critical. What was critical, however, was the railroad at Manassas Junction. During this time, railroads and rivers were the only way to transport materials quickly, or sometimes at all. Control or disruption of these arteries usually meant control of the enemy's supplies, food, ammunition, and means of communication.

The Fort Ward Museum and Historic Site is home to preserved earthworks and exhibits on Civil War Alexandria.

At Manassas Junction, two of Virginia's most important railroads came together. One of these was the Orange & Alexandria Railroad, which provided a connection to practically all of Virginia. The other was the Manassas Gap Railroad, which ran due west to the town of Strasburg, right in the heart of the Shenandoah Valley. Not only did the valley contain bountiful food stores to feed the Confederate armies, but also the thousands of fighting men who had come together at Harpers Ferry. So, on May 6, the day after the Confederates left Alexandria, the commander of Virginia's military forces—Robert E. Lee—ordered that the Confederacy start preparations to defend the critical railroad junction at Manassas.

As the armies on each side of the Potomac began to form, commands were assigned. Generals who had gone to West Point together, had served together, and sometimes even fought together in previous wars were now set to fight each other. On the Union side, control of the Union's Department of Northeast Virginia was given to Brigadier General Irvin McDowell by General-in-Chief Winfield Scott on May 27, while Major General Robert Patterson took command of Union forces in Chambersburg, Pennsylvania, near Harpers Ferry, on June 2. For the Confederates, Lee assigned Major General Joseph E. Johnston to command the men training at Harpers Ferry on May 15, and on May 27 Major General Pierre Gustave Toutant Beauregard—the captor of Fort Sumter and the Confederacy's most celebrated hero to this point—was put in charge of the defenses at Manassas.

In addition to strengthening the defenses at Manassas Junction, one of Beauregard's first actions was to reorganize the troops between Manassas and Alexandria. These troops, stationed at towns such as Fairfax, Vienna, and Centreville, were not meant to hold these positions. Beauregard knew McDowell was coming to Manassas; he just did not know when. Knowing what the Union army was doing—and more importantly, where and when they were moving—would give the Confederates as much warning as possible before the attack.

FAIRFAX

> *From here, you will continue on to Fairfax. From Fort Ward, turn right out of the parking lot, drive for 0.4 mile, and turn left on North Van Dorn Street (VA 401). Return to King Street (VA 7, Leesburg Pike) and drive 3 miles until reaching Arlington Boulevard (US 50 West). Head west on Arlington for 7.1 miles until you reach the Fairfax Museum and Visitors Center.*

Late on May 31, McDowell sent Union cavalry westward in an attempt to scout the Confederate positions. When they reached the town of Fairfax Court House at 3:00 AM the next day, they found them, opening the first skirmish on Virginia soil. Although likely first fired upon by civilians in the town, the cavaliers quickly rode

The Fairfax Museum and Visitors Center.

through the town, turned back, and eventually ran into the Warrenton Rifles, commanded by Captain John Marr. The Union cavalry charged the Confederates twice without success, then raced back to Alexandria. On the Union side, one soldier was killed; for the Confederates, it was Marr who gave his life.

Here at the Fairfax Museum & Visitor Center, you will find a variety of exhibits on the Civil War period and the skirmish here. The history of Fairfax is rich, so be sure to check out all of this small but well-done museum.

❯ *Turn left out of the museum and drive 0.4 mile. Find a place to park, then walk to the southwest corner of Main Street and the Chain Bridge Road, where a memorial sits on the lawn of the old Fairfax Court House.*

A memorial to Captain John Marr, the first Confederate officer to be killed in the Civil War, rests on the lawn of the old Fairfax Court House.

It was at this corner that the actual skirmish took place. The memorial on the courthouse lawn, flanked by two cannons, is to Marr, memorialized as the first soldier to be killed in action during the Civil War.

VIENNA

> *From the courthouse intersection, proceed north along Chain Bridge Road (VA 123) for 4.9 miles, staying on the road when it changes to Maple Avenue. Turn left on Lawyers Road, then take the first right onto Church Street Northwest, driving 0.3 mile to the Freeman's Museum.*

On June 17, the 1st Ohio, led by Brigadier General Robert Schenck, was performing some telegraph work along the Loudoun & Hampshire Railroad. As they steamed toward the town of Vienna, the engineer inexplicably blew his whistle, letting everyone know of their approach. This included the 600 or so Confederates under Colonel Maxcy Gregg who were in the area to disrupt Union railroad activities. They were being presented a golden opportunity to do just that.

Positioning his men and two pieces of artillery, Gregg and the 1st South Carolina Volunteers waited patiently until the train came around a sharp turn in the track just before the town. As soon as the train came into view, they opened fire. The Union troops quickly jumped off the train to fight, only to have the engineer detach the cars they were riding on, throw the engine in reverse, and hightail it back to Alexandria, stranding the soldiers. The Confederates, thinking that the Federals were an advance unit of a larger force, quickly retreated. As for the Union soldiers, they were forced to make a long march back to Alexandria.

Here in front of the Freeman's Museum is a Virginia Civil War Trails sign that briefly mentions the fight. Also, in the park across the street, you will see a biking/walking path, a caboose, and several signs. The path is part of a rails-to-trails program and follows the former railroad. If you walk up the path to the signs, you will find a more thorough description of both the battle and the history of the railroad.

> *From the Freeman's Museum, continue on Church Street, taking the second right onto Park Street Northeast. Drive southeast on Park Street for 0.4 mile and pull into the parking lot of the Vienna Community Center.*

This is the area in which the fight actually occurred, at the time just outside the town. Along this section of the path, on the west side of the street, you will find a stone marker commemorating the first railroad battle in history. Looking down the path, you can see the bend in the old track and the direction from which the Federals came.

> *At this point in your tour, you may either pick up the story and head northwest to the Shenandoah Valley or stay in the Manassas area. You may also prefer to pick*

up the valley sites after touring all of the Manassas area. If you decide to stay near Manassas, follow the directions below to Signal Hill.

On June 29, Scott and McDowell presented their plans for Manassas to Lincoln and his cabinet. Although McDowell and Scott both felt the still-green army was not ready, and Lincoln was sympathetic, political demands required that the Union army act immediately. The plans were approved, and McDowell began making preparations.

A major part of McDowell's plans concerned the large gathering of Confederates in the Shenandoah Valley, 70 miles to the west. Both Scott and McDowell knew early on that the Union force around Washington outnumbered the Rebels in Manassas, but if the Confederate force under Johnston was able to combine with Beauregard's, it would be an even fight. To keep this from happening, Scott assigned Patterson, an old veteran, to take command of the Union troops in that area and hold Johnston right where he was—far from Manassas.

Patterson arrived in Chambersburg, Pennsylvania, in early June and began to form his army, taking them into Maryland. Here began a series of movements—and lack of movement—that would accomplish little and would eventually cost the Union army dearly.

On June 16, Patterson marched his army into Harpers Ferry unopposed. Johnston had withdrawn south to Winchester, leaving the town for the Federals. However, the very next day, Patterson heard rumors that Johnston was threatening his rear, and he withdrew back into Maryland on June 18. Patterson stayed north of the Potomac River until July 2, when he recrossed at Williamsport, Maryland. Just south of Williamsport, near the small hamlet of Falling Waters, Patterson finally saw the enemy in action.

FALLING WATERS (HOKE'S RUN)

> *If you decide to follow the complete tour to the valley, from Vienna get onto I-66 west to Front Royal, following for 4.1 miles before exiting to Lee-Jackson Memorial Highway (US 50). Follow the highway for 52 miles until you reach I-81 in Winchester, Virginia. Drive north on I-81 for 30 miles to Martinsburg, West Virginia, and Exit 20, Spring Mills Road. Head east on Spring Mills Road for 0.2 mile until reaching US 11, then pull into one of the many surrounding parking lots.*

When Patterson crossed into Virginia, Johnston immediately sent Colonel Thomas J. Jackson, who was in camp with his brigade of Virginians at Martinsburg, north toward Falling Waters to gauge the Union force. Jackson's men advanced up the Valley Turnpike—now US 11—and set up a line of battle on a small ridge facing north toward the Union army, which was advancing south down the turnpike. Spring Mills Road runs roughly along the Confederate line, with their artillery—four guns—

Falling Waters. The stones at the top of the falls are remnants of the original Valley Turnpike.

placed squarely on the Valley Turnpike. From this ridge, they would easily have been able to see the Federals emerging from the tree line in the distance.

❯ *Drive south on US 11 for 0.5 mile. On the east (left) side of the road, you will see a stone monument along with a West Virginia Civil War Trails sign. Pull into the parking lot.*

The position you are now standing in is the area from which Jackson observed the battle. You will notice a slight ridge behind you, which would have given him a commanding view of the battlefield.

There is an interesting story about Jackson that emerges here, one that rings true at least in some form. As the battle commenced, Jackson was writing a dispatch to Johnston while Federal artillery screamed overhead. A Union cannonball struck a tree under which Jackson was either sitting or was astride his horse, raining debris down upon the commander. The unflappable Jackson calmly finished what he was doing, barely acknowledging what had happened, then suggested to his men that it was probably a good time to move on.

❯ *Return north on US 11 for 0.7 mile, toward and through the intersection with Spring Mills Road. Pull over to the east (right) side of the road opposite the white house.*

The white house on the west side of the turnpike, still privately owned, was known as the Porterfield House at the time of the battle. The house itself is quite old, and was actually built by David Crockett, grandfather of famed Tennessean Davy Crockett. The Porterfield Farm found itself in the center of the battle, and Jackson's infantry advanced as far as this house while Union troops lined up in front of the tree line to the north. The farm's barn was destroyed, but the house remains.

❯ *From the Porterfield House, continue north on US 11 for 1.2 miles, then turn right onto County Route 11/16 (CR 11/16), a small road that passes through the former village of Falling Waters. Follow the road for just 0.1 mile through the curve until you reach a gravel pull-off containing a West Virginia Civil War Trails sign.*

Here at this gravel pull-off is a small but quite beautiful waterfall from which the battle got its name. The current US 11 swerves just west of these falls, but the old Valley Turnpike used to cross right atop the falls, and some of the roadbed of the original pike is still easy to spot. The Union soldiers marched over the falls and followed the turnpike out to the open ground you saw before.

The heart of the battleground is the open land around the Patterson House. The much larger Union force pushed the Confederates back steadily. Jackson, however, was not looking for a victory; he followed orders, and was able to stall the Federals, making them think twice before moving farther south.

> *From the falls, return on US 11 1.5 miles south to the intersection with Spring Mills Road. Turn right (west) and drive for 0.7 mile. Pull over in the median at Stumpy's Hollow.*

This is the area known as Stumpy's Hollow. Although the Confederates left the field to the Federals, they did not come away empty-handed. Lieutenant Colonel J. E. B. Stuart, commanding Confederate cavalry, came across a small group of Union skirmishers that had gotten lost, stopping to stack their arms and rest while their captain rode off to find the proper route. Still wearing his U.S.-issue blue uniform (as was common early in the war), Stuart approached the soldiers and asked them to take down part of a rail fence so that his cavalry could come through. The soldiers, thinking he was a Federal officer, quickly obliged. Finally, as the rest of the Confederate cavalry appeared behind him, Stuart drew his pistols and said, "Surrender, or you are dead men." Though the story is often exaggerated to say that Stuart single-handedly captured an entire company of infantry, it is not far from the truth.

Following the battle, Jackson withdrew south on the Valley Turnpike through Martinsburg to the town of Darkesville, where Johnston brought the rest of the Confederate army in the valley the next day. They prepared for an attack by Patterson, but to their surprise, it never came. After waiting several days, Johnston brought his entire force back to Winchester on July 7.

Patterson, in the meantime, held his position at Falling Waters and waited for more troops, finally advancing to the outskirts of Winchester on July 15. However, after running into Confederate cavalry north of the city on July 16 and receiving bad intelligence, Patterson became convinced that he faced 42,000 Confederates and 60 pieces of artillery in Winchester—almost four times the size of Johnston's actual force. On July 17, Patterson did order an advance into the town, but was talked out of it by his staff. He instead sent his command east to Charles Town, Virginia, occupying it without a fight. From Charles Town, he traded several telegraph messages with Scott in Washington, who ordered him to attack Johnston immediately. On July 18, Patterson again considered then rejected an advance toward Winchester, telegraphing Scott that Johnston was being held in Winchester, exactly where he wanted him.

He couldn't have been more wrong.

PIEDMONT STATION

> *From Martinsburg, drive south on I-81 for 31.1 miles to Winchester, getting onto US 17 South at Exit 313A. Follow US 17 south for 23.4 miles to the town of Delaplane, Virginia. When you reach the Delaplane Grade Road (CR 712), turn left, drive for 0.1 mile, and pull over.*

Joseph Johnston's men traveled the rails from Piedmont Station to Manassas, the first time in history that trains were used to transport troops for battle.

On July 18, while waiting in Winchester for Patterson to attack, Johnston finally received the order from Richmond that he knew was coming. He was to take his entire force—11,000 men—and join forces with Beauregard at Manassas as quickly as possible.

Early that morning, he sent his command, led by Jackson's brigade, south through Winchester toward the town of Piedmont Station to the southeast. Among the ranks, hearts sank; they were heading south, apparently in retreat, and were giving up the Shenandoah Valley. What they did not know, however, was that Johnston had ordered that their destination not be revealed until they were all well on their way. Along the march, at some point of rest along the way, the units heading for Piedmont Station learned their true destination, instantly putting an extra spring in their step.

Marching through the night, the first Confederates reached Piedmont Station in the wee hours of the morning on July 19. At approximately 2:00 AM, Jackson's men boarded a train and headed east along the Manassas Gap Railroad to join Beauregard. Throughout July 19 and 20, the train (there was only one engine for most of the two days) ran back and forth between Piedmont Station and Manassas, eventually delivering Johnston's entire command. It was the first time in history that a railroad was used to transfer troops for battle.

Although the station itself is gone, Piedmont Station, now known as Delaplane, hasn't changed all that much, and the location of the former station is clearly marked by a historical marker and a Civil War Trails sign. The railroad itself is still in the place it was during the war. Looking to the west, one can see some of the open fields where thousands of Confederates waited their turn to ride the rails to Manassas.

It was not until July 20 that Patterson discovered the Confederates were no longer in Winchester. When he realized his blunder, he telegraphed Washington that the Confederates were no longer in his front and were on their way to Manassas. Within a week, he was permanently relieved of command and honorably discharged from the U.S. Army.

❯ *From Delaplane, return to US 17 and drive south for 1.3 miles before getting onto I-66 East. Drive east on I-66 for 28.5 miles until Exit 52, US 29 South toward VA 28. Drive south on Centreville Road (VA 28 South) for 5.8 miles until the intersection with Manassas Drive. Turn left on Manassas Drive and follow for 1.5 miles, then turn right on Signal View Drive. Follow Signal View Drive for 0.7 mile, passing Signal Bay Water Park on your right, then making the first possible U-turn. Return approximately 0.4 mile to a pull-off and memorial just before you return to the water park. You are now at Signal Hill.*

While Patterson avoided the Rebels in the Shenandoah Valley, McDowell prepared to meet the Confederates gathered at Manassas. His plans approved and preparations made, McDowell set his Army of Northeastern Virginia—35,000 inexperienced soldiers—in motion on July 16.

The army consisted of five divisions. Each was to march on separate roads, converge on Fairfax and trap the Confederate brigade there under General Milledge Bonham, then turn their attention toward the rest of the Confederates at Manassas. The First Division, commanded by Brigadier General Daniel Tyler, was to march toward Vienna, then emerge west of Fairfax Court House. The Second, led by Brigadier General David Hunter, was to follow the Fifth Division under Colonel Dixon Miles toward Annandale; here, Miles would turn onto one road, while Hunter stayed on the same path. The Third Division, under the command of Brigadier General Samuel Heintzelman, would follow the Orange & Alexandria Railroad, and then head south of Manassas. Finally, Brigadier General Theodore Runyon would lead the Fourth Division, primarily a reserve unit.

McDowell's plan was a good one. However, it depended heavily upon speed—an element that is often lacking in the green troops that made up his army. Soldiers constantly fell out of the line of march for reasons ranging from fatigue to blackberry picking. This lack of speed meant that Bonham, waiting in Fairfax to detect any approach of Union troops, easily detected the oncoming Federals and withdrew behind the Confederate line along Bull Run in the early hours of July 18.

Bull Run is a fairly small creek, but it provided a perfect, natural line of defense. With its steep banks, Bull Run could only be crossed at a handful of well-defined places, and the Confederates placed strong defenses at each. Well to the south of Manassas Junction was the Union Mills Ford, where a railroad bridge also crossed the stream. To the north and closer to the town of Manassas, McLean's, Blackburn's, and Mitchell's Fords were all very close to each other and had good roads leading to them. They also all occurred at sharp bends in the creek and came from three different directions. Proceeding upstream, three smaller fords—Island, Ball's, and Lewis's—provided good crossing points. Finally, farthest north of the Confederate line, a stone bridge crossed Bull Run along the Warrenton Turnpike. The bridge was an excellent crossing and was wide enough for an advancing army. North of the stone bridge, practical crossings of Bull Run were few and far between.

SIGNAL HILL

> *From Vienna, drive west on I-66 for 9.3 miles to the exit for VA 28 South and Centreville. Follow VA 28, Centreville Road, south for 5.8 miles until its intersection with Manassas Drive. Turn left on Manassas Drive and follow for 1.5 miles, then turn right on Signal View Drive. Follow Signal View Drive for 0.7 mile, passing the Signal Bay Water Park on your right, then making the first possible U-turn. Return approximately 0.4 mile to a pull-off and memorial just before you return to the water park.*

A monument at Signal Hill explains the first use of battlefield telecommunication.

In addition to the distribution of troops at the crossings, Beauregard employed a fairly novel instrument in his defense plan. Not long before the Civil War started, the use of signal flags, or *wig-wagging,* to communicate over long distances came into practice. One person with a visually distinctive flag in each hand would use a system of motions to signal phrases or even spell out words to another signaler within eyesight. Beauregard built four wig-wag towers: one north of Bull Run at Centreville, one at the stone bridge, one near his headquarters at the McLean Farm, and the main one just east of the town of Manassas.

Although the signal tower at Centreville was lost early, the other three towers were all used, and wig-wagging would feature prominently in the battle to come. You are now located at the site of the primary wig-wag tower, which was perched on the hill in front of you as you face the monument. Note the inscription—it will reveal itself to be very important as you proceed on your tour.

MCLEAN FARM

❯ *Return the way you came down Signal View Drive, then turn left on Manassas Drive, returning to Centreville Road (VA 28). Follow Centreville Road for 1.5 miles to the intersection with Yorkshire Lane. Turn left on Yorkshire Lane and pull into the parking lot on your left.*

This is the former site of the farm of Wilbur McLean, for which McLean's Ford is named. Beauregard, a man who was very sure of himself, was absolutely convinced that the Union army would attempt to cross Bull Run using Blackburn's and Mitchell's Fords. They were on good roads, were close to each other, and were the closest crossings to the railroad junction. Although he scattered troops all along Bull Run and defended the crossings well, he concentrated his forces—seven divisions, 22,000 men—here, around the McLean Farm, which stood roughly in between the three fords at the bend in the river.

On one occasion, as Beauregard and his staff were about to sit down to dinner, a cannonball tore through the house, nearly killing the general. Over the course of the war, the farm was virtually destroyed, and today, nothing remains of the home except for this historic marker. However, after the two large battles that raged around his Manassas home, Wilbur McLean moved to a location that he thought would be well removed from the fighting. He was wrong. His other former homestead, in Appomattox, Virginia, is quite well-preserved. It was in the parlor of this home that Lee surrendered his Army of Northern Virginia in 1865, effectively ending the Civil War.

❯ *Pull left out of the parking lot back onto Yorkshire Lane and drive 0.6 mile to the intersection with Old Centreville Road. Turn right on Old Centreville Road and drive another 0.6 mile. You will drive over a bridge crossing Bull Run.*

This bridge across Bull Run is in the approximate location of Mitchell's Ford. The south bank is now part of a residential complex. While the north bank is part of the Occoquan Water Trail, a 20-mile trail system that runs all the way to the Occoquan River, there are no markings to indicate the location of the ford.

BLACKBURN'S FORD

❯ *After crossing the bridge at Mitchell's Ford, continue 1 mile on the Old Centreville Road, now called Ordway Road, to its intersection with Centreville Road (VA 28).*

Turn right on Centreville Road and drive 0.4 mile. Just before recrossing Bull Run, you will see a small gravel turnoff on the right just before the bridge. Pull in here and park next to Bull Run.

Upon reaching an abandoned Fairfax Court House on July 18, McDowell reset his battle plan to account for the lost element of surprise. The Union divisions would now converge at Centreville, just northeast of Manassas. Tyler's division had already been ordered to move ahead of the rest of the army to occupy the town, and then advance cautiously down the Warrenton Turnpike to feel out the Confederate positions. McDowell's orders to Tyler were explicitly clear: "Do not bring on an engagement, but keep up the impression that we are moving on Manassas."

Upon entering Centreville at about 9:00 AM on July 18, Tyler's division found many signs that the Confederates had left in a hurry, and not long before they had arrived. With Colonel Israel Richardson's brigade in the lead, Tyler turned south toward Manassas. Upon reaching a crest overlooking Blackburn's Ford, both Tyler and Richardson viewed the landscape and determined that nothing was in their way; in fact, they thought that they were able to see clear to Manassas. Deciding that the opportunity to win the day lay before him, Tyler decided to work his way across the seemingly undefended ford. He brought up the rest of Richardson's brigade along with two pieces of artillery.

It is not likely that Tyler actually saw Manassas Junction, which was still 4 miles in the distance. It is certain, however, that he did not see Confederate general James Longstreet's brigade concealed in the woods on the opposite bank of Bull Run. When the Union infantry began to advance through the woods shortly after noon, they promptly ran into a wall of musketry that seemed to come from nowhere. Indeed, the woods around the ford were so thick that both sides were virtually firing blind.

If you are facing the bridge, you are looking south across the ford at the Confederate position. Longstreet's soldiers were in woods to your right, now mostly lost to development. Behind you, you can still see the slope atop which Tyler placed his artillery.

When the first Federals ran into heavy fire, instead of following McDowell's orders to not bring on an engagement, Tyler immediately called for more men and artillery to be brought up. Despite objections from a member of McDowell's staff who was present, Tyler ordered a barrage of canister fire from the Union artillery to be directed at the woods. This resulted in a return volley from the Confederates, revealing the Confederate strength and position.

Tyler ordered Richardson to line his troops along the crest and prepare for a charge—three regiments to the right of the guns and one, the 12th New York, to the left. Finally, however, Tyler decided to heed his orders and stop the engagement, calling off the attack. Unfortunately, however, the New Yorkers did not receive word in time and were caught in the open by Longstreet's men. They were able to hold their ground for 30 minutes before retreating. The Confederate pursuit then ran into the 1st Massachusetts, inflicting similar damage to that regiment.

Finally, Tyler ordered all of his infantry to withdraw behind his guns on the hill, and the Rebels returned to the south side of Bull Run. An artillery duel lasted until about 4:00, by which time McDowell himself had reached the field. Extremely angry at Tyler for disobeying his orders, he nevertheless felt compelled to command Tyler to reoccupy the crest overlooking the ford, then left for Centreville to rejoin the rest of his army. Remarkably, Tyler again disobeyed orders, and soon sent his entire command marching back to Centreville.

In terms of bloodshed, the Battle of Blackburn's Ford was small; the Union suffered 85 casualties, the Confederates 68. However, in terms of importance, this decisive Confederate victory yielded immeasurable results. The supposed ragtag band of Rebels had successfully repulsed an assault from the U.S. Army. Confederate morale shot through the roof, and they would continue to ride this wave all the way through the battle at Manassas.

Blackburn's Ford, where Union forces attempting to cross Bull Run ran into a wall of Confederate musket fire.

MANASSAS NATIONAL BATTLEFIELD

❯ *Pull out of the parking area at Blackburn's Ford and turn right, driving south on Old Centreville Road for 0.8 mile. Turn right at Yorkshire Lane and follow for 1.5 miles, turning left on Amherst Drive. Follow Amherst Drive for 0.6 mile, then turn right on Lemond Drive and continue 1.6 miles until reaching the intersection with Sudley Road (VA 234). Turn right and head north on Sudley Road for 2.1 miles. You are now within the boundaries of Manassas National Battlefield. Turn right and stop at the park's Henry Hill Visitors Center.*

The mess at Blackburn's Ford sent McDowell searching for a new plan. The original plan, to flank the southern portion of the Confederate line, was out; Beauregard knew too much about the Federal position and strength. The new plan would be the reverse, and would be a complete surprise. The Union would flank the northern part of the line, the Confederate left. There were no Confederates north of the stone bridge, and although it would be the farthest route from Manassas Junction itself, coming in from the Confederate left and rear would enable the Federals to roll up the line quickly.

On the evening of the 18th, McDowell planned his attack for July 20, and ordered his chief of engineers, Major John G. Barnard, to find a crossing north of the stone bridge, saying that he must have the information by the evening of the 19th. However, poor weather and Confederate pickets—advance outposts for sizable forces— hampered Barnard's mission, and it was not until noon of the 20th that he was able to deliver.

And deliver he did. Well north of the Confederates was a crossing of Bull Run at Sudley Springs, fairly well concealed from Confederate view, but still within a seemingly easy march from the Union position in Centreville. Another smaller crossing existed in between. McDowell held a Council of War on the evening of the 20th, and the final plan of attack was determined. Tyler's division would demonstrate heavily at the stone bridge and the other lower fords, focusing Confederate attention there.

VISITOR'S TIP

While you are at the visitors center, check out the day's tour schedule. Manassas National Battlefield offers two ranger-led tours concerning First Manassas, one at Matthews Hill and one at Henry Hill. The times and frequency are seasonal, although the Henry Hill tour is given at least daily. If you are able to take one, take the guided tour of Henry Hill; if you can take both, try to take the tour of Matthews Hill first. The tours are free.

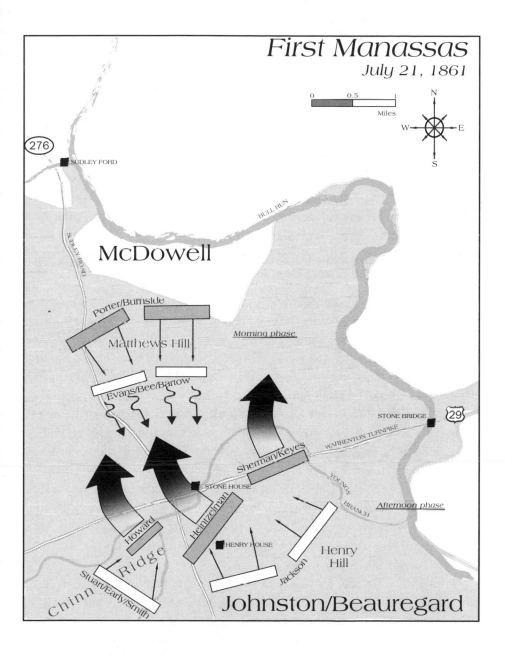

Meanwhile, Hunter's division would cross at Sudley Springs and move south, with Heintzelman's division to follow. The march was set for 2:00 AM, July 21. The eve of the first major battle of the Civil War was at hand.

The visitors center is located on a part of the battlefield known as Henry Hill. You will return here for the climax of the battle, but for now, enter the visitors center and view the exhibits. Practically the entire museum is dedicated to the first battle here, and the 45-minute film shown in the park's theater is recent and well done.

After you have finished touring the visitors center, be sure to get a brochure of the park, which contains self-guided tours of both the First and Second battles at Manassas. The tour for the first battle is a walking tour, while the tour for the second is by car; your tour will take in parts of both.

Stone Bridge

> *From the visitors center parking lot, turn right on Sudley Road (VA 234) and drive 0.5 mile to the intersection with the Lee Highway (US 29). Turn right and drive east on US 29 for 1.5 miles, crossing Bull Run and pulling into the parking area on the left immediately following. Walk down to the stone bridge.*

After a late start and a sluggish march, the first Federal troops—Tyler's brigade—reached the stone bridge before 6:00 AM and began the engagement. They quickly pushed the Confederate pickets back across the bridge and began their demonstration. A 30-pound rifled cannon was kept in the rear of Tyler's line; the gun was fired three times in quick succession, signaling to the other units that the fight was on, and that they could now cross Bull Run.

The stone bridge that exists today is a reconstruction of the original, which was in the same place as the current Warrenton Turnpike crossing. You can see that the bridge was a nice, wide lane, and would have made an ideal choice for an army trying to cross a major stream like Bull Run.

Unfortunately for the Union, neither Hunter nor Heintzelman were near their crossing at 6:00 AM when the signal gun was fired. Getting to Sudley Ford had proven much more difficult in execution than on paper, due to poor maps and poor roads. It wasn't until 8:45 that the lead of Hunter's division, General Ambrose Burnside's brigade, finally made its way across.

By that time, Colonel Nathan "Shanks" Evans, commanding the Confederate troops at the stone bridge, was well ahead of the game. At about 7:30, while Evans continued to fight Tyler at the stone bridge, a report was received that Union troops were seen marching well to their left flank. At almost the same time, Captain E. P. Alexander, manning the main Confederate signal tower at Signal Hill, saw two odd things as he looked north toward the bridge. The first was large clouds of dust rising

The current stone bridge over Bull Run is a re-creation of the original.

north of the fighting; were these troops on the march? The second was unmistakable. The glint of the sun off brass artillery and thousands of Union bayonets convinced him that Federal troops were attempting to flank the Confederate line. Alexander signaled "Look out for your left—you are turned" to the signal tower at the Van Pelt House, which immediately relayed the message to Evans. As you previously noted on the monument at Signal Hill, this was the first time that a message had been transmitted during battle by telecommunication.

That message was an important one. Evans had barely over one regiment around the stone bridge, while nine were at or south of Mitchell's and Blackburn's Fords. He knew he was badly outnumbered, and he had every excuse to pull back. Instead, Evans played along. Keeping four companies at the bridge to face Tyler, Evans took the rest of his command to meet the oncoming threat, setting up to the left on Matthews Hill.

Sudley Springs

❯ *Turn right out of the parking area and return west on Lee Highway (US 29) 1.5 miles back to the intersection with Sudley Road (VA 234). Turn right on Sudley Road and drive north 1.7 miles to Stop 5 on the park driving tour, the Sudley*

Cemetery. Please be sure to respect the Sudley United Methodist Church's parking lot, particularly if it's a Sunday.

The crossing at Sudley Springs is really two crossings, as it occurs just before Catharpin Creek comes into Bull Run. The first, which crosses Bull Run, is Sudley Ford; the second, across Catharpin Creek, is known as Sudley Springs Ford. As Burnside's men filed across, a number of frightened citizens looked on, wondering what would come with the day. Many of these were at Sudley Church, attending their Sunday services in the same location as the current church.

Sudley Ford is upstream of the current bridge, and is actually surrounded by private property on both banks, so it is not viewable. Sudley Springs Ford is accessible by park trail, and runs along the current route of Sudley Road.

Matthews Hill

> *Turn right out of the parking area and drive 0.9 mile. Pull into the parking area for Tour Stop 4 of the park driving tour on your left.*

Evans had set up the Confederate line atop Matthews Hill, a large ridge south of Sudley Ford. In place at 9:00 AM, Evans waited as Burnside's brigade formed. When they emerged from the tree line north of Matthews Hill at 9:15, Evans opened fire. The surprised Federals moved toward the crest, but the small group of Rebels was able to inflict enough damage that they stalled the advance. Hunter was even wounded in the exchange, passing command of the division to Burnside.

Walk up the trail to the crest of the hill and then turn around to face north. The height of the ridge becomes much more obvious looking back down the hill (and, of course, after climbing it).

At the McLean House, Beauregard got wind of what was occurring on the left, finally abandoning his plans for keeping his army concentrated around the McLean Farm. (Johnston, now in Manassas with his army, was the ranking officer, but he was still asleep when the battle started.) He sent the brigades of General Bernard Bee, Colonel Francis Bartow, and Jackson north to reinforce Evans as soon as possible.

Evans fought fiercely to keep the Federal advance in check, but after 45 minutes, the rest of the Union force was beginning to draw into line on the field, preparing to swallow the small band of Confederates. At 10, however, Bee's brigade came up, forming on the right and finally giving Evans's men a rest. Bartow followed soon afterward, more than doubling the Confederate strength on the hill. This new Confederate line was able to hold for another 45 minutes before the Union numbers—even without Heintzelman's division, which wouldn't cross Sudley Ford until 11—were becoming too much to overcome. The Confederates conducted a charge before Bee ordered them to fall back to the south bank of a small stream known as Young's Branch at 10:45.

Not long after this initial retreat, the Confederates saw another Union unit coming into view unexpectedly on their right. It was the brigade of Colonel William Tecumseh Sherman. Sherman, part of Tyler's division, had reconnoitered Bull Run earlier in the day by himself after the fighting began and found a small but usable ford not far north of the stone bridge. (The Confederates had noted a red-haired Union officer dash through heavy fire on horseback early in the battle, thinking he was crazy; this was probably Sherman.) When Tyler received an order to advance over the bridge, even though the original plan was to wait until Hunter had driven the Confederates past, Sherman led his troops to the newly found ford and crossed.

With Sherman's appearance and both sides of the Union line enveloping their flanks, the Confederates were once again forced to fall back, this time across the Warrenton Turnpike and up the northern slope of Henry Hill. In short order, Tyler brought the rest of his division over the stone bridge and onto the field, while Heintzelman finished his crossing at Sudley Ford. Fresh Federal troops now flooded

The southern slope of Matthews Hill as seen from the Henry House.

the battlefield. McDowell, now on the field himself, watched the retreating Confederates and rode among his men, shouting, "Victory! The day is ours!"

If you turn around again and face south, you will see the tree line and stream running by the stone house at the bottom of Matthews Hill. Beyond, in the distance, you should be able to see Henry Hill and the park visitors center. The ford that Sherman used to cross Bull Run, now known as Farm Ford, is to your left; a park trail that you can use to access it is best accessible from the stone bridge site. If you wish, continue on the trail down the south slope of Matthews Hill, then return to your car.

Henry Hill

❯ *From Matthews Hill, return to the visitors center. Turn left out of the parking area and drive 1.2 miles south on Sudley Road. Proceed to the back of the visitors center, then follow the walking tour of First Manassas in the National Park Service brochure. As you walk, note the commanding view that Henry Hill provides of the entire battlefield.*

The original monument to the Union soldiers who fought at first Manassas still stands at Henry Hill; a similar one for the second battle can be found at the Deep Cut.

As McDowell proclaimed his victory—and certainly from the Union viewpoint, it appeared to be just that—a new unit quietly filed onto the battlefield. It was the First Virginia, Jackson's brigade. They arrived from south of Henry Hill at about 11:30 AM. Setting two batteries of artillery in the center, Jackson directed his infantry to form a line just behind the crest of the hill—out of sight of the Union troops—and to lie in wait, while the rest of the Confederate troops gathered and began to re-form near the site of the former Robinson House.

❯ *Face north toward Matthews Hill. Note the Henry House in front of you, with the Stone House and Young's Branch just beyond the Warrenton Turnpike.*

During this small lull in the battle, the Union troops (who, for all their elation, had still taken quite a beating), began to re-form their own line. Facing south, Heintzelman's division took the right of the line, just west of Sudley Road. From his left onward stood Porter's brigade, then Sherman's (on Sudley Road), Burnside's, and finally Keyes's brigade on the Union left. The artillery of Charles Griffin and James B. Ricketts set up behind Keyes. Although all of the Confederates were visibly falling back, the Federals still had to push past Henry Hill, then on to Manassas Junction in the distance.

As the Federals crossed the turnpike and made their way up the northern slope of Henry Hill, they could see only the disorganized group of Confederates behind the Robinson House, falling back to the right of the concealed Jackson. Bee, seeing Jackson lying there, rallied his men with the cry, "There stands Jackson like a stone wall! Let us determine to die here, and we will conquer. Follow me!" Thus was born a legend. Stonewall Jackson received his famous name, and the First Virginia would forever be known as the Stonewall Brigade.

Despite Bee's eloquence and success rallying the Fourth Alabama, he would un-fortunately follow his words to the letter. Riding at the front of the Alabama troops as they surged and then quickly retreated, Bee was left practically alone on the field. He soon fell, mortally wounded.

At 12:30 PM, Beauregard and Johnston finally arrived at Henry Hill to personally direct the action. They immediately began to start rallying and re-forming the Con-federate line. Before long, it was agreed that Beauregard would stay at the front, while Johnston went to the Lewis House, Portici, to retain overall command and direct the oncoming reinforcements to the proper position. Among these, just barely off the train from Piedmont Station, was the cavalry of J. E. B. Stuart.

❯ *Proceed to the Henry House. As you walk, note the short distance between the house and the crest of the hill, along with the location of the artillery placed around you.*

At the beginning of the Civil War, it was commonly accepted military practice—a tactic of Napoleon's—to set one's artillery slightly in front of the infantry at the early stages of an engagement. At 1:00, as the Union troops were steadily marching up Henry Hill, McDowell did just that, sending Griffin's and Ricketts's batteries toward the crest of Henry Hill, near the Henry House. Griffin objected heavily, thinking the position too far in front of the line, but he was assured that the infantry would be there to support him. Ricketts arrived first, setting his guns just southwest of the house, with Griffin arriving soon afterward. Eleven heavy guns were now firing on the Confederates.

Thinking that Confederate sharpshooters were in the Henry House, Ricketts turned one of his guns around and poured a heavy fire into the building. Unfortunately, the only people in the house were the Henry family, including 85-year-old widow Judith Carter Henry. Her family had tried earlier to move the bedridden Henry

Henry House, where 85-year-old widow Judith Carter Henry was killed during the battle.

DID CITIZENS REALLY COME FROM WASHINGTON
TO PICNIC AND WATCH THE BATTLE OF MANASSAS?

Yes, although it wasn't quite the joyful outing that legend has made it out to be. Indeed, some important citizens, including senators, congressmen, and other Washington dignitaries, began arriving in Centreville as early as two days before the battle. None of these spectators were actually near the field during the battle, although quite a few did get tangled up in the ensuing flight to Washington. A number of Confederate citizens also watched from a distance, and after news of the victory was transmitted, many began to arrive from Richmond to view the triumphant army.

to a neighbor's house, but the journey proved too much, and they returned at her insistence. The fire from Ricketts's guns killed the poor widow, and she was the only civilian casualty of the battle. She is buried in the family plot next to the house.

At 2:00, with Ricketts and Griffin set less than 100 yards from Jackson's front, Union infantry finally did come in the form of the 11th New York Zouaves. As they appeared among the guns, Jackson's men were finally ready to make their presence known. They rose as a unit and began to pour a devastating fire into the Zouaves at close range. The Zouaves tried to hold for a time, but eventually withdrew down the hill toward the relative safety of Young's Branch. However, just as they reached the foot of the hill, Confederate cavalry led by Stuart—directed to the Confederate left by Johnston and concealed in the woods—charged into them, hitting them again.

At about the same time, the 33rd Virginia, left of Jackson's line, marched toward the two exposed Union batteries. Griffin immediately turned his guns toward Jackson, but his chief of artillery, Major William Barry, ordered him not to fire, thinking that they were more infantry coming to support them. It was a mistake made many times that day and at other places early in the war; blue uniforms mixed with gray on both sides of the line, and it was often difficult to discern friend from foe. The Virginians tore into the artillerymen, and although Griffin was able to withdraw three of his guns to safety, the rest had to be abandoned; the Confederate fire was so devastating that there were not enough surviving horses to save the other guns.

Seeing the Federal guns in danger, Heintzelman ordered a volley fired toward them, which temporarily cleared the Confederates from the area. Jackson, however, immediately ordered another charge to keep the guns. For the next two hours, the heat of the battle was centered here, with both armies fighting viciously to gain and hold possession of these two critical batteries.

Late in the afternoon, around 4:00, Confederate brigadier general Kirby Smith's

Fifth Brigade arrived on the field and moved to the left of the Confederate line, where the heaviest fighting was. Almost immediately, Smith was wounded, and command passed to Col. Arnold Elzey. Elzey moved into the woods to his left, followed quickly by Early's Sixth Brigade and Stuart's cavalry. The Confederate line eventually moved far enough to the left that when they emerged from the woods they overlapped the Union right considerably. Elzey moved toward the front of Howard's brigade at Young's Branch, while Early and Stuart attacked Howard's exposed right flank.

The Federal right was crushed by the unexpected attack. Beauregard ordered a general charge across the entire line, beginning with the left. For the next 30 minutes, unit by unit, the Union troops began to run—some toward the stone bridge to the east, others toward Sudley Ford to the north. Although McDowell was able to re-form a few of the Union troops at Centreville, most choked the roads leading to Alexandria and Washington in complete disorder. McDowell and his command eventually decided to continue the movement and also eventually headed back toward the capital. Although the Confederates did pursue the Union troops for a short time, it was not a concentrated effort, and Beauregard ordered all of his troops behind Bull Run at 7:00.

What had looked like a sure Union victory had turned into a complete rout. The demoralized Federal troops staggered into Washington over the next two days. By all accounts (Confederate included), McDowell's battle plan had been brilliant. Its downfall was the expectation that green troops, barely able to complete a march let alone effectively fight a battle, would be able to carry out that plan. McDowell became the scapegoat for the fiasco, and lost his command to Major General George B. McClellan on August 15. McClellan would rename his new command the Army of the Potomac and would drill his men into a massive and effective fighting machine.

> ### CASUALTIES
>
> **Confederate:** killed, 387; wounded, 1,582; missing or captured, 13; total: 1,982.
>
> **Union:** killed, 460; wounded, 1,124; missing or captured, 1,312; total: 2,896.
>
> **Total Casualties: 4,878**

On the Confederate side, this great victory had proven to both the soldiers and to both nations that the Rebels could fight, and that this would not be a short war. Nor would it be a bloodless war. Confederate resolve, bravery, and creativity had won them a hard-fought but costly first victory.

On the afternoon of the battle, as the Federal line was beginning to crumble, an anxious Jefferson Davis arrived in Manassas, unable to sit in Richmond and await the result. He returned to Manassas on September 30 to confer with Johnston and Beauregard about their next move. It was decided that the Rebels would not advance to

Washington; they would continue to hold Manassas until either the expected Federal advance in the spring or, in the best case, European recognition of the Confederacy. They stayed until March 1862, when they quickly and quietly withdrew without a fight in the face of overwhelming Union numbers.

On October 21, 1861, Johnston was given command of the newly created Department of Northern Virginia, encompassing all of the state north of the James River and the Shenandoah Valley. The decision as to who would command Johnston's Valley District was a simple one. Jackson, who had been promoted to major general two weeks earlier, would head west to the Shenandoah to further cement his growing legend.

CHAPTER 2

Stonewall Jackson in the Shenandoah Valley

BEFORE LEAVING MANASSAS, Stonewall Jackson bid farewell to his command, the First Virginia, known now and forever after as the Stonewall Brigade. "In the Army of the Shenandoah, you were the First Brigade," he told his men. "In the Army of the Potomac, you were the First Brigade. In the Second Corps of this army, you are the First Brigade. You are the First Brigade in the affections of your general, and I hope by your future deeds and bearing, you will be handed down to posterity as the First Brigade in this our Second War of Independence!" He then left for his new assignment—commander of the Shenandoah Valley District, Department of Northern Virginia. (He would soon ask that the Stonewall Brigade be transferred to the valley, and the approval of his request was enthusiastically received by his soldiers.)

Jackson arrived and assumed command on November 4, 1861, and immediately set to work whipping his new soldiers into shape, just as he had done at Harpers Ferry six months ago. It wasn't long before he began active operations during the winter of 1861–1862, many of which not only ended in failure, but began to quickly drain the strength and morale of his army, leading many to question his generalship and even his sanity.

As Jackson maneuvered within the valley in the spring of 1862, to the east, Union general George B. McClellan finally began his long-stalled campaign for Richmond. With overwhelming forces approaching the Confederate capital, Jackson's Army of the Shenandoah took on a new importance. Union troops in and around the valley would surely soon be moving to join McClellan and increase his strength—that is, unless Jackson could somehow keep them busy enough to force them to remain in

Old Court House, Winchester.

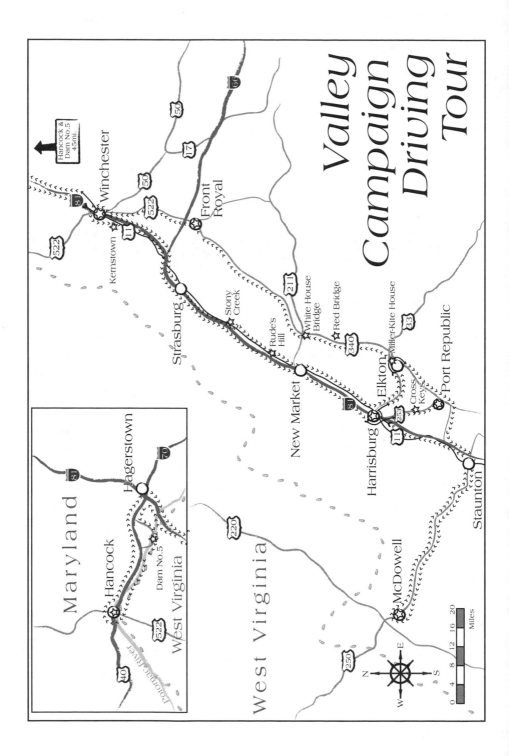

the Shenandoah Valley. If this mission was not accomplished, it just might spell the end of the Confederacy.

Jackson's Shenandoah Valley Campaign, particularly May and June 1862, is now the stuff of legend. Largely regarded as nothing short of brilliant for many years, it has been studied, dissected, and debated by historians, and generals the world over have taken tactics from Jackson's playbook. The campaign was, without question, a success, and even though Jackson forced his men to endure hardships beyond belief for any military force, they were forever proud to have served under him.

Was Jackson a genius? Or was he lucky? It's time to see for yourself.

BEFORE YOU GO

» PLANNING YOUR TRIP

Like many things, there are easy and—well, less easy—ways to tour Jackson's valley campaign. The shortest, easiest way would begin in Winchester and end in Port Republic, skipping a few smaller sites and seeing them out of order. Besides the fact that it's a hard campaign to grasp without seeing the topography of the valley up close, it also leaves you in a fairly isolated area, and you'd probably end up driving back the way you came anyway. A better way to do it would be to perform a loop through the Shenandoah Valley around a prominent ridge, Massanutten Mountain. This would mean hitting a few of the sites out of order, but it would save time and miles.

The best way, however, is to make an additional loop through the valley, just as Jackson did during his famous campaign. It would only mean one more trip through the valley, and the sites would, for the most part, be seen in the order that the Confederates saw them. Seeing the Shenandoah Valley this way also makes the importance of the roads, gaps, and valleys, as well as the reasoning behind Jackson's movements, much more clear. The longest route is the one presented in this chapter, but it's your tour.

If you would like to take a shorter version of the tour, it won't be difficult to pick up—most of the important sites are centered near Winchester and Front Royal in the north and Harrisonburg in the south. You also might want to consider beginning at the southern end of the valley, near Harrisonburg or Staunton, but getting to these cities may be a bit more difficult than making the relatively short drive from Washington, D.C., to Winchester.

> **STONEWALL JACKSON'S VALLEY CAMPAIGN**
>
> **Number of sites:** 17
>
> **Total miles:** 508
>
> **Estimated time:** 3–4 days
>
> **Must-sees:** Kernstown, Winchester, Cross Keys/ Port Republic
>
> **Close seconds:** Front Royal, McDowell

Although there are plenty of places to stay in the valley, you may want to plan ahead at least a little bit as you make your drive. Some of the cities and towns may have hotels but few restaurants, and vice versa. Your best bets will be Winchester, Front Royal, and Harrisonburg. Also available if you're the outdoor type is Shenandoah National Park. Besides its breathtaking beauty, the park offers many options for both camping and fine lodging.

There is one more piece of information that is essential not only for your trip planning but also for understanding the campaign. The southern end of the valley is higher in elevation than the northern end, and both the North and South Forks of the Shenandoah River flow northward. Therefore, if you are driving south, you are moving *up* the valley; if you are driving north, you are moving *down* the valley. While these terms don't mean quite as much today as they did during the Civil War, you will still come across them, so don't let them send you in the wrong direction.

» RECOMMENDATIONS

Jackson's valley campaign, like any other military movement, is best studied with the aid of a map. However, for this trip, it will be very helpful to take a good look at both the geography and the towns and roads of the valley before you set off on your journey.

The valley lies between two sets of mountains: the Alleghenies to the west, and the Blue Ridge to the east. There are few gaps through either range, but those of the Blue Ridge were more strategically important to the armies. Also, between these two formidable ranges lies Massanutten Mountain. It is around this prominent ridge that the Shenandoah River is split, with the North and South Forks meeting at the northern end. These two forks, along with the numerous creeks that feed them, would prove to be obstacles for both the Union and Confederate armies. The valley formed between Massanutten Mountain and the Blue Ridge, and through which the South Fork flows, is known today as the Page Valley (as it runs through Page County), but is still called and was historically known as the Luray Valley (for the town of Luray).

IN DEPTH

Peter Cozzens—*Shenandoah 1862: Stonewall Jackson's Valley Campaign*
Robert G. Tanner—*Stonewall in the Valley: Thomas J. "Stonewall" Jackson's Shenandoah Valley Campaign, Spring 1862*

"Both are great books, presenting contrasting views on Jackson in the valley. Tanner focuses on the Confederates, and is laudatory of 'Stonewall,' while Cozzens examines both sides and scrutinizes Jackson much more closely. Read both."

—*Tom Trescott, Abraham Lincoln Book Shop, Chicago*

Winchester, Virginia, is the largest city at the northern end of the Shenandoah Valley, with Staunton at the southern end of the area Jackson traversed. Most of the major cities in between were connected by the Valley Turnpike, which ran straight down the heart of the valley to the west of Massanutten Mountain. Present-day VA 11, for the most part, directly follows the trace of the old turnpike. It is also important to remember that in 1862, the state now known as West Virginia did not exist, and was still part of Virginia until it essentially "seceded" from Virginia the next year.

Many of the sites noted in this chapter have very limited operating hours; in some cases only a few hours per week or only a few months of the year. If there is something that you know you want to see, call ahead first to double-check that it will be open. If you are going off-season, you can visit many of the locations by appointment. Just remember that, for the most part, these sites are staffed by volunteers, so be sure to show your appreciation.

Last but not least, be sure you stop frequently and enjoy everything the Shenandoah has to offer. Both the landscape and the people are unforgettable, and you will find plenty to distract you from your Civil War tour as you wind your way through.

THE CAMPAIGN TOUR

WINCHESTER

❭ *Begin your tour at the Shenandoah Valley Civil War Orientation Center. The center is located within the Winchester-Frederick County Visitor Center at 1400 Pleasant Valley Road, just west of Exit 313 on I-81.*

Here at the Shenandoah Valley Civil War Orientation Center, you can pick up information about sites, food, and lodging in the valley, as well as watch a short video designed to introduce you to the valley's extensive Civil War history. The Shenandoah Valley Battlefields National Historic District has done a tremendous job helping to preserve and interpret those sites in the valley that remain, and one more broad look at the valley will help as you begin your drive.

Old Court House Civil War Museum

❭ *Turn left from the parking lot onto Pleasant Valley Avenue, then turn right at the stop light onto Millwood Avenue. Drive 0.6 mile and turn right onto Cameron Avenue, then drive another 0.6 mile to Boscawen Street. Find parking (be sure to feed the meter, if necessary) and walk to the Old Court House.*

When Jackson met his army, he set his headquarters in Winchester, the northern gateway to the valley. While the valley as a whole had very mixed feelings about the war

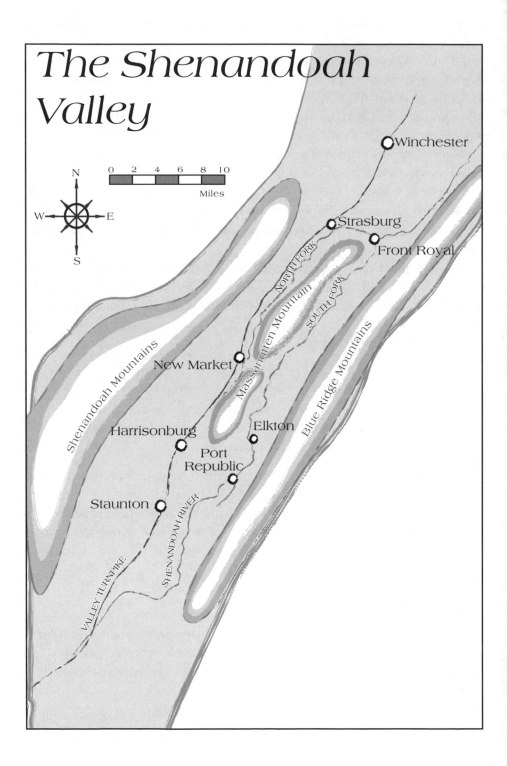

The Shenandoah Valley

N
W — E
S

0 2 4 6 8 10
Miles

Winchester

Strasburg

Front Royal

NORTH FORK

SOUTH FORK

Massanutten Mountain

New Market

Shenandoah Mountains

Blue Ridge Mountains

Harrisonburg

Elkton

Port Republic

Staunton

SHENANDOAH RIVER

VALLEY TURNPIKE

(a large segment of the population was Amish, and did not support slavery or the war), Winchester was very much a "secesh" city, and was fully supportive of the Confederate army's presence.

The Old Court House, along with many other buildings downtown, existed when the possession of Winchester changed hands again and again. Today, the Old Court House Civil War Museum houses a fine collection of Civil War artifacts and displays, with big plans for future additions to its exhibits. Also present, all over the walls, are well preserved and fascinating examples of graffiti that soldiers from both armies left during its various occupations.

The Old Court House in Winchester now houses a Civil War museum.

When you leave the Old Court House, take a walk up and down Loudoun Street, which is now a pedestrian walkway. Not only are there dozens of great boutiques and restaurants, but you can also imagine the townsfolk standing at their doors, cheering the Confederate army as it marched by—or making remarks and even taking potshots at the Yankees as they made their way down the street.

Stonewall Jackson Headquarters

❯ *From the Old Court House, drive north on Cameron Street, then take the next left at Piccadilly Street. Take the next right onto Loudoun Street and drive 0.3 mile to North Avenue. Turn left on North, then take the next left on Braddock Street, driving 0.1 mile to Stonewall Jackson's headquarters.*

While his army was based in Winchester, Jackson preferred to stay at this cottage, which was then north of the city, rather than the hotel downtown. The cottage belonged to Lieutenant Colonel Lewis Moore, who invited Jackson to use it as his headquarters.

Stonewall Jackson used this cottage as his headquarters when his army was based in Winchester.

The two rooms that Jackson used as a bedroom and an office during his stay have been restored to their 1862 appearance. Other rooms of the house have displays on Jackson, his family, his staff, and the Civil War in general, and the cottage includes a very nice collection of his personal items, including his prayer book and prayer table. Although the home and exhibits can only be seen through a guided tour, it is well worth the time.

DAM NO. 5

❯ *From the Jackson headquarters, return to US 11 North and drive 2.5 miles to I-81. Take the ramp onto I-81 North and drive for 33 miles, getting off at Exit 1 as soon as you cross over the Potomac River and into Maryland. Turn left on MD 68 West (Conococheague Street) and follow it for 5.6 miles, then left onto MD 56 (Big Pool Road). Drive another 0.5 mile until reaching Dam Number 5 Road. Turn left here and drive for 2.9 miles. Pull into the parking area for Dam Number Five and Chesapeake & Ohio National Park.*

North of the Potomac River, the primary consideration of the Union's Department of the Shenandoah during that winter of 1861–1862 was the Baltimore & Ohio Railroad and, to a lesser extent, the Chesapeake & Ohio Canal. Leading the effort to keep these two lines open was Major General Nathaniel Banks. Heading a group that was technically a division of McClellan's new Army of the Potomac, Banks moved his headquarters from Harpers Ferry to Frederick, Maryland, after taking command in July 1861. Despite several requests by Banks to attack Jackson in the valley, McClellan ordered him to put the better part of his force into winter camp in Frederick.

Throughout the history of warfare, it has generally been accepted that winter campaigns are to be avoided, and this was certainly the case during the Civil War. Besides freezing temperatures, the roads so essential for moving an army with any speed can very quickly become at best an obstacle and at worst a hazard. Thousands of marching soldiers and hundreds of horses, wagons, and pieces of artillery traveling over a muddy winter road will turn that road into a quagmire, forcing soldiers to spend most of their energy on hauling equipment out of the muck every time it gets stuck. Perhaps worst of all, the combination of all these factors can very quickly destroy an army's morale.

None of this, however, meant that winter campaigns, however risky, were completely out of the question. With most of the Federal troops north of the Potomac River, Jackson thought that the time was right to try his hand at a winter campaign against the railroad and the canal.

You are now looking at Dam No. 5, about 7 miles upstream from the town of Williamsport, Maryland. On December 7, 1861, Jackson sent a unit to this dam in an attempt to destroy it and disrupt traffic on the Chesapeake & Ohio Canal. The dam

Dam No. 5, upstream from Williamsport, Maryland.

was well guarded, however, and after several days the force returned to Winchester, reporting that they were unable to complete their mission.

Undeterred, Jackson personally led a larger force to the dam on December 18. Again, several attempts to break the dam as Confederate soldiers entered the icy waters waist-high were unsuccessful. Finally, on December 20, Jackson's men were able to cause a breach in the dam, and with mission accomplished, Jackson returned to Winchester. The dam, however, was completely repaired by the next evening.

The area you are now standing in would have been the Union position during the scuffle for the dam. The Confederate troops were across the river, where you can now see the powerhouse and other elements of the modern-day structure.

HANCOCK

> *Turn left out of the parking lot onto Dam Number 5 Road and drive 0.6 mile, then turn right on Ashton Road. Drive 2.6 miles (through a number of curves) until you reach Clear Spring Road (MD 68), then turn left to get onto I-70 West toward Hancock. Follow I-70 West for 14.1 miles until you reach Exit 3 for MD 144. Take Exit 3 and turn right onto Main Street (MD 144) at the end of the ramp, then drive for 1.5 miles. You will see a parking area for the Chesapeake & Ohio Canal National Historic Park on your left.*

Jackson returned to Winchester after finally breaking Dam No. 5, but not for long. On December 25, Jackson was reinforced by Major General William Loring's Army of the Northwest, bringing his total force to about 10,000 men. Jackson set out on another winter campaign, one that would be cursed for years by every Confederate who took part—the Romney Campaign.

The Army of the Shenandoah left Winchester on January 1, 1862, bound for the town of Bath, Virginia. From the outset, and throughout the entire campaign, the conditions were terrible—wet, cold, and muddy. The army would not reach Bath until January 4, and only after a rather cold relationship had developed between Loring and Jackson. The Confederates just barely caught the tails of the withdrawing Federal troops, and they pursued on all three roads leading out of town, finally concentrating on Hancock, Maryland. By the evening of January 4, Jackson had set artillery on the Virginia side of the Potomac and began lobbing shells into the town. The shelling was supposedly in retaliation for Union troops firing on Shepherdstown, Virginia, but it had little effect.

From where you are standing, looking across the river, you can see the heights on which Jackson placed his artillery. This piece of the Chesapeake & Ohio National Historical Park also has some interpretive signs that explain the battle and the campaign. Turning around, you will see the small and rather picturesque town that was the target of Jackson's bombardment laid out before you on the hillside.

Jackson asked for the town's surrender on January 5, and when it was refused, he continued to fire until finally withdrawing on the morning of January 7 and heading for Romney, Virginia. For the next two weeks, the army would jump several times between Romney, Unger's Store (now simply called Unger), Martinsburg, and the mountain gaps surrounding the area, with Jackson all the while marching his troops hard and draining their morale. Finally, on January 23, Jackson took most of his men back to Winchester, leaving Loring's division in Romney and other units scattered about for the time being. After being commanded by Richmond to recall Loring back to Winchester, Jackson complied and immediately resigned, citing interference with his command from afar. A political scramble ensued to convince Jackson otherwise, with the end result being that Jackson stayed on and Loring after receiving a promotion to major general—was transferred to Georgia. However, even his most loyal troops were beginning to wonder exactly what "Old Jack" had meant to accomplish with the Romney Campaign.

KERNSTOWN

❯ *From the parking lot in Hancock, turn right and drive east on Main Street for 1.6 miles, taking the ramp onto I-70 East. Drive east on I-70 for 22.1 miles to Exit 26, I-81 South. Drive south on I-81 for 40.1 miles until you are back in Winchester, then take Exit 313B. At the end of the exit, bear left onto Jubal Early Drive and drive 1.1 miles to Valley Avenue (US 11), then turn left and drive 2.1 miles to Opequon Church Lane on your right. Turn onto the lane and drive 0.2 mile to the end, parking in the gravel area in front of Opequon Presbyterian Church.*

By February, the Confederates' effective fighting force was weakened approximately by half due to a combination of sickness (no doubt helped along by the conditions of the Romney Campaign) and soldiers taking leave. Jackson asked Joe Johnston for 9,000 reinforcements, something Jackson was not accustomed to doing. Meanwhile, across the Potomac, Banks was preparing to do some early campaigning of his own. Knowing that Jackson was stretched rather thinly, Banks started massing troops to cross the river and regain complete control of the Baltimore & Ohio Railroad.

On February 6, Union troops retook Romney, and on the 10th they scattered a group of Rebels at Moorefield, Virginia. Several other towns came into Federal possession before Harpers Ferry was reoccupied on February 26. The next day, Jackson was forced to evacuate Martinsburg, which the Union took on March 2. By March 7, Banks's force was skirmishing with Confederate colonel Turner Ashby's cavalry only 7 miles north of Winchester. Finally, on March 11, with the Union army pressing hard from the north and his troops scattered ineffectively, Jackson was forced to evacuate Winchester.

As Jackson encamped near Mount Jackson north of the town of New Market on March 16, contemplating his next move, higher powers to the east were unknowingly shaping his decision. McClellan had grandly marched into Manassas to take possession, only to find that the Union army had been held at bay by "Quaker guns," logs painted black and mounted to look like cannons. Johnston had given him the slip and was headed south. Upset at this humiliation and McClellan's stalling in getting his campaign for Richmond under way, President Lincoln reorganized McClellan's command. Part of that reorganization was the transformation of Banks's command into the Fifth Corps of the Army of the Potomac, consisting of two divisions. One of these divisions was to be sent to defend Washington from Manassas Junction, leaving only one in the Shenandoah Valley.

On March 22, Ashby, after probing the Union forces south of Winchester, reported to Jackson that the Federals were leaving. In truth, Brigadier General James Shields's division was mostly camped north of Winchester, out of Ashby's sight, and there was only a skeleton guard set up south of town watching the Valley Turnpike. Jackson, however, saw a chance to reclaim Winchester and command of the northern end of the valley, and he was not about to pass it up.

Banks knew that there had been some skirmishing with Ashby's cavalry south of town along the turnpike that morning. He wasn't overly concerned; Ashby, a bold cavalier, was known for appearing out of nowhere and causing a ruckus. Still, as a result, he redistributed his troops a bit more evenly. One brigade remained camped just north of Winchester; the second was in Winchester itself; and the third was at Kernstown, near a commanding height known as Pritchard's Hill and watching over the Valley Turnpike. Banks then prepared to leave for Washington, D.C.

One significant development of the skirmishing on the March 22 was that Shields, commander of Banks's division, was hit in the arm by a shell fragment, and although he was wide awake and aware, was bedridden in town. Command of the division fell to Colonel Nathan Kimball. With Banks and Shields out of the picture, Kimball would essentially be left in command of virtually the entire Shenandoah Valley.

On the morning of March 23, Ashby appeared again, and the skirmishing continued. On this morning, however, the 8th Ohio, meeting Ashby's advance, soon discovered that he was supported by infantry, and at 9:00, R. P. Chew's Battery opened up on the Federals. This sounded the alarm, and soon Federal reinforcements were being pushed to Kernstown. Kimball placed 12 pieces of artillery atop Pritchard's Hill and started directing troops there as well. Ashby's forces, which had been pushing northward on the east side of the Valley Turnpike, made a concerted effort to advance, but a reinforced Federal counterattack swept them back to their original position by 11:00.

Two miles to the south of the fighting, Jackson was advancing up the turnpike with the rest of his men. Reaching a grove known as Bartow's Woods on the west side of the turnpike, Jackson halted his troops for a rest while he personally went through the woods and scouted the Federal positions.

Jackson quickly noticed the artillery placed atop Pritchard's Hill, seemingly unsupported, along with another prominent position to the west known as Sandy Ridge. He had not intended to attack this day; it was a Sunday, and the pious Jackson did not like to fight on Sundays. What he saw in front of him, however, was too grand an opportunity to pass up. He quickly ordered his men through Bartow's Woods and called for an immediate attack.

Unfortunately for Jackson, it was what he did *not* see that spelled trouble. He did not see the now 3,000 infantry holding Ashby at bay. Worse, he did not see the three full regiments behind Pritchard's Hill that Kimball was directing into position.

From where you stand at the Opequon Church (the structure has been replaced with a modern building), looking to the north you can see Pritchard's Hill, although it is difficult to discern from here how commanding a position it is. Running to the west and northwest is Sandy Ridge. From here, the most important thing to note is the distance from where you are standing to the ridge—along with the fact that it is completely open.

You are a bit north of where Bartow's Woods stopped and opened to the fields around Kernstown. At 2:30 PM, when Jackson's men reached the edge of the woods, they were immediately hit with artillery fire from Pritchard's Hill. Jackson sent his men to the woods at the base of Sandy Ridge—three-quarters of a mile in the distance. As his men got across the fields as quickly as they could, they soon discovered not only the artillery that was placed in addition to that on Pritchard's Hill, but also the 84th Pennsylvania Infantry, one of the units deployed out of Jackson's view. Taking heavy fire, the Confederates raced to the far side of Sandy Ridge and took their positions.

Rose Hill

❯ *From here, return to the Valley Turnpike and turn left (north), driving 1.6 miles to Cedar Creek Grade (VA 622), then turn left. Drive 1.9 miles until you reach Jones Road, then turn left and drive 0.6 mile. Immediately after a sharp left in the road, you will come upon a large home with historical markers; pull into the gravel area in front of the home.*

You are now in front of William Glass's former home, known as Rose Hill. The house and farm are on the northern end of Sandy Ridge, and looking to the south you can see the west side of the ridge extending down the road. The property is now owned by the Museum of the Shenandoah Valley and is being restored. At present the property is only open once per month for self-guided tours of the estate, which includes significant portions of the battlefield, including that part of the field which we

Looking south at Sandy Ridge from Rose Hill.

will see contained the most intense and decisive fighting of the battle. It is hoped that, in time, Rose Hill will be more accessible, but for now, if you want to see this part of the battlefield, plan well ahead.

Kernstown Battlefield

> *From Rose Hill, return 0.6 mile north on Jones Road, then turn right and retrace your path back on Cedar Creek Grade 1.9 miles until you reach the Valley Turnpike (VA 11). Turn right on the Valley Turnpike and drive 1.3 miles. On your right, just after passing an auto dealership, you will see Battle Park Drive. Turn right here and follow the road to Kernstown Battlefield. Drive around the Pritchard Home to the gravel parking lot and park near the visitors center.*

The large hill to your left, as you face the Pritchard House, is Pritchard's Hill, and you can easily see why this hill would become the centerpiece in the battle that was about to happen. Before you take a hike up the hill, explore some of the exhibits in the visitors center.

As a diversion, Jackson again sent Ashby forward to take pressure off his side of the line. By 3:00, the Confederate artillery was in place on Sandy Ridge and was driving the Federal troops back behind Pritchard's Hill. It was at about this point in the battle that Jackson was told by his reconnaissance force that there were approximately 10,000 Union soldiers behind Pritchard's Hill. Jackson, who had been planning a general assault, called off the attack, but decided that his troops were already fully committed, and that he would continue the fight.

Soon, from the north, the Union brigade of Colonel Erastus B. Tyler appeared, along with eight companies of cavalry. Jackson sent the 27th Virginia ahead at the same time, and the two collided at the northern end of Sandy Ridge. Falling back, just before 4:00, the Confederates took up a position behind a low stone wall just east of the Glass House.

At this point, begin your climb up Pritchard's Hill. It will take you a few minutes; there are a few benches along the way for you to take a rest if needed. Once you get to the top, however, you will have most of the battlefield spread before you.

From the top of the hill, looking back toward the farm, turn right to again view Sandy Ridge. Directly to your west at the north end of the ridge (well within artillery range, but out of sight with today's tree line) is the stone wall that the Confederates used as a defensive position. From here, the Federal artillery continued to fire at the Confederates, but the fighting at the wall would soon become so close that the bombardment could not be continued.

Tyler's men advanced against the stone wall, and at 4 PM, the Confederates unleashed a murderous volley from behind their formidable defensive position. Almost

Pritchard's Hill at the Kernstown Battlefield.

immediately, the focus of the battle shifted to this wall. Jackson sent more men here as reinforcements, and many Confederates took up the position on their own, driving all of Tyler's advances back. At 4:45, Kimball also began ordering charges against the position from here on Pritchard's Hill.

At approximately 5:30, the Federals were gaining ground, inching closer and closer to the wall, and much of the fight at this point was hand-to-hand. Kimball sent the 14th Indiana against the Confederate right, starting to break the line. At the same time, the Confederates, who had kept up a constant fire, were running out of ammunition. By 6:00, some of the units were completely out of ammo and were forced to withdraw, weakening the line. Tyler's brigade and the 14th Indiana pressed, and the withdrawal soon turned into a rout. As darkness fell, Jackson attempted to make a stand, but it was useless, as his men were completely scattered. Many of them were captured in the twilight, and Jackson was forced to take his entire army—or at least the parts of it he could find—south down the Valley Turnpike. The field and the battle belonged to the Union army; Confederate casualties amounted to 718, while the Federals suffered 590.

The effects of the Battle of Kernstown, however, would be felt much further than just the battlefield. Banks immediately returned to his command at Winchester, as did the division that had left earlier. A few weeks later, as it became evident that McClellan had not defended Washington as earnestly as promised, Lincoln made Banks's Department of the Shenandoah independent of McClellan's command. He did the same with General Irwin McDowell's troops at Fredericksburg, denying McClellan their use and keeping them in the vicinity of Washington should the Confederates attack through the valley. Jackson's aggressiveness was attracting a lot of attention.

STONY CREEK

❯ *From the Kernstown battlefield, turn right onto the Valley Turnpike (VA 11) and drive south 1.6 miles, then take the exit for I-81 South. Drive 30.7 miles south on I-81 to Exit 279 at Edinburg. At the bottom of the exit, turn left onto Stony Creek Drive (VA 185 East) and drive for 0.9 mile until with the road ends at Main Street (Valley Turnpike, VA 11). Turn right, cross the bridge, then pull into the parking lot for the Edinburg mill immediately to your right.*

The day after the battle at Kernstown, Banks ordered Kimball to pursue Jackson as he moved up the Valley Turnpike, and he did so through March 26, pushing the Confederates south of Strasburg. Jackson again camped near Mount Jackson, but on the advice of one of his new staff members, Jedediah Hotchkiss, moved to a better position farther south called Rude's Hill. Jackson ordered Ashby to form a defensive line north of their position at Stony Creek and hold it, giving him infantry support from the Stonewall Brigade. On April 1, Banks made a strong effort to push Ashby back, but with his supply wagons east of the Blue Ridge Mountains and Ashby having burned the bridge, he was forced to stop here.

Exit your vehicle, read the Virginia Civil War Trails sign at the mill about the artillery duel here, and then walk over to view the creek. (There are some easy trails down to the shallow creekbed; if you choose to climb down, use care getting there.) One look at the creek will tell you why Hotchkiss chose this position for defense. Its

"MAKE ME A MAP OF THE VALLEY . . ."

Maps are essential tools of any military campaign, and they can make or break an army in the field. This was particularly true during the Civil War. Stonewall Jackson understood this, and knew that knowing every last ridge, road, gap, and creek in the Shenandoah Valley was key to success in such a limited theater. On March 26, Jackson summoned Jedediah Hotchkiss, a cartographer who had grown up in the area. Jackson asked him to make "a map of the Valley, from Harpers Ferry to Lexington, showing all the points of offense and defense in those places." Hotchkiss immediately went to work, and within two days his observations were influencing the army's movements. Hotchkiss's map of the Shenandoah Valley has since become recognized as one of the most important and influential maps ever created.

The Confederates used Stony Creek as a defensive line following the Battle of Kernstown.

steep banks and width provide a considerable obstacle for an army to cross. Ashby was able to hold this position for more than two weeks in the face of repeated harassment by Federal troops.

RUDE'S HILL

> *Turn right out of the mill's parking lot onto the Valley Turnpike (US 11). Drive south on the turnpike for 10 miles. On your right will be a gravel area with several historic markers and signs; pull over here.*

You are now at Rude's Hill. Jackson's army encamped on the hills around here from April 2–17, and although the soldiers may have gotten some rest, events were happening rapidly during their stay. During this period, due not only to returning enlistments but also the initiation of the Confederate draft, Jackson's army doubled in size from 3,000 to 6,000 men. On April 12, Jackson asked for Major General Richard Ewell's division at Brandy Station, another 3,000 soldiers. Even though McClellan was pushing up the peninsula, General Robert E. Lee approved Jackson's request, knowing that his mere presence in the valley reduced the Federal force pressing Richmond.

On April 16, Banks decided to push the Confederates even farther up the Shenandoah Valley, and elected to make a night march on the Stony Creek line. When he got to the line, however, the only thing he caught was a glimpse of Ashby as the Confederate cavalry burned the new bridge over the creek. (Actually, it was more than a glimpse; Ashby, well known for his bravery and with it his recklessness, was very nearly captured.) The next day, Banks expected Stonewall Jackson to make a stand at the excellent defensive position that was Rude's Hill, but the Confederates were gone, having pulled back up the valley. Banks pushed forward to occupy the town of New Market, then Harrisonburg on April 25.

MILLER-KITE HOUSE

> *Return north on the Valley Turnpike 0.3 mile to Caverns Road, then turn left and drive 0.6 mile to I-81 South. Drive south on I-81 for 21.4 miles to Exit 247B at Harrisonburg. After you get off the ramp, you will need to make a U-turn, then follow US 33 East for 16.1 miles to the town of Elkton. Take the ramp for Exit for US 340 North, then drive 0.3 mile to Rockingham Street. Turn right onto Rockingham Street and drive 0.4 mile to the Miller–Kite House.*

> *As you drive from Harrisonburg to Elkton, note the prominent ridge you are driving around. This is the southern end of Massanutten Mountain, which runs north all the way to near Strasburg and Front Royal and virtually divides the Shenandoah Valley in two.*

After leaving Rude's Hill, Jackson took his army around the southern end of Massanutten Mountain, then headed northeast into the Luray Valley to Conrad's Store, now known as Elkton. The army camped east of the South Fork of the Shenandoah River, near Swift Gap in the Blue Ridge Mountains, on April 19. Jackson took up headquarters at this residence, now known as the Miller–Kite House. During this time, Jackson planned his next movements, frequently calling on his staff, particularly his new mapmaker, Hotchkiss.

Part of Jackson's planning included the burning of several bridges across the South Fork of the Shenandoah, at White House, Red Bridge, and Columbia Bridge. The assignment was given to Ashby's cavalry, and while they completed the burning of Red Bridge, Ashby's men were too intoxicated to complete their mission. It was here, at the Miller–Kite House, that Jackson and Ashby got into a heated confrontation, resulting in Ashby's command being split temporarily. However, recognizing that he needed his able cavalry commander, Jackson relented, but with clear expectations for Ashby on the discipline of his troops.

When you tour the Miller–Kite House, you can see the bedroom Jackson used, as well as several exhibits on the war, Conrad's Store, and Elkton. Although the exhibits are relatively small, there are some remarkably interesting pieces in the collection, so take a close look.

The Miller-Kite House, which served as Stonewall Jackson's headquarters in April 1862.

Jackson stayed here in the Elk Run Valley from April 19–30. Before he left, he ordered Ewell to bring his troops to Swift Run Gap, then headed south to Brown's Gap in the Blue Ridge, exiting the Shenandoah Valley. To Banks, the meaning of Jackson's movement was quite clear: Jackson was evacuating the valley and moving toward Richmond. Banks sent telegrams to Washington saying that Jackson had "abandoned the valley of Virginia permanently," and that there was "nothing more to be done by us in the valley." Secretary of War Edwin M. Stanton ordered Banks not to push any farther than he already had, and on May 1, Lincoln ordered Banks to pull back north to Strasburg, then send Shields's division to Irvin McDowell in Fredericksburg so they could join McClellan near Richmond.

The trouble was that Jackson had not quit the valley.

MCDOWELL

You will now be heading for the battlefield at McDowell. Before you go, please read this carefully. Although the distance is not great, you will be driving through the mountains for much of the journey, and the roads, though good, are winding. You will be driving through absolutely beautiful country, and should stop to take it all in, but because of this and the extra care you will need to take, your travel time to

McDowell will probably be at least two hours. Once you get to McDowell, there are not many options for lodging outside of a tent, so plan accordingly.

❯ *From the Miller–Kite House, drive west 0.6 mile back to the exit for US 340. Drive on US 340 South for 16.1 miles until reaching VA 256 West, then turn right and drive 6.7 miles to I-81. Enter I-81 South and drive for 9.5 miles, then take Exit 225 for VA 262 South. Continue on VA 262 South for 4.9 miles until reaching the ramp for US 250 West. Drive (with caution!) for 21.9 miles on US 250 West. You will then see a pull-off area with parking and some facilities, part of George Washington National Forest. Park here and enjoy the view.*

The Union army had taken the bait. Jackson had intended to appear that he was headed for Richmond. Instead, when he exited the valley at Brown's Gap, he headed for the rail depot at Mechum's Station. Although slowed getting to the station by poor weather, he was able to quietly transfer his entire army back to Staunton by rail on May 4 and 5. There, he joined forces with the small but experienced Confederate force of Brigadier General Edward "Allegheny" Johnson from western Virginia.

West of Staunton, in the Allegheny Mountains, was John C. Fremont and the Union's Mountain Department. Jackson pushed west from Staunton into the mountains, with Johnson, now second in command, leading the way. On May 7, Johnson encountered Union skirmishers on Shenandoah Mountain. Johnson pushed them

The view from Fort Johnson.

over the mountain and back through one of their own original fortifications, Fort Johnson, but the advance was slowed by heavier resistance at Shaw's Ridge. Soon, the Union commander, Brigadier General Robert H. Milroy, withdrew west to the town of McDowell, where he could join forces with Brigadier General Robert C. Schenck and bring the Federal force to approximately 6,000.

You are now standing on Shenandoah Mountain. Part of the wonderful vista before you, the closest ridge directly in front of you, is Shaw's Ridge. The town of McDowell lies just beyond the ridge.

Portions of the earthworks of Fort Johnson remain, and the trail to your left will not only take you through the old entrenchments, but will also give you another wonderful view of the mountains and the valley below. The trail, though not very long, is not an easy one, and the first half is all uphill, but it is well maintained and worth the time to hike.

> *Pull right out of the parking lot back onto US 250, watching carefully for oncoming traffic coming around the bend in the mountain. Drive 9.2 miles to the town of McDowell, turning left then right onto VA 645. Pull over and enter the Highland County Museum.*

By 4:00 AM on May 8, Milroy's Union soldiers were in ranks in the fields of McDowell, behind the Bull Pasture River and facing east toward dominating Bull Pasture Mountain. They were particularly focused on a knob on the western portion of the mountain known as Sitlington's Hill, next to the Staunton-Parkersburg Turnpike that Jackson would have to take to get to McDowell. They were certain that an attack was coming, and they would be ready for it. So here they waited—and waited and waited—with no sign of the Confederates.

At 10:00 AM, Schenck arrived with his 1,500 men, including cavalry and artillery. Schenck, now the ranking officer, and Milroy conferred on what to do when the Confederates appeared. They quickly decided that an assault up the mountain was the only solution; with the Confederates atop the mountain and the Federals at the bottom, cavalry and artillery would be virtually useless. This battle would have to be fought by the infantry, and the only effective way to do that was to climb. So Schenck and Milroy adjusted their lines . . . and waited.

Finally, at about noon, movement was detected atop Sitlington's Hill, and as soon as it was confirmed that they were Rebels, Union skirmishers began their advance. The climb was difficult and long, but soon they were within firing range.

They were correct in that there were Confederates atop Sitlington's Hill. But those Confederates certainly weren't prepared for an attack. In fact, the Confederates atop the hill were Jackson, Johnson, and Hotchkiss. Hotchkiss had ascended earlier to sketch the mountain and the Federal positions below, and the two generals were

The field east of Sitlington's Hill, where Union forces waited for the Confederates.

surveying the field. Jackson did not intend to fight this day, but the next. But now, with the Union soldiers moving up the mountain, Johnson called his force forward to take a position at the top of the hill.

From your position here at the Highland County Museum (or anywhere else in town, for that matter), Bull Pasture Mountain dominates the landscape. For now, enter the museum and explore its exhibit on the battle. The museum also serves as a Civil War Orientation Center for the Shenandoah Valley Battlefields National Historic District. There is also a very well-done video on the battle and its significance. The home itself was an inn, and stood during the battle; walking through it presents its own interesting history.

> *Drive (or walk) 0.3 mile back toward the mountain down US 250 until you come to its intersection with VA 678 at the McDowell Presbyterian Church. There is a park behind the church where you can get out and walk.*

You now have a wonderful uphill view of the battlefield. There are several historic signs, Virginia Civil War Trails signs, and other markers that will help you orient yourself, so get out of your vehicle and take a good look around. Looking at the mountains, you can see US 250 coming through toward you; to the right of this is Sitlington's Hill, the focus of the battle. Also in front of you is the Bull Pasture River, and looking to your right are the open fields where most of the Union troops set their ranks before advancing to the hill. Thanks to a great cooperative effort by several preservation groups, these appear much as they did at the time of the battle, and will stay that way.

At 4:30 PM, the Union finally made its first coordinated advance across the river, 2,400 men making up five regiments. The Confederates, waiting at the top of the hill, watched as they advanced and began to climb, keeping their ranks as best they could. But they held their fire until the last possible moment.

> *From here, return to US 250 and drive 1.6 miles to a gravel pull-off for the Civil War Trust's McDowell Battlefield Trail. Read the interpretive signs here at the trailhead, and if you have the time and stamina, make your way up the mountain. The trail contains several signs along the way, and reaching the top will be worth the effort. Know, however, that the trail is 1.5 miles long, and it is quite a steep climb. Before you go, be sure not only that you are prepared for a mountain hike, but also that you will be back before the sun goes down—there isn't a lot of light here in the mountains (which is part of its beauty).*

When the Union soldiers had come well within musket range, the Confederates began a sustained and devastating fire from behind the crest of the hill. Still, the Federals kept coming, and by 5:30 PM, the fighting had become heavy all along the line. Bullets buzzed through the thick trees of the mountain, hitting their marks all too often through what seemed to be adequate cover. At 6:15, Johnson caught a Federal flanking movement, and adjusted his troops to the right to counter it. This occurred throughout the fight, with Schenck and Milroy continually attempting to get around the Confederate flanks. But the Confederate position, along with the sheer weight of numbers from continuous reinforcements, ensured that the Rebels would not budge. As the sun went down, there was one last concentrated effort at both flanks, but again it ended in repulse.

The soldiers kept fighting through the darkness, even though both sides were running very low on ammunition. The fight finally died down at about 9:00 PM, and within the hour Milroy began to pull his men off the hill to begin a retreat west to the town of Franklin. Jackson began a halfhearted pursuit the next day, but did not follow them far. Jackson had seemingly appeared out of nowhere and delivered a decisive Confederate victory. As was his nature, he attributed the victory to divine providence, sending the message to Richmond that "God blessed our arms with victory at McDowell yesterday."

By the time of the battle at McDowell, Banks was beginning to have his doubts about Jackson's presence in the valley, and began to express his concerns to Washington. Still, on May 12, Shields's division left the valley to join the Union forces at Fredericksburg as planned. Several days later, Stanton ordered Banks to reorganize his troops. The result of these movements was that Banks had only 6,000 Union troops and 16 guns at his new base in Strasburg.

Jackson took his men east through the mountains and on toward Harrisonburg, stopping just southwest of the town on May 19. On May 18, he had ordered Ewell to camp just north of New Market. There, with their two commands barely 20 miles apart, the two generals met to discuss their next disappearing act.

❯ *From here, if you plan on taking the shorter tour of the Shenandoah Valley, skip to the section on Harrisonburg, follow through to the end of the chapter, then resume your tour here, finally stopping at Strasburg, just south of Winchester. Otherwise, continue on to Red Bridge and the Luray Valley.*

To the east, outside of Richmond, the Confederate line that had held George B. McClellan's Army of the Potomac in place for a month had finally withdrawn, and the Rebels were pulling back up the Peninsula. The Federals were right behind them, inching toward Richmond. Anything that could be done to relieve pressure on the Confederate capital had to be done now. Knowing McClellan's caution as a general and Lincoln's desire to keep Washington safe, Lee pressed Jackson to do whatever he could to keep Union troops in the valley. Nothing would better accomplish that than a movement to the north, down the Shenandoah. Throwing in a bit of panic would only help further.

Near New Market and the center of Massanutten Mountain is the Luray Gap. Connecting New Market and the town of Luray, this Gap was the only practical way over the mountain. From the current positions of Jackson's and Ewell's forces, it would have been simple and practical to advance north to Strasburg and confront Banks there. But if the army were to pass through Luray Gap, they would be able to advance unseen and undetected before rounding the northern end of Massanutten Mountain at a prominence known as Signal Knob. From there, the Confederates would be virtually the same distance from Winchester as the Federals—and could possibly even cut the smaller force off before they could reach safety. If successful, this plan would send alarm bells off in Washington that could slow, and possibly even stall, McClellan's advance on Richmond.

RED BRIDGE

You are now about to enter the Luray Valley, formed by Massanutten Mountain to the west and the Blue Ridge to the east. As you proceed down the valley (i.e., drive north), you will make a few stops along the way at points that you have already heard mention of, but that will mean a great deal more at the end of the tour.

Also, as you drive, note the presence of Massanutten Mountain to your left. Driving up the Luray Valley, you can appreciate the shielding that the mountain provided for Jackson's army. The entire Shenandoah Valley east of the mountain is completely obscured, and the Luray Valley—ranging from only 3.5 to 10 miles wide— becomes a perfect avenue to advance undetected.

> *Drive east back through the mountains on US 250 for 29 miles until you come to the intersection at VA 262. Bear left onto VA 262 North and drive for 5.4 miles until you reach I-81. Take the ramp for I-81 North and drive 21.8 miles to Exit 247A at Elkton for US 33. Follow US 33 East for 15.7 miles until you reach the ramp for US 340 North. Drive on US 340 North for 9.6 miles. Turn right here onto Grove Hill River Road (VA 650) and drive 1 mile. On your left will be a gravel parking lot with a boat launch; pull in here and park.*

This boat landing is near the former site of Red Bridge. Earlier in the campaign, this was the one bridge that Ashby's cavalry did burn down before drunkenness prevented them from destroying the other two that Jackson had assigned to them. There are a few historic markers and signs here that tell the story of the incident. In front of you is the South Fork of the Shenandoah River, which runs north through the Luray Valley to join the North Fork at the town of Front Royal on the other side of Massanutten Mountain.

WHITE HOUSE BRIDGE

> *From the Red Bridge site, return 1 mile on Grove Hill Road to US 340 and turn right (north). Drive north on US 340 for 10.6 miles (taking care not to take US 340 Business Route). Just past the 10-mile point, you will cross the South Fork of the Shenandoah River. Just past the bridge, to your left on the other side of the divided highway, you will see a set of historic markers. Make the next possible U-turn and drive 0.2 mile south, then pull over in the gravel area at the markers.*

White House Bridge crossed the Shenandoah's South Fork near where the modern bridge does today.

From this pull-off area, you can not only see the former site of White House Bridge, but you can actually partially see the building it was named for—White House, in the distance to your right. Read the Virginia Civil War Trails sign here, and then proceed down to the bridge.

〉 *Pull out of the gravel parking area and drive several hundred feet, turning right at the next road, Kaufman's Mill Road. If you continue down the road, you will arrive at the riverbed and see the formidable width of the river at this point. Continuing up around the bend to your right, you can actually drive near White House itself—but do not approach it; it is on private property.*

FRONT ROYAL

〉 *From White House Bridge, return to US 340 North and drive 28.2 miles directly into the town of Front Royal. Once you are in the town, turn right on East Main Street (the Warren County courthouse will be on your right at the intersection). Drive 0.2 mile down Main Street, then park in the lot next to the restored railroad depot that is the Front Royal Visitor's Center.*

The drive you just took, from the town of Luray (at Luray Gap) to Front Royal, was the same route that Jackson's Army of the Shenandoah took through the Luray Valley. From May 21–23, Jackson's combined force marched north down the Luray Valley and stopped just short of the town of Front Royal, where you now are. As they marched, part of Ashby's cavalry stayed in the Shenandoah Valley, providing an additional screen for the army—not only to keep the Federals from moving south,

---

DID BELLE BOYD HAND STONEWALL JACKSON A VICTORY AT FRONT ROYAL?

Belle Boyd was well-known to the Union army as one of the Confederacy's most effective spies. Boyd, just turned 18 at the time of the battle, was staying at a hotel in Front Royal (now known as the Belle Boyd Cottage) which was run by relatives. When Boyd heard that Jackson was approaching, she ran through enemy fire to the Confederates, finding Jackson and telling him that if he moved quickly enough, he could "bag them all." She then ran back over the fields, taking more fire, before reaching safety in the town.

It does seem that most, if not all, of the story is true. How much of a difference her efforts made, however, are much less certain. It is probable that Boyd didn't tell Jackson anything he didn't already know, and he didn't alter his original battle plan. Still, it makes a great story, and Boyd was certainly one of the more interesting figures of the war.

The Warren Rifles Museum. The Belle Boyd Cottage sits on the same property, behind the museum.

but also to give the impression that Jackson's entire Army of the Shenandoah was right behind them.

Before you begin your tour of Front Royal, visit the Front Royal Visitor's Center and pick up a copy of its driving tour of the Battle of Front Royal. It's remarkably well done and does a great job of pointing out the most prominent features of the battlefield, many of which are still easy to pick out of the landscape. You can also download the driving tour from the Front Royal Visitor's Center website, discoverfrontroyal.com, and it is also posted on a Virginia Civil War Trails sign outside of the center. The route below will take you to all of the major points of the battle, but you may choose to follow the other driving tour to visit other points of interest.

While you are here in town, you might want to visit two related sites located right around the corner from the visitors center. One is the Warren Rifles Museum, which contains a large collection of artifacts gathered by valley residents over the years. (When you consider not only how much fighting took place here but also how many of the valley's residents had ancestors who fought in the war, you can imagine how sizable the collection is.) Right behind the museum is the Belle Boyd Cottage, the residence where the infamous Confederate spy was staying when she allegedly sped to the Confederate army and alerted it to the weak Union presence in the town.

Asbury Chapel

> *From the visitors center, return to US 340 via Main Street, then turn left. Head south on US 340 for 4.2 miles. On your right, you will see the Asbury Chapel. Pull into the parking lot here. (If you arrive on a Sunday, be respectful, as Asbury Chapel is still an active church.)*

This is the point at which Jackson stopped his army, somewhere near 8:00 AM. The head of the Army of the Shenandoah was near your current position, and was strung along the Luray Road (US 340) for miles. Jackson called for a soldier who was familiar with the countryside and asked if there was any other way into town besides Luray Road. The soldier told him that there was a little-known road nearby that would take them east to the Gooney Manor Grade Road, which swept indirectly around the main route but would bring them into the town.

From here, Jackson formed his battle plan. He sent Ashby's cavalry west to find a crossing over the South Fork of the Shenandoah, with the mission of cutting off any telegraph or rail traffic coming to or from Front Royal. Next, now knowing that Front Royal was garrisoned by the First Maryland Infantry of the Union army, Jackson sent a courier to the end of his column to summon his own First Maryland Infantry to the front to lead the attack. (This movement actually stalled the Confederates for an hour, as the unit had to move up the road through Jackson's entire army.) Finally, he diverted his army onto the small forest road that had been shown to him, ultimately coming out on the Gooney Manor Grade Road and advancing toward Front Royal.

Although from here you may choose to return to Front Royal using the quicker US 340, it would probably be worth your time to take the same alternate route that Jackson found. Rocky Lane, just to your south, is that same path, and although it has been widened a bit, for the most part the countryside around retains its original appearance. You will eventually come out on the Browntown Road, which was the Gooney Manor Grade Road that Jackson used on his final approach.

Prospect Hill

> *Turn right out of the church parking lot, then take the immediate left onto Rocky Lane (VA 607). Drive on Rocky Lane for 1.6 miles until reaching Browntown Road, then turn left and drive for 1.9 miles until you reach US 340 at the south edge of Front Royal. Turn right on US 340 and drive for 1 mile, turning left on Prospect Street. From here, drive into Prospect Hill Cemetery and proceed to the top of the hill.*

At about 1:45 PM, Jackson was in position to begin his attack. His army swept northward through the town, quickly capturing the pickets and advancing street by street.

Jackson quickly took possession of Prospect Hill, the large hill on which you now stand, for its commanding view of the town. A battery of artillery was sent to the top of the hill, but it was soon found that the Union guns had all been placed on Richardson's Hill, north of town, and were well out of range of the Confederate artillery.

At the time of the battle, this area was virtually treeless (although it was a cemetery), and it provided an excellent observation post for the battle. It is possible that Jackson himself observed part of the battle from here, although it is not known for certain. Although your view is a bit more obstructed, you can still easily see the town and the hills to the north that would become critical points of the fight. A bit more difficult to see, just north of the town, are the North and South Forks of the Shenandoah. It is here, just above Front Royal, that the two forks join to form the Shenandoah River.

Richardson's Hill

> *From the cemetery, use Prospect Avenue to return to US 340 and turn left. Head north on US 340 for 1.1 miles, turning right on North Commerce Avenue. You will see a park immediately to your left; pull into the parking lot.*

At about 2:30 PM, the Union commander, Colonel John Kenly, was summoned from his tent more than a mile north of Front Royal. A black civilian had ridden into the Union camp, breathlessly telling Kenly's officers that the town was being overrun by the Confederates. Although for a time Kenly and his staff simply mocked the man, it was not long before they accepted the truth. Kenly commanded his men to form a line on Richardson's Hill north of the town.

At the foot of the hill, very near where you now stand, was a stone wall. The advance line of Federals formed behind this wall and began to form an organized defense. Meanwhile, as the Confederates moved north, they also began to take fire from the Union artillery posted on Richardson's Hill. For a short time, their advance was slowed, but Kenly was eventually forced to pull back.

> *From the park, return to US 340 (you may need to make a U-turn) and follow North Royal Avenue for 0.6 mile, bearing right when US 340 veers off. Pull over at the Virginia Civil War Trails sign on your left.*

From this position, near the top of Richardson's Hill, Kenly formed a second, reinforced line at approximately 4:00 PM. However, by 4:30, Kenly realized he was being flanked to his west. He could no longer stay on this side of the river, and he ordered an immediate withdrawal north of the two forks of the Shenandoah to his rear.

As you look south down Royal Avenue and US 340, you can see the rolls in the landscape that made this such a commanding position. By turning around, you can also see why Kenly had no choice but to retreat; with the river at his back and the Confederates attempting to get in his rear, he would not have been able to hold this position for any length of time.

South Fork Bridge

> Continue north on Royal Avenue for 0.3 mile to the end of the road. There is another Virginia Civil War Trails sign here; pull out and stop.

As Kenly retreated, he ordered the bridges over both forks burned, no small feat considering the size of the bridges. The small walking path you can see here, along with Royal Avenue, was the old Front Royal–Winchester Turnpike, where the bridges crossed over both forks of the river. Although the view from here is somewhat obscured (you are looking at the South Fork), you can still see the former bridge embankments in the river. (Don't bother climbing down the bank to view them here; you will have a better view of what's left of the old bridge from the North Fork.)

Guard Hill

> Drive south on Royal Avenue for 0.2 mile, turning right on 18th Street, then driving another 0.3 mile back to US 340. Turn right on US 340 and drive for 0.9 mile, crossing both forks of the Shenandoah River. As you cross, note the large

The embankments of a bridge that once crossed the South Fork of the Shenandoah River are clearly visible today.

prominence in front of you; this is Guard Hill. After you cross the North Fork, take the next right onto Riverton Road. Follow Riverton Road for 0.1 mile until you come to a public access boat ramp. Pull into the area and park. (Take care not to get in the way of people putting their boats in the water or taking them out, as they will need a lot of room to do so.)

When the Confederates saw the smoke coming from the bridges, they immediately advanced and put the flames out as best they could. While the Union attempt to burn the bridges did not stop the Rebels, it did slow them, and Kenly formed a new defensive line on Guard Hill.

Turning your back to the river, you can see Guard Hill rising in front of you. From this commanding position, the Federals were able to hold off the Confederates until about 6:00 PM. Soon, however, Kenly discovered that Confederate cavalry had found crossings to both his left and right. About to be outflanked, he ordered yet another withdrawal, this time toward the town of Cedarville.

If you walk down to the river, you can easily discern the old embankments of the bridge that used to run over the North Fork of the Shenandoah, along with a great view of the very scenic river.

Fairview

> *From the boat launch, turn left and drive on Riverton Road to return to US 340. Turn right and drive north on US 340 for 3.2 miles. On your right, you will see a boarded-up, run-down white house; just beyond the home is a gravel parking area. Carefully pull off the highway and park here.*

The white house you see before you was once known as Fairview, and was a prominent landmark along the Front Royal–Winchester Turnpike. As the Federals retreated, Jackson's Confederates were close behind and began to catch stragglers along the way. With darkness beginning to fall, Kenly decided to make a final stand on this ridge, knowing that he needed to buy time for Banks in Strasburg, who by now surely must have heard of the Confederate attack here.

This desperate attempt by the Federals was all for naught, as the Confederates mounted a final charge up the ridge from the south. Kenly himself was wounded in the resistance, and the Union troops finally surrendered. The fighting ended around 7:00 PM in the area spread out around you. Almost the entire Union command of 1,000 men were casualties, mostly captured, although a good portion were able to escape in the darkness.

Jackson had completely surprised the Front Royal garrison. With his victory came spoils, as the Federals had established a fairly well-stocked depot here. However, most importantly, Jackson had gained a clear path to Winchester by getting behind the Union forces at Strasburg.

For his part, Banks retained a fairly cool head at Strasburg, listening to the piecemeal reports and trying to discern fact from fiction. He did not receive his first reports that something had happened at Front Royal until 4:00 PM that day, and it was not until 10:00 PM that he felt he had enough information to start moving his army north to Winchester. His first complete and reliable report came at midnight from one of the escapees. Meanwhile, reports started flooding into Washington from all corners, throwing the government into a temporary panic over the safety of the capital.

Still, the consensus of Banks and his staff was that the Confederate force that had captured the garrison at Front Royal was Ewell's, and that Jackson was still to the south near Harrisburg, but probably pushing north down the Valley Turnpike. At the same time, Jackson did not know exactly where Banks was, either—whether he had left Strasburg, started moving north, or had even possibly already withdrawn to Winchester.

At 6:00 AM the next day, the Confederates started leaving Front Royal, and all were out of town and on their way north by 10:00 AM. Around this time, Confederate cavalry ran across a Federal wagon train heading north down the Valley Turnpike. This gave Jackson the confirmation he needed that Banks was headed for Winchester. He decided to split his army in order to take advantage of the roads and try to cut Banks off before he could reach the town. Ewell was to head north along the Front Royal–Winchester Turnpike. Jackson would enter the turnpike at Middletown, hoping to get there before Banks.

Fairview was once a Front Royal landmark.

Neither party would be able to get in front of Banks's force, which also had split to take advantage of the roads. For the rest of the day and through the night, both Jackson and Ewell would push northward, fighting the Federal rear guard the entire way. It was not until 2:00 AM on May 25 that the last Union troops entered Winchester. Jackson finally halted his men at Kernstown at 3:00 AM, with Ewell arriving to the east some time earlier. It was late, and it had been a long, hard day, but neither army would get much sleep that night.

FIRST BATTLE OF WINCHESTER

Camp Hill

⟩ *From Fairview, turn right onto US 340 North and drive 4.9 miles. At this point, keep going straight, following US 522 North for 7.4 miles. (You are now roughly following the former Front Royal–Winchester Turnpike, the same path that Ewell used to approach Winchester.) When you reach the Millwood Pike (US 17 North/US 50 West), turn left and drive 0.3 mile, then bear left onto Jubal Early Drive for another 0.2 mile. Take a quick right at Apple Blossom Drive and drive 0.2 miles to Pleasant Valley Road, turning right. This will take you back to the starting point of your tour, the Winchester-Frederick County Visitor Center.*

Camp Hill, one of the few remaining open spaces of the First Winchester battlefield.

After only a few hours' sleep (sunrise was just before 5:00 AM that day), the fight was to resume. Jackson had sent a simple order to Ewell: Attack at daylight. Even though their commands had marched and fought through the night, Jackson found it imperative to keep the pressure up.

Banks's men had set up their defenses on two major hills south and southwest of the city—Bowers Hill, west of the Valley Turnpike, and Camp Hill, rising between the Valley Pike and the Front Royal–Winchester Turnpike. However, they had left major gaps in their line. Unfortunately for the Federals, almost all of the commanders were not out at the front line, but were in the city, unable to see the problems in their defense that were so obvious to both Ewell and Jackson.

Today, most of both of these hills are inaccessible and difficult to view beneath the growth of Winchester. However, keeping your eyes out for changes in the landscape will aid your view of the battle. The Valley Turnpike is still present as US 11, and the Front Royal–Winchester Turnpike is US 522, which you drove into town on. As you stand in the parking lot of the visitors center, face toward the main road and look to your left. You will notice a rise in the landscape; this is Camp Hill, right in front of you.

Ewell was only a mile southeast of Winchester when he began to move up the turnpike, but heavy morning fog made any action slow. He soon scattered the pickets from his front, and advanced along the road to the Millwood Pike intersection—the same major intersection to your left as you look toward Camp Hill.

> Turn left out of the visitors center parking lot and drive 0.2 mile to the intersection with Millwood Pike. Turn right on Millwood Pike and drive 0.5 mile to Kent Street. Turn left on Kent Street and drive just 0.1 mile. You will see a cemetery on your right; pull off to the side of the road.

You are now atop Camp Hill. At the time of the battle, the Front Royal–Winchester Pike had stone walls lining both sides, and the Federals took advantage of it. Under the cover of the fog, Union troops in the area where you stand quietly formed behind both walls. When the fog lifted, Ewell ordered the 21st North Carolina Infantry, commanded by Colonel William Kirkland, to advance up the road. Inexplicably, Kirkland did not send pickets in front, and marched the entire unit forward. They were consequently caught in a sudden crossfire, with four Federal regiments firing from both sides of the road and the only escape being back down the walled road to the south. The North Carolinians were decimated, and the slaughter continued until the fog came back onto the field. If you continue looking down Kent Street, this attack occurred just to your left.

When the fog returned, the firing stopped for about 30 minutes. Ewell, having seen his opportunity, moved his troops to the east to flank the Federals on Camp Hill.

Bowers Hill

> ❯ *From the cemetery, make a U-turn and then an immediate left onto Bond Street. Drive 0.3 mile on Bond Street. Turn left onto Valley Avenue, then make a quick right onto Miller Street. Drive 0.4 mile on Miller Street, then turn left on Seldon Drive, following it for 0.6 mile to its intersection with Meadow Branch Avenue. Turn right onto Meadow Branch, then right again onto Ramseur Lane. You will see a bend in the road in front of you; drive to the bend and pull over.*

On the western front of the battlefield, the fog had lifted earlier for Jackson. When it did, he saw that the Federals had taken a strong position atop Bowers Hill. After the Confederates had swept through the Federal pickets, Jackson set his artillery—14 guns—and commenced an artillery duel with the Union guns on the crest of the hill that lasted for two hours.

Through the small clearing in front of you, in one of the few empty spaces in this sparkling new subdivision, you can see that there is indeed a hill here. The water tower in the distance—you can only see the top—is at the crest of Bowers Hill, the Federal position. Unfortunately, this is probably the best view you will get of the hill short of a helicopter ride. As you try to sneak a peek at the history in front of you, take care not to disturb the property of the residents.

At 7:00 AM, with the battle going nowhere, Jackson finally determined to make his move. He sent Brigadier General Richard Taylor's Louisiana Brigade marching left to face the Union right flank, being held by the 2nd Massachusetts Infantry. Taylor had quickly established himself as one of Jackson's favorites, a hard and aggressive fighter whose command possessed remarkable discipline and remained cool under fire. (He had likely picked up at least a few tips from his father, General Zachary Taylor, hero of the Mexican War and 12th president of the United States.) At 7:30, every eye on the battlefield watched as Taylor's men steadily marched up the western side of Bowers Hill. Halfway up the hill, Taylor suddenly and finally shouted for the charge. The effect was immediate. Taylor's charge ran right over the Federal right flank, sending all resistance fleeing to the rear.

Meanwhile, back on the eastern front, the fog did not lift again until 9:00 AM. Ewell's flanking movement had gone undetected, but he saw little resistance in front of him. Banks had given the order for all Federal units to withdraw and regroup north of Winchester. With the 15th Alabama leading the way, Ewell took up the pursuit, sending the remaining units through the town. On the west, Jackson was doing the same, and by 9:30, all Federal forces had been cleared from his path.

As the Union soldiers retreated through the town, they met resistance not from the Confederate soldiers—who were slowed by the chaos in the town, as well as fatigue from the previous days—but from the women of Winchester. Although for the most part the Union troops had treated the residents of Winchester with dignity and civility during their occupation, many of the women did not return the sentiment, throwing objects and even shooting and killing some of the fleeing soldiers. It was behavior that would not be forgotten during the many times the Federals reoccupied Winchester.

Banks was able to reach Martinsburg by 1:30 PM, and then called a halt until 5 to collect the rest of his men. After sending a wire to Washington saying that his army had been defeated but was intact (he had conducted a particularly effective retreat), his men resumed the march, and by 11:00 PM went into camp across from Williamsport, where they would cross the Potomac River into Maryland the next day.

Unable to mount an effective pursuit, Jackson stayed in Winchester, granting his exhausted men a day of rest and thanksgiving on May 26. He would keep his headquarters here through May 31.

HARRISONBURG

> *From your position near Bowers Hill, turn around and return to Meadow Branch Avenue, then turn left. After 0.3 mile, continue onto Jubal Early Drive, then drive another 1.8 miles to I-81. Take I-81 South for 66 miles until you reach Exit 247B. From the exit, merge onto East Market Street (US 33 West) and drive 1.6 miles. Turn left on Federal Street and drive 0.2 mile to Franklin Street, turning right and then taking the next right onto Main Street. After you turn onto Main Street, pull over and park, then walk to the Hardesty–Higgins House Visitor Center.*

While Jackson and Banks were engaged in the northern end of the valley, other arrangements were being made in Washington. Late on May 23, Lincoln heard the first news from Front Royal, and although the details were being sorted out, he knew action had to be taken. On the afternoon of May 24, Lincoln informed McClellan that McDowell's force in Fredericksburg would not be going south to Richmond; instead, his 20,000 men would head for the Shenandoah Valley to deal with Jackson. Additionally, Fremont's Mountain Department, west of the valley, would head for Harrisonburg and attempt to cut off Jackson's route of retreat. Both forces began their movements on May 25, the day of the battle at Winchester. Although Fremont, through a combination of fatigue, poor supply lines, and bad conditions, would not head for Harrisonburg but to Strasburg instead, he would be there by June 1. Shields's troops, the lead division of McDowell's force, were in Front Royal by May 30. Jackson didn't know it, but two Federal armies were about to converge from the east and west below him, trapping him in the Shenandoah Valley.

Beginning May 27, with Banks out of the way, Jackson began spreading his army all over the northern end of the valley. He sent troops to Harpers Ferry, Front Royal, Berryville, and Martinsburg, partly to take advantage of their position, but also to find out where the enemy was and feel out its strength. Shortly, however, he received unexpected news. On the evening of May 29, Jackson learned that Fremont was headed for Strasburg, and that Shields was on his way from the east. There was also a considerable Union force in Harpers Ferry, currently having an artillery duel with the Confederates, as well as Banks's army, which was in relatively good condition despite its recent defeat. All of a sudden, Jackson's scattered Army of the Shenandoah—16,300 men strong—was in the midst of more than 52,000 Union troops.

The next morning, May 30, Jackson ordered all of his troops to concentrate just north of Winchester. The same day, his garrison at Front Royal was routed by Shields, who had marched overnight to catch the Rebels off guard. Fremont was also close by, just to the west. The two Federal pincers of Fremont and Shields would close on Jackson's army unless he moved immediately.

The march began at 8:00 AM on May 31. Jackson ended the day's march just north of Strasburg; it was soon discovered that Fremont's advance guard was only 5 miles west of him. Fighting began at 7:00 AM the next morning and would continue on and off for the next several days, with Jackson moving as fast as possible up the valley and Fremont right on his tail. At the same time, in Front Royal, Shields suggested a new plan to McDowell; as Fremont chased Jackson up the Valley Turnpike, Shields would move south up the Luray Valley, emerging at New Market and in Jackson's path, trapping him. The plan was approved, and Shields began marching that afternoon.

On June 2, anticipating Shields's movement, Jackson sent cavalry under Major Samuel Coyner into the Luray Valley, with the mission of burning the White House and Columbia Bridges, the only two remaining bridges over the South Fork of the

Shenandoah River for miles. In the meantime, Jackson kept moving, his rear guard busy not only with fighting off Fremont's advance but also with burning bridges along the Valley Pike in the army's wake, slowing the Federals as much as possible. On June 4, this reaped a huge reward at the bridge over the North Fork. As Fremont began to cross the newly repaired bridge, the river rose 12 feet in less than four hours, and the bridge

The Harrisonburg visitors center is housed in a building General Nathaniel Banks once used as his headquarters.

become so dangerous that it had to be cut away. Fremont's army was stuck on the wrong side of the river for a day and a half.

Jackson's exhausted army reached Harrisonburg on June 5, moving too swiftly to be caught at New Market as Shields had envisioned. He sent his wagons south toward Staunton, while the infantry headed southeast, finally stopping to get some rest near the hamlet of Cross Keys. The next day, Jackson set up camp near Port Republic, a small town on the South Fork of the Shenandoah, while Ewell's division stayed near Cross Keys.

Here in the town of Harrisonburg, you are now at the Hardesty–Higgins House. Banks used this house as his headquarters while his army was this far up the valley, before he knew that Jackson was headed for the battle at McDowell. It is now home to the Harrisonburg visitors center, as well as the Valley Turnpike Museum and a Civil War Orientation Center for the Shenandoah Valley Battlefields National Historic District. Harrisonburg is also home to many other attractions, as well as some fine boutiques and restaurants, so if you have the time, take a stroll around the downtown area.

Turner Ashby Monument

❯ *From the visitors center, head north to Market Street, then turn right and drive 1.3 miles to Cantrell Avenue. Turn left on Cantrell and drive 0.2 mile, then turn right on Reservoir Street for 1.1 miles. Then turn right on Neff Avenue. Follow Neff Avenue for 0.4 mile to Turner Ashby Lane. Follow Turner Ashby Lane to the parking area at the end of the road and walk up the very short trail. (Note: If your map or GPS is out of date, it may not show the correct roads; a building development near this site has obscured the old Turner Ashby Lane, necessitating the new one you are driving on.)*

On the afternoon of June 6, Fremont's army occupied Harrisonburg and went into camp, not knowing exactly where the Confederate army was. Fremont searched for information and sent cavalry in several directions, including southeast down the Port Republic Road. They did not have to ride far before they rode into a Confederate trap set for them and were driven back. They resumed their advance, slowly this time, and again began to approach the Confederate cavalry. Ashby, promoted to brigadier general only days before, saw an opportunity and ordered a charge, leading the way as he always did. Inexplicably, none of the Confederate troopers obeyed, and Ashby was left all alone between the lines. He was soon quickly gunned down and killed by the Federals. A sharp fight ensued, lasting for about an hour, and although they held the field at the end, the Confederates had lost an exceptional cavalier in Ashby, who had become a legend not only among his own troops but among Union soldiers as well for his daring.

THE LOSS OF TURNER ASHBY

Turner Ashby's bravery and daring had become legendary among both his own men and the enemy. Riding a white horse, Ashby often appeared to be some-what of a ghost, defying capture and seemingly oblivious to danger. When he finally fell on June 6, his loss was felt deeply both by his men and his fellow officers, who recognized Ashby's zeal and passion for the Confederate cause. This included Stonewall Jackson; though the two had their quarrels, Jackson always trusted his cavalry commander and was thankful to have him.

A monument to Confederate brigadier general Turner Ashby.

The park here is right in the middle of the battleground, and there are interpretive signs that tell the story of the battle and help you orient yourself. A large granite monument sits on the spot where Ashby fell. Although development is springing up all around the area, it seems that Harrisonburg has at least recognized the importance of this site, and is determined to protect it, even if some of the view around it becomes a bit cluttered.

CROSS KEYS

Union Church

❭ *From the Ashby Monument, return to Neff Avenue and turn right, then drive 0.6 mile to Port Republic Road (VA 253 East). Turn left, then drive 4.3 miles on Port Republic Road to Cross Keys Road (VA 276). Turn right on Cross Keys Road and drive 0.8 mile to Battlefield Road (VA 679). Turn left at this intersection. You will see a small white church on your right and a cemetery on your left. Pull into the parking lot of the church. This is still an active congregation, so be respectful if you arrive on a Sunday.*

As a result of the cavalry clash the day before, Fremont ordered Milroy to do further reconnaissance down the Port Republic Road. A half mile outside Cross Keys, he ran into Confederate skirmishers and returned to Fremont. His estimate of the size of the Confederate force was that it was approximately 20,000 men. That night, at a

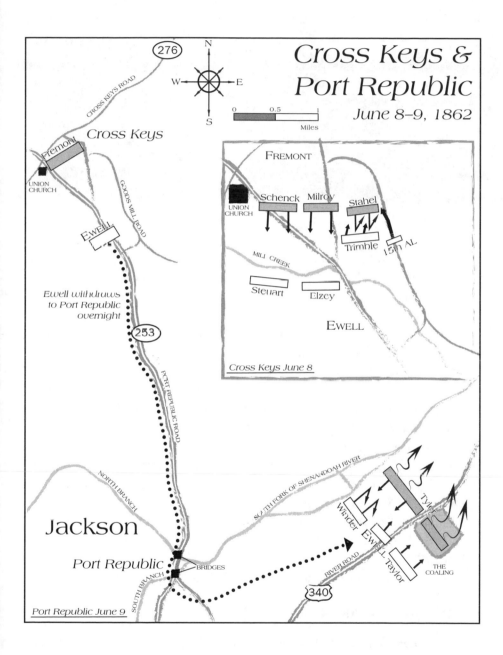

Cross Keys & Port Republic
June 8–9, 1862

276

N
W · E
S

0   0.5   1
Miles

CROSS KEYS ROAD

Cross Keys

Fremont

UNION CHURCH

GOODS MILL ROAD

Ewell

Ewell withdraws to Port Republic overnight

253

PORT REPUBLIC ROAD

NORTH BRANCH

Jackson

Port Republic

SOUTH BRANCH

BRIDGES

Port Republic June 9

SOUTH FORK OF SHENANDOAH RIVER

RIVER ROAD

340

Winder

Ewell Taylor

Tyler

THE COALING

FREMONT

UNION CHURCH

Schenck   Milroy   Stahel

Trimble   15th AL

MILL CREEK

Steuart   Elzey

EWELL

Cross Keys June 8

The Cross Keys cemetery.

council of war, most of Fremont's staff agreed with him. Their conclusion was that Jackson needed to cross the South Fork of the Shenandoah at Port Republic to reach safety, and had turned his army to face them until the crossing could be made. It was decided that Fremont's army of just over 14,000 would attack the next morning.

In reality, Milroy had not run into Jackson at all; in fact, Jackson was already at Port Republic. Milroy had run into Ewell's division, which was encamped southeast of Union Church. Ewell did not have 20,000 soldiers with him, but only 6,620. Jackson, meanwhile, had set up at Port Republic, sending pickets north in order to detect any movement by Shields, who he knew was heading south toward him.

By 7:00 AM on June 8, 1862, Fremont's entire army was heading south on Port Republic Road (the same one you just drove) and headed for Cross Keys. First contact was made just after 8, slightly north of the Union Church where you are now standing. These were pickets from the 15th Alabama, set up around the Union Church and well ahead of the main Confederate line. After putting up a token resistance to Fremont's advance, the Alabamians passed around the church and cemetery and through the fields to your right as you face the road, heading southeast to join the rest of Ewell's line. As the Federals advanced, they would eventually form their line with the right established at the cemetery in front of you, then advance over the same fields.

Confederate Right—Goods Mill

> *Turn right onto Battlefield Road and drive 1.3 miles. As you drive, the area to your right is where the Confederates had set up the left of their line and where most of the fighting near the end of the day took place (it is all on private land now). You*

will then continue on Port Republic Road another 0.5 mile until you reach Charlie Town Road, then turn right. Follow Charlie Town Road for 0.4 mile (making sure to bear right at the 0.1 mark), then turn left onto Goods Mill Road (VA 708). Drive for 0.9 mile and keep your eyes out for a pull-off area to your left; there will be a Virginia Civil War Trails marker here. Park here (be careful not to leave any part of your car in the roadway), exit your vehicle, and enjoy the beautiful scenery as you walk the short interpretive trail.

At 10:00 AM, Ewell's line was set, posted on a ridge facing north. It was a good defensive position; directly in front of the line was Mill Creek, creating a steep ravine that would slow down any attacker. The ground in front of them was open, and both flanks of the line were anchored in heavy woods. On a knoll in the center of the ridge were four batteries of artillery, 16 guns. The right side of the line, General Isaac Trimble's brigade, was set a half mile ahead of the line out of necessity; the woods were simply too thick to maintain ranks. Because of this, General Arnold Elzey gave him two of his brigades, the 13th and 25th Virginia under Colonel James Walker, to extend east of the woods. By day's end, they would prove critical.

Fremont arrived at approximately 10:30 and formed a line directly opposite Ewell's. The battle began with an artillery duel that lasted through most of the battle. Satisfied that his line was well set, Fremont headed for the rear; apparently, he did not see a need to observe the fighting.

After the Union line was formed, attacks began across the fields, but were piecemeal and disorganized (which tends to happen when there is no one in command present). During this time, Trimble took advantage of an opportunity. In front of him was a low wooden fence, and he sent his three brigades—one of which was the 15th Alabama that had already seen action at Union Church—crawling toward it so as not to be seen by the enemy. There they waited, until at noon, the 8th New York Infantry began advancing right toward them, through the open fields to your right as you walk the trail. The Confederates waited until the New Yorkers were within only 40 yards of the fence, then rose as one and fired. The volley was devastating, and the survivors immediately ran back, having no cover in the open fields.

Trimble immediately saw a prize in the field beyond: a Union battery, only a half mile distant. He sent part of the 15th Alabama to go get them, but their attack was repulsed. At about the same time, the two Virginia regiments, which had moved around the woods on Goods Mill Road, appeared on the Union left. By the end of the day, this side of the Union line was pushed back more than a mile.

The rolling landscape you see in front of you was the New Yorkers' final position before retreating. Walker's two brigades passed over the ground where you now stand to get on the Federal left. If you continue to walk the trail all the way around, you will

The rolling fields on the Confederate right at the Cross Keys battlefield.

be walking along the area where Trimble advanced his brigade (although the actual area of the wooden fence and the advance is beyond the trees along the trail).

On the other side of the line, little was accomplished until midafternoon when Milroy decided to advance against the Confederate left. Although he was able to make some progress over the rest of the afternoon, it came at a heavy price. Hearing of the advance from a distance, Fremont ordered Milroy to disengage and return to his original position on the line.

The firing stopped shortly after 6:00 PM. Milroy, on the Union right, went to the rear to find Fremont, and when he did, begged for a chance to renew his assault. Fremont was about to do so when he received a dispatch from Shields inferring that he had captured the bridge at Port Republic. With this new information, Fremont decided to give his men, who had primarily been marching and fighting for almost two weeks, a rest. He would renew his assault in the morning.

On the other side of the line, the Confederate right, it was Trimble who begged to continue the fight. He asked Ewell at twilight, then again after dark, and even went to Jackson himself, but his request was refused each time. Ewell's Confederates had accomplished their mission: Hold Fremont where he was and make him think twice about advancing farther. There would be fighting the next day, but it would not be here. Overnight, Ewell's men slipped out of their lines, undetected, and headed for Port Republic.

PORT REPUBLIC

Kemper House

> *Carefully pull out of the parking area and turn right (south) onto Goods Mill Road. Drive 0.9 mile on Goods Mill Road to Charlie Town Road, then turn right and follow Charlie Town Road for 0.4 mile. At the intersection with the Port Republic Road, turn left and drive 3.2 miles to the town of Port Republic. On your left will be the Kemper House; pull into the small parking area here.*

Shields's mission of catching Jackson at New Market had not exactly gone as planned. Shields had left Front Royal on June 1 and advanced south up Luray Valley using the Luray Road, as it was the only major road in the narrow valley. The next day, he found both the White House and the Columbia Bridges burned, and knew that the Red Bridge upstream was also gone. This was a major problem for Shields. The only way he could possibly get through the Luray Gap and on to New Market was to cross the South Fork of the Shenandoah River, but as he advanced, he found that he had no options. Deciding to march past Luray, on June 4 he reached Conrad's Store and found that bridge destroyed as well. The next bridge to the south was at Port Republic.

On June 8, before Fremont and Ewell began their fight on the other side of the river, a small force of Union cavalry and artillery quietly approached Port Republic. At the town, two branches of the South Fork converge. There was a bridge over the north branch, while Middle Ford allowed a crossing of the south branch in the town itself. Unwisely, before the Federal cavalry could surprise Jackson's Confederates in and around the town, their artillery sounded, alerting everyone to their presence. The cavalry attempted to burn the bridge but was unsuccessful, and they were eventually driven off. As they headed back north, they met Erastus Tyler of Shields's division, and the entire division went into camp not far north of Port Republic.

In the Confederate camp, Jackson's entire staff assumed that after Ewell had held off Fremont, Jackson was ready to make his escape from the Valley. He also could have resumed the fight against Fremont. But Jackson, who was not one to share his plans with anybody, including his staff or generals, had other ideas. He would fight Shields. He had several reasons for doing this. Shields was closer to his army than Fremont was, and his Union force was smaller. The Confederate position at Port Republic was closer to their supply base, and in case of disaster, a retreat through Brown's Gap would be simple. Fremont also had an easy escape route, while Shields's division, which had fought terrible road conditions all the way through the narrow Luray Valley, did not. Jackson ordered the bridge over the North Fork prepared for firing, while a temporary bridge was built over the south branch to ease movement.

The Kemper House, where Turner Ashby's body was brought after his death, in the town of Port Republic.

The small bridge you just crossed over the North Fork is in the same location as the 1862 bridge. The Kemper House where you are parked is home to the Port Republic Museum. It is usually open for a few hours on Sunday and by appointment; it contains exhibits on the battle, as well as a guide for a walking tour of the town. The Kemper House is also sometimes referred to as the Turner Ashby House; it was here that Ashby's body was taken after he was killed.

The Coaling

> *From the Kemper House, turn left onto Port Republic Road and drive 1.2 miles. Turn left onto US 340 North and drive 2.1 miles to Ore Bank Road.*
> *As you drive along US 340, you are heading down the same road and in the same direction as the Confederate advance. To your left, the fields are still open; to your right, the woods are still thick, just as they were at the time of the battle.*
> *On your right at the intersection, you will see a large hill. Park in the gravel area across the street and climb the hill. It is a steep but short climb, and there are*

benches along the way to allow you to take your time. The view of the battlefield from the top will help you understand why this position was so important.

Shields marched his troops overnight in order to be in a position to attack the next morning. At 4:00 AM, Union pickets from Shields's division, who were watching the north bridge, reported that they had seen no one cross. The reason for this was simple: Jackson already had his entire command, except for Ewell's division, across the north branch by that time. At 5, with only part of the army across the temporary south bridge, General Charles Winder was already advancing the Stonewall Brigade a mile down the Luray Road. Under the cover of the morning fog, Winder put two divisions, the 2nd and 4th Virginia, in the thick woods to the right of the road to advance on a commanding hilltop known as The Coaling. The Coaling was already in Union possession, and seven guns loomed over the field. In the open fields left of the road, Winder placed the 5th and 27th Virginia.

You are now standing atop The Coaling, the focal point of the Battle of Port Republic. You can see quite a distance from the top, and looking to your left down the highway, have an only slightly obscured view of the battlefield. It is obvious why the Union chose this position for their artillery; at this elevation, their guns could command any part of the field. This hill has been preserved by the Civil War Trust, and is really the only piece of the battlefield from which to study it; it also happens to be the best.

The fog lifted by 6:00 AM, and artillery from both armies began to pepper the field. The Confederates pushed through the woods toward The Coaling and came within 100 yards, but found that the woods were crawling with Federal troops. Their lines were soon shattered with volleys of grapeshot and the men fled toward the rear. On the left, while the Confederates were advancing, it was a very slow push, and every inch of ground cost them heavily.

As Taylor's brigade crossed the south branch, they were almost immediately ordered into the fight. While the 7th Louisiana went to the left, the rest of Taylor's men went to the far right to support the attack against The Coaling.

By 8:30 AM, the fight was not going well for the Confederates. The infantry could not advance with any regularity, and the Federal artillery atop The Coaling provided a devastating fire. Winder launched a charge against the Union right about this time, but it was repulsed with heavy losses. At 9:30, the Confederates, low on ammunition, began to pull back. However, by this time, Ewell's division arrived on the field. Still weary from the previous day's fight against Fremont, Ewell went to the right and hit the Union left flank. While his men took a lot of casualties, they also took a great amount of pressure off Winder's advance on the Confederate left.

Near 10, with Ewell now over the bridge, Jackson ordered it burned, and being well-prepared, it went up quickly. Taylor's full force was now on the field, and he ordered a massive charge against The Coaling, actually taking two Federal batteries. Two Ohio regiments were immediately sent from the Union right to the left to counter Taylor's action, and the fighting became hand-to-hand. At some point, someone in the Louisiana brigade began to shout for the Federal horses to be killed so that they could not pull the guns away. The Confederates did this to great effect, but they were eventually pushed back. Taylor soon received reinforcements from Ewell's division, and he resumed the charge. Finally, the Union line at The Coaling broke. The Rebels, now possessing the hill, turned the Federal guns toward Winder's part of the line, hitting the Federals with their own artillery from the rear. Winder pressed again, and soon all of Shields's Union troops were routed and heading for the rear.

Around the time the fighting at Port Republic was at its heaviest, Fremont, after some searching, finally realized that there were no Confederates in front of him and that Ewell had given him the slip. He marched his army toward Port Republic, reaching the town at noon, only to find the bridge burned. The battle was mostly over at this point, but he still ordered artillery set up on the bluffs overlooking the South

A view from the top of The Coaling.

Fork. It was a token gesture. There was nothing he could do from the wrong side of the river.

Had Fremont's and Shields's forces been able to combine, they almost certainly would have spelled Jackson's doom. Instead, Jackson's forethought in burning the bridges over the South Fork of the Shenandoah prevented them from doing so. Instead of fighting one large force, he was able to fight and defeat two smaller Union commands in two days. Shields was in retreat. Fremont was standing helpless across the river. And Jackson, his work done, finally took his army to Brown's Gap in the Blue Ridge Mountains, which he would leave on June 18 to join the new commander of the Confederate Army of Northern Virginia, Robert E. Lee, in the defense of the capital at Richmond.

CHAPTER 3

The Peninsula Campaign and the Seven Days Battles

UPON TAKING COMMAND in August 1861, General George B. McClellan began to whip the Union forces around Washington into shape. He inherited an army that was inexperienced, undisciplined, and completely demoralized after its rout at Manassas. McClellan, named general-in-chief over all Union armies, immediately took hold of his new command and began to drill, drill, and drill again. Within months, his Army of the Potomac—the largest army ever assembled on the continent—was a massive, well-oiled fighting machine whose soldiers would do anything for their beloved commander. To be sure, this was partly due to the fact that he had lifted the morale of his troops to new heights. Another contributing factor may have been that he never actually made them fight any battles.

By March 1862, Abraham Lincoln and others in Washington also began to notice that the juggernaut being compared to Napoleon's Grande Armée in the press had not gone anywhere. It certainly wasn't going to Richmond, which was where most thought it should go as quickly as possible to bring the war to an end. Most also thought that the best way to get to Richmond was by a direct march due south.

McClellan thought otherwise. For months, he had been working on a plan to invade Richmond from the east, landing his army by sea near West Point and Urbanna, Virginia, and then marching west to the Confederate capital. In McClellan's plan, one great battle at the outskirts of Richmond, rather than a long campaign, was to decide the war once and for all.

Seven Pines National Cemetery, one of the few reminders of the battle here.

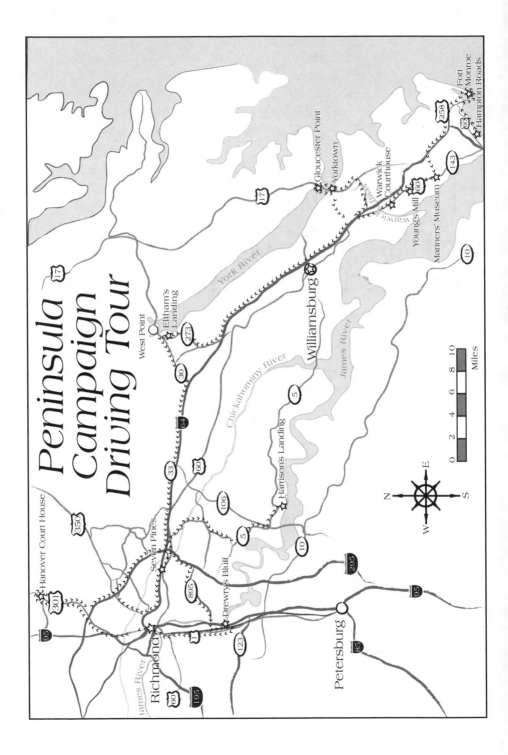

Peninsula Campaign Driving Tour

Tired of indecision, Lincoln finally cornered McClellan in the White House on March 7, 1862, and demanded that he take action. McClellan pled his case for his Urbanna Plan, and although Lincoln didn't like it, he decided that it was better than no plan at all. The decision would be made by McClellan's generals; if they agreed with McClellan, Lincoln would follow their lead. A council of war was held that afternoon, with the 12 generals present voting 8–4 to approve the plan, not without some political pressure from a few of McClellan's appointees. The generals explained their vote to a stunned Lincoln, who reluctantly gave the go-ahead under the condition that Washington remain well-defended from any possible Confederate advance.

Within the next week, significant events would alter the plan. The appearance of the Confederate ironclad CSS *Virginia* (formerly the USS *Merrimac*) caught everyone off guard. This was followed by the discovery that there were no longer any Confederates in Manassas; tens of thousands of Rebel troops had moved south undetected. Ultimately, the Urbanna Plan was scrapped and McClellan decided on a new base of operations. He would instead land his army at Union-occupied Fort Monroe, on the tip of the peninsula formed by the York and James Rivers. On March 17, the first ships carrying troops and supplies left Washington, and McClellan's long-awaited drive on Richmond, henceforth known as the Peninsula Campaign, had finally begun.

BEFORE YOU GO

» PLANNING YOUR TRIP

There's really only one way to take this tour, and that's to follow the Union army's path up the peninsula. The tour begins at the very tip of the peninsula, Hampton Roads. Although there will be a little winding here and there, you will head straight northwest to the Confederate capital at Richmond, then end your tour on the outskirts of the city. Don't even think about doing the tour backward, retreating down the peninsula. Not even McClellan did that.

With only a few exceptions, the majority of the battlefields you will come across are not completely intact. However, don't let that keep you from stopping at the sites that are left. Al-

> **THE PENINSULA CAMPAIGN**
>
> **Number of sites:** 26
>
> **Total miles:** 262
>
> **Estimated time:** 3–4 days
>
> **Must-sees:** Richmond National Battlefield, Museum and White House of the Confederacy, The Mariners' Museum
>
> **Close seconds:** Fort Monroe, Williamsburg

though they are scattered and often small, the remaining pieces of the Peninsula Campaign are many, and what has been preserved is usually in excellent condition. Following the path of these small sites is the best way to understand the story of this campaign.

There is another great bonus to touring the Peninsula Campaign. With only a few exceptions, almost all of the sites on this tour are public areas. This means that you generally aren't restricted to operating hours—as long as the sun is up, you can visit anytime you like. You can see things at your own pace and not have to worry about skipping sites or rushing to see something before it closes. (The few sites that do have operating hours, though, are all exceptional, so you might want to plan ahead just a little bit.)

» RECOMMENDATIONS

This small piece of the U.S. is full of history. Besides the great events of the Civil War, the first successful English settlement on the continent, Jamestown, is here, only a few miles from Yorktown, the battlefield that clinched our separation from the mother country. There are also numerous historic homes and estates of presidents and statesmen, and the former Virginia capital of Williamsburg is a remarkable place to visit. If you are an American history buff, prepare to be sidetracked from time to time.

Once you get close to Richmond, you will have virtually unlimited options for food and lodging. Though a bit less crowded on the peninsula, you shouldn't have any problems finding what you need between Hampton, Newport, and Williamsburg.

If you have family in tow and they need a break from our country's fascinating history (although they're guaranteed to be wowed at the nearby Hampton Roads Naval Museum), you can always head down to Virginia Beach. Only 40 miles southeast of Hampton, the city provides great beaches and a number of attractions. If you are considering this option and you plan on going during the summer months, expect some crowds and make reservations.

THE CAMPAIGN TOUR

HAMPTON ROADS AND FORT MONROE

Hampton Roads

> *Your tour begins at Christopher Newport Park, a public park along the water in Newport News. Proceed to the intersection of West Avenue and 26th Street, then turn west on 26th Street. The park will be on your right. Note that getting to the intersection can be a bit tricky—one wrong turn and you may find yourself on an on-ramp for one of the many highways in the area, so drive slowly and make sure you don't miss a turn.*

When the Civil War broke out, almost all of the U.S. military's forts, bases, armories, and other properties in the seceding states were seized by those states and eventually handed to the Confederacy. One of the few exceptions was Fort Monroe. The largest of many fortresses built following the War of 1812, Fort Monroe provided important advantages for the Union. For one, its size dominated the waters known as Hampton Roads, not only the naval avenue to the capital at Richmond but also home to the Gosport Navy Yard in Norfolk, which was under Confederate control. Any ships built at Gosport would have to pass the numerous and massive guns of Fort Monroe to reach open water. Second, possession of the fort gave the Union a toehold in Virginia. It would become the starting point of military operations that would eventually reach as far south as Georgia, as well as a base for the naval blockade of the Confederate coast. While it is some distance from Richmond, Fort Monroe provided an extremely safe and secure point of entry into Virginia.

However, the day after McClellan's Urbanna Plan was approved, even the safety that Fort Monroe could provide was in doubt. On the afternoon of March 8, 1862, the Union gunboats *Congress, Cumberland,* and *Minnesota* were anchored in Hampton Roads when a very strange object came steaming from the direction of the nearby Elizabeth River. It was the CSS *Virginia,* an ironclad warship constructed from what was left of the USS *Merrimack* after the Federals evacuated and torched Gosport Navy Yard. Her approach was completely unplanned; she was on her maiden voyage, and her captain simply decided to try taking a run at the Union ships.

The affair was completely lopsided. With cannonballs bouncing off her sturdy sides, the *Virginia* rammed the *Cumberland,* which began to sink instantly (although

MERRIMACK OR VIRGINIA?

Both. The ship was commissioned the USS *Merrimack* (and not Merrimac, as it is often misspelled) in 1856. When the Federals evacuated Gosport Navy Yard, they tried to burn everything they could, but didn't do a very good job of it. What was left of the *Merrimack* was sound, so the Confederates turned her into an ironclad and rechristened her the CSS *Virginia.* Still, on both the Union and Confederates sides, she was still widely known and referred to as the *Merrimack.*

The famous Battle of the Ironclads occurred at this area of Hampton Roads on March 9, 1862.

she was able to get off a few more volleys before disappearing under the waves). The *Virginia* next turned toward the *Congress,* which had run aground, and quickly forced the ship to surrender after tearing her to pieces. Once the crew was taken off, the *Congress* was set afire and burned well into the night. The *Virginia* then began to make a run at the *Minnesota,* which had also run aground, but because the *Virginia* had a deep draft and the tide had gone out, the Confederates decided to finish the job the next morning.

The view of the water from Christopher Newport Park overlooks the area of Hampton Roads where the fighting of March 8 took place. Just offshore, under the waves in front of you, lies the USS *Cumberland.* To your left is where the USS *Congress,* run aground, burned until the flames hit her powder magazine and blew her to bits.

❯ *From the park, return to West Avenue and turn right, driving 0.1 mile to Martin Luther King Jr. Way (23rd Street). Turn left here; after 0.2 mile, keep left at the fork in the road toward Roanoke Avenue, then keep following Martin Luther King Jr. Way (now 25th Street) for another 1.4 miles to Roanoke Avenue. Turn right on Roanoke Avenue and drive for 0.5 mile to 16th Street (VA 167). Turn left and drive 0.5 mile on 16th Street. After crossing a small bridge, you will see a small park with a parking lot and a fishing pier on your right. Pull into the parking lot.*

The next morning came too late for the Confederate Navy. Arriving on the scene just in time was the USS *Monitor,* the Union's first ironclad warship, having left New

York only three days before. The *Monitor* had an extremely shallow draft, and she sat aside the *Minnesota* to protect her. As the *Virginia* steamed forward, the *Monitor* went to meet her, and the ironclads dueled for hours, eventually fighting to a draw. Neither ship had done significant damage to the other, but they had made history as the first ironclad warships to meet in battle.

Even though the *Virginia* had been fought off, she survived, and her mere presence caused great concern among the Union high command. Could the *Virginia* pass Fort Monroe and reach open water? How could McClellan land his army at Urbanna with virtually no protection if the ironclad appeared? Although assurances from the U.S. Navy over the next few days eased anxieties a bit, concern in Washington over this new element of warfare—even with the presence of the *Monitor*—was high.

From this park, you can see where the USS *Monitor* and the CSS *Virginia* met at Hampton Roads, the famous Battle of the Ironclads. The Virginia Civil War Trails sign here will help orient your view. Across Hampton Roads, the U.S. Navy's legacy lives on at the Norfolk Naval Base, which you can also see clearly from the park.

Fort Monroe

> *From the parking lot, turn right and follow VA 167 for 4.3 miles, continuing with 167 as it veers left and changes from Chesapeake Avenue to LaSalle Avenue. Turn right at West Pembroke Avenue and drive for 2.1 miles to Mercury Boulevard. Turn right onto East Mercury Boulevard and drive 1.7 miles, bearing left onto In-galls Boulevard and entering Fort Monroe.*

> *Through 2011, Fort Monroe will remain an active military installation, so be sure to drive with caution in and around the fort, and pay close attention to the rules and regulations. The original fortress itself, within the interior of the base, is easily accessible; simply pull up to the gate and tell the guard you would like to visit the fort and the museum. The guard will give you a day pass and a map to the museum so you can tour the grounds at your leisure (within reason). Proceed first to the Casemate Museum. A word of caution: As you drive, keep an eye out for one-way streets—there are many, and they are small and well traveled.*

On the same day the CSS *Virginia* appeared at Hampton Roads, another piece of the Confederate military began to disappear. The Confederates had occupied Manassas Junction since the battle at Bull Run, and had stayed there unchallenged. They knew, however, that the Union army would be coming as soon as the spring weather allowed. So on March 8 and 9, the entire Confederate force in and around Manassas quietly began to move south.

The withdrawal was skillfully executed—and well timed. On March 10, with much pomp and circumstance, McClellan led his troops to Manassas, expecting to meet at

The Casemate Museum tells the rich history of Fort Monroe.

least some resistance. The only thing the Federals found was that they had been held at bay with "Quaker guns"—logs, painted black, mounted on wheels to look like cannons.

McClellan's march, with the press invited to watch, was an extreme embarrassment. Lincoln summoned McClellan to the White House the next day; McClellan refused his commander-in-chief, saying he was too busy in the field. He probably regretted that decision when he read in the newspaper on March 12 that he had been relieved as general-in-chief. The president explained to McClellan that he needed to concentrate on Richmond and not worry about the other armies across the country. But the fact that the Confederate army had slipped away undetected right under McClellan's nose probably had something to do with the decision.

McClellan could come to only one conclusion: that the movement of his army had been leaked by spies. If this were true, those same spies must know of his Urbanna Plan. He immediately called another council of war. The landing at Urbanna was out; not only did the Confederates know the plan, but the presence of the *Virginia* made such a move too risky. It would have to occur at a much safer location, and the safest place on the coast was under the mighty guns of Fort Monroe.

As you drive to the museum and pass through the walls of the fortress, you can't help but notice the sheer mass of its earth and stone construction. Once inside, however, you may be surprised at just how spacious it is. This was the largest fortress in the country, and there is quite a community inside.

The star attraction of the Casemate Museum is the cell of Confederate president Jefferson Davis, imprisoned here after the war. However, you will find that the museum contains the entire fascinating history of the fort, from before its construction through its use today. A large part of the exhibit, of course, includes its Civil War history.

As you leave the museum, pick up the brochure for the walking tour of Fort Monroe. Just across the street from the museum you'll find the former home of engineer Robert E. Lee, stationed here early in his career during the fort's construction. Walking to your right will take you to the Flagstaff Bastion. Climbing the pathway to the top will reward you with a wonderful view not only of Hampton Roads in front of you, but also the rest of the fort behind you. When you climb back down, you may either continue the excellent walking tour or drive out of the fort. When you leave, however, be sure to drive back to the outside of the fortress along Fenwick Drive. From here, you will get a sense of the fort's impregnability, with its huge walls and deep moat.

From March 17 through early April, ships, barges, and converted canal boats brought troops and supplies to the shores around Fort Monroe. Over three weeks, the tally came to 121,500 men, 14,592 animals, 1,224 wagons, and 44 batteries of artillery. The force being assembled to take Richmond would come together all around where you stand, filling the huge fortress to capacity and spilling onto the shorelines.

The exterior of Fort Monroe.

THE MARINERS' MUSEUM

❯ *From Fort Monroe, bear left onto Mellen Street and drive 0.7 mile to Mallory Street. Turn left on Mallory Street, then drive just 0.2 mile before you merge right onto I-64 West toward Williamsburg/Richmond. Continue 9.8 miles on I-64 until you reach Exit 258A for US 17/J. Clyde Morris Boulevard. Follow J. Clyde Morris Boulevard for 3.1 miles. By this time, you will have entered The Mariners' Museum Park. Turn left on Museum Drive and drive 0.3 mile to the parking lot for the museum.*

The Mariners' Museum is not on the ground of any significant battlefield (although some skirmishing did take place on and around the museum park's land). Still, this is a stop that can not be missed. While the mission of the museum is to cover all things maritime (which it does unbelievably well), it is also the home of the USS *Monitor* center. If you ever wanted to see, touch, and walk through history for yourself, this is the place to do it.

The *Monitor* sank on December 31, 1862, off Cape Hatteras, North Carolina. The ship was finally rediscovered in 1973 and was declared America's first National Marine Sanctuary. Since that time, numerous research expeditions, all carefully restricted,

A full-size replica of the USS Monitor *at The Mariners' Museum in Newport News, Virginia.*

have been conducted at the site. The crowning moment, certainly, was in 2002, when the distinctive gun turret of the *Monitor,* along with her twin Dahlgren guns and carriages, was raised from the ocean floor.

Touring the museum takes some time, only partly because of its vast collection. It is mostly because the experience has been so well laid out and presented that it seems every moment is more stunning than the next. You see the *Monitor's* anchor. Then you see her lantern, the last visible piece before she disappeared beneath the waves. You move on to a walk-through reproduction of the gun turret, and then step out onto the deck of a full-size reconstruction of the entire ship. After walking up, down, and around the ship, you come back inside the museum to actually touch a piece of the iron plating that made her so famous and see her propeller, fully restored and on display. Finally, for the grand finale, you walk by the USS *Monitor* Center's research lab, where you can view scientists working on the original turret, guns, and steam engine. The exhibits are interactive, interesting, and thorough, and it is the kind of museum that children love as well.

YOUNG'S MILL

❯ *Leave The Mariners' Museum parking lot and return to the main entrance, driving 0.4 mile to Warwick Boulevard (US 60). Turn left on Warwick Boulevard. You are now driving along the old Warwick Road, one of the Union army's main avenues up the peninsula. Drive 3.5 miles on Warwick Boulevard, after which you will see a small white building on your left and across the median; this is Young's Mill. Take the next safe U-turn (about 0.2 mile), then return to Young's Mill at the intersection of Warwick Boulevard and Old Grist Mill Lane. Pull into the parking lot.*

Twelve miles north of Fort Monroe, the Confederate Army of the Peninsula was waiting. In fact, they'd been waiting since winter. Commanded by Major General "Prince" John Magruder, the 10,000-man army had been entrenching and building fortifications, trying to find any way to prevent a Federal force from advancing up the peninsula. Their work, seemingly meaningless at the time, paid off.

Magruder had created three lines of defense on the peninsula. The first of these was more or less a screen to keep an eye on the Federals and prevent them from seeing what was going on farther north. The right flank of this line was centered where you are now standing, at Young's Mill, and scattered eastward to the York River. It was not a very strong line, but it was not intended to be. Magruder's second line, stretching from Yorktown to Mulberry Island, was heavily fortified, as was his third line, a fallback line at Williamsburg.

On April 1 (April Fools' Day, as it so happened), McClellan sent his arrangements for the defense of Washington to the War Department, then immediately boarded a

Confederate forces put up little resistance at Young's Mill.

ship to Fort Monroe. According to his calculations, McClellan had left 55,500 men to defend Washington, enough to satisfy the president's concerns. He arrived at Fort Monroe the next day, and after meeting with Flag Officer Louis M. Goldsborough on the USS *Minnesota* to discuss the naval situation, he immediately began preparations for the army to move. Only two days later, on April 4, the Union army began to move north toward Magruder's first defensive line.

Here at Young's Mill, the Army of the Potomac's IV Corps, commanded by General Erasmus Keyes, met some resistance as it advanced up the Warwick Road and over the dam that formed the mill's pond. The Confederates didn't put up much of a fight, quickly abandoning their earthworks and falling back to Magruder's second line. If you walk across the road from the mill and look through the trees, you can still see some remnants of the Confederate fortifications that Keyes encountered.

As the Federals kept marching, Lee, now serving as military adviser to Davis, ordered Joseph E. Johnston to take his army, which had withdrawn from Manassas, to the peninsula as quickly as possible. Although Magruder had received some reinforcements, bringing his army to 15,000 men, it seemed that they would be no match for what was approaching.

WARWICK COURTHOUSE

❯ *From Young's Mill, turn right onto Warwick Boulevard, then make the first safe U-turn so that you are once again heading north. Drive 2.3 miles on Warwick Boulevard to Denbigh Boulevard. Turn left onto Denbigh Boulevard and drive 0.2 mile to Old Courthouse Way. Drive another 0.2 mile on Old Courthouse Way; you will see the courthouse, a small brick building, on your left. Pull into the parking lot behind the building.*

When Keyes's IV Corps reached Warwick Courthouse, it was not somewhere they intended to stay for very long. On April 5, however, Keyes ran into Confederate resistance up the road at Lee's Mill. It was not the same virtually insignificant resistance that he had brushed aside at Young's Mill the day before; this was different. Keyes set his headquarters here at Warwick Courthouse, and would remain for almost a month.

One of the most significant happenings here at the courthouse was the use of an innovative way of observing the enemy. The army had employed an air balloon corps, and a base for aerial observation was centered here. Two balloons, the *Intrepid* and the *Constellation,* were used to get a bird's-eye view of the Confederate defenses, with the first flight taking place on April 6. Although the observers on the *Intrepid* couldn't see much that day (or, for that matter, during most of the campaign), within a short time both sides were using some form of aerial reconnaissance.

LEE'S MILL

❯ *From Warwick Court House, return to Old Courthouse Road, turning left and driving 0.2 mile to Warwick Boulevard. Turn left onto Warwick Boulevard and drive 2.8 miles to Lee's Mill Drive. Drive 0.2 mile and turn left on Rivers Ridge Circle, then drive another 0.1 mile. Pull into the small parking area on your left.*

While making his plans for the campaign, McClellan assumed that the Confederates would hold a strong position at Yorktown, and he was right. What he did not anticipate was that Yorktown would only be part of a very strong line stretching across the entire peninsula and across the York River. It was here at Lee's Mill on April 5 that the Federals first discovered elements of the Confederate defenses—Magruder's second line, also known as the Yorktown line.

The army started the day's march in a heavy rain. It had been reported that the roads on the peninsula were very good, but that quickly proved to be incorrect. The Federals were slowed to a crawl at every location by deep mud, and conditions only became worse as more troops and wagons went over the roads.

Keyes's IV Corps, forming the Union left as it advanced, was to flank the Confederate position at Yorktown, while General Samuel Heintzelman's III Corps on the right approached it directly. Advancing along the Warwick Road, Keyes soon found the Confederates where they were not supposed to be—in front of him and behind heavy earthworks. After some skirmishing and observation of the Confederate position, Keyes stopped his advance and relayed the information back to McClellan. His estimate of the Confederates in front of him was 2,000 to 3,000 men, and he added that he did not believe the fortifications could be taken "without an enormous waste of life."

As you walk around the earthworks here at Lee's Mill, you can understand Keyes's reluctance to attack. They are indeed heavy, and as you proceed along the trail to the wetlands around the river, you can imagine what the Union force would have to overcome—crossing the open, swampy ground on one side of the trail and then storming the high embankment on the other, all while under artillery and musketry fire. For those who looked at the position you are now in from the other side of the swamp, it was an easy conclusion to reach.

SKIFFES CREEK

❭ *From the parking lot at Lee's Mill, turn right and head 0.2 mile back on Rivers Ridge Circle, then turn right on Lee's Mill Drive and drive 0.1 mile to Warwick Boulevard. Turn left on Warwick Boulevard and drive 1 mile until reaching Enterprise Drive. Turn left on Enterprise Drive and drive 0.4 mile to the Skiffes Creek Historic Park on your left. Pull in and walk the short trail around the redoubt.*

Here at Skiffes Creek, you are near the extreme right of the Confederate Yorktown line. Though strong, these redoubts, placed here on Mulberry Island to prevent a flanking movement, could not receive the support that those in the center did. This had been an early worry for Magruder, but it became a nonissue. With the CSS *Virginia* at anchor nearby in the James River, this side of the line would be well protected.

Confederate earthworks such as these were not the only physical obstruction that McClellan would run into on April 5. In addition to fortifications, poor roads, and unexpected Confederates, he also found the Warwick River. The river did not even appear correctly on most maps of the peninsula, as it was a seemingly insignificant obstacle. Magruder, though, saw an opportunity. After building his line behind the Warwick, he constructed three dams in addition to several existing ones, flooding the river and creating an almost impassable obstacle to his front.

Perhaps most significantly, Magruder, long known in the army for his antics, pulled off one of the most effective deceptions of the entire war. Magruder took his 15,000 soldiers and, by marching them up and down the line, having them make a lot of noise, and shifting their positions, made them look several times their actual size. It was a desperate ruse, but it worked extremely well.

As if these were not enough, McClellan also received distressing news from Washington. Secretary of War Edwin M. Stanton, after receiving McClellan's report of the troops defending Washington, had his staff do some accounting. They soon discovered why McClellan had boarded the boat to Fort Monroe before the dispatch was received by the War Department. Following Stonewall Jackson's attack at Kernstown in the Shenandoah Valley on March 23, McClellan considered that part of the army— situated more than 60 miles west of Washington—in his calculations, and other parts of the defenses were counted twice or more. Stanton's more careful estimate was significantly less than McClellan's; in fact, it was precisely 26,671, less than half. A furious Lincoln, whose orders had been directly disobeyed, held Irvin McDowell's I Corps in Fredericksburg, keeping them near Washington in case they were needed.

With both the Confederates and, in McClellan's mind, the U.S. government against him—he considered Lincoln's decision a "fatal error" that imperiled his entire campaign—McClellan formed a new plan. One of his undeniable strengths as a commander was in siege warfare. He ordered the roads repaired and his siege guns brought up to the front. He would not fight his way through the lines. He would pound the enemy at Yorktown into submission, just as George Washington had done 81 years before.

DAM NO. 1

> *From Skiffes Creek Park, turn right onto Enterprise Drive and drive 0.4 mile back to Warwick Boulevard. Turn right on Warwick Boulevard (heading south this time) and drive 0.7 mile to the exit onto VA 105 East/Fort Eustis Boulevard. Take the exit and drive 1.3 miles to Jefferson Avenue. Turn left on Jefferson Avenue and drive 0.3 mile to Newport News Park and Constitution Avenue. Turn right on Constitution Avenue and follow it for 1 mile into the park. On your left will be a picnic area and a walkway across the water. Park here.*

On April 6, Johnston's army began arriving in Richmond and immediately began to move to Magruder's line by ferry and railroad. By April 11, more than 34,000 Confederate troops had been added to the defenses. Magruder's army, as well as that of General Benjamin Huger at Norfolk, would now be rolled into Johnston's command, forming the new Army of Northern Virginia. As they hurried men to the front, a bewildered Johnston wondered why the attack had not come yet.

By now, there were two reasons why the Federals had not attacked. One, of course, was that McClellan had decided on siege tactics rather than a direct offensive. The other was a trait that was not exclusive to McClellan, but one that would forever be associated with him. Taking estimates of the enemy's size from Rebel prisoners as gospel, McClellan now believed that at least 100,000 Confederates were on the other side of the Yorktown line. Lincoln's reply to this estimate, on April 7, was clear—"you must act"—but McClellan, who always resented outside meddling with his strategies, continued the siege. He may have had fewer men (which he didn't; he actually outnumbered the enemy by almost 10-to-1 on April 5), but he knew that his heavy artillery, particularly his siege guns, dwarfed the Confederates' ability to defend against them.

During the siege, only one significant offensive action took place, and it was right here at the Dam No. 1 site. This dam was one of the three that Magruder had built to flood the Warwick River. On April 16, after a prolonged artillery bombardment, 200 Union soldiers from Brigadier General William "Baldy" Smith's division splashed across the wide, flooded plain toward the Confederate position. Although they were able to reach the first part of the Confederate line, they were soon forced back across the water, as they had not been supported by any other troops. Later in the afternoon, another attempt was made with similar results.

Take a look at the monuments here (the men of the Third Vermont took the brunt of the Confederate response), then walk out onto the walkway across the water. As you look across the river, the attack happened just to the left of your view.

GLOUCESTER POINT

❯ *From the Dam No. 1 parking lot, turn left onto Constitution Avenue and follow it for 1 mile (it will change names to Clubhouse Way halfway through) until you reach Fort Eustis Boulevard (VA 105). Turn left on Fort Eustis Boulevard and drive 2.4 miles, then turn left onto US 17, George Washington Memorial Highway. Stay to the left and follow US 17 for 5.2 miles, crossing the York River (you will have to pay a toll on the bridge). Almost immediately after coming off the bridge, turn left on Lafayette Heights Drive and drive 0.2 mile to River View Street. Turn left on River View, then take the next left on Battery Drive, and finally the next right onto Vernon Street. Park at Tyndall's Point Park on your right.*

In planning his campaign, McClellan had counted on support from the U.S. Navy. The peninsula was narrow enough that gunboats on both the James and York Rivers would be able to cover the army's advance. Unfortunately for the Federals, though, neither one of these approaches were readily available. On the James River, of course, the CSS *Virginia* still loomed large, and although she had attempted to pick a few fights over the weeks, the Union Navy was unwilling to engage.

North of the peninsula, as on land, the primary obstacle to accessing the York River was at Yorktown. At this small port, as well as across the river at Gloucester Point, the Confederates had amassed a fairly sizable amount of heavy guns, most salvaged from Gosport Navy Yard when they occupied it. They were older, generally, and not the most effective weapons, but the twin batteries along the river here made any

The view toward Yorktown across the York River from Gloucester Point

passage extremely hazardous. Although the ironclad USS *Galena* eventually did successfully run the gauntlet, the batteries remained in Confederate hands until the siege was lifted.

Here at Tyndall's Point Park, the remaining earthworks of the Gloucester Point batteries are in excellent condition, and the local historic society has done an exceptional job interpreting them. Although often overlooked because of Yorktown's fame, there is a good reason that these fortifications were continuously occupied for almost 200 years before the Confederates arrived. The stroll through the works is short, easy, and pleasant, so get out of the car and take it.

YORKTOWN

〉 *From Tyndall's Point Park, return to US 17 by following Vernon Street back to Battery Drive, then right on River View Street to Lafayette Heights Drive. Turn right onto Lafayette Heights Drive and drive 0.2 mile to US 17. Turn right on US 17 and drive 1.3 miles, going back across the bridge over the York River. Once you cross the river, turn right at Mathews Street, drive 0.1 mile, then turn right onto Water Street. You are now passing through historic Yorktown, which became a very busy port for the Union army during and after the Peninsula Campaign. Follow Water Street for 0.6 mile to Comte de Grasse Street, turning right, then take the next left at Main Street. Bear left onto Colonial Parkway and follow it for 0.2 mile to reach the Yorktown Victory Center.*

As the Federal siege drew on and on, the Confederate army took the opportunity to get stronger and stronger. More soldiers came down the peninsula to reinforce the lines, and at its height, 26 brigades—more than 56,000 men—were on the Yorktown line.

The Confederates strengthened and enlarged earthworks at Yorktown that were built by the Americans, French, and British during the Revolutionary War.

During both Magruder's initial construction of the line and its use during the Peninsula Campaign, the Confederates took advantage of what work had already been done for them. Much of both the British and American earthworks still existed from the 1781 siege that ended the Revolutionary War. These were strengthened, built upon, and joined to Magruder's line, creating a very strong position around the port of Yorktown and the left of the Confederate line.

Although the focus of Colonial National Historical Park is the Revolutionary War, there is an existing park driving tour of Civil War-related sites. In addition, the park does plan to add, as it is able, more emphasis on the Civil War history of the Yorktown defenses. When you enter the visitors center, simply ask for Civil War information in addition to the regular park tour, and you will be able to tell which parts of the defenses had significance during McClellan's siege. There is also Yorktown National Cemetery, created after the Civil War to accommodate many of the dead from the Peninsula Campaign.

WILLIAMSBURG

Redoubt No. 1

> *From Yorktown, take VA 238 West (Goosley Road) out of the park from its intersection with Cook Road. Drive 1.7 miles on Goosley Road, then turn left on Old*

Williamsburg Road and continue to follow VA 238 for 3.3 miles to Jefferson Avenue. Turn right on Jefferson Avenue and drive 0.8 mile to I-64 West. Take I-64 West for 4.7 miles to Exit 242A. Exit onto VA 199 West and drive 1.4 miles to the ramp for US 60. Turn left at the end of the ramp and drive 1.4 miles on US 60 West to Quarterpath Road. Turn left at Quarterpath Road and drive 0.8 mile. On your left will be Redoubt Park; pull into the parking area.

As the Union line inched toward the Confederates, Johnston knew he would soon have to abandon his position at Yorktown. He also knew that once in motion, the Confederates would have to fall back all the way to their defenses at Richmond. This long retreat would also mean that the Confederates would no longer be able to hold the Gosport Navy Yard.

Still baffled by McClellan's inaction but seeing signs that he would attack soon, Johnston warned Davis on April 27 that the Confederates would have to abandon the line. Two days later, he planned his withdrawal for the night of May 3. Alerting Huger's Confederates at Norfolk that they would have to evacuate, Johnston prepared his army of 56,600 and 36 batteries of artillery to retreat up the peninsula as quickly as possible.

Johnston couldn't have timed his movement better. McClellan had almost all of his pieces in place. His siege guns were at the front, his naval support was ready, and his infantry was eager to move after sitting in front of the Confederate defenses for almost a month. McClellan intended to begin his bombardment of the Confederate works on May 5.

On the morning of May 4, Heintzelman, commander of the Union III Corps that was to lead the ground assault on the Confederate works, went up in the *Intrepid* to get an aerial view of the defenses. He found the works completely empty. Probing carefully into the Confed-

erate fortifications, it was soon confirmed that Johnston had again slipped away undetected, leaving only empty tents and his old, scavenged naval artillery at Yorktown and Gloucester Point. By that afternoon, most of the Rebel army had passed Williamsburg, slowed only by rain and occasional cavalry clashes in the rear.

The first of 14 redoubts that form the Williamsburg Line.

Not about to let him

get away again, McClellan called for a pursuit. By the morning of May 5, the Federals were pressing enough that a Confederate rear guard was formed at Magruder's original fallback defense, the Williamsburg line.

You are now looking up close at the first of 14 redoubts, numbered southeast to northeast, that formed the 3-mile-long Williamsburg Line. Though unfinished and not as strong as the line at Yorktown, this line was still formidable, and pieces of it have survived through the years. Although it was unoccupied and saw little action during the Battle of Williamsburg, Redoubt No. 1, where you now stand, is the best preserved and most accessible fortification. The design of the park will take you right into the earthworks, as well as give you a good view of the former Quarterpath Road it overlooks.

Fort Magruder

〉 *Return 0.8 mile down Quarterpath Road to US 60. Turn left onto US 60 West and drive 0.6 mile, then bear right onto Page Street. Drive 0.2 mile on Page Street, then turn right on Penniman Road. Drive 1.7 miles on Penniman Road; you will first see a church, then a small, fenced-in park. Find a place to park, then walk to the fenced-in area.*

Johnston correctly anticipated that McClellan, who now had possession of the York River, would attempt to cut him off before he reached Richmond. At the northern end of the peninsula was the town of West Point, which not only contained a port but was also the terminus of the Richmond & York River Railroad. The Federals could now move their troops by boat to West Point and attempt to get between the Confederates and the safety of the capital defenses. With Federals already close to the rear, the Rebels had to move quickly to keep them from their front.

On May 5, while three of the four Confederate divisions pushed north through rain and mud, General James Longstreet's division remained behind, manning the Williamsburg Line and acting as rear guard. His troops filled as many of the 14 redoubts as they could, but were forced to leave positions on both ends of the line empty. The strongest part of the line was near the center at Redoubt No. 6, better known as Fort Magruder.

You are now at the site of Fort Magruder. Around the fencing, you can see that some of the original earthworks still remain, although they are considerably reduced from their once towering height of 15 feet. These works, along with most of the line, also had swampland and abatis in front, dissuading enemy attempts to storm the fortifications. Located near the former junction of the Warwick Road and the Yorktown Road (about 0.2 mile south of you, roughly following Penniman Road and Government Road), Fort Magruder's position necessitated that it be the largest and strongest fortification on the line.

South of the junction, the two roads were separated by thick woods and wetlands, enough so that communication between them was virtually impossible. With additional confusion caused by scattered troop positions, Union coordination in the area was confused throughout the Battle of Williamsburg on May 5. Overall command at the front belonged to General Edwin Sumner, commander of the Union II Corps, none of which was nearby. The

The site of Fort Magruder, center of the Williamsburg Line.

only two divisions in the area belonged to General Joseph Hooker, whose division belonged to Heintzelman's III Corps, and Smith, whose division was part of Keyes's IV Corps. The total Federal force came to 18,500, but they would remain mostly separated.

At 7:00 AM, Hooker's division took a position on the Warwick Road, with his artillery in the road and adjacent cornfield, and his infantry in woods to his left. As soon as his artillery unlimbered, the guns of Fort Magruder opened up and Hooker was pinned down, waiting for elements of Smith's division to arrive. Longstreet, seeing that Hooker was not moving, directed troops through a ravine to the west and into the woods in front of Hooker's men. With the Federals caught off guard, the fighting raged in the west woods, particularly in an area later known as Bloody Ravine. Over the course of the day, Hooker's left was slowly bent backward, parallel to the Warwick Road. Hooker begged for reinforcements, but Sumner ordered him to hold until the other division of the III Corps, commanded by General Phil Kearny, arrived.

Finally, at 3:00 PM, the Union left could bear no more, and Hooker's men began to break for the rear. However, just as the Confederates moved forward, a quick series of events occurred. First, the Confederates were stopped in their tracks by a deadly volley of Union canister at only 150 yards from artillery that had pulled back earlier. Heintzelman, just up from the rear and trying desperately to rally his III Corps troops, ordered the regimental band to begin playing "Yankee Doodle." Finally, at what seemed that very moment, Kearny's division heroically arrived from the rear. It was a combination of events that the Confederates had no answer for. Hooker's inspired men instantly rallied and joined Kearny's, and the Rebels were soon pushed behind their line. The furious fighting at Fort Magruder would continue through the rest of the day, but neither side gained any more ground.

Redoubt Nos. 12 & 13

❯ *From Fort Magruder, turn around and return the way you came, driving north on Penniman Road for 0.4 mile to Hubbard Lane. Turn right on Hubbard Lane and drive 0.9 mile just past the Colonial Parkway to Lakeshead Drive. Follow Lakeshead Drive for 2.2 miles, staying with it as it enters New Quarter Park. Park in the lot near the softball field.*

Within a short walk of the parking lot here in New Quarter Park are Redoubt Nos. 12 and 13 of the Williamsburg Line. Neither of these two fortifications saw any action during the May 5 battle at Williamsburg; however, they both survive, mostly intact, and are easily accessible. (Almost too much so; you are permitted to climb on and around both redoubts here, an activity forbidden in most parks to protect the historic earthworks.) Their nearby companions, Redoubt Nos. 11 and 14, still exist and are not far away, but they are on the other side of the Colonial Parkway and are inaccessible.

Longstreet simply did not have enough men to fill the Williamsburg Line, so some of the redoubts at each end, including Nos. 12 and 13, were simply not manned. Although the Confederates were able to hold the line fairly successfully during the battle, it would be their unprotected flanks, particularly here on their left, which ultimately led to their greatest losses.

Cub Creek Dam

❯ *Return to Lakeshead Drive and leave the park, driving 2.2 miles to Hubbard Lane. Turn left on Hubbard Lane, then immediately take the sharp left onto the ramp for the Colonial Parkway. Turn right onto the parkway and drive 1.8 miles. You will cross over a dam, and on your right after the dam will be a small parking area. Pull in here.*

On this side of the line, the Union right, Smith's division had met little resistance. Hearing of a small road over the dam at Cub Creek in front of him, Smith asked Sumner for permission to advance. Exercising caution, Sumner allowed Smith to send only one brigade. Smith sent Brigadier General Winfield Scott Hancock, who quickly found two Confederate redoubts—completely empty.

From this parking area, you are looking at Cub Creek Dam, now with the Colonial Parkway riding on top of it. The mill pond in front of you was also present at the time of the battle. Hancock's men would have crossed over the dam and moved just to the left of the parkway, which is where they found the first empty fortification, Redoubt No. 14. Only slightly farther along, still left of the parkway, is Redoubt No. 11.

When Hancock reached Redoubt No. 11, he immediately relayed his findings back to Smith and took up a position with his 3,400 men in this ready-made fortification about a mile east of Fort Magruder. Smith soon sent Hancock another brigade, but remarkably, Sumner ordered Hancock to fall back to the other empty redoubt. Both Hancock and Smith protested, but Sumner had made up his mind.

Longstreet had asked for reinforcements for the Confederate left, opposite this position, and received General Daniel Harvey Hill's division. Hill sent General Jubal Early to the far left, while he lined up just to Early's right. At 5:00 PM, Hill and Early, with two brigades each, began their advance, but soon became separated marching through the thick woods. Early emerged from the woods first, just to the right of Redoubt No. 11, and immediately wheeled left and charged.

Hancock, who was about to proceed with his withdrawal, immediately abandoned his orders and opened up on the advancing Rebels. The fortified Federals tore into the Confederates, repelling their charge and wounding Early in the process. At nearly the same time, Hill emerged from the woods far to Early's right and moved left to support him. Hancock turned his guns and repeated his vicious unloading on Hill's men, who were also repulsed. It was a mismatch from the beginning—3,400 Federals in a

Cub Creek Dam, to the right; Redoubt Nos. 11 and 14 lay just beyond in the trees ahead.

fortified position with eight cannons versus 1,200 Confederates out in the open with no artillery. In the wake of these two devastating blows, Hancock ordered a counterattack and drove the Confederates back with force.

As the fighting died out with the daylight and McClellan finally appeared on the field, the casualties for the Battle of Williamsburg were counted—2,283 on the Federal side, 1,682 for the Confederates. More importantly, though, for the Confederates, the rear guard had held the Union forces—at least by land—and bought time for the rest of the army to retreat toward Richmond.

ELTHAM'S LANDING

❯ *From the Cub Creek Dam parking area, turn left onto the Colonial Parkway and drive west for 2.6 miles. Take the ramp right onto Parkway Drive and proceed 0.4 mile, following it to Capitol Landing Road. Turn right and drive 0.8 mile on Capitol Landing Road to Merrimack Trail (VA 143). Continue on Merrimack Trail 0.8 mile to I-64 and take the ramp onto I-64 West. Drive for 11.4 miles on I-64 to Exit 227 for VA 30. Take the exit and bear right, then drive 2.8 miles on VA 30 North until reaching Farmers Drive (VA 273). Turn right on Farmers Drive and drive 3.8 miles. On your left will be a small clearing with a parking area and historical signs. Pull over here.*

Just as they had at Yorktown two days before, the Federals advanced to the Confederate earthworks at Williamsburg and found them empty. Longstreet had moved to catch up with the rest of the army overnight. Johnston had kept his men moving, and although not all of his forces were past West Point, he was now in a position where the Federals could not cut him off from Richmond.

Still, on May 6, McClellan sent General William B. Franklin's division to West Point by boat. The troops went ashore at Eltham's Landing, part of the sprawling Eltham Plantation, and disembarked throughout the night. Knowing that most of Johnston's army was near, Franklin directed his men to remain on the defensive.

Johnston, not knowing exactly what part of the Federal force had landed, directed General John Bell Hood to feel out the Union forces, then fall back to the main army. Hood, never known to be timid on the battlefield, led his brigade of Texans north toward Eltham's Landing. Supported by Colonel Wade Hampton's South Carolinians, Hood did a bit more than "feel out" Franklin's forces. He drove through the Federal pickets, sending the Union troops running for Eltham's Landing and the safety of the gunboats in the York River.

The point where you are now standing is approximately where Hood's men first encountered the enemy. They quickly drove them north, and pushed them for almost a half mile before breaking off the engagement at about 2:00 PM.

> *Continue north on Farmers Drive for 1 mile to its intersection with Plum Point Road. On your right will be a small clearing with a gravel parking area. Pull in here.*

The Federals used the road beside you, now Farmers Drive, in their retreat back to Eltham's Landing. To the north, at the landing, Franklin's entire division was ashore, thousands of soldiers, along with artillery, animals, and wagons. Hood's strike to drive the Federals back to the landing allowed Johnston to lead his army back to the Richmond defenses without further harassment, and by May 9 the last part of the Confederate army had reached safety.

DREWRY'S BLUFF

> *From the park near Eltham's Landing, turn right onto Farmers Drive and drive north 0.8 mile to VA 33 West. Turn left and drive 5.8 miles on VA 33 West until reaching I-64. Take the ramp for I-64 West and drive 18.7 miles to Exit 200 for I-295 South. Pay close attention to the signs and follow I-295 South for 5 miles to Exit 25 for VA 895 West. Take VA 895 West and drive 8.4 miles (you will have to pay a toll) until reaching the exit ramp for the Jefferson Davis Highway (US 1 South) toward Petersburg. At the end of the ramp, merge onto US 1 South and drive 2.5 miles to Chester Road. Turn left on Chester Road, then merge almost immediately onto Bellwood Road and drive 0.5 mile to Fort Darling Road. Turn left on Fort Darling Road and drive 0.4 mile. On your right, you will see a sign for Richmond National Battlefield Park and Drewry's Bluff (Fort Darling). Pull in here and park, then walk down the trail to the fort.*

On May 6, Lincoln, along with Stanton and Secretary of the Treasury Salmon P. Chase, arrived at Fort Monroe to see the effects of the campaign firsthand. McClellan begged off seeing them, saying that he was too busy at the front, even though he was usually anywhere but there. The president and his party settled for General John Wool, commander at Fort Monroe, and Goldsborough to get the Navy's perspective. As they spoke, Lincoln, studying a set of maps, wondered aloud why Norfolk had not

---

PRESIDENT LINCOLN'S RAID

On the evening of May 9, Abraham Lincoln, along with a small party, personally conducted a reconnaissance of the Virginia shoreline near Norfolk. Unable to resist the temptation, the president directed the boat to go ashore. Lincoln strolled up and down the beach for some time, gleefully enjoying his personal invasion of the South. Thus Lincoln became the only sitting president to ever set foot on enemy territory.

---

yet been taken. Receiving no satisfying answer, Lincoln, Chase, and Stanton personally rode out to Norfolk to find a good landing spot for the troops. On May 10, the Federals did land and retook Gosport Navy Yard, which the Confederates had abandoned days before.

The abandonment of Norfolk had bigger consequences than just the loss of the navy yard. It also meant that the CSS *Virginia* had lost a home base. The deep draft that had hampered her since her maiden voyage also prevented her from going very far up the James River, and she could not be made light enough to get over the river's sandbars. With no other option, on the night of May 10, the captain of the *Virginia* ran her aground near the mouth of the Elizabeth River and set her on fire. The flames reached the powder magazine just before dawn on May 11, and the CSS *Virginia,* so critical to the Confederacy's otherwise insignificant navy, exploded, ending her short but successful run.

With the *Virginia* out of the way, the Federals suddenly had unhampered control of the waters. By this time, they had received two other ironclad ships, the USS *Galena* and the USS *Naugatuck.* On May 15, the three ironclads, along with two other warships, advanced up the James River with the goal of bombarding Richmond from the river. There was only one seemingly small obstacle in the way.

The interior of Fort Darling at Drewry's Bluff.

You are now standing in that obstacle—Fort Darling, which sits atop Drewry's Bluff, 7 miles downriver of Richmond. Take note of the fort's extremely large earthworks, but the most important feature of the fort is its position atop the bluff. Walk around the fort until you come to one of the views of the river; one is a viewing platform, while the other holds a piece of heavy artillery. As you look downriver (to your right), notice the two great advantages that the position at Drewry's Bluff has. First, you can see more than a mile of the mostly winding James River, meaning that the Confederates in the fort would have plenty of time to take careful aim, then fire shot after shot at any Federal ships as they approached. The second advantage is its height. Drewry's Bluff sits 110 feet above the waters of the James River.

Artillery looks downriver from Drewry's Bluff.

At 7:45 AM, the *Galena* anchored at broadside about 600 yards away from the fort. She was almost immediately hit twice by the heavy artillery on the bluff. The much more versatile *Monitor* attempted to get in position to fire, but her captain soon discovered that neither of the ship's two guns could elevate enough to hit the fort. In addition, the Confederates had sunk pilings, ships, stone, and other debris in the river, making navigation any farther than Drewry's Bluff extremely risky. Finally, after 3½ hours, the Federal gunboats withdrew. The *Galena's* iron had kept her afloat, but she was hit 44 times and suffered heavy damage. The small but perfectly placed Fort Darling had driven off the mighty Federal navy with only eight guns while barely suffering a scratch. The Federals would not attempt to pass Drewry's Bluff again.

RICHMOND

Richmond National Battlefield Park/Tredegar Iron Works/ American Civil War Center at Tredegar

> *From Drewry's Bluff, turn right out of the parking area onto Fort Darling Road and drive 1.3 miles to Marina Drive. Turn left on Marina Drive and proceed 0.5 mile to the Jefferson Davis Highway (US 1). Turn right on US 1 and drive 7.2*

miles, crossing the James River and heading into downtown Richmond. When you come to Byrd Street shortly after crossing the river, turn right and drive 0.5 mile to South Fifth Street. Turn right on Fifth Street and drive 0.2 mile to Tredegar Street. Turn right on Tredegar Street. On your right will be the large brick buildings of the Tredegar Iron Works. Pull into the parking lot.

On May 10, the Union army, now reunited at West Point, resumed its march to Richmond. In the Confederate capital, citizens started evacuating, and a quiet panic began to reign, with everyone seemingly expecting the Federals to enter the city at any moment. Even Jefferson Davis put his wife and children on a train to go stay with relatives, and the government made preliminary plans to relocate if necessary.

Johnston arranged his forces as best he could. He placed the entire Confederate army behind the Chickahominy River, which begins northwest of Richmond and runs southeast to the James River. The Chickahominy was a formidable obstacle and was directly in McClellan's path. The army was placed in a line right in front of the capital, facing east toward the oncoming Union army, the entirety of which was on the other side of the river.

There were other threats to Richmond as well. Though Lincoln was still holding them back for the moment, McDowell's I Corps remained in Fredericksburg, and could move south on the capital or join McClellan at any time. A greater distance away but seemingly unoccupied at the moment were the Federal forces in the Shenandoah Valley under General Nathaniel Banks. Although Stonewall Jackson had recently caused a stir at McDowell, it was thought by the Union that he had left the valley and was headed for Richmond, leaving Banks to join McClellan's campaign.

While the city of Richmond watched and worried, McClellan did advance—very, very slowly. From Eltham's Landing, the Federals next occupied White House Landing, on the Pamunkey River at the point where the Richmond & York River Railroad crossed, and established their supply base there. Only 23 miles from Richmond, it not only gave the advantage of being easily accessible by water, but also provided a railroad to aid McClellan's latest strategy. Knowing that McDowell was about to receive troops from Banks in the Valley and would soon be joining him, McClellan—still thinking that he was heavily outnumbered—decided that instead of one grand battle, he would besiege Richmond. This meant moving his massive siege guns to the front, and having a railroad rather than using the unpredictable roads made that option much easier.

McClellan also took some time to reorganize his army. He created two new corps and decided that each corps would be made up of two divisions. The commanders of the II, III, and IV Corps—Sumner, Heintzelman, and Keyes—would remain unchanged. General Fitz John Porter would command the new V Corps, while the VI Corps fell to Franklin, a personal favorite of McClellan's.

For almost two months, the Confederate capital of Richmond endured a terrible waiting game as the two armies faced each other. The story of Richmond, during both this campaign and the rest of the war, is best interpreted at Richmond National Battlefield Park. The park is large and contains many units, but you are now standing at the main visitors center, the former Tredegar Iron Works. The old iron works produced artillery and shells for the Confederates throughout the war, and survived long after as an iron foundry. Walking the grounds to see the remnants of the furnaces and mill runs and reading the interpretive signs about the foundry's history and operations provide a glimpse into the past of Richmond, a large city of industrial might that was a center of Southern culture. Although these descriptions still ring true today, the city has changed a great deal since (and because of) the Civil War.

There are two interpretive centers on the site. One is operated by the National Park Service and is free to visit. This center contains numerous maps, signs, and exhibits to help you interpret and decipher the swirl of activity that surrounded Richmond during the war, including the Peninsula Campaign. This is also the place to learn about any park programs happening here or at the park's other units and visitors centers.

The other museum, the American Civil War Center at Tredegar, is a privately run site. Although its collection is good, the real strength of this museum is helping visitors

The former Tredegar Iron Works now serves as the main visitors center for Richmond National Battlefield Park.

understand the Civil War as a whole, presenting as many viewpoints as possible and putting you in the position of the people who had to make some very tough decisions during the period. The highly interactive center makes a concentrated effort to interpret sensitive and not necessarily politically correct issues as historical conditions and debated viewpoints rather than indisputable facts. Although there is a charge for the museum, it is an hour or two well spent, and children will enjoy the exhibits.

Museum and White House of the Confederacy

❯ *From Tredegar Iron Works, turn left out of the parking lot onto Tredegar Street and drive 0.2 mile to South Seventh Street. Turn left on Seventh Street, then take the next right onto Byrd Street, and then the next left onto Ninth Street. Drive 0.7 mile on Ninth Street to East Leigh Street. Turn right on Leigh Street and drive 0.2 mile to 12th Street, then turn right again. At this point, the Museum and White House of the Confederacy will be 0.1 mile directly in front of you. You may find a place to park on the street, but your best bet is to park in the nearby parking garage that is shared with the hospitals of the Medical College of Virginia (you can have your parking validated at the museum).*

The Museum of the Confederacy in Richmond, Virginia.

As the Federals prepared, the Confederate leaders conferred, observed, and strategized. Johnston would be patient, but looked intently for any opportunity to strike. Lee did the same, and Davis, a West Point graduate and former U.S. secretary of war, paid close attention to the happenings at the front.

In addition to the events happening immediately before them, Davis also had a much bigger picture to view—and it was not pretty. The Civil War was not only being fought on the outskirts of Richmond. It was being fought in Kentucky, Missouri, Tennessee, Mississippi,

Louisiana, and on the seas. The early part of 1862 did not bode well for the fledgling nation. In just the first four months, Ulysses S. Grant had captured Fort Donelson and Nashville as a result, then reversed an almost certain Confederate triumph into a disaster at Shiloh. On the Mississippi River, the Federals had gained control as far south as Memphis while simultaneously moving north and capturing the South's largest city, New Orleans. Finally, along the Atlantic Coast, the fall of Fort Macon gave the Union a significant toehold in North Carolina, while Fort Pulaski—thought practically impregnable—had been taken apart within a day by the experimental and highly successful use of rifled artillery. In May 1862, the war was not going well on any front, and Davis had much to keep him occupied.

The anchor of the CSS Virginia *sits outside The Museum of the Confederacy.*

While he did travel to the capitol building down the street, for the most part Davis did his business and conferred with the generals of his army here—at the White House of the Confederacy. This is the home that the Davis family, hailing from Mississippi, used during their stay in Richmond. Besides the obvious strain of the war, the Davis family suffered personal tragedy here as well, including the loss of a child, Joseph, who died after an accident at the mansion.

The guided tours of the home are conducted by well-trained staff who seem to have an answer for every question fired at them, whether it be about the Davis family or the origins of the wallpaper in each room. The tours are very entertaining and the stories told are both historically and personally intriguing. Tickets for the tour are obtained through the home's companion piece, the museum.

Together, the Museum and White House of the Confederacy are a true treasure trove of the history of the short-lived nation. If the Confederate States had anything comparable to the Smithsonian, this is it. The museum is not exceedingly large, and you will find it fairly easy to get through quickly, but you may catch yourself gaping at some of the artifacts you see. While most museums seem to display only one or two truly significant pieces, it seems this museum carries at least one in every single display. For instance, that's not just any anchor sitting out in front of the museum; it's the CSS *Virginia's,* along with her propeller shaft. That tent on display? It's Lee's. Those leather riding gloves? Jackson's. That plumed hat? Yes, it's the one made famous by J. E. B. Stuart, sitting on his field desk. It seems that personal effects of virtually every significant Confederate commander, east to west, are represented. Be sure to buy the combination ticket to see both the museum and the White House. This combination of artifacts and unique historic site are must-sees.

HANOVER COURTHOUSE

> *From the Museum and White House of the Confederacy, drive south to Broad Street, then turn right. Drive approximately 1.2 miles on Broad Street to US 301 (North Belvidere Street). Continue on US 301 for 14.4 miles. Once you get outside the city, you will eventually be driving through farmland, so keep your eye on the odometer. When you get to the intersection with Peake's Road, turn left and find a safe place to pull over.*

On May 20, Silas Casey, leading a division of Keyes's IV Corps, crossed to the south of the Chickahominy River. The crossing went uncontested, so the next day, McClellan ordered the rest of the IV Corps across and had Keyes advance to the town of Seven Pines, due east of Richmond, to anchor the left of what would be his line. On the right, Smith's division of the VI Corps advanced to Mechanicsville, northeast of Richmond, on May 24. Over the next few days, McClellan formed his line between these two points. Although additional bridges were built over the Chickahominy for quick passage, McClellan had his army split by the river; the II, V, and VI Corps on the north side, and the III and IV Corps on the south.

McClellan had also lost McDowell's I Corps yet again. On May 23, Jackson appeared in the Shenandoah Valley from nowhere and surprised the Union garrison at Front Royal, then routed Banks's command at Winchester two days later. Lincoln ordered McDowell west to meet the threat. Jackson had accomplished his mission of keeping Federal troops in the Valley. In fact, he even had the Union commander-in-chief wondering about other arrangements. On May 25, the day Banks was driven from Winchester, Lincoln wired McClellan and told him that he had been taking too long, and that the time had come for him either to act quickly or to bring the army back home.

McClellan, already delusional about how much smaller his army was than the Confederates', took the news as essentially sealing his fate. Furthermore, he took hold of every chance he got to reinforce his own fears and demonstrate the incompetency of those meddling with his campaign. So when a rumor arose that 17,000 Confederates were bearing down on his right and rear from Hanover Court House, he was quick to believe it. On May 27, he sent Porter's V Corps, 12,000 men, to clear them out.

There were indeed Confederates at Hanover Court House, but the number was closer to 4,000, and they were not going to attack anybody. They were there to guard the Virginia Central Railroad, garrisoned 4 miles southwest of the town near a point known as Peake's Crossing. Porter's skirmishers appeared at noon, with the rest of the infantry coming up about an hour later. After about an hour's fight, the Confederates retreated, with many of them going toward Hanover Court House. Porter pursued, leaving only three regiments as a rear guard. Porter's thought was that there must be more Confederates ahead, but there weren't. In fact, there were enough who retreated the other way—down Ashcake Road—that they launched their own attack on the rear guard.

Outnumbered, the three Federal regiments put up a very strong fight, but they were taking heavy casualties. Word was sent to Porter, who returned just in time to drive off the rest of the Confederates. The Federals then returned south to their place in the Union line facing Richmond. McClellan, as was his habit, proclaimed a great victory in the face of superior numbers, further reinforcing his belief that although he had the better fighting force, he would have to continually overcome great odds to lead his army to victory.

There isn't much in the area that tells of the battle today, although there is a Virginia Civil War Trails Marker in the town of Hanover that discusses the battle. Most of the land around the original battleground can still be seen, however. The battle was fought mostly on farmland, just as it appears today, and the roads and railroad are roughly in the same spot they were at the time of the battle. Most of the heaviest fighting took place south of Peaks Road (the former Ashcake Road), between its intersections with Hanover Courthouse Road to the west and Hillcrest Road to the east. The Kinney House, still standing, was a focal point of the battle, and it was Dr. Kinney's farm where much of the action occurred. However, all of this is private property today, so you will have to observe from the roadside. If you travel a bit farther west on Peaks Road, you will cross a set of railroad tracks—the same set of tracks that the Confederates were guarding that day.

SEVEN PINES

> *From Hanover Courthouse, drive on US 301 South for 6.8 miles until you reach I-295. Take the ramp for I-295 South and drive 11.4 miles to Exit 28B for US 60, which will eventually trace the Old Williamsburg Road. After you get off the ramp, continue 4 miles on US 60 West. The Sandston Public Library will be on your left; pull into the parking lot.*

It did not go unnoticed by Johnston that the Union army was split across the Chickahominy River. While he did not know its exact disposition and strength, he knew part of the army was isolated, and that was enough. It was just the opportunity he was looking for: a chance to fight only half of the Army of the Potomac and defeat them while the other half was trying to cross the Chickahominy.

On May 28, with his entire army south of the river, Johnston decided to hit the Union left flank at Seven Pines. According to reports from D. H. Hill, opposite that part of the line, only the Federal IV Corps was facing him (although he apparently did not know that the III Corps was behind them). Johnston decided to attack immediately, setting the date for May 31. It would be the first offensive action of the war for the Confederate army in the east.

Johnston planned to use three roads—Nine Mile Road on the left, the Williamsburg Road in the center, and Charles City Road to the right—to converge on Seven Pines with 15 of his 22 brigades. The other seven brigades would hold the line of the Chickahominy to ensure that Federal reinforcements could not cross. The main attack was to come from Longstreet on the right, with Hill in the center and G. W. Smith on the left. The assault would begin at 8:00 AM.

As often happens with military plans, it didn't quite turn out the way Johnston intended. Through a combination of mixed and misunderstood orders and a torrential rain that began the night before, the morning of May 31 found all three forces on the same road, four hours behind schedule. The only one who was even close to being in position was Hill on the Williamsburg Road in the center, and his orders were to wait for word from Longstreet.

Finally, at 11:00 AM, Hill could wait no longer. Nobody even seemed to know where Longstreet was, so Hill decided to take the initiative. He began to move through the White Oak Swamp in front of him, and at 1:00 PM, although not all of his units were in position, Hill began his assault along the Williamsburg Road.

That Williamsburg Road is the same one that you are now standing next to. The Union forces, Casey's division of the IV Corps, were lined up across the road right where you are standing. As you face the road, turn left and you will see the area from which Hill's Confederates were marching. While most of the surrounding area was woodland at the time of the battle, there was a clearing here, and the Union had built earthworks and obstructions, as well as deployed several batteries of artillery, to guard it. This was the first of three lines the Federals had set.

Just south of where you are, a large redoubt holding several guns had been built. This redoubt became a focal point of the fighting. While at the beginning of the battle the Federal guns here poured devastating fire into the Confederates, it would eventually fall and be used by the Confederates themselves.

> *Exit the library parking lot, turn left on Williamsburg Road (US 60 West) and drive 0.2 mile. Pull over into the parking lot on your right next to the historical markers.*

The site of George McClellan's first line at the Battle of Seven Pines.

This is the area from which Hill's Confederates emerged from the woods on the opposite side of the clearing from the Federals. Hill had set two brigades on each side of the road, but the right was not in place when the left began marching, meaning that when those two brigades on the left came out of the woods, all of the Federal fire was focused on them. While the brigades on the right did eventually appear, the fighting became heavy and raged for two hours. Finally, about 3:00 PM, the Federals were forced to fall back to their second line.

❯ *From this parking lot, turn left and return to Williamsburg Road (US 60 East). Drive 0.8 mile to the Seven Pines National Cemetery on your left. Traffic is heavy here, so be careful as you pull into the cemetery. Once you enter, there is very little room; in fact, you will probably have to back out onto Williamsburg Road, so think ahead.*

While the Federal IV Corps was engaged in a heavy fight, McClellan was on the other side of the river, sick with malaria and resting in his tent. At 1:30 PM, both he and Heintzelman of the III Corps heard the sounds of battle. McClellan issued orders to Sumner's II Corps to be ready to cross the Chickahominy if necessary, while Heintzelman sent a courier to find Keyes for a report. Hearing nothing, at 2:30 he sent Kearny's division toward the sound of the fighting to reinforce whatever was happening. Heintzelman finally did receive confirmation at 3:00 PM and sent word to McClellan, who immediately ordered Sumner to cross.

Here, at the second Union line, Kearny arrived in time to reinforce the IV Corps and try to keep Hill's Confederates at bay. The intersection of the Williamsburg and Nine Mile Roads adjacent to the cemetery was the center of the town of Seven Pines. Hill sent one of his brigades, commanded by Colonel Micah Jenkins, far to the left to attempt to flank the Federal line. Jenkins eventually found Nine Mile Road and advanced down it, surprising and quickly clearing out every Federal unit in his path and eventually getting in their rear. The Union troops were forced to abandon the town and retreated more than a mile east of Seven Pines.

Seven Pines National Cemetery is one of the few relatively clear pieces of ground left of the battle. Many of the dead from the Peninsula Campaign's battles now lie here, with a large number of them—more than 1,200—unknown. Though small, the cemetery is still in use today, and there are burials here as recent as the conflicts in Iraq and Afghanistan.

❯ *From the cemetery, return to Williamsburg Road and drive west, taking the right turn on Nine Mile Road immediately past the cemetery entrance. Drive 1 mile on Nine Mile Road, just past its intersection with Hanover Road. Pull over into one of the nearby parking lots.*

The Battle of Seven Pines is also known by the name Fair Oaks, and it is in that area where you are now standing. While the heaviest fighting occurred along the Williamsburg Road, it was here along Nine Mile Road that one of the most critical events of not only the battle but the entire Civil War occurred.

Unbelievably, even though he was only 2.5 miles away, Johnston did not know about the fighting at Seven Pines. He was in what is scientifically termed an "acoustic shadow," and could not hear the fight going on. When he finally received word at 4:00 PM, he decided to send G. W. Smith's division down Nine Mile Road to join the battle.

It was around this time that Lee appeared on the battlefield. Apparently, in all of his hurried preparation for the battle, Johnston had forgotten to notify either Lee or Davis, both of whom had heard the battle from Richmond and rode out to see what was going on. Johnston did not take the time to explain himself, however; he was heading to the front with G. W. Smith's division, which was being led by General Chase Whiting (G. W. Smith had claimed illness and begged off joining the fight). Shortly after the division left, Davis rode up, incensed, as was Lee, that an offensive was taken without the courtesy of even notifying the high command.

On this day, though, neither Davis nor Lee would reprimand Johnston for his actions. At 5:30 PM, Whiting's Confederate division ran into Sumner's II Corps, which had had trouble crossing the river because of flooding caused by the rains of the previous night. General John Sedgwick's division was in front and met the Confederates first. By this time, however, it was late in the day, and although both sides received reinforcements, darkness soon ended the fighting, most of which occurred just north and east of Fair Oaks Station, your current location.

At dusk, in the last moments of the day's fighting, Johnston, who had insisted on seeing the battle up close, was severely wounded, taking a bullet in the shoulder and a shell fragment to the chest. It was a seemingly devastating blow for the Confederates. Johnston was taken to the rear, where both Davis and Lee assured Johnston they would take care of his army. Command fell to the next officer in rank, G. W. Smith, who had earlier declined to join the fighting. G. W. Smith had impressed neither the president nor Lee, and as they rode together back to Richmond, it was decided that G. W. Smith's command would last only through the current battle, and that he would be relieved immediately afterward.

Fighting did resume at first light the next day, June 1, but not much came of it. By this time, the Union II, III, and IV Corps had all taken strong positions in line. Hill resumed the attack down the Williamsburg Road, but was given green troops who were easily pushed back by Hooker's division, which had not fought the previous day and was fresh. The fighting died out before noon. The Confederates had suffered 1,132 casualties in their assault and had cost the Union 1,203, and by the next day, both armies were in the same positions they were in before the battle had started. But one major change had occurred. On the afternoon of June 1, Davis informed G. W. Smith of his decision to relieve him, and at 2:00 PM, Smith transferred command to the new leader of the Army of Northern Virginia: General Robert E. Lee.

THE SEVEN DAYS: DAY ONE—OAK GROVE (FRENCH'S FIELD)

❯ *From Fair Oaks, drive southeast on Nine Mile Road for 0.2 mile, then turn right on Naglee Avenue. Drive 0.4 mile to Williamsburg Road (US 60) and turn right. Drive 0.9 mile and turn left on Airport Drive, then drive another 0.9 mile and make a U-turn. Drive 0.3 mile; there will be a historic marker on the right side of the road. If you cannot pull over here (it is rather difficult), continue down Airport Drive and park at the Virginia Aviation Museum.*

After gathering the opinions of all his generals—something Johnston (or many military commanders, for that matter) was not one to do—Lee immediately determined his plan. To Lee, seizing the initiative was the most important aspect of fighting, and McClellan was certainly not going to put up much of a fight yielding it. New entrenchments were dug around the capital while the entire Confederate army in Virginia was reorganized. After his poor showing at Fair Oaks, G. W. Smith was out, having suffered a nervous breakdown. Part of his division, along with other reinforcements, was sent to Jackson in the Shenandoah Valley, 7,900 men in all—moving in plain sight of the Union army. The other part of the command went to newly promoted major general A. P. Hill, who was now commanding his own division, which he called his "Light Division." Magruder also gained another division, while reinforcements from Georgia and the Carolinas went to Huger and D. H. Hill. Including Jackson's army, Lee had 92,400 men at his disposal—the most he would ever have during the entire war.

On the other side of the line, McClellan, whose Army of the Potomac was 105,900 strong, was now convinced that he was outnumbered 2-to-1. He had been hearing rumors—Jackson was coming, Jackson was in his rear, even that P. G. T. Beauregard had brought his army from Corinth, Mississippi—and he seemed to believe them all. Not even Lee, who had purposely sent stragglers and "deserters" into the Union lines to spread misinformation, could predict the lengths to which McClellan would let his imagination take him. While begging for reinforcements and repeatedly preaching his imminent doom to Washington, he began to fortify his positions.

As McClellan geared up for another siege, Lee prepared for an attack. His plan was to hit the Federal right, the part of the army north of the Chickahominy River. After Seven Pines, McClellan had eight additional bridges built over the river, but left one corps—Porter's V Corps—on the north side to guard the right flank and the supply line to White House. Lee's intent was to bring Jackson from the valley to take a position on the Union right, but first he had to confirm that Jackson had a clear way through. To do this, he sent his cavalry commander, Stuart, with 1,200 horsemen to investigate. At 2:00 AM on June 12, Stuart woke his staff and told them to mount up. His cavalry rode 22 miles the first day. On June 13, after making steady progress, Stuart decided to go through with a plan that Lee had not exactly approved, but that he had not forbidden, either. Stuart decided to ride completely around the Army of the Potomac. Over the next few days, the Confederate cavalry would destroy supplies near White House, fight some small actions, and even build its own makeshift bridge over the Chickahominy River. Returning to Richmond on June 15, Stuart's "Ride Around McClellan" soon became part of his growing legend.

More importantly, though, Stuart's ride gave Lee all the intelligence he needed for his battle plan. On June 16, he recalled Jackson to Richmond, cautioning him to come quickly and quietly. While his army was still marching, Jackson rode ahead to meet with Lee and his other generals on June 23 to work out a plan to drive McClellan from Richmond. The entire plan revolved around Porter's V Corps, and while it would leave Richmond exposed south of the river, Lee counted on McClellan's caution to hold him in place (along with an encore performance by Magruder to exaggerate his strength). Jackson would lead his army to Porter's flank and rear. A. P. Hill's division would cross the Chickahominy upstream and move along the bank, then link with the forces of Longstreet and D. H. Hill, which would cross closer to the Federals but later in the day.

A VERY IMPORTANT CAPTIVE

The White House from which the Union supply base took its name was the home of "Rooney" Lee, son of Robert E. Lee. The general's wife, Mary, was staying there when the Federals approached. In her flight, she left a note on the door, signed by "a Grand-daughter of Mrs. Washington," asking that the home where George Washington courted Martha Custis be protected. She moved to another local home, but the Federals quickly caught up with her there, too. Under guard, making much fuss about her treatment, and becoming an embarrassment to McClellan, she was gallantly escorted through the lines under a flag of truce to be reunited with her husband.

The V Corps would be outnumbered, cut off from the rest of the army, and swept to the York River. The movement was set for 3:00 AM June 26.

Meanwhile, McClellan was hearing rumors again. To counter the movements that he believed would seal the fate of his army, he decided to launch a series of attacks along the lines. The first would occur just west of Seven Pines, down the Williamsburg Road to a location known as Oak Grove. Although Lee was the one seizing the initiative, McClellan would begin the first of what would later be known as the Seven Days Battles.

At 8:30 AM June 25, Hooker sent two of his brigades west down the Williamsburg Road and through the White Oak Swamp to the south. Dan Sickles's brigade, moving through wet ground and Confederate abatis, soon fell behind Cuvier Grover's, which appeared in a large clearing known as French's Field and immediately took fire from the Confederates of Huger's division. Eventually, the fighting became heavy and more men were brought up on both sides, but at 10:30 AM an order to withdraw came from McClellan himself. Three miles away from the fighting (he was almost never near the actual fighting during this or any other campaign of the war), McClellan had misinterpreted the telegraph communications coming into his office. At 1:00 PM, McClellan did actually come to the field himself, ordered the attack renewed, and rode away. The fighting went on until dark, with the end result a gain of approximately 600 yards for the Union. This was enough for McClellan to claim victory; he had gained his objective, Oak Grove, and moved just a bit closer to being able to bring his siege guns to the front.

However, that night, McClellan received news from an escaped slave that both Jackson and Beauregard were present, and that the Confederate strength was surely greater than 200,000 men. He promptly sent a telegram to Stanton that his army would soon be attacked and destroyed. He then went to Porter and told him that he should prepare to be attacked. For once, even if only partially, McClellan had correctly anticipated the Confederates' plans.

The battlefield at Oak Grove has been almost completely lost to Richmond International Airport. If you are on Airport Drive, most of the heaviest fighting occurred to the east, where the terminal now sits, and north through the airfield near the Virginia Aviation Museum. There is one Confederate earthwork still existing and accessible at the airport, at Airport Drive and Clarkson Road. However, if you decide to risk seeing this earthwork, use extreme caution, as there is nowhere to pull over, and all of the streets in the area are one-way. There is also a historical marker in front of the museum.

THE SEVEN DAYS—DAY TWO: BEAVER DAM CREEK (MECHANICSVILLE)

Chickahominy Bluffs

〉 *From the Virginia Aviation Museum, turn right onto Airport Drive and follow it for 1.1 miles to I-64. Take the ramp for I-64 West and drive 5.5 miles to Exit 192 for US 360/Mechanicsville. Turn right onto the Mechanicsville Turnpike (US 360) and drive 2 miles. On your right you will see a National Park Service area for Chickahominy Bluffs. Pull into this area, park, and walk to the overlook.*

As planned, on June 26, all elements of the Confederate assault on the Union right were in place, except for the most critical piece, the piece that the entire operation hinged upon: Jackson's army. Not only was Jackson six hours behind schedule, but the rest of the Confederates weren't exactly sure where he was. In fact, even Jackson didn't know where he was. Although he moved slowly and cautiously, he eventually became confused by the roads and got lost. At 5:00 PM, Jackson finally gave up, going into bivouac until he received more information. His army would not fight this day, and this would only be the first of several questionable performances by the legendary Stonewall over the Seven Days.

Porter, heeding McClellan's warning, had taken a very strong defensive position behind Beaver Dam Creek. Besides the obstacle of the creek itself, the woods in front had been cleared, and abatis had been placed in front of the line. The Union troops were posted on high ground, occupying entrenchments that the Confederates had built prior to their arrival. Porter placed General George McCall's division here, 9,500 men with six batteries of artillery, 32 guns in all. The line ran along the creek for 2 miles.

South of the Chickahominy, every Union soldier was expecting an imminent attack. This was part of Lee's plan—for Magruder and Huger to demonstrate along the line, holding the Federals in place while exaggerating their numbers to prevent other units from supporting the attack against Porter. Though the "threat" continued throughout the day, the attack never came.

A. P. Hill crossed the Chickahominy River as planned, but after waiting for Jackson to appear on his right for some time, became impatient. A. P. Hill was a man of action and did not like to sit while there was battle to be done. He decided that something must have gone wrong with the plan, and at 4:00 PM he advanced.

The overlook and view that you now have from Chickahominy Bluffs is the same view that Lee, Davis, and other Confederates observing the movements had on June 26. There are many more trees obstructing your view today than there were in 1862, but you can get an idea of the commanding view that the bluffs provided at the time, and why Lee chose to observe from here. As you look straight out from the viewing platform, the crossing of the Chickahominy River used by Longstreet and D. H. Hill is approximately a half mile to the northwest in front of you. The Union line at Beaver Dam Creek is slightly to your right (east and northeast).

Still wondering where Jackson was, Lee observed a large group of infantry moving in front of him. After studying them for a short time, he realized they were A. P. Hill's Light Division. Ideally, Jackson would be present to hit the Union right and turn them, but Lee knew that he had to keep the Federals on this side of the river occupied to prevent them from moving on Richmond. Turning to Longstreet, he calmly told him, "General, you may now cross over."

The observation platform at Chickahominy Bluffs.

Beaver Dam Creek

> *From Chickahominy Bluffs, turn right onto the Mechanicsville Turnpike (US 360) and drive north 1.6 miles, bearing right onto the Mechanicsville Bypass to the exit for VA 156 South. Take the exit, then turn right on Cold Harbor Road (VA 156 South) and drive 0.6 mile. On your right, you will see a National Park Service area for Beaver Dam Creek. Pull into this area and drive to the parking area.*

This area is just a small portion of the Union line at Beaver Dam Creek that existed along a well-known landmark, Ellerson's Mill. The trail is easy and very short (less than 0.2 mile); walk over to the bridge to put yourself between the Union and Confederate lines, then look out over the open area around the creek.

As soon as A. P. Hill's Confederates reached the clearing, which was to your left, McCall's division of Pennsylvania Reserves on the high ground to your right greeted them with a withering fire. Without the support of Jackson's flank attack, A. P. Hill's assault was direct against the center of a heavily fortified line, and the Confederates paid dearly for it. A. P. Hill would eventually direct all of his efforts on the far right of the Union line, but these assaults were also thrown back with ease. The last Confederate assault of the day was here around Ellerson's Mill. The results were the same.

At the end of the Battle of Beaver Dam Creek (also known as the Battle of Me-

Despite decisive victory at Beaver Dam Creek on the second day of the Seven Days Battles, George McClellan decided that night that he would withdraw the Union army from Richmond.

chanicsville), McClellan rode up to survey the field. He was elated with the Federal success: the Union had suffered only 361 casualties, less than a quarter of the Confederates' 1,475. It was an undisputed Union victory, and best of all, McClellan thought, it had to have come against the mighty Stonewall Jackson.

Later that evening, he learned the truth: that the Federals had not been fighting Jackson, and that Jackson was probably still off somewhere to his right or, worse, in his rear. This was the last straw. McClellan, after many months of stalling and planning, launched his grand campaign, then took almost two months to approach the Confederate capital. Finally, on the outskirts of Richmond, he scored his first decisive victory over the Confederate Army of Northern Virginia, which he outnumbered approximately 2-to-1, nearly three months after his army left Fort Monroe and began marching up the peninsula. And on the night of that victory, McClellan decided that his army, which he perceived to be in grave danger, must evacuate its position immediately. Lee had sought the initiative, and he was receiving it in spades.

THE SEVEN DAYS—DAY THREE: GAINES' MILL

❯ *From Beaver Dam Creek, turn right back onto Cold Harbor Road (VA 156). Drive for 1.6 miles, then turn right to continue following Cold Harbor Road and VA 156. Drive 3.1 miles to the visitors center for the Cold Harbor/Gaines' Mill unit of Richmond National Battlefield Park (there will be a sharp left turn shortly before reaching the center). Park and enter the visitors center.*

Late on the night of June 26, McClellan began making arrangements to evacuate his supply base at White House to a safer point along the James River, rather than the York. He also issued orders to Porter, telling him to evacuate his position at Beaver Dam Creek and cross the Chickahominy River as soon as possible. McClellan had not provided a reason for the move, and Porter assumed that McClellan simply wanted to get his entire army on the same side of the Chickahominy. While Porter argued, unsuccessfully, that he should hold his current position, both generals agreed that it was too late to cross the river that night. Porter quietly withdrew from his earthworks to a position 4 miles to the east on a high plateau east and south of Boatswain's Creek.

At sunrise on June 27, with the Federals already far away and almost in their new defensive position, the Confederates woke to find empty earthworks in front of them. They immediately began pursuit, with Longstreet on the right, A. P. Hill in the center, and Jackson, who had been found, on the left.

Lee suspected that the Union had taken its new position at the next logical place, which was Powhite Creek, not far in front of them. Lee also wanted to stick with his plan of the day before, and sent Jackson, with D. H. Hill now part of his command, off to flank the Federal right. A. P. Hill's division would lead the assault.

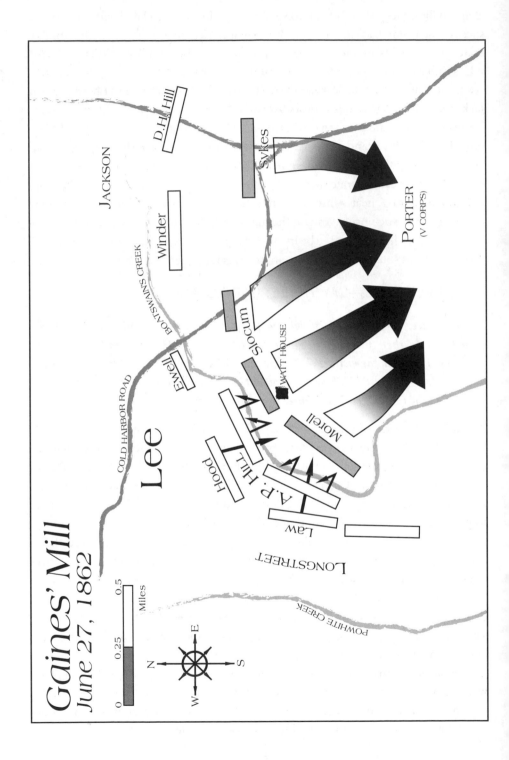

Gaines' Mill
June 27, 1862

JACKSON

D.H. Hill

Sykes

Winder

BOATSWAIN'S CREEK

PORTER
(V CORPS)

Slocum

Ewell

WYATT HOUSE

COLD HARBOR ROAD

Lee

Hood

A.P. HILL

Morell

Law

LONGSTREET

POWHITE CREEK

0   0.25   0.5
Miles

N
W   E
S

The position of the Union left during the Battle of Gaines' Mill.

The visitors center for Gaines' Mill, shared with the adjacent Cold Harbor battle-field of 1864, will orient you to the events of June 27, 1862. Inside, you will find a short electric map program that will give you a concise explanation of the Battle of Gaines' Mill. You can also find out here whether any tours of the Gaines' Mill battlefield will be conducted that day. If you are able to take a ranger-guided tour, jump at the chance; the National Park Service tours are thorough, informative, entertaining, and best of all, free.

❯ *From the visitors center, turn right onto Old Cold Harbor Road and drive 0.3 mile, then turn left onto Watt House Road. Drive another 0.2 mile and carefully pull over when you reach the clearing on your right. (This is private property, so do not enter the clearing.)*

Porter had indeed left a few troops at Powhite Creek, but only to keep an eye on the Confederate advance he knew was coming. At noon, Maxcy Gregg's brigade of A. P. Hill's division reached the creek and traded a few shots with the Federals, but by the time they crossed the creek the enemy had disappeared.

Gregg pressed forward through the woods and soon came upon a clearing at the base of a long hill, known locally as Turkey Hill. As soon as they entered the clearing, they were hit hard by Union artillery and went back into the woods. Lee and A. P. Hill immediately came up to the front to take a look, and what they saw was not what they had hoped for. In front of them was the large clearing that Gregg had found, with a creek (Boatswain's Creek) on the other side that was not on any of their maps. On the other side of the creek, atop Turkey Hill, Porter had set himself in an excellent defensive

The thick forest and steep bank leading from Boatswain's Creek to the Union line at Gaines' Mill.

position, perhaps better than the one at Beaver Dam Creek, where the Confederates had been slaughtered the day before. It was evident they were in for a very hard fight.

The clearing to your right is, roughly, the same clearing that the Confederates found and would have to charge across during the Battle of Gaines' Mill. Boatswain's Creek is to your left, and the Confederates set their battle lines just inside the tree line to your right. Just like at Beaver Dam Creek, this clearing represents only a small portion of the line, but during the battle, nearly all of the Confederate assaults would have to begin with crossing a quarter mile of open ground such as this.

❯ *Continue on Watt House Road for another 0.5 mile to the Gaines' Mill battlefield and park in the designated parking area.*

The defensive position of the Union V Corps was indeed excellent. The Federal line was 2 miles long and 1 mile deep. Porter had arranged his troops in an arc along Turkey Hill. The men were arranged into two lines. The first was set just behind the swamp created by Boatswain's Creek, and the second was about halfway up the hillside. The V Corps was the largest in the Army of the Potomac, and Porter had 27,160 men at his disposal, along with 96 guns arranged into 17 batteries of artillery. In front of all this was the creek itself, which had steep, overgrown banks and swampland on both sides of it. Beyond the creek was the large clearing that any attacker would have to cross first, completely exposed to Federal artillery.

The Confederates did have one element of the battle to their advantage: numbers. The present portion of Lee's army (Jackson included) totaled 54,300. Beginning at 1:00 PM, Lee began to set his battle lines, again with A. P. Hill's division to lead the assault.

As for Jackson, he had again had difficulty reaching the battlefield. D. H. Hill had found it, quite by accident, when he stumbled onto Boatswain's Creek (which was not on his map, either) and was met by heavy Federal fire. He fell back to wait for Jackson, whose guide to the battlefield had made a wrong turn, forcing them to backtrack for several miles.

Seeing the Confederates setting up in front of him, at 2:00 PM Porter called for Henry Slocum's division of the VI Corps, which was at the ready, expecting the call through previous arrangement. McClellan, again miles from the battlefield, sent them forward from his headquarters south of the Chickahominy. Slocum's division arrived by 2:30 PM, increasing the Federal strength to 36,400. Soon afterward, McClellan began to receive word of heavy enemy movement along the entire Union line—again, the antics of Magruder and Huger. McClellan, who had not yet told his generals of his plan to withdraw, began packing up his headquarters.

At 2:30, A. P. Hill's men finally began the assault. Going directly against the Union center, some of his units were able to briefly cross the creek and meet the first Union line, with some fighting even becoming hand-to-hand. A. P. Hill's repeated assaults, however, did not budge the Federals. At 3:30, General Richard Ewell's division of Jackson's army reached the Old Cold Harbor Road, and they were immediately sent to the center of the line, only to meet the same result. Longstreet was ordered by Lee to attack the Union left to take pressure off the attack in the center, but it was not enough. In two hours of fighting, the Confederates suffered an estimated 2,154 casualties, heavy losses they could not afford.

The Federals were also taking losses. The center of their line, though it had repelled every attack, was being hit hard and running low on ammunition to boot. At 5:00 PM, Porter asked for more reinforcements, and McClellan, who was slow to get the order, sent two brigades from the II Corps, three hours' march from the battlefield.

The area you are now in only covers a small section of the 2-mile front of the Battle of Gaines' Mill. You are now in the center of the line, the portion that withstood the heaviest attacks throughout the day. In front of you is the Watt House, which was present at the time of the battle. It is a private home, so please do not disturb the residents, but feel free to walk up to the house and read the interpretive signs.

In the open fields to the north, the tree line to the left runs along the creek, with the Union battle line facing it as it winds around. But to really get an idea of what the Confederates had to charge through to get to the first Union line (the portion you see in front of you), walk the trail down to Boatswain's Creek. It does go down and then up again, but the trail is well formed and the walk is not strenuous. Combining the

Site of the Union center at Gaines' Mill battlefield and Watt House, which is now a private residence.

heavy growth around the creek with the large open field you saw previously, you can now sense the tremendous task the Confederate soldiers were asked to perform.

Near dark, with A. P. Hill's men used up, Jackson's divisions, led by Generals Chase Whiting and Charles Winder, reached the battlefield. At 7:00 PM, D. H. Hill was also ready to move, and he launched an attack on the Federal right, slowly pushing them back. Longstreet kept up his pressure on the left, holding them in place. Whiting's division was brought to the center, and hearing of the previous efforts to take the line, he decided on another tactic.

Arranging his men, Whiting ordered them not to fire their weapons until they had overrun the enemy line. The thought was simple: Firing the weapon, then stopping or slowing to reload cost valuable time and momentum. Whiting's men began the charge, and within 100 yards of the swamp, fixed their bayonets and started a dead run for the Union line. Disappearing down one side of the creek and quickly appearing atop the other, the Federals immediately fired—and couldn't reload fast enough. The first line broke and ran, completely obscuring the firing line of the second line, which had to wait until their fleeing comrades got out of the way. By the time this happened, it was too late, and the second line was also overrun. Now the Confederates were ready to fire.

As you walk the trail and begin to climb back up the slope of the ravine, you will be following the path that Whiting's men took to hit the Federal center. You will also see, at the top, several markers denoting the point at which the Union line, after repulsing repeated assaults, finally broke.

Almost simultaneously, Longstreet carried the Federal left, and D. H. Hill the right. The entire Union line broke at once, and the Federal soldiers began streaming toward the crossings of the Chickahominy River in complete disarray. Unfortunately for the Confederates, darkness prevented a more thorough pursuit, but they were able to capture many of the enemy, along with 22 cannons. Soon after the line broke, the two Union divisions from the II Corps arrived and were able to help cover the retreat, probably saving many others from being captured as well.

The Federals continued crossing the river overnight, burning the bridges when they were finished. For the first time in weeks, the Army of the Potomac was all on the same side of the Chickahominy River. They had been routed, but the V Corps had fought the good fight. The Confederates had won the field and the day, but it had cost them 7,993 men, more than the Union's 6,837. Moreover, 2,829 of those Union casualties were captured, while virtually all of the Confederate losses were killed or wounded.

At 11 that night, McClellan called his generals together and told them of his plan. They were headed for the James River. In fact, Keyes's IV Corps was already on the move, McClellan having spoken to Keyes earlier in the night. The Union navy had been asked to bring their gunboats up the James to provide cover for the retreating army. Shortly afterward, McClellan sent a telegram to officials in Washington, berating them for the lack of support they had given his army and blaming the imminent destruction of his force on Lincoln's administration.

THE SEVEN DAYS—DAY FOUR: GARNETT'S AND GOLDING'S FARMS

❯ *From the Watt House, drive north (the direction from which you came) on Watt House Road 0.7 mile back to the Old Cold Harbor Road (VA 156). Bear left onto Old Cold Harbor Road, drive 1.6 miles to Creighton Road, and turn left. Drive 1 mile on Creighton Road and take the ramp for I-295 South. Drive 3.3 miles on I-295 South to Exit 31B, VA 156 South/North Airport Drive. Merge onto VA 156 South and drive 1.5 miles to East Washington Street (you will pass a historical marker for Golding's Farm on the left). Turn left onto Washington Street and drive 0.5 mile, then pull over.*

Clearly possessing the initiative now, Lee saw more than an opportunity to drive the Federals from Richmond. He now believed he could crush them, possibly ending the war. To do that, however, he needed to determine what the Union army would do. They could fight for the supply line to White House, possibly successfully. They could retreat back down the peninsula. They also could try to get to the James River. Needing more information, on the morning of June 28 Lee sent Stuart's cavalry, along with infantry support from Richard Ewell's division, to capture White House and the York River & Richmond Railroad, as well as keep an eye on the crossings of the lower Chickahominy River. Until Lee knew where to move, he would keep most of his army north of the river.

In the afternoon, Lee received his answer. White House was burning; the Federals had set fire to all stores left at the port, leaving nothing to the Confederates. Union troops also were seen burning the bridges across the lower Chickahominy at the approach of Confederate cavalry. Now it was certain: McClellan was headed for the James.

Around this time, the soldiers of the Army of the Potomac were beginning to come to the same conclusion. Always the last to know, the men on the ground were not told of their destinations. But as they marched south and then began building bridges over the White Oak Swamp, it became apparent that they were on the retreat. By noon, bridges had been built and the IV Corps began to cross, followed by Porter's beat-up V Corps.

The portion of the Confederate army south of the James River still needed to keep the Federals occupied and, they hoped, in their lines. On June 27, as part of Magruder's demonstrations, Brigadier General Robert Toombs had been ordered to do a reconnaissance in force, and advanced over the farm of James Garnett, only to be beaten back. The next day, Toombs tried it once more. His orders were again to perform a reconnaissance in force, but Toombs went beyond this, pushing into Union general Baldy Smith's territory on the farm of Simon Golding. Smith beat him back soundly, and Toombs's brigade suffered heavily as a result.

Practically the entire battlefield at Garnett's and Golding's Farms has been lost. There is a highway historical marker, but it is some distance southeast of the actual battleground. The closest you will be able to get is within this subdivision, which now covers the old ground, although driving around the streets probably won't help you much as you try to interpret the battle. Toombs's brigade would have been coming generally from the northwest, while Smith's division would have come from the southeast, with the two colliding in the area where you stand.

This small battle was the only significant engagement of the day, as the armies maneuvered and tried to decipher each other's movements. McClellan set up a temporary headquarters at Savage's Station while the IV and V Corps finished crossing to the south side of White Oak Swamp. At 2:00 AM, McClellan himself made the movement, packing up his headquarters and crossing south, closer to safety.

THE SEVEN DAYS—DAY FIVE: SAVAGE'S STATION

> *Drive 0.5 mile back down Washington Street to VA 156 and turn left, then drive 1.9 miles on VA 156 North to Old Hanover Road. Turn right on Old Hanover, then after only 0.1 mile, take a quick left onto Grapevine Road and drive 1.4 miles to Meadow Road. At Meadow Road, turn left and drive 0.1 mile. On your right will be a gravel pull-off area with several historical markers; pull over here.*

By June 29, the Army of the Potomac was practically in full flight. Evacuating Savage's Station, a small depot on the Richmond & York River Railroad, they burned massive amounts of supplies in order to keep them out of Confederate hands. Worse, as they began to leave, the wounded soldiers scattered among the grounds soon realized that they were going to be left to the Confederates; if they could not get out under their own power, they would be captured.

To add to the confusion, McClellan did not assign rear guard duty to any part of the army. (It's possible that this was deliberate; protocol dictated that command would fall to Sumner, and McClellan had not trusted Sumner since his performance at the Battle of Williamsburg.) The II, III, and VI Corps of the army were essentially on their own, knowing only that they needed to reach the other side of the swamp.

Lee, by now, had developed his plan to destroy the Union army. Part of his force would attack McClellan's rear (where it existed), while the other part focused on the crossroads at Glendale. The objective was to pin as much of McClellan's army as possible against White Oak Swamp, where they would be forced to stand and fight. Longstreet and A. P. Hill were to take the long way around the whole army, heading for Glendale, while Huger's force, which was much closer, would take Charles City Road. Magruder was to advance along the Williamsburg Road against the rear guard. Jackson and D. H. Hill would quickly rebuild the Grapevine Bridge over the Chickahominy, then go to Magruder's left and assist his attack.

The three Union corps north of the swamp moved in concert as best they could, but it would not last long. Heintzelman's III Corps was on the left. Sumner's II Corps, in the center, was well out in front of the others. On the right, Franklin's VI Corps quickly fell behind, and asked Sumner to wait.

At 9:00 AM, Magruder ran into the rear of II Corps, and although a sharp fight occurred, it was quick, and the Federals quickly moved on, while Magruder exercised caution and did not push. In the afternoon, the three corps did come together again to form some semblance of a rear guard, but soon Heintzelman led his III Corps to White Oak Swamp, failing to tell the other two commands.

Around 5:30 PM, Franklin and John Sedgwick, one of Franklin's division commanders, saw troops approaching and thought that the III Corps had finally found them. They had been found, but it was not by Federal troops. It was Magruder again, biting at the heels of Sumner and Franklin. Magruder, without the support he was supposed to receive from Jackson (who had received poorly written orders and stayed north of the Chickahominy River), launched an assault, and the Federals sent reinforcements to the rear and turned their artillery on him. The fighting was heavy, at some points hand-to-hand, but was over by 9:00 PM.

The Confederates had come out well ahead in the casualty count—473 to the Union's 1,038—and, most importantly, had gotten the Federal troops to momentarily halt their retreat. Lee, however, was greatly displeased, and unleashed his fury on Magruder for attacking. In truth, Magruder, who happened to be heavily sedated with morphine that day due to an upset stomach, had fought fairly well, other than being a bit cautious. Most of the fault actually lay with Lee, or at least his staff, for issuing unclear orders to Jackson, and perhaps with Jackson himself.

Most of the battlefield at Savage's Station lies within the close proximity of the large cloverleaf formed at the intersection of I-64 and I-295. As you stand at the historic markers in front of you, the open farmland in front of you would have been the Union side of the field. Just beyond the trees on the far side of the field is the former Richmond & York River Railroad, and just slightly behind is the Old Williamsburg Road. The Confederates came from the east, and the two lines collided north to south, approximately along where I-64 runs. This viewpoint, which has been improved in the past few years, is really the only safe way to see the ground, or at least come close to it.

THE SEVEN DAYS—DAY 6: GLENDALE AND WHITE OAK SWAMP

Glendale National Cemetery/Glendale Visitor Center

〉 *From the Savage's Station overlook, turn right (east) onto Meadow Road and drive 2.5 miles, at which point it becomes VA 156. Continue on VA 156 and drive another 4.9 miles as it becomes Elko Road. Here, turn right on Charles City Road, continuing to follow VA 156, and drive 1.2 miles to Willis Church Road, still VA 156. Turn left on Willis Church Road and drive 0.7 mile. On your left, pull into Glendale National Cemetery. The building here also serves as a visitors center for the Glendale/Malvern Hill Unit of Richmond National Battlefield Park.*

Throughout the night, the Union army continued its march south toward the James River. It was not easy. Often later referred to as the "blind march," units struggled to keep together in the darkness and confusion. In fact, the entire V Corps got lost and began heading west, straight toward Richmond; it wasn't until after they had marched for miles that Brigadier General George G. Meade, observing the stars, suggested that perhaps they should turn around. Still, by daybreak of June 30, the entire

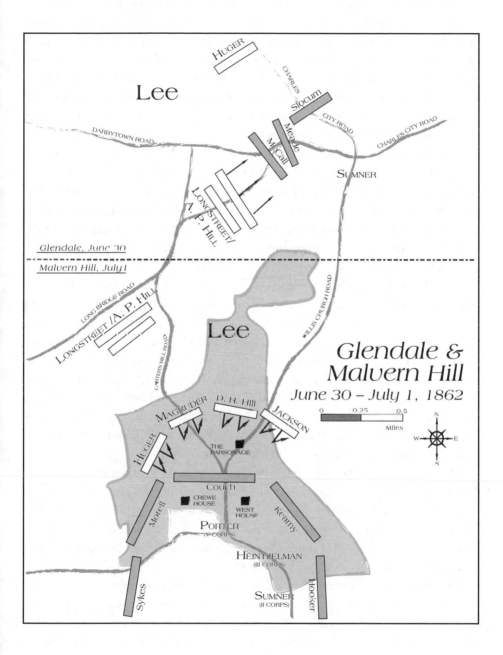

HUGER

Lee

CHARLES

Slocum

CITY ROAD

DARBYTOWN ROAD

Meade

McCall

CHARLES CITY ROAD

SUMNER

LONGSTREET/
A. P. Hill

Glendale, June 30

Malvern Hill, July 1

LONG BRIDGE ROAD

WILLIS CHURCH ROAD

LONGSTREET /A. P. HILL

Lee

CARTERS MILL ROAD

**Glendale &
Malvern Hill**

June 30 – July 1, 1862

0   0.25   0.5

Miles

N
W   E
S

MAGRUDER   D. H. HILL   JACKSON

HUGER

THE
PARSONAGE

Couch

CREWE
HOUSE

WEST
HOUSE

Kearny

Morell

PORTER
(V CORPS)

HEINTZELMAN
(III CORPS)

Sykes

SUMNER
(II CORPS)

Hooker

Federal army had gotten past its last major obstacle, White Oak Swamp, burning its main passage, White Oak Bridge, behind it.

This did not mean that the Federal army was no longer in danger. Keyes's IV Corps and the majority of Porter's V Corps were well ahead of the rest of the army, stopping on a plateau to the south known as Malvern Hill. The other units had a clear path to Malvern Hill using Willis Church Road, also known as Quaker Road (one of several in the area; the multitude of "Quaker Roads" in the area would cause confusion among the Confederate commands that day). However, a large number of wagons still needed to pass, clogging the roads in front of the other corps. All of these roads leading toward the James River eventually converged at a crossroads near the Glendale Farm. So, to reach safety, they would have to hold this crossroads until the road was clear.

Lee also knew that the Federals would have to pass through Glendale. It wasn't just a hunch. No matter how it got through White Oak Swamp, the Army of the Potomac had to pass through the crossroads at Glendale. So Lee sent his entire army there to crush the Federals once and for all. It would later be said by many that if the Confederacy had one chance to destroy the Union army and win the Civil War as a result, it was quite probably June 30, 1862, at Glendale.

All of Lee's forces, including Jackson, were now available and on the field. Jackson would take over for Magruder, who would be in reserve, following the Federals' path over the swamp at White Oak Bridge with 25,300 soldiers. General Theophilus Holmes, whose 7,200 men had been guarding the North Carolina coast, would circle around to the west, taking River Road to meet the head of the Federal column. The rest of the army would converge on Glendale: Huger, on Charles City Road, with 12,000; Longstreet and A. P. Hill, using Long Bridge and Darbytown Roads, with 19,200; and Magruder's reserve of 13,600 Confederates supporting Longstreet. The sound of Huger's guns would be the signal to open the battle. If the Federals could be cut off and surrounded, it would be the end of McClellan's army.

Here at Glendale National Cemetery, you will find the visitors center for the Glendale/Malvern Hill Unit of Richmond National Battlefield. The center is only open during the summer months; however, a visit to the cemetery is worth taking a few moments. The cemetery was created in the months after the war, and many of the dead are from McClellan's Peninsula Campaign, including the surrounding battles of Glendale, White Oak Swamp, and Malvern Hill.

Inside the center, there are a few exhibits related to the surrounding battles. The most useful exhibit is the electric light map program that displays and explains the movements of both armies on June 30 and July 1, 1862. Finally, you may want to pick up the park's driving tour brochure for the battles of Glendale, White Oak Swamp, and Malvern Hill. It is very inexpensive, and following the roads on the 19-mile drive will give you a very thorough understanding of the events of these two critical last

Glendale National Cemetery is the final resting place of many Union soldiers who died during George McClellan's Peninsula Campaign.

days of the Seven Days Battles. (If you come during the off-season, the brochure can be picked at the Tredegar or Cold Harbor/Gaines' Mill visitors centers.)

Just outside the cemetery gates is the Willis Church Road (aka Quaker Road) that the Federals were so desperate to protect. As you look at the road, almost all of the battle occurred up the road to your right around the crossroads. Also to your right, you will see a historic marker on the opposite side of the road. This marker denotes the location of the former Glendale Farm, for which the battle is named (although, like many other Civil War battles, it is also known by several other names).

Glendale Crossroads

> *From the cemetery, turn right onto Willis Church Road and drive 0.7 mile to the next intersection. Go through the intersection and pull over in the gravel area next to the historic markers on your right.*

This is the Glendale crossroads, focal point of the Battle of Glendale. It will help if you have a map with you, because the roads do get confusing. The historical markers where you pulled over are north of the intersection. As you face the intersection, Charles City Road will come from the northwest, your extreme right, and will bend around to your extreme left to head due east. To your right front is Darbytown

Road, and just down this road is its intersection with Long Bridge Road. To your left front is the road you just came from, Willis Church Road.

The Federals placed themselves in a very wide arc around this intersection to block all the roads from any oncoming Confederate advance. The placement of the different units was done by McClellan with the advice of his generals and staff. Shortly after, he left for the rear, again leaving no one in charge. The army's commander spent most of the rest of the day on the USS *Galena,* purportedly to take a look at the probable site for his new supply base, Harrison's Landing.

Slocum's division of the VI Corps was placed astride Charles City Road, approximately 1.5 miles northwest of the intersection (to your extreme right). His men were placed at a strategic clearing near the Brackett Farm, and had felled trees across the road to slow any Confederate advance.

Except for two divisions at White Oak Bridge, the remaining units were spread widely west of the crossroads across Darbytown and Long Bridge Roads (to your front right). Kearny's division of the III Corps was farthest north on the Union right, not far from Slocum. His III Corps counterpart, Hooker, was farthest south and formed the Federal left. In the center and well in front of these two units was McCall's division of the V Corps, astride Long Bridge Road. Slightly behind him and to his left, also in the center, was Sedgwick's division of the II Corps. This 2-mile line contained large

The Glendale crossroads were the focal point of the Battle of Glendale.

gaps, and where there were no gaps, the units intermixed, which would cause confusion later in the battle. In total, the line held 13 batteries of artillery and 36,300 men, and every one of these men knew battle would be coming.

Confederate Advance

> From the historic markers, pull out to your left toward the intersection, then take a right turn down Darbytown Road. Drive 1.3 miles west on Darbytown Road until reaching Carters Mill Road, then turn left. Drive 0.6 mile on Carters Mill Road, then turn left again onto Long Bridge Road. You are now following the Confederate advance of Longstreet's and A. P. Hill's divisions. Drive slowly, as there are few places to pull over here. If you do choose to pull over, use extreme caution.

From the start, the Confederate attack at Glendale crossroads was botched in almost every way by almost every commander on the field. Huger, advancing very slowly and cautiously southeast down Charles City Road, eventually came to the felled trees and other obstructions that Slocum's Union division had placed in the road. Instead of moving the trees, Huger decided it would be quicker to cut a new path through the forest around the road. When he finally did come in sight of the Federals in the late afternoon, he thought their position too strong and commenced a long-range artillery duel, advancing no farther. Huger was out of the fight.

Holmes, taking River Road, eventually came upon Malvern Hill, well south of Glendale, where most of the Union IV and V Corps were already forming defensive positions. When Holmes came up from the west at 3:00 PM, he decided to set up his six pieces of artillery to drive the Federals away. Holmes apparently did not see that not only were most of the V Corps on the western edge of the hill, but also that the Federal reserve artillery—36 guns in seven batteries—were also facing him. Before he could fire a shot, the dust cloud that his men created was spotted, and the Union artillery opened up, followed shortly by the heavy naval artillery of the USS *Galena* and USS *Aroostook* on the James River. Holmes was quickly forced to retire, and he too was out of the fight.

Magruder and the reserve force had been ordered by Lee to support Holmes's advance, but because of poor maps, they arrived far too late to do any good. Magruder then went to support Longstreet and A. P. Hill, but again, by the time he arrived, he could not contribute. Magruder was out.

That left Longstreet and A. P. Hill. They were accompanied by Lee and Jefferson Davis, and were on time, coming onto Long Bridge Road before noon. There they waited for the signal of Huger's guns. Finally, at 2:00 PM, they heard firing—it was actually Jackson, not Huger—and answered with a signal of their own. That signal immediately brought Federal shells crashing all around them. For some reason, it took a few moments to notice that Lee, Davis, Longstreet, A. P. Hill, and their staffs were all conferring with each other in the same place during the bombardment; one of the many shells exploding in their vicinity could have taken out most of the Confederate high command in an instant. A. P. Hill finally ordered Lee and Davis to the rear, then had to do it a second time, a bit more sternly.

While Lee ordered the artillery battle maintained, he stalled Longstreet's advance until hearing from Huger and Jackson. Finally losing his patience, he ordered Longstreet forward around 5:00 PM.

This short stretch of Long Bridge Road, between Carters Mill and Darbytown Roads, is where the heaviest fighting of the Battle of Glendale took place. In front of Longstreet's forces was McCall's division, stretched across the road in their path. Kearny and Hooker were too far away to support him, and Longstreet's half-mile-wide line enveloped the Federals. Soon the Confederates flanked a Union battery, charging out of the woods to claim six pieces and pushing back McCall's left. As Longstreet pressed forward, the fighting grew very intense, eventually becoming hand-to-hand. The two lines went back and forth along this road, charging and countercharging, trying to gain control of the artillery in the center. The only significant movement in the lines came on the Union left, where Hooker was steadily driving the Confederates back.

To the north, Kearny soon heard the sound of battle. After determining what was in his front, he wheeled his division around to the left, eventually forming almost a right angle with McCall's division. Kearny had to advance through thick woods, and it took him some time to reach the fighting. When he did, the Confederates immediately launched a charge, then another and finally a third, all of which were repulsed. Eventually, Slocum's division, which had nothing to do with Huger standing still, was also called into the fight. The struggle lasted until after dark. At 8:30 PM, A. P. Hill threw his last reserves into the fight, but the Union line held. The Confederates would not destroy the Union army at Glendale. And again, throughout the battle, everyone had the same question on their mind: Where is Jackson?

Unlike the large battle at Gaines' Mill, the casualty count here was about the same on both sides—3,797 for the Union, 3,673 for the Confederates. However, like that battle, a disproportionate amount of the Confederate losses were due to killed and wounded, practically all of their casualties, while almost half the Union number, about 1,800, were captured, along with 18 pieces of artillery.

While at the moment there is not a great deal of interpretation on the Glendale battlefield itself, that situation is changing. Several years ago, Glendale was largely regarded as "lost," with housing already existing on the field and more subdivisions to come. Now, however, both Glendale and Malvern Hill are wonderful success stories in battlefield preservation. The Civil War Trust, in partnership with other groups, foundations, donors, the National Park Service, and local landowners, has protected hundreds of acres at each of these two battlefields, including much of the portion where Longstreet and McCall collided along Long Bridge Road. While significant work remains to preserve the rest of the area, and further development continues to encroach on the battlefield, the transformation over the past few years is nothing short of remarkable.

White Oak Swamp

❯ *Continue on Long Bridge Road until reaching Darbytown Road, then turn right. Drive 1.7 miles straight ahead, first on Darbytown Road and then Charles City Road as you pass through the Glendale crossroads. At Elko Road, bear left and drive 1.3 miles, crossing the small bridge over White Oak Swamp. There will be historic markers on your left immediately after you cross the bridge; you may find it easiest to proceed up the road to turn around and come back, then park in the gravel area adjacent to the bridge.*

After the Federals had finished crossing White Oak Swamp and burned the White Oak Bridge, Franklin, commander of the VI Corps, stayed behind to guard the crossing. He kept Baldy Smith's division with him, and was also given Israel Richardson's division of the II Corps. They set the artillery on a hillside overlooking the bridge site, with their infantry slightly behind a bend in the road and some of the rolling terrain of the area. Franklin's total force was about 25,200 troops.

Jackson, tasked with pushing through the crossing and converging with the rest of the Confederate army at Glendale, got an early start that morning, but was slowed when his troops began picking through the still-smoldering temptations left behind by the Federals at Savage's Station. When his first units finally made their way to the bridge, they found it burned, and immediately saw the strength of the Federal position across the river. Knowing it would take some creativity to get past the Union guns, Jackson began setting his artillery behind a ridge on the north side of the swamp and waited for the rest of his command to arrive—25,300 men, almost exactly matching the Federal strength.

You are now standing at the site of the White Oak Bridge, and you can see what's left of the White Oak Swamp in front of you. Although development has taken away pieces of the swamp in this area over the years, much of the terrain remains as it was during the battle. Across the bridge on the left side of the road, almost directly in front of you, you can see the high ground on which the Union placed its guns. Behind you and to your right is the ridge behind which Jackson placed his artillery (you may have noticed this ridge if you had to drive past and then turn around to get to the bridge location).

At 2:00 PM, with all of his artillery ready to go, Jackson quickly rolled his guns into position and surprised the Federals. (This was the firing that Lee and Longstreet thought was Huger's signal.) The Union artillery pulled back on its ridge, stunned by Jackson's sudden appearance. Encouraged by his progress, Jackson sent the Second Virginia Cavalry to find another crossing of the swamp, and he and D. H. Hill accompanied the party. However, soon after they set out, they discovered that in addition to the Union artillery, the infantry was in force, too. Previously obscured by trees and the terrain, the Union troops opened up on the cavalry, forcing them back in a hurry.

As a last resort, Jackson actually sent some of his men down to the bridge in an attempt to build a temporary crossing, but the Union fire was far too intense and concentrated on the same spot. Although in numbers it was an even fight, the Federals had a much better position and had had the time to strengthen it. Jackson settled for an artillery duel that lasted the rest of the day but did little damage. In later years, he would receive much criticism for his performance at White Oak Swamp; Longstreet, for one, quite plainly said later that he could have used Jackson's men at the crossroads and that he should have either moved or found another crossing. Whether true or not, it is only one of many questionable decisions by the legendary general during the Seven Days, and his troops' lack of involvement effectively neutralized a third of Lee's army.

If you walk across the bridge, or as you drive across, Baldy Smith's division was on the hill to your left, with Richardson's division to the right. It was Richardson's men, in woods and behind this large hill, that Jackson did not see when he and his cavalry reconnoitered for another crossing at the bridge.

THE SEVEN DAYS—DAY SEVEN: MALVERN HILL

The Parsonage

❭ *From White Oak Bridge, continue south across the bridge and drive 1.3 miles, then turn right onto Charles City Road. Drive 1.7 miles to Long Bridge Road, going through the Glendale crossroads, and turn left. Drive 1.1 miles to Carters Mill Road, then turn left. Drive 1.4 miles on Carters Mill Road; as you drive, observe the landscape on your right. You are now heading up Malvern Hill; before long, you will see several cannons marking the Confederate position. Note not only that you are going uphill, but also that Malvern Hill is more of a plateau than a hill, with several spots where the elevation changes drastically. When you reach Willis Church Road, turn left and drive 0.2 mile, then pull into the gravel parking area to your right.*

During the night, well after the fighting at Glendale had ceased, the Union VI Corps headed south down Willis Church Road, followed by the II and III Corps. All of them, without orders, went to a rise called Malvern Hill, where the IV and V Corps had already begun preparing defenses the day before. It was a short march, and by daybreak on July 1, 1862, the entire Army of the Potomac, for the first time during the Seven Days Battles, was united and on the same field.

Here at the Parsonage parking area, face away from the road and slightly to your right; this is Malvern Hill. It is a very gradual elevation, but its long slope of open ground (which you are now on) belies its height, 130 feet above the James River. At that height is a plateau, 1¼ miles north to south and three-quarters of a mile east to west.

To a trained military eye, Malvern Hill provides an ideal defensive position. When Porter's V Corps arrived on the hill the day before, he formed on the west side with his left on River Road. His artillery and infantry followed the arc of the plateau, and when the IV Corps arrived behind him, they simply filled in next to him, extending the line. When the other three corps arrived, they did the same. Soon the Union artillery bristled around the crest of the hill in a horseshoe shape from west to east. If there was a weak spot, it was to the north, where the hill was narrowest, but this is not to say that the line was weak at all. With troops holding the high ground with large open fields in front of them, an enemy attacking Malvern Hill from any direction would find it a daunting task.

McClellan came to that conclusion very quickly. He arrived on the field at approximately 8:30 AM to observe the defensive positions, and made a few adjustments, extending the line slightly. By 9:15 he was safely back on board the *Galena* to again sail to Harrison's Landing. As he had done the previous days, he left no one in command.

Lee was extremely frustrated. Even though he had sent the Union army fleeing from the gates of Richmond, he had had his chance to crush them and let it slip away. To say he was unhappy with his generals would be quite an understatement; though he almost never lost his cool, several accounts exist of Lee venting his frustrations on his generals and staff over these two days. Still, Lee saw that his army had one more chance for victory here at Malvern Hill, and though it was against long odds, he had to take it.

A VERY SHORT REST

By July 1, Robert E. Lee was, to say the least, exhausted. In a telling indicator of just how severe a toll the Seven Days had taken, Lee asked General James Longstreet to remain at his side throughout the battle—not as adviser, but to take over command of the army if Lee could not continue. Later that day, when one division commander came to deliver a report, he found Lee sleeping under a tree—with President Jefferson Davis standing guard over him, making sure he would remain undisturbed.

Longstreet and A. P. Hill's divisions, which had fought so hard the day before, would be kept in reserve. Jackson, Huger, and Magruder, who had done very little and had relatively fresh troops, were to make this fight. Jackson would lead on the Confederate left, advancing toward Malvern Hill down Willis Church Road, with Magruder following him. Huger was to advance across the open farmland on the Confederate right.

It took some time for the Confederate line to form, and for once, it was Jackson who was in place first. His position was in the area around you on the south side of Willis Church Road. D. H. Hill, still part of Jackson's command, lined up his division on Jackson's right astride the road, making up the center of the Confederate line; many of them lined up just to the south of you, and they often sought cover in the woods across from the parking area.

As had happened too often for the Confederates during the Seven Days, another Confederate command went missing at the wrong time. This time it was Magruder, who had poor maps and took the wrong road, delaying the battle for three hours. Huger's division was not much better; two of his brigades, along with Huger himself, could not be found. What was present of Huger's division lined up to D. H. Hill's right.

The ruins of the Willis Creek Parsonage, present at the time of the battle, are across Willis Church Road. D. H. Hill used the house during the battle, and shells ex-

A view from the Malvern Hill plateau.

ploded throughout the yard. Also in this area was the Poindexter Farm. As you look to the south, away from the road, you will notice a rise in the terrain. Lee noticed this as well, and thought that it would make a good artillery position. To the west, in the open fields along Carters Mill Road, Longstreet found a similar rise. Lee and Longstreet conferred, and came up with a new plan of battle. Virtually all of the Confederate artillery would be placed here, on the Poindexter Farm, and on the rise near the Carter House. These two massive batteries of artillery would provide a converging fire on the front of Malvern Hill, the Union center. After softening the line with artillery, the infantry would be able to charge and possibly break the line. Lee immediately started making arrangements.

Still looking south, you will notice a small white house in the field. This is the West House, and was a landmark during the battle. The Federal artillery was lined up almost directly in front of this house, extending in both directions across Malvern Hill. To the right of the West House is the point on the Union line where Lee and Longstreet would focus their artillery.

There is a walking trail that circles virtually the entire battlefield at Malvern Hill, and it can be picked up here at the Parsonage. The trail is just over 1.5 miles, with an extension to an overlook that brings the total length close to 2 miles. It is a long walk, but if you have the time, take it. It is the best way to understand the terrain of Malvern Hill and how it affected the battle. If you do take the trail, be sure you are well prepared for a long hike.

Malvern Hill

❯ *From the Parsonage parking area, turn left, back onto Willis Church Road. Follow the road for 0.4 mile, bearing left, then park at the parking area and kiosk on your right.*

Atop the hill, many of the Federals were catching what rest they could, except for the artillerymen, who were regularly launching shells toward the forming Confederates. Throughout the entire Civil War, with only a few exceptions, Union artillery was vastly superior to the Confederates' in number, size, and accuracy. This battle would be no different.

When the Confederates rolled their guns out at the Poindexter Farm, it was not exactly the grand battery that Lee had envisioned. Of the 17 batteries under Jackson's command, because of their scattered nature and the fact that they had fired a great deal of ammunition the previous day at White Oak Bridge, the Confederates could only gather 16 cannons for the left side of the line. As soon as the Federals saw them, they trained their 37 guns on them and quickly took most of them out of the fight. The same happened on the other side of the field at the Carter Farm, where each of the six Confederate batteries that were gathered were formed piecemeal and were taken out one at a time almost as soon as they appeared.

At the kiosk next to the parking lot, you are standing near the Union center. To your right, across the road, is the West House, with cannons marking the Federal artillery line, which extends across the road in front of you and then to your left. During the battle, the Union guns became so hot from repeated firing that they were rotated in and out. To your right, you should be able to see the ruins of the Parsonage; a short distance in front of it is the ridge the Confederate artillery used. To the left, far in the distance, cannons are placed in the position of the other Confederate battery at the Carter Farm.

Lee's plan, as written, was that Brigadier General Lewis Armistead would determine the proper time for the Confederate advance. Armistead's command would be closest to the Union center and could see how well the Confederate artillery was doing; when the Federal line was soft, Armistead would give the rebel yell, and the rest of the infantry would charge.

Armistead's brigade was one of the two from Huger's division that made it to the field. Huger's division had not fought during the Seven Days, and Armistead was leading a brigade into battle for the first time in his career. In addition, Lee's orders, written by his staff, were confusing, and nobody seemed to consider that, with massive amounts of artillery firing at once, no one would be able to hear anyone give the rebel yell. Together, these factors were a recipe for misinterpretation and disaster, and that's exactly what happened for the Confederates.

By 3:00 PM, it was evident that the Confederate artillery assault was not effective. In fact, Lee was already discussing moving units far to the left, to be in position to outflank the Union right the next day. At the same time, on the field far from these discussions, Union skirmishers were giving Armistead's brigade a hard time, and they began to press the Confederates. Armistead pushed back, moving forward into a small ravine in front of the Federal line and becoming pinned down.

An hour later, at 4:00 PM, Magruder, with his own division still far behind him, and the rest of Huger's brigades—without Huger—arrived on the field and lined up to the right of Armistead. Magruder saw Armistead in the ravine, as did Lee, who was just then receiving a false rumor that McClellan was in retreat. Lee ordered Magruder to advance, even though Magruder would be leading soldiers not under his command—and not all of them agreed to follow him. What Lee did not make clear to Magruder was that he should charge when signaled. Magruder interpreted the order to mean that he should charge immediately.

At 5:30 PM, Magruder led 5,000 men of Huger's division in a charge against the Union line. General Ambrose Wright's brigade, moving quickly, ended up well in front of the others, and although they got within 500 yards, they were badly torn up. D. H. Hill, seeing Magruder's advance, thought that Armistead's signal had been sounded and sent his five brigades in, with one of them getting within 200 yards of the Federals.

Suddenly and without warning, Lee had an infantry fight on his hands. He did his best to direct the battle, but units kept throwing themselves against the Union line one at a time, enabling Federal artillery to concentrate on one regiment at a time and mow them down with canister. At 8:30 PM, the last charge was made, and although these men came closest to the line, they met the same fate as the others.

The Federals had not gotten away without a scratch, suffering 3,007 casualties during the Battle of Malvern Hill, 818 of them missing (probably most of them rounded up as stragglers on the next day's march). But for the Confederates, it had been a nightmare. In a battle that had really only been fought less than half the day, they had lost a staggering 5,650 men. In later years, D. H. Hill estimated that more than half of these casualties came not from the Union infantry but from artillery, a remarkable and distinctive feature of this terrible battle.

Still at the kiosk, looking straight in front of you as well as slightly to your right, you are viewing the wide open fields that D. H. Hill's men charged over. If you elected not to take the entire walking trail, you may find it worth your while to follow part of it into the woods to your left. This will take you to the location of the Crewe House and, more importantly, give you a good view of where Armistead's and Magruder's men came from. This is probably the best spot on the battlefield from which to appreciate the difficulty the Confederates faced in climbing the hill. None of the trees around you were present at the time of the battle; the Confederates rushing against the mass of Federal artillery had no cover.

HARRISON'S LANDING

> *From Malvern Hill, turn right onto Willis Church Road (VA 156) and drive 0.2 mile, then turn right to stay on Willis Church Road. Drive another mile to the intersection with VA 5. Turn left onto VA 5 East and drive for 8.5 miles, keeping with it as it winds through the woods. You will then reach Herring Creek Road (VA 633) and will begin to see signs for Berkeley Plantation. Turn right onto Herring Creek Road, then bear right onto the entrance road for Berkeley Plantation.*

By daybreak of a very rainy July 2, the Union army was on its way to Harrison's Landing, a safe site within a short march where the army could encamp under the protection of the gunboats in the James River. More than a few of McClellan's generals were outraged at the fact that they were evacuating an excellent defensive position from which they had whipped the Rebels; Kearny, never one to mince words, said that it must be "cowardice or treason." McClellan, who was still on board the *Galena*, paid no heed. He sent a telegram to Lincoln saying that the move was simply a move to "a different base of operations," and the use of the term "change of base" as a substitute for retreat soon became fodder for many a joke, Union and Confederate.

The Peninsula Campaign, however, had been anything but funny. Over a three-month period, McClellan had taken the Army of the Potomac a very short distance, fought one offensive action, and turned around. The estimated cost of this less-than-grand expedition: 25,370 Union soldiers.

With the rains and the army destroying the roads, the meager Confederate pursuit did not reveal much to Lee about the Union army's intentions. It was decided that Stuart's cavalry would conduct a reconnaissance, which was completed the next day. After a short skirmish and a close call, Stuart reported that the camp was approximately 4 miles long and stretched a full mile from the bank of the James River, and that there were heavy creeks on two sides of the camp. Seeing the strength of the position and considering the Federal navy's presence, Lee took the Army of Northern Virginia back into the Richmond defenses.

Although the Union casualty numbers were terrible, they were nothing compared to the Confederate losses. Their casualties over the Seven Days in defense of their capital amounted to 22 percent of the total force, a number that would not allow the Confederates to last long in this war. Further, the Confederates had suffered "hard" casualties, few captured and almost all killed and wounded; in fact, the Union losses of missing or captured were six times higher. They had driven the enemy away, but it was not without great cost.

CASUALTIES (SEVEN DAYS)

Confederate: killed, 3,494; wounded, 15,758; missing or captured, 952; total: 20,204.

Union: killed, 1,734; wounded, 8,066; missing or captured, 6,055; total: 15,855.

Total Casualties: 36,059

Total Estimated Casualties During Peninsula Campaign: 55,820

Berkeley Plantation was the home of Benjamin Harrison, signer of the Declaration of Independence, father to President William Henry Harrison, and great-grandfather to President Benjamin Harrison. One of the reasons McClellan chose the site for his new base was the wharf that extended into the James River to serve the plantation, making it a perfect place for his army. Today, touring the home provides a wonderful mix of history from the colonial period through the present day, and the grounds are beautiful, providing a great place to spend a quiet afternoon.

Of course, there is plenty of Civil War history here. Still stuck in the wall of one of the buildings is a Confederate cannonball, courtesy of Stuart during his July 3, 1862, reconnaissance. The basement of the home serves as a museum, with a considerable portion dedicated to its use as a Union camp. Also on the grounds, down a

Visitors to Berkeley Plantation can still see a Confederate cannonball fired by J. E. B. Stuart lodged in one of the outbuildings on the property.

short path to the family graveyard, is the site where the somber "Taps" was composed, and there is a memorial there to commemorate the event.

On July 8, Lincoln arrived at Harrison's Landing to see McClellan's new base. He conferred with McClellan about the new Union army, the Army of Virginia, commanded by John Pope. When asked if the two commands should be combined, McClellan said no; he should keep his army here, be reinforced with 55,000 men, and advance on Richmond when he was ready. Lincoln went back to Washington and sent his new general-in-chief, Henry Halleck, for his assessment. After speaking with McClellan and his generals, Halleck advised Lincoln to bring the army back. On August 3, McClellan was ordered to bring his army home. In a last desperate attempt, McClellan sent Hooker to reoccupy Malvern Hill, but Lee quickly countered the move, and Hooker was recalled.

Seeing the Federals give Malvern Hill up so quickly for a second time had provided Lee with just the information he needed. He was now certain that McClellan was not going to advance on Richmond under any circumstances. Lee had been considering another plan, but was reluctant to leave Richmond exposed. Now, he saw another chance to seize the initiative—by moving north.

CHAPTER 4

The War Moves North: The Second Manassas Campaign

ON JUNE 26, 1862, in the midst of the Seven Days Battles around Richmond, Abraham Lincoln created a new Union army. It would be commanded by General John Pope, who had achieved success in the western theater. Patched together from the fractured, demoralized, and poorly supplied commands spread across northern Virginia, the army consisted of 51,000 men and was organized into three corps. The I Corps would be commanded by Franz Sigel, who replaced John Fremont after he refused to serve under Pope. Nathaniel Banks's forces in the Shenandoah Valley would form the II Corps. The III Corps would be led by Irvin McDowell, still near Fredericksburg. The new army's name would be the Army of Virginia.

Almost immediately upon taking command, Pope began shaking things up, both north and south. On July 14, Pope issued a message to the men now under his command. On the face of it, it might have sounded like a rallying cry, but to most of his men it was an arrogant insult. Pope boasted of the Union victories in the western theater, "where we have always seen the backs of our enemies," and decreed that this new army would not use terms like "line of retreat" or "taking strong positions and holding them," because "success and glory are in the advance, disaster and shame lurk in the rear." While it may not have been Pope's intention, the majority of officers in Virginia saw it as a direct slap in the face to the fighting men of the east and, particularly, George McClellan.

Soon afterward, Pope issued a series of vague orders setting harsh policies for the

Union and Confederate forces fought near Chapman's Mill in Thoroughfare Gap.

treatment of civilians in Virginia. The orders earned criticism from Union officers because they antagonized civilians, and while they allowed Union forces to feed and supply themselves from the land, further denying supplies to the Confederacy, they also destroyed discipline, as soldiers had virtually free license to plunder or to arrest civilians with little cause.

In the south, the orders were regarded as barbaric. Robert E. Lee went so far as to write a letter to Union general-in-chief Henry Halleck to inform him that if Pope were captured, he would be treated as a criminal rather than a prisoner of war. However, Lee had already been working on his own plans to deal with the new Army of Virginia. As McClellan's Army of the Potomac stood frozen at Harrison's Landing, Lee knew that they would eventually combine forces with the new army. If he moved north quickly enough, he might be able not only to hit Pope's army before that happened, but to create an opportunity to invade the north, bringing relief to Virginia's citizens and dealing a severe blow to Union morale.

The end result of this great campaign would be what was, to that point, the bloodiest battle of the war. Lee's first campaign of the war would reveal many of the maneuvers that would mark him as one of history's great military commanders. It would also bring the Union army in the east to one of its lowest points. Often overlooked, the Second Manassas Campaign provides great drama, entertaining stories, and some of the most spectacular movements of the Civil War.

BEFORE YOU GO

» PLANNING YOUR TRIP

While there are a number of stops on this tour, you are likely to spend most of your time at the first (Cedar Mountain) and the last (Manassas National Battlefield). The city nearest to the battlefield at Cedar Mountain is Culpeper, where there are plenty of hotels and restaurants. If you would like a bit more variety in your choices, however, you might want to stay in Fredericksburg, an hour's drive east but loaded with options.

At the other end is Manassas. As you saw in Chapter 1, Manassas is on the edge of the Washington, D.C., metro area, and it offers many options for food and lodging. Remember also, though, that the area is congested, and you should be sure to allow yourself a bit of leeway in your travel times to account for traffic.

SECOND MANASSAS CAMPAIGN

Number of sites: 12

Total miles: 155

Estimated time: 2 days

Must-sees: Cedar Mountain, Manassas National Battlefield Park

Close seconds: Thoroughfare Gap, Chantilly

In between, you will be visiting mostly small sites in rural areas. To be frank, with only a few exceptions, there isn't much left of most of them. Still, with the help contained here, you should be able to decipher the different areas of battle, and passing through Thoroughfare Gap as the Confederate army did is an almost essential part of the tour. While not all of these sites present a lot to see, you would be doing yourself a disservice by skipping most of them. Be forewarned, though, that there isn't much left of the Rappahannock Crossings except for the crossings themselves, and you may wish to skip these sites altogether, shortening your tour by about 50 miles and quite a bit of time.

» RECOMMENDATIONS

As noted in the first chapter, staying in Manassas gives you many options, but the other small cities in the area offer convenient and pleasant places to stay as well. If you plan to visit Washington or other parts of Northern Virginia during your trip, Alexandria or Arlington may be the best options.

Also, don't forget to visit the website for Manassas National Battlefield to check the tour times and to see if any special events might be coming up. The anniversary of the battle is in August, and there are almost always commemorative events surrounding it. Be sure to also look at the options and times for the ranger-guided tours, all free and always worth your time.

The Confederate army was briefly split into two during this campaign, and both parts covered the same ground. Because of this, a handful of the stops—particularly Catlett's Station, Bristoe Station, and Thoroughfare Gap—don't exactly match up chronologically with the events of the campaign. The same applies to the sites within Manassas National Battlefield Park to some degree. However, they are all fairly close together, so if you choose to follow them in a different order, you won't lose much. While they are presented here in the easiest order to see, you may want to change your route after reading ahead a bit.

Finally, a repeated word of warning: Take care as you drive around Manassas National Battlefield. The roads running through the park are very busy highways. Be extremely careful as you enter and exit the roadways in this hilly area.

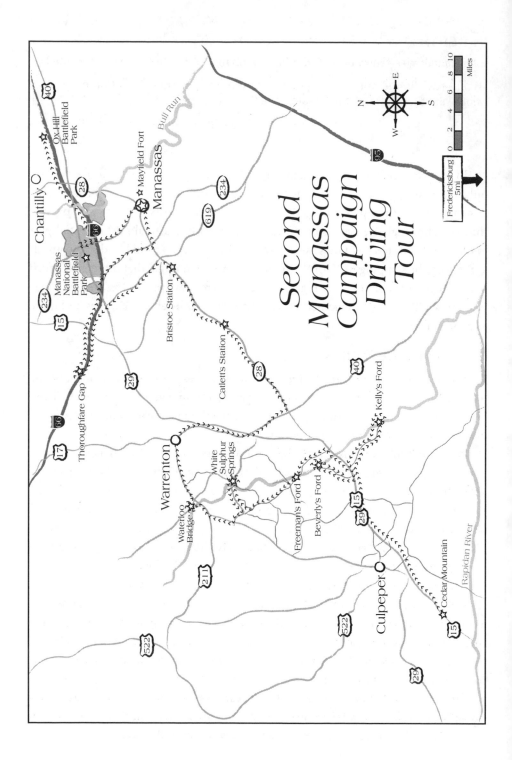

THE CAMPAIGN TOUR

CEDAR MOUNTAIN

Cedar Mountain Battlefield

> *Your tour begins in Rapidan, Virginia, just southwest of Culpeper. From Culpeper, drive south on US 15 (James Madison Highway) for about 4.5 miles until you reach General Winder Road (VA 657). Turn right here and drive 0.2 mile to the sharp bend in the road. You will see several signs and historic markers; pull into the gravel area.*

In early July, while Pope commanded the army from Washington, he directed several cavalry raids against the Virginia Central Railroad, the Confederate lifeline to the bountiful supplies of the Shenandoah Valley. The raids, originating from Culpeper, were not particularly successful—most of the track that he was able to destroy was repaired within days—but they did provide Pope with valuable intelligence, confirming rumors that Stonewall Jackson was in nearby Gordonsville. Further probes by Federal cavalry estimated Jackson's strength at 30,000.

Lee had indeed sent Jackson to Gordonsville, northwest of Richmond, with 14,000 men. Lee was still uncertain at this point about the intentions of McClellan's Army of the Potomac, but was looking for any chance to break out of the Richmond defenses and head north. Seeing a possible opportunity, Lee sent A. P. Hill's Light Division to Gordonsville on July 27 as reinforcement, with the caveat that Jackson attack quickly so that Hill could return to defend Richmond, if necessary.

Two days later, as Hill arrived at Gordonsville, Pope arrived at Culpeper, ready to advance against Jackson's forces. He began to concentrate his forces at Culpeper, looking for an opportunity to advance on Jackson's left. However, Pope soon learned that the Army of the Potomac had been ordered to withdraw from the peninsula, and that Ambrose Burnside's force would also be arriving from North Carolina. Halleck, Lincoln's new general-in-chief, ordered Pope to form a line along the Rappahannock River, with his left at Fredericksburg, and wait for the coming reinforcements.

The Union army's troop movements, however, were no longer a mystery to Lee. One of the fruits of Pope's intelligence-gathering expeditions was the capture of Confederate captain John Singleton Mosby, who was riding to join Jackson with a letter of recommendation from General J. E. B. Stuart. Not knowing that Mosby would later turn out to be one of the Confederacy's most effective raiders, earning the nickname "The Gray Ghost," they shipped him to Fort Monroe and then paroled him only days later, sending him on his way. Mosby was able to gather valuable intelligence while at Fort Monroe, and was able to confirm for Lee not only that McClellan would be leaving the peninsula, but that Burnside was headed to Alexandria, not near Richmond to support McClellan as feared. Lee was now convinced: It was time to take the army north and destroy the villain Pope before he could be reinforced. As Lee so simply and subtly put to Jackson, "I want Pope to be suppressed."

On August 7, having learned that Pope's forces were moving but that they were still strung out on the roads leading to Culpeper, Jackson immediately prepared to attack. Banks's corps was already in the area; if Jackson could attack before the rest of the army was there, he could deal a major blow to the Federals. His army was on the move from Gordonsville that evening, and although traffic jams and miscarried orders would slow the march, the head of the Confederate force— Major General Richard Ewell—would be within 8 miles of Culpeper by August 8, his division camping near Cedar Mountain.

Pope, meanwhile, knew that Jackson was heading northeast. General Samuel Crawford's brigade was already between Culpeper and the Rebels, and Pope ordered Banks, who was approaching Culpeper with his two divisions, to support him. Banks reached Culpeper that night, while Crawford camped only 4 miles north of the Confederates.

The next morning, August 9, after having received orders from Halleck not to at-

Monuments and interpretive signs commemorate the action at Cedar Mountain Battlefield.

tack until more troops arrived, Pope sent General Benjamin Roberts to verbally relay orders to Banks that he was to occupy a strong position and wait. Pope should have written the order down, because by the time it reached Banks's ears, he thought he was to move forward and attack immediately if Jackson advanced. Skirmishing had been occurring all morning, and Crawford had started taking artillery fire at 11:00 AM. Banks pushed his corps to Cedar Mountain, with General A. S. Williams's division arriving at noon and General Christopher Augur's division coming up at 2:00 PM. By 3:00, the line was formed, with Williams's division and artillery on the Union right and Augur on the left, facing southwest astride Culpeper Road with cavalry guarding both flanks. The Federal force totaled 9,000 men.

On the other side of the field, things were moving a bit slower. Jackson didn't expect to fight that day, mostly because of the lack of progress during the previous two. General Jubal Early's brigade, part of Ewell's division, received orders at 8:00 AM to advance and take control of the crossroads of Culpeper and Madison Court House Roads. Seeing Federal cavalry in full presence, Early formed his men in some nearby woods and put several pieces of artillery on the north slope of Cedar Mountain to drive them off. (These were the guns that the Union troops heard at 11:00 AM.) Jackson came up to the front to take a look at the Federal position, and thinking that he greatly outnumbered them, decided to attack. Early would move forward to hold the center while Ewell, with two brigades, would flank the Federal left. General Charles Winder, who had been put in command of the Stonewall Brigade that morning, would turn the Federal right. Early was to wait until Winder was in position before advancing. Preparations having been made, Jackson and Ewell left the field to nap.

Where you now stand, at the Civil War Trust's well-tended site, is the intersection of the old Culpeper Road and the west end of the Crittenden Farm lane, where the front gate became a landmark of the battle. Both are now part of General Charles Winder Boulevard. If you are looking at the historic markers, Culpeper Road ran behind you and into the fields to your right. Winder Boulevard then takes a turn to the east to continue down what was the Crittenden Farm lane. The farm lane generally formed the Confederate line, with the Union line across the fields to your left as you look down the lane. Also as you look down the lane, you can see Cedar Mountain rising distinctly from the farmland.

At 2:00 PM, Early began to move forward. Scuffling with Federal cavalry (sent in front as Banks formed his lines), Early discovered Union artillery only a half mile to his front and ordered his own four pieces placed to his right in a grove known as "The Cedars." At 4:00 PM, Winder also saw the artillery and ordered a brigade forward to investigate. Finding that the Federal right reached much farther than previously thought, Winder and the Confederates suddenly realized that they were facing a significant amount of Union troops.

Shortly after Winder's discovery, Ewell ordered five guns to Culpeper Road, opening an artillery duel that lasted an hour. During this exchange, Winder, who was helping to direct the Confederate artillery fire, was struck by a shell and killed, and command of the Stonewall Brigade fell to General William Taliaferro. Meanwhile, far to the rear, Hill heard the rising sounds of battle and sent four pieces of artillery forward, where they were placed to Early's left front.

During this time, Banks had still been watching and waiting for Jackson to move. Although the artillery fire had certainly increased, neither army had yet made a significant movement. Banks reported as such to Pope at 4:25 PM, but added that the Confederates seemed to be taking up position for an attack. Finally, at 5:00 PM, Banks decided to make his move. On the Union left, east of Culpeper Road, Augur's division advanced, leaving one brigade behind to watch Ewell's two brigades on the north slope of Cedar Mountain. While one brigade became somewhat confused marching through the tall August corn and was driven back, General John Geary's brigade, with his right on Culpeper Road, moved forward against Taliaferro's Confederates. Although the brigade received both frontal and flanking fire from Confederates west of the road, Geary advanced steadily and put up a fierce fight. Both Geary and Augur would be wounded in this part of the field.

Still standing at your position near the historic markers, if you face the fields to the north you can see the area where Augur's division made its advance. The trace of Culpeper Road is still visible in front of you, and Geary's brigade would have been just to the right of it, moving toward you from across the field.

At this point, you will probably want to take the Civil War Trust's trail through Cedar Mountain Battlefield. It is a half-mile loop trail over easy terrain with the option of taking a detour to a monument to the Third Wisconsin Infantry. There are markers along the trail that explain where you are on the battlefield and interpret the events in concise detail. If you don't want to take the trail, walk just a bit ahead to the first visible trail sign.

The Union right, west of Culpeper Road, began to move at 5:15 PM. Crawford's brigade, with its left along the Culpeper Road, advanced against Lieutenant Colonel Thomas Garnett's Confederates. At 6:00 PM, with their lines only 100 yards apart, Crawford's men lunged forward, and although they were hit with a staggering volley, they kept going. Meeting the line and engaging in hand-to-hand combat, Crawford finally drove one of Garnett's regiments back in retreat. He had punched a hole in the Confederate center.

Seeing the opportunity he had, Crawford immediately moved to his right, flanked another of Garnett's regiments, and drove them off the field. He then wheeled about and moved to his left. Coming up behind the Confederates who had been firing at Geary's division across Culpeper Road, the Federals sent a fierce volley into their rear,

The fields at Cedar Mountain. The old Culpeper Road ran to the left of the split-rail fence.

shocking and scattering them. One by one, Garnett's remaining regiments, then Taliaferro's, and then Early's were rolled up as Crawford crossed Culpeper Road and kept moving down Crittenden Lane. The Confederate line was disintegrating, and it seemed as if nothing could stop the Union attack.

The trail marks the point at which Crawford's men first met the Confederates. If you are standing near the beginning of the trail, the Union advance would have come from your front left. The Virginians who had been firing into Geary's troops across Culpeper Road were lined up along the road right in front of you; when the Union troops wheeled to their left (toward you), they found themselves right behind these Confederates, and continued down Crittenden Lane to your right.

Crittenden Lane

> *Drive west down Samuel Winder Road 0.2 mile back toward US 15. Pull over briefly at the intersection.*

Unfortunately for the Union, however, General George Gordon's division, which was supposed to follow Crawford's and provide support, stayed where it was, safely in the woods at the north end of the field. Meanwhile, Hill had sent Lieutenant Colonel Edward Thomas's brigade to the Confederate right, setting the troops at an angle to the line. By the time Crawford's men reached the fresh Rebel troops, they were exhausted, and the hole that had been created in the Confederate line had not been filled by Federals, as it should have been, but was instead occupied by two more of Hill's brigades. In addition to these fresh troops, Hill and Jackson were able to rally Garnett's crushed regiments, with Jackson gallantly waving his sword in the air to inspire his men forward. (This instance is famously known as the only time Jackson ever drew his sword in battle. Not many noticed at the time, but because of this lack of use, it was actually rusted into its scabbard, remaining there as he waved it.)

Looking in front of you, you can see the continuation of Crittenden Lane across US 15. Crawford's brigade had advanced well down this lane before they were forced to pull back.

Union Right

❯ *From the intersection, turn left on US 15 and drive 0.3 mile to Dove Hill Road, then turn left and drive 0.4 mile. You will see a pond to your left; carefully pull over here (there isn't much room) and look to your left, south of the road.*

You are now between the lines. Looking south of the road, Crawford's fight took place to your front, while Gordon remained behind you. By this time, it was Crawford's brigade that was being attacked from the rear, receiving volleys from Hill's brigades. Soon after, Taliaferro's re-formed troops were delivering flanking fire into the Union brigade. The Federals were forced to pull back past where you now stand, covered by the 10th Maine Infantry, which had been kept back to protect the Federal artillery. Still, Gordon did not move, and would not until 7:00 PM, but he soon withdrew as twilight began to darken the field. By 7:15 PM, the fight west of Culpeper Road was over.

Union Left

❯ *Carefully turn around and drive 0.4 mile back to US 15, then turn left. Drive 0.6 mile on US 15 until you reach Cedar Mountain Drive (VA 649) on your right. Turn right onto VA 649 and drive 0.2 mile to its intersection with VA 692, then pull over.*

On the east side of the battlefield, Crawford's presence had severely distracted most of the Confederates on the Crittenden Farm lane, but Ewell's two brigades on the far Confederate right had not done much. As the Federals on the Confederate left were being pushed back, Ewell brought his men off the north slope of Cedar Mountain and advanced against Augur's division, driving it back steadily. Soon all of Banks's corps was in full retreat.

Looking toward the cornfield to the south (tall August corn was part of the reason for confusion in the Union advance that day), you will see Cedar Mountain to your front left. Ewell had been in position on the low forward slope of the mountain. The Union advance at the beginning of the battle came from right where you are standing, the former Mitchell's Station Road (now VA 649). VA 692, behind you, is a continuation of the old Culpeper Road.

Final Position

> *Turn left to drive on VA 692 for 0.4 mile. You will cross over Cedar Run; pull into the gravel area near the cemetery on your left.*

Jackson attempted to pursue the Federals all the way to Culpeper, but Pope had brought up a division from McDowell's corps to assist Banks, and they soon found themselves fighting a rear guard action for Banks. Forming a line astride Culpeper Road, the Federals stopped the pursuing Rebels in their tracks and settled into an artillery duel that lasted well into the night. Jackson's troops advanced slightly beyond the creek down Culpeper Road (which you just drove on) to a point not far from where you stand.

The lines faced each other for two more days, but nothing more came of it. Jackson withdrew to Gordonsville on the evening of August 11, with the Confederates having suffered 1,400 casualties. While the Federals had suffered many more, 2,500, Pope was not displeased. His Army of Virginia, with only a few exceptions, had fought well at Cedar Mountain. Furthermore, he had only Banks's corps fighting against all of Jackson's and Hill's forces, and although they were defeated, they were able to stop the Confederates from advancing. This early victory in the Bull Run Campaign would be the first validation in Pope's mind that not only could he defeat Jackson, but he needed to. Within a few weeks, this focus on Jackson would lead to near disaster for the Army of Virginia.

There was one thing that Pope had lost, however: his aggressiveness. In the days following the Union defeat at Cedar Mountain, Pope began mentioning words like "retire" and "retreat" in his correspondence with Halleck in Washington. It seemed that Pope, so boastful in the previous weeks, was suddenly becoming cautious. For Lee, that caution was like blood in the water. Pope, like McClellan before him, was abandoning the initiative, and Lee was happy to seize it.

THE CROSSINGS OF THE RAPPAHANNOCK RIVER

Note: For the most part, the various crossings of the Rappahannock River are accessible only by viewing them from the highway, and none of the locations, except for

Kelly's Ford, are developed for visitors. In short, there isn't much to see here. If you do choose to visit, be very careful as you pull over to see these sites.

Kelly's Ford

〉 *From the gravel parking lot, turn left onto VA 692 and drive 1.2 miles to return to US 15. Turn right and follow US 15 north for 2.1 miles, then merge right to stay on US 15 and US 29, and drive another 10.3 miles. At Kelly's Ford Road (VA 674), turn right and drive 4.9 miles. Turn left here to stay on Kelly's Ford Road, approaching the bridge; pull into the gravel parking lot on your right immediately before the bridge.*

On August 13, Lee began shifting the rest of the Army of Northern Virginia to join Jackson, leaving only two divisions and a brigade of cavalry to protect Richmond. Upon Lee's arrival, he gathered Jackson and General James Longstreet to form their campaign plan. The Confederate army would be split into two wings. Longstreet would command the right, with five divisions and 30,000 men. Jackson would take the left, with three divisions and 24,000 men. Pope had set his defensive line along the Rapidan River; if the Confederates could catch his army between the Rapidan and Rappahannock Rivers by attacking his left and sending cavalry to burn the bridges to his rear, he could be trapped and destroyed before McClellan could join him.

Even though his army had now been reinforced with two divisions from Burnside's force, Pope's movement was still limited. The Union right was exposed, but the left needed to stay close to Fredericksburg. Any reinforcements would come through there, as would supplies from the nearby depot at Aquia Landing. Because of poor management behind the lines, Pope's army was growing hungry, and the connection needed to be maintained.

Remaining cautious, Pope sent cavalry south of the Rapidan to scout the Confederate positions. Both wings of Lee's army were by now moving to trap the Federals, but there had been delays, as well as one major incident of insubordination. On the evening of August 17, Longstreet intended to send General Robert Toombs's brigade to Raccoon Ford on the Rapidan to screen the Confederate movements. Unable to find Toombs, as he was off visiting a friend, Longstreet relayed the order to one of Toombs's lieutenants, who promptly obeyed the order. When Toombs returned, however, he was outraged that his command had been ordered to move without his knowledge—even by Longstreet—and withdrew them from the ford. Shortly after, the Union cavalry crossed, promptly capturing a member of Stuart's staff who happened to be carrying important papers to General Fitzhugh Lee. The next morning, August 18, Stuart, who was resting on the porch of a nearby house, saw cavalry riding up and assumed it was Fitz Lee. Instead, it was 1,000 Union troopers, and Stuart only barely escaped. The Federals captured more valuable intelligence, as well as Stuart's prized plumed hat. Longstreet, incensed not only that the Union had captured information but that his orders were disobeyed, had Toombs arrested.

Pope now had the entire Confederate battle plan, and confirmed that his right, as expected, was in danger. He immediately wired Halleck that he was withdrawing across the Rappahannock River. That night, August 18, the Federals lit their campfires, then quietly began slipping out of their positions at 11:00 PM. Lee would not discover their absence until the middle of the next day, after much of the Army of Virginia had escaped north of the Rappahannock.

On August 19 and 20, Pope took defensive positions along the Rappahannock, starting at Kelly's Ford and stretching 9 miles upriver to Waterloo Bridge. Kelly's Ford and the bridge of the Orange & Alexandria Railroad at Rappahannock Station were Pope's strongest positions, defended primarily by McDowell's and Sigel's corps. The others were held by strong pickets. Because of the need to keep close to Fredericksburg, and because Pope now suspected Lee would try to creep around his left, his positions accordingly grew weaker as the line stretched northwest to (in order) Beverly's Ford, Freeman's Ford, Fox's Ford, White Sulphur Springs, and finally Waterloo Bridge.

From the gravel parking lot, you can either walk down to the river or walk up to the bridge to overlook the river. (In either case, use caution.) The location of the ford is not at the bridge itself, but by looking downstream (to your right) you can just see the shallows of the Rappahannock where the ford was located. Although the land around the ford is privately owned, you can always spend a night at the Inn at Kelly's Ford, which owns the property on the south bank of the Rappahannock.

Beverly's Ford

⟩ *From the parking lot at Kelly's Ford, turn left, then turn right onto Kelly's Ford Road. Drive 4.8 miles on Kelly's Ford Road, then bear left onto Elkwood Crossing (VA Route 678) and drive another 0.3 mile. Turn right onto Berry Hill Road (VA 676) and drive 1.1 miles to Beverly Ford Road (VA 677). Follow Beverly Ford Road for 1.8 miles, passing the airport and going through the winding curves until you cross a stream. Shortly after this stream, the road takes a left turn and becomes Glenna Lake Road. Follow the road for another 0.2 mile, then take an extremely sharp right, almost doubling back, to continue on Glenna Lake Road. Continue another 0.5 mile to the end of the road.*

Lee's intention was not to move around Pope's left, but rather his right. However, from the intelligence he had gathered, the Federals were no farther west than Rappahannock Station. On April 21, as Jackson approached Beverly's Ford to cross, he quickly drove off the small Union force there. However, other units in the area were quickly alerted, and Federal reinforcements rushed to the scene. While the Confederates did cross briefly, they pulled back after one of Sigel's brigades and his cavalry arrived. The first of what would be many artillery duels over the Rappahannock River began, and by the end of the day, it was obvious to Pope that the Confederates were moving northwest to his right, not his left.

Although trees obscure much of the area today, you are on the Confederate side of Beverly's Ford. Confederate artillery was placed in the fields around you, and it was in these fields that Jackson's troops formed to make their short excursion across the Rappahannock. The banks of the river, off the roadway, are private property; the river is right in front of you (in fact, you can probably hear it), and the ford is at your location.

Freeman's Ford

❭ *From the end of the road at Beverly's Ford, travel 0.5 mile down Glenna Lake Lane, then take a sharp left and continue another 0.4 mile. As the road turns to Beverly Ford Road (VA 677), continue another 2.8 miles to US 15/US 29 North (James Madison Highway). Turn left onto US 15 and drive 2.9 miles to the intersection with Freeman's Ford Road (County Road 651). Turn left on Freeman's Ford Road and drive 4.8 miles until you reach a bridge over the Rappahannock River. Carefully pull over before or after the bridge.*

From August 21–23, the Confederates slowly inched northwest. One unit would move left to take the next unit's place, enabling the army to move sideways along the river. As they moved, Union forces would also move, reinforcing each crossing and preventing the Rebels from coming over. An almost incessant artillery duel occurred along the Rappahannock at each of the various crossings.

Here, at Freeman's Ford, Stuart tried to cross at 10:00 AM on August 22, but found it too well guarded and moved on. The same day, when Confederate firing from the south bank at Freeman's Ford died down around 3:00 PM, Sigel noted the sudden quiet and sent troops across the ford to investigate. One regiment reported back to Sigel that they could see a Confederate supply train in motion, and Sigel immediately sent General Henry Bohlen's brigade across the river to attack. Unfortunately for the Federals, Jackson had assigned General Isaac Trimble's brigade to guard the wagon train. Trimble remained out of sight until the Federals were exposed, then hit their right with a tremendous fire, routing them and sending them back across the Rappahannock.

The land around Freeman's Ford is all private property. The location of Trimble's attack, on the south bank, is difficult to distinguish from the current landscape. The bridge does cross over the original ford, though, and although there's not much to see, the ford itself is fairly easy to spot from the bridge. Be very careful, though; while there isn't much traffic, an oncoming driver's view will be obscured by the trees and bends in the road.

Sulphur Springs

❭ *At the bridge, the name of the road changes to Lakota Road/VA 621. Continue across the bridge on VA 621 for 3.1 miles, then turn left where it changes to Jeffersonton Road to continue on VA 621 for another 1.6 miles. Turn right onto Springs Road and drive 2.6 miles to another bridge across the Rappahannock. Pull over very carefully before the bridge.*

In the late afternoon of August 22, Jackson began to cross the river at Sulphur Springs, which to this point was only lightly guarded. The crossing was delayed briefly by a heavy rain, and the lead brigade, Early's, was not able to cross until it died down at 5:00 PM. Soon it was dark, and Ewell decided to continue the crossing the next day. However, during the night, the heavy rains came back, and before long the Rappahannock River had risen by 6 feet, stranding Early on the north bank. With the rest of Jackson's force watching helplessly from the south bank, Early set up a defensive position and waited for the Federals he knew would soon be coming.

The next morning, Pope sent Sigel, with support from Banks and General Jesse Reno's IX Corps, recently arrived from the Army of the Potomac, to attack the Confederates at Sulphur Springs. While Jackson scrambled on the south bank to build a makeshift bridge and evacuate Early's troops, the Federals hurried to catch the brigade before it could reach safety. Sigel, however, didn't reach Early's skirmishers until the end of the day, and although they drove them back, they went no farther. As darkness fell and the Confederate bridge was completed, Jackson decided to send the rest of Ewell's division to the north bank. Early eventually convinced Ewell that he could not stay where he was. Jackson's entire wing was once again south of the Rappahannock early on August 24.

The nearly 30-hour delay that Jackson's Sulphur Springs crisis caused permitted Pope to refocus his troops to the north and west, where Lee was still trying to get around the Federal right. In addition, Pope was now finally beginning to receive some of the reinforcements he had been promised. The focus now shifted upriver, from Beverly's Ford and Rappahannock Bridge (which the Federals burned at noon on August 23) to Sulphur Springs and Waterloo Bridge.

The land on the north and west side of the river where Early had his brief meeting with Sigel's troops is now private property. The bridge here at Sulphur Springs, which was a popular hot springs retreat before the war, is in the approximate location of the original bridge, long since gone.

Waterloo Bridge

> *From the bridge at Sulphur Springs, make a U-turn and drive west on Springs Road 2.6 miles, then bear right onto Jeffersonton Road and continue another 1.2 miles. Turn right onto VA 229 North and drive 2.1 miles to US 211 (Lee Highway). Turn right on US 211, then take a quick left onto Old Bridge Road (VA 622). Continue for 1.3 miles until reaching Waterloo Bridge. There is very little room to pull over here, so you may want to settle for driving across. If you do pull over, be very careful.*

On August 24, Lee knew he had to break the stalemate along the Rappahannock. Time was not on Lee's side; the longer Pope held the strong positions north of the Rappahannock, the more reinforcements he would receive. Although he did not know the details (General Fitz John Porter's V Corps and General Phil Kearny's division of the III Corps of the Army of the Potomac would arrive on August 24), Lee did know that Pope's army was growing.

Lee came up with a bold plan that, if not executed perfectly, could destroy his army. Lee, however, was not one to pass on a bold plan. He would send Jackson upriver, far beyond the Union right, to cross out of reach of the Federals and then cut their supply line at the Orange & Alexandria Railroad, forcing Pope to fall back. Longstreet would remain along the Rappahannock to continue the artillery duels that had been going on for three days, holding Pope in place, and would follow Jackson's route the next day. This would put the two halves of the Confederate army 50 miles apart, with the entire Union Army of Virginia in between. Further, Jackson would have only one option for crossing the Bull Run Mountains in his path—a narrow pass known as Thoroughfare Gap. If the Federals were to take the gap between the passages of Jackson and Longstreet, Lee's army would be permanently separated. However, if it worked, the Confederates would end up between Pope and Washington, D.C., with a chance to destroy Lee's entire army. Naturally, Jackson and Longstreet loved the plan, and by 6:00 PM that night, Longstreet's men began replacing Jackson's at Sulphur Springs and Waterloo Bridge.

At 3:00 AM on August 25, Jackson's troops were given orders to march. As was often the case with Jackson's army, the soldiers did not know where they were going, but by now had learned to expect something interesting. Ewell's division was in front, followed by Hill's Light Division and then Taliaferro's bringing up the rear. The 24,000 Confederates of the left wing of Lee's army, along with three battalions of artillery totaling almost 80 guns, marched northwest along the Rappahannock. One of Jackson's staff who came from the area knew of a crossing north of their position called Hinson's Ford (inaccessible today, except by river). The Rebels crossed here and then moved north to the town of Salem, halting the march at midnight. They had traveled 25 miles that day, and although the men were tired, they also knew that Jackson had something special in mind.

The Federals, meanwhile, were beginning to scatter themselves all over the area north of the Rappahannock. Pope attempted to shift his line to the southwest, but it did not go well. McDowell's corps was now in Warrenton, east of Sulphur Springs. Sigel, finding Early's brigade gone from the north bank on the morning of August 24, moved to Waterloo Bridge to take possession. Porter's V Corps was all alone at Kelly's Ford, awaiting orders from Pope.

To make things worse, other Federal reinforcements were stalled. One reason was that Halleck was in over his head, overwhelmed with the task of moving men and supplies to Pope. The other reason was far more troublesome; it was George McClellan. Having been ordered to bring his army north on August 3, McClellan, still bristling at his perceived lack of support from Washington, was moving very slowly. In later years, it would be clearly evident in his correspondence to other officers and to his wife that McClellan was practically reveling in Pope's distress, thinking it was proving him right and the Lincoln administration wrong. Consequently, he not only took his time in moving his army north, but deliberately prevented some of them from assisting Pope during the campaign.

The historic Waterloo Bridge that you see today dates from well after the Civil War, but it is in the same location as the original. Like the other Rappahannock crossings, there isn't much left to see, although the existing bridge is quite interesting.

CATLETT'S STATION

> *From Waterloo Bridge, continue 0.2 mile to CR 688 (Leeds Manor Road), then turn right and drive 0.7 mile to US 211 East. Drive 5 miles on US 211 East to US 17/US 29 Business Route South (James Madison Highway). Turn right and follow US 17 for 10.6 miles to VA 28 North (Catlett Road). Turn left at VA 28 North and drive 8.8 miles to Elk Run Road (County Road 806); after 8.2 miles, note the railroad bridge to your right as you cross Cedar Run. Turn right onto Elk Run Road and drive 0.2 mile to a Virginia Civil War Trails sign on your right.*

Before Lee had decided on his flanking movement, he authorized Stuart to take his cavalry behind Union lines on August 22. While intelligence-gathering would be critical, the primary objective of the raid was to cut the Orange & Alexandria Railroad, cutting off Pope's supply line and probably forcing him to abandon the Rappahannock line. Stuart took 1,500 troopers across Waterloo Bridge and into Warrenton, where Stuart learned that the most vulnerable spot on the railroad was where it

Confederate forces attacked a Union Camp near Catlett's Station on Aug. 22, 1862.

crossed Cedar Run at Catlett Station. At 7:30 PM, as the column approached the station, Stuart sent a scout ahead and learned that not only the railroad but a large number of Federal supply wagons lay ahead.

With their movements obscured by the rain and thunder (the same storm that stranded Early at Sulphur Springs), the Confederates were able to quietly capture the Union pickets and come within yards of the camp. Finally, Stuart sounded a charge, and his cavalrymen raced through the camp, causing mayhem and destruction. Among the wagons found was Pope's headquarters wagon, which contained not only Pope's papers, but also his dress coat and hat, which Stuart gladly took.

Despite their best efforts, because of the heavy rain and the soaked timbers, the Confederates were not able to burn the Cedar Run Bridge. Although they left Catlett's Station at 3:00 AM August 23 with prisoners and other captured goods, the raid,

AN EXCHANGE OF PRISONERS

General J. E. B. Stuart, still unhappy about losing his trademark plumed hat to Union cavalry on August 18, now had General John Pope's best dress uniform coat as a result of the raid at Catlett's Station. Although he had gotten even, he also saw an opportunity. Stuart sent Pope a note through the lines, describing the situation and proposing "the fair exchange of the prisoners." Receiving no response from the humorless Pope, Stuart sent the coat to Richmond, where it was displayed in the capitol building for all to enjoy.

though celebrated in later years, was not a success. Not only was the bridge left intact, but even Pope's papers only served to confirm what Lee had already deduced for himself. Lee would hope that Jackson's attempt to cut the Orange & Alexandria—a far riskier endeavor—would bring better results.

The Virginia Civil War Trails marker here tells the story of Catlett's Station. The Union depot was around your current position, and turning to your right, you can see the same tracks where the Orange & Alexandria Railroad went through. The former location of the bridge over Cedar Run, which you saw on your drive, is about a half mile south of where you are now standing.

Bristoe Station

❯ *Drive 0.2 mile on Elk Run Road to return to VA 28. Turn right on VA 28 and drive 6.4 miles to Aden Road. There will be a Virginia Civil War Trails marker on your right; pull over here.*

Jackson's Confederates were up and marching again early on August 26, heading east from Salem through White Plains. At noon, they passed through Thoroughfare Gap with no opposition—a promising sign—and kept moving toward the town of Haymarket. By 4:00 PM, the Confederates had reached Gainesville, the Orange & Alexandria Railroad only 5 miles beyond. While Jackson's men took a brief rest (they had certainly earned it after covering 50 miles in 32 hours), Stuart's cavalry joined the column to watch Jackson's right, the flank nearest Pope's army, as they rapidly approached their target.

Along the Rappahannock River, Longstreet kept up the charade of the Confederate presence on the south bank. Occasionally showing force to let the Federals know they were still there, Longstreet's wing did its best to keep the Union army focused on the river and divert attention from Jackson. Finally, in the late afternoon, Longstreet left General R. H. Anderson's division and one battery at Sulphur Springs and Waterloo Bridge to demonstrate while he took the rest of his army along the same path that Jackson took, across Hinson's Ford and through Thoroughfare Gap.

At 6:00 PM, a regiment of Confederate cavalry approached Bristoe Station and found it only lightly guarded. They were able to approach to within 100 yards of the Federals and then charged, with the infantry following up their success and sending the small Union company to flight. Suddenly, in the distance, a train whistle was heard from the west. Jackson's men tried to tear up the track in front of it, but weren't able to do so in time, and although they did pepper the engine with musket fire, the train roared through and headed for Manassas.

When the next train approached, the Confederates were ready, and the train was easily derailed. With that train still sitting on the track, the third train since their arrival approached Bristoe Station. The Confederates extinguished the lights on the disabled train and stood well back to watch the oncoming train smash into the rear of the one before it. They were hoping to catch one more, but the engineer of a fourth train, sensing trouble, slowed and threw the engine into reverse, retreating to Warrenton as fast as possible.

Shortly after the destruction at Bristoe Station was complete, Jackson was persuaded by Isaac Trimble to let him have a go at Manassas Junction, only 5 miles away. At dawn, Jackson would order Hill's and Taliaferro's divisions to reinforce Trimble, leaving Ewell behind at Bristoe with three brigades to keep an eye out for the Federals.

At 8:00 PM, Pope received a telegram from Manassas. (The Confederates, apparently having too much fun smashing trains, had for the moment forgotten to cut the telegraph wires.) An engineer who had just pulled into the station reported that he had been fired upon by Confederates, saying that it was probably some cavalry. Shortly after receiving the message, the wire from Manassas went dead. Over the next few hours, Pope would receive other reports that a large number of Confederates had passed through Thoroughfare Gap and various towns that day. By midnight, it was apparent that although the exact situation was unknown, the Confederate army—or at least a good part of it—was between the Union Army of Virginia and Washington.

Before dawn on August 27, Pope had issued orders for his entire army of 60,000 men to leave the line of the Rappahannock River and march to Gainesville, just west of Manassas. Deducing correctly that Lee had to have split his army, Pope's plan was to destroy the lead element before the two parts could reunite. The entire Army of Virginia did an about-face—making the Union left its right, and vice versa—and headed for Gainesville in three columns. McDowell and Sigel's corps were on the left using the Warrenton Turnpike; Kearny's division of the III Corps of the Army of the Potomac, along with Reno's corps, made up the center; Joseph Hooker's division of III Corps, along with Porter's V Corps, took the right, moving along the Orange & Alexandria Railroad toward Bristoe Station.

Sending cavalry ahead, Hooker soon learned that the Confederates were still at Bristoe Station in large numbers. Those same cavalry alerted Ewell that the Federals were approaching, and he placed his three brigades to meet them, one on each side of the railroad facing west, and the third facing northwest. Hooker ran into the first Confederates 2 miles west of the station at Kettle Run, where the Confederates burned the railroad bridge and withdrew to the main force. Meeting heavy resistance, Hooker sent three regiments against Ewell's line while two others went to the left. The Federals took heavy casualties in the center, but the Confederates were soon outflanked. After an hour's fight, seeing that the Confederates were in trouble, Ewell withdrew his entire force across Broad Run by 6:00 PM and burned the bridge behind them, leaving the Union troops stranded.

You are now standing just behind the Confederate center, where the heaviest fighting took place. The railroad is to your left, and to your right is the direction from which Hooker sent his flanking force, forcing Ewell back. The location of the Confederates' train-wrecking activities, Bristoe Station, is behind you, to the northeast near where the railroad crosses Bristow Road. (Bristoe Station Battlefield Heritage Park, located near the crossing, preserves part of an October 1863 battlefield, and it is worth visiting if you have the time.)

THOROUGHFARE GAP

> *Turn right back onto VA 28 and drive 1.4 miles, then turn left onto VA 619 West (Linton Hall Road). Follow VA 619 West and then continue onto VA 55 (John Marshall Highway) for 10.8 miles. Turn right onto Turner Road and drive 0.1 mile, crossing under the interstate, then take the next left onto Beverly Mill Drive. Follow Beverly Mill Drive for 1 mile until you reach the mill on your right.*

From Washington, Halleck ordered William Franklin's VI Corps of the Army of the Potomac, which had been sitting in Alexandria, to march toward Gainesville on August 27. With Franklin's 10,000 men and Pope's army, Jackson soon had Union forces converging on him from several different directions. The problem was that no one knew with certainty where Jackson was. A strong clue appeared later that night as an orange glow of flame emanated from Manassas, and Pope was now certain that Jackson was burning Union supplies at Manassas Junction. He issued orders at 9:00 PM that would shift all of his forces in that direction at dawn the next day.

In making this movement, Pope made two assumptions. The first was that Jackson must be at Manassas Station. The second was that he would catch Jackson at Manassas before the other half of the Confederate army could join him.

Unfortunately for Pope, these two assumptions that he banked his entire army on were both incorrect, and they would prove to have great effect on his campaign. He virtually ignored the fact that the other half of the Rebel army even existed, and he sent no troops to intercept them or even discover where they were.

Irvin McDowell did think enough of the missing half of Lee's army to send a unit to Thoroughfare Gap, which they would have to pass through to reach Jackson. It was all of one division, General James B. Ricketts's 5,000 men, waiting in Gainesville to see if anyone showed up. (He had intended to leave Sigel's entire corps there, but the late marching orders from Pope prevented him from doing so.) At 9:30 AM on August 28, Longstreet's wing began its passage through the gap and was spotted by Federal cavalry, alerting Ricketts of its presence.

Ricketts hit the Confederates' front just as they were emerging from the east side of the gap, temporarily trapping them in the steep narrows. The gap itself could barely fit the Manassas Gap Railroad and Broad Run, both of which ran through it, let alone half an army. However, the Confederates rushed troops to the front, forming a line with their left at Chapman's Mill and sending other units climbing precariously along the gap's sides. Ricketts was able to hold his position until nearly dark, but in the end, the Federals were too small and too late, and Longstreet's entire force passed through Thoroughfare Gap that evening.

MANASSAS STATION

The Manassas Museum/Downtown Manassas

❭ *From Chapman's Mill, return 1 mile on Beverly Drive to Turner Road. Turn right on Turner Road to cross the interstate, then take the next left onto VA 55 East (John Marshall Highway). Turn left on VA 55 East and drive 2.7 miles until reaching US 15 North (James Madison Highway). Turn left and take the ramp to I-66 East. Drive 3.8 miles on I-66 East to Exit 44 for VA 234 South (Prince William Parkway) toward Manassas. Continue on VA 234 for 5.3 miles to the exit for VA 28. Take the exit for VA 28 North (Nokesville Road) toward Manassas. Follow VA 28 for 3.1 miles, taking you into downtown Manassas. Take a right turn on Battle Street, after which you will see the Manassas Museum in front of you. Turn left onto Prince William Street and then right into the museum's parking lot.*

Late on August 26, Trimble quietly approached Manassas Junction with his "two 21's"—the 21st North Carolina and the 21st Georgia. They approached through the dark to within 100 yards of the junction and charged, easily capturing the 115-man Union garrison within five minutes. When the rest of Jackson's command (minus Ewell's division at Bristoe Station) came up on the town the next morning, they were greeted with a sight that instantly energized the tired, hungry, worn-out troops.

Although Manassas Junction was strategically important when the war began, by August 1862 the Manassas Gap Railroad was unusable, making the junction itself meaningless. The town of Manassas was now used as a supply depot—a very large one. Massive amounts of stores of every kind were kept here, and to the Confederates, who were virtually always for want of something, it could barely be believed. Knowing that there was far too much to take with him, Jackson turned a blind eye as his men treated themselves to new rifles, new artillery, new clothes, new shoes, and best of all, enormous amounts of food. The men gorged themselves on everything they could get their hands on, much of it beyond luxury for the Confederate soldier. (Knowing that things could easily get out of hand, Jackson did ask a cavalry unit to quietly find and destroy the liquor as soon as possible.)

There is a walking trail in downtown Manassas that highlights not only Jackson's

A more modern building now marks Manassas Station.

raid but also how the town coped with the Civil War. The signs, all part of the Virginia Civil War Trails system, are located along Prince William Street and Center Street in the downtown area. Your best bet, though, would be to visit the Manassas Museum first. The museum presents a complete history of the town, including, of course, a thorough examination of its Civil War history. If you happen to visit during off hours, another Civil War Trails marker outside the museum will guide you through the walking tour.

Mayfield Fort

> *From the museum parking lot, turn right onto Prince William Street and take an immediate left onto Main Street. Drive 0.1 mile, crossing the railroad tracks, then take the next right onto Center Street. Follow Center Street for 0.5 mile, including a sharp bend to the left, until reaching Quarry Road. Turn right on Quarry Road; you will drive 0.3 mile, then will have to make a right turn to stay on Quarry Road for another 0.3 mile. At this point, you will see Battery Heights Boulevard on your right. Turn right onto Battery Heights Boulevard, then immediately pull into the parking area for Mayfield Fort on your left.*

There was still some business to attend to at Manassas. A New York regiment, on its way to support the small guard at the supply depot, heard about Trimble's attack as it passed through Centreville. The regiment proceeded to Manassas to take care of the "guerrillas" who had raided the depot, crossing Bull Run at Mitchell's Ford and marching toward Manassas. When they came upon enemy cavalry, the Union force—

about 1,000 strong—fired upon them, not knowing that Jackson's entire command was present. Jackson immediately sent Hill's division to occupy earthworks built during the winter, and soon 9,000 Confederates stretched in a long arc around the Federals, who quickly retreated. Another Union unit, patched together the night before in order to protect the railroad, also approached, meeting the same result and withdrawing after 15 minutes. After repulsing this last effort, the Rebels went back to their feast.

The site and some of the earthworks at Mayfield Fort have been preserved as part of the Manassas Museum system. The fort is maintained as a public park and contains a boarded walkway that leads up to the top of a knoll, where you will find interpretive signs about the fighting here.

MANASSAS NATIONAL BATTLEFIELD PARK

Brawner Farm

❯ *From the Mayfield Fort parking area, turn right onto Battery Heights, then left onto Quarry Road, driving 0.3 mile before turning left to stay on Quarry Road for another 0.3 mile. At Prescott Avenue, turn right and drive for 0.1 mile, bearing left to join Sudley Road. Continue on Sudley Road for 5.8 miles; you will enter Manassas National Battlefield Park, pass the visitors center, then come upon US 29 (Lee Highway). Turn left on US 29 and drive 2.6 miles to Pageland Lane. Turn right onto Pageland Lane and drive 0.4 mile; the entrance to the Brawner Farm Interpretive Center will be on your right. Turn here and follow the road to the parking area, then take the short walk to the Brawner House.*

Even while his troops were looting the supply base at Manassas Station, Jackson knew he could not stay there long. He knew as little about Pope's location as Pope knew about his. He did know, though, that the Federals would have to pass through Gainesville to get to him. Had Jackson left the Union stores burning and headed northwest toward the Bull Run Mountains, or north to reunite with Lee near the town of Aldie or Leesburg, he hardly could have been thought the worse for it. But Jackson knew that this moment was the Confederates' best chance to defeat Pope's Army of Virginia before it joined forces with the Army of the Potomac, and he would take advantage.

Jackson not only had the opportunity to draw the Union army into battle, but also to pick the battleground, a rare luxury for a commander in the field. His experience during and after the first battle at Manassas gave him knowledge of the field and its surroundings. It could make a nearly perfect place to battle again. Gainesville was only 4 miles to the west, and Thoroughfare Gap was only 6 miles farther, simplifying the

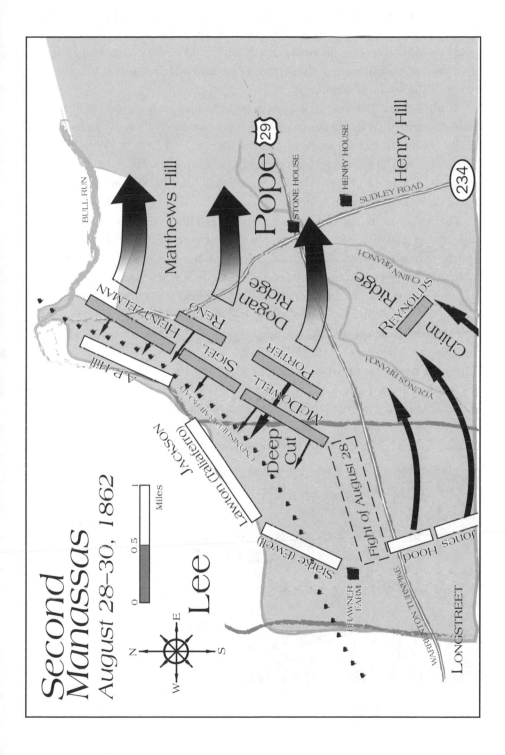

Second Manassas
August 28–30, 1862

BULL RUN

Matthews Hill

Pope 29

STONE HOUSE

HENRY HOUSE

SUDLEY ROAD

Henry Hill

234

Dogan Ridge

CHINN BRANCH

Chinn Ridge

Reynolds

YOUNGS BRANCH

HEINTZELMAN

RENO

SIGEL

PORTER

McDOWELL

A.P. Hill

(UNFINISHED RAILROAD)

JACKSON

Lawton (Taliaferro)

Deep Cut

Fight of August 28

Starke (Ewell)

BRAWNER FARM

Hood

Jones

WARRENTON TURNPIKE

LONGSTREET

Lee

Miles
0   0.5   1

N
W — E
S

junction of the two wings of the army. The field was well beyond the Union left. In the very worst case, if the battle did not go well, the roads leading north to Aldie would provide an easy escape route. Best of all, thanks to the presence of an unfinished railroad embankment of the Manassas Gap Railroad, Jackson could conceal his men until the last possible moment.

As night came, Jackson had his troops gather whatever last precious items they could carry and then set fire to everything left at Manassas Station. (Pope had gotten this part right, but Jackson would not remain there to wait for him.) With Hill, Taliaferro, and Ewell all using separate routes, Jackson's force headed to the small hamlet of Groveton just west of the old battlefield. Many of his men, veterans of that battle, would sleep on Matthews Hill that night.

The next morning, August 28, Jackson arranged his line behind the unfinished railroad. The embankment ran very close to the Warrenton Turnpike at Groveton and stretched toward the northeast to Sudley Springs, where the Federals had made their crossing of Bull Run during the first battle. Taliaferro's division held the right of the line, only 0.25 mile from the turnpike, while Ewell held the center and Hill the left. Cavalry was sent out to picket, and although there was skirmishing with the head of Sigel's column, most of the day was quiet, and the Confederates relaxed behind the embankment wherever they could find shade.

You are now at the site of the Brawner Farm. The Brawner House here is the same one that existed during the battle, although there have been significant improvements. For many years, the interpretation at Manassas National Battlefield Park was largely centered on the first battle. However, the Brawner House now holds an entirely separate visitors center for the interpretation of Second Manassas, long overdue. Inside you will find an electric map that explains the battle and the events around it, as well as exhibits on Groveton, various units that fought in the battle, and the aftermath of the Union defeat, which reached far beyond the massive number of casualties. The Brawner House is also the starting point for some tours of the battlefield, so be sure to ask if there are any programs that day.

The fighting at Groveton, which opened the Second Battle of Manassas, took place at Brawner Farm.

For the Federals, August 28 started out as a frustrating day. Pope had expected to hear the sound of battle at Manassas Junction by early morning, but all was quiet, and his scattered units could not find the Confederates. At noon, Kearny's division reached Manassas Station, only to find the wreckage from the previous day, and by the early afternoon most of the Union army, except for McDowell's force, was at Manassas Station. Pope set up his new headquarters near Blackburn's Ford at Bull Run and ordered his army toward Centreville, well to the east of Jackson's new position.

McDowell received his orders while his men halted at Gainesville. After checking on his lead division, commanded by General Rufus King, he rode off to confer with Pope, leaving orders to continue a direct march to Centreville via the Warrenton Turnpike.

Confederate cavalry kept a close eye on King's division as it made its way east. The Federals would have to march up a steady grade, and would then pass the Brawner Farm and the Confederate right. The fields surrounding the position were mostly clear, other than the embankment, the Brawner House itself, and a 30-acre stand of trees known as Brawner's Woods.

Just before the Federals reached the Brawner Farm, an unfortunate, untimely, and somewhat unbelievable event occurred. King had had an epileptic seizure several days before, and after much pleading with McDowell was allowed to remain in the field, commanding his division from an ambulance. At this moment, King decided to leave his ambulance and almost immediately suffered another severe seizure, taking him out of action for several hours. Before King's staff could inform his generals that their commander was out of commission, a lone Confederate on horseback appeared north of the turnpike, studied the Federals for a few minutes, and then disappeared.

It was Jackson. Riding calmly back to his staff, he gave a simple order: "Bring out your men, gentlemen." With these words, the Battle of Second Manassas began.

King's division, unaware that it had no leader, proceeded east past the Confederates. The lead brigade was commanded by General John Hatch, followed in order by the brigades of John Gibbon, Abner Doubleday, and Marsena Patrick. Hatch was the first to see Confederate movement to their left, north of the turnpike, and halted the column to bring up his artillery. The Confederates were quicker to fire, though, and they quickly found their range. Hearing the commotion a quarter mile ahead, Gibbon rushed to the front, and on the way saw other Confederate artillery appearing just south of the Brawner Farm, lining up to fire into not only his brigade but Doubleday and Patrick behind him.

Gibbon immediately ordered his infantry to find cover in the Brawner Woods, just ahead to their left, and Doubleday's brigade followed. Patrick's brigade moved into the woods south of the turnpike. After a short conference, Gibbon and Doubleday deduced that this must be Stuart's force; after all, they had been told that Jackson was in Centreville. They decided on a charge of the Confederate artillery. Riding in front, Gibbon led one regiment, the Second Wisconsin, through the woods toward the Confederate line.

The 450 men of the Second Wisconsin arrived just in time to see the Confederate artillery pull back and be replaced by infantry, seemingly from nowhere. It was the Stonewall Brigade, 850 strong by this time, a year into the war. Greatly outnumbered, most regiments would have withdrawn with these odds, but not this regiment. They held their ground as the Confederates unleashed their first volley, then returned fire at 150 yards. The Virginians advanced to a rail fence and fired again. For 20 minutes, standing only 80 yards apart, the two units stood toe-to-toe and slugged it out, each taking a devastating toll on the other.

As you exit the Brawner House, you can easily see the Warrenton Turnpike (now US 29), where King's leaderless division advanced until being surprised by Jackson's Confederates. As you look at the road, to the left, you will see a small forest. Although much larger today than it was at the time of the battle, these are the Brawner Woods that sheltered Gibbon's and Doubleday's brigades.

Turning to your left, you are now looking at the area where the two sides faced each other. It will be worth your time to take at least the short walk to the trailhead, if not the entire loop trail around the Battle of Groveton area. The placement of interpretive signs and the creative preservation of the landscape here make it very clear where the two lines were during the firefight. It is truly striking to see the short distance that separated the men on that terrible August evening, making one wonder how anyone could have managed to make it out alive.

Each side began throwing troops into the fight, although it was not easy. Gibbon sent up the 19th Indiana to the left, then the Seventh Wisconsin and Sixth Wisconsin to the right. Jackson, furious that the rest of his infantry seemed not to be moving, began personally leading troops into the fight, sending Trimble's brigade and other men from Ewell's division in. The line grew longer, the fight grew hotter, and the casualties mounted.

Gibbon, seeing a gap forming in the Union line, went back to the other brigades for help. He had already sent all of his men in and needed reinforcements. But without King present, the other brigade commanders were almost criminally unwilling to assist. Hatch offered only a handful of troops, while Patrick said he could spare none, even though his entire brigade had not fired a shot. Doubleday, thankfully, saw the Union distress and sent two regiments, the 76th New York and 56th Pennsylvania, into the fight. The gap was filled, and the Confederates were not able to gain advantage.

By 7:30 PM, it was growing dark and no more units were brought into the fight, but that did not stop the slaughter. Jackson ordered a charge, but not all of the units received the order, so those who did charge went unsupported and suffered heavily

IS THIS MANASSAS OR BULL RUN?

Both . . . and neither. Civil War battles often had more than one name, and this one was known both as the Second Battle of Manassas and the Second Battle of Bull Run. In addition, some regard the action here on August 28, 1862, as a separate battle altogether, calling it the Battle of Groveton. It is not uncommon to run across battlefields with three, four, or even five different names, depending on geography, who fought there, or events during the battle, and there is no standard naming convention, so they can all be considered correct.

for it. Ewell was shot in his left knee and eventually lost his leg. Taliaferro was also wounded, but not as seriously. Eventually, the firing died down in the darkness, but the lines did not move, remaining within a stone's throw of each other.

After the fight, Gibbon was able to find King and his brigade commanders and let them all have it for their lack of support. But this was not a time for argument. After initially deciding that they should continue on to Centreville per McDowell's orders, Gibbon was able to convince the others that they had found Jackson. Prisoners and other evidence supported the theory, and King sent a courier to Pope in Manassas saying they would hold their position. Receiving no response, King quietly withdrew his men from their lines at 1:00 AM and headed for Manassas Junction.

Upon receiving the news at 9:30 PM that Jackson had been found, Pope was elated. Still ignoring Longstreet's existence, he ordered all of his forces to Groveton, thinking he had Jackson cut off. (King never received these orders, hence his withdrawal.) Pope had a chance to move to the protection of the earthworks at Centreville, which would have ensured both his joining the Army of the Potomac and the protection of Washington. Instead, he was so convinced that he was about to "bag" Jackson, as he had previously boasted, that he decided to stay and fight. Jackson's bait, though costly, had worked perfectly. He had drawn battle on his ground and under his terms, and needed only wait for Longstreet's wing to arrive, completing the Confederate plan to defeat and possibly destroy the Union Army of Virginia.

Sudley Springs

> *From the Brawner Farm parking area, turn left onto Pageland Lane and drive 0.4 mile to US 9. Turn left on US 9 and drive 2.7 miles to the Sudley Road intersection. Turn left onto Sudley Road and drive 1.6 miles. As you drive north on Sudley Road, Matthews Hill is on your right; the Federals formed their lines of battle in the fields to your left.*

Dawn of August 29 found both armies on the move. Most of the Union troops were moving toward the Confederate left near Sudley Springs, retracing their steps over Henry Hill from the previous summer's battle. Although they knew Jackson's general location, they still had not determined exactly where he had formed his lines, and they moved with caution, Sigel's corps in the lead.

Watching from a distance, Jackson shifted the strength of his line to his left, remaining behind the unfinished railroad. Hill's division, which had not fought the day before, remained where it was. With the wounding of Ewell and Taliaferro, command of their divisions fell to Generals Alexander Lawton and William Starke. Only two of Lawton's brigades remained in the center, while the other two went to the Brawner Farm to guard the Confederate right flank and watch for the approach of Longstreet's wing. Because of the heavy woods and poor fields of fire along most of the line, Jackson put virtually all of his artillery on his right near Groveton.

Before long, first contact occurred near Sudley Springs on the Confederate left. Confederate general Maxcy Gregg's brigade, holding the extreme left, had taken a position on Stony Ridge behind the railroad embankment, and as the Federals approached, he sent a regiment to meet them. Gregg's men were quickly driven back by General Carl Schurz's division, but Confederate reinforcements came to support them. Before long, each side was throwing units into the fight, which remained heavy for more than an hour.

You are now standing at the Sudley Church, Jackson's extreme left. Just to the north of your position are the fords that were Jackson's escape route to the north, the same fords the Union used to enter the first battle here. The Sudley Church, though rebuilt since the battle, remains in its original spot. The most obvious and prominent feature here, though, is the end of the unfinished railroad embankment. An interpretive sign here gives a short explanation of why the embankment was here in the first place, but its importance to Jackson is obvious: It is a perfect ready-made breastwork, extending all the way to Groveton, and was also high enough to conceal his entire wing during the first day's action.

Union general Robert H. Milroy, whose brigade held Sigel's center, heard fighting to his right, and he immediately sent two of his four regiments in support. Unfortunately, instead of moving directly to their right, the two regiments, the 82nd Ohio and the 5th West Virginia, moved to their right front and ran almost straight into the Confederate line. Remarkably, although the West Virginians took a heavy volley, the Ohioans had found a gap in the Confederate line around a cut in the embankment known as "The Dump" and rushed into it. They were able to hold for a while, but Milroy did not get his other two regiments there in time to support them, and all were eventually forced to withdraw with heavy losses.

By 10:00 AM, Sigel had a pretty clear picture of Jackson's line. Although his center

(Milroy's brigade) had taken a beating, he saw that if he could take the Sudley Ford, Jackson might be cut off from escape. Soon, Hooker and Kearny's divisions, both from General Samuel Heintzelman's III Corps of the Army of the Potomac, were on the field. Sigel put Hooker into his damaged center while Kearny went to the right of Schurz. All were in place by 11:00 AM, just as the Confederates mounted a successful charge that broke the Union line temporarily. The Federals sealed the breach and countercharged, and for another two hours the fight at Sudley Springs was heavy, waning just as Pope arrived on the field at 1:00 PM.

At the time he arrived, Pope thought the fighting on the Union right unimportant. He expected to soon hear heavy sounds of battle to his left, where he had ordered McDowell and Porter to attack the Confederate right flank. Accordingly, as he rode down the line to inspect it, he told his men they simply needed to hold their positions and Porter's corps would do the rest. Around 2:00 PM, Pope began a series of attacks that were to serve as a diversion to his main effort, but all they served to do was extend the bloodshed along the northern part of the unfinished railroad. At 3:00 PM, it was General Cuvier Grover's brigade of Hooker's division that suffered; at 4:00 PM, General James Nagle's brigade of Reno's IX Corps; and at 5:00 PM, Kearny's division. All inflicted damage, but all took heavy losses and were repulsed, with Kearny's due to a timely and fortunate reinforcement from Early's Confederate brigade. By the time the

A portion of the Unfinished Railroad at Manassas near the center of the line. It was at this spot that Union general Cuvier Grover's forces suffered heavy losses.

battle died down on the Confederate left, both armies held the same positions they had when they started fighting more than 10 hours earlier.

All the while, Pope awaited the sound of battle from Porter's and McDowell's attack on the Confederate right, but it never came. Had he ridden to the left of his line during his afternoon inspection, Pope would have discovered that neither Porter nor McDowell were anywhere near the Warrenton Turnpike, where he had expected them to crush the Confederates and win the day.

Unfinished Railroad

> *From the Sudley Springs parking area, turn left and drive 0.2 mile to Featherbed Lane. Turn left onto Featherbed Lane and drive 1.3 miles; pull into the parking area on your left, then walk up to the trailhead for the Unfinished Railroad loop trail.*

James Nagle's 4:00 PM attack on August 29 against the Confederate center occurred in this area, west of Groveton Road. Although the field is now almost completely obscured by trees, this is an excellent place to view the unfinished railroad and explore it easily without taking too difficult a hike. Taking the short loop trail around the embankment will also take you to the location of Grover's earlier attack. On both sides of the embankment, throughout its length from this point all the way to Sudley Springs, men from both sides engaged in terrible fighting throughout the second day of battle. If you wish to explore further, there are good trails that will take you along the entire embankment.

Deep Cut

> *Turn left from the Unfinished Railroad trail parking area onto Featherbed Lane and drive 0.3 miles. Pull into the parking area for the Deep Cut on your right.*

The reason Pope kept expecting Porter and McDowell to attack the Confederate right is that he thought he had ordered them to do so. Wanting to ensure that Jackson could not escape to the west, on the morning of August 29 Pope directed Porter's V Corps and Hatch's division (formerly King's) to Gainesville, west of the Confederate position, using the Manassas-Gainesville Road, well south of the battlefield. McDowell was also with him. At 11:00 the Federals stumbled onto Confederate cavalry at a small creek called Dawson's Branch, and taking caution, Porter halted the column. At almost the same time, a courier arrived to deliver "clarification" of Pope's instructions.

In later years, this rambling, confusing, and controversial document would simply be known as the "Joint Order." Pope's intention was for Porter to keep moving toward Gainesville and then join with other Federal forces that would be coming down the Warrenton Turnpike. At the same time, if Porter established communications with

A view of the Union soldiers' steep climb to the Deep Cut.

those forces, he was to halt. Pope also added that it would probably be necessary to fall back to Centreville that same night. Finally, to top it all off, the order closed with a statement saying that if Porter or McDowell might be better off not following the order, then they should not. It was not exactly the stuff of decisive leadership.

In their front, the skirmishing was growing heavier, and large dust clouds could be seen rising ahead of them. (It was actually Stuart's cavalry, dragging brush to create the illusion of a large force.) McDowell then received a report from General John Buford's cavalry. At 9:00 AM, Buford had counted 17 Confederate regiments, 500 cavalry, and one battery of artillery marching toward Centreville. This was enough to convince both Porter and McDowell that Longstreet was in front of them. McDowell advised Porter to fall back behind Bull Run, per Pope's order, while he would take Hatch's division and ride north to support the fight there. Incredibly, McDowell did not forward Buford's remarkably detailed report to Pope until late that day.

Porter held his position until almost 9:00 PM, when he received more direct orders from Pope. Enraged because he did not advance, Pope considered putting Porter under arrest, then sent his corps north to take a position on Dogan Ridge, east of the unfinished railroad. At 11:30 AM the next morning, August 30, Pope ordered his troops to attack the Confederate line. By this time, Pope was under the illusion that the Confederates were in retreat. Porter moved his 10,000 men through the Groveton Woods in front of the ridge and began taking heavy Confederate artillery fire even before they emerged. Waiting for promised support on their right, the V Corps remained stalled in the Groveton Woods for more than an hour.

Across the road from the parking area is the site of the Groveton Woods, where Porter's men waited and took Confederate artillery. Although some of this land is private property, the forest can be seen, and one can imagine the whistling of the shells through the tall trees as the Union soldiers stood there, anticipating what was to come.

Six hundred yards in front of the Federals was a cut in the railroad embankment, now well known as the Deep Cut. The last 150 yards of the approach to the Confederate line was a steep upward slope. Worse, Confederate artillery at the Brawner Farm to the south controlled the entire field. Twice Porter asked for reinforcements, and twice he received no answer. At 2:30 PM, Federal sharpshooters emerged from the Groveton Woods, crossed the Groveton–Sudley Road, and rushed forward to take shelter in a creek halfway up the ridge known as Schoolhouse Branch. Although there were comparatively few of them, the sharpshooters took out a good number of Confederates at the embankment.

From the parking lot, walk the trail along the Groveton road and then up the embankment. Most of the trees on your left as you make your way up were not here at the time of the battle, but the tree line on your right is mostly what existed then. Remarkably, not long ago, this entire area was densely wooded, and viewing the Deep Cut was virtually impossible without taking a fairly strenuous cross-country hike. Today, however, much of the original area has been restored to its 1862 appearance, making one of the most important events of the Second Battle of Manassas accessible again. (Oddly, some local residents are resisting further restoration of the landscape. For them, Manassas National Battlefield Park is as much recreational as it is historic.)

A view of the Deep Cut from the Confederate artillery position at Groveton.

As you make your way up the slope, you will pass Schoolhouse Branch. There is an interesting anachronism here, a monument to some of the sharpshooters who fought at the Deep Cut. But instead of the usual granite monument so common on Civil War battlefields today, it is a simple wooden sign indicating the significance of the spot for posterity. This is how many of these locations were marked in the first years after the war, and the sign serves to humbly remind the visitor that those who fought here were not just historical statistics.

Finally, at 3:00 PM, the V Corps emerged from the woods in a rush. The Confederates were startled, but their artillery, 18 guns, opened up almost immediately. The Union troops raced across the pasture in front of them, stopping shortly at Schoolhouse Branch to take shelter and then continuing up the hill. As they pushed, they took incredible losses, but they were able to reach the Confederates at the unfinished railroad.

Now that you have climbed to the top of the ridge, you can imagine the difficulty of thousands of Union soldiers as they raced to the Deep Cut as fast as they could, dodging Confederate artillery and facing a wall of fire from the infantry behind the embankment. There is a memorial here, identical to one on Henry Hill near the visitors center, erected not long after the battle by its survivors. You can look up and down the embankment from here; note the distinctive rocky terrain, adding one more hardship to what the men who fought here were already facing. As you face the embankment, if you walk to your right, after a short hike you will also eventually come to "The Dump," site of heavy fighting on the second day of the battle.

The fighting here was unbelievably desperate, often becoming hand-to-hand. The Confederates poured reinforcements in from wherever they could, while the Union soldiers were able to use the railroad embankment as their own breastwork in certain parts of the line. The heavy losses on both sides concerned both Jackson and Porter; if there were any point where the outcome of the battle was in doubt, this was it. On some parts of the line, the Confederates ran out of ammunition and began to throw large rocks at the Federals, which were often thrown right back at them.

Unfortunately for the Union men, they were stuck between two evils. The pasture that they had crossed was now totally dominated by Confederate artillery, and the number of guns covering the field seemed to grow by the minute. No reinforcements could be sent. At the same time, any retreat back down the slope and across the pasture would also meet with devastating results. So the Federals fought on until, finally, many of the men took it on their own to retreat from the Deep Cut. Porter eventually withdrew his entire corps back to Dogan Ridge.

As you face the embankment, turn to your left. Although difficult to see because of the existing trees (which were not there at the time of the battle), the Brawner Farm and the site of the Confederate artillery is only a short distance from where you now stand. (If you have the time, the trail from the Deep Cut to the Brawner Farm clearly illustrates just what Porter's men were up against.) If you now turn to your left again, before you make your way back down the slope, take note of the open, rocky field in front of you, in particular the long distance between your position and the Groveton Woods. This entire area was blanketed with heavy Confederate artillery fire during the fight, and it was this gauntlet of fire that held many a Federal soldier at the Deep Cut rather than heading back down the slope.

Confederate Artillery

❯ *From the Deep Cut parking area, turn right onto Featherbed Lane and drive 0.5 mile to US 29. Turn right on US 29 and drive 0.5 mile to the parking area for Battery Heights on your right.*

On August 29, despite what Pope may have believed, Longstreet's wing of the Confederate army was present. At 10:00 AM that day, the lead elements of the right wing of the Confederate Army of Northern Virginia began to arrive from near Thoroughfare Gap. Lee called for Jackson to join him and Longstreet to determine their battle plan. Jackson would hold his position behind the unfinished railroad, stretching northeast. Longstreet's men would join with Jackson's right, near the Brawner Farm, and form a line heading southeast. The two lines would form what would later be described as a set of jaws around the Union army. The upper jaw, Jackson, would remain in place, while the lower jaw, Longstreet, would stay concealed in the woods until it was time to snap shut on the Federals.

This is one of several spots from which the massed Confederate artillery did so much damage to the Union attackers at the Deep Cut, which can be seen in the distance. This point, along with the nearby Brawner Farm, was one of the few spots on the Confederate side of the field where artillery could be effective, and when Longstreet's artillery arrived, much of it was placed on this rise.

Longstreet began deploying his men immediately. One brigade was north of the Warrenton Turnpike to connect with Jackson's line, while the next, John Bell Hood's Texas Brigade, set its left on the turnpike, with the rest of the brigades forming from there. By noon, the entire Confederate line was in place—more than 3 miles long— and the generals were discussing the best time to close the jaws and destroy the Federals. Just then, however, Stuart rode up, telling of a large Union force in front of Longstreet's line. An unexpected development, Lee himself went out to inspect the situation, and not knowing what was in front of them or their intentions, agreed that it would be prudent to delay the advance.

The Federals to their front were Porter's V Corps, still holding their position. Pope did not know it, but Porter's decision to stay where he was may have saved his army.

His mere presence here gave the Confederates second thoughts about making any movement south of the Warrenton Turnpike until late that evening.

At 6:30 PM, Lee and Longstreet finally decided that a forced reconnaissance should be conducted. Hood's Texas Brigade would lead, supported by the surrounding units. At almost the same time, Pope received a report of Confederate wagons heading west down the Warrenton Turnpike in retreat. (These were actually ambulances, evacuating the wounded.) Believing this report but dismissing the innumerable reports before it that a large number of Confederates was now amassed south of the turnpike, Pope ordered Hatch's brigade to "pursue" them. Hatch advanced down the turnpike until he ran right into Hood and the rest of the Confederates. A sharp fight ensued, with Hatch holding as well as he could but sending a message back that no Confederates were retreating. His report, like the others, was dismissed. The Federals were eventually forced to retreat at 8:00 PM in the darkness. The Confederates followed, taking a position only yards away from the Federals, ready to spring Lee's trap at a moment's notice. However, with units intermingling and becoming confused in the darkness (as well as the still undetermined intentions of Porter's men to their right), Lee ordered all of Longstreet's units back to their original positions just after midnight.

Back at Union headquarters, Pope thought the fight on the Warrenton Turnpike unimportant. He was, by now, beginning to accept that perhaps the entire Confederate army was present. Still, he was convinced the Federals were winning the battle, the Confederates were in retreat, and Longstreet would only be reinforcing Jackson. Pope decided to renew his attack in the morning, and he would make his battle plan then.

Longstreet's Advance

> *Turn left back onto US 29 and drive 0.7 mile. After heading up a slope, you will see a park road on your right; pull in here and park in the lot on your right. Walk up the slope toward the monument and cannons at the top of the hill.*

When the Union officers met at 7:00 AM on August 30, none of them shared Pope's opinion that the Confederates were in retreat. After meeting for an hour, the generals agreed on the day's plan: keep hammering at the Confederate left near Sudley Springs. The line had now been bolstered by the 8,000 men of Porter's V Corps, and considering the near successes of the previous day, that should be enough to ensure Union victory. Despite the efforts of Porter and General John Reynolds to sway his opinion, Pope still dismissed the notion that the Confederates could be south of the Warrenton Turnpike in any force.

Despite the general agreement on the plan of attack, Pope failed to issue orders to his commanders. This astonished not only the Union generals, but the Confederates as well; although Lee would remain patient, he too was wondering what was going on. The field remained mostly quiet until about 10:00 AM, when Reynolds's division advanced toward Groveton on the south side of the turnpike. Taking possession of a commanding hill in a meadow just east of the town, Reynolds set artillery here and then waited, like the rest of the armies, for something to happen.

At 11:00 AM, the trigger for the chaos that would rule the Union army for the rest of the day walked into Porter's lines. The man, a Confederate straggler, reported that Jackson was retreating westward to join Longstreet. Porter did not believe him, but per protocol, sent the man to Pope's headquarters along with his opinion of the straggler's story. Despite all evidence to the contrary, despite the repeated warnings of his generals, and despite all logic, Pope bought the straggler's story without question. By 11:30 he had issued orders to Porter to attack the Confederate line, initiating the fight at the Deep Cut.

As both sides struggled at the Deep Cut, reports continued to pour in about Confederates on the Union left. Just after noon, Sigel reported Confederates moving to the left, and the same report came from Reynolds around 1:00 PM, with McDowell ordering Reynolds to fall back to Chinn Ridge to guard the left flank. Still, Pope was unfazed, but he finally relented and authorized Sigel to send a brigade south to "that bald hill." Pope had meant Henry Hill, site of the climax of the first Battle of Manassas, but Sigel sent them to Chinn Ridge just to the west. It would be one of the few fortunate mistakes the Federals would make that day.

The Confederates, even as they kept an eye on the Deep Cut, prepared for their movement to snap the jaws shut on the Federals. Preparations began at 2:30 PM, with Longstreet scheduled to move at 5:00 PM.

Just before the Deep Cut fight, Colonel Gouverneur Warren, guarding artillery on Dogan Ridge, noticed that Reynolds was no longer in his position atop the hill east of Groveton. Knowing that it was an important position, Warren moved forward to take it. Although they did receive some artillery fire, most of the Confederates were watching Porter at the Deep Cut, so Warren's artillery took up position on the crest of the hill. Skirmishers (the 10th New York Zouaves) and fallback infantry (the 5th New York) were set around the artillery, with the 10th lined up along Lewis Lane to the front.

The monument here at the top of the hill marks the point where Warren placed his artillery. As you look ahead, the intersection to your right was the center of the small hamlet of Groveton. The road directly in front of you was Lewis Lane, where the 10th New York formed its line. From this vantage point, you can see why Warren considered this an important part of the field; you have a commanding view of the turnpike, which would have made this an effective artillery position.

More than just Confederate artillery was focused on the Deep Cut. McDowell saw that Porter was in deep trouble and sent Reynolds's division to the Union center,

Colonel Gouverneur Warren's artillery overlooking Groveton.

leaving only 1,200 men on Chinn Ridge. Both Longstreet and Lee also observed Porter's failure to break the line. Instantly recognizing the opportunity, both generals knew that now was the time to shut the jaws. The Federals had been either ignoring or denying the fact that Longstreet was on the field. Soon they would not be able to do so any longer.

The main objective of Longstreet's advance was to possess Henry Hill, east and south of the Federal position. From here they would command both the Warrenton Turnpike and virtually all of the fords across Bull Run except for Sudley Springs, which Jackson would take. Their most important obstacle was time. If the jaws could not be shut by sundown, the Union army would escape. At 4:00 PM, the Confederate movement began, with Hood's Texas Brigade advancing toward Henry Hill and keeping its left on the Warrenton Turnpike. Approximately 24,000 Confederate soldiers were south of the turnpike; only 2,200 Federals lay in their path.

When the Texas Brigade emerged from the woods in front of Lewis Lane, the 10th New York did not stay long. Knowing that they did not have a chance, they quickly abandoned their position as well as the artillery on the crest of the hill. (Remarkably, the Confederates moved past the artillery so quickly that the Federals were able to virtually walk in and retake it shortly after it was overrun.) They fell back in confusion toward the right of the 5th New York, lined up in the thick woods 200 yards behind Warren's guns.

New York Infantry Monuments

> *Return down the hill to your vehicle and continue down the park road for 0.2 mile to the next parking area.*

The 5th New York had no idea what was heading its way. Its arms were stacked and it was not in any sort of battle formation. Its first and only warning was the 10th New York rushing out of the woods to its front. Quickly falling in, the 5th readied itself for whatever was coming. It was a remarkably disciplined regiment; almost any other unit certainly would have taken its cue from the 10th and gone to flight.

The 5th was in line on the west bank of Young's Branch with a steep ravine behind them. When Hood's Confederates appeared in front, the men of the 5th were not able to fire because too many of the 10th, still in flight, were in their way. By the time their field of fire was cleared, the Texas Brigade was only 40 yards to their front and unleashed a devastating volley. Warren issued an immediate retreat, but it could not be heard over the roar, and the regiment was too disciplined to fall back without orders. The New Yorkers held their line until the punishment became too great, and were fi-

A monument to the 5th New York Infantry. More than half the regiment was killed, wounded, or captured within five minutes at Second Manassas, the largest single regimental loss of the entire war.

nally forced to flee down the embankment. The Confederates quickly took the ridge-line and fired down into the ravine, easily picking off the retreating Federals.

In barely more than five minutes, the 5th New York—which had begun the day with more than 500 men in its ranks—suffered 120 men killed and 175 wounded or captured. It would be the largest single regimental loss of the entire Civil War.

Here, monuments to both the 5th and the 10th New York have been placed in the area where the 5th made its brave stand. Facing away from the monuments, you are looking in the direction from which first the fleeing 10th New York and then the Texas Brigade appeared. Behind the monuments, one can easily see the steep ridge from which the Texans delivered their deadly fire as the New Yorkers retreated.

Chinn Ridge

❯ *Drive around the loop in the parking area and return 0.2 mile down the park road back to US 29. Turn right onto US 29 and drive 1 mile to Sudley Road. Turn right onto Sudley Road and drive 0.5 mile. Turn right onto the park road and drive 0.8 mile, taking a right turn to the Chinn Ridge parking area.*

Although the destruction of the two New York regiments did not slow the Confederate advance in the least, it did have one electric result. Pope was now acutely and painfully aware that despite his previous denials, the Confederates were not only south of the Warrenton Turnpike, but in overwhelming numbers. Instantly, the Union army jumped to adjust to its newfound threat.

McDowell, like Lee and Longstreet, knew that the key to Union escape was Henry Hill, and the only thing between the Confederates and Henry Hill was the 1,200 Federals on Chinn Ridge. Chinn Ridge is about 500 yards west of Henry Hill, angled slightly to the northwest with Young's Branch to the west and Chinn's Branch to the east. The Chinn Farm itself was on the south end of the ridge. Colonel Nathaniel McLean's brigade, sent by Sigel to "that bald hill" earlier, quickly formed on the ridge facing west while McDowell scrambled to send units to aid McLean (possibly, in part, to correct his gross mistake of sending Reynolds's division north only hours before, leaving the hill virtually empty). McLean's four regiments were set in two lines, one behind the other, with their four guns on the right.

As the Confederates emerged from Young's Branch, which was obscured by a tree line, the Federal artillery let forth a volley of canister. They mostly missed their mark, but it was enough to make Hood's Texans think twice about charging up the ridge, and they fell back into the trees. When they emerged again, it was Union musketry that stalled the advance. The Confederates fell back into the woods to the Union left, using them as a screen to move toward the Chinn Farm in an attempt to flank the Federals.

Walk to the end of the parking lot and face west so that the paved pathway is to your right and the parking spaces are to your left. You are now looking in the direction of Young's Branch. While much of the area in front of you was clear of trees, the woods to your left are the same woods that Hood's Confederates moved through. Before you walk the pathway, you may want to explore what's left of the Chinn Farm—the foundation of the home, as well as a small cemetery.

Federal units tried to move south, but Jackson's men, as well as the Confederate artillery at Groveton, continued to keep them occupied. Besides the Union fire from Chinn Ridge, though, the Confederates were slowing themselves down. Hood, being nearest the "hinge" of the jaws, not only had the least distance to cover but also moved very quickly, and he had to hold and wait for the units to his right to catch up with him. Soon he faced an additional four regiments from Ohio along with artillery, and the Union line was now at an angle facing both west and south toward the Chinn Farm.

General James Kemper's division eventually came up on Hood's right, with the lead brigade, Nathan Evans's, moving through the Chinn Farm and taking shelter behind the farm's outbuildings. After several piecemeal attacks and remarkable defiance by the Federals, the Confederates made a concerted effort toward the Union left, rolling up several Ohio regiments and a battery but eventually losing momentum and falling back. After once again driving the Confederates back, McLean saw a large group of soldiers in dark uniforms coming from his new left, east of Chinn Ridge. While he thought they were the enemy, he was told they were actually reinforcements, and he directed his attention back to the battle in front of him. It was actually the rest of Kemper's division.

Walking down the paved pathway at the end of the parking lot will take you along the crest of Chinn Ridge. As you walk, the Union positions were to your right, with the Confederates coming initially from your left and then from behind you. When the first Union line fell back, a new line was formed at the rail fence you see here. Keep walking until you get to the two cannons placed to the right of the pathway.

Remarkably, McLean was able to stall the Confederates by himself for 30 minutes, enough time to allow more than 7,000 Union troops to begin moving south to protect the Union left. Just as McLean's line was collapsing around 5:00 PM, two other Federal brigades arrived. The Confederate fire made it difficult to form, but the Federals were able to put up enough resistance to slightly slow the Confederates. Soon, the focus of the fight was over the battery of the Fifth Maine, and the two lines pushed each other back and forth over these critical guns. In the end, however, the Confederate numbers were overwhelming. When D. R. "Neighbor" Jones's division appeared from the ravine of Chinn Branch, almost completely enveloping the Federals, the fight was over. The Union line finally broke around 6:00 PM, with the Federals retreating in good order to the northeast along the ridge.

The two guns you see here are in the position of the Fifth Maine artillery, scene of

Chinn Ridge trail at Manassas National Battlefield Park.

the fiercest fighting on the ridge. From this position, you also have a good vantage point of the ravine at Chinn Branch, from which even more Confederates entered the last stages of the fight. When the Federals withdrew, they left in the direction of the rest of the pathway. From here, you may either continue on or walk back to your vehicle; most of what lies ahead is related to the first battle at Manassas, although the forestation of the ridge over the years has made it very difficult to interpret.

The Confederates had gained Chinn Ridge, but the fierce fight put up by McLean's brigade and the rest of the Union troops had stalled their advance considerably. For all their superior numbers, they had taken a beating and had been slowed enough for Federal troops to begin moving not only to secure Henry Hill, but also off the fields of Manassas.

Portici/South Cavalry Field

❭ *From the Chinn Ridge parking area, drive 0.7 on the park road back to Sudley Road. Turn right on Sudley Road, then take an immediate left onto Battlefield Parkway. Drive 0.9 mile on Battlefield Parkway until reaching the park road to Portici on your left. Turn left and drive 0.2 mile to the trailhead to Portici.*

At the far southern end of the battlefield, Buford's cavalry had been patrolling the roads since midafternoon, watching over the Union left. When Longstreet's advance began, Buford pulled his cavalry back to the Lewis Farm and Portici, the home that had been a Confederate staging area during First Manassas. At 6:00 PM, Beverly

Robertson's Confederate cavalry, which had followed the Federals, was assigned by Stuart to intercept the retreating Union army as it made its way across Bull Run. Buford was intent on preventing that.

Buford stacked his four regiments of cavalry behind a low ridge. When Robertson approached, all he could see was a small squadron of cavalry, and he promptly ordered a charge by the Second Virginia. As they moved across one ridge, the Union squadron quickly gave way, but as they crossed the second ridge, they suddenly found an entire brigade of horsemen in front of them. They quickly retreated and rejoined the rest of Robertson's command.

When Robertson brought up the rest of his brigade, the Federals were in line on the crest waiting for them. A sharp fight ensued, but having lost the element of surprise, the Union cavalry quickly scattered. Although the Confederates were dominant once again, Buford's resistance marked one of the first times Federal cavalry stood up to the usually far superior Confederate horsemen and gave them a good fight. Within a year, Union cavaliers, with the help of commanders like Buford, would begin to turn the tide of the war on horseback.

From your vehicle, drive to the end of the most well-kept part of the road and keep your eyes peeled for the trailhead to the site of Portici. The trail is a bit more than a quarter mile there and back and makes its way through a nicely mown meadow, so make sure you have some good shoes on. At the end of the short trail, just past the tree line, you will find several interpretive signs for Portici and the cavalry battle that occurred in the fields around you.

Henry Hill

〉 *Return to Battlefield Parkway and turn right, driving 0.9 mile back to Sudley Road. Turn right on Sudley Road and drive 0.5 mile. Pull into the parking area for the Manassas National Battlefield Park visitors center.*

Orders were rapidly moving up and down the Union lines at 4:30 PM, shortly after the destruction of Warren's regiments. Some units were directed to move south to meet Longstreet's threat, while others made preparations for a fighting withdrawal. While some went to aid McLean's defense on Chinn Ridge, others went to Henry Hill, knowing, as did every commander on the field by this time, that that location was the key to either the escape or the destruction of the Union Army of Virginia.

The first troop placements were made by Pope himself, whose headquarters were at the Stone House north of Henry Hill and the Warrenton Turnpike. Federals began lining up facing west along Sudley Road, most of them slightly up the slope of the hill. By 6:00 PM, the time the Federals finally withdrew from Chinn Ridge, a half-mile-long line consisting of four brigades was on the western slope of Henry Hill. More troops were on the way, and artillery was soon placed atop the crest of the hill. It was, actually, almost identical to the strong defensive position the Confederates had taken during First Manassas.

With the defense starting to take shape, Pope turned command of Henry Hill over to McDowell and went to the business of withdrawing the rest of the army to the strong earthworks at Centreville. All of his corps commanders, still on the right facing Jackson, were ordered to pull back fighting to the east across Sudley Road, keeping their extreme left on Henry Hill to prevent a break in the line. Although Jackson did keep the Federals occupied as they moved, his pursuit was not enough to keep them pinned in place. Franklin's VI Corps of the Army of the Potomac, only now arriving in Centreville due to McClellan's resistance to let them go, was ordered to remain in Centreville and prepare a strong defense.

While virtually all of the interpretation that currently exists on Henry Hill is related to the first Battle of Manassas, the features that played a role in the second can easily be spotted. Sudley Road remains in its original place, and looking to the west toward the road, you can see where the Federals lined up both on the road and behind it. The area across the road was much less forested than it is today, but the majority of the fighting would be just around and on your side of the Sudley Road.

Even with the strong Union position, the Confederates were far superior in number to the Union defenders. Yet another Confederate division, R. H. Anderson's, lined up to the right of Jones, and the Confederate right extended well past the Union left. However, this put many of Anderson's troops in the woods, and in the growing darkness it was difficult to tell how many of the enemy were in front of them. The Federals were eventually pushed off Sudley Road, and the center and left of the line began to give slowly. As reinforcements poured in, the fight went back and forth on the west slope of the hill, with the Union troops holding just enough to buy time for the rest of the army to cross Bull Run at the stone bridge and head west to Centreville.

The woods you see to your left are in approximately the same position they were at the time of the battle. Much of the heaviest fighting on the left, however, actually occurred on the campus of the Northern Virginia Community College, just south of the park boundary.

At 7:00 PM, with the field growing dark, the last group of Federal reinforcements—

> **CASUALTIES (ESTIMATED*)**
>
> **Confederate:** killed, 1,400; wounded, 7,500; missing or captured, 1,400; total: 10,300.
>
> **Union:** killed, 1,700; wounded, 8,400; missing or captured, 6,000; total: 16,100.
>
> **Total Casualties: 26,400**
>
> *The various casualty counts for this battle vary greatly.

Colonel Edward Ferrero's brigade of Reno's Corps—arrived on Henry Hill. The men lined a bit farther back on the hill along a crest, where they lay down and kept silent. The rest of the Union troops on Henry Hill pulled back fighting, leaving only Ferrero. The Confederates began to follow, led by Richard Toombs, who had been released from arrest just to lead this final advance. His glory was short-lived, however, as the Federals waited for Toombs's men to come close. Reno then ordered a devastating volley out of the darkness, sending the Confederates running back to the west.

At 8:00 PM, Pope finally issued the final orders for the Army of Virginia to retreat to Centreville, and by 11:00 PM almost all of the Federals were across Bull Run. The second battle at Manassas was finally over. Although badly damaged, Pope had managed to withdraw his army to the safety of the Centreville defenses.

CHANTILLY (OX HILL)

❯ *From the visitors center, return to Sudley Road and turn left. Drive 0.8 mile, then take the ramp to I-66 East. Drive 7.8 miles on I-66 East to Exit 55 for the Fairfax County Parkway. Merge onto the parkway and drive 1.2 miles to Monument Drive. Follow Monument Drive for 0.8 mile to Ox Road; you will see part of the Ox Hill Battlefield Park on your right. Turn right on West Ox Road and turn right into the parking area for the park.*

When Pope finally settled in Centreville, he immediately wrote to Halleck to tell him of the day's events. At 9:45 PM, he telegraphed that the Union army had indeed been forced to withdraw, but they had managed to inflict great damage on the Confederates in the process and that the army was safe.

Although he may still have been in a small state of shock to spin the story so positively, Pope's assessment was mostly true. It was a close shave, but the Army of Virginia had emerged intact. Their position in Centreville would resist any attack. The Confederates had paid a heavy price for their victory. Perhaps most important—and this is something Pope would probably not have acknowledged—the mood of the Federal troops was not the same as it had been after their first defeat at Manassas. Just over a year ago, that army, full of green soldiers, had fled the field in panic. Now these veterans, in a much more terrible battle, had withdrawn in good order. And they were not scared, sullen, or sad. They were angry—at Pope, at McDowell, at the rest of the Union generals who had been outgeneraled once again. Adding fuel to the fire, as the men marched into Centreville, Franklin's VI Corps greeted their fellow soldiers not with encouragement but with mocking jeers, prompted by Pope's boasts of the previous months.

Pope's rose-colored view did not last long. The 13,826 Federal casualties, when combined with 8,353 Confederate, made Second Manassas the bloodiest battle of the Civil War up to that time. Wiring Halleck the next morning, August 31, Pope actually

Ox Hill Battlefield Park in Chantilly, Virginia.

managed to ask Halleck his thoughts on whether the Washington defenses would hold should his army be destroyed. Pope was whipped.

Happiness was not in great supply on the other side of Bull Run, either. Lee, for one, was upset. Although his army had performed well, he had had another chance to crush a Federal force, just as he had outside Richmond, and he had failed. His men, even in victory, were not jubilant. They were tired. They had marched hard to get to Manassas, and then were engaged in the longest, hardest fight of the war.

As was his trademark, Lee was not about to give up easily. He knew exactly where Pope was, and although a frontal assault on Centreville was out of the question, he might be able to trap him between his current position and the defenses of Washington. The strategy was not very different from that of the previous parts of the campaign; Longstreet would keep the Federals occupied at Centreville while Jackson went on a flank march around the Union right using the Little River Turnpike, intercepting Pope along his escape route, the Warrenton Turnpike. Longstreet would follow a half day behind. Jackson left the afternoon of August 31, although his progress was slowed considerably by the weather and the fact that his men were completely spent. On this one rare occasion, Jackson, for the most part, let it slide.

Lee was not the only general who thought the Confederates should attempt a flank march. Most of the Union generals had already made the assumption that Lee would do exactly that, and were stunned that they were not yet on their way to Washington.

By the afternoon, virtually all of Pope's generals had lost faith in him. When he finally received a report from his cavalry that Jackson was trying to move around the army, Pope sent two brigades from Franklin's VI Corps to Fairfax to stop them.

The next morning, September 1, Pope's attitude had changed again, this time to rage. Writing Halleck, he accused several of his generals of "unsoldierly and dangerous conduct" on the field of battle. He mentioned no names, but it was obvious that most of his attack focused on Porter, with indirect implications of others as well. He further stated that the army should be brought into the defenses of Washington and completely reorganized. This assessment was correct; the divisive jealousies between the McClellan faction (such as Porter) and the Pope faction (such as McDowell) had completely disrupted the army. For Pope, it was time to shift the blame to those McClellan men. And McClellan, for his part, seemed to find every available excuse not to aid the Army of Virginia with his own men of the Army of the Potomac. As he said, it was Pope's mess to get out of.

At 11:00 AM, Pope began moving troops toward Germantown to protect his retreat route, then sent the IX Corps (under Isaac Stevens's command, because Reno was ill) to a point on the Little River Turnpike to intercept Jackson. By 3:00 PM, finally, much of the Union army was headed east to safety, with the rest of the army following later in the day.

Lee's instructions to Jackson on his flank march were clear: Do not engage the enemy unless victory is certain. It was understandable; Lee had separated his army again, and there was some risk involved. So when Jackson noticed Union cavalry frequently appearing on his right, realizing he had lost the element of surprise, he decided to wait for Longstreet to come up, reuniting the Confederate army. He stopped his march at 2:00 PM just 2 miles short of Germantown near Chantilly, at the crossroads of the Little River Turnpike and Ox Ford Road.

The Chantilly crossroads were the destination of Trimble's force, although they had a hard time getting there. Traveling cross-country, they had become lost along the way and approached Ox Hill at the crossroads from the southwest. There were other units now coming up to assist him, as Pope ordered Heintzelman's III Corps—Kearny's and Hooker's divisions—to the crossroads, but Pope had neglected to inform Stevens. In any case, the III Corps would not be able to find the IX Corps until battle had already begun.

Here within the Ox Hill Battlefield Park, you are now located near the original crossroads. Most of the battlefield has been lost to the development and sprawl you fought through to get here. However, what you see before you may be one of the better efforts you'll find at interpretation of a battlefield in the middle of a city. In the past several years, the park has undergone a wonderful transformation from being a mostly isolated green space to a very nice memorial to the events that occurred here. Start with the interpretive kiosks at the beginning of the trail to orient yourself to the landscape.

Stevens approached the crossroads at 4:00 PM and immediately began forming a line at the south end of Reid's cornfield, 0.25 mile south of the turnpike. (Reno, on the field but too sick to command, did not approve of the plan, but deferred to Stevens.) Jackson, in turn, deployed his entire command at the north end of the cornfield, extending well beyond the Union right and straddling Ox Ford Road.

At this point, begin to make your way around the loop trail heading clockwise. The signs along the trail will tell the story of the battle chronologically and will also give you an idea what the surrounding area once looked like, making interpretation of the battlefield much easier than you might think at first glance.

Stevens, unfortunately for the Federals, did not realize the size of the Confederate force when he sent his men across the field at 4:30 PM. They initially met heavy resistance, but because of their concentration on the portion of Jackson's line at the cornfield, advanced steadily. Early in the battle, Stevens decided to lead the 79th New York by himself. It was a fatal decision. Moving to the front and taking the colors of the 79th, he led them in a charge but was soon shot and killed. The 79th, inspired, reached the Confederate line and began to break it.

At almost the exact time of Stevens's death, the skies opened and brought a terrible thunderstorm, with heavy lightning and rain that cut visibility on the field considerably. The New Yorkers began to lose track of each other in the stormy darkness and, without a leader, were forced to pull back. The other Federal regiments, though, were making good progress, and at 5:00 PM were steadily pushing the Confederate center back. The weight of the Confederate numbers began to reverse the tide around 5:30, but just at that moment, Kearny's division of the III Corps arrived on the field.

Before his death, Stevens had asked for support, and Kearny, receiving the message, had rushed his division into the fight. Taking the front as the men of the IX Corps re-formed, Kearny sent his lead brigade, General David Birney's, to attack the right of the Confederate line. His attack was successful, but he was unsupported on his right and asked for help. Trying to arrange support, Kearny rode ahead to inspect the right and came upon the captain of the 21st Massachusetts, which had been badly beaten in the previous fighting. Kearny ordered them to re-form and fight; the captain initially refused, but changed his mind when Kearny threatened to turn the Federal artillery on their regiment. Still, they advanced slowly, and the captain again said the advance was too dangerous.

Kearny would never be accused of cowardice, and despised those who exhibited the trait. So at 6:15 PM, to show the 21st Massachusetts that it could be done, Kearny rode forward to the north end of the cornfield. In the darkness, he approached another unit and asked it to identify itself, and it did—the 49th Georgia. Kearny replied "OK," and began to slowly ride away. When one of the Georgians realized Kearny was a Yankee officer and ordered him to halt, Kearny put the spurs to his horse and tried to escape. He was shot dead off his horse, which wandered back into the Confederate lines.

By 6:30 PM, the fight began to die down with the dusk. Reinforcements arrived for both sides, but the fight was not renewed, and by 2:30 AM the Federals had withdrawn to the east toward the rest of their army.

Continuing around the trail, you will pass through part of the cornfield. Although the point at which Kearny fell is just outside the park boundary, there is still a monument to his memory here, as well as one for Stevens. The approximate spot where Stevens fell is marked with a quartz stone, laid by a former Confederate soldier who owned the land following the battle.

The Battle of Chantilly, or Ox Ford, was mostly seen as a useless battle for both sides. Neither had gained from the fight, and the Union had lost two major generals in Stevens and Kearny. The loss of Kearny was particularly mourned on both sides of the line. His body lay on the field through the night, and was recognized the next day even though his uniform had already been picked over for souvenirs. Hill was notably upset at the loss. Upon learning of Kearny's death, Jackson reportedly said in alarm, "You have shot the most gallant officer in the United States Army!" Lee took personal charge of Kearny's body, sending it back into the Union lines the next day with a note for Kearny's widow. A month later, Lee would also send on Kearny's missing personal effects as well as his horse.

On the morning of September 2, Lincoln, along with Halleck, endured one of the most humbling moments of his presidency. Visiting McClellan at his home, Lincoln

Monuments to Union generals Phil Kearny and Isaac Stevens, both of whom died at the Battle of Chantilly.

offered him command of the entire army. There was no better alternative, as he explained to his shocked cabinet later that day. Pope could not be given another command. McClellan was excellent at defense, and the capital was nervous. Perhaps most important, the soldiery loved him, and they needed a leader they could trust. It was a hard pill to swallow, but McClellan was the best choice. Pope's Army of Virginia simply ceased to exist, with his forces instantly being merged into the Army of the Potomac.

The Confederates had no such leadership crisis. Although his forces had taken a beating, jeopardizing the success of their planned movement into Maryland, Lee had established himself as a force to be reckoned with. He had demonstrated tactical brilliance, his movements were bold but calculated, his subordinates had executed their tasks precisely, and he had shown patience. He had taken control of the Army of Northern Virginia on June 1 when the Federals were within 10 miles of the Confederate capital. In three months, Lee had not only repelled the invaders from the outskirts of Richmond, but had driven them from Virginia soil altogether.

As Pope's army marched into the defenses of Washington, McClellan was there to greet them in full dress uniform. The two commanders exchanged salutes and Pope transferred control of the army. Within earshot of Pope, Hatch raised three cheers to the return of McClellan, and the news spread rapidly down the line. In an instant, the Union troops were reenergized, tossing hats and knapsacks into the air. Mac was back. Surely, he would lead them to whip Bobby Lee.

CHAPTER 5

Lee's First Invasion and the Road to Antietam

ROBERT E. LEE HAD LEFT RICHMOND in early August with the intention of invading Maryland and, perhaps, Pennsylvania. His army had achieved astounding victories, and, although they had been costly, they were giving the Confederacy hope. Only months after seemingly being pushed back on every front, fortunes were beginning to turn both east and west. Furthermore, across the ocean, foreign intervention—particularly by France or England—was becoming more likely with each Confederate victory.

Even with these brightening prospects, the Confederate Army of Northern Virginia could not stop now even if it wanted to. The army was hungry, and there was no food where they were. Moving west into the Shenandoah Valley would only temporarily feed them, and moving south toward Richmond would mean further burdening Virginia's already depleted farmland. Either direction would allow the Union forces to recover. The capital at Washington was within striking distance, but Lee knew that the city's defenses were impregnable.

On September 3, 1862, Lee informed Confederate president Jefferson Davis that it was time to take the army onto Union soil. There was food there, and moving to the north would relieve pressure on Richmond and Virginia's farmers. It might also bring Maryland, which held strong Confederate sympathies, into the fold. From their position, the army could harass Washington, Baltimore, or even Philadelphia. In the very

The IX Corps monument to Jesse Reno at Fox's Gap.

worst case, Lee would have an easy escape route through the Shenandoah Valley, and Braxton Bragg's Confederate army in Kentucky could be brought east if necessary.

Lee was also counting heavily on the Union army, and particularly George B. McClellan, to play their part. With McClellan once again in command, the Confederates could count on the Federals moving slowly and cautiously, something that the tenacious Lee could take advantage of. Further, the Union had been badly beaten at Manassas, and Lee surmised that they must be completely demoralized.

While Lee's assumptions made sense, there were factors that Lee did not consider, and in some cases could not foresee. The only real error he made was in his assessment of Union morale. For all his faults, McClellan was well loved by his troops, and after the poor generalship shown by John Pope and Irvin McDowell, the Federals were ready to prove themselves under his command. Other fortunes in the following weeks would virtually fall into McClellan's lap, giving him tools that led to sudden and unexpected aggressiveness by the Union army.

The most significant thing riding on this invasion and the great battle that would end it was known only by a small group of men in Washington. On July 22, President Abraham Lincoln had informed his cabinet that he would free the slaves in the rebellious states. There were military reasons for emancipation; slaves were doing much of the Confederacy's labor, allowing white men to fight. The most compelling argument, though, was that while the war was still about preserving the Union, too much had happened to simply revert to the way things were. There would be no compromise. Slavery, one way or another, would end. The cabinet was in general agreement, but it was proposed that unless it could be tied to Union victory, emancipation might be seen as an act of desperation. So Lincoln agreed to withhold his proclamation until that victory came. That September, on what remains the bloodiest day in American history, the question of slavery would be settled along the banks of Antietam Creek.

ANTIETAM CAMPAIGN

Number of sites: 8

Total miles: 120

Estimated time: 2–4 days

Must-sees: Antietam National Battlefield, Harpers Ferry National Historic Park

Close second: South Mountain

BEFORE YOU GO

» PLANNING YOUR TRIP

The distance of this tour is not great, but be sure not to cheat yourself. Allow yourself plenty of time. While you can take the auto tour at Antietam National Battlefield in a very short time, you should not. The battlefield is well preserved, almost every piece of it is easily accessible, and the beautiful countryside and easy terrain practically beg that you take your time. Allow yourself at least a day at Antietam.

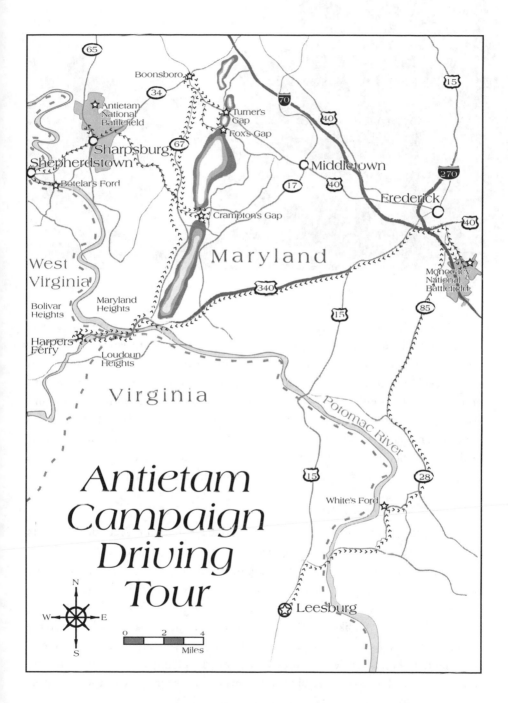

65

Boonsboro

34

Antietam
National
Battlefield

67

Sharpsburg

Shepherdstown

Botelar's Ford

Turner's
Gap

Fox's Gap

70

40

15

Middletown

17

40

270

Frederick

Crampton's Gap

40

Maryland

Monocacy
National
Battlefield

340

West
Virginia

Maryland
Heights

15

85

Bolivar
Heights

Harpers
Ferry

Loudoun
Heights

Virginia

Potomac River

28

White's Ford

15

Antietam
Campaign
Driving
Tour

N

W   E

S

0   2   4

Miles

Leesburg

Civil War museum at Harpers Ferry.

Chances are good that you'll want to spend a fair amount of time in Harpers Ferry. The battlefield here is only part of the story; in fact, until recent years, much of it was not even part of the park. Even if you just focus on the Civil War, there is enough here to keep you busy for many hours, and the park's analysis of John Brown's raid here just before the war is quite compelling. Besides that, both Jefferson and Washington spent significant time here, and the history of the arsenal, slavery, and the postwar period are fascinating. The town itself has plenty to keep anyone occupied. Finally, the sheer beauty of the place—from the incredible natural features to the quaint town itself—is entrancing. Allow yourself at least a half day here.

» RECOMMENDATIONS

Finding a place to stay or to eat won't be an issue on this tour. Frederick, Harpers Ferry, Hagerstown, and most points in between have plenty of hotels and restaurants. You may, however, want to consider staying in Sharpsburg and using that as a home base. There are three great advantages to doing this. First, with the possible exception of Frederick, almost every point on the tour will be within a very short drive. Second, as noted above, you will likely want to spend extra time at the battlefield, and having it there at your convenience is a big plus, particularly if you choose to walk some of the trails after the Visitor Center closes. Finally, much of Sharpsburg has been around since the war, and there are several great bed & breakfasts that have historical significance related to the battle and other pieces of the Civil War.

At both Antietam National Battlefield and Harpers Ferry National Historical Park, be sure to see what ranger programs are being held on the day of your visit. You may also want to consider using a personal guide to take you through Antietam. Arranged through a contractor that works with the park, the tours charge by the hour and can be as broad or as detailed as you'd like. In fact, you don't even have to stick to the battlefield itself. You can hire a guide to see other parts of the campaign, and this can be particularly helpful when touring the battlefield at South Mountain. If you do plan on using the services of a guide, be sure to arrange your tour as far in advance as possible so that a guide can be made available to you.

If you have the opportunity, visit the park during the Annual Antietam National Battlefield Memorial Illumination. Once a year, as darkness falls, the battlefield is covered with one candle for each of the 23,000 casualties that occurred here. Although the practice is now conducted in many places around the country, it is particularly special here—haunting, sad, and beautiful all at the same time. It is sure to be a sight that you will not forget.

THE CAMPAIGN TOUR

LEESBURG

❭ *Your tour begins in Leesburg, Virginia, northwest of Washington on the south bank of the Potomac River. Start at the Loudoun Museum, 16 Loudoun Street SW, on the northeast corner of Loudoun and Wirt Street SW.*

On September 3, the Army of Northern Virginia began its movement toward Leesburg. The army was 50,000 strong with reinforcements on the way. But there were also complications. First and foremost, the army had been either fighting or marching for almost a month without rest, and the men were extremely hungry. Straggling had become commonplace, and Lee set forth strict orders to prevent his army from shrinking any further. There was also the matter of "invasion" itself. Many soldiers

IN DEPTH

John M. Priest—*Antietam: The Soldiers' Battle*
Stephen W. Sears—*Landscape Turned Red: The Battle of Antietam*

"Together, this pair of tremendous works gives you both a complete guide to the historical aspects of Antietam and a remarkable view of it through the eyes of the soldier in the thick of the fight."

—*Tom Trescott, Abraham Lincoln Book Shop, Chicago*

A view of downtown Leesburg.

supported the southern cause to defend their homes, but pushing into enemy territory was not part of the bargain. They would defend to the death, but invasion was out of the question, and some units refused to cross the Potomac.

As the army prepared to cross, Lee set up his headquarters at the Harrison House and met with Stonewall Jackson, James Longstreet, and J. E. B. Stuart to discuss the upcoming campaign. Even though Lee didn't hide anything about his movement into

The Loudoun Museum.

Maryland, he still did not expect the Union Army of the Potomac to be able to pursue him for three to four weeks. The Confederates would make it clear to the citizens of Maryland that they were not there to invade. Foraging would not be permitted; while the army would live off the land, anything that was taken would be paid for, and the people would be treated with the utmost respect. Many Marylanders sympathized with their cause, after all, and the Confederates could expect some support along the way. The crossing would begin at White's Ford the next day.

Here at the Loudoun Museum, you will find exhibits on the rich history of the area, and much of the collection obviously pertains to the Civil War. The museum contains a nice garden, and visiting the many shops and restaurants in Leesburg is a pleasant way to spend the afternoon. The Harrison House where Lee stayed still exists, at 205 North King Street, but it is now owned by a private business and can only be viewed from the outside.

WHITE'S FORD

> *From the museum, turn right around the corner to head north on Wirt Street SW, take the next right on Market Street, and then the next left onto US 15 BR (North King Street). Drive 1.8 miles on US 15 BR, then continue another 1.5 miles on US 15 (James Madison Highway). Turn right at White's Ferry Road (MD Route 655), then drive 1.2 miles to White's Ferry, where you will pay a small toll to ride the ferry across the river. (The ferry runs continuously, and driving around the ferry will add 40 miles to your trip.) After exiting the ferry, drive 0.2 mile and turn left to continue on White's Ferry Road, then drive 2.6 miles to Martinsburg Road. Turn left at Martinsburg Road, drive 0.4 mile, and then bear right to continue on Martinsburg Road, following it another 2.3 miles. The entrance to White's Ford will be on your left; it can be hard to spot in the deep forest here, so watch your odometer and keep your eyes open. Drive 0.3 mile to the parking area.*

Beginning Thursday, September 4 and throughout the weekend, the Confederates crossed the Potomac here at White's Ford, then used the canal towpath of the Chesapeake and Ohio Canal to march 23 miles north toward the city of Frederick. As they crossed, the soldiers knew that this was a momentous occasion, and several regimental bands played a popular tune of the time, "Maryland, My Maryland," as the troops waded through the Potomac's strong current.

Although the Potomac is not far from you—less than 200 yards to the west— it is difficult to see or access the ford itself from the parking lot. This area, however, is preserved as part of the Chesapeake and Ohio Canal National Historical Park, and you can see a remnant of the old canal in the still water in front of you. If you walk across the blocked portion of the canal at the end of the parking lot, you will reach the old canal towpath, the same one that Lee's troops used after they crossed. Today, the towpath is used as a long scenic and historic trail than runs more than 180 miles along the river from Washington to Cumberland, Maryland.

FREDERICK/BEST FARM

Monocacy National Battlefield Visitor Center

> *From White's Ferry, return 0.3 mile down the park road back to Martinsburg Road, then turn left. Follow Martinsburg Road for 1.6 miles, then turn right to*

A view of the Confederate and Union camp site at Monocacy National Battlefield.

stay on the road for another 0.5 mile. At this point, you will bear left onto MD 28 West (Dickerson Road) and drive 4.8 miles. Bear right onto MD 85 North (Buckeystown Pike) and drive 9.6 miles, entering the city of Frederick. Turn right on Grove Road and drive 0.2 mile to MD 355 (Urbana Pike), then turn right on MD 355 and drive 1 mile. You will see the Visitor Center for Monocacy National Battlefield on your left. Pull into the parking lot.

In Washington, military matters were moving with uncharacteristic speed. Certainly some of it was fear-generated. Citizens in Washington, Baltimore, Philadelphia, and Harrisburg were pleading for Union troops to defend themselves as word of Lee's crossing spread. Undoubtedly, McClellan's return to command was strong motivation as well, both for him and for his men. On September 5, just days after taking control, McClellan ordered his corps commanders to have their troops cook three days' rations and be ready to march the next day. The Federals did leave on schedule, and McClellan joined them on September 7, setting up field headquarters in Rockville, Maryland.

McClellan had not only the veterans who had fought on the peninsula and at Manassas but also fresh recruits. No fewer than 35 new regiments were encamped around Washington, some of them not having yet received any training. The veterans, meanwhile, were scattered across the city after the rematch at Manassas. Organization, however, was one of McClellan's specialties, and it took him little time to put the army back into condition to move.

Other Federal troops to the west were not so fortunate. Union garrisons existed at Harpers Ferry, Martinsburg, and Winchester, Virginia. McClellan urged their evacuation, but General-in-Chief Henry Halleck allowed only the Winchester post to leave, saying that Harpers Ferry was defensible enough to hold the Rebels off. The former armory was guarded by nine regiments, seven of which were green, and they were under the command of Colonel Dixon Miles. Miles had recently been found guilty of drunkenness during First Manassas over a year ago, and although he kept a command, he was sent far to the West, where, supposedly, he would sit out the war.

Among other people surprised that Harpers Ferry would be held was Lee. In fact, he needed Harpers Ferry. His army, by now camped in the fields east of Frederick, now had plenty of food, but it still needed supplies to come through the Shenandoah Valley. Lee did not share Halleck's assessment of the defensibility of Harpers Ferry; he knew, in fact, that it could be easily taken, and although it slightly altered his timeline, it did not alter his plan.

The citizens of Baltimore and Washington did not need to worry; Lee was planning no occupation of Union cities, at least not yet. He would stay here at Frederick, briefly, hoping to draw the Federals into a fight while threatening those cities. West, however, was where the army would go—away from the Federal supply bases at Washington and over Catoctin and South Mountains. South Mountain was particularly important. Only two well-worn passes large enough for an army to move through existed. Once the Confederates were on the other side of the mountain, Confederate cavalry could guard the passes and screen the army's movements, making it virtually invisible. The army could rest, resupply, and plan for the next phase of the campaign.

On September 9, Lee issued his orders. The plan was risky, dividing his command into four parts. Longstreet, always the most cautious of Lee's lieutenants, greatly objected to this division; 26 of the army's 40 regiments would be away with Jackson. But if all went well, the Confederates would not only reopen the Shenandoah Valley but also would have the supplies of Harpers Ferry, further relieving the troops' needs for basic necessities like shoes and blankets. Jackson's wing, split into three divisions, would attack the 10,500 Federals at Harpers Ferry on September 12, while Longstreet would cross South Mountain and remain in Boonsboro, just west of South Mountain, and await Jackson's return. The plan, written up in detail as Special Orders No. 191, was given to Lee's assistant, who made copies and distributed them among the Confederate high command. The march began at dawn the next day, and by that evening the entire Confederate army, except for Stuart's cavalry, had left Frederick.

Here at Monocacy National Battlefield Visitor Center, you can see the fields where Lee's men camped before they made their way west. Although the exhibits here are focused on the 1864 "Battle that Saved Washington," you will find that the rangers here are well versed in the area's link to the Antietam campaign as well. The Visitor

Center is only a few years old and is a vast improvement over the old building, now used as park offices. Be sure to take the walk up to the second floor to get a wonderful panorama of the Maryland fields, and if you have time, take a tour of Monocacy Battlefield.

Best Farm/Special Orders No. 191

> *From the Visitor Center, turn left out of the parking lot, then carefully pull over to the set of monuments and markers on the right side of the road, less than 0.1 mile away.*

The Union Army was quick to the march, but once under way, that march was characteristically slow. McClellan divided his army into three wings. On the left was William Franklin's VI Corps, along with Darius Couch's division. In the center, Edwin Sumner was in overall command of his II Corps, along with Alpheus Williams's XII Corps (the remnants of Nathaniel Banks's corps from Pope's army). Taking the right, Ambrose Burnside led his former IX Corps, under command of Jesse Reno, as well as Joseph Hooker's I Corps, formerly McDowell's command from John Pope's Army of Virginia. In total, the force comprised 85,000 men in 15 divisions, with another 72,500 defending Washington.

In typical fashion, McClellan soon declared that he did not know enough about the enemy to advance. Although he accompanied this with his usual gross overestimate of Confederate strength, he actually had this one right. The intelligence he received in Virginia came from his network of Pinkerton spies, professionals operating in enemy territory. Here in Maryland, Federal intelligence consisted almost completely of reports from citizens and from McClellan's own cavalry, from which Stuart had been successfully screening Confederate movements. Finally, on September 11, McClellan felt confident enough to move. He wired Henry Halleck and reported the enemy's strength at over 120,000, near Frederick. Consequently, he needed more men, or his army would surely be destroyed. Within 10 minutes, Lincoln himself responded, saying that he was sending Fitz John Porter's V Corps from the defenses of Washington to him, and also placed Miles's Harpers Ferry garrison under his command.

By 10:00 AM on September 12, the Federal army began filing into Frederick, making camp in the same place that the Confederates, long since gone, had before them. As the Union men settled in, the citizens of Frederick welcomed their appearance—at least, at first. Although the border state of Maryland did have heavy Confederate sympathies to the east in Baltimore, the western portion of the state was decidedly pro-Union, and the Federals were greeted with cheers. To their dismay, however, the citizens realized that the Yankees' treatment of their property, and indeed the citizens themselves, was sadly lacking, and that the hated Confederates had not plundered or harassed nearly to the degree that the Federals did.

The Union forces made their way into camp over the next two days. Each unit was assigned a campsite on the various fields. One of those fields was the farm of David Best, where you now stand, and the 27th Indiana infantry, part of Williams's XII Corps, was one of the units. On September 13, two members of Co. F of the 27th, Sgt. John Bloss and Corp. Barton W. Mitchell, made camp and began to relax alongside a fence. Mitchell, seeing something poking out of the grass, went to investigate and found a truly grand prize—three cigars, wrapped in paper. Excited about their treasure, the men briefly looked at the paper the cigars were wrapped in. They didn't really know what the paper said, but they recognized the names on it—Lee, Jackson, Longstreet, Stuart—and it was addressed to D. H. Hill. It was Lee's Special Orders No. 191.

Bloss and Mitchell took the paper to their company commander, who took it to the 27th Indiana's headquarters. Recognizing its importance, the regimental commander skipped the brigade and division commands and went straight to XII Corps commander Alpheus Williams. The order had been signed by the aide who transcribed the order for Lee, R. H. Chilton. One of Williams's aides, Colonel Samuel Pittman, knew Chilton well from previous service in the old army and verified that the order was in Chilton's handwriting. It was authentic.

At the headquarters of the Army of the Potomac, McClellan was entertaining some of the local citizens visiting the camp. Shortly before noon, the found order was discreetly handed to him. McClellan scanned the paper and, with a start, immediately excused himself from his visitors, saying that he had business to attend to. After verifying the origins and authenticity of the order, McClellan excitedly raced to the telegraph station. That day, Lincoln had twice asked for a progress report, receiving no response; now he would get it. Lee had made a "gross mistake." The overly cautious McClellan had had the Confederate battle plan dropped into his lap. Here before him

---

SPECIAL ORDERS NO. 191—WHOSE FAULT WAS IT?

It is probable that we will never know exactly how Special Orders No. 191 fell into Union hands. We do know that Jackson received his copy, then transcribed it for D. H. Hill, temporarily with Longstreet's command. Hill received this copy and kept it for the rest of his life as he maintained his innocence, swearing that it was the only copy he ever received. Chilton stated that he must have received the original and signed for it, or it would have been noted as missing. One would think that the cigars might have provided a clue, but that part of the story was untold for more than 20 years, and the cigars jogged no one's memory.

were Lee's troop dispositions and their movements, and although he still thought he was outnumbered, every step of the Confederate army was laid out in detail. As he told General John Gibbon, "Here is a paper with which if I cannot whip Bobby Lee, I will be willing to go home!" (Despite discovering intelligence that could have led to the annihilation of the enemy, Bloss and Mitchell were not allowed to keep the cigars wrapped in the order.)

The exact spot of the Union's good fortune has been lost to time, but there is a monument on the Best Farm to denote it as the site of the famous Lost Order. You can drive up to the farm using the park road, but there is no further information on the order. More interpretation is available at the park Visitor Center.

HARPERS FERRY

Harpers Ferry/Maryland Heights

❭ *From the Visitor Center at Monocacy National Battlefield, turn right out of the parking lot. (If you are at the memorials on the Best Farm, pull up to the entrance road to the farm and turn around.) Drive 1.6 miles on MD 355 North (Urbana Turnpike) to MD 85. Turn right here and drive 0.4 mile, then turn left to merge onto I-70 West. Drive 1.9 miles to Exit 52 for US 340 West/US 15 South. Continue on US 340 West for 19.6 miles. You will wind through Maryland near Maryland Heights just before you cross the Potomac River into Virginia (and Loudoun Heights), then will shortly cross the Shenandoah River into West Virginia (and Bolivar Heights). Turn left to enter the parking area for Harpers Ferry National Historical Park. Visit the Visitor Center to check the park's activities that day, then board a park shuttle to reach the town of Harpers Ferry.*

Contrary to Halleck's beliefs, Harpers Ferry was practically indefensible. The town and former armory is located in a mountainous area at the confluence of the Shenandoah and Potomac Rivers, creating three points of high ground. To the northeast, north of the Potomac River in Maryland, is Maryland Heights, a steep embankment formed by the southern end of Elk Mountain. Southeast of the town and the confluence of the rivers is Loudoun Heights. Finally, between the two rivers (in what is West Virginia today) is Bolivar Heights, along with the town of Harpers Ferry, which begins at the confluence and works its way up the mountainside, first to a rise known as Camp Hill and then to the heights themselves. Control of either Maryland or Loudoun Heights would provide a commanding point from which to bombard Harpers Ferry.

The view from Bolivar Heights. Maryland Heights is on the left, Loudoun Heights on the right.

The plan to take Harpers Ferry, as Lee laid out so clearly in Special Orders No. 191, was for a simultaneous assault on the town from all three of the heights, preventing the Union garrison from escape. John Walker's division had the easiest assignment; he would cross the Potomac River and approach the relatively undefended Loudoun Heights from the south. Lafayette McLaws's division, along with Richard Anderson's, may have had the most difficult task in taking the Maryland Heights. Maryland Heights could be easily defended, as accessing them meant either looping around the base of Elk Mountain or snaking along the ridge at the top. Jackson's three divisions had the most demanding work, if not the most difficult. They would have the longest march, approaching Bolivar Heights and Harpers Ferry from the west. All three commanders—Walker, McLaws, and Jackson—were to attack on the morning of September 12.

Almost immediately after setting out, Jackson discovered that the Union garrison at Martinsburg, 2,500 men, had not evacuated their position as expected. Jackson would have to take Martinsburg to clear his approach from the west, adding considerable distance to his already-long march. Although the extra distance did not make things pleasant, clearing the garrison at Martinsburg was practically effortless, with the Union troops quickly retreating to join their counterparts at Harpers Ferry. Jackson continued on with his march, sealing off Bolivar Heights on September 12.

Walker's division was also delayed. Part of their mission was to destroy an aqueduct

The Union defensive line at Bolivar Heights.

of the C&O Canal over the Monocacy River along their march. It sounded like an easy enough task, but the Confederates spent almost an entire day trying to take down the massive stoneworks, finally giving up and moving on. They, also, would not approach their objective, Loudoun Heights, until September 12. (The aqueduct still stands in defiance today, not far from White's Ford, as part of the Chesapeake & Ohio National Historical Park; it is impressive and picturesque enough to be worth the diversion, if you have time.)

Monocacy Aqueduct.

McLaws knew from the start that his assignment, Maryland Heights, would not be easy. Oddly, though, the worst potential part of the mission—fighting through the Union defenses to get to the heights—was not an issue. McLaws sent two brigades to the top of the mountain to advance along the ridge while the rest of the division closed in from the east to prevent any Federals from escaping, but there were no Federals, at least not where it mattered. Solomon's Gap, the best approach to the ridge, was completely undefended. McLaws was ready to assault the heights on the evening of September 12. The delays encountered by Jackson, Warner, and McLaws set the Harpers Ferry mission 24 hours behind schedule.

By the time the shuttle from the Harpers Ferry National Historical Park Visitor Center reaches the town, you will have noticed the impressive beauty of the place. The rugged mountains and the whitewater of the rivers frame the town and quickly take you out of the present. Allow yourself plenty of time to roam. From a historical standpoint, both Washington and Jefferson spent time here, and both commented on its beauty. It became one of only two U.S. armories in the country, the other being in Springfield, Massachusetts. This, of course, made it the center of John Brown's raid and attempt at starting a slave insurrection in 1859, an event that sharply divided the nation and pushed it toward civil war. All of this history is right in front of you, and to boot, the town contains numerous wonderful shops and restaurants, all within a short walk of each other.

To orient yourself, walk toward the town and the confluence of the rivers. On your right is the Shenandoah River, and on your left is the Potomac. The town behind you extends up Camp Hill, eventually reaching Bolivar Heights. The rise to your right, on the other side of the Shenandoah, is Loudoun Heights, and Maryland Heights is to your left, across the footbridge that extends the Appalachian Trail from Maryland to West Virginia.

The first word that the Federals at Harpers Ferry received that they were under assault was from the fleeing Martinsburg garrison, saying that Stonewall Jackson was right behind them. Soon afterward it was learned that Confederates were approaching Maryland Heights as well. Colonel Miles had only 1,600 troops there, and they were almost all green. Although massive naval artillery had been placed on the face of Maryland Heights in front of you, they were placed to defend Harpers Ferry and were useless against an attack on the heights themselves. To add to the sense of doom, the Harpers Ferry garrison had little faith in Miles. Although he had stopped drinking, there were definitely residual effects of his battle with the bottle, and his judgment was not always sound.

On September 13, McLaws advanced along the top of Elk Mountain toward Maryland Heights. The Federals had formed a breastwork in the woods atop the ridge, but they were no match for McLaws's veterans. Men began to head for the rear, and after their colonel was shot, they were all in full flight. Upset with their poor showing, Miles ordered Maryland Heights evacuated. The Federals either spiked the artillery they left behind or sent it tumbling into the Potomac below, then crossed a pontoon bridge into Harpers Ferry.

Crossing the footbridge in front of you will take you to the Maryland Heights trail. Be aware before you set off that this is not an easy trail to hike. Depending on which paths you would like to follow, it is a loop of from 4.5 to 6.5 miles, and parts of that loop are strenuous to say the least. (One look up the mountain should tell you that!) There are no facilities or water along the trail, so be sure you're prepared. Having said all that, the reward for the hike is worth the work. You will get some wonderful views, and many of the earthworks, stone fortifications, and powder magazines from the war still remain to be explored.

Across the Potomac, Walker's men had a very easy go of it. Advancing on September 13, they found Loudoun Heights unoccupied and immediately proceeded to begin placing their artillery where it could best menace the Federal garrison. There is a park trail of Loudoun Heights, but while it is certainly a great hike, you won't find much history here. The trail is an 8-mile loop and, like the Maryland Heights trail, is strenuous.

Although much of the interpretive material in the town discusses the Civil War, you will find two small museums dedicated to the battles that occurred here, one of them focusing only on the September 1862 battle. They are right across from each other on High Street and should not be missed. Inside you will find not only descriptions of the battle but also maps and models that make interpretation of the landscape simple.

Bolivar Heights

› *When you are finished at Harpers Ferry, board the shuttle to return to the Visitor Center. Drive out of the main parking lot and go through the main intersection with US 340 onto Washington Street. Follow Washington Street for 0.2 mile as it curves to the right, then turn left onto Whitman Avenue and drive 0.2 mile to the parking area for Bolivar Heights.*

Jackson lined his men up on Schoolhouse Ridge, opposite Bolivar Heights, on September 13. Miles concentrated his Union forces here to face them, lining up along the ridge with his right on the Potomac River. As Jackson's men filed in and artillery began appearing from all directions, Miles knew that it was only a matter of time, but he held out. Thinking that he could hold Harpers Ferry for another 48 hours, Miles asked a small group of cavalry to break out and get help.

You are now standing atop Bolivar Heights. You have several options for trails from here. There is a very short 0.6-mile round-trip trail through the meadow in front of you that will take you along the Union battle line, with some interpretation along the way, as well as remnants of the rifle pits the Federals used. If you feel like walking a bit farther, you can also hike the longer trail, which will take you down the heights toward Schoolhouse Ridge. If you have the time, take this easy hike that provides great views. Otherwise, much of the ground covered by the trail is accessible by car along nearby Bakerton Street.

Schoolhouse Ridge

❯ *From the Bolivar Heights parking area, return down Whitman Avenue 0.2 mile, then turn right onto Washington Street, following the curve to the left that will take you back to the intersection with US 340. Turn left onto US 340 and drive 0.9 mile to Millville Road on your left. (On your right is Bakerton Street, the area in front of the Bolivar Heights hiking trail.) Turn left onto Millville Road and drive 0.7 mile; pull into the parking area on your right.*

The rise in front of you is Schoolhouse Ridge. On September 14, Jackson spent most of the day arranging his artillery around the trapped Federals. At 1:00 PM, the Federals fired the first shots, attempting to hit a Confederate position on Loudoun Heights. This prompted an immediate response from the Confederate artillery, which thundered throughout the night. Miles's Federals were being shelled from three directions and could do little to stop the bombardment.

For a long time, Harpers Ferry National Historical Park was focused on the town's history. In recent years, however, the park administrators have been able to acquire pieces of the surrounding battlefield land, blending it nicely into the park. Interpretation of Schoolhouse Ridge is being developed, and trails will be established to better

Schoolhouse Ridge.

interpret the Confederate positions here. In the meantime, feel free to walk the fields in front of you and climb the ridge to get the Confederate soldiers' view. The park, local groups, and the Civil War Trust put great effort into preserving this land, and a battlefield that not so long ago was difficult to visit up close and personal will now be kept for posterity.

Murphy House

> *Pull out of the parking area and turn left onto Millville Road, then drive 0.7 mile back to US 340. Turn right onto US 340 and drive 0.9 mile, turning right into the entrance to the park. However, instead of driving straight toward the Visitor Center, take an immediate right onto Campground Road. Drive 0.2 mile on Campground Road, then turn left at Murphy Road, following it for 0.3 mile and stopping in front of the Murphy House.*

Overnight, Jackson moved part of his line forward from Schoolhouse Ridge to flank the Union left. Under A. P. Hill's command, the artillery was set here around the Murphy Farm, with Hill's infantry in the surrounding fields.

At dawn on September 15, the Confederate artillery resumed their bombardment. With Hill's new position, the Federals were now taking additional close-range artillery fire to their rear. At 8:00 AM, as the Confederate infantry prepared to assault the Bolivar Heights line, flags of truce began popping up along the Union lines. They had had enough. Unfortunately, it took several minutes for the Confederate firing to stop completely. Miles was out in front of his men after the surrender when a stray Confederate shell burst nearby. Miles was hit in the leg and died the next day.

The Union surrender of Harpers Ferry was the largest of the war, and it would in fact remain the largest surrender of any United States troops until the surrender at Bataan during World War II. The Confederates captured 11,500 men, 13,000 small arms, 200 wagons, and 73 pieces of artillery. Now that the fighting was over, Jackson needed to hurry his men back to the rest of Lee's army. A. P. Hill's division would stay behind to complete the surrender and begin shipping the spoils south to Richmond.

The Murphy Farm walking trail will take you through the Confederate battle lines around the house, and at 1.3 miles round-trip on easy ground is a very nice stroll, offering several great views and a few preserved earthworks from the war. Also along the trail is the former site of John Brown's Fort, which had been moved several times after the war ended. It is now very near its original location in Harpers Ferry.

BOONSBORO

> *From the Murphy Farm House at Harpers Ferry, drive 0.3 mile and then turn right onto Campground Road. Drive 0.2 mile on Campground Road to Shenandoah*

A view of the old National Pike as it runs through Boonsboro.

Street, then turn left to access US 340. Turn right onto US 340 and drive 3.9 miles, exiting onto MD 67 North. Drive 12.8 miles on MD 67 North. As you drive, South Mountain will be to your right, stretching across the horizon for your entire drive. When you reach US 40 (Main Street/National Pike), turn left and drive 1 mile to the intersection of North Main Street and Shafer Park Drive. Park in the lot near the Virginia Civil War Trails marker on the left.

As Jackson's wing of the army left for Harpers Ferry on September 10, Longstreet's command crossed South Mountain at Turner's Gap and set up camp in Boonsboro, only 15 miles to the west but behind the screen of South Mountain. They received a very cold reception from the citizens of Boonsboro, whose sympathies lay very much with the Union.

Soon after they arrived, a report was received that Federal soldiers were approaching Hagerstown, Maryland, to the north, not far from their position. This sudden development could potentially derail many of Lee's plans. It was decided that Longstreet would immediately march for Hagerstown with two divisions, while D. H. Hill's division would stay in Boonsboro with the supply train, half of the reserve artillery, and Stuart's cavalry, which would continue to hold the South Mountain gaps. Again Longstreet objected—the army was now divided into five parts—but Lee was still counting on McClellan and the Army of the Potomac to take their time getting across the mountain.

As it turned out, the report of troops approaching Hagerstown was a false alarm. Still, on September 12, Lee decided to wait in Hagerstown until news from Harpers Ferry arrived. D. H. Hill would hold the line in Boonsboro.

Boonsboro is a nice little community today that embraces its past, but there isn't much to see here regarding the Antietam Campaign except for a Virginia Civil War Trails marker. It is located on the historic National Road, the same one that both armies used several times during the war. Going through Boonsboro, the road is Main Street, and the marker is near its intersection with Shafer Park Drive.

SOUTH MOUNTAIN

Turner's Gap

> *From the parking lot, turn right onto US 40 (Main Street) and drive south for 2.1 miles. As you drive, you will be climbing South Mountain, and Turner's Gap will open right in front of you. Turn left at Zittlestown Road, the entrance to Washington Monument State Park, and drive 0.9 mile to the road for the park's Visitor Center, which is another 0.3 mile. Pull into the lot.*

The Union Army of the Potomac had everything it needed. It had four full corps and parts of two others, 87,000 soldiers in all—twice the size of the Confederate force it faced. It had precise and reliable information on exactly what the enemy was doing and where they were doing it. To top it all off, they had a commander known for his cautiousness who was certain that he had the Confederate army in his grasp. Unfortunately for the Union, though, General George McClellan, despite his newfound aggressiveness and the extraordinary circumstances, did not do anything with speed.

After wiring President Lincoln that the army would move immediately after finding the Confederates' Special Orders No. 191, McClellan planned and prepared to move—for 18 hours. Not knowing that D. H. Hill was all by himself in Boonsboro (and he could not have) with only one division, McClellan deduced that the Confederates had approximately 30,000 waiting for him beyond Turner's Gap, dwarfing Hill's actual numbers of around 4,500. The plan called for the Union army to pass through Turner's Gap the next day, September 14, with battle coming on September 15. There would be no attempt at surprise. At the same time, Franklin's VI Corps would cross South Mountain through Crampton's Gap, on the south end of the mountain, and head west to Harpers Ferry to rescue the Federal garrison by approaching Maryland Heights from the rear. For all this planning, no marching orders were issued. Had they been, it is likely that Harpers Ferry would have been relieved in time.

On the evening of the 13th, as Lee waited in Hagerstown for news from Harpers Ferry, some interesting intelligence arrived. The assumption was that the Federals, having just arrived at Frederick, would stay there for a while, as per McClellan's modus operandi. However, at 10:00 PM, Stuart informed Lee that something was going on in the Union camp. A citizen who had been visiting the camp (one of those at McClellan's tent when he received his copy of the lost order) was a Confederate sympathizer, and although he didn't know what the paper that caused so much excitement said, he did realize that it must be important. That afternoon, he was able to cross the lines and find Stuart to relate his story. (The citizen's name has been lost to history.)

Unlike his Union counterpart, Lee began issuing orders even though he lacked information. He did not want to give up on the operation at Harpers Ferry, as the potential rewards were too great. He would send a courier to Jackson asking for the status of the operation, as well as giving him a prod to hurry. General McLaws, on Maryland Heights, would receive a similar message, although since his command was the most exposed to a potential Federal advance, he needed to be prepared to shift his troops rapidly. Stuart's cavalry would hold the gaps and gather as much intelligence as possible. Longstreet would leave Hagerstown the next morning for Turner's Gap to aid in the defense effort.

That left only D. H. Hill in Boonsboro. Hill was to block any attempted Federal advance with his single division. The next morning, Hill would join Stuart at Turner's Gap and plan their defense.

Washington Monument State Park, in conjunction with Gathland State Park, is part of Maryland's South Mountain State Battlefield. The small museum you see before you is the best place on South Mountain to begin your exploration. Inside, you will find displays of artifacts as well as interactive displays, a computer map program, and information on thoroughly exploring the South Mountain battlefield. (Much of the battlefield is on private property today, so respect the locals' rights.) The Friends of South Mountain State Battlefield have developed a 23-mile, 14-stop tour that highlights all the details of Turner's, Frostown, Fox's, and Crampton's gaps. This tour can be picked up here at the museum or online at the group's website. It follows a few mountain roads, so make sure your car is in proper shape.

❭ *From the museum, drive 0.3 mile back to Zittlestown Road. Turn left, then make an immediate right onto Washington Monument Road. Drive 0.9 mile to the park exit at US 40. Across the intersection, you will see a large tavern and hotel, the Old South Mountain Inn. Turn left onto US 40 and pull into the inn's parking lot.*

General Daniel Harvey Hill arrived at Turner's Gap on the morning of September 14 and quickly realized that there was a lot of work to be done. Stuart, who was to meet him here, was instead at Crampton's Gap, which he thought the more immediate threat to the Harpers Ferry operation. The only Confederates at Turner's Gap were 200 cavalry, with one brigade, Alfred Colquitt's, at the eastern foot of the mountain. In addition, defense of the gap would not be easy. Although the National Road, which ran through the gap, was in itself easy enough to hold, there were other roads—the Old Hagerstown Road and the Old Sharpsburg Road, in addition to several farm lanes—that would enable the Federals to hit the Confederate position on both flanks with ease. These roads also enabled the Federals to use Fox's Gap to the south as a point of access. In all, Hill had five roads to cover to hold Turner's Gap.

Hill's first move was to bring Colquitt's brigade back to the top of the mountain. He then sent for another brigade from Boonsboro, Samuel Garland's, to move to Fox's Gap, and ordered the rest of his division to come up. Additionally, he sent a courier to Longstreet, telling him of the situation and informing him that he should hurry. Hill knew that his small force could never hold the ocean of blue uniforms that he saw east of South Mountain.

You are now in Turner's Gap, and the road in front of you is the old National Road. As you face the road, if you turn to your right, you will see that the Appalachian Trail crosses the road here; this was formerly the road that led right to Fox's Gap, 1 mile south, and which the Federals would use to hit the Confederate right. (You can walk the trail and walk to Fox's Gap from here.) Also to your right, on the left side of the road as you look east, is Dahlgren Road; this would have been the road used by the Federals to hit the Confederate left.

Turning around to look to the west, you can't help but notice the Old South Mountain Inn. In continuous operation for more than 250 years, the inn has seen a whole lot of history pass through the gap, from the colonial period to the present. During the Battle of South Mountain, D. H. Hill used the inn as his headquarters; it was a natural choice because it sits right at the crest of the mountain along the gap and the National Road.

Although Turner's Gap was the main focus of the battle, most of the day's fighting occurred 1 mile to the south at Fox's Gap. It wasn't until 4:00 PM, seven hours after the first shots, that Hooker's I Corps approached Turner's Gap from Frostown to the northeast. Three Federal divisions—led by John Hatch on the left and George Meade on the right, with James Ricketts's division in reserve—advanced toward the Confederate left along a farm road. When they approached the crest of the mountain, Robert Rodes's Confederate brigade of 1,200 men appeared, and the Federals began to push them back steadily. Rodes's men fought stubbornly, though, and were able to hold the Federals for four hours before they were finally forced to give up the high ground. Darkness eventually ended the fighting, and Hooker's corps never did reach Turner's Gap on September 14.

The area where most of the I Corps fought is to your front right as you face the road, obscured by the trees. As the sun went down, Burnside decided to attack the gap head-on as a diversion for the two ongoing flank attacks. Gibbon's brigade was chosen for the assault. Gibbon—who was D. H. Hill's best man at his wedding—was able to reach Colquitt's main line but could go no farther. As the fighting died down with the darkness and the depletion of ammunition, the sounds of musketry were replaced by taunting, as both sides went at each other verbally for the next several hours.

Fox's Gap

❭ *From the parking lot, turn left onto US 40 and drive 0.2 mile to Moser Road. Turn left on Moser Road and drive 1.1 miles to Reno Monument Road. Turn left on Reno Monument Road and drive 0.6 mile. You will see a dirt pull-off to your right, along with several historical markers; park here.*

Although Hill was right to be alarmed, the urgency of the Federals was not exactly on the same timetable as the pace of the Confederates. What Hill saw from the mountain was Reno's IX Corps. McClellan, whose multiplication of enemy troop levels was reflex at this point, was confident that Turner's Gap could be taken easily by only Alfred Pleasanton's cavalry, along with one brigade from the IX Corps. If that brigade encountered resistance, three of Reno's four brigades were close enough to support them. After that, the Army of the Potomac would simply walk through the gap. In fact, the corps that was to lead the march, Hooker's I Corps, was still east of Frederick, 12 miles away.

Eliakim Scammon's brigade began their movement up the mountain at 6:00 AM, with division commander Jacob Cox accompanying them. Cox soon began gathering clues telling him that the passage may not be such a cakewalk, so he sent for a second brigade, commanded by George Crook, and informed Reno of the situation. After consulting with Pleasanton, it was decided that Scammon would take the Sharpsburg Road to Fox's Gap, with Crook behind him.

At 9:00 AM, after they had begun to take some light artillery fire, the Federals came upon a small pasture with a stone wall on the other end. Behind that stone wall was Garland's Confederate brigade, who had hurried up the mountain. It quickly grew into an extremely hot fight. The Confederates were outnumbered 3,000 to 1,000, and Garland knew it, but he also knew that he needed to hold this position, just south of Fox's Gap, until the rest of D. H. Hill's division could come up.

As Cox pushed his division forward, Garland's green Confederates held as best they could. Finally, a charge from Scammon at 10:30 broke the Confederate right, sending them down the west side of the mountain. (Wounded in the charge was Lt. Colonel Rutherford B. Hayes of the 23rd Ohio; behind the lines, Supply Sergeant William McKinley, of the same regiment, was unhurt. Both would go on to be elected president of the United States.) Cox then turned the division toward Fox's Gap to the north. During this movement, Garland was mortally wounded, dying later that day. By noon, the Federals had reached Daniel Wise's farm just south of the gap. Scammon's brigade, however, had been fighting hard for three hours after climbing the east face of South Mountain, and Cox decided to pull back and wait for the rest of the IX Corps to arrive.

Although Reno had received Cox's earlier message at 8:00 AM and immediately sent the rest of the corps, the first units, after getting lost, would not arrive until 2:00 PM. Orlando Willcox's division arrived first, followed by Samuel Sturgis's and Isaac Rodman's divisions. A lull in the fighting occurred as the units consolidated and re-formed. Reno himself, along with Right Wing commander Ambrose Burnside, also arrived on the field. Burnside, in charge of the movements of both the I and IX corps, decided to hold Sturgis's and Rodman's divisions until Hooker's men could get into place, enabling a coordinated attack on both Confederate flanks.

The Confederate force, meanwhile, was growing. Hill's division was on the mountain, and elements of Longstreet's command began to appear at 3:00 PM. They formed behind another stone wall, this one on the Wise homestead. At 4:00, they advanced on the Federals, unaware that Willcox's division was now present, and they were soon thrown back. The fighting again grew more intense, centered on the Wise field and the Sharpsburg Road. By 5:00, as Willcox and Cox began to surround them, the Confederates were finally forced to pull off the mountain.

Unfortunately, the fight was not over. At 6:00, John Bell Hood's Texas Brigade arrived on the field and renewed the attack. With the sun setting and visibility already poor because of the smoke of battle, Reno rode to the front to see the fighting. In almost the same spot where Garland had been mortally wounded earlier, General Reno was hit by a Confederate sharpshooter. He was taken to the rear, where he called out to Sturgis, "Hallo, Sam, I'm dead!," then said good-bye. Although Sturgis refused to believe him, his commander was correct, and within minutes Reno died. He was the first Union corps commander of the war to be killed in action.

After Hood's assault, the lines settled where they were. Hill, Longstreet, and Lee knew that they would have to fall back, and after dark the Confederate lines at Turner's and Fox's Gaps were abandoned. Although the Union held the field, and McClellan wired Washington exclaiming a "glorious victory," the Confederates had been able to prevent the Federals from passing through the gap for one crucial day. McClellan's sluggishness crossing South Mountain at Turner's Gap would allow Lee to concentrate his divided forces, leading directly to the massive bloodletting at Antietam.

Here at Fox's Gap, a monument to Reno sits surrounded by mostly woodland and an open meadow. This monument sits in the approximate spot where Reno fell, and is also very near the spot where General Garland was mortally wounded. The road you drove in on, Reno Monument Road, was the Sharpsburg Road at the time of the battle. The pasture you see across the road is Wise Field, and you are now standing on the Wise homestead. After reading the several historical markers in this area, if you have time, take the walking tour of Fox's Gap created by the Friends of South Mountain Battlefield (the text of the tour can be picked up at Washington Monument State Park or found online). The walking tour does an excellent job of interpreting the action here from the first shots to the last. The Civil War Trust has helped to acquire some of the land that was part of the battlefield, and more of it should be accessible in the future. For now, though, be sure to stay on the trail, as all of the surrounding land is private property.

Crampton's Gap

> *From the Reno Monument parking area, turn left onto Reno Monument Road to head west. Follow Reno Monument road for 2.2 miles until reaching the intersection with MD 67 (Rohrersville Road). Turn left onto MD 67 South and drive 4.4 miles to Townsend Road on your left. Turn left on Townsend Road and drive 1.3 miles toward Crampton Gap, which should now be appearing in front of you. When you reach the intersection with Arnoldstown Road and the massive brick arched memorial, turn left and park in the designated parking area.*

Stuart thought he had reason to worry about Crampton's Gap. If the Federals were moving across South Mountain to rescue the garrison at Harpers Ferry, surely they would pass this way. But all that Stuart could see was one Union brigade in the town of Burkittsville, east of the mountain. Leaving his cavalry to watch over the Federals, Stuart rode to Maryland Heights at 2:00 PM to discuss the situation with McLaws, who would be most exposed to a Union movement through Crampton's Gap.

What Stuart did not see in Burkittsville was that behind that brigade was the entire VI Corps of the Army of the Potomac. Franklin had started their march at 6:00 AM and reached Burkittsville at noon. After entering the town, the Federals began to take artillery fire, and Franklin, taking a cue from his commander, decided to stop his advance and plan his next movement. His orders did not mention anything about moving quickly. For 90 minutes, the 12,300 men of the VI Corps sat in Burkittsville.

At Crampton's Gap high above, fewer than 1,000 Confederate soldiers waited behind a stone fence for the Federals to come up. Although puzzled as to why the Union troops were not moving, they knew that eventually an assault would come. Upon receiving word that the Federals were in force, McLaws sent General Howell Cobb's brigade to support the small group of Confederates at the gap.

At 2:00 PM, with Henry Slocum's division on the right and most of Baldy Smith's division to the left, the Union forces attacked up the mountain toward the Confeder-

The War Correspondents Memorial Arch dominates Crampton's Gap.

ates at the stone wall and quickly sent the Confederates back to Crampton's Gap. Franklin, somehow thinking himself outnumbered, informed McClellan at 3:20 that he had been "severely engaged" and would have to renew the attack in the morning. Apparently, General Slocum did not get this message, because at 4:00 he led a charge against the Confederate fallback position at the gap. Cobb's brigade was arriving at just this moment, but it was a little bit too late. The Confederates dropped everything when Slocum charged, abandoning Crampton's Gap in full flight.

McLaws and Stuart were extremely concerned with this development. With an entire Federal corps only a short march away, the entire Harpers Ferry operation was in jeopardy. However, when they went to observe the Union position at Crampton's Gap, they found that the Union force was not going anywhere. Franklin was satisfied; he had control of the gap, and had been able to show his men something that few of them had seen before—the sight of Confederate soldiers fleeing.

The battle at Crampton's Gap was technically a total victory for the Union, but Franklin's failure to move through the gap virtually guaranteed the fall of Harpers Ferry, which surrendered the next morning. Combined with the inability of the Federals to get through Turner's Gap at the other end of South Mountain, they had given the Confederates enough time to capture a major garrison, reunite their heavily divided army, and choose their own battleground rather than be taken in pieces by the much larger Army of the Potomac. The opportunity that had come with Special Orders No. 191 had been a gift, and although it slightly disrupted Confederate plans, McClellan's slowness had mostly let it go to waste.

Not completely, however. McClellan's sudden aggressiveness was puzzling to Lee; it was certainly unlike all his previous behavior. For once, the Union army had taken the initiative, even if they did it slowly. Lee knew that he needed to reunite his army as quickly as possible. After receiving a message from Jackson saying that Harpers Ferry would fall the next day, he ordered all of his units to march, as soon as their missions were complete, to the town of Sharpsburg, Maryland.

Crampton's Gap is contained within Gathland State Park. The dominating feature of the site, the War Correspondents' Arch, was constructed by George Alfred Townsend, a Civil War journalist who bought the land around Crampton's Gap after the war. The Gathland Museum does not discuss the fight here, but there are numerous interpretive panels and historical markers around the house that very clearly paint the picture of the battle. Much of the final action, the actual capture of Crampton's Gap by the Federals, occurred at this intersection and in the fields surrounding the arch and house. If you go down the east side of the mountain to Burkittsville, you will find two churches that were used as hospitals after the battle, and on your way back toward the gap you will see the area of the Union advance along the hillside on both sides of the road.

ANTIETAM

Antietam National Battlefield Visitor Center/Dunker Church

❭ *From the parking area at Crampton's Gap, turn right onto Townsend Road and drive 1.3 miles to MD 67. Turn right on MD 67 North and drive 0.5 mile, then turn left onto Trego Road. Trego Road will eventually turn into Mt. Brier Road; follow this road for 2.1 miles, then turn left onto Porterstown Road. Drive 2.9 miles on Porterstown Road to MD 34. Turn left onto MD 34 West and drive 1.5 miles. You are now in the town of Sharpsburg. Turn right on North Church Street (MD 65) and drive 0.9 mile to Dunker Church Road. Turn right here and drive another 0.2 mile to the Antietam National Battlefield Visitor Center.*

The dawn of September 15 found the Confederates gone from Turner's and Fox's Gaps, and the Union army immediately began pursuit. The I, II, and XII corps would take the National Road through Turner's Gap, while the IX Corps, now commanded by Jacob Cox, and part of the V Corps using Fox's Gap. Franklin's VI Corps, hearing artillery fire and then a mighty cheer, deduced that Harpers Ferry had fallen, and remained where they were per McClellan's orders. As for the commanding general, he remained at his headquarters east of South Mountain gathering conflicting intelli-

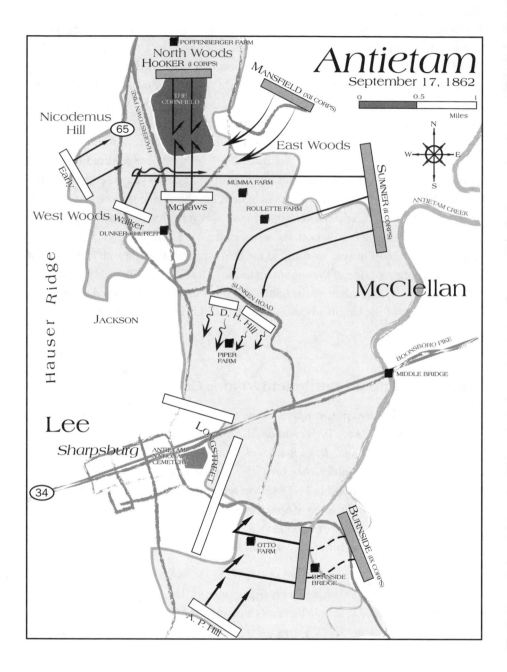

POFFENBERGER FARM

North Woods
HOOKER (I CORPS)

THE CORNFIELD

MANSFIELD (XII CORPS)

Antietam
September 17, 1862

0   0.5   1
Miles

Nicodemus
Hill

65

HAGERSTOWN PIKE

East Woods

N
W   E
S

Early

MUMMA FARM

SUMNER (II CORPS)

ANTIETAM CREEK

West Woods Walker

McLaws

ROULETTE FARM

DUNKER CHURCH

Hauser Ridge

JACKSON

SUNKEN ROAD

D. H. Hill

McClellan

PIPER
FARM

BOONSBORO PIKE

MIDDLE BRIDGE

Lee

Sharpsburg

ANTIETAM
NATIONAL
CEMETERY

LONGSTREET

34

BURNSIDE (IX CORPS)

OTTO
FARM

BURNSIDE
BRIDGE

A. P. Hill

gence reports—Lee was in full flight across the Potomac, Jackson and Longstreet had been wounded, Lee had told a citizen that their army was "whipped." As was his habit, the choicest bits were forwarded to Washington, where many found McClellan's exclamations of glorious victory wearily familiar.

By the time solid intelligence started to come in around 1:00 PM, the reality of the situation began to sink in. Lee had not crossed the Potomac. He had formed a defensive line 1.5 miles long running north to south in front of Sharpsburg and behind Antietam Creek. Finally deciding to ride to the front to take a look for himself, McClellan observed the Confederate lines from the east side of the creek with Fitz John Porter at 3:00. McClellan decided that an attack that day was out of the question; it was too late in the day, and not all of the Confederate dispositions were yet known. McClellan even suspected that Lee was bluffing, making it appear than he had more troops than he actually did. He was; Jackson's entire wing was not on the field. The Army of the Potomac had left Turner's Gap at dawn and traveled a total of 8 miles to Antietam Creek. Yet somehow, again, there would not be an attack on that day.

The next day, September 16, would bring more reports of the Confederates crossing back into Virginia in full flight, but as the morning dawn lifted, it was evident that they were still in line across the fields. McClellan had told Halleck that if the Confederates were still there when the fog lifted, he would attack. He did not. In fact, he could not. Having arrived 18 hours earlier, McClellan had not issued a single order to his commanders, had not set any positions, and did not have enough information to launch an attack, saying that more reconnaissance needed to be done. One thing, though, was very clear to him. Even though there was no mountain in front of him and no cavalry screening his movements, McClellan was convinced that he was now outnumbered.

By noon on the 16th, Jackson's men began to join the Confederate line. Lee now had six of his nine divisions on the field, with two more (McLaws and Anderson, coming from Harpers Ferry) on the march. Only A. P. Hill's division, still seeing to the surrender in Harpers Ferry, was not immediately available. McClellan's stalling had allowed the Army of Northern Virginia to reunite to nearly its full strength. Over the course of the day, the Confederate line would grow to over 4 miles in length, par-

---

POINTING THE FINGER AND NOT THE THUMB

"(General Lee is) too cautious and weak under grave responsibility . . . wanting in moral firmness when pressed by heavy responsibility and is likely to be timid and irresolute in action."

—*Union General George B. McClellan, giving President Abraham Lincoln his opinion of the command abilities of Confederate General Robert E. Lee*

---

alleling the Hagerstown Turnpike, with Jackson's wing on the left and Longstreet's on the right.

Also at noon, McClellan finally issued orders to his commanders. The attack would occur the next day. Three stone bridges crossed Antietam Creek near Sharpsburg: the Upper Bridge, farthest north; the bridge of the Boonsboro Turnpike, also known as the Middle Bridge; and the Rohrbach Bridge, farthest south, where the Sharpsburg-Rohrersville Road crossed. The Confederates had focused their lines on the lower two bridges, so the Federal attack would concentrate on the Confederate left, farthest to the north.

McClellan also shuffled his command in preparation for the assault. Hooker's I Corps would cross the Upper Bridge that night and lead the main Union attack at dawn; Joseph Mansfield's XII Corps would follow later that night to support Hooker. II Corps, commanded by Sumner, would be ready to cross at the Upper Bridge if necessary. The IX Corps, still under the command of Jacob Cox after Reno's death at South Mountain, would take up a position at the Rohrbach Bridge and attack the Confederate right. (In McClellan's organization, Burnside, who had commanded the IX Corps previously, was left without a command; however, Cox still reported to him, and his orders had to come through Burnside.) Franklin's soon-to-arrive VI Corps, as well as Porter's V Corps, would be kept in reserve.

Oddly, McClellan chose to group his entire cavalry force in the center of his line, meaning that they could not perform the two primary functions of cavalry: protect the army's flanks and gather intelligence. It was an old Napoleonic tactic to finish battles with a cavalry charge down the center, but it was a practice that had been made obsolete by modern weapons.

At 4:00 PM, Hooker crossed the Upper Bridge, and although there was some Confederate resistance, he was able to set his position for the next day, with Lee making adjustments accordingly. Mansfield followed with his corps around midnight. The stage was set for the bloodiest day in America's history.

The Visitor Center at Antietam National Battlefield is a necessary stop to get you oriented to the battlefield. Check in at the desk to find out when the park rangers will be giving talks on the battle; there are usually short overviews given continually throughout the day. There are also two films shown about the battle. The shorter one, 26 minutes cleverly centered on Lincoln's visit to Antietam, is shown on the hour throughout the day. The other is an excellent hour-long explanation of the battle and its consequences, and is shown only at noon. Both are worth seeing.

After you've gone through the center itself, head toward the rear of the building, where an observation area will help you understand the battle and the landscape. The Confederates understood the value of this view, as they massed artillery near this spot. Likewise, from your elevated position you can see virtually the entire northern portion of the battlefield with ease. After you've finished inside the glass observation area, walk outside onto the plateau and take in a slightly different view, this time with the rolling countryside under your feet. From both views, the critical part that the landscape played in this battle becomes much clearer, from the ridges around the Sunken Road in front of you to the woods and open ground to your left near the Cornfield. In front of you, in the distance, South Mountain rises from the landscape.

Before you leave the Visitor Center, take a walk back around the building to the north toward the monuments, lines of cannons, and the small white building across the road. Although it is a large battlefield, and the auto tour is indispensable (much of your route here will follow the same path), Antietam is best explored on foot. So much of the battlefield has been preserved, making the fields quiet even on the busiest days, that the many easy hiking trails throughout the park are not only educational but also very pleasant walks.

As mentioned previously, in the beginning stages of the battle, Confederate artillery under Colonel Stephen D. Lee was massed on this plateau, commanding the fields to the north and east. The artillery you see in front of you represents a hodgepodge of the different kinds of artillery used in the battle. Also present are the monuments to the New York and Ohio regiments that distinguished themselves in this

Confederate artillery, set atop the plateau near the Dunker Church (background).

area and the grand monument to the many fallen sons who shed their blood here on their own Maryland soil.

Carefully cross the road to the white building, the Dunker Church, a prominent landmark during the battle. Although this is not the original, it was reconstructed using much of the material from the original. This conspicuous white building, both during and after the battle, was used as a reference point, and it is now a well-recognized part of Antietam's history, featured in many a photograph from the time of the battle to today. Behind it and to the north is an area known as the West Woods. The road that you crossed to get to the Dunker Church was, at the time of the battle, the Hagerstown Pike.

North Woods

> *Your tour will largely follow the National Battlefield's driving tour, although there will be a few detours along the way. From the Visitor Center, turn right onto Dunker Church Road (the old Hagerstown Pike) and drive 1 mile to Mansfield Avenue. Turn right here and drive 0.2 mile to the small parking area on your right.*

As dawn broke on September 17, Joseph Hooker's I Corps was up and ready to move. The army formed in the fields of Joseph Poffenberger's farm. As you face the field across from the parking area, the Poffenberger farmhouse is behind you to your right. Directly in front of you, where today you see open field, was a grove of trees that came to be known as the North Woods; at the time of the battle, they served as a light screen for the Federals as they formed. The woods are currently being restored by the Park Service to their 1862 appearance. Looking to your front left, you will see another small grove of trees; this marks the area of the East Woods, some of which has been deforested since the time of the battle.

Confederate infantry was mostly lined up on the west side of the Hagerstown Turnpike (now Dunker Church Road), with artillery near the Dunker Church to the south and on a rise known as Nicodemus Hill to the west. (Nicodemus Hill is not on the park grounds, but the site is on the heights across the highway.)

Hooker had formed a solid plan. He would take two of his three divisions straight down the Hagerstown Turnpike. Abner Doubleday's division would form the right, west of the turnpike, and move south toward the West Woods; Ricketts's division would be left of the turnpike and would pass through the North Woods and, behind it, the cornfield of the Miller Farm. George Meade's division would be in support, with some units moving through the East Woods. Their target was the Dunker Church, the approximate center of the Confederate line. If Hooker's 8,600 men could break through at the Dunker Church, the Confederate line would fold.

The Confederate line, held by Jackson's 7,700 troops, was mostly in and around the West Woods and south of the Miller cornfield, stretching as far east as the Smoketown Road. John R. Jones's division, four brigades, was in the woods, just north of the Dunker Church, while Alexander Lawton's division held the southern portion. Most of these troops were obscured from Hooker's vision, either by the West Woods themselves or by the numerous ridges and rock shelves running through them.

East Woods

> *From the parking area at the Poffenberger Farm, follow Mansfield Avenue around the bend 0.5 mile to Smoketown Road, then turn right. Drive another 0.2 miles to Cornfield Avenue; turn right and pull into the parking area.*

Artillery fire began almost with first light. The Confederates fired from Nicodemus Hill and the Dunker Church, while much of the Federal fire came from massive artillery placed east of Antietam Creek. As the bombardment began, Hooker's troops began moving through, with Meade's units in the East Woods being the first to appear in front of the Confederates.

You are now at the southern end of the East Woods, where the Federals emerged in front of Isaac Trimble's Confederate brigade, deployed in the Samuel Mumma Farm. As you face away from the parking area to look south, the Mumma Farm is across the intersection to your front left, while the East Woods are behind you.

Meade and Trimble's early encounter here was the first sharp fighting of the day. After trading volleys for some time, the Federals began to run low on ammunition and pulled back into the East Woods for cover. At almost the same time, to the west, the first Union troops were emerging from the southern edge of Miller's cornfield.

The Cornfield

> *From the East Woods parking area, pull back onto Cornfield Avenue and drive 0.3 mile to the next parking area on your right.*

At 6:00 AM, Ricketts's division began to move south through Miller's cornfield, with Abram Duryea's brigade of 1,100 in the lead. The September corn had not been harvested yet, and it was tall enough to hide the Union troops as they moved south.

Still, Colonel Marcellus Douglass's Confederates, south of the cornfield, knew that they were coming. Douglass ordered his men to lie down, pick out a row of corn to aim at, and await the order to fire. The order came as soon as Duryea's brigade reached the edge of the field, and they were instantly hit with a deadly volley. Other Federal troops rushed through the corn while Trimble moved most of his troops from the Mumma Farm to support the Confederates.

Even with Trimble's brigade, Douglass did not have enough men to hold his po-

A view across the infamous Cornfield at Antietam.

sition. He was also running low on ammo and taking flanking fire from Meade's men in the East Woods. Eventually, he was forced to pull back. But this would only be the first of many deadly firefights in this area on that day. It would be known forever after as simply the Cornfield.

As you face the Cornfield, turn to your left to look toward the Hagerstown Pike and the West Woods. As Ricketts's division moved through the Cornfield, Doubleday's division of 2,200 men also moved south on the other side of the Pike. Hooker rode with them, commanding from the front. They moved cautiously, not knowing the disposition of the Confederates to their right. Their caution was justified at 6:30 AM when the lead unit, John Gibbon's Iron Brigade, was suddenly hit hard on the right, with fire coming from the West Woods and the Miller pasture. Far from being slowed, Gibbon quickly moved forward, and Doubleday rushed another brigade to the front to aid him. Soon, Gibbon's men were in the West Woods, with the rest of Doubleday's division lining up along the turnpike near the Cornfield. This area is just to the left of where you are now standing.

Confederate division commander John Jones, stunned by an artillery shell, had been replaced by General William Starke, and Starke, leading his division from the front, emerged from the West Woods to meet the Federals. Rushing to a rail fence along the turnpike, Starke's Confederates quickly formed and began trading volleys with Doubleday's men. The lines were only 30 yards apart and tore into one another ferociously. Starke was able to stop Doubleday's advance, but the Confederates paid dearly for it, taking converging fire from the Cornfield, the pasture to their north, and Gibbon's Federals in the West Woods. Starke was shot three times and died within the hour. Eventually, both the Confederates and most of Doubleday's division were forced to fall back.

At 7:00 AM, just as Hooker's corps began to press south, more Confederate reinforcements were brought in. Hood's division came up, forming a line south of the Cornfield. Lawton's division had been decimated. Hood's men waited until they passed through their ranks and then fired a volley into the Federals, forcing them back into the corn. At the same time, Confederates on the right of the line broke into the East Woods. Hood's line pushed forward into the Cornfield.

Now it was time for Hooker to call for help. Throwing his last reserves into the fight, Hooker asked for Mansfield's XII Corps. (As McClellan and his staff watched the carnage from the Pry House, 2 miles away, he had still not issued any orders to any other commander on the field.) As the Confederates reached the north end of the Cornfield, they met the same reception that the Federals had at the south end. Hooker's two reserve brigades, part of Meade's division, hit them as soon as they reached the edge of the Cornfield. In addition, Federal artillery, which had not been effective for much of the morning, received a simple correction in their fire by General Gibbon, a former artillerist. They made this correction and switched to double loads of canister shot. Hit with both musketry and artillery at only 30 yards, the Confederates were cut down in bloody fashion. The 1st Texas, part of Hood's famed Texas Brigade, suffered a staggering 82 percent casualty rate in the Cornfield, the highest regimental loss of any Confederate unit in the Civil War.

At 7:30 AM, the XII Corps began to form to support Hooker. Hood wisely pulled his Confederates back and called for reinforcements while Mansfield formed his brigade. As Mansfield placed units near the East Woods, another Confederate unit approached and fired. Mansfield was shot in the chest, mortally wounded. He was taken to the rear and died the next day. Command of the XII Corps fell to General Alpheus Williams.

The carnage continued here for hours in the same fashion, with both sides trying desperately to break the bloody stalemate. Seeing that the Federals were doing nothing on the Confederate right, Lee began pulling units from there and sending them to Jackson on the left. D. H. Hill, in the center, also pushed units toward the East Woods. The Union I Corps was practically finished, except for Gibbon's men, who were still pushing for the West Woods.

It would take a unit of the XII Corps to finally bring the bloodbath on the north end of the field to a stop. After Confederates had made yet another push into the East Woods, George Greene's division was sent in by Williams to flank them. A descendant of famed Revolutionary War general Nathaniel Greene, George Greene wheeled a brigade to hit the Confederates, who by this time were at the north edge of the East Woods and Cornfield, on their right flank at point-blank range. Another Federal unit charged simultaneously, and the Confederates broke. Greene, his troops fresh, did not stop, and pushed every Confederate unit in their path toward the West Woods, moving all the way to the Dunker Church. The Confederate artillery here was forced to fall back, and Hooker ordered his own artillery support. Fighting from the front as usual, Hooker soon paid for it; he was shot in the foot and carried to the rear, out of the battle.

It was 9:00 AM. Dead and wounded were littered across the fields—in rows at the north and south edge of the Cornfield, along the Hagerstown Pike, in the East Woods. In three hours of fighting, the two sides had suffered more than 8,000 casualties. The Union held this part of the field, but the fighting was not over.

The site of most of the carnage just described is easily within your view here at the southwest edge of the Cornfield. There is a Cornfield hiking trail, 1.6 miles long, which will take you through various parts of the corn and near the East Woods and clearly points out areas where troop movements occurred. The ground is mostly level, but the Cornfield is still used as farmland, so watch your footing if you decide to take the trail. (The trail actually starts from where you stopped at the Poffenberger Farm but can easily be picked up here.)

General John Mansfield Monument

› *From the Cornfield parking area, carefully make a U-turn and drive 0.3 mile east down Cornfield Avenue, near your stop at the East Woods. Turn left at Smoketown Road and drive 0.1 mile, stopping at the intersection with Mansfield Road. Pull over to the right.*

This is the area where General John Mansfield, commander of the XII Corps, was mortally wounded. A career soldier, age 58, Mansfield had been given command of XII Corps only two days prior to the Battle of Antietam. The memorial you see here, a cannon with the muzzle pointed down, is a traditional way of marking the deaths of generals or other important people in battle. Usually a much more singular occurrence, on this battlefield, you will see several instances of these monuments.

› *From the Mansfield memorials, make another U-turn and drive 0.1 mile back to Cornfield Avenue. Turn right on Cornfield Avenue and drive 0.4 mile to Dunker Church Road. Turn left on Dunker Church Road and drive 0.2 mile. Turn right into the roundabout for the park's Tour Stop 5, the West Woods.*

West Woods

At 6:00 AM, Edwin "Bull" Sumner's II Corps, like Hooker's I Corps, was up and ready to move. Sumner, an experienced veteran, had earned quite a reputation as a brave, tough, and perhaps somewhat dim-witted commander. Usually one who thought with his guts rather than his brains, McClellan thought so little of Sumner that he had continually made decisions through various campaigns to prevent Sumner from being in charge of too many troops at once. Still, it could never be said that he was not ready to fight. After time went by, and he had still received no orders, Sumner went to the Pry House, where McClellan was watching the battle from easy chairs brought out to the lawn for comfort. Sumner asked to see the general commanding and was refused, McClellan's aide telling Sumner that he was too busy.

By 7:20 McClellan had changed his mind. Although there were parts of the battle-field he could not see—most of the Cornfield was obscured by the East Woods—he knew that the fighting was heavy. Seeing Hood's Confederates emerge from the West Woods, McClellan reluctantly sent two of the II Corps' three divisions. John Sedgwick immediately forded Antietam Creek east of the Dunker Church with his division and brought them onto the field. Sumner accompanied them to the East Woods.

The Second Division, William French's, was 20 minutes behind, and by the time they made it to the East Woods, Sedgwick was gone. Seeing Union troops off to the southeast, French went to join them. Most of the units on the field by this time, 9:00 AM, were from the XII Corps, and although they held good positions, they were quite scattered. As for the I Corps, they had been almost completely used up, particularly Doubleday's and Ricketts's divisions, although some of Meade's units were still in fighting condition.

When Sumner was sent back to the field, he was to report to Hooker. However, by the time he got there, McClellan's worst nightmare had come true. Hooker had been wounded and taken off the field, meaning that the ranking officer, 65-year-old Bull Sumner, was in charge. Sumner received a report from a completely demoralized Ricketts and quickly concluded that both the I and XII corps were out of the fight. Minutes later, when XII Corps commander Williams tried to give Sumner a more thorough and accurate briefing, he was brushed aside.

With French still behind, Sumner came up with his battle plan. From this position, he certainly must be farther north than the Confederate left flank. All he needed to do was take Sedgwick's division straight to the West Woods, wheel to the left, and come down hard on the enemy from behind. The division left immediately.

The Confederates had made some adjustments as well. Lee had brought McLaws's division, which had marched all night from Harpers Ferry, to the left of the line after a very brief rest. Jubal Early's brigade, which had been protecting artillery, also came up to join the line. Finally, Lee had repositioned artillery from the Dunker Church and Nicodemus Hill to Hauser's Ridge, well to the west but having a commanding view of the western part of the field.

Sedgwick approached the West Woods just north of the Dunker Church with his three brigades set in three parallel lines, 50 yards apart. The front of the division was 500 yards wide, a massive and impressive front for the 5,400 soldiers on the march. The front line was made up of Willis Gorman's brigade, followed by that of N. J. T. Dana, then Oliver O. Howard's in the third line. When the division finished crossing the Cornfield and emerged on the Hagerstown Pike at 9:00 AM, they immediately began taking artillery fire from Hauser's Ridge.

At the entrance of the park area for the West Woods, if you turn to face the open fields to the east, Sedgwick's three lines would have been coming straight toward your position. The front of the Union force would have stretched from near the Dunker Church, to your right, all the way to the intersection near the Cornfield, to your left.

Sedgwick had moved about a quarter mile into the West Woods when the first shots came, more artillery fire from Hauser's Ridge. Sumner remained in the front, riding with Sedgwick. Suddenly, a heavy fire, followed by the rebel yell, came from their left and rear. It was McLaws, supported by all the other units Lee had poured into the area. They had been able to conceal themselves in the thick woods south of the Federals and were able to begin the attack undetected. What's more, the formation that Sedgwick's division was in—three parallel lines facing west—did not provide a good defense for an attack on the flanks, and the Federals had great trouble trying to get their regiments wheeled to the left to meet the oncoming Confederates, particularly in the middle of a forest.

Sumner, in the front, did not completely know what was happening in the first few minutes of action. After several minutes, he rushed to the rear. He found brigade commanders Dana and Howard trying to turn their troops left, but being overwhelmed, one regiment at a time, before they could accomplish anything. Soon, regiments began moving rearward—some in good order, some not. (Many of the men of Sedgwick's division would later credit Sumner's cool under fire for enabling them to escape the Confederate attack.)

Some Union units resisted for a time—particularly Gorman's brigade, in the front—but soon another of McLaws's brigades was hitting the Federals from their front to the west. As the rest of the Union units moved north through the Miller Farm to safety, the Confederates pursued as best they could, moving their artillery to keep up with the retreat. As they passed, those men of the I and XII corps who were still on the field often picked up and went with them. The Confederates were finally slowed by Gibbon's Iron Brigade, who formed a makeshift defensive line out of several units in front of the North Woods. Eventually, the Confederates pulled back to the West Woods. Sedgwick's division of the II Corps had suffered 2,300 casualties, most of them in the first 10 to 15 minutes of fighting. The Confederates did not escape unscathed, having suffered 1,000 casualties, but they did, in the process, virtually eliminate an entire division from combat for the day.

As you stand in the roundabout in the West Woods parking area, if you face away from the Hagerstown Pike, you will be facing west, the same direction that Sedgwick's division was facing. Turning to your left, you will see where the initial Confederate attack came from. Although the restoration of the West Woods isn't quite complete, it has been a big success story for the park, and you can get some idea of how well the Confederates were able to conceal their position as they approached the Federals. Your position in the roundabout is the approximate center of the rear Federal line, Howard's brigade. Also here is another monument with a cannon, muzzle down, memorializing the death of Confederate general William Starke in earlier fighting here.

There is also a park hiking trail that explores the West Woods. The trail is 1.5 miles and will take you through the woods, giving you a somewhat better idea of how the fighting in the West Woods was affected by the terrain. Also on the trail is the rock ledge that Gibbon's Iron Brigade encountered when they assaulted the West Woods earlier that morning. Williams would direct another assault against the West Woods at 9:45 AM, but his two regiments were driven back by Confederates firing from behind this wall.

As for Greene's position near the Dunker Church, he held his exposed position, eventually getting artillery support. At 10:00 AM the Confederates attacked his position from the West Woods, but Greene's artillery hit them with canister at 70 yards, and they were forced back into the trees. Greene's Federals pursued to a point 200 yards past the Dunker Church, forming a line and asking for reinforcements. By this time, however, the fighting had shifted to the east.

Mumma Farm

❯ *From the West Woods roundabout, turn right onto Dunker Church Road and drive 0.2 mile to Smoketown Road. Turn right on Smoketown Road and drive 0.2 mile. The first right will be Mummas Lane; turn right here and drive 0.1 mile to the Mumma Farm.*

French's division, lost from the moment they reached the East Woods, began to move southeast at 9:30 AM, to the left of Greene's position on the plateau near the Dunker Church and toward the center of the Confederate line. Robert E. Lee, along with Longstreet and D. H. Hill, watched French from a raised position near the Hagerstown Pike. As French made his way through the Mumma Farm, where the day's action had begun, it became clear that he was headed right for Hill's line. Hill had put his two brigades in a sunken farm road southeast of the Dunker Church. The road zig-zagged its way from the Hagerstown Pike and eventually met the Boonsboro Pike, and one of these angles formed the split between the two brigades, with Rodes's on the left and George Anderson's on the right. The angle was very slight, and they were both facing north, well protected by the ready-made breastwork that the road provided.

French's division of 5,700 men moved through the west part of the Mumma Farm, then on through the Roulette Farm's pasture and orchard. Max Weber's brigade was in front, followed by Colonel Dwight Morris's brigade and then Nathan Kimball's. After crossing the open ground of the Roulette Farm, the Federals came upon a low rise in front of them. The Confederates, right behind that rise, watched and waited.

The farm you see before you is the Mumma Farm. The house did not survive the battle; Confederates burned the house as they passed through the grounds before the battle to prevent Union sharpshooters from using it. Shortly after the war, however, the Mumma family rebuilt the home. Farther in the distance, beyond the Mumma Farm, is the Roulette House, which from this vantage point is somewhat obscured by trees. As you look at the Mumma Farm, turn to your left to look north; you will see the south end of the East Woods, from which French's division began their march, passing over the ground in front of you. If you now turn to your right to look south-east toward the observation tower, you are looking through the fields of the Mumma Farm to the pasture of the Roulette Farm beyond. The observation tower is at the far end of the Sunken Road. French's division kept moving until they reached the ridge right in front of the road.

Sunken Road/Bloody Lane

> *From the Mumma Farm pull-off, continue 0.5 mile down Mummas Lane. Turn right at Bloody Lane and drive 0.1 mile, then turn right on Richardson Avenue to reach the parking area.*

As French's men neared the ridge, they fixed bayonets and prepared to charge. Many soldiers on both sides later remarked that in this brief moment, the battlefield was almost completely silent. Then it began.

The Confederates waited, as instructed, until the Union troops were over the ridge far enough that their belt buckles could be seen. When Weber's brigade was within 80 yards of the Sunken Road, the Confederates fired. Few missed. The Federals who were still standing stumbled backward behind the cover of the ridge as quickly as they could. The ridge was the only cover they had; there was nothing else around but pas-ture. French's Second Brigade, led by Morris, came up to the left of Weber. Longstreet, seeing that the Union troops were reeling, ordered a charge, but Greene's artillery near the Dunker Church cut them down. When Kimball's brigade, French's last, came up to the line, they too attempted a bayonet charge, and they too were slaughtered. This was a different kind of firefight. As a veteran of the 8th Ohio later described, "What we see now looks to us like systematic killing."

Soon, Lee brought in his last reserve unit, Richard Anderson's division of 3,400 men. The Confederate reinforcements moved north through the Henry Piper Farm, behind Hill's division, to get to the Sunken Road. The farm had mostly been plowed for the winter, with the exception of a small orchard and 25 acres of corn immediately behind George Anderson's brigade. Richard Anderson's men tried to find cover where they could, mostly in the orchard, but they took heavy firing from both the Union line in front and the artillery across Antietam Creek. As they moved up, Richard Anderson was wounded, and command of the division fell to Roger Pryor, one of the comparatively few politician generals in the Confederacy. In the Sunken Road, George Anderson, commander of the right brigade, was hit and carried off the field, mortally wounded.

It was not long before the II Corps reserve division, Israel Richardson's, was brought into the fight. By the time his 4,000 soldiers reached the Sunken Road around 10:30, French's men were badly beaten up. Both Richardson and his division were well known for their toughness, particularly the famous Irish Brigade, led by Thomas

A view of the Sunken Road from near the Antietam Visitor Center.

Meagher. The Irish Brigade led the division, but when they formed to the left of French and attempted a charge, they met the same disastrous results.

Take a walk to the Sunken Road, now known just as commonly as Bloody Lane. As you stand in the road and walk its length, look to your left and see what the Confederates saw as the Union troops appeared over the ridge, thousands of close-range targets silhouetted perfectly against a clear sky. It is not unlikely that you will sense something indescribable here. Many do, from veteran battlefield stompers to first-time visitors. And no matter how many times you may visit, the feeling is always there. There are certainly other places on other battlefields where a similar feeling occurs for many, but here, in this humble road, it is virtually guaranteed.

Walk a bit to your left to find the angle in the road, then look down the two sections of the Sunken Road. As you face south, toward the Confederates, Rodes's brigade was lined up to your right and George Anderson's to your left. If you turn around and face north, toward the Union line, French's division overlapped the angle, with most of his men coming up to the line to your left. Richardson's division, beginning with the Irish Brigade, lined up on the portion of the road to your right.

There is a park walking tour available that begins at the Visitor Center (not far from your current position) that follows the Union advance through the Mumma and Roulette farms and takes you through the fighting at the Sunken Road. While you could pick up the trail here, you should consider taking it from its original starting point. Seeing what the Federals saw as they came up on the road will clearly demonstrate how they were able to march into such devastating fire without knowing what was coming, and it is also an excellent example of how even very subtle variations in terrain can affect the outcome of a battle.

Observation Tower

> *From here, either walk down the Sunken Road to the observation tower or return to your car and drive there, 0.2 mile down Richardson Avenue.*

As the rest of Richardson's division filed neatly into line north of the road, Pryor's division of reinforcements was anything but neat. His four brigades were scattered all over the Piper Farm, with only parts of one of them actually reaching the Sunken Road quickly. As the others eventually popped into the crowded road in piecemeal fashion, commands became mixed, attacks were suddenly uncoordinated, and confusion reigned. Slowly, the strong Confederate position was beginning to collapse.

Around noon, the Union line began to extend, overlapping the Confederate right. As the Confederates seemed momentarily awestruck by the sight of even more blue uniforms forming in front of them, the 29th Massachusetts, part of Meagher's Irish Brigade, pounced. The startled Confederates began to break, but the crowded Sunken Road would not allow free movement. Soon, in the confusion, many of the Confederates began to try to head for the rear. Except for two regiments, the entire Confederate right broke, and those two regiments—the 2nd and 14th North Carolina—did not stay long.

On their left, the Confederates were suddenly taking enfilading fire from the Federals across the angle. As Rodes tried to maintain order, one of his regimental commanders asked for instructions. Rodes ordered the commander to pull his regiment down the line, away from the angle, and then rushed to attend to another matter. When he returned only minutes later, to his horror he found that the commander had misunderstood the order and turned his regiment around to march for the rear. All five of Rodes's remaining regiments followed suit, abandoning the Sunken Road.

As the Confederates poured rearward through the Piper Farm, the Federals followed, taking their own position in the Sunken Road and firing into Piper's cornfield and orchard. The Confederates were able to rally many of their troops and began to receive more artillery support. (After one gun crew was shot down by Union sharpshooters, Longstreet's own staff began to work the pieces, with Longstreet himself holding their horses and directing fire.) By 1:00 PM, the Federal attack began to stall, and Richardson ordered his division to fall back behind the ridge north of the Sunken Road. They were running low on ammunition, and elements of William Franklin's VI Corps—Baldy Smith's division—were beginning to arrive on the field.

One thing that Richardson did not have was artillery. Asking for at least a battery or two, he was told that none could be spared, even though 44 guns sat unused near the East Woods, as did all of the I Corps artillery at the Poffenberger Farm. As Richardson went searching on his own for more guns, he was hit by Confederate artillery near the east end of the Sunken Road. Richardson fought his wound for six weeks, but in the end, it was mortal.

Richardson was replaced in command by Winfield Scott Hancock, a brigade commander in Baldy Smith's division of the newly arrived VI Corps. After the Federals were all back behind the ridge in front of the Sunken Road, Hancock called off the attacks on the Confederate center. They would hold this position for the rest of the day.

In this portion of the Sunken Road, you will find monuments to both Union General Israel Richardson and Confederate General George Anderson. The observation tower, built in 1896 by the War Department, enabled the Army to use Antietam as a case study for its officers. Its purpose today is much the same, and climbing to the top will give you an excellent view of virtually the entire field. From the tower you will have an excellent view of not only the Sunken Road but also the fields of the Mumma and Roulette farms, over which the Federals had to advance, as well as the Piper Farm, through which the Confederates retreated.

Burnside Bridge

❭ *From the observation tower, continue on Richardson Avenue for 1.1 miles, crossing MD 34 (where the name changes to Rodman Avenue). At the T intersection, turn left onto Old Burnside Bridge Road, then drive 0.5 mile to the parking area for the bridge.*

Since 7:00 AM, Burnside and Cox, on the east side of Antietam Creek at the Rohrbach Bridge with the rest of the IX Corps, had been watching Confederate units march to the other side of the battlefield. Burnside had been told to expect orders, but as it was for almost every other commander on the field, nothing had come. McClellan did not want to risk sending the IX Corps into battle. Throughout the day, he would continue to wonder where the rest of Lee's army was. He was looking at all of it, of course (except for A.P. Hill's division at Harpers Ferry), but he was quite convinced that half of the Army of Northern Virginia was still hidden.

Finally, at 9:00 AM, McClellan learned that Franklin's VI Corps, which had stayed near Crampton's Gap at South Mountain, would soon be arriving to join the rest of his army. This gave him the confidence to order Burnside across the Rohrbach Bridge to attack the Confederate right. The order was issued at 9:10, when the Union army had finally gained possession of the cornfield. By the time Burnside and Cox received that order at 10:00, Sedgwick's division in the West Woods had been torn apart, and French's division was fighting desperately at the Sunken Road. McClellan still needed Burnside to attack, however. The initial command was to keep the Confederate troops in front of him, and by this time, most were already gone. But McClellan still needed to give Lee's hidden forces something to think about, and feinting an attack on their right would do just that. McClellan promised reinforcements as well.

Even with a numeric advantage of better than four-to-one, crossing the bridge would be no easy task. The Rohrbach Bridge itself was only 12 feet wide, and 125 feet

EXTRA INCENTIVE

A common part of the Union soldiers' rations was a bit of whiskey. One of Edward Ferrero's two regiments to first cross Burnside Bridge, the 51st Pennsylvania, had had their ration taken away from them as punishment. When Ferrero told his men that they had been selected to charge the bridge, at least one of the men asked if their whiskey would be returned if they took the bridge. Ferrero promised that it would. It did not make the job any easier, but the 51st Pennsylvania (along with the 51st New York) did eventually take the bridge, and they were rewarded as promised.

long, with steep banks on both sides of the creek. Defending it would be simple. David "Neighbor" Jones's numbers had dwindled to 3,000 Confederates, but all 3,000 of those guns were trained on the same small area. Further, his men had a stone wall to use as a breastwork, and 400 of them were within 100 yards of the bridge.

Burnside had 12,500 men, but he also had no cover on the approach to the bridge, only open farmland. The bridge would create a severe bottleneck for his men, only allowing more time for the Confederates to pick them off. So with this numerical advantage, Burnside and Cox came up with a plan. While one of the IX Corps' four divisions pinned the Confederates down at the bridge, two others would use Snavely's Ford, found just a bit downstream the previous day by McClellan's staff, to cross Antietam Creek, then would turn back to the north to hit the Confederates from behind.

The operation began immediately. Isaac Rodman's division, along with part of Colonel Eliakim Scammon's, moved south to Snavely Ford. The other part of Scammon's division, Colonel George Crook's brigade, would assault the bridge directly, with Samuel Sturgis's division to follow him. Willcox's division would remain in reserve.

From the beginning, things went wrong for the Federals. Crook's brigade, which was supposed to run straight downhill to the bridge and take it in force, got lost and ended up being pinned down 350 yards upstream, where they stayed for hours. When Rodman got to the ford, he discovered that it wasn't a ford at all. The actual Snavely's Ford was another 2 miles downstream; the location sited by McClellan's engineers had bluffs 160 feet high. They would have to find another way to cross. Finally, Sturgis's division took a shot at assaulting the bridge. The lead brigade, James Nagle's, was immediately torn up and forced to retreat.

By noon, Burnside and Cox had still not crossed the bridge, and McClellan was growing impatient. Now with increased artillery support, Sturgis sent half of his other brigade, Edward Ferrero's, to assault the bridge with 670 men. They were still not able to cross, but the two regiments that charged split at the bridge and were able to take cover at the bank, keeping up a fire for the next hour. Finally, at 1:00, the Confederates began to run low on ammunition, and the combined fire of the artillery and infantry was taking its toll. Jones withdrew his men to a stone wall 0.5 mile west of the bridge, as the Federals poured across, then formed a line along the west bank of the creek. Sturgis's entire division crossed at the bridge, while Crook finally found a ford for his brigade once the Confederates pulled back. By that time Rodman had also found a suitable crossing and had made his way north to join the line. In no time, the Federals had reunited practically the entire IX Corps on the western side of Antietam Creek. The Rohrbach Bridge, another marker of Union inefficiency and hesitation at Antietam, would forever be labeled "Burnside Bridge."

The bridge that you see today is the original bridge, and in fact it was open to

The Rohrbach Bridge over Antietam Creek, now forever known as Burnside Bridge.

traffic until 1966. The walk down to the bridge—or rather, back up from it—can be a bit challenging, but there are places to stop and rest along the way, so you can take your time. If you don't want to walk all the way down to the bridge, there is an overlook that provides an excellent view of it. The path points out the Confederate positions, then ends right at the bridge. The setting is very peaceful here, with Antietam Creek running by and the steep banks of the creek isolating the area from the rest of the park. Do not let the peaceful atmosphere fool you; on September 17, 1862, the fighting here was as hot as anywhere else on the field.

There are several walking trails that begin in the area of the bridge. One of them is the Union Advance trail, 1 mile over mostly easy terrain, except for two moderately steep hills (but still on a good pathway). The trail shows the Confederate positions, where the Federal charges came from, the location where Crook tried to cross, and, of course, the bridge itself, rather beautiful in its setting.

The other two trails, the Snavely Ford Trail and the Final Attack Trail, are a bit longer and more difficult, but by no means rugged. Still, you should be prepared for a hike, with good shoes, water, and all the other necessities. The Snavely Ford Trail is 1.8 miles and follows Antietam Creek as it winds southward, going down one side and looping back up the other to the bridge. The Final Attack Trail, 1.7 miles, will take you through the comparatively rugged landscape to the west of the bridge, where the final scenes of the Battle of Antietam were played out. It is a wonderful and often over-looked part of the battlefield, and the drama that occurred here is no less than any other portion of the field. If, however, you don't want to hike the trail, you will over-look the area at the next stop and read about the conclusion of the battle.

South Battlefield

〉 *From the Burnside Bridge parking area, return 0.5 mile on Old Burnside Road. Keep following the road as it curves to the left and becomes Branch Avenue for an-other 0.2 mile, then pull over in one of the designated parking areas on either side of the road.*

The Union line on the south side of the battlefield was now formidable. Ready to advance, Burnside sent a message to McClellan that he was across Antietam Creek in strength. He was surely expecting information about the reinforcements he was prom-ised, but the only response he received was that he must advance at once.

Unfortunately for the Federals, there were complications. Sturgis's division had been used up, and would have to be replaced by Willcox's reserve division. This took time with the bottleneck at the bridge. Further, it was soon discovered that there would be no reinforcements. McClellan, expecting Lee to mass his supposedly unused troops (which did not exist) for an assault on the Union center, put Federal troops from the V Corps to brace that part of the field near the Middle Bridge. None of them would aid the IX Corps, which would not be ready to move until 3:00 PM.

That was too late. At 2:30 PM, A. P. Hill, whose division had left Harpers Ferry that morning, rode up to the Confederate command and informed them that they were near, crossing the Potomac. Lee ordered him to place his troops on the right to sup-port Neighbor Jones for the oncoming assault.

The 8,500 Union troops under Cox and Burnside began their advance with Rodman's and Willcox's divisions of fresh troops in the front, along with 22 pieces of artillery that had been brought across the bridge. Jones had only 2,800 Confederates to cover not only the town of Sharpsburg but also the critical road to the Confederate escape route at Botelar's Ford. Two brigades were on Cemetery Hill (where Antietam National Cemetery is today) to hold the right, with another three on the left. The Confederates also had artillery present, 28 guns, with Lee looking for more.

As you face the broken ground in front of you, you can see that the Union advance was not easy. The landscape here makes for a difficult walk in itself, let alone under fire. To your right is the farm of John Otto, just southeast of Cemetery Hill, to your right rear. The Otto Farm, particularly its orchard, saw heavy fighting during the late stages of the battle. Not far behind you is the town of Sharpsburg, the size and look of which has not changed much since the battle.

CASUALTIES

Confederate: killed, 1,546; wounded, 7,752; missing or captured, 1,018; total: 10,318

Union: killed, 2,108; wounded, 9,540; missing or captured, 753; total: 12,401

Total Casualties: 22,719

Burnside's plan was to flank the Confederates and ultimately block that escape route to Botelar's Ford, converging on the town from the east and the south. As they pushed through the rocky, uneven ground, Confederate artillery took a deadly toll on the Union soldiers, but the Union artillery, more powerful and with longer range, soon dominated the Confederate guns. Soon the Federals were on the eastern edge of Cemetery Hill, forcing them to fall back to a stone wall just east of the town.

By 4:00, the Union IX Corps had advanced over most of the field. The fighting had been hard, but they had advanced steadily, and the Confederate right flank was beginning to collapse into the town of Sharpsburg. However, just as the Federals seemed on the brink of victory, A. P. Hill's division arrived on the field. They had covered 17 miles in less than eight hours, and although they were tired, they were ready to fight. When General Isaac Rodman began to see Hill's troops arriving, he rushed to give warning, only to be mortally wounded.

There was no time for organization; Hill's men were placed piecemeal as they came in and given orders as they fell into line. Hill pulled up his artillery to the Harpers Ferry Road, behind where you now stand, and began to hit the Federals with canister shot at 60 yards. In a rather sudden reversal, the Federals were forced to fall back over the rough terrain.

By 4:30, the fight on the southern part of the field was at its peak. Cox had pulled troops back to form a line facing south to protect the Federal left, which was suddenly exposed with Hill's appearance. Other units tried to hold at the Otto Farm, fighting desperately not to lose the ground they had fought so hard to gain. To their dismay, however, they were not supported; McClellan never sent the reinforcements he had promised. The Confederates saw the advantage, pushing east toward Burnside Bridge. In their pursuit, brigade commander Lawrence O'Bryan Branch was mortally wounded, the sixth general—three on each side—to die at Antietam.

As Cox and Burnside formed a line to protect the bridge, the Confederates held them there, but made no further attacks. The field finally became quiet as darkness approached. As the numbers were reported throughout the night, the awful reality of the day began to sink in. The killing had simply gotten out of control. The Union Army of the Potomac had taken 25 percent casualties, while the Confederate Army of Northern Virginia had lost 31 percent of their men. In total, 22,719 Americans fell on the fields of Antietam, on what is still the bloodiest single day in American history.

As you drive down Branch Avenue, you will see a number of memorials to your left. Among them is the Isaac Peace Rodman memorial, near the site where he was killed. As you turn to your right and drive up the Harpers Ferry Road, on your right will be a trailhead; this short path will take you to the site where Lawrence O'Bryan Branch fell.

Pry House

> ❯ *From the parking area, continue on Branch Avenue 0.7 miles as it turns to the right. Turn right on Harpers Ferry Road and drive 0.8 miles to MD 34 (East Main Street). Turn right onto MD 34; very soon, to your right, will be Antietam National Cemetery, which is an impressive and humbling place, not to mention the location of a key battlefield feature—Cemetery Hill. It will be worth your time to stop and pay your respects. Drive 2.4 miles on MD 34 to the entrance to the Pry House, which will be on your left.*

Here at the Pry House, General McClellan and his staff watched the battle. It is obvious, from this elevated position, that much of the action can be seen. However,

Pry House, McClellan's headquarters and now a museum of Civil War medicine.

the contrast between McClellan's style of command and that of Lee, riding from point to point on the battlefield, is striking.

Also here at the Pry House, during certain parts of the year, the home is open, and you can view exhibits related to Civil War medicine and the treatment of the wounded. No one was prepared to deal with the unrealistic number of casualties at Antietam, and the advancement of medicine throughout the war because of battles like this is extremely interesting. The exhibit is an annex of the National Museum of Civil War Medicine in Frederick, a fascinating museum that brings home the awful and often unrecognized toll that disease and even treatment took on the armies.

Botelar's Ford

❭ *From the Pry House, turn right onto MD 34 West and drive 5.4 miles to Canal Road, just before the Potomac River. Turn left on Canal Road and drive 1.3 miles. Pull over at the historic marker on your left.*

The next morning, September 18, nearly everyone expected the fighting to resume. The men had held their lines and were awaiting the dreadful order to attack. McClellan, though, would not attack. It has been argued that had he done so, he may have crushed the Confederate army. Between the V and VI corps and other units, the Union still had over 62,000 troops in reserve that never fired a shot. Still, holding on to his belief that Lee had many more troops than he had already shown, McClellan denied repeated requests by his generals to renew the attack.

General Lee's main concern was taking his army to safety across the Potomac. Throughout September 18, the wounded were taken across Botelar's Ford to Virginia soil. Confident that McClellan would not attack again, Lee fed his men in their lines, then began to pull them out of their positions after dark, crossing the Potomac overnight. By the time dawn broke on September 19, the Confederates were gone, on their way to Martinsburg, Virginia.

Lee did leave some infantry and artillery as a rear guard at Botelar's Ford, and he was wise to do so. Late on September 19, Union troops of the V Corps under Fitz John Porter fought their way across the ford, pushing the Confederates back. The troops he had, however, were mostly fresh recruits. When A. P. Hill arrived the next day, September 20, to drive them back across the ford, they were quickly and easily routed. The fight at Botelar's Ford ended Lee's Maryland Campaign.

The view from your position is probably the best and easiest view of the ford itself, which played such a critical part in the campaign. Not only was it the Confederate escape route, but Jackson's movement from Harpers Ferry to Sharpsburg also used this ford, as did A. P. Hill when he came to the Confederates' rescue on September 17.

➤ *Make a U-turn and drive 1.3 miles back to MD 34. Turn left at MD 34, which becomes WV-480 South as you cross the Potomac River, and drive 0.8 miles to German Street. Turn left at German Street and follow it for 1.7 miles as it eventually becomes the River Road. Pull over at the historic markers located at the intersection of River Road and Trough Road.*

You are now opposite the position you were at across the river. The ground around you is where most of the fighting took place on both September 19 and 20. Although thick and overgrown today, it is easy to see how Hill's Confederates, from the bluffs above you, could easily drive the green troops off the field and into the river.

The Battle of Antietam is often referred to as a Union victory, but in reality, it was a draw. Both sides had taken enormous casualties. In McClellan's eyes, though, the victory was obvious and complete. Thinking afterward that he suddenly had great leverage because of his success in saving the country, he attempted to demand supplies and more men, and even began to arrange for General-in-Chief Henry Halleck and Secretary of War Edwin M. Stanton to be pushed out.

The Federals did hold the ground, and for Abraham Lincoln, it was also victory enough. On September 23, the Emancipation Proclamation was issued, declaring that on January 1, 1863, all slaves in areas of rebellion would be free. Although the release of the Proclamation certainly had its detractors—George McClellan among them—it gave the war a new cause, providing the Union with a higher moral ground. In addition, the Union's new direction and the victory at Antietam once again delayed foreign intervention. England, France, and other countries would only back the Confederacy if they would clearly win the war; now, however, it was not so clear, and the thought of siding with slavery was unthinkable.

On October 1, Lincoln arrived at Sharpsburg, unannounced, to meet with McClellan and view the battlefield. Lincoln stayed four days, attempting to persuade McClellan to move into Virginia to pursue the Confederates, and McClellan agreed to do so. In characteristic fashion, however, excuses were made; the Army of the Potomac was still outnumbered, in McClellan's eyes, and supplies were not being received quickly enough. Winter was coming quickly, and all wondered whether there would be any more fighting in 1862. The answer would soon be revealed along the familiar banks of the Rappahannock.

CHAPTER 6

Hollow Victories: Fredericksburg and Chancellorsville

THE SLOW SPEED with which the Union Army of the Potomac moved had become habit. On the Peninsula, at Second Manassas, and at Antietam, its prime mover was not to create situations but rather to react to them. Following Antietam, the army and its commander, George B. McClellan, faced a new test. This time it was the Confederates who had left the field. It had been costly, but by the time the bloodbath of September 17, 1862, had ended, the Union held the initiative. What would they do with it?

The question was answered quickly as Robert E. Lee escaped to Virginia practically unhindered. The Federals remained in camp around the fields of Antietam, resting and recuperating, but still inactive. A visit by the commander in chief, intended almost solely to get the army to move, was not successful. Even when President Lincoln ordered an advance into Virginia on October 6, McClellan did nothing. Finally, only after unrelenting pressure from Washington and another embarrassing "Ride around McClellan" by J. E. B. Stuart's Confederate cavalry, the Federals crossed the Potomac River and once again trod upon Virginia soil on October 26.

In repeated messages, McClellan assured the War Department that he was moving at the best possible speed. In fact, the average distance covered during the first eight days of the campaign was little more than 3 miles per day. Finally, on November 5, Lincoln's patience had run out. General Ambrose Burnside was ordered to take command of the Army of the Potomac; General McClellan was relieved of duty. Burnside at first refused the order, but then accepted after learning that if he did not take it the

---

The Meade Pyramid marks the point of the Union breakthrough at Fredericksburg.

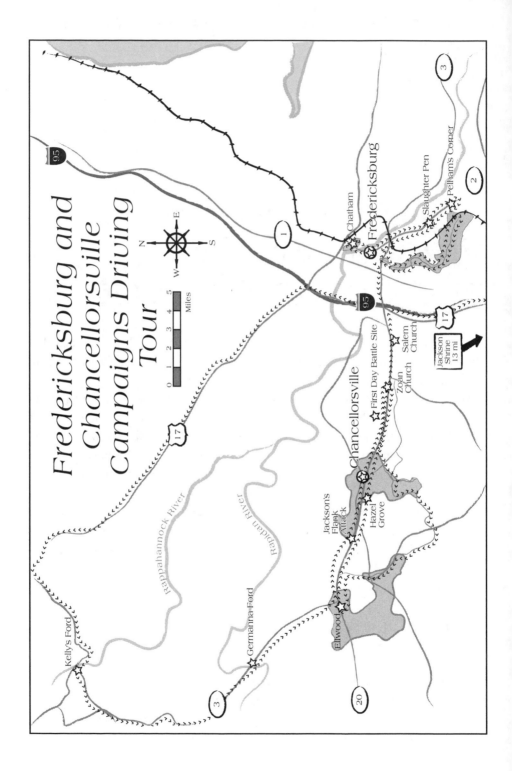

Fredericksburg and Chancellorsville Campaigns Driving Tour

N E S W

Miles
0 1 2 3 4 5

95

1

Chatham

Fredericksburg

Slaughter Pen

Pelham's Corner

3

2

17

95

17

Jackson Shrine
13 mi

Salem Church

Zoan Church

First Day Battle Site

Chancellorsville

Jackson's Flank Attack

Hazel Grove

Ellwood

20

Rappahannock River

Rapidan River

Germanna Ford

Kelly's Ford

3

army would be given to General Joseph Hooker. On November 11, after a grand and pompous farewell during which many of the soldiers wept openly, McClellan boarded a train for New Jersey, not to tread onto another battleground until his 1864 presidential campaign—against Abraham Lincoln.

From the moment he was offered command, Burnside repeatedly told anyone and everyone within earshot that he was not fit to command the army, and there were those who believed him. Many thought that McClellan should have remained in command. Others thought that if a change was to be made, it was Hooker who should have gotten the appointment, not Burnside. Although almost everyone liked him personally, many were skeptical of his abilities. He would have to prove himself not only on the field but also in the backbiting politics that had pervaded the Army of the Potomac for months.

For the Confederates, even though they had suffered badly at Antietam and were dreadfully short of food, shoes, and other critical supplies, morale was good and getting better. After giving his men time to rest, General Robert E. Lee divided his army, moving General James Longstreet's command, now known as the I Corps, to Culpeper, Virginia, while General Stonewall Jackson's wing, the new II Corps, remained in the Shenandoah Valley. In typical fashion, Longstreet, whose troops had a much longer route than the Federals, was in Culpeper by November 4, far outpacing what McClellan had been able to do.

For the next eight months, both armies would remain in the vicinity of Fredericksburg, eyeing each other across the Rappahannock River. During that time and for the rest of the war the fighting would return to this place, again and again, making it the bloodiest ground in the country. Brilliant strategy, great drama, and terrible disaster abound in this piece of the war, and it is difficult to appreciate or understand fully what happened here until you have walked the ground for yourself.

BEFORE YOU GO

» PLANNING YOUR TRIP

The battlefield at Fredericksburg is deceptively simple. There are many who consider Marye's Heights the entire story of Fredericksburg, but it is not, not by a long shot. While what happened there may be the most tragic episode of the battle (and possibly the Civil War), events on the other fronts, which were intended to be the focus of the battle,

---

FREDERICKSBURG AND CHANCELLORSVILLE CAMPAIGNS

Number of sites: 11

Total miles: 100

Estimated time: 2–3 days

Must-sees: Fredericksburg & Spotsylvania National Military Park

Close second: Kelly's Ford

---

are just as compelling. Make sure that you spend time exploring the Confederate right, south of the town, particularly Slaughter Pen Farm.

In contrast, the Battle of Chancellorsville is deceptively complex, and some would rather not study the tactical aspects of the battle. The Battle of Chancellorsville is so much more than the death of Stonewall Jackson, so don't fall into that trap. On a similar note, Robert E. Lee's brilliant maneuvering at Chancellorsville led many to call Chancellorsville his finest hour. However, the battle plan of Union General Joseph Hooker was also not only brilliant but also perfectly executed in the days preceding the battle. Be sure to include the Federals' remarkable movements to Chancellorsville Tavern; they are a large part of the story, and make Lee's achievement all the more fascinating.

» RECOMMENDATIONS

This one's an easy one. Stay in Fredericksburg. Every hotel, restaurant, and convenience you can imagine is here, and the only two sites not in the immediate area—Kelly's Ford and the Jackson Shrine—are both within 25 miles. The amount of sprawl here is overwhelming, and unfortunately, that sprawl has taken (and continues to take) significant portions of the battlefield. The variety it creates, however, is great for travelers.

Better yet, stay *in* Fredericksburg—as in the original old town. Although the growth of the town has swallowed a great deal of that battlefield as well, the town still looks very much like it did 150 years ago. Although many of the town's buildings were destroyed during the war, most were rebuilt, and many have been around since the Colonial period. There are several wonderful choices for bed & breakfasts in town that have historical significance, and the shops and restaurants will have you exploring the town's streets for days. Best of all, the town is well removed from the sprawl, and the people here are wonderful. Odds are good that you will at least look at a real estate brochure while you're here—it's that great.

IN DEPTH

Francis Augustin O'Reilly—*The Fredericksburg Campaign: Winter War on the Rappahannock*

George C. Rable—*Fredericksburg! Fredericksburg!*

"Both of these books are excellent sources on the Federal fiasco. O'Reilly's book is a bit more detailed, while Rable's is a sweeping narrative. Both are superb pieces of scholarship."

—*Tom Trescott, Abraham Lincoln Book Shop, Chicago*

THE CAMPAIGN TOUR

FREDERICKSBURG VISITOR CENTER

❯ *Your tour of the Fredericksburg and Chancellorsville campaigns starts at the Fredericksburg Unit Visitor Center of the Fredericksburg & Spotsylvania National Military Park. Pull into one of the parking lots near the Visitor Center.*

On November 7, 1862, the first heavy winter storm of the season began to fall in Northern Virginia, 4 inches of wet snow and sleet. For several days, the storms continued, with the ground freezing as night fell and then thawing when the sun came, turning the Virginia roads into mud. Thus the soldiers of the Army of the Potomac learned a lesson that has been known to great military minds for millennia: winter campaigns are fraught with danger, sap morale, often yield no results, and should only be begun if the advantages are certain.

All over the country, though, the press and the public cried for a winter campaign. Certainly, the Confederates were hurting after Antietam, and could be dealt a death blow. Further, more victories were needed to prevent foreign intervention in the war. The Emancipation Proclamation, it was hoped by some, would be vindicated with another victory, while others hoped that a quick end to the war would bring a settlement that somehow restored the old republic, slavery and all.

As it happened, November 7 was also the day that command of the Army of the

The National Park Visitor Center at Fredericksburg.

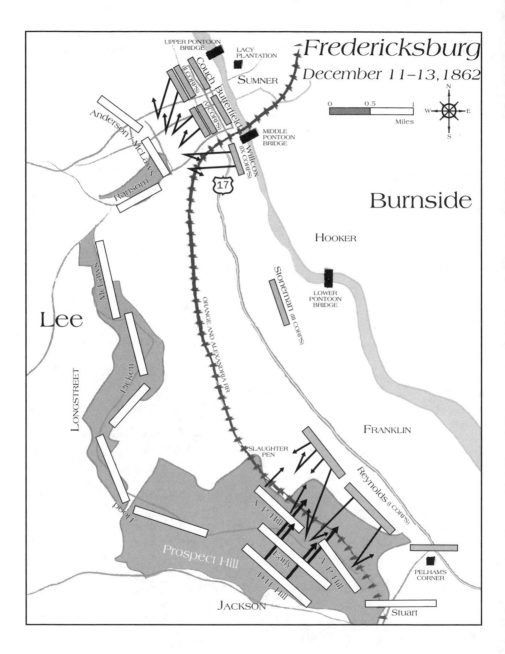

Fredericksburg
December 11–13, 1862

UPPER PONTOON BRIDGE

LACY PLANTATION

Couch (II CORPS)

Butterfield (V CORPS)

SUMNER

0   0.5   1
Miles

N
W — E
S

MIDDLE PONTOON BRIDGE

Anderson

McLaws

Willcox (IX CORPS)

Ransom

17

Burnside

HOOKER

McLaws

Lee

Stoneman (III CORPS)

LOWER PONTOON BRIDGE

LONGSTREET

Pickett

ORANGE AND ALEXANDRIA RR

Pendl

FRANKLIN

Reynolds (I CORPS)

SLAUGHTER PEN

A. P. Hill

A. P. Hill

Prospect Hill

Early

A. P. Hill

PELHAM'S CORNER

D. H. Hill

JACKSON

Stuart

Potomac was transferred to Ambrose Burnside. Knowing that his predecessor was dismissed largely for his lack of speed, and feeling the pressure coming from all sides, Burnside immediately began preparations for a winter campaign. Setting his headquarters in Warrenton, Virginia, by November 9 Burnside had already planned his campaign, sending the details to General-in-Chief Henry Halleck in Washington.

Burnside's plan abandoned McClellan's strategy of following the Orange & Alexandria Railroad and drove the army straight for Fredericksburg, then Richmond, with all rapidity. This would not only place the Federals outside the Confederate capital but, if executed properly, would put them between the capital and Lee's Army of Northern Virginia. Halleck did not approve of the plan, but it was the campaign that everyone in the north had wanted all along—no end-around movements, no sieges, simply straight "On to Richmond" to end the war. On November 14, Lincoln gave his approval to the plan, adding simply that he thought it would "succeed, if you move rapidly; otherwise, not."

The first step in getting to Richmond quickly was crossing the Rappahannock River, and the most direct route for that crossing took the army through Fredericksburg. A small city of about 5,000 (with one third of the population either enslaved or free blacks), Fredericksburg was an old city, having already risen and fallen because it was not on a railroad. Although the bridges had already been destroyed, crossing the Rappahannock would be easy enough through the use of pontoon bridges, floating passages that could be stretched across a river in a matter of hours. It was agreed that Halleck would arrange for the pontoons while Burnside concentrated on moving his army.

As had most of the army's previous commanders, Burnside reorganized his force to his liking. Although the corps structure remained intact, another layer of command (and bureaucracy) would be added, which Burnside called "Grand Divisions." The Right Grand Division, consisting of the II and IX corps, would be commanded by Edwin Sumner. The Left Grand Division would hold the I and VI corps under the watch of William Franklin. The Center Grand Division, under Hooker's command, would be made up of the III and V corps. Additionally, the XI Corps, now commanded by Franz Sigel, would remain in reserve.

At 5:00 AM on November 15, the day after Lincoln's approval was received, Sumner's Right Grand Division began their march to Falmouth, on the Rappahannock opposite Fredericksburg. The other two Grand Divisions would leave the next two days, and by November 17, the first Federal troops were already on the Rappahannock. Despite poor weather and poorer roads, the Grand Divisions had indeed moved rapidly, as promised. The soldiers, the press, and the citizens, whether they were McClellan supporters or not, all seemed to approve of Burnside. His men were moving, and "On to Richmond" suddenly looked like a reality.

The first stop on your tour is the Visitor Center for the Fredericksburg Unit of

Fredericksburg & Spotsylvania National Military Park, one of two visitor centers in the park. You will eventually return here later in the tour, but for now, be sure to check the times for ranger-led programs for Fredericksburg and, perhaps, Chancellorsville to help you plan your tour. The small museum here is also worth checking out, as it contains some interesting artifacts. You can also view the park's 22-minute film on the battle and take a look at some of the maps of Fredericksburg to orient yourself. Finally, before you leave, pick up a brochure for the estate at Chatham and be sure to ask about the hours and tour schedule there. Whether the home is open or not, you will want to see the grounds of the estate, which is your next stop.

CHATHAM

> *From the Visitor Center parking lot, turn left onto Lafayette Boulevard and drive 0.7 mile to Caroline Street. Turn left onto Caroline Street and drive 0.4 mile to William Street. Turn right on William Street and follow it for 0.4 mile as it changes to Kings Highway. Watch for Chatham Heights Road on your left and carefully turn onto Chatham Heights, then drive 0.1 mile to Chatham Lane and take another left turn. The parking area for Chatham will be on your right.*

As you leave your car, notice the large fields around you. In 1862, this was only a fraction of the open land here, and as the Union army began arriving on November 17, the fields quickly filled with tents and shelters of all kinds. If you have time, proceed to the home, known as the Lacy plantation at the time of the battle but built almost 100 years earlier as Chatham. This mansion and the grounds around it would be the center of much activity before and during the Battle of Fredericksburg.

As the Federals began to gather on the north bank of the Rappahannock, Robert E. Lee was still not certain what the new Union commander's intentions were. Fredericksburg was certainly a possibility, but so was Culpeper, as it had been weeks before. On November 17, Lee ordered Longstreet to send two of his five divisions to Fredericksburg. After seeing the situation at Fredericksburg for himself on November 20, Lee sent for the rest of Longstreet's command. Jackson's men were already on the march from the Shenandoah Valley and began to arrive in Fredericksburg on December 3, having covered 175 miles in 12 days. Lee presumed that even with his entire command present, he would not be able to stop the Federals and would eventually have to fall back. Still, the Confederates began to construct defensive works, awaiting the Union army's inevitable crossing.

Although the Confederates could not prevent the Federals from crossing the Rappahannock, Washington bureaucracy could. Burnside arrived at Falmouth on November 19 expecting his army to be making preparations to cross the river, but there was a problem. The pontoon bridges, which were supposed to come in time for the soldiers to cross immediately, had not arrived. Immediately, blame began to be distributed, mostly between Halleck, Captain Ira Spaulding of the 50th New York Engineers, and another engineer, General Daniel Woodbury. On November 7, the order had been given to send the pontoons to Washington for shipment. The order was sent by regular mail, however, and did not reach Berlin, Maryland, where the pontoons were built, until November 12. Two days later, Spaulding was able to get 36 of the pontoon boats to Washington, but had assumed that there was no great urgency to the order. On the same day, November 14, Burnside's chief engineer, Lieutenant Cyrus Comstock, wired Woodbury twice asking about the bridges, and was finally told that the first bridge would be shipped overland on November 16, with the second probably coming by water sometime later. That first pontoon actually left November 19 and would not arrive until November 24. The rest of the bridges were finally at Falmouth on November 27, 10 days behind schedule. Burnside, in a letter to Halleck, sternly reminded him that "The President said that the movement, in order to be successful, must be made quickly, and I thought the same." Halleck responded that it wasn't his fault and that Burnside should talk to General Woodbury.

Across the Rappahannock, as citizens fled the town and the Confederates continued to improve their defenses, Lee could not understand why he had not yet been attacked. As Jackson's troops arrived, he placed them at various points downriver, not knowing where Burnside would choose to cross. As they waited, the Confederate defenses became stronger and more versatile, enabling them to better defend any potential threat. A military road was constructed behind the lines to move troops quickly from one part of the battlefield to the other, and a telegraph system was also set up to run the length of the line, which out of necessity was miles long and very thin at several points. Entrenchments were built for long-range artillery, while lighter guns were placed within the woods to protect them from counterbattery fire.

On November 26, Lincoln arrived at Falmouth to confer with Burnside. Not knowing of the pontoon fiasco until he arrived, and seeing the growing number of Confederates across the river in Fredericksburg, both Lincoln and Halleck assured Burnside that they would not force him to fight a battle he was not ready for. Still, Burnside could feel the pressure to attack. In the camps, in the White House, and across the country north and south, the question was the same, and everyone wanted an immediate answer: Would the army, which had been braving freezing temperatures and wet conditions, go into winter camp, or would it attack?

The mansion at Chatham served as a headquarters and communication center for the Federals before and during the Battle of Fredericksburg. If you have time to tour the home, it is full of surprises. George Washington certainly spent time here, as he grew up just south of the mansion at Ferry Farm. Other presidents later visited, including Thomas Jefferson, William Henry Harrison, and, of course, Lincoln. In the early 1800s, some of the slaves at the plantation rebelled and were later executed. After the battle, the home was used as a hospital, and both Clara Barton and Walt Whitman served here as nurses. Outside the home, the grounds, impeccably kept, provide not only several wonderful gardens to walk through but also, as you go around the home, a magnificent view of Fredericksburg. As you look at the town, the three dominant church spires that punctuate the skyline today were all present at the time of the battle, and Fredericksburg looks much the same today as it did in 1862.

This view was more than just pretty. The rise that the home is placed on is known as Stafford Heights. The heights run far south of this position, along the Rappahannock well below the town. With its obvious commanding view, Union heavy artillery, including massive siege guns, were placed here at Chatham and along the length of Stafford Heights. Sumner, commander of the Grand Right Division, set his headquarters here, and it was the primary command and communications center during the battle. From these heights, the Union command watched the battle unfold for three days in Fredericksburg and beyond.

Finally, note the heights beyond the town of Fredericksburg. This rise, known as Marye's Heights, was where Longstreet's Confederates had developed their line to great strength. Troops and artillery were massed all along the heights, as well as the high ground to either side. The heights would be the focus of the Union assault in Fredericksburg on the final bloody day of the battle.

A view of Marye's Heights from the Confederate line at the Sunken Road.

THE CITY OF FREDERICKSBURG

Middle Pontoon Bridge Site

❯ *From Chatham, drive 0.1 mile on Chatham Lane to Chatham Heights Road, then turn right and drive another 0.1 mile to Kings Highway. Turn right onto Kings Highway and drive 0.3 mile, crossing the river and taking the first left onto Sophia Street. Drive 0.6 mile on Sophia Street to the parking area for City Dock Park.*

By the end of November, news had spread about the delay of the pontoon bridges. Many in the War Department—Halleck, in particular, as well as Quartermaster General Montgomery C. Meigs—took abuse in the press for the pontoon failure, although Burnside was kept largely out of the blame game and retained public support. It was universally recognized, though, that getting the Union army across the Rappahannock at Fredericksburg would be a very tough feat.

Still, the question remained—would the Union army cross, or would they go into winter camp? Those most affected, the soldiers on both sides of the river, mostly just wanted the matter decided one way or the other. As for those who would make the decision, Burnside and his lieutenants, they were divided. Sumner favored a crossing downstream of the town to turn the Confederate right, while others favored crossing upstream to turn their left. General John Gibbon, saying that winter conditions made an assault on Fredericksburg impossible, even proposed moving the entire army by sea toward Petersburg, Virginia, similar to the previous campaign on the Peninsula. Rumors took hold of the camps as the men wondered why the decision was taking so long, particularly on the Union side as they watched the Confederate defenses grow stronger.

General Lee had made his mind up. The Confederates would not be falling back. The Confederate defenses were now so strong that he believed they would hold, despite their inferior numbers. He still could not prevent the Federals from taking Fredericksburg, but they would not be able to take the Confederate position. Every man in the Army of Northern Virginia, from Lee down to the lowliest private, was confident that if the Yankees crossed at the town, they would be slaughtered. Jackson, for one, did not approve of the position—although the Federals would be beaten back, a victory would bear no fruit, as the Confederates could not attack the Union positions on Stafford Heights. Still, with the Rappahannock River and high ground in between the Federals and the 80,000 Confederates, along with their 60 batteries of artillery, they were in a good spot.

Finally, in early December, Burnside made his decision. Of all the possible crossings, the least expected was at Fredericksburg itself, so that is where he would cross. Six pontoon bridges would be built. Two would be just below the heights at Chatham, one at the City Dock on the south side of Fredericksburg, and three a mile downstream near a creek called Deep Run. Sumner's Right Grand Division would cross in the town while Franklin's Left Grand Division crossed to turn the Confederate right. Hooker's Center Grand Division would be in reserve, ready to move in whatever direction it was needed. Once across, the Federals would surge forward and gain control of the Confederate military road, dividing their army.

On December 9, the soldiers were ordered to cook three days' rations and fill their cartridge boxes. The next day, at Chatham, Burnside held a meeting for his generals to review the details of the plan. He knew that few of them supported it, and when he raised the matter, General Winfield Scott Hancock was quick to state that no one disapproved of the general himself, but that many of them thought the plan faulty. Burnside's response was that he had not wanted command of the army, but now that he had it, he had made up his mind and would not change it now, adding that he only asked that his commanders carry out his plan to their best ability. All in the room either agreed or stood silent. The building of the pontoon bridges would begin at 3:00 AM the next morning.

City Dock Park marks the spot where the town's steamboat wharf was located, left over from its heyday as a point of export. It was also where the Union chose its middle pontoon bridge site. Directly across the river from you is Ferry Farm, the boyhood home of George Washington, where many Union troops camped in the weeks before the battle. You can visit Ferry Farm today and walk down to the location where the middle pontoon bridge was started in the early morning hours of December 11, 1862. As you stand at the historical markers in the parking lot and look away from the river, you will see an old stone passageway. This is Rocky Lane, left over from colonial days of the ferry crossing located here.

Fredericksburg Civil War Walking Tour

❯ *From the park, turn around and drive down Sophia Street to the first left onto Princess Elizabeth Street, then the first right onto Caroline Street. Drive 0.3 mile to the intersection of Caroline Street and Charlotte Street. Find a place to park in one of the surrounding lots or on the street; you will be walking the streets of Fredericksburg from here. Begin at the Fredericksburg Visitor Center on the northwest corner of the intersection.*

The Fredericksburg Visitor Center is your best bet for gathering information about what you'll find in the town. Now a National Historic District, Fredericksburg has a wonderful feel to it—lots of shops, restaurants, inns, and historic sites, but anything but the tourist trap that places like this often become. Stop in the Visitor Center first to pick up a map of the town and the two brochures titled "Fredericksburg 1862—A Walking Tour," Parts I and II. These two walking tours, developed in concert

The upper pontoon site at Fredericksburg.

with the National Park Service, provide an excellent blow-by-blow description of the crossing of the river and the fighting in the town. In addition, grab anything else that catches your eye, as you'll have the opportunity to see plenty along the way. If you don't want to follow the entire Part I walking tour (about 1.5 miles), your best bet is to drive from here to the intersection of Sophia Street and Hawke Street, the upper pontoon bridge site.

With map in hand, walk north on Caroline Street (away from Charlotte Street and toward Hanover Street). Take your time and soak in the feel of the town. Many of the buildings on each side of the street date back to the time of the battle or well before, although during the three days of the battle most were heavily damaged.

When you reach Amelia Street, turn right and walk toward the river, then turn left on Sophia Street, strolling until you reach the historical markers on your right between Fauquier and Hawke Streets. As you walk, look across the river. You should be able to see the mansion at Chatham. From your position on the riverbank you can get a sense of just how commanding the Federal position on Stafford Heights was. Turning around, you can also see that Stafford Heights runs well downriver, stretching miles below Fredericksburg. Note also the homes and buildings along the riverbank on your side of the Rappahannock, stretching south of you for the length of the town.

The early morning hours of December 11 were cold and draped in a dense fog. Union engineers quietly moved down to the riverbank here below Chatham, at the middle bridge site, and at the lower crossing near Deep Run. The building of the pontoon bridges began at 3:00 AM, with the engineers muffling their tools using cloth and attempting to remain as quiet as possible. The work went on until about 5:00, when two sudden blasts of artillery sounded.

The Confederates, surmising that the Federals were crossing this day, were prepared to meet them. William Barksdale's brigade, consisting almost entirely of Mississippians, had two regiments in the town, concealed in the buildings along the riverfront. Two other brigades were held in reserve on Marye's Heights. The artillery blasts were a signal that the building of the pontoon bridges had begun. As soon as their dark shapes could be discerned through the fog, Barksdale's men began sniping at the engineers and picking them off. Although they had made good progress to this point—one of the upper bridges and the middle bridge were two-thirds complete, with the second upper bridge about one-quarter finished—the engineers took heavy casualties as they tried to complete their work and were eventually forced off the bridges. Time and again, the engineers would venture back out, as would Federal infantry later, and each time they were forced back to the riverbank.

Lee knew that eventually, the Union bridges would be completed and the army would cross, but he needed time. Jackson's divisions were still scattered as far as 20 miles south of the town and needed time to consolidate now that the locations of the

The Sunken Road at the base of Marye's Heights.

crossings were known. Barksdale's mission was to harass the bridge-builders and delay them for as long as possible.

To Burnside, the delay was intolerable. From the beginning, his campaign depended upon speed. In developing his battle plan for Fredericksburg, speed and surprise were again the key elements. Now, with everything seemingly in place, his advance was slowed again. Burnside turned to his chief of artillery and angrily ordered him to bring every gun "to bear upon the city and batter it down."

From the heights across the river from you, the artillery bombardment was a spectacular thing to watch. Beginning at 12:30 PM, when the fog lifted, it continued for two hours without reprieve. There was hardly a building that emerged unscathed, and most were hit multiple times; many were either set aflame or were completely knocked down.

At 2:30 PM, the firing stopped. Fredericksburg was in ruins. Entire blocks had been leveled. The Union engineers went back out onto the pontoon bridges to finish their work, only to discover that as seemingly complete as the bombardment was, there were still plenty of Confederates to continue shooting at them, except that now there was no fog. The engineers retreated to the riverbank again; a new plan was needed.

Two Union regiments, the 7th Michigan and the 19th Massachusetts, piled into three of the pontoon boats from the brush along the riverbank on the opposite side. With engineers rowing, the infantrymen laid low in the boats. Although the Confederates fired at the approaching boats, they could not stop them, and all three boats managed to make it across. The site where the boats landed is right in front of you on the lower part of the bank. The rise in the bank that exists today was also there when the Federals landed, and they used this ridge to establish their landing site and allow other units to cross while the engineers continued their work.

From this point on, the fighting would be from street to street, house to house. The Federals quickly deployed and took control of the houses along the riverbank, forcing Barksdale to fall back to Caroline Street.

From here, walk to Hawke Street and turn left, moving away from the river, walking to Caroline Street. The 19th Massachusetts formed to the right, while the 7th Michigan took the left, and both units advanced uphill into to the town, just as you are. All along Caroline Street, the two sides were shooting at each other at very close range from buildings facing each other. As this fighting continued, however, the engineers were able to resume their building of the bridges. A similar operation occurred at the middle bridge, and Barksdale sent reinforcements there, but it was not enough. By 4:30 PM, the first bridge of the upper crossing and the middle bridge were complete, enabling more Union troops to enter the town.

Continue up Hawke Street to Charles Street, then turn left and walk four blocks to William Street. On the northwest corner of this intersection, a remnant of the past

THE HORRORS OF WAR

The Union pillaging of Fredericksburg, though the largest and most extreme example of such behavior during the Civil War, was not an isolated incident. Earlier in the year, orders issued by General John Pope essentially permitted plundering the Virginia countryside in order to feed the army. At the time, Pope was viewed as a barbarian, even by some Union generals, but it was not long before the results of these orders began to weaken the Confederacy. Robert E. Lee was twice forced to move north to relieve Virginia's farmers and was twice defeated. The Army of Northern Virginia was continuously in want of food, and by war's end they were thoroughly beaten. The policy of bringing the war directly to the citizens of the south was tragic but effective.

remains—a former auction block where slaves were sold. Although it has little to do with the battle, its presence and relevance here cannot be ignored.

Cross William Street and turn left, toward the river, and walk one block to Princess Anne Street. This is the location of the Market House and Market Square. Barksdale controlled operations from the building, and his reserve troops, brought down from Marye's Heights, were gathered in the Square. After fiercely contesting the Federal advance for hours, Barksdale's Mississippians re-formed here at approximately 7:00 PM and fell back to the safety of Marye's Heights, mission accomplished.

During the night and throughout the following day, as Burnside observed the Confederate positions, the occupying Union troops began to ransack the town. While most of the Union soldiers did not participate, the pillaging was widespread, and although much of the raiding was simply in search of a good meal, the vast majority was outright vandalism perpetrated by soldiers venting their frustration and showing their contempt for the southern aristocracy that pervaded much of this genteel town. The liquor discovered during the mayhem did not help things, and the Union revelry continued through the night of December 12. From Marye's Heights above, the Confederates had already been angered by the sight of the women and children of Fredericksburg fleeing their homes during the Union bombardment. Now their blood boiled as they watched Yankee troops taking pleasure in destroying the town.

Continue on Princess Anne Street three blocks to Charlotte Street, then turn left. You have now returned to the Visitor Center. From here, you may wish to continue with Part II of the Fredericksburg Walking Tour, which would lead you along the path of the Union assault and up to Marye's Heights. It's a bit longer at 2.7 miles, and much of it will be slightly uphill, but there is no better way to see what's left of what the Union troops saw as they advanced on the final day of the battle. Otherwise, your tour of the final day of battle—December 13—will begin at the south end of the battlefield.

FRANKLIN'S LINE AND PELHAM'S CORNER

> *From the Fredericksburg Visitor Center, proceed on Caroline Street (one-way) two blocks to George Street, then turn left. Take the next left onto Princess Anne Street and drive 0.5 mile to US 17 (Dixon Street), then turn right. Follow US 17 for 3.5 miles as it changes from Dixon Street to Tidewater Trail. This road was known as the Richmond Stage Road at the time of the battle, and Franklin's Right Grand Division formed on the left side of the road. At the intersection with Benchmark Road, pull into the mini-mall on the southwest corner and park in the parking lot, close to the intersection.*

Burnside awoke after only a few hours' sleep and finally drafted his orders for the day. They were issued at 6:00 AM, and Franklin received the orders for his Left Grand Division at 7:30. He had expected them to arrive the previous evening, and after reading the order, there was no doubt that it would have been better for everyone if they had.

The Union assault would be a two-pronged attack, as previously determined, even though all element of surprise was lost. Sumner's Right Grand Division would assault Marye's Heights, while Franklin's force would attack the Confederate right, formed on a ridge in front of him known as Prospect Hill and running north toward the other Confederate position. Beyond that, however, the order was vague and confusing. Franklin, never one to take initiative when it came to matters on the field, did not seek clarification of the order. In his eyes, he was to create a diversionary attack on this part of the line. Accordingly, he prepared one division—George Meade's, of John Reynolds's I Corps—to make the assault. The other two divisions of the I Corps, Abner Doubleday's and John Gibbon's, would support Meade's flanks.

Burnside's intent was not to create a diversion. In fact, Franklin's attack was to be the main assault. When Franklin gained the Confederate Military Road, he would head north toward Marye's Heights, giving the Federals in the town a fighting chance against that position. In later years, blame for this gross misinterpretation would be passed around between many. In the end, however, it underscored the fact that Burnside, who had barely allowed himself to rest over the previous weeks, was fatigued to the point of being unfit to command on December 13.

Meade, receiving his orders, warned Franklin that his attack could not be successful. He was confident that he could break the Confederate position, but with only one division and limited support, he knew he could not hold it. Franklin shrugged off his concerns; orders were orders. At 9:00 AM, as the fog began to lift slightly, Meade's three brigades began to form along the Richmond Stage Road. It would take almost an hour to get into position.

From your vantage point at the intersection, as you look north along Tidewater Trail, the Federals were setting up just a bit down the road on the opposite side, about

400 yards, with the rest of Franklin's forces behind. Tidewater Trail was the old Richmond Stage Road. The other road creating the intersection was an old country road that led to Hamilton's Crossing, the far right of the Confederate line.

Guarding the Confederate right, along with Stuart's horsemen, were 18 guns under Stuart's artillery commander, 24-year-old Major John Pelham. Pelham was already gaining a favorable reputation, having proven his mettle at Second Manassas and Antietam. Pelham proposed a bold and rather reckless venture to Stuart. He wanted to take one or two cannons far in front of the rest of the Confederate artillery and enfilade the Federal line. Stuart, himself known for daring exploits such as these, gave his approval. Pelham took a 12-pounder Napoleon, along with an artillery crew, forward to the corner where you now stand and gave birth to a Confederate legend.

Armed with solid shot, Pelham placed his gun in a low area obscured by hedges and what was left of the fog. At 10:00 AM, just as Meade's division was about to advance, Pelham fired his first round, drawing an immediate response from the Union artillery. The problem for the Federals was that they could not find Pelham. Pelham's crew, with their single piece, would fire a shot and then hit the ground to try and avoid any incoming fire. His crew did take casualties, but they continued firing as five full Union batteries attempted to stop the Confederate artillery, which many assumed must have been at battery strength. Before long, Stuart ordered Pelham to withdraw, saying he had done enough, but Pelham refused the order. Stuart gave the order a second and then a third time, but Pelham held his ground and kept firing. It was only when he finally ran out of ammunition that Pelham removed his gun and rejoined the Confederate line. Pelham, with his lone cannon, had delayed the Federal advance for almost an hour. Writing of the event the next day, General Lee, who observed the action with admiration, referred to Pelham's heroism and gallantry. To this day, you will find that virtually any mention of the young major will label him "the gallant Pelham."

You are now standing at Pelham's Corner, and as you can see, the mini-mall has graciously been named in his honor. It may not exactly be fitting of his exploits, but the corner where his single gun was placed has been preserved, memorialized by an old stone marker and several interpretive signs. The Confederate position is far to your left as you look at the intersection; you will have a much better look at it from the next stop, the Slaughter Pen.

Pelham's attack had more than a delaying effect on the Federals. The men of Meade's division, never able to discern exactly where the firing had come from, were a bit shaken. Doubleday's division, which was to support Meade's left during his assault, was now kept behind the Richmond Stage Road and angled to the southwest to protect the seemingly exposed Federal left. Meade, already concerned about the support he would receive, would have to move with even less than before.

The Slaughter Pen

> *From Pelham's Corner, return north on Tidewater Trail 1.1 mile. On your left, you will see the entrance to Slaughter Pen Farm, preserved by the Civil War Trust. Pull into the farm and park just past the interpretive signs.*

Jackson's Confederates, having had time to get in position, now waited for the Federal advance. The line consisted of 35,000 men and 54 guns, although the thick woods made artillery placement difficult. Still, all of those positions had the cover of the woods, and they would inflict plenty of damage that day. Jackson had stacked his divisions, creating a deep line running from Hamilton's Crossing, where the Richmond, Fredericksburg & Potomac Railroad curved to the west, to Deep Run, one of two streams between the position here and the town of Fredericksburg. A. P. Hill's division was in front, with William Taliaferro's and Jubal Early's divisions behind. Hill's brigades were lined up just behind the railroad, 1,000 yards west of the Richmond Stage Road.

At 11:00, after the excitement caused by Pelham's attack had died down, Meade and Gibbon re-formed their lines as an artillery duel opened. Although the Confederate guns that opened the fight had the upper hand for a time, soon all of the Federal guns were brought to bear. The barrage lasted for an hour, with the Confederates eventually pulling back. The Rebel batteries had taken such damage that part of Prospect Hill, which was hit particularly hard, became known as "Dead Horse Hill."

Slaughter Pen Farm, now preserved by the Civil War Trust.

The Union infantry finally advanced at noon. The 8,000 men in Meade's and Gibbon's divisions looked at a mostly open field in front of them, but unfortunately, it would not be a simple crossing. Drainage ditches crossed the plain, along with hedgerows and plenty of mud, not to mention Confederate artillery blanketing almost the entire area. The ground descended slightly to the railroad, after which it gradually rose to Prospect Hill, 65 feet above the plain, through thick, swampy woods. Only one stand of trees extended east beyond the railroad, almost directly across from where Meade lined up his division.

Behind that stand of trees, unknown to almost everyone, was the Union army's best possible chance of victory at Fredericksburg. A 600-yard gap existed in A. P. Hill's line between James Archer's and James Lane's divisions. Although the gap was pointed out to Hill, he thought the terrain in front enough to prevent any Federal progress there.

Meade's three brigades, commanded by Colonel William Sinclair on the right, Brigadier General Conrad Jackson on the left, and Colonel Albert Magilton behind, made their way across the field, taking casualties from the converging fire of the Confederate artillery and, as they approached the railroad, infantry. Before long, the neat lines of each unit did not exist; the broken terrain and Confederate fire scattered regiments and brigades easily. The advance continued, though, all the way to the railroad. Sinclair's brigade entered the stand of trees in front of the railroad and, to their surprise, found no Confederates. They kept advancing through the woods until they found some, eventually running into Maxcy Gregg's brigade in the second Confederate line.

Gregg, seemingly well behind the lines, had had his men stack their arms, hoping to prevent them from accidentally inflicting "friendly fire" casualties on any retreating Confederates. When firing did begin on his right, Gregg raced there to command his men to stop firing at what must be Confederate soldiers. By the time he finally realized in the limited visibility that they were indeed Union troops, Gregg had been mortally wounded.

Sinclair himself had been wounded and Colonel William McCandless was now in command of the Federal brigade. With some assistance from Conrad Jackson's brigade, the Union was now astride the Military Road, just as Burnside had designed. Gibbon's division, meanwhile, had come up to the right of Meade's. Meade's Third Brigade, Magilton's, struck at Lane's Confederate brigade while Gibbon assaulted the front at the railroad, attempting to flank the Confederates to the right. McCandless and Jackson went the other way, attacking to the left and hitting the left flank of Archer's brigade.

Meade's brigades began to roll up Confederate regiments as they moved down the line, catching them in crossfire between the two brigades. (Jackson was soon killed on the field, but his brigade fought on.) Unfortunately for George Meade, his premonition had come true. Although he had found a monstrous gap in the Confederate line, he and Gibbon could not hold the position by themselves. Franklin had ordered David Birney to line up his III Corps division on the Richmond Stage Road to be ready to support the assault, but there they stood. Meade, who had been at the railroad watching his attack lose momentum, sent three requests for Birney's division to come up but did not receive a response. Finally riding back to the line, a furious Meade tore into Birney, who replied that he was ordered by his superior (George Stoneman, commander of the III Corps) to take his orders for the day from John Reynolds, commander of the I Corps. Meade was not part of the bureaucratic picture. Thus the costly Federal breakthrough, which had accomplished exactly what Burnside had intended, went unsupported.

You are now standing in an area known after the battle as the Slaughter Pen. It was across this ground that Gibbon advanced to the right of Meade and attacked General James Lane's Confederates. The Civil War Trust has preserved this critical portion of the battlefield, which now contains a long walking trail, along with interpretive signs, that will explain the action on this often overlooked part of the field. The trail is 1.8 miles long, but is mostly along nice even ground. Make sure you're prepared for the hike; allow about 90 minutes to cover the trail. There is no shade along the way, so wear sunscreen.

Only one of Gibbon's brigades was able to cross the railroad, just to the left of where the trail will take you at its westernmost point. At this far end of the field, looking to your left, you will see a stand of trees crossing the railroad; although altered a bit over time, this is where Sinclair's Union brigade found the breakthrough point. (This land belongs to the National Military Park, but is currently undeveloped; made sure that as you tour the Slaughter Pen, you stay on the marked trail.)

Soon, Confederates from Early's division, held behind A. P. Hill's line, began to fill the gap and push the Federals back. The fighting became hand to hand around the railroad for both Meade's and Gibbon's divisions, but they were exhausted and running out of ammunition and soon headed for the rear. Early's men pursued them, sensing that they were triggering a rout of the Federals. Meade attempted to rally his men, but it was no use; Gibbon had been wounded and taken off the field, and the men were spent. The Confederate counterattack was uncoordinated, and although they did damage, its piecemeal nature could not gain any success. By this time, Birney's division was on the field, and Federal artillery began to tear the Confederates down as they attempted to cross the ground east of the railroad. As Early's battered men returned to their lines, he greeted them with pride, but then tore into their commanders for making the foolhardy attacks. Many of those who fell did so here at the Slaughter Pen.

At 2:15 PM, after receiving cryptic messages that seemed to indicate that the attack on the Confederate right had been going well, General Burnside received a dispatch saying that that was not the case. Burnside ordered Franklin to advance to his right front, but Franklin refused, saying that all his men were engaged. (In truth, the majority of his men had only taken some artillery fire, if that, and did not fire their weapons.) Franklin sensed that his left was threatened, and he asked for reinforcements. In the meantime, he had called up Sickles's division from the III Corps, and Sickles was mostly able to drive the rest of the Confederates back across the railroad.

Stonewall Jackson, seeing the Federal failures, had thoughts of an assault on the Federal position, but botched orders and the oncoming darkness led to the end of the fighting on the south end of the field. Artillery hammered on for a short while, but before too long the Federal guns had all but silenced the Confederates. The primary piece of Burnside's plan of attack, the assault on the Confederate left, did not fall into place. No ground was gained, and much blood was spilled needlessly. Unfortunately, the failure here was only a domino for what would become one of the Civil War's most infamous disasters.

THE CONFEDERATE RIGHT

Telegraph Hill/Lee's Hill

❯ *From Slaughter Pen Farm, turn left onto US 17 Business Route North (Tidewater Trail) and drive 2.0 miles to the ramp for VA 3. Take the ramp to your right for VA 3 West and drive 1.1 miles to Lafayette Boulevard. Turn left on Lafayette Boulevard and drive 0.2 mile to the park road at Lee Drive. Turn left on Lee Drive to reenter the National Military Park and drive 0.2 mile to the parking area on your left.*

The view of Fredericksburg from Lee's Hill.

This is Telegraph Hill, from which General Lee observed the battle on December 13. A quarter-mile climb to the top is rewarded with a view of Fredericksburg. The view is somewhat obscured by trees, but it is still lovely, particularly in winter when the leaves have fallen (and when the Battle of Freder-

Guns at Howison Hill.

icksburg took place). As he watched his men repeatedly repulse the Union attacks, it was here that Lee made a famous remark to Longstreet regarding war, saying that "It is well this is so terrible! We should grow too fond of it!" After the battle, the rise was much more commonly referred to as "Lee's Hill."

In addition to your view at the top, you will find a sheltered kiosk with interpretation not only of Lee's activity on the hill but also of the Second Battle of Fredericksburg, closely tied to the battle at Chancellorsville the following spring. Although the trail is short and the path is good, it is steep, so don't be afraid to stop to catch your breath on the way up.

Howison Hill

> *From Lee's Hill, continue on Lee Drive for 0.5 mile. Pull into the parking area on your left.*

Howison Hill held several pieces of Confederate artillery during the attacks on December 13. The artillery here would have been directed at the plain below Marye's Heights, only a mile to your north.

Union Breakthrough

> *From the parking area at Howison Hill, continue on Lee Drive for 3.5 miles. Pull into the parking area and then walk to the two interpretive signs on the left side of the road.*

The road that you have been driving on, Lee Drive, is what's left of the military road that Lee used to enable his command to move behind the lines. It was also one of the objects of Burnside's attack plan. You are now on Prospect Hill, the small rise where Jackson's forces were centered. This is the area where Meade's division found the gap in the first Confederate lines between Lane's and Archer's brigades, and where they ultimately found Maxcy Gregg's brigade in the second Confederate line.

Gregg was mortally wounded in the woods before you. During the battle, the visibility in these woods was usually no better than 50 yards, and you can see that it hasn't changed much, with thick undergrowth all around. It is no surprise that the Federals were able to approach Gregg's brigade with little warning.

Prospect Hill

> *Pull back onto Lee Drive and drive 0.5 mile to the end of the tour road. Pull into the parking area at Prospect Hill.*

This area marks the far right of the Confederate line, with the exception of Stuart's cavalry and artillery. This area of Prospect Hill, held by Colonel Reuben L. Walker's artillery, was that part of the field referred to as "Dead Horse Hill" for the many horses that fell here during the Union artillery barrage. The earthworks from Walker's position are fairly well preserved and plainly show how the artillery was placed in one of the few spots on the battlefield where it actually had some freedom to maneuver.

It may be somewhat difficult to see from this position, but as you look out at the open field, the tracks of the former Richmond, Fredericksburg & Potomac Railroad, still in use today, are not far in front of you and curve very close to your right. The fields beyond the tracks are where Conrad Jackson's (in front) and William Sinclair's (to your front left) brigades of Meade's division reached the railroad, fighting desperately with Archer's and then Early's Confederate brigades.

In the distance, alongside the railroad tracks to your left, you will see a stone pyramid standing alone. This marker is known as the Meade Pyramid, built in 1897 by the Richmond, Fredericksburg & Potomac Railroad as part of a project requested by the Confederate Memorial Literary Society. The railroad erected the marker to denote the spot of Meade's breakthrough for those riding the rails. The pyramid is meant to resemble a similar but much larger memorial at Richmond's Hollywood Cemetery, where 18,000 unknown Confederate dead lay at rest. (You may get a better

Earthworks remain at Prospect Hill, the far right of the Confederate line.

glimpse of the pyramid as you return down Lee Drive, where an interpretive marker stands on the right side of the road heading northwest.)

There is a very short walking trail at the end of the parking lot that will take you to Hamilton's Crossing. The crossing was a small rail depot where the railroad intersected an old mine road from the area's iron mines. Today, it will take you very near the still-active railroad tracks, so if you go, beware of trains passing by.

THE UNION ASSAULT AT MARYE'S HEIGHTS

Western Edge of Fredericksburg

❯ *From the parking lot at Prospect Hill, return down Lee Drive, driving 4.7 miles to Lafayette Boulevard (US 1). Turn right and follow Lafayette Boulevard 1.1 miles to Prince Edward Street/Kenmore Avenue, then turn left. Bear right onto Prince Edward Street and drive 0.2 mile to Charlotte Street. Turn left around the corner onto Charlotte Street and pull over.*

Burnside anxiously awaited word on the progress of the Union attack on the Confederate right. Everyone in the town of Fredericksburg had heard the assault begin hours before, but only short, incomplete messages gave any indication of the army's progress. Burnside's plan had called for Franklin's Left Grand Division to roll up the Confederate right before the attack on Marye's Heights by Sumner's Right Grand Division began, but it was already approaching noon. In Burnside's eyes, it could wait no longer. Every indication was that things were well on the left; it was time to assault the Confederate position in front.

The men in the town of Fredericksburg, most of whom had been staring at the strong Confederate works atop Marye's Heights for days, had done their best to arrange their lines within the town's narrow streets. Finally, the order to advance came. Sumner directed II Corps commander Darius Couch to begin the movement. Couch selected French's division to lead the assault, with Hancock's division in support. French's men began their advance at noon.

Before reaching the heights, the Federals had little in front of them, but were not without obstacles. Your location here at Prince Edward Street was approximately the western edge of the town. Today, it is very difficult to appreciate exactly what the men had to advance through because of the great amount of development that has occurred over the years. At the time of the battle, however, virtually the entire area from this point up to the heights, with the exception of a handful of buildings and fences, was open pasture.

The First Brigade of French's division—Kimball's—was essentially a massive skirmish line, designed to drive any Confederates on the plain back to the main Confederate line at Marye's Heights. As soon as they stepped out from the town onto the large plain that led to Marye's Heights, they began taking artillery fire, seemingly from every direction. Struggling to maintain their lines and with nothing to hide behind, Kimball's men advanced first to a canal ditch that ran across the fields. Quickly reforming in the shelter of the ditch and a small rise in front of it, the Federals were soon back out onto the field and on their way toward the Confederate line.

Canal Ditch

> *Proceed 0.1 mile on Charlotte Street to the next right at Kenmore Street. Turn right onto Kenmore Street and drive 0.1 mile to the five-way intersection with Hanover Street. Pull over near the intersection.*

Kenmore Street roughly follows the path of the former canal ditch, the remnants of which are mostly gone. The canal was approximately 15 feet wide and 5 feet deep. Union engineers had tried to drain the ditch before the battle, but fairly deep ice-cold water remained. There had been a few small plank bridges across the ditch, but most of these had been taken up by the Confederates. When the Federals came upon them, they either tried to slowly make their way across on what was left over or simply waded through the cold water.

If you walk to the intersection and turn left to go up Hanover Street, to your left you will see some semblance of the rise in the ground that protected the Federals after they emerged from the canal ditch. From this position, it is a bit easier to discern your distance from Marye's Heights, about 500 yards. Looking back toward the town, the tough climb that the attackers had—a low but long slope—becomes more obvious.

Kimball's men proceeded up the slope—near Hanover Street, where you now stand—and advanced toward the base of Marye's Heights, coming within 100 yards of a stone wall protecting the Confederate infantry. Kimball himself was wounded in the assault. Near the wall, a small swale provided just a bit of cover for this first group of Union attackers. Unfortunately, they would be far from the last to seek whatever cover they could get.

Only a portion of the original stone wall at the Sunken Road remains.

Marye's Heights

❯ *From the intersection, turn left onto Hanover Street and take the first left turn onto Weedon Street. Drive 0.3 mile on Weedon Street to Lafayette Boulevard. Turn right on Lafayette Boulevard and drive 0.2 mile to return to the National Park Visitor Center on your right.*

You are now at the base of Marye's Heights. The large rise in the ground on your left, as well as the ground that now holds Fredericksburg National Cemetery behind you, is where Longstreet placed his artillery. The Confederate infantry were lined up along the base of the heights in a sunken road, behind the stone wall you see before you.

If you aren't able to catch one of the guided park tours, there is a Sunken Road/Marye's Heights Walking Trail, as well as a walking tour of Fredericksburg National Cemetery, that will guide you through this small but critical piece of the Fredericksburg battlefield. Although virtually all of the area where Union blood was so senselessly spilled is now lost to development, the preserved Confederate position here at Marye's Heights helps to explain how, if not why, so many men were killed in such terrible fashion.

Start your tour at the large sign behind the Visitor Center that shows the Fredericksburg landscape as it was in 1862. From here, if it was difficult before, you may be

Fredericksburg National Cemetery.

able to get a sense of where you are on the battlefield. If you choose to take the trail up Marye's Heights, you will more easily be able to discern your location relative to the Union assaults, but this picture will help if you choose not to make the climb.

Walk through the parking area and onto the Sunken Road to your left. Looking up and down the road, one can see why this was such an obvious position for lining up infantry. The depth of the road makes the stone wall running front of it a perfect height for a breastwork. To be sure, Confederate blood was spilled behind this wall, but it was nothing compared to the slaughter below. As you walk along the lane, occasionally take a glance downhill toward the town (particularly when you reach Mercer Street and Kirkland Street), and imagine yourself firing at oncoming troops from behind the protection of this wall. It is no wonder that the Confederates had such confidence in their position.

Robert Ransom's division was behind the wall here in the center of the line at Marye's Heights. To his left was Richard Anderson's division, and to his right that of Lafayette McLaws. As the Federals became pinned down at the swale in front of the stone wall, the Confederates at the wall fired into them furiously at close range. Meanwhile, the next Union brigade, commanded by Colonel John Andrews, made their way up the hill. Andrews's brigade met the same result, with Andrews being wounded. Next up was Colonel Oliver Palmer's brigade, the last in French's division, and they, too, were stopped before the wall.

Crossing back in front of the stone wall, the former foundation of the Stephens House, present at the time of the battle, is outlined. Just a bit farther on is the original

Innis House. During the assault, although many did not even come close to driving this far up the hill, these homes, and the others existing at the time, soon had dozens and then hundreds of Union soldiers trying to take cover behind them. One look inside the windows of the Innis House might make you wonder how the home is still standing; the walls are still peppered with bullet holes from the battle.

At the northern end of the park boundary, you will find the Richard Rowland Kirkland Monument. After the fighting stopped on December 13, as wounded Union soldiers lay by the thousands on the slope in front of the wall, Kirkland and the other Confederates heard their cries as they suffered through the bitterly cold night. Most cried simply for water. Kirkland, a sergeant in the 2nd South Carolina, was unable to sit idle and asked permission to bring water to the wounded. Permission was denied, but he was told in not so many words that if he did venture out onto the field to be careful not to be shot, either by the Federals or, more likely, the Confederates still holding the line and watching for any movement in the darkness. Lading himself with canteens full of water, Kirkland ventured out beyond the Sunken Road and brought water to many of the wounded, at least temporarily relieving them in their anguish. Although it is likely that there were other Confederates who did the same, Kirkland's name is the one that has been passed down through history, becoming known on both sides of the line as "The Angel of Marye's Heights." Less than one year later, Kirkland was killed at the Battle of Chickamauga, September 20, 1863.

The monument to Richard Kirkland, the Angel of Marye's Heights.

Although most of the wall you see today has been reconstructed (part in the 1930s, part in 2004), the northernmost portion of the wall, near the Kirkland Monument, is the original stone wall from the battle. Walk around the end of the stone wall and then proceed down the Sunken Road. The large home atop the hill, Brompton, was present during the battle, but it now belongs to the University of Mary Washington and is private property, so do not attempt to climb the hill here. As you keep walking, you will soon come upon a path that you can take to climb Marye's Heights and see the vantage point of the Confederate artillerists. Before you climb the hill, though, just slightly past the paved path up Marye's Heights is a monument to General Thomas Cobb, mortally wounded during defense of the heights. Cobb and his brigade, better known as Cobb's Legion, had performed admirably throughout the early part of the war.

Although General Cobb was wounded near the Sunken Road, the vast majority of Confederate casualties on the Confederate left happened on Marye's Heights, not at the base. Confederate artillery suffered numerous casualties. Many Confederate infantry units were kept in reserve here, and as Confederates began to pour into the Sunken Road to increase their firepower, many were killed or wounded descending Marye's Heights to get to the road.

Walk up the paved path toward the rear of the white Richardson House, built after the war. The Marye's Heights trail will take you along some of the Confederate artillery positions. Although it may still be somewhat obscured, you should be able to see part of the old town of Fredericksburg, easily discernible by the church spires piercing the sky. (The view is somewhat better during the winter, when the trees have been cleared of their leaves.) Even with the blocked view, you can see that the position on Marye's Heights was, as many knew going into the battle, virtually impregnable.

With all three of French's brigades now on the hill, either killed, wounded, or pinned down, next in line was Hancock's division. His lead brigade got to within 50 yards of the stone wall, but no closer. Next up was the famous Irish Brigade, who made their assault at 12:30 PM, and although they may have gotten the closest to the wall at 25 yards, they too could not reach it. The last of Hancock's brigades was also cut down in the enfilading crossfire of Confederate artillery and musketry that blanketed the field below. Thus far, French's division had suffered approximately 1,160 casualties; Hancock's division, roughly 2,000, a 40 percent casualty rate.

As more Union soldiers made their way toward Marye's Heights, those who came before were barely, if at all, able to withdraw. The fire was so heavy that retreating down the hill was just as likely to get one killed as running up it, so those who survived often stayed right where they were as the assaults continued.

As the futility of these attacks became more apparent, the Federal commanders grew more resistant to sending their men up the hill. After French's and Hancock's divisions, Howard's division—all three brigades—met the same result. That was the last of the II Corps divisions to make the attempt; they were all spent. Sturgis's division of two brigades from the IX Corps moved to the left of the other divisions, trying to flank the Confederates out of the Sunken Road, but with no better luck. By 2:00 PM, ten brigades had assaulted the stone wall, and all ten had been destroyed.

At 2:15, Burnside received his first somewhat accurate report from the attack on the Confederate right. The report was not good, indicating that Franklin had made no progress and may have been in need of reinforcement. Still, Burnside saw a need to press the attack on Marye's Heights, his judgment clouded by stubbornness and fatigue. Burnside ordered Hooker to take his Grand Center Division into Fredericksburg to continue the assault on Marye's Heights. Observing the ground and quickly conferring with the division commanders who had already attempted the maneuver, Hooker sent back a request that the order be canceled. When Burnside would not do so, Hooker rode back to Burnside's headquarters to protest in person, receiving the same reply. Livid, Hooker went back to Fredericksburg and ordered Daniel Butterfield's V Corps into the fray.

Unfortunately, the story does not change. Butterfield's V Corps, Stoneman's III Corps, and Willcox's IX Corps all sent brigades in, only to have them torn apart. Even after sundown, which thankfully came early on this December 13, brigades were being sent against the wall. Thousands of Union troops—dead, wounded, and living— became obstacles, covering the ground and making advance difficult.

At 5:00 PM, Colonel Rush Hawkins's brigade of George Getty's division, IX Corps, made their assault. Hawkins's brigade took only half the number of casualties the others did, but only because the darkness prevented the Confederates from seeing

THE "AWFUL ARITHMETIC"

Unlike their Confederate counterparts, Union generals were often unwilling to put their troops at risk, moving slowly and cautiously. The longer this went on, the less the American people would tolerate results like those at Fredericksburg. Lincoln, however, knew that although aggressive action caused higher casualties, it would also win the war more quickly. In what he called the "awful arithmetic," Lincoln realized that even though the Union had suffered 50 percent more casualties than the Confederates at Fredericksburg, if that battle were fought with the same result over seven days, the Confederate army would be wiped out, while the Federals would still have a sizable force. It would not be until Ulysses S. Grant took control that any general in the east would subscribe to Lincoln's view, and ultimately it is that strategy that won the war for the Union.

them. Still, they could not approach the wall. Although Confederates at the wall sniped at the moving mass of Union soldiers just in front of them, the fight was over.

From atop Marye's Heights, you can either retrace your steps back the way you came or, better yet, return through Fredericksburg National Cemetery. The cemetery was established in 1865 and contains more than 15,000 fallen Union soldiers, most of whom remain unknown, from Fredericksburg and other battlefields. To return to the Visitor Center, bear to your left and walk through the cemetery gate. If you have time, however, take a stroll through the peaceful cemetery to reflect on those who paid with their lives the terrible cost of both Fredericksburg and the Civil War.

The night of December 13, many of the Union soldiers slept on the hill, unable to move lest they be seen and shot. Those who survived the cold night, and many did not, found what little sleep they could between the bodies of their dead comrades. Remarkably, Burnside wanted to continue the assault the next morning, but his generals, to his shock, unanimously recommended against it. On December 14, the Confederates expected and hoped for a renewal of the attack, but it did not come. At the south end of the field, Jackson allowed a temporary cease-fire so that each side could retrieve their wounded, and in Fredericksburg, the same happened the next day, December 15. Remarkably, as the two sides walked through the dead, fraternization was common; those who were mercilessly butchering each other only hours before found common ground in the senseless horror they had just witnessed, even if it was of their own doing. The night of December 15, Burnside mercifully gave the order for the Federals to retreat to the other side of the Rappahannock, leaving Fredericksburg to the Confederates.

On the night of December 14, a brilliant display of the aurora borealis, or northern lights, appeared in the skies above Fredericksburg. Under the circumstances, it was difficult for many not to interpret such a rare and spectacular event as having some meaning. The butchery at Fredericksburg would not be permitted to simply go unnoticed by any higher power. The Union suffered 12,653 casualties at Fredericksburg. Although the Confederate total was large at 5,309, it was well less than half the Federal total. Worse, few could find sense in the slaughter. The Union attacks had been repulsed and stubbornly repeated, time and time again, and lives had been wasted. While the Confederates had scored a well-earned victory, it was little else. As Stonewall Jackson opined before the battle, the simple killing of Yankee soldiers, who could and would be replaced, was a hollow victory if unac-

> **CASUALTIES**
>
> Confederate: killed, 595; wounded, 4,061; missing or captured, 653; total: 5,309
>
> Union: killed, 1,284; wounded, 9,600; missing or captured, 1,769; total: 12,653
>
> **Total Casualties: 17,962**

companied by strategic gain, as this battle was. Confederate morale was high, and they had much to be proud of, but they had gained nothing in the process.

KELLY'S FORD

Kelly's Ford Site

❯ *From the Fredericksburg Visitor Center, pull right out of the parking lot onto Lafayette Boulevard and drive 0.4 miles to the ramp for VA 3 (Blue and Gray Parkway). Continue on VA 3 for 1.7 miles and then take the ramp for I-95 North. Drive 2.7 miles on I-95 North to Exit 133 for US 17 North/Warrenton Road. Continue on US 17 for 17.1 miles to CR 634 (Courtney's Corner Road). Turn left and drive 5.4 miles, staying with the road as it changes to Country Road 651 (Sumerduck Road). Turn left at CR 620 (Edwards Shop Road, Kellys Ford Road) and drive 0.4 miles. As soon as you cross the bridge over the Rappahannock River, pull into the parking area on your left.*

After Fredericksburg, the armies remained where they were, facing each other across the Rappahannock. The soldiers resumed what had been an unspoken truce for picket duty, not shooting at each other and even trading newspapers, coffee, tobacco, and, of course, verbal jabs across the river.

The Rappahannock River near Kelly's Ford.

In the high command on the Union side, politics reigned. The entire army, from top to bottom, had lost confidence in Burnside. Several generals complained openly about their commander, never a good practice for building troop morale. Burnside was furious, but he attempted to stay above the fray. Knowing the administration was under great scrutiny, on December 22, he even went so far as to write a letter to the press putting the responsibility for Fredericksburg squarely on his own shoulders. Standard behavior for a good leader, to be sure, but considering the conduct of other generals, it was remarkable.

In late January, Burnside sealed his fate. On January 20, 1863, Burnside's Left and Center Grand divisions broke camp and began to move, resuming the winter campaign. By afternoon the roads had thawed. A light rain began that evening and soon turned to a downpour. The resulting mud made the roads unusable. Wagons and artillery were lost over embankments. Horses and mules were killed, breaking their legs, becoming too stuck to move, even drowning in the mud. With the element of surprise lost and his army's morale sinking even lower than his wagons, Burnside called for a return to camp, only to have the armies go through the same ordeal on the return trip. It went down in history as the "Mud March." Throughout, many generals continued to openly lambaste their leader.

Upon his return on January 24, Burnside took a train to Washington to meet with Lincoln, handing him two documents. One was General Order No. 8, not yet enacted, which called for the dismissal of a good number of his generals, including Franklin, Hooker, and others who had been openly critical of Burnside. The other document was his resignation. Burnside could not continue leading the army unless the general order was enacted. Lincoln agreed with the order but asked Burnside to return the next day. After sleeping on the decision, Lincoln relieved Burnside of command and placed Hooker in charge of the Army of the Potomac, but agreed to execute much of General Order No. 8. He would not accept Burnside's resignation, though, and gave him a 30-day furlough. A much-relieved Burnside returned to Falmouth to give Hooker command, as well as deliver new orders to other generals. William Franklin, Baldy Smith, and other generals were either relieved of command or reassigned. Edwin Sumner was also relieved, mostly because of age.

The men of the Army of the Potomac were glad to see a change made, but were mostly indifferent to Hooker as the new commander. Within a short time, that would change. Hooker practically remade the army, conducting a thorough reorganization and enacting strict disciplinary but morale-building rules. Tackling perhaps the most severe problem, Hooker reduced desertions from 30 percent of his absentees to 4 percent. Furloughs began to be granted by lottery and by merit. More inspectors were authorized, and they were given greater authority. Mandatory rations—soft bread four times per week, fresh or desiccated vegetables three—were enacted, and supply sergeants were held accountable for providing them. Indeed, the entire supply system was revamped, and up to 140 railroad cars of supplies were now reaching the army per day. Within two months, Hooker took the Army of the Potomac from its lowest point ever to being happy, fit, disciplined, and proud.

For the Confederates, morale was not the problem; in fact, the Confederates were overconfident, at this point thinking they were practically invincible. The problem was food, or rather getting food to the men. The army was supplied by a one-track railroad, meaning that they only received two trains of supplies per day. To relieve the pressure, Lee sent much of his artillery and cavalry south so that the horses could have fresh forage. To meet a potential threat on the peninsula (the Union IX Corps had been shipped there temporarily), Lee sent Hood's and Pickett's divisions south, along with Longstreet, reducing the number of mouths to feed by 20,000.

This did not completely quiet Confederate activity, however. Stuart's cavalry still conducted frequent raids. On February 24, cavalry under Fitzhugh Lee, in an attempt to gather information about the Union strength, charged through the Federal picket lines and made it all the way to the main infantry before turning back.

Before he left, Fitz Lee left a note for William Averell, now leading a division in the new cavalry-only corps Hooker had created as part of his reorganization. Averell and Lee had been classmates and good friends at West Point. Lee's note said, "I wish you would put up your sword, leave my state, and go home. You ride a good horse, I ride a better. If you won't go home, return my visit, and bring me a sack of coffee."

For Hooker, it was the last straw. Since the beginning of the war, Confederate cavalry had been superior to the Union's to the point of embarrassment. Now was the time to put his new cavalry corps to the test. Averell volunteered to launch a cavalry attack right at them, with him in command. Hooker quickly gave his approval.

On the evening of March 16, Averell took two brigades of cavalry, along with their light artillery, north along the Rappahannock. The 2,200 troopers gathered at Morrisville for the night and sent a scouting party ahead to Kelly's Ford. The next morning, March 17, Averell's men arrived at the ford to discover his scouting party in a shootout with a small party of Confederates. The Confederates knew that Union cavalry had left the camp; they just didn't know where they were heading. There were not many of them—about 85—but they were in a strong defensive position and had lined the ford with abatis. Averell decided that a forced crossing of the ford would be best. Three times the cavalry charged the crossing, and three times they were repulsed. After some of the Federals braved the fire to clear much of the abatis, however, the fourth crossing was successful, and they captured many of the Confederates.

From the gravel parking lot, you can either walk down to the river or walk up to the bridge to overlook the river. (In either case, use caution.) The location of the ford is not at the bridge itself, but by looking downstream (to your right) you can just see the shallows of the Rappahannock where the ford was located. Although the land around the ford is privately owned, you can always spend a night at the Inn at Kelly's Ford, which owns the property on the south bank of the Rappahannock.

Averell's troopers were on the far bank, while the Confederates were on the side of the river where you parked. If you approach the bank of the river from the parking area, you may notice an old stone millrace. That same millrace, downstream of you, was what the Confederates guarding the ford used for cover as they repulsed the initial Union charges.

Stone Wall/Pelham Monument

> *From the parking area at Kelly's Ford, pull out to the left and take the immediate right onto Kellys Ford Road. Drive 0.8 mile on Kellys Ford Road to a gravel area on your right. Pull into this area and park.*

Knowing full well that his good friend Fitz Lee would arrive with the intention of attacking, Averell decided to put his cavalry into a defensive position. A stone wall on the farm of C. T. Wheatley seemed to be a good choice for a position, so the Federals set themselves up behind the wall.

A marker at the spot where the gallant John Pelham was mortally wounded.

At 7:30, in Culpeper, Fitzhugh Lee learned of the Federal crossing at Kelly's Ford and raced to get his cavalry in order. Although Union intelligence had placed the Confederate cavalry at approximately 3,000, it was actually closer to 800. Also in Culpeper, somewhat by chance, were Stuart and John Pelham, both of whom decided to ride along. Stuart left Lee in command.

You are now standing at the old Wheatley Farm. As you face away from the paved road and look down the gravel road in front of you, the land to your left was where most of the action took place early in the fight. In 1863, however, the area was clear of trees. If you walk down the gravel road, on your right, you will occasionally see piles of stone. These are the remnants of the stone wall that the Federals formed behind, and while most of it is gone (it was much taller at the time of the battle), it is still easily discernible.

Lee and his Confederates arrived at noon. As Averell predicted, Lee immediately formed a cavalry charge against the Federal position at the wall using the Third Virginia, one of his five regiments present. As they charged in column, four abreast, they headed straight for the wall and then turned left. Averell's stationary cavaliers, along with his artillery, easily took out many of the Confederates, who attacked mostly with pistol and saber. As the Third Virginia moved along the wall, they eventually found the gate and were met there by the Fifth Virginia. Also waiting at the gate was Pelham, acting as cheerleader. When one of the Federal shells burst overhead, Pelham was hit in the back of the head with an artillery fragment. He was carried to the rear, where he soon died of his wound.

If you keep walking along the gravel road, you will eventually reach a point where it curves to the right. Not far beyond that curve is a stone monument to mark where Pelham was mortally wounded. The walk is about 1 mile there and back, but the trail is easy and usually well cared for.

After the Confederates made it through the gate, they lunged at the Union right, but the Federals repulsed the charge as they rode between the outbuildings of the Wheatley Farm. Meanwhile, Colonel Alfred Duffie, an experienced French horseman leading Averell's First Brigade, countercharged the remaining three Confederate regiments. Fitz Lee had no choice but to withdraw his cavalry through some trees and into the next field.

Final Charge

> *From the parking area at the stone wall, pull out to your right and drive 2.0 miles on Kellys Ford Road. Carefully pull over to the right before the stream (Carter's Run). There is not a lot of room here, so use extra caution.*

The field on the right side of the road is where the final stages of the battle played out. Fitzhugh Lee's Confederates and Averell's Federals lined up facing each other, 600 yards apart. As you face the field, the Federals were to your right, the Confederates to your left.

Again, Averell correctly predicted that his old friend would charge. Just as before, Averell's stationary horsemen and his artillery easily outgunned the rushing Confederates, quickly breaking up the charge. Instead of countercharging, though, Averell hesitated. One of the captured Confederates indicated that Stuart was on the field,

The scene of the final charge at the battle of Kelly's Ford.

and a train whistle was heard from the nearby Orange & Alexandria Railroad. (Fitz Lee had asked an engineer to run his train back and forth, blowing the whistle.) These two factors led Averell to believe that reinforcements were coming, and he withdrew his forces. Although a stunning victory over the Confederate cavalry was given away, the showing by the Federal cavalry was a remarkable turn of events. From this point on, the Confederates would have to take Union cavalry seriously.

Two Union horsemen, too seriously wounded to make it back to camp, were left, along with a Federal surgeon. Also left was a sack of coffee with an attached note. The note read, "Dear Fitz. Here's your coffee. Here's your visit. How do you like it?"

GERMANNA FORD

❯ *From the Kelly's Ford battlefield, continue north on Kellys Ford Road 0.4 mile, then turn left on Newbys Shop Road (SR-673). Drive 1 mile on Newbys Shop Road and then turn right on Thoms Road (SR-675). Drive 2.3 miles to Carrico Mills Road (SR-669) and then drive 3.7 miles. Turn left onto VA 3 (Germanna Highway) and drive 5.5 miles. Immediately after crossing the Rapidan River, pull into the parking area for the Germanna Visitor Center on your left.*

The organizational changes that Hooker made after taking command were significant. Burnside's Grand Divisions were scrapped, leaving Hooker with seven corps of infantry plus his new cavalry corps, led by George Stoneman. At the corps and divisional level, many were being promoted to fill the holes that were created by the housecleaning after Fredericksburg, leaving Hooker with leaders who were good fighters but whose command potential was still unknown. The protection of Washington, which had been a severe restriction on the army's previous commanders, was now its own separate, unattached department. Finally, one of Hooker's stipulations upon taking command was that he would only work directly with the president, not through Henry Halleck.

Perhaps the most significant change, however, was the creation of the Bureau of Military Intelligence (BMI). Hooker chose Dan Butterfield, former commander of the V Corps, to be his chief of staff, and Butterfield recommended Colonel George Sharpe to head up the new intelligence network. Previously, McClellan had relied on the Pinkerton Agency to provide his intelligence. The biggest problem with the information provided—besides the fact that it was often incorrect—was that it was given only in the form of raw data. The BMI would change that. Sharpe created a network of spies, cracked codes, executed ruses, and performed other intelligence-gathering methods that would be overseen by military personnel, not civilians, who could verify the information coming in. The result was instant and remarkable. Within the first few months of his command, Hooker knew almost precisely where every unit of the Army of Northern Virginia was located, how strong they were, and when they moved. Only days before the battle, BMI put Confederate strength at 54,600, underestimating by only 1,600 men, and their artillery at 243 guns, 23 over the actual total. Other security practices were also put into place: the press was stifled and pickets were accompanied by officers to prevent fraternization with Confederates. It was an amazing contrast to previous practice.

On April 12, following a week where President Lincoln personally reviewed the troops and conferred with Hooker in Falmouth, Butterfield arrived at the White House to personally deliver the general's plan for the spring campaign. It was for the president only; even Secretary of War Edwin Stanton was excluded.

From his intelligence, Hooker knew that the Confederates were starving and relied only on the single-track Richmond, Fredericksburg & Potomac Railroad for supply. If this line were to be cut, Lee would be forced to leave the Fredericksburg defenses, either to fall back or attempt to move west to Culpeper. Therefore, the key to Hooker's plan was to have Stoneman's cavalry corps quietly move south of the Confederate army to cut the railroad. The infantry, also in concealed movements, would cross the Rappahannock upstream of Lee's position, turning the Confederate left. Once out of the Fredericksburg defenses, Hooker could fight them on a battleground of his choosing. Stoneman's 10,000 horsemen would be between Lee and Richmond, keeping him away from the capital. Lincoln gave his assent, and explicit orders were issued to Stoneman to leave the very next day.

As part of Stoneman's raid, Butterfield threw off the Confederates with a simple but devastatingly effective ruse. Knowing from the BMI that the Confederates had cracked the Union signal flag code, Butterfield had a signalman deliver a message down the line that the Federal cavalry was moving out toward the Shenandoah Valley. The Confederates, including Lee, bought it hook, line, and sinker, moving most of their cavalry 20 miles west of their army to intercept the "oncoming" cavalry. When Stoneman was stalled for some time crossing the Rappahannock, it was assumed that he had simply run into complications, but was still going to head west.

Knowing that the Confederates were guarding Banks' Ford and U.S. Ford heavily, three corps of Hooker's infantry—his flanking wing, conducting the main attack—would cross the Rappahannock River at the relatively unguarded Kelly's Ford, then cross the Rapidan River at Germanna and Ely's Fords. Two other corps would demonstrate heavily against the Confederate right, downstream of Fredericksburg, while the final two would temporarily remain in camp, giving the impression that the Federals had not moved, and would later serve as a reserve. Hooker's flanking wing would then move through unguarded Chancellorsville and hit the Confederates on their exposed left and rear.

On paper, the plan was brilliant, but it still needed to be executed. On April 27, the Union soldiers got their chance. The V, XI, and XII corps, just under 40,000 strong, set off from camp in complete secrecy, leaving their shelters up and traveling light, with little artillery and few wagons, the soldiers carrying eight days' rations. Along the way, civilians were sequestered by advance parties so that they would not see the army's movements. They made a good march and reached their designated stopping point, 14 miles short of Kelly's Ford.

At 4:00 AM the next morning, the flanking wing set off for their next point, 1.5 miles from Kelly's Ford, arriving at 4:30 PM. At 6:00 PM, a group of sharpshooters filled a number of pontoon boats 500 yards downstream from the ford and stormed the opposite bank, with the few Confederates present quickly scattering. (The pontoon was brought overland, again in secrecy, and arrived at the same time as the soldiers.) The bridge was completed and the XI Corps was over the Rappahannock by 10:30 PM, with the other two corps to cross in the morning. On the same day, April 28, the Union I and VI corps moved their corps downstream, remaining behind Stafford Heights and lighting no fires. The II and III corps moved slightly upriver, with the exception of John Gibbon's division of the II Corps, who stayed in camp and kept up business as usual—picket duty, lighting fires, raising a reconnaissance balloon, even conducting a review for some citizens.

Thus far, over two days, Hooker's disciplined soldiers had performed marvelously. The first slip-up only came on the evening of April 28 when a captain from the XI Corps became lost in the dark and was captured. He freely told the Confederates what he knew—which wasn't much. Hooker had not even filled in his corps commanders on the complete plan yet. He did reveal, though, that the Union XI Corps had crossed the Rappahannock with 14,000 men. J. E. B. Stuart, in Culpeper, found out at 9:00 PM, but because the telegraph stations were down for the night, he could not get the information to General Lee until the next morning.

That morning, August 29, downstream of Fredericksburg, the I and VI corps began building five bridges to cross the Rappahannock in two areas—Franklin's crossing, where General Franklin had crossed during the Battle of Fredericksburg, and Fitzhugh's Crossing, about 1 mile downstream. The building of the bridges, which was supposed to be completed by 3:30 AM, was far behind schedule, and the Confederates were alerted to the Union presence before they crossed. This had much to do with the fact that the chief engineer for both operations, Henry Benham, was so drunk he could not even stay on his horse, and several times shouted at his men from the bank of the river. Still, all five bridges were complete by noon, the two corps united, and soon 16,800 Federals were across the river, facing Stonewall Jackson's entire corps, which had been called up to face the sudden Union threat.

Even when Lee heard about the "division" that had crossed at Kelly's Ford—the XI Corps was the smallest in the army, and Stuart labeled them incorrectly based on their number—he still surmised that the attack would be at or below Fredericksburg. Stoneman's cavalry would probably move to cut the Orange & Alexandria Railroad, near Gordonsville, and the Federal infantry was only there to support them. Three days into Hooker's plan, it was working better than anyone could have hoped.

After the XII and V corps crossed at Kelly's Ford, the army split into two. George Meade's V Corps would cross the Rapidan at Ely's Ford, while Henry Slocum's XII and Oliver Howard's XI corps would cross at Germanna Ford. The three corps commanders now had their orders: gain control of the two fords and proceed to the crossroads at Chancellorsville as swiftly as possible.

You are now at Germanna Ford. The ford is located on the north side (downstream) of the bridge you drove over before you pulled into the Germanna Visitor Center. The Federals of the XI and XII corps approached from the same direction as you did. Here at the Visitor Center there are several historic markers, but most of them have to do with General Grant's crossing of Germanna Ford in 1864. It is possible to view the ford itself from the bridge over the Rapidan, but if you choose to do this, be extremely careful; you would have to drive in the opposite direction and pull onto the shoulder after crossing the bridge.

Confederate engineers were working on a bridge here on April 29 when a citizen came running toward them at 11:00 AM shouting that the Yankees were coming. In disbelief, the engineers sent one man down the road on horseback. Just as he was about to turn back, he spotted a squadron of Union cavalry and raced back to warn his men. It was not quite quick enough, however, and the Federal infantry came up and easily took the ford. By nightfall, the entire Union column was camped on the south bank of Germanna Ford.

The crossing of the V Corps at Ely's Ford was much less eventful; it was guarded by only 12 Confederate pickets, all of whom ran before a shot was fired. Meade's corps was in camp on the south bank of the Rapidan by 10:00 PM. Ely's Ford is located near where Ely's Ford Road (CR 610) crosses the Rapidan River, just a few miles northwest of Chancellorsville Tavern. There is a boat launch on the east side of the road on the south bank that is at the location of the original ford. If you would like to see Ely's Ford, the exact location can be found in Appendix A.

CHANCELLORSVILLE

Chancellorsville Visitor Center

❭ *From Germanna Ford, continue on VA 3 East (Germanna Highway) for 9.3 miles. The Visitor Center for the Chancellorsville Unit of Fredericksburg & Spotsylvania National Military Park will be on your left.*

The Visitor Center for the Chancellorsville Unit of the Park shows a film on the battle and is the central point for touring the battlefield. It also serves as the ranger station for the Wilderness and Spotsylvania battlefields. In addition to a small museum, you'll find information about the park's ranger-guided programs as well as the

The Visitor Center at the Chancellorsville battlefield.

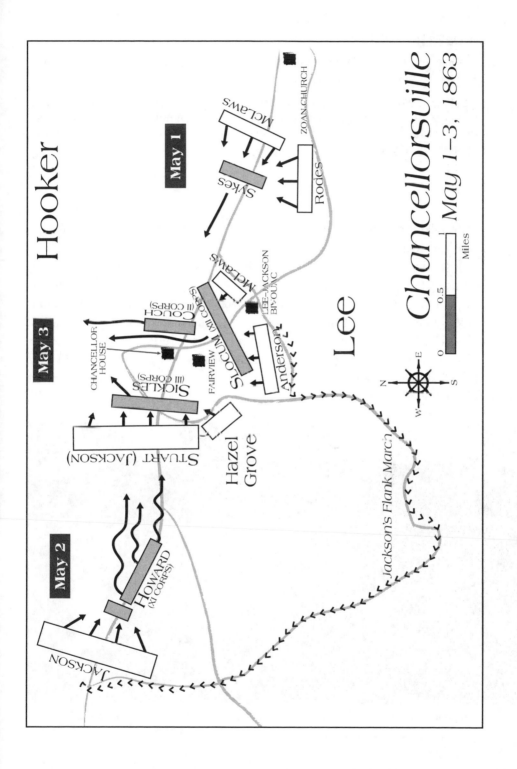

Chancellorsville
May 1–3, 1863

Hooker

Lee

May 1

May 2

May 3

ZOAN CHURCH

McLAWS

RODES

SYKES

McLAWS

LEE–JACKSON
BIVOUAC

ANDERSON

SLOCUM (XII CORPS)

COUCH (II CORPS)

CHANCELLOR
HOUSE

FAIRVIEW

SICKLES (III CORPS)

STUART (JACKSON)

Hazel
Grove

HOWARD
(XI CORPS)

JACKSON

Jackson's Flank March

Miles

0   0.5

N
W   E
S

many walking and driving tours that will take you through the rather large Chancellorsville battlefield.

Just behind the Visitor Center is the site where Stonewall Jackson was mortally wounded. If you listen to the short ranger-guided program while you are here, you will visit the site. Otherwise, you will see it later on your tour. There is also a long walking tour called the Chancellorsville History Trail that begins and ends at the Visitor Center. The trail is 4 miles long and covers a good portion of the battlefield, particularly the third day's fighting, and will take you to the Chancellorsville Inn and through the Union and Confederate lines. The brochure can be picked up inside the Visitor Center.

Little remains of the Chancellor House, focal point of the battle of Chancellorsville.

Chancellor House

⟩ *From the Visitor Center, return to VA 3 East (watch the one-way roads). Turn left onto VA 3 East and drive 0.8 mile to Ely's Ford Road (CR 610). Turn left on Ely's Ford Road and pull into the parking area on your left.*

The early morning hours of April 30 found Meade's advance cavalry on the move, headed south on the Ely's Ford Road for the Chancellorsville crossroads. After briefly skirmishing with and driving off Confederate pickets, the soldiers took possession of the crossroads here. By noon, the rest of the V Corps had arrived. The XI and XII corps arrived midafternoon, making the junction of the flanking wing complete. Meade wished to press east and keep going, but Slocum, placed in charge of the flanking wing as Hooker attended to matters on the other side of the line, said that their orders were to wait here until the II and III corps arrived. They were to form a defensive position around the Chancellor House and wait for the Confederates to be forced out of their Fredericksburg defenses.

The stone foundation you see before you is what's left of the Chancellorsville Inn. The Inn was the home of the widow Chancellor, along with seven of her nine children. Having entertained Confederate officers many times in the previous months (six of the seven Chancellor children were attractive young ladies, the seventh a son), their reception of the Federals was cold, to say the least, especially after hearing that their home would be taken over for General Hooker's headquarters.

Virginia Route 3, which you used to get to Chancellorsville Inn, was the Orange Turnpike at the time of the battle. The Turnpike itself was a replacement for another road, the Orange Plank Road, which runs mostly to the south, although the two roads do overlap for a portion, as they do here at the crossroads. Knowing that the crossroads provided direct routes not only to Fredericksburg but also to several of the fords, Hooker arranged for the Federals to form a defensive line around this spot. One of Meade's divisions formed a line 2 miles north of the crossroads on the Ely's Ford

The view toward Fairview from Hazel Grove.

Road, while his other two faced east, spanning the Orange Turnpike. Slocum's XII Corps formed to their right and curved south and west across the Orange Plank Road, while Howard's XI Corps finished the curve, crossing the Turnpike west of the crossroads.

Walk around the ruins of the Chancellorsville Inn and read the interpretive signs to learn more about the Chancellor family and how they survived the war. The Inn would not survive the battle; it would be set aflame by Confederate artillery. It was rebuilt shortly afterward, but again burned to the ground in 1927. Notice also, across the highway, a long clearing in the trees leading up to a hilltop. Near the bottom of the hill stood Fairview, a large estate, while at the top was the Hazel Grove Farm. You will visit both of these sites on your tour, but for now, remember your clear view of them from the Chancellor House.

Although delayed in their bridge-building efforts at U.S. Ford, which was now unguarded with the Federal advance, the II Corps (minus Gibbon's division, who was still in camp keeping up the ruse) crossed the Rappahannock and camped just north of Chancellorsville. The III Corps would be crossing at 7:00 AM the next morning. Finally, at 6:00 PM, Hooker arrived to establish his headquarters. For three days, the Federals had been executing their movements perfectly. It was now just a matter of time before Stoneman's cavalry cut off the Confederate supply line and they were forced into the waiting arms of the Union army.

Zoan Church

> *From the parking area at the Chancellor House, turn right to get to the intersection with VA 3 and then turn left onto VA 3. Drive 3.6 miles to the Zoan Baptist Church on your right; pull in and drive to the end of the parking lot.*

Atop Telegraph Hill, already being called Lee's Hill, Robert E. Lee scanned the horizon, looking at the nearly 3-mile-long line of Federal soldiers along the Rappahannock. They stood opposite Prospect Hill, south of Fredericksburg, where Jackson placed his corps for the Battle of Fredericksburg and where they stood today, awaiting the Union attack on the Confederate right. After watching for several minutes, Lee closed his spyglass, turned to his aide, and said, "The main attack will come from above."

Above meant the Confederate left—not here, where masses of Union soldiers were in plain view, but where hints of Federal activity had been arising for the last two days. Stuart had gathered some intelligence, although much of it had been delayed. W. H. F. "Rooney" Lee, Robert E. Lee's son, had been watching Stoneman's cavalry, which was now surely not advancing to Gordonsville. As a cautionary measure, Lee had sent Richard Anderson's division toward Chancellorsville the previous night, April 29, to meet any threat to the exposed Confederate left. After considering all the evidence, he was now certain in his determination.

Anderson had formed a line just west of the Chancellorsville crossroads that night, but as dawn came on April 30 he realized that his defensive position was not exactly ideal. His location, encompassing Chancellorsville and most of the surrounding area, was in the Wilderness, an area characterized by its deep forest and thick, tangled underbrush. Visibility was poor and there was not much room to maneuver, so Anderson pulled his division to a clearing 3.5 miles east of Chancellorsville near the Zoan Church.

The Zoan Baptist Church you see here is the descendant of the former, and today the church building sits in the same location as the previous one did. Although it takes an informed eye today, it is apparent why Anderson chose this position for his line. As you look across the highway at the shopping center, look at the area just left of it (west) where another church sits today. You will notice the ground rises suddenly and significantly, forming a nice ridge right across the former turnpike. It was this feature, along with the surrounding open field, that made this position so attractive to the Confederates.

As the situation became more apparent to Robert E. Lee, he realized that more than just one division would be needed to hold off the Federals, whose size had grown from one division to the three corps that they actually were. He sent Anderson his chief engineer to prepare defensive works around his line and wired Richmond to hurry E. Porter Alexander's artillery that had been sent south for the winter. Lafayette McLaws's division moved west that night to reinforce Anderson, arriving at 1:00 AM on May 1. Finally, Jackson would leave only Early's division below Fredericksburg and one brigade on Marye's Heights in the town. The rest of his corps—three divisions— would leave at dawn to join the rest of the Confederates on the left. Lee was shifting almost all of his army to meet what he was certain was their biggest threat, leaving just a shell to face the diversion in front of him. Although the Confederates were now faced in the right direction, they were also doing exactly what Hooker wanted them to.

First Day at Chancellorsville Battlefield

> *Pull out of the parking lot for Zoan Church and make a U-turn on VA 3 so that you are heading west. Drive 1.5 miles on VA 3. On your right, you will see a Civil War Trust sign, as well as the Lick Run Community Center. Pull into the parking lot.*

Stonewall Jackson arrived at Zoan Church at 8:30 AM on May 1, well ahead of his three divisions. Having been briefed by Lee, Jackson knew what lay to the west, although he didn't know where the Federals were. He immediately ordered Anderson's and McLaws's men to abandon their works and fall into line. They would not be defending anything today. They would be on the attack, and they would not be waiting for the Confederates behind them.

The Confederate line that Anderson and McLaws had formed stretched across the Orange Turnpike and the Orange Plank Road. The two roads merged before they reached Chancellorsville, so Jackson decided to send columns on both. McLaws would command the column on the turnpike, totaling 13,000 men, while Jackson took command of the other column. With the upcoming reserves from his corps, this column would have 27,000 troops. By 10:30 AM both columns were heading west into the Wilderness.

Hooker had known better than to fight in the Wilderness. In fact, his primary goal on May 1 was to clear the way so his army could get out of the Wilderness and in position to attack Lee's flank and rear just west of Fredericksburg. But since the previous afternoon, when Slocum had denied Meade's request to keep heading west, the army had stayed at Chancellorsville while it waited for the II and III corps to join them. The Union army spent almost 24 hours surrounding the Chancellorsville Crossroads.

As far as Hooker knew, Jackson was still south of Fredericksburg, so the forces he sent out to gain the Union positions in the late morning on May 1 were comparatively light. Meade took two divisions northeast on the River Road, 10,850 men. Two other divisions under Slocum, 13,450 men, marched southeast down the Orange Plank Road. The center column, marching due east on the Orange Turnpike, was George Sykes's division. It would be Sykes's division who would collide with McLaws's Confederates on the Turnpike, opening the Battle of Chancellorsville.

You are now standing at the center of that collision, thanks to the Civil War Trust. This is the First Day at Chancellorsville battlefield, rescued from almost certain development and maintained by the Trust. As you look at the highway (VA 3, the old Orange Turnpike), the Confederates came from your left and the Federals from your right. There is a nice walking trail and a good number of historical markers to help you interpret the battlefield. The trail is well kept and is just over 2 miles long. Be prepared for a hike before you go, however—there are no facilities along the way. Although the tree lines have changed over the years, most of the area where you stand—and where the fighting took place—was open field north of the turnpike.

At about 11:30 AM, barely a half mile west of Zoan Church, first contact was made when the advance unit of McLaws's force—William Mahone's brigade, of Anderson's division—met Federal cavalry on the turnpike, just to the east of the parking lot. The cavalry raced back to Sykes's upcoming division, and Sykes sent Colonel Sidney Burbank's brigade of only 1,500 men forward while the rest of the division came up. The two sides formed on either side of the field, with the Federals advancing toward the Confederates and taking casualties as they moved uphill.

The high ground east of Chancellorsville where Lafayette McLaws formed his Confederates.

By 1:00 PM, all three of Sykes's brigades were on the east end of the field, slugging it out with the three Confederate brigades of McLaws and Anderson that had been brought up. The Confederate left was taking a beating but holding, and McLaws, knowing that the column on the Orange Plank Road was not far to the south, sent a messenger to ask Jackson for support from that end. Sykes was not only outnumbered but also isolated, and the Confederate line overlapped his flanks on both ends. He too sent a messenger, back to Joe Hooker, asking for reinforcement.

By the time Hooker heard about Sykes's troubles, he had an idea of what he might be up against. Intelligence was now coming in that Jackson was no longer in his position south of Fredericksburg and was on the march, although his whereabouts were unknown. Hooker arranged for Hancock's division of the II Corps to move to Sykes's position and allow him to fall back. In fact, Hooker, suddenly on the defensive and somewhat in the dark because of BMI's sudden battlefield communication problems, issued a command for all three columns—Meade's, Sykes's, and Slocum's—to return to Chancellorsville.

In the meantime, Sykes's brigade was beginning to take heavy fire on their right from Robert Rodes's Confederate division, which had moved up through the Wilderness from the Orange Plank Road. As Hancock's troops arrived to cover them, Sykes fell back under fire as quickly as possible all the way across the field. Both Sykes and Hancock then made their way west back to Chancellorsville.

McLaws's Line

From the parking lot at the First Day at Chancellorsville Battlefield, turn right onto VA 3 and drive 0.9 mile to McLaws Drive. Turn left at McLaws Drive and drive 0.3 mile; there will be a parking area on your right.

After the Federals' quick retreat, the Confederates were eager to pursue. McLaws followed the two Union divisions toward Chancellorsville, while Jackson's column to the south, which had only barely begun to tangle with Slocum's column before he received the order to withdraw, followed the Federals closely.

As Sykes and Hancock retreated, they noticed the ridge running along what is now McLaws Drive. Both generals wanted to make their stand there, but were directed to keep moving back toward Chancellorsville. Instead, McLaws's Confederates, somewhat bewildered that the Union troops had left the high ground, occupied it and held the position through the three-day battle. While they did launch several assaults against the Union defenses around Chancellorsville from here, they soon realized that they were far too strong to carry by a direct assault.

Here at McLaws's Line, the National Park has created a walking tour that will take you along what's left of McLaws's entrenchments (mostly east of McLaws Drive, across the street from the parking area) and tell the stories of the fighting that happened here. At the time of the battle, the fields you see before you were forested. However, thanks to another great preservation effort, this one spearheaded by the Central Virginia Battlefields Trust, this battlefield land is not the strip mall that it easily could have been. The trail here, a loop just under 2 miles, is on fairly even ground and is a nice walk. Like the others, there are no facilities on this trail, so be prepared before you set out.

The area where Slocum's column ran into the Confederates is just past the parking area and to your left down the Orange Plank Road, although it is mostly private property now. Upon hearing Hooker's order to withdraw back to Chancellorsville, Slocum, Sykes, Meade, and Couch, whose II Corps was now at the crossroads, were all beside themselves. Four days of perfectly executed maneuvering were suddenly being tossed aside for caution's sake.

Jackson's aggressiveness had suddenly stuck the Army of the Potomac right in the middle of the Wilderness. Further, Hooker—who, as both sides would later acknowledge, had created a brilliant battle plan—had committed the same fatal error as the Union commanders who preceded him. To be sure, Hooker's plan was still intact. The Confederates were out of the Fredericksburg defenses, and his army was in force south of the Rappahannock. But now they would be fighting defensively. Robert E. Lee had been forced back at Antietam and was then dug in at Fredericksburg, and for over seven months had been looking for any opportunity to seize the initiative again. By withdrawing to Chancellorsville, Hooker had just handed Lee exactly what he needed to score one of the most astounding victories of the war.

Lee-Jackson Bivouac

> *From the parking area, turn right onto McLaws Drive. Drive 0.4 mile to the next intersection, the Old Plank Road. You will see historic markers at the intersection on your right; park to the right side of the road in one of the designated parking spots.*

On the evening of May 1, the picture of the Federal lines was becoming clearer to the Confederates. Stuart's cavalry had been poking at both of the Federal flanks and had encountered only minimal resistance from infantry pickets rather than cavalry. (They obviously did not know yet that Hooker had committed almost his entire cavalry corps to Stoneman's raid.) One thing was obvious to all: the Union position around Chancellorsville was exceedingly strong.

As the day drew down, Jackson and Lee eventually made their way to the small clearing you see before you, at the intersection of the Orange Plank Road and the Catherine Furnace Road (which McLaws Drive will become as you continue your tour). Although the conversation was only heard in bits and pieces by staff and other onlookers, it was clear that retreat or defense were not part of the discussion. The discussion centered on how to attack the Yankees.

Lee and Jackson talked into the night as various intelligence reports came in, and it was quickly decided that the Union right was the most likely place for success. At that moment, the right was unprotected, making it the obvious target. How to get there through the entanglement of the Wilderness was another matter. Jackson's chaplain, Reverend Beverly Lacy, knew the area well, and he was summoned to recommend any roads, large or small, that could get around the Federal right undetected. The two generals eventually bedded down for the night here.

The first two to rise the

The Lee-Jackson Bivouac, site of the final meeting between the two generals.

next morning, well before daylight, were Jackson and Lee, and they sat alone around a small fire discussing the day's plans. Some changes were made to the route of the march, but the plan remained the same. How to conduct the march was apparently an easy decision. Lee and Jackson quickly agreed that Lee should divide his army (again, since Early's division still overlooked the Rappahannock at Fredericksburg), leaving the two divisions from Longstreet's corps (still under Lee's direct command) where they were, with Jackson taking his entire corps on the flank march. It was bold, but it was also in character. After orders were written, Jackson left immediately to prepare his men. As his column later passed the intersection, Jackson saluted Lee for the final time. The two would not meet again.

It was only in hindsight that the significance of the early morning conversation between Lee and Jackson on May 2 was realized. It has often been depicted in various forms of art, some well, some not. Here at the Lee-Jackson bivouac site, their final meeting is remembered with markers, monuments, and tributes. In one of the more interesting and touching ones, two cedar trees were planted side by side in 1937 to mark the meeting, and they have grown handsomely.

Catherine Furnace

〉 *At the intersection, McLaws Drive becomes Furnace Road. Continue down the Furnace Road 1.4 miles to the T intersection. Pull into the parking area for Catherine Furnace to your left.*

In 1863, Catherine Furnace, which had lain dormant for several years, was once again making iron, having been pressed into service for the Confederacy. The remains of the furnace itself are all that remain today, with the many production buildings long gone. Catherine Furnace was only one of several iron operations that had been operating in the area for over 150 years before the battle, but their presence had a direct impact on this battle in particular. The furnaces required massive amounts of wood and charcoal to reach the necessary temperatures, and the abundant timber that was here at the time served that purpose. The timber was replaced by the harsh undergrowth that soon characterized the Wilderness and played such an important role in the Battle of Chancellorsville.

Jackson's flank march took him past Catherine Furnace, and it was here that he turned south to continue on the Catherine Furnace Road. Not far from this position, Federal troops first saw Jackson's men moving at 8:00 AM and reported it to Hooker. Not acting quickly on the information, Hooker sent Sickles's III Corps from their works at nearby Hazel Grove to investigate, but did not issue the order until noon. Here at Catherine Furnace, the Federals caught the rear guard of Jackson's flanking column at 1:30, almost six hours after they were first sighted. Sickles found that

Jackson had turned south and leaped to the conclusion that the Confederates were on the retreat. His removal of the III Corps would only make Jackson's operation more effective when it was launched.

Jackson's Flank March

> *To follow the route of Jackson's famous flank march, pull out to the right and follow what is now called Jackson Trail East for 2.8 miles. Turn left at Brock Road and drive 0.3 mile before turning right onto Jackson Trail West. Follow Jackson Trail West for 2.3 miles until rejoining Brock Road. Turn left on Brock Road and continue north 2.7 miles to VA 3. You have now followed the march route; from here, continue on to Ellwood.*

Jackson's column totaled 33,000 men, three full divisions plus cavalry and artillery. Rodes's division led the column, followed by Raleigh Colston's and then A. P. Hill's. The march on this very narrow road was almost 12 miles long. With his men only able to march four abreast at the most, Jackson's column became very long, stretching out for miles. The march route led southwest from Catherine's Furnace toward the Brock Road, where it turned northwest on a country road, out of sight, until it rejoined the Brock Road and went north to cross the Orange Plank Road and the Orange Turnpike. It would be early afternoon before the head of Jackson's column would reach their destination west of the Union right flank.

Today, the route of Jackson's flank march is preserved by the Park Service. The road you have to drive on, however, is much wider and more comfortable and makes a great short drive. The road is gravel but well maintained, and you will not have to worry about traffic or other hindrances until you regain Brock Road, just as Jackson's men did.

Ellwood

> *From the end of the Jackson's Flank March route, turn left onto VA 3 West and drive 1.1 miles to VA 20 (Constitution Highway). Turn left on VA 20 and drive 0.6 mile. On your left, you will see signs for Ellwood; pull into the parking area. If you are visiting in the off-season or during off-hours, you must obtain a free parking pass at the Chancellorsville Visitor Center.*

The farm at Ellwood holds a fascinating history, but it is the Civil War that made its mark here. Ellwood was owned by the Lacy family, the same family that owned the large estate of Chatham overlooking Fredericksburg from across the Rappahannock. It was a summerhouse for the wealthy family of Virginia's upper elite. Social status, however, means little when thrust into the middle of a war.

After the battles of Chancellorsville and the Wilderness the next year, Ellwood was used as a field hospital, and several Union generals used Ellwood as headquarters during the Wilderness campaign. For many visitors, though, the mark of distinction that sets Ellwood apart as a destination lies in the Lacy family cemetery.

After Jackson was wounded late on May 2, he was taken to a field hospital well behind the lines, where his arm was amputated. Jackson's personal chaplain, Reverend Beverly Tucker Lacy, just happened to be brothers with the owner of Chatham and Ellwood. The reverend thought it an honor to bury Jackson's left arm in the family cemetery at Ellwood, where it remains today in a marked grave, far from where Jackson died at Guinea Station and from where he is buried in Lexington, Virginia.

The home at Ellwood is open for tours during the summer months, and it is a great tour if you are able to take it. When the home is not open for tours, the road to the home is usually chained off. However, that doesn't mean that you can't visit the grounds. While you are at the Chancellorsville Visitor Center, ask a member of the staff for a parking permit to visit Ellwood, and they will gladly grant you a free one-day pass that will allow you to park outside the gate and walk to the home and the cemetery. Ellwood was a simple farm compared to the estate at Chatham, but the grounds here make for a wonderful stroll.

Ellwood, summer home of the Lacy family, who also owned Chatham in Fredericksburg.

Stonewall Jackson's arm lies buried in the family plot at Ellwood.

Jackson's Flank Attack

❯ *From the parking area at Ellwood, turn right onto VA 20 and drive 0.6 mile to VA 3. Turn right onto VA 3 East and continue for 2.8 miles, then make a U-turn. Drive 0.2 mile on VA 3 West to the gravel road on your right leading to Jackson's Flank Attack.*

On the evening of May 1, in the Chancellor House, Hooker met with his corps commanders to plan their next steps. When he asked all of his corps commanders about their present dispositions, all replied that their current defensive positions were solid. Hooker was particularly concerned with the position of Howard's XI Corps on the far right, which was deployed right where they had ended the day's march, strung out along the Orange Turnpike. Hooker asked Howard to turn his right at an angle across the road to defend against an attack from that direction. Howard, though, concerned for the morale of his men after the day's retreat, begged Hooker not to make the change, and Hooker relented. Howard's men remained along the turnpike, facing south, except for three regiments that were brought to an angle as a precaution.

Hooker was worried about his right. Oliver Howard was the least experienced corps commander he had, and the XI Corps itself was considered the army's weakest. To shore up the right flank, Hooker sent for John Reynolds's I Corps, still watching the Confederates south of Fredericksburg, to march immediately to the right flank

It was here that Jackson's famous flank attack routed the Union right at Chancellorsville.

and extend it all the way to Ely's Ford on the Rapidan River. The message was sent at 1:55 AM, May 2, and Hooker expected Reynolds to be in position by midafternoon. However, because of the communication problems that were plaguing the Federal army throughout the entire battle, Reynolds did not receive the order until three hours later, long after he should have started his march.

With Reynolds's I Corps still on the move and Sickles's III Corps chasing Jackson's tail at Catherine Furnace, Howard's XI Corps was isolated along the Orange Turnpike within the thick growth of the Wilderness. At the same time, Jackson was forming his men a half mile to the west. He would attack in three massive lines straddling the Orange Turnpike. Four brigades from Rodes's division would be in front, while the second and third lines were composed of a mixture of Rodes's, Colston's, and Hill's divisions. Most of Hill's division, bringing up the rear of the column, would not be on the field in time for the initial assault, nor would most of the artillery, which would not be of much use in the Wilderness anyway. But the 21,500 men Jackson had would be enough.

Most of the Federals were lounging or cooking supper at 5:45 PM when suddenly an exodus of animals began to appear from the forest to their right—birds, rabbits, deer. For a very short time, it was amusing. Then the Confederates appeared in a rush. Charles Devens's division was at the end of the Federal line, and within minutes the entire division was in flight down the Orange Turnpike. Those few regiments who stood their ground were quickly killed or captured.

You are now standing at the spot where the line of the XI Corps ended and where

Jackson's Confederates surprised them. As you face the turnpike, the Confederates came from your right, with the center of their three lines on the turnpike itself. The majority of the Federals were on the turnpike, strung out for a mile and a half to your left. Near this spot, two regiments attempted to make a stand against the oncoming Rebels, but were soon forced to fall back with the others. The immediate area around was forested wilderness at the time of the battle.

Jackson's men kept pressing, soon reaching a clearing at the Wilderness Tavern. There they encountered the next division in line, Carl Schurz's. Schurz attempted to make a stand and formed a line, but it was only a few minutes before they too were forced to flee. By this time Howard had appeared on the field, trying to rally his men, but most of them didn't hold much feeling for Howard. Much of the corps was composed of German immigrants, so when Franz Sigel had been replaced with Howard only a month earlier, the morale of the entire corps sank. Howard wasn't going to rally anyone under the circumstances.

Looking to your left down the field, the farm you see is the approximate area where Schurz made his brief stand against the Confederates. This vast area, once under heavy threat of development, was rescued, like many other parts of the park, by the Civil War Trust and the Central Virginia Battlefield Trust. Acquired in pieces, it is now all part of the National Military Park, and additional parcels south of the turnpike are slated to be preserved by these groups.

Before long, the Confederates were through this clearing and again pressing through the forest, this time to meet with the only remaining intact brigade of XI Corps, Adolphus Buschbeck's, along with the few soldiers who had been rallied. Howard was able to form a solid line of 4,000 men, but within 20 minutes they were outflanked and pushed back. The Confederates were within 2 miles of Chancellorsville and had completely routed an entire Union corps. After an hour and a half of forcing their way through the Wilderness, however, the lines were disorganized, and some of the Confederates had stopped along the way to feast on leftover supper and to search for new equipment. Sunlight was growing scarce, and Jackson did not want to waste any of it.

Jackson's Wounding

> From the flank attack site, pull right onto VA 3 West and drive 0.3 mile, then make a U-turn. Drive 2.3 miles on VA 3 East, then turn left to enter the parking area for the Chancellorsville Visitor Center.

Rodes saw the need to stop and reorganize his division, but many of the Confederates kept moving forward, including his own men in the front. This had much to do with Jackson. Jackson was continuously issuing the same order to everyone within earshot: "Press forward! Push ahead!" Jackson knew that victory was far from certain at this point, and he wanted to make it so. As for Rodes, he knew A. P. Hill's division had arrived and would carry the momentum forward.

From the opposite direction, Hooker was now fully aware of the situation, with thousands of panic-stricken Germans surrounding the Chancellor House. Hooker immediately leaped to his horse and began barking out orders. One of those orders was to call for his old division, now belonging to General Hiram Berry, to stop the flow of Confederates. He may not have liked his nickname, but "Fighting" Joe Hooker was just that, and he could certainly inspire his men like few others.

Before long, men of the III and XII corps had formed a strong line that stretched well beyond the flanks of the oncoming Confederates. As darkness fell, the fighting between the lines grew more confused by the minute. Although it was nearly a full moon, this mattered little in the tangled Wilderness. Units became lost behind enemy lines and were captured or were hit by friendly fire in the confusion. Still, the Federals were now forming counterattacks from their now-strong position, particularly with cavalry.

A remnant of the Orange Turnpike, where Stonewall Jackson was mortally wounded.

One of the Confederate units that had stuck together fairly well during the flank attack was Nathan Lane's brigade of A. P. Hill's division. Advancing to the Bullock Road (which runs just to the west of the Visitor Center), Lane posted two regiments north of the road and two south, readying them for a night attack. His fifth regiment was posted in front as skirmishers. In the darkness, Lane's brigade—all North Carolina regiments—had several encounters with Federal units, and firing continued sporadically in front of them. To be sure, they were on the alert, with an attack by Federal cavalry almost likely.

Jackson, as was his habit, was determined to lead his men from the front, no matter what the circumstances. At 9:00 PM, joining A. P. Hill, he and his staff rode east on the Orange Turnpike. Ordering Hill to press the attack now that he was on the field, he continued to ride, with Hill and his staff not far behind. Even though they rode along the turnpike, they went unseen by Lane's entire brigade.

By this time, the field was mostly silent. Suddenly, a shot rang out on the right. To this day, no one knows whether it was fired by a Union soldier or a Confederate. But that single shot was enough to garner a response from Lane's brigade. Two regiments from south of the turnpike fired a scattered blast, hitting the staffs of both Hill and Jackson. Several men were wounded or killed by the blast. Instinctively, those who were left spurred their horses back toward their own lines and into the trees surrounding the turnpike, including Jackson, who was unscathed. To the men of Lane's brigade, it sounded as much like a brigade of Union cavalry as anything else, and was undoubtedly the most likely assumption.

The firing continued, now mostly by the two regiments closest to the road on either side. By this time, several members of Hill's staff were running toward Lane's line shouting that they were firing into their own men. The reply from Major John Berry, now commanding the 18th North Carolina, would change history. "Who gave that order? It's a lie! Pour it into them!"

Jackson was hit three times, in the right hand, the left forearm, and the upper left arm. Once order was restored, Jackson's personal physician, Dr. Hunter McGuire, was sent for, and what was left of his staff tried to get him to the rear as quickly as possible. Jackson was aware enough to put Hill in command before being taken off. Soon met by Dr. McGuire, he was moved to a hospital near Wilderness Church along the Orange Turnpike. Early the next morning McGuire amputated Jackson's left arm.

The volley that had taken Jackson had attracted the attention of the Federals also,

A TERRIBLE COINCIDENCE

Jackson's wounding at Chancellorsville was a terrible blow to the Confederate army. Indeed, Confederate generals were often unwilling to stay away from the front, and although they were often more effective on the battlefield, they would suffer mightily for it. In fact, the circumstances of Jackson's wounding were eerily repeated almost exactly one year later only 5 miles away. On May 6, 1864 during the Battle of the Wilderness, James Longstreet—Lee's most valued and capable general after Jackson—was also hit by friendly fire and was seriously wounded in the throat. Longstreet would survive but was out of action for a considerable amount of time, depriving Lee of one of his best lieutenants during the decisive campaign of the Civil War.

and they placed a battery on the turnpike only 100 yards away from Lane's brigade. They unleashed several volleys of canister as Jackson was carried off, and soon other artillery in the area was pounding the Confederate position. One of the casualties of this barrage was A. P. Hill, hit in the back of the legs. Hill transferred command again, this time to Robert Rodes, temporarily, until Stuart arrived.

There are several monuments around the Visitor Center that commemorate where Jackson was mortally wounded, placed there over the years by various groups. If you walk around to the rear of the Visitor Center, you will see several of these along the turnpike. The first and most prominent was placed by Jackson's staff 25 years after the battle, and was placed along the turnpike so that it would be visible, not to mark the spot of the wounding. Another marker, nearby and barely discernible, is a boulder placed by Jackson's chaplain, Reverend Beverly Lacy, and J. Horace Lacy, wartime owner of the estates at Chatham and Ellwood. This was supposed to mark the location of Jackson's fall, but accounts of the incident from those who were there have rendered it inaccurate.

In a wonderful feat of forensic history, in 1996, the park's chief historian, Robert Krick, came upon a document from Private David Kyle. Kyle lived at the Bullock House, just north of Chancellorsville, and was accompanying Jackson as his personal

One of several monuments to Jackson's wounding at the Chancellorsville Visitor Center.

guide during the battle. Kyle was present during the wounding, and through the document he left and other accounts, Krick was able to pinpoint exactly where the wounding took place. If you are able to take the guided ranger tour around the Visitor Center, it will be pointed out to you; if not, ask for the short brochure for the Wounding of Stonewall Jackson trail.

Slocum's Line

> *From the Visitor Center, return to VA 3 and turn left onto VA 3 East. Drive 0.8 mile to CR 610 (Old Plank Road) and turn right, then drive 0.1 mile to Slocum Drive. Turn right onto Slocum Drive and drive 0.3 mile, then park near the historic markers on your left.*

General Hooker was not giving up. Although he insisted on fighting a defensive battle, he had reason for hope. Lee's army, as he could now see, was divided. He still had Sedgwick's VI Corps below Fredericksburg, as well as Gibbon's division at the former camp, and from his intelligence there were relatively few Confederates in front of him. If Sedgwick could move as swiftly as possible, he would come upon the rear of Lee's force from the east, crushing it between his and Couch's II Corps in their defensive line. Orders went out immediately for Sedgwick and Gibbon to move without hesitation, and he also sent a member of his staff, Gouverneur Warren, to make sure that Sedgwick understood the importance of his mission. By daybreak, Gibbon's division held the town of Fredericksburg, but Sedgwick, who did not act on his orders in time, would be held up in his advance.

There was also the matter of Stoneman's cavalry raid. For days, the Union high command had awaited word from Stoneman about his progress. Still, every day, Confederate trains continued to appear at Hamilton's Crossing. It would later be known that Stoneman, whose orders could not possibly have been spelled out more clearly, had practically ignored them. His huge cavalry force—leaving Hooker with little cavalry, which would have proven very valuable during Jackson's flank march—moved slowly and cautiously. When they finally did act on their mission, to cut the Richmond, Fredericksburg & Potomac Railroad, they did so in the wrong places and with ineffective methods. Lee's supply line was temporarily slowed, but not cut, and the delays did not last long. Stoneman's failure was massive and his absence catastrophic.

With the aim of strengthening his position, Hooker withdrew his lines slightly. Sickles's III Corps was to abandon their position at Hazel Grove and withdraw to the estate at Fairview, not far from the Chancellor House. This left Slocum's XII Corps exposed on the right, but they had been holding their line and strengthening it for three days. Across the field from them was Richard Anderson's division, one of the two divisions under Lee's direct command.

Slocum's Line, site of heavy fighting on May 3 at Chancellorsville.

Lee knew that before long, he would have to unite his divided army. Stuart's corps (formerly Jackson's) was west of the Federal army, while he was east. It appeared, though, that the Federals were extended in the center, Hazel Grove, and the area held by Slocum's XII Corps. If Stuart could press the attack from his right, he could push those Federals back, allowing his forces to reunite with Lee's.

Early in the day, Hooker aided Lee's efforts by abandoning the position on Hazel Grove. On his side of the Union position, Lee ordered Anderson to assault Slocum's line. After repulsing an initial charge, Slocum's men held their strong position and then countercharged. For the next several hours, the two lines fought fiercely, going back and forth, with the Federals slowly gaining the upper hand.

Unfortunately for the Union, the decision to evacuate Hazel Grove would haunt them in another way. Soon that high ground was covered with Confederate artillery, and some of this was focused on the XII Corps line. At 8:30, the Federals had held their ground well and repulsed every attack fiercely. By 9:00, however, they were being hit from the rear by artillery and running out of ammunition to boot. Finally, Slocum called for his men to withdraw toward Fairview.

This part of the National Military Park has only recently been developed, but the interpretation of the area will improve sooner rather than later. Along the roadway you can see the remnants of Slocum's entrenched line; the Federals would have been on the same side as the road, while the Confederates attacked from the woods in front.

Hazel Grove

❯ *From the historic markers, continue on Slocum Drive 0.5 mile to Stuart Drive. Make a sharp right turn onto Stuart Drive and drive 0.4 mile to the parking area for Hazel Grove just past the clearing. The parking is along the opposite side of the road, so you will have to turn your car around to park; use caution.*

When Sickles withdrew from Hazel Grove in the early hours of May 3, he had vacated one of the most important pieces of the battleground at Chancellorsville. Hooker did not yet realize its advantages, but the Confederates, once they occupied the crest, saw them immediately. Hazel Grove was on high ground and overlooked one of the largest clearings in the area. Most important, the clearing was a practically direct line to the estate at Fairview, where the Federals had concentrated many of their guns.

After Archer's brigade of A. P. Hill's division drove off the Federal rear guard at Hazel Grove by 6:45, the Confederates began massing their artillery atop the hill, eventually bringing 28 guns to bear. Archer's brigade formed the far right of Stuart's corps, with the rest of A. P. Hill's division, now under the command of Henry Heth with Hill's wounding, falling in line down the slope. Behind Hill's division were Colston's and Rodes's divisions, but it would be Hill's men who took on the worst of the fighting.

If you walk over to Hazel Grove and look down the clearing, you can see what an important position this was. Oddly, even the Confederates did not appreciate it until they had actually gained it. In the distance, the road that you see is VA 3, the old Orange Turnpike. In front of the road and slightly to the right is the location of Fairview,

Artillery at Hazel Grove.

A view from Hazel Grove toward Fairview and the Chancellor House.

the center of the Federal line on the morning of May 3. Just beyond the road, also on your right and slightly obscured by trees, is the Chancellor House. The clearing both atop the hill and down the slope was slightly larger at the time of the battle, but today you can see enough to appreciate its advantages.

In the trees to your left, A. P. Hill's division lined up to advance toward Fairview in an attempt to take the Union position there. The Federals had 44 guns at Fairview, and they soon began pounding the artillery at Hazel Grove. The Confederate line stretched well beyond the turnpike, and Sickles's III Corps fought desperately to keep them from advancing. Hiram Berry, commanding Hooker's old division, was killed just south of the turnpike. Soon units from the II Corps and the XII Corps were in the fight, desperately trying to keep hold of Fairview.

An excellent walking tour of Hazel Grove and Fairview begins here at Hazel Grove. Approximately 1 mile, the tour will take you all the way down the slope to Fairview and the areas of the most intense fighting. You will see the former site of the Fairview House along with the all-important artillery position.

Fairview

> *From Hazel Grove, you may elect to use the Hazel Grove/Fairview Walking Trail to reach the next stop on the tour by foot. If you wish to drive, from the Hazel Grove parking area, drive 0.2 mile on Stuart Drive back through the clearing to Berry Paxton Road, then turn left. Drive 0.4 mile to the Fairview parking area at the end of the road.*

As the fierce fight continued on both sides of the turnpike, Hooker again called for Sedgwick's VI Corps to come up on Lee's rear. He knew that if he could hold until that was accomplished, the Confederates could still be defeated in detail—Lee first, then Jackson's corps—and a Union victory secured. Hooker did not realize, unfortunately, that Sedgwick was still poking around in Fredericksburg, preparing for an assault on Marye's Heights.

Both sides began to throw everything they had into the fight. Much of Couch's II Corps, which had no Confederates in front of it, was brought west. Stuart, meanwhile, moved his second and third lines into the battle. Soon the Confederates had pressed so close that the Federal artillery could no longer fire at them for fear of hitting their own men. Finally, the Union artillery at Fairview had no choice but to pull back into the fields around the Chancellor House. The Federals were on the retreat.

From the parking lot, walk to the site of the Fairview House and, nearby, the marker for the Union artillery position. The fighting along the Union center in the fields around you cost more than 17,000 casualties over a five-hour period. From here, you can clearly see not only up the slope to Hazel Grove but also across the roadway to the nearby Chancellor House.

As soon as the Union artillery left their position, the Confederate artillery swooped down from Hazel Grove to take the same position at Fairview. Almost immediately, they turned their guns on the Chancellor House, from which Hooker was conducting his retreat. Hooker was leaning on a pillar of the house when it was struck by a Confederate cannonball. He was struck senseless. With Union lines collapsing all around him, suddenly the Union general in command was out of the fight.

Apex of Hooker's Line/Bullock House

> *From the Fairview parking area, return 0.4 mile to Stuart Drive. Turn right on Stuart Drive and drive 0.7 mile to the intersection with VA 3. Continue across VA 3, where the road becomes Bullock Road, then drive another 0.8 mile to the parking area on your right.*

For nearly an hour, the Union army was without a leader. Command should have fallen instantly to Darius Couch, the senior officer on the field, but it was not until 10:00 that Couch was notified and placed in command. During that hour, the Union lines were steadily collapsing in on themselves. Meade now brought his V Corps into the fight, shoring up the right side of the Union position. By 10:00 nearly every Federal unit was north of the Orange Turnpike. When Hooker, only semiconscious, handed command to Couch, he ordered him to withdraw the army to a position already marked out on a map.

Had Couch been able to take command earlier, he may have been able to save the battle. The Confederates had by no means won it, and Meade had proposed a flank attack from his V Corps and Reynolds's I Corps that, if successful, would have been devastating. Unfortunately, Hooker would not give approval. Almost any other commander would have, but Hooker did not have his wits about him at the time. It is quite possible that Couch would have encouraged the assault. But he had his orders from the commander himself.

The new Federal position was to be along the lines of the Ely's Ford Road and the Bullock Road, which converged just north of the Chancellor House. This new position was not only strong defensively but would leave several routes of retreat open across the Rappahannock and Rapidan Rivers, particularly U.S. Ford. The II Corps, now commanded by Hancock with Couch's taking the army, would cover the retreat of the other units while they filed onto these roads. The movement was begun immediately, with the Federals taking heavy losses as they withdrew under fire. The Confederates pressed from all sides now, with the two parts of the army reunited. By noon, the Union forces were in their lines, strongly entrenched, and the Confederates were suddenly alerted to a new and more pressing threat. Had they advanced as intended, it is likely that they would have suffered enormously for it; the Federals had fresh troops at the front and more than 150 guns at the ready, with 140 more in reserve. Thankfully for everyone, the fight at Chancellorsville was over.

As you walk away from the parking area, you will see the site of the Bullock House, a landmark for the Federals as they made their withdrawal. Bullock Road used to cross through the Ely's Ford road, but only a trace of the road is left now. However, across the intersection in front of you, you can see the defensive earthworks that formed the apex of Hooker's defensive line at the former intersection. Three corps were spread down each road, with the left flank resting on the Rappahannock River and the right flank on the Rapidan.

Salem Church

> *From the parking area at the Bullock House Site, continue on to the intersection and turn right onto Ely's Ford Road (CR 610). Drive 0.7 mile on Ely's Ford Road to VA 3. Turn left onto VA 3 East and drive 5.8 miles to Salem Church Road. Turn right on Salem Church Road and drive 0.2 mile to General Semmes Boulevard. Turn left on General Semmes Boulevard and then another immediate left onto Old Salem Church Road. Drive 0.2 mile to the parking area for Salem Church on your left.*

To the east of Chancellorsville, Sedgwick's VI Corps, which Hooker so badly needed that May 3, stared up at the imposing position that was Marye's Heights. No one could ever forget what had happened there five months ago at the Battle of Fredericksburg, and no one wanted to repeat the slaughter of that day. When Gibbon crossed over into Fredericksburg with his division, Sedgwick's force totaled only 27,100 men and 66 guns to overtake the place that simply could not be taken last December.

Atop the Heights, Early saw the Federals below but considered their presence here a ruse. Accordingly, of the 12,700 men and 46 guns in Early's division, only 1,200 were at Marye's Heights with eight guns, while the rest of his force was set on his right, where Sedgwick and Reynolds had crossed the Rappahannock days before.

After poking at the flanks of the Confederate position atop Marye's Heights, Sedgwick finally decided on a direct assault of the Heights and the dreaded stone wall in front of it. Before the assault began, the Federals waved a flag of truce to their front, hoping to retrieve the wounded that they had already left in front of the stone wall. The wall was manned by two regiments of Barksdale's brigade, the same Mississippians who had fought so bravely to stop the Federals who were building bridges on the first day of the Battle of Fredericksburg. Remarkably, the commander of one of the regiments agreed to the truce. It was an honorable move, but not a smart one. As the Union soldiers went to retrieve their fallen comrades, they got a good hard look at exactly how few Confederates they faced. Although the Federals still took a good number of casualties and several attempts to take the stone wall, they did finally take it, driving the Confederates over Marye's Heights and taking control by 10:30 AM. The assault, often referred to as the second Battle of Fredericksburg, cost the Federals 1,100 casualties and the Confederates 475, with many captured.

In Chancellorsville, as General Lee prepared to finish off the Army of the Potomac, one of Early's staff members rode up to inform Lee of the fall of Marye's Heights. Lee immediately sent McLaws's division, along with one of Richard Anderson's brigades, to the east to meet Sedgwick's belated advance.

A view of the stone wall from Marye's Heights, site of the Second Battle of Fredericksburg.

There was a more immediate solution to Sedgwick's breakthrough. Cadmus Wilcox's brigade, which had been left with Early's division, was posted on the heights north of Fredericksburg. Seeing that Sedgwick had a clear shot to the rest of Lee's force, Wilcox swiftly moved his troops between the two on the Plank Road. He positioned his troops on a ridge 4 miles west of Fredericksburg near Salem Church facing east.

The Salem Church that you see here today is the very same one that witnessed the battle. A closer examination of the building will tell you that, as it is still pockmarked by bullet holes. Although difficult to detect today because of the massive amount of suburban sprawl surrounding it, the ridge is still somewhat discernible here, mostly at the location of the church itself, still on high ground. The ridge ran north to south in front of open ground, but much of that ground has now been bulldozed, taking the battlefield and its character away.

General William "Bully" Brooks led the first Union assault with his division, a brigade on each side of the Plank Road with two batteries of artillery in the middle. First contact was made at 3:25 PM, well after the fighting at Chancellorsville had ended, with the Federals firing on the Confederate skirmishers and advancing quickly. The Confederates fell back into a long line of trees and awaited the oncoming column. The line of trees was broken only by the Plank Road and Salem Church. Also hidden in the trees was McLaws's division, which had been given plenty of time to arrive on the field.

The Federals entered the woods cautiously, maintaining their lines and taking the bait leading them into Wilcox's trap. Just before they reached the clearing on the other side, the Confederates appeared and fired. Along a half-mile front, the two lines opened on each other. After a Federal charge briefly pierced the Confederate line, Wilcox ordered a countercharge that drove the surprised Federals from the woods. Retreating across the open ground, Brooks's division withdrew under the cover of the rest of the Federal infantry and artillery to the rear. The Confederates, emerging from the woods and seeing the massed Union force, slowly backed into the woods, and the Battle of Salem Church was over. The Federals had taken the worst of it with 1,523 casualties to the Confederates' 674, with the Rebels firing from behind covered positions. Wilcox's countercharge, however, was what won the field.

Now the Union Army of the Potomac was divided—Hooker's six corps, just below the Rappahannock, and Sedgwick's VI Corps, seemingly all alone near Fredericksburg. Lee's plan was for McLaws and Early to unite and crush the VI Corps on May 4, but miscommunication on the Confederate side led to Confederate delays, giving Sedgwick time to form a strong defensive position around Banks' Ford. A seething Robert E. Lee rode east to try to coordinate activity, but the Confederates moved slowly and could not open the attack until 5:30 PM. Sedgwick's men held, and after dark he constricted his lines more tightly around the ford.

At Chancellorsville on May 4, Hooker was up and alert and once again riding among his men. The Federals were in a strong position and still outnumbered the enemy. Furthermore, if Sedgwick could hold Banks' Ford, Hooker could cross the Rappahannock at U.S. Ford behind him and recross at Banks' Ford the next day to take the offensive. Indeed, Hooker was eager to retake the initiative from the Confederates. So when he heard late that night that Sedgwick had decided to cross to the north bank of the Rappahannock and leave Banks' Ford to the Confederates, he was quite dismayed. At midnight, Hooker called a meeting of his corps commanders to ask their opinions about either renewing the offensive or ending the campaign. Hooker left his generals to discuss the matter for a time, then rejoined the conference to gather opinions. The commanders had voted three to two to renew the offensive. Still, Hooker ultimately decided, on his own, to withdraw.

On May 5 the Union wounded and the reserve artillery began crossing the Rappahannock at U.S. Ford. At 4:00 PM a heavy rain began to fall, halting the already delayed Confederate plans for a renewal of the attack on Hooker's position. Lee rescheduled the assault for May 6, but as he was writing the orders, a courier arrived to tell him that the Federals were gone.

The Chancellorsville campaign was over. To be sure, Lee's strategy had been brilliant, and Chancellorsville is often referred to as his masterpiece. Lee, however, was not satisfied. In his eyes he had lost yet another opportunity to crush the Federals. But perhaps the most costly loss for Lee and for the Confederate cause would come a few days after the battle.

> **CASUALTIES**
>
> **Confederate:** killed, 1,724; wounded, 9,233; missing or captured, 2,503; total: 13,460
>
> **Union:** killed, 1,694; wounded, 9,672; missing or captured, 5,938; total: 17,304
>
> **Total Casualties: 30,764**

Stonewall Jackson Shrine

❯ *From the parking area at Salem Church, turn right onto Old Salem Church Road and drive 0.2 mile. Turn left at General Semmes Boulevard and then left again immediately onto Salem Church Road, driving another 0.2 mile to VA 3. Turn right onto VA 3 East and drive 1.3 miles to the ramp for I-95 South. Drive 11.5 miles on I-95 South to Exit 118 for CR 606/Mudd Tavern Road. At the end of the exit ramp, turn left onto Mudd Tavern Road and drive 4.6 miles, continuing with it as it becomes Stonewall Jackson Road. Immediately after crossing the railroad tracks, turn left into the entrance for the Stonewall Jackson Shrine and drive 0.3 mile to the parking area.*

The room in which Jackson died.

The farm office building where Stonewall Jackson spent his final days.

On May 4, Jackson was taken by ambulance to Guinea Station, a good distance behind the Confederate lines. He could recuperate there until he was well enough to travel by rail to Richmond. The farm at the station was Fairfield, home of a friend of Jackson, Thomas Chandler. Jackson was put up in the farm office in a comfortable room on the ground floor. On May 5 and 6, Jackson seemed in better health, but May 7 brought a marked downturn. Dr. McGuire quickly diagnosed the condition as pneumonia, made much the worse by Jackson's weakened state.

The farm office building still stands, and the room in which Jackson died is preserved in almost exact detail, down to the clock on the mantle. Not all of the pieces are original, but the feeling re-

The Stonewall Jackson Shrine at Guinea Station.

mains; there is a palpable, empty sadness about the place. In the upstairs portion of the building you can view the rooms where other members of Jackson's staff stayed, some of them also injured in the same barrage of friendly fire that felled Jackson. Be sure to check at the Chancellorsville Visitor Center about the hours for the site.

Back on April 20, Jackson had met his wife Anna and their five-month-old daughter Julia, who he was seeing for the first time, right here at Guinea Station. It had been a happy few weeks, as it always was when the Jacksons were together. Now Anna was called back to Guinea Station to attend to her husband. On May 10, it was evident that Jackson would not survive the day. Jackson said his good-byes to little Julia and Anna, then slipped into delirium for a short time, followed by sleep. At 3:15 PM, Jackson awoke and spoke his final words: "Let us cross over the river, and rest under the shade of the trees." He then passed away.

Jackson's death brought the entire South to grief, including Robert E. Lee, who said several times that, in the name of the Confederate cause, he sincerely wished that he could have fallen in Jackson's place. Now, Lee would have to find a way to press on to his next objective—his most ambitious and most decisive—without his most gifted and most trusted lieutenant at his side.

CHAPTER 7

High Water: The Gettysburg Campaign

Rᴏʙᴇʀᴛ E. Lᴇᴇ's ᴍᴀsᴛᴇʀꜰuʟ ᴠɪᴄᴛᴏʀʏ at Chancellorsville had come at a very high price. He had lost more than 13,000 men, including his trusted lieutenant, Stonewall Jackson. He was disappointed in his victory, but he was not about to sit idly, waiting for the Union Army of the Potomac to make the next move. Although he had been soundly defeated, the new Federal commander, Joseph Hooker, had proven himself a much more capable field general than any of his predecessors. He was also willing to fight.

While not as grim as the previous year, the first part of 1863 did not look good for the Confederacy. The invasion of Kentucky had been a failure, and Braxton Bragg's army was stalled in central Tennessee. At the all-important stronghold of Vicksburg, the Federals were making yet another attempt to complete their conquest of the Mississippi River. Charleston remained under siege, and the long-hoped-for prospect of foreign intervention was fading fast. Even the great victory at Chancellorsville was muted by the loss of Jackson.

The greatest problem Lee's Army of Northern Virginia faced was the same as it had been through virtually the entire war: food. Both men and horses were growing weaker with every day of meager rations. The farms of Virginia, hard-hit by Federal occupation, were under great strain to feed the population, let alone the army; indeed, Richmond and other locations had already experienced food riots. There were other supplies that the Confederacy had great need for—shoes, in particular—but food remained the overwhelming problem.

Nine months ago, Lee had attempted to remedy this problem by taking his army across the Potomac River into Maryland. Although the campaign ended with the

The picturesque town of Gettysburg.

bloody battle at Antietam, the benefits of taking the army where they could eat the product of Union farmland had made themselves readily apparent during their short stay. Had Lee been able to gain the battlefield of his choosing, as he had intended, Antietam may not have happened. With all of these in mind, Lee decided that it was once again time to take his army onto Union soil.

Lee had another problem with the loss of Jackson. His army had had only two corps, one led by Jackson and the other by James Longstreet. Lee reorganized his army evenly and systematically, creating a III Corps. Each corps would consist of three divisions and each division four brigades (with two exceptions of five). Longstreet would remain in command of his I Corps. Richard Ewell, who had lost a leg at Second Manassas, was now ready to take the field again, and took the II Corps, Jackson's former command. The new III Corps would be commanded by A. P. Hill. Hill had proven himself a more than capable field commander as well as a difficult, impetuous subordinate for many, including Longstreet and Jackson; bringing him to the level of corps command relieved this problem.

The Union army did not share Lee's impressions of Hooker. Almost immediately, Abraham Lincoln began to look for a replacement. Hooker had brought the army to the peak of its morale after the disaster at Fredericksburg, but the loss at Chancellorsville deflated that morale quickly. In addition, few still had confidence in Hooker. Although he almost immediately began tinkering with plans for his next movement, he no longer garnered the praise and cheers that he had only weeks before. Even Lincoln, who visited the army on May 7, suggested that there was little need to cross the Rappahannock just now.

When the Confederates began to trickle northward on June 3, 1863, the now-capable Federal intelligence network took notice. At first, Hooker determined that it was the beginning of a grand cavalry raid behind his lines, and possibly an attempt to get between him and the capital, forcing him to move. Hooker made arrangements to stop the raid before it started. It would be the first of a series of attempts by the Federals to determine what the Confederates were up to while simultaneously keeping their own intentions concealed. The two armies would continue these movements for almost a month before meeting, almost by chance, at a small college town in Pennsylvania to fight a battle that would come to define not only the Civil War but also, in its aftermath, the nation as we know it.

BEFORE YOU GO

» PLANNING YOUR TRIP

The two great battles of this campaign, Brandy Station and Gettysburg, took place more than 100 miles from each other. In between, there are numerous smaller actions

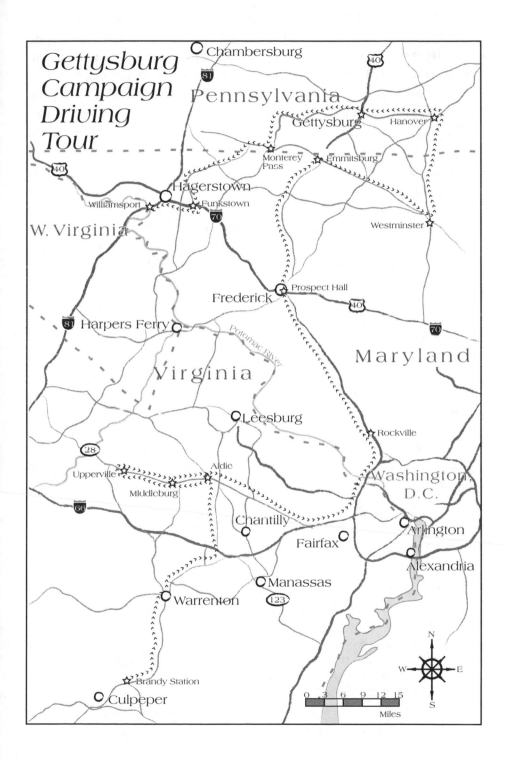

Gettysburg
Campaign
Driving
Tour

Chambersburg

Pennsylvania

81

40

Gettysburg

Hanover

Monterey Pass

Emmitsburg

Hagerstown

Williamsport

Funkstown

70

W. Virginia

Westminster

40

Frederick

Prospect Hall

40

70

81

Harpers Ferry

Potomac River

Maryland

Virginia

Leesburg

Rockville

28

Upperville

Aldie

Washington, D.C.

Middleburg

66

Chantilly

Fairfax

Arlington

Alexandria

Manassas

123

Warrenton

N

W   E

S

0   3   6   9   12 15

Miles

Brandy Station

Culpeper

that run through beautiful parts of the Virginia countryside, but where you might feel that the significance of the battles is not enough to warrant a visit. This often leads to the common and unfortunate decision of skipping Brandy Station altogether and heading straight for Gettysburg. If you're able, please resist the temptation. Brandy Station is not only the beginning of the story of Gettysburg but also the beginning of the turning of the tide of the war in the east. Besides, the battlefield is a great visit, and there are plenty of other things to see and do nearby.

If you or anyone in your party are looking for distractions during your trip, the area around Aldie, Middleburg, and Upperville is Virginia's wine country. There are numerous quaint, quiet towns along the way, along with the usual tours and tastings. The area also offers plenty of great places to stay, particularly Middleburg, a famous retreat for President Kennedy, among others.

While you're at Gettysburg, a good map and a set of binoculars will take you a long way, particularly if you climb the observation towers. Also, if there was ever one battle you wanted to study up on before you visit the field, this is it. If you know just a little bit about the terrain and the names before you go, the enjoyment of your visit will increase tenfold.

» RECOMMENDATIONS

You will have a fairly good amount of open-road driving on this tour. Still, with small detours, you can quickly get to major population centers. Look for food and lodging

IN DEPTH

Edwin B. Coddington—*The Gettysburg Campaign: A Study in Command*
Noah Andre Trudeau—*Gettysburg: A Testing of Courage*
Bradley M. Gottfried—*The Maps of Gettysburg: An Atlas of the Gettysburg Campaign, June 3–July 13, 1863*

"There are so many good books on every aspect of the Gettysburg campaign that it's a bit overwhelming. Coddington is probably the best single-volume work on the battle, but Trudeau's is a great narrative—a real page-turner. Additionally, Gottfried's collection of the maps of the campaign is a great resource."

—*Tom Trescott, Abraham Lincoln Book Shop, Chicago*

in Fredericksburg and Culpeper, Virginia, around the Washington, D.C. area, Frederick, Maryland, and Gettysburg itself.

If you're stuck with only a couple of days and simply can't make the time, a good option might be to stay at Gettysburg for the trip and try to soak in as much as you can. After you understand the battle a bit better, taking the campaign tour might make more sense, and certainly a second, fifth, and twentieth visit to Gettysburg will still bring you something new.

If you go during the summer or on a weekend, be prepared for crowds. There's a reason that this is the nation's premier battlefield site, and the park receives hundreds of thousands of visitors each year. If you're looking for a good time of year to go to avoid the crowds, your best bet might be September or October, when summer vacations are over and the weather is still great. Also, consider getting to the park very early, right after sunrise, and driving to the more popular sites such as Little Round Top or the Copse of Trees. Time it right and you just might have the whole place to yourself, a splendid rarity.

THE CAMPAIGN TOUR

BRANDY STATION

Graffiti House

> *Your tour of the Gettysburg campaign starts at the Graffiti House near the Brandy Station battlefield.*

On June 1, 1863, Robert E. Lee met with his new corps commanders, James Longstreet, Richard Ewell, and A. P. Hill. At that meeting, Lee laid out the plan for his upcoming campaign. It was simple enough. The army would move, in pieces to avoid detection, northwest to Culpeper, then into the Shenandoah Valley. A. P. Hill's III Corps would move last, keeping the Federals along the Rappahannock in front of Fredericksburg while the other two moved. J. E. B. Stuart's cavalry would provide the essential job of staying between the two armies, screening the Confederates' movements. While the Confederates moved north through the valley into Maryland and possibly Pennsylvania, the Union forces would eventually discover that they had been flanked. This would force them out of their position in front of Fredericksburg and probably out of the state altogether, thereby relieving Virginia's farmers from the devastating Union foraging that had been occurring since the previous summer.

The first unit to move would be Lafayette McLaws's division of Longstreet's corps on June 3. Longstreet's other two divisions, which had been held in Richmond, would meet them in Culpeper. Ewell's corps left the next night, June 4, moving under cover of darkness to avoid detection. By June 7, both Ewell's corps and McLaws' division, as well as John Bell Hood's division from Richmond, were in Culpeper. Lee arrived the same day. Lee decided that the movement to the Valley would begin June 9.

Also in Culpeper was the entire Confederate cavalry force. Stuart had staged a grand review for Lee, demonstrating his majestic horsemen. The fact that all of the Confederate cavalry were massed in one spot did not go unnoticed by Union intelligence, which reported that the Confederates were likely to stage a massive raid behind Union lines. Stuart had made a habit of using his cavalry to embarrass Union commanders, and Hooker was not about to let it happen to him. He directed his new cavalry commander, Alfred Pleasanton, to meet the threat directly.

On June 8, Union cavalry approached Beverly's and Kelly's Fords on the Rappahannock River. They had also brought infantry with them to support, a brigade at each ford, but they would not be needed in this fight. The Federals bedded down within close range of the fords, quietly and without fires, and waited for the morning's battle in Culpeper.

Unbeknownst to the Union troopers, the Confederate cavalry was not in Culpeper. On the same night, June 8, Stuart had moved his cavalry to Brandy Station, directly across the river. Setting his headquarters on Fleetwood Hill, a commanding

Some of the hundreds of messages and drawings uncovered at the Graffiti House.

rise just north of the station, Stuart also turned in. The last thing he or any of the 9,700 Confederate cavalry expected was a Union attack.

You are now at the Graffiti House, the main source of information for the Battle of Brandy Station. The home, located next to the former Orange & Alexandria Railroad, dates back to 1858 and was used by both sides many times throughout the war as a hospital, an office, and even a headquarters. During the war, soldiers in the upper portion of the house did a real number on the walls of the various rooms—writing messages and poems, drawing pictures, even documenting events. Eventually wallpaper was put over the

The "Dancing Lady," one of the Graffiti House's more popular drawings.

graffiti and it was soon forgotten. In 1993, while renovating the home, the owner peeled back the wallpaper and found a remarkable surprise—a virtual time capsule of the thoughts, feelings, and whimsies of soldiers at war. Thankfully, that owner recognized the treasure for what it was and kept what was left of it intact (the building had not been used for many years).

In 2002 the Brandy Station Foundation, a community-based organization dedicated to preserving the adjacent Brandy Station battlefield, bought the home to use as its headquarters. Here you will find a museum, gift shop, a film on the battle, and of course the graffiti, which is still being revealed and preserved in painstakingly delicate fashion. The foundation also arranges tours of the battlefield and lectures about the area's rich Civil War history. The Graffiti House is only open seasonally, so be sure to plan ahead if you wish to see it.

Grand Review Site

> *From the Graffiti House, pull out to your left onto Brandy Road (VA 762). Drive 2.0 miles to the Virginia State Police headquarters on your right at State Police Road (VA 342). Turn right and park in the station's visitor parking area.*

It was in the fields behind and surrounding the State Police headquarters that Stuart staged two grand reviews of his cavalry. The first review, on June 7, was for General Lee and prominent citizens, but Lee was held up in Fredericksburg, temporarily distracted by Union movements across the Rappahannock. So the next day, June 8, the entire review was performed again for Lee's benefit. Worried about the toll that parts of the review might take on the already-weakened horses, Lee forbade the more strenuous activities that accompany similar reviews such as mock charges. When the review was over, Lee went back to the army in Culpeper, while Stuart's cavalry remained at Brandy Station preparing to lead Lee's army north the next day.

Initial Union Assault

> *From the police station, turn right onto Brandy Road and drive 0.5 mile to US 15/US 29 (James Madison Highway). Take the ramp to your right onto US 15/US 29 North and drive 4.7 miles to Beverly Ford Road (VA 676). Turn left onto Beverly Ford Road and drive 2.8 miles until reaching a small creek, then turn your car around.*

This is the area from which the Federals began their attack at Brandy Station, although they didn't know it until they arrived. Union intelligence had told them that Stuart's cavalry was at Culpeper with the rest of the army. So when they splashed across the Rappahannock River at Beverly's Ford (just under a mile to the northeast) around 4:00 AM they were surprised to find a strong Confederate presence. This column, commanded by John Buford, expected to cross the ford and make their way to Brandy Station, where they would meet a second column commanded by David McMurtrie Gregg crossing at Kelly's Ford. From there the combined command of 8,800 cavalrymen would seek out the Confederates and bring them to battle.

The first Confederates that Buford confronted were sound asleep at the time of the crossing, and they were easily scattered. However, the noise soon roused the other nearby Confederate camps. As the Federals moved south down the Beverly Ford Road, Buford's column, with Benjamin "Grimes" Davis's brigade in the lead, collided with the scrambling Confederates in the road to your front. Near the slight bend in the road, Davis was killed, causing some confusion in the Union ranks. The Confederates formed defensive lines to the south near St. James Church and to the east behind a stone wall. Buford hurried the rest of his command across the river and prepared to assault the Confederates at 7:00 AM.

Buford's Knoll

> *Drive 0.8 mile south on Beverly Ford Road. Just past the airport, pull into the gravel parking area with historical markers on your right.*

The main brunt of Buford's force was directed south at St. James Church, but after several direct assaults would not budge the resistance there, Buford attempted to flank the Confederates on their left. Sending troopers to the north and then west, the Federals came across W. H. F. "Rooney" Lee's brigade, dismounted and in position behind a stone wall. Both Confederate flanks were protected, with the Hazel River to the north and Ruffans Run to the south. The Federals charged the wall repeatedly and eventually brought their accompanying infantry up to attempt to break Lee's line, but the Confederates would not budge, holding their position behind the wall. Finally, after hours of fighting, Rooney Lee was forced to pull his men back; other developments were arising on the field.

From the gravel parking area, a trail will take you to Buford's Knoll, which overlooks the area of the stone wall that Lee's men held so firmly. Interpretive markers along the trail will tell you where Buford's men were and also explain the opening stages of the battle. The trail itself is easy and the grounds are well kept, although climbing up Buford's Knoll at the end of the trail may present a challenge to some. The trail is not a loop, however, and is about 2 miles total, so be sure to set aside ample time to reach the site.

This area is one of several on the battlefield protected by the combined efforts of

The fields at Brandy Station, looking west toward Buford's Knoll.

the Civil War Trust, the Brandy Station Foundation, and other groups. Only a few years ago, the battlefield was slated for major development, including a large shopping center, an entertainment complex, an ice rink, and even a lighted golf course. Now, however, a great portion of the land is either publicly accessible or will be in the future. Efforts continue to reclaim this monumental piece of history, acre by acre, and hopefully much of the battlefield will be joined together in one piece.

St. James Church

❯ *From the gravel parking area, turn right onto Beverly Ford Road and drive 0.8 mile to St. James Church Road (VA 676). Turn right, and then pull into the gravel parking area on your left.*

When Buford's men were organized in the early hours of the fight after the initial clash, they proceeded south toward the Confederate line at St. James Church. The Confederates were lined up along the St. James Road, stretching east across where the airport now sits, as well as up the Green Mill Road (now also part of the St. James Road) that angles to the northwest. In your position at the parking lot, you would have been near the center of the Confederate line. As you face St. James Road, the Federals were lined up before the far tree line to your front, which also ran east across the present airport.

Walk across St. James Road to the trailhead for the Civil War Trust's St. James Walking Trail. The trail is an easy loop trail of 1 mile. This piece of the battlefield saw

The interpretive trail for the St. James Church site at Brandy Station.

much of the early fighting; if time restricts you to choose between taking the trail to Buford's Knoll and the St. James Church trail here, choose this one.

At 7:00 AM, the Federals began making charges across the field against Confederate cavalry, infantry, and artillery. Like much of the day's fighting, the scene would often be described as grand in later years, much like the ideal cavalry charge is often pictured. After realizing that breaking this line would take considerable effort, Buford shifted much of his command to Rooney Lee's position at the stone wall in a continued effort to break the Confederate left. Stuart oversaw the fighting here, conducting charges and countercharges that frustrated the Federal efforts. The fighting continued here until 10:30 AM, when suddenly the sounds of battle began to erupt in the rear of the Confederate positions. Soon, almost the entire battle would shift to new ground.

Fleetwood Hill

> *From the parking area, turn right onto St. James Road, and then take the next right onto Beverly Ford Road. Drive 0.4 mile on Beverly Ford Road to Cobb's Legion Road on your right. Turn right on Cobb's Legion Road and drive 0.2 mile to Fleetwood Heights Road (VA 685). Turn right on Fleetwood Heights road and drive 0.8 mile. On your left is an old historic marker with steps leading up to it; carefully pull over here and walk to the monument.*

This monument, placed by the Daughters of the Confederacy, was one of the first to be placed on the battlefield and remains one of the few today. It may seem an odd and inconvenient place for a monument, but at the time it was placed, it was the perfect

Several modern structures mar the top of Fleetwood Hill, the critical ground at Brandy Station.

spot. Here, at the crest of Fleetwood Hill, is where the engagement became more than just a regular cavalry fight.

After David Gregg crossed Kelly's Ford with the second column of Federal cavalry, it wasn't long before he met pockets of Confederate buildup along the straight route to Brandy Station. Not wanting to be detected, he went around the Confederates and eventually approached Brandy Station from the south, behind schedule but still holding the element of surprise. As soon as Gregg reached the area and heard the fighting, he immediately directed his force to what was obviously the most commanding spot on the field—Fleetwood Hill.

Gregg's arrival was indeed a surprise to the Confederates. The Union cavalry force suddenly doubled and the enemy was in their rear. Upon Gregg's entrance at 10:30, virtually all of the Confederate units facing Buford at the stone wall and at St. James Church withdrew to defend Fleetwood Hill, the site of Stuart's headquarters.

You are now at the crest of Fleetwood Hill. Even from this somewhat obscured position, it is easy to see that where you stand commands both directions down the Fleetwood Heights Road. To your south, where the two large modern homes now stand, is where much of the fighting took place. Also located along this ridge was Stuart's headquarters. Although this small section of the battlefield has been developed, much of the surrounding land has been protected.

> *Return to your car and continue 0.5 mile on Fleetwood Heights Road. Pull over in the gravel area next to the historical markers on your left.*

A historic marker at the crest of Fleetwood Hill.

As Gregg's Federals neared the crest of Fleetwood Hill from the south and west, the Confederates came charging from their position at St. James Church. The two forces clashed, and what followed, from virtually every account, was a cavalry battle that was as picturesque as those depicted in so many paintings. Sabers flashed, pistols fired, horses charged and reared as more and more troopers entered the fight. Soon Brandy Station had become the largest cavalry battle ever seen on the continent.

The fighting went on at Fleetwood Hill for hours until finally, in the late afternoon, Wade Hampton's Confederates made several decisive charges that secured the crest of Fleetwood Hill. At the same time, Stuart ordered Rooney Lee, now some distance behind the stone wall, to charge the Union right at 4:00 PM. Although the Federals weren't routed, the charge was effective, and Buford decided to withdraw his men back across Kelly's Ford, ending the fight.

You are now standing on the west slope of Fleetwood Hill. Thousands of horses filled the fields around you as the cavalrymen fought desperately. By the time it was over, the Union had suffered 868 casualties to the Federals' 515. This battle, though won by the Confederates, marked a turning point in the war for cavalry. Since the beginning of the war, the Confederate cavalry had dominated, with better leaders, better horses, better riders, and better organization. Hooker's changes in early 1863 began to turn the tide somewhat, instilling some pride into the Union units. Also playing a large part was that the Confederate horsemen were running out of steam. It was becoming harder and harder to keep their horses fed, and as the war went on, those who replaced fallen cavalrymen were not of the same quality. The Federals had put up a good fight at Brandy Station. The battle at Kelly's Ford three months earlier was an indication of things to come; Brandy Station was a definitive statement that the new Union cavalry had arrived.

ALDIE

Aldie Mill

❯ *From the Fleetwood Hill parking area at Brandy Station, pull out to your left (west) onto Fleetwood Heights Road and drive 0.5 mile to Alanthus Road. Turn left on Alanthus Road, then take the next left onto US 15/US 29 North (James Madison Highway). Drive 26.2 miles on US 15/US 29 North, then turn left to stay on US 15 for another 13.7 miles. When you reach US 50 (John S. Mosby Highway), enter the roundabout and drive west (third exit of the roundabout) on US 50. After 1.1 miles, you will see the Aldie Mill Historic Park on your left; pull into the parking lot.*

Although Lee's plans to take his army north were delayed by a day, there were no changes. On June 10 Richard Ewell's II Corps left for the Shenandoah Valley, passing through Chester Gap, near Front Royal, the next day. Four days later, June 15, two of Ewell's three divisions scattered a Federal force at Winchester, clearing the way for the rest of the Army of Northern Virginia to move north. Longstreet's I Corps left Culpeper on the same day, with A. P. Hill's III Corps leaving Culpeper on June 18.

Not far behind the Confederates was Hooker's Army of the Potomac. On June 13, after information gathered from the Bureau of Military Intelligence and at Brandy Station confirmed that most of Lee's army had been in Culpeper, Hooker put the army in motion. Immediately, the I, III, V, and XI corps were all headed north along the Orange & Alexandria Railroad. Within two days, almost the entire army was near Fairfax, with Hooker setting his headquarters there.

Also on June 15, Robert Rodes's division, the third of Ewell's three divisions, had made his way through Martinsburg and to the Potomac River. With very little fanfare, Rodes's division began crossing into Maryland at Williamsport. By the end of the day, the cavalry accompanying Rodes, commanded by Albert Jenkins, had already reached Chambersburg, Pennsylvania.

The Confederates were moving quickly, and the Union army knew little about their whereabouts. This was due in large part to Stuart's capable cavalry. Providing a solid screen for the Army of Northern Virginia all along its route, the Federals were

Aldie Mill, witness to much of the battle of Aldie.

The battlefield at Aldie along the Snickersville Turnpike.

forced to rely on citizen reports and rumors, all of which conflicted. Once the Confederates were in the Valley, Stuart needed only to guard the gaps through the Blue Ridge Mountains to keep the army's movements secret.

Desperate to gain reliable information, Alfred Pleasanton led his cavalry corps through the Bull Run Mountains at Aldie, Virginia, on June 17 to see what the Confederates were up to. David Gregg's division was in the lead, with Judson Kilpatrick's brigade in front. At 2:30 PM, Kilpatrick was met at Aldie Gap by Confederate cavalry commanded by Colonel Thomas Munford, coming from the other direction. After first chasing Confederate pickets west on the Ashby's Gap Turnpike, Kilpatrick was soon met by one of Munford's regiments, which quickly chased him in the other direction. For the moment, though, they were the only Confederate regiment in the immediate area, and as the rest of Gregg's division came up, the Rebels withdrew to the northwest.

The Ashby's Gap Turnpike is now called the John Singleton Mosby Highway, US 50. Along the highway is the Aldie Mill, built in 1807, which witnessed much of the early fighting of that day as the two sides pressed each other up and down the turnpike. Today the mill is a living history park, open on the weekends seasonally and still operating as a flour mill. As you face the road, the Union advance came from your right, while the Confederates came from your left. You will find several Virginia Civil War Trails signs here, as well as a few museum exhibits devoted to the Civil War, with an emphasis on Mosby. The tour of the flour mill, as well as the grounds around it, is quite fascinating if you have the time to stay.

Furr Farm/Snickersville Turnpike

〉 *From Aldie Mill, pull out to the left onto US 50 and drive 0.6 miles to the Snickersville Turnpike (VA 734). Turn right on the Snickersville Turnpike and drive 1.3 miles to a small gravel area, just around a bend in the road, with a stone monument and several historical markers. Pull into the gravel area.*

Aldie Gap was more than just a way through the Bull Run Mountains. The Ashby's Gap Turnpike passed through the gap, and just to the west, the Snickersville Turnpike diverged to the northwest. These two roads led to Ashby's Gap and Snickers Gap in the Blue Ridge Mountains, behind which Lee's army was moving. By breaking through Aldie Gap, Alfred Pleasanton now had two choices for breaking the Confederate cavalry screen. This also meant that Stuart had two roads to block instead of one.

Along and just north of the Ashby's Gap Turnpike, the Confederates formed a well-defended line in a ditch running across one of the area farms, holding repeated Federal charges back. Soon Gregg was on the field, and he and Kilpatrick sent several units north along the Snickersville Turnpike in an attempt to flank the Confederate left. Anticipating the movement, Munford brought up the rest of his brigade, giving him a total of 2,000 cavalrymen—five regiments—against Kilpatrick's 1,200 men.

Two Federal regiments—the First Massachusetts and the Fourth New York cavalry—made their way up the Snickersville Turnpike and through the fields to the south, fighting fiercely with the Confederates until they reached the Furr Farm. Waiting for them there were portions of the Second, Third, and Fourth Virginia cavalry, dismounted and behind a low stone wall. When the Union troopers came close to the wall, the Virginians unleashed a deadly volley. The Federals held and attempted to get around the stone wall, but soon additional Confederate cavalry arrived and pushed them back through the fields and down the turnpike to the south.

The monument here to the First Massachusetts cavalry, erected in 1883 as the first Union monument south of the Mason-Dixon line, marks the spot where the Federals tried in vain to get by the stone wall. As you face the monument, if you turn to your left you will see the remnants of that same stone wall, still in place after all these years. The Confederates were on the other side of the wall. If you keep turning left to face the road, the Snickersville Turnpike, the Federals came from the road to your left as well as the fields directly in front of you, the Furr Farm. After you read the historic markers here, carefully cross the road and see where most of the battle at Aldie took place. At the time of the battle and as you can see today, fences, ditches, and tree lines were obstacles throughout the day's fighting.

Just as Kilpatrick's Federals were retreating at 5:00 PM, David Gregg's other brigade arrived, commanded by his brother, Colonel J. Irvin Gregg. Also with the brigade were Alfred Pleasanton and one of his aides, Captain George Armstrong Custer. With these fresh troops, Custer and Kilpatrick countercharged back up the Snickersville Turnpike, reaching this same position at the Furr Farm. Beaten back and receiving word from Stuart that Federal cavalry had appeared in his rear at the town of Middleburg, Munford withdrew. Although they held the ground, Union losses came to 305 casualties. The Confederates had lost 198 men, but they had also bought time for Stuart, who by now was calling additional troopers in to meet the threat.

The Union troops in Middleburg were a regiment sent by Pleasanton through Thoroughfare Gap; only 280 men strong, most of them were easily captured by the next morning. However, the Union cavalry would soon be arriving there in force, continuing their push toward the Blue Ridge Mountains.

MIDDLEBURG

❯ *From the Furr Farm Site, carefully pull back onto the Snickersville Turnpike and make a U-turn, being very careful about traffic coming from the direction of Aldie. Drive 1.3 miles south on the Snickersville Turnpike to US 50 West (John S. Mosby Highway). Turn right on US 50 and drive 4.6 miles to North Madison Street. Be sure to slow down as you enter Middleburg, as the pedestrian tourist traffic is often high. Once you have turned on Madison Street, pull up to the small pink house on the left (the Pink Box) and find a place to park.*

After taking a day to maneuver their cavalry into a more defensible position, the Confederates formed a defensive line on the Ashby's Gap Turnpike just west of Middleburg. The Federals, however, seemed to be taking their time, with Pleasanton requesting infantry support to push farther west toward the Blue Ridge and, he hoped, the Confederate army. At 6:00 AM on June 19, Union troops from Colonel J. Irvin Gregg's brigade left their position at Aldie and rode toward Middleburg on the Ashby's Gap Turnpike. After quickly blowing through Confederate pickets in the town itself, Gregg occupied Middleburg while the Confederates retreated to their stronghold, a position called Mt. Defiance.

Within the town of Middleburg, you will find much reference to Civil War history, but as in the rest of the area, much of this is focused on the exploits of John Mosby. One of the few references to the battle is a Virginia Civil War Trails sign opposite the Pink Box, the town's Visitor Center, but the main part of the battle happened west of the town. Middleburg is a great place to stop and spend an afternoon. One stop you might want to make is the Red Fox Inn, near the spot where Stuart established his headquarters before the Battle of Aldie and only a few blocks from the Pink Box.

Mt. Defiance

> *From the Pink Box, turn around and return to US 50. Turn right onto US 50 and drive 1.5 miles. As you approach the gravel median, notice the gradual ascent you are making. Carefully pull into the median, or proceed to Upperville.*

Your drive to this point brought you up the eastern slope and just over the crest of Mt. Defiance, where Stuart formed the Confederate line. His 3,200 troopers were in a long line straddling the Ashby's Gap Turnpike, with artillery on the turnpike itself and the troopers dismounted. In the fields on either side of the turnpike, stone walls provided a strong defensive position as well as converging fire for any force that decided to assault the position from the road.

Before Colonel Gregg brought his men against Stuart's Confederate wall, he wisely took his time forming his units, placing artillery and waiting for reinforcements. Before long, about midmorning, General Gregg brought up the rest of his division and took command of the field. Soon the Federal line, 4,500 strong, overlapped the Confederates north of the turnpike. When the Union cavalry advanced in a coordinated movement, both flanks of the Rebel line were soon forced to fall back. The center held for a time, but eventually it too felt the weight of Federal numbers. The fight was heavy but decisive. Skirmishing continued throughout the day, but the Union held the town of Middleburg. Pleasanton was hesitant to move on without infantry support. Had he done so and been able to keep pressing toward the Blue Ridge Mountains, he would have found two thirds of James Longstreet's I Corps; on June 19, one division camped at Ashby's Gap, while a second camped at Snickers Gap.

Aside from a rather elaborate construction commemorating the battle that is on private property (seen only from the eastbound lanes), no memorials exist at Mt. Defiance. The crest of the ridge is still quite easy to pick out of the landscape, but it is difficult to even slow your car to view it. When you do reach the crest, however, a look both east and west will tell you why Stuart chose this position for the fight.

UPPERVILLE

Rector's Crossroads

> *From Mt. Defiance, continue 2.5 miles on US 50 West to Atoka Road (CR 713). Turn left on Atoka Road and park in the gravel area to your left.*

While the seven Union infantry corps made their way north toward the Potomac River, Pleasanton's cavalry corps was still trying to find the enemy. He certainly knew where their cavalry were, as his men had been fighting them for four days. As for the Confederate infantry, all he knew—all anyone in the Army of the Potomac knew—was that they were somewhere, or at least had been somewhere, in the Shenandoah Valley.

June 20 was filled with rain, and the dawn of June 21 found both cavalry forces where they had stopped fighting two days before. Stuart's cavalry had regrouped at the Bittersweet Farm, while Pleasanton's cavalry held the commanding ground at Mt. Defiance. Pleasanton, though, had finally been able to pry a brigade of infantry from the V Corps, Colonel Strong Vincent's brigade of James Barnes's First Division. The Confederates, for their part, were able to bring fresh troopers to the fight as Wade Hampton's brigade replaced the fought-out brigade of Colonel John Chambliss.

The morning began with H. Judson Kilpatrick's brigade of cavaliers slowly advancing westward, staying just north of the Ashby's Gap Turnpike. Before long, at 7:30 AM, an artillery duel erupted at fairly short range, lasting an hour. As the shells burst overhead, however, the Federal infantry quietly moved to Kilpatrick's left, south of the turnpike, and made their way through the woods until they found the Confederate right and rear. As Hampton's men focused on Kilpatrick on their left, the Federal infantry appeared from nowhere on their right and sent the surprised Confederates toward the rear. Hampton's entire line was soon streaming down the turnpike toward Upperville. For two hours, as the Confederates formed lines behind fences and in ditches, the Federals would use the same successful pattern—cavalry pressing on the right, followed by the infantry flanking the left—to keep Hampton's brigade moving backward down the turnpike.

Rector's Crossroads, where the 1st SC cavalry stalled the Federal advance toward Upperville.

Just to the west of your position (your left, as you face US 50) is Goose Creek, where Stuart and Hampton would form a strong defensive position. In order to do that, however, they needed time. Here, at Rector's Crossroads, the First South Carolina Cavalry came up from the rear to hold the Federal advance for as long as possible. With only 200 troopers, the regiment took severe losses but enabled the Confederates to gain a more defensible position. The South Carolinians set themselves on the high ground to your left.

Also at the crossroads is the Rector House, now home to the Mosby Heritage Area Association, which you have been passing through since Aldie. This portion of the Virginia countryside was known as "Mosby's Confederacy" during the war, and his raids and further exploits have become legendary. Two days after the battle at Upperville, Stuart would set up headquarters here in the Rector House to prepare for what would be his most infamous cavalry expedition.

Goose Creek Bridge

❭ *From Rector's Crossroads, turn left onto US 50 and drive 0.9 mile to Lemmon Bottom Road (CR 832). Turn right on Lemmons Bottom Road and drive 0.2 mile to a gravel road on your right; pull onto the gravel road and drive down to the parking area near the Virginia Civil War Trails sign.*

Slightly to your left, as you face the field, is Goose Creek Bridge. Over 200 years old, the bridge still supports traffic today. The former Ashby's Gap Turnpike left the straight course that US 50 follows today to cross Goose Creek at the bridge, and it was around this picturesque structure that Union and Confederate cavalry fought for over two hours on June 21.

After the Federals had made their way through Rector's Crossroads, they advanced west on the turnpike to the Goose Creek Bridge, where they were met with a heavy barrage of horse artillery. Soon Pleasanton brought the Federal artillery to answer, and a two-hour artillery duel ensued, with the Union cavalry making several attempts to rush over the bridge, only to be repulsed each time. Finally, again, it was the infantry's turn to make the difference in the fight. Colonel Vincent sent part of his brigade, the 83rd Pennsylvania, upstream of the bridge and around the Confederate right. The Pennsylvanians waded through the stream and outflanked Hampton's Confederates, forcing their artillery to be pulled back. At the same time, the rest of Vincent's men rushed down the steep banks of the creek with Kilpatrick's cavalry right behind them. The Confederates were again forced to abandon their position and head farther west.

As you face the field, the Federals were on the high ground opposite you, while the Confederates were on the high ground to your rear. The 83rd Pennsylvania would

Goose Creek Bridge, at left, and the adjacent battlefield.

have come from your right, crossing the low fields here and coming up on the right flank of the Confederates behind you. The rest of the Federals would have streamed down the bank opposite you, as well as over the bridge.

Following their fight here, Vincent's infantry was done for the day; they had marched more than 13 miles over a very short time. From here on out, it was a cavalryman's fight.

Vineyard Hill

⟩ *From the Goose Creek Bridge parking area, return up the gravel road to Lemmons Bottom road and turn left, then drive 0.2 mile to return to US 50. Turn right on US 50 and drive 2.8 miles to Upperville. On your left, you will see Upperville Park; drive to the gravel entrance at the far end of the park, across from a cemetery, and pull in to park.*

The high ground upon which you now stand is known as Vineyard Hill, scene of some of the most intense fighting of the Battle of Upperville. On this well-defined plateau (slightly altered over the years with the development of the surrounding park)

A view of the northern part of the Upperville battlefield from Vineyard Hill.

was a square vineyard, 250 yards on each side, bounded by thick hedgerows that provided good cover for dismounted cavalry. Hampton's brigade formed south of the turnpike in and around the vineyard, while Beverly Robertson's brigade took up position on the north side of the road. Stuart sent all but two pieces of artillery to the rear and the safety of Ashby's Gap.

H. Judson Kilpatrick's brigade, once again in the lead of David Gregg's division, was the first Federal unit on the field. Kilpatrick deployed into three columns, one north of the turnpike, one south, and the third directly on it. Kilpatrick ordered a charge along the line. On the Confederate left, the fight was over almost before it began; Robertson's brigade had spotted John Buford's cavalry division flanking their left, not knowing that Buford had no way to cross Panther Skin Creek between them, and began to fall back. Kilpatrick's men pursued, but Hampton sent a regiment into their flank from the south, stopping their advance.

South of the turnpike at Vineyard Hill, the Federal charge was put in piecemeal, and Hampton's well-protected troopers easily beat back the initial charges of the rest of Gregg's division. Although both sides had sheltered positions from which to fire, mounted charges and countercharges dominated the ground around Vineyard Hill. When the last of the Union cavalry finally took cover behind a stone wall, Confederate cavalry pursuing them were sent back to their position as well by well-timed rounds of canister fire from the Federal artillery. Finally, Hampton's brigade covered Robertson's withdrawal to the west, with Hampton then taking his men to the rear.

As you look out in almost every direction, heated cavalry fighting was taking place on every inch of ground. The grounds immediately in front of the hill as well as the open fields across the highway were filled with horsemen on June 21. Soon after the fighting began here, Buford's men met resistance to the north, only 1 mile away, and their fight could also be seen from this position.

Trappe Road

> *From Vineyard Hill, turn left onto US 50 and drive 1 mile to Trappe Road (VA 619). At the intersection, on your left, you will see several historic markers; pull into this area.*

The intersection here, where Trappe Road meets the old Ashby's Gap Turnpike, is the scene of the final action in the Battle of Upperville. Throughout the day, John Buford's division had been paralleling the movement along the Ashby's Gap Turnpike and had been continually thwarted in their efforts to hit the Confederate left by flooded streams, bad roads, and the action of Colonel John Chambliss. Finally, Buford found an opportunity to head south as his division neared the Trappe Road, crossing over the Thomas Farm. After a short but hard fight, Buford got the best of Chambliss, but soon William "Grumble" Jones's brigade appeared to reinforce the Confederates. Here, also, a great cavalry battle ensued, with mounted clashes occurring all over the Thomas Farm. Eventually, Chambliss's brigade could not continue any longer and began to head south toward the Ashby's Gap Turnpike, with Grumble Jones not far behind.

Here at the crossroads, the two separate battles would finally converge as the Confederates retreated and the Federals pursued. Robertson's brigade of Rebels formed a line behind a stone wall at Trappe Road, stopping the first Union unit, J. Irvin Gregg's brigade. The Federals took up their own position behind a stone wall north of the turnpike, hitting every Confederate unit as they passed. Soon the fight moved toward Ashby's Gap, now only a few miles in the distance, as the Union cavalry doggedly pursued and Robertson's brigade put up a desperate rearguard action. Unfortunately for the Federals, though, darkness was coming, and after a long day's fight they were not able to keep pushing toward the gap.

Five days of fighting had seen repeated victory by the Union cavalry, but in the end it was all for naught. Pleasanton was not able to gather any information regarding Lee's army, much of which by now was already crossing the Potomac. In the process, he had lost 827 men. Stuart, who had been repeatedly pushed rearward for almost 12 miles between Aldie, Middleburg and Upperville, had lost 510 Confederate troopers, but had completed his mission. On June 22, the day after the battle at Upperville, Pleasanton took his cavalry back to Aldie Gap without seeing so much as a shadow of the Army of Northern Virginia.

ROCKVILLE

❯ *From Trappe Road in Upperville, pull onto US 50 East. Continue on US 50 East through Middleburg, Aldie, and beyond, following it for 21.3 miles until you reach VA 606 (Loudoun County Parkway) near Dulles International Airport. Turn left onto VA 606 and drive 5.8 miles to the ramp for VA 267 East. Take the ramp and drive 14.7 miles on VA 267 East (a toll road) until reaching I-495. Exit to your right and then bear left to enter I-495 North and drive 7.5 miles to I-270 North. Bear left onto I-270 north and drive 3.7 miles to Exit 5 for MD 189/Falls Road. (The exit ramp itself is 1.1 miles long.) At the end of the exit ramp, bear right onto MD 189 but take an immediate left onto Great Falls Road. Drive 0.7 mile on Great Falls Road. Just after the intersection with MD 28, turn left onto North Van Buren Street. Take the next right onto West Middle Lane and pull into the parking area at the Beall-Dawson Historical Park on your right.*

The day after the Federal cavalry withdrew to Aldie Gap, Stuart advanced to Middleburg, establishing his headquarters at the Rector House and resting his horsemen for what he knew would be a massive operation. Both Stuart and Robert E. Lee knew

The Beall-Dawson House, centerpiece of the historical park in Rockville.

that the Confederates would need to know the exact whereabouts of the massive Union army just as much as the Federals needed to know theirs. The primary functions of cavalry were to screen an army's movements, protect its flanks, and gather intelligence. There had been nobody better than Stuart at gathering intelligence. There was no discussion or debate as to whether the mission was too risky; it was a no-brainer. It had to be done.

On June 25, as the first elements of the Army of the Potomac and the last of the Army of Northern Virginia found their way into Maryland, Stuart began his mission. He left two of his five brigades of cavalry with the army to maintain the screen on their right flank while leading the other three from Salem, Virginia, at 1:00 AM. After running into the trailing elements of the Union army near the town of Haymarket, Stuart moved south and east to find a longer way around the army. The Federals continued to cross the Potomac over next two days, and Stuart gave them a wide berth as he circled back toward Washington. His men finally crossed the flooded Potomac overnight at little-used Rowser's Ford on July 27. The next morning the cavalry headed northeast to Rockville, Maryland.

Rockville was a prime example of a torn town in a border state. Both Union and Confederate sympathies were strong here, even though the capital at Washington was just to the south. At the time Stuart's men entered the town, holding slaves was still legal in Maryland, and there were plenty throughout the town (although many fled upon the Confederates' arrival). Though virtually no combat occurred in Rockville during the Civil War, to say that families, neighbors, and the community as a whole suffered from the fallout of their divided loyalties is a vast understatement.

Your first stop in Rockville, at the Beall-Dawson Historical Park, begins to tell the story of the town during both Stuart's short occupation and the war as a whole. Although there are exhibits here, such as the Beall-Dawson House, other historic buildings, and interpretive signs, the most effective aspect of the block-sized park is its feel. Living history reenactors roam the grounds seasonally, helping to convey a sense of the feelings of the time. Strolling through the peaceful gardens and quiet neighborhood streets show you how close the neighbors were, while interpretive signs along the way remind you just how badly they were torn apart when the war came.

When Stuart's cavalry entered the town, one of their first activities was to round up the town's Union sympathizers and take them prisoner to prevent them from alerting the Federals to their presence. Across the street from the Beall-Dawson House, on Adams Street, is the former home of John and Dora Higgins, a pro-Union family. Stuart's men came to arrest Higgins, but as it was Sunday, he had already left for Christ Episcopal Church. Sneaking away when she got the chance, Dora ran toward the church to warn her husband and other Union sympathizers of the Confederates' presence.

> From the parking lot at the Beall-Dawson House, pull out to your right onto Middle Lane and take the next right on Adams Street. Drive two blocks on Adams Street to Jefferson Street (MD 28) and turn left, then take the first right onto South Washington Street. A large church will be on your right; find a place to park on the street.

This is Christ Episcopal Church, where John Higgins and his fellow vestrymen were preparing for the Sunday service. Dora Higgins arrived in time to alert her husband and others in the group to remain in the vestry, out of sight of the Confederate troopers combing the town for Union sympathizers. She succeeded in her mission and warned several other men on her way home to boot. However, after Stuart's cavalry left with their prisoners at the end of the day, Dora returned to the church to let her husband know that it was safe to come out. It was not. Dora had been followed by the Confederate rear guard, who arrested the men and took them with the rest of Stuart's command.

The story of the Higgins family, though one of the more dramatic, was a common one in Rockville. Virginia Civil War Trails signs throughout the town further tell the

The Higgins House, home of one of Rockville's strongest Unionist families.

story of Stuart's occupation and how it forced the town to make hard choices on the spot. Neighbors betrayed one another while simultaneously standing strong for each others' fair treatment and well-being. It was not often that the Civil War directly touched Maryland, but when it did, the effects were powerful.

> *Turn around on South Washington Street and drive north back to Jefferson Street. Turn right onto East Jefferson Street (MD 28) and drive 0.1 mile to the next left at Maryland Avenue. Turn left on Maryland Avenue, then take the next left turn after that onto Montgomery Avenue/Courthouse Square. Find a place to park on the street (watch the parking meters) and walk to the old courthouse.*

This is Rockville's old courthouse, dating back to 1840 and still in administrative use today, although the town has grown considerably. In the jails of the courthouse and on the town square, the Confederates rounded up prisoners while also gathering what spoils they could from a nearby Federal army railroad car and a captured wagon train. At 6:00 PM, Stuart finally left Rockville and headed north, dragging his spoils and more than 400 prisoners—most civilians—with him. Needless to say, the Confederate column, already well behind the Union army's advance north, moved slowly. (After the Confederates were a good distance away from the town and other means of spreading intelligence quickly, the prisoners were paroled and set free.) Stuart may have gained a few temporary prizes from his daylong stay in Rockville, but it would significantly compromise his mission of keeping Lee informed of the Union army's location.

PROSPECT HALL

> *Continue on Rockville's Court House Square one block to South Washington Street and turn left. Drive one block and take the next right onto West Jefferson Street (MD 28) and drive for 1 mile to I-250. Take the ramp for I-250 North and drive 26.6 miles to Frederick. Take the Jefferson Street exit to US 15 South/US 340, turning left at the end of the exit ramp. Follow US 340 West for 0.4 mile, then take the MD 180 Exit. At the end of the exit ramp, continue straight 0.2 mile on Himes Avenue, then pull into the drive to the left next to the monument and historic signs.*

Irvin McDowell. George McClellan. John Pope. George McClellan again. Ambrose Burnside. Joe Hooker. All of these men had taken their turn at the helm in the eastern theater and none had found success. The war was more than two years old now, and although things were going well in every other theater, the eyes of the world were continually on the Union Army of the Potomac, wondering who would be next in the carousel of generals who could not find a way to defeat the much smaller and poorly equipped Army of Northern Virginia.

Hooker had been in command for five months but was already fighting an uphill battle to maintain his position. Most of his generals no longer had faith in him. Secretary of War Edwin M. Stanton wanted him out. General-in-Chief Henry Halleck, a bitter enemy of Hooker's since before the war, was back in the loop after Hooker initially requested that he deal only with the president. It seemed that the only one left with any faith in Hooker's abilities was President Lincoln, who would always have the final say but who also felt political pressure to replace the man who had been so soundly outgeneraled at Chancellorsville.

On June 27, the last elements of the Union army crossed the Potomac River into Maryland. The headquarters of the army was accordingly moved to Frederick, as was George Meade's V Corps. Hooker, meanwhile, was headed west to Harpers Ferry. He had been successful at prying troops away from the Washington defenses, but had been stymied by Halleck in his efforts to take control of the troops at Harpers Ferry. Hooker had hoped to bring at least some of the 10,000 men of that garrison to join his force, but Halleck's answer was already waiting for him when he arrived: No.

For Hooker, this was the last straw. In his eyes, 10,000 fresh and fit soldiers that he needed were being put to little use at Harpers Ferry, while in Washington, a man who was not fit for desk duty and who disliked him personally was making field command decisions for him. Never one to shy away from the alluring game of politics, an im-

Prospect Hall, where George Meade took command of the Army of the Potomac.

petuous Hooker wired Halleck that because he was not being given the tools he needed to do his job, he could not do it, and was therefore tendering his resignation. Halleck received the message and delivered it to the President, who held counsel with both Halleck and Stanton.

Despite Hooker's tendency to get caught up in the politics of the military, Abraham Lincoln liked him. He was aggressive, and Lincoln was convinced that Hooker deserved another chance. Hooker also had many allies in Washington who would not be pleased with his removal. Still, it was painfully obvious that Hooker could no longer work with Henry Halleck. Hooker had presented Lincoln with a me-or-him decision, although all he really wanted was the Harpers Ferry garrison.

On the evening of June 27, the Union V Corps was camped on the fields around Prospect Hall, the grand building atop the hill next to you. General George Meade's headquarters tent was also here with the rest of his corps. At 3:00 AM on June 28, Meade was awoken from a sound sleep by a courier from Washington who told him that he had come to give him trouble. He then handed him an order from the president. Lincoln had called Hooker's bluff. He was being relieved of duty, joining the dubious list of those who preceded him. Major General George Meade was now in command of the Army of the Potomac.

Along with the interpretive signs here, there is a monument, placed on the 100th anniversary of the change in command, which commemorates Meade's taking the army. Meade would go on to lead the army through the end of the war, though for much of that time General Ulysses S. Grant would be looking over his shoulder. Still, here on the grounds of Prospect Hall, that carousel of commanders for the Federal army finally came to a stop.

EMMITSBURG

> *From Prospect Hall, turn left onto Himes Avenue and take the ramp for MD 180/Jefferson Pike. As you take the ramp, keep bearing right through the cloverleaf on MD 180 until you reach US 15 North. Drive 0.7 mile on US 15 North, then take the ramp for US 15 North/I-270 West and continue on US 15 North. Now that you have gotten through the maze of entrance and exit ramps, follow US 15 North for*

The Union I and XI Corps camped here on the grounds of St. Elizabeth Anne Seton's Daughters of Charity at Emmitsburg.

22.9 miles. As you approach Emmitsburg, turn left onto South Seton Avenue (US 15 Alternate Route North). Drive 0.8 mile to the entrance to the Shrine of St. Elizabeth Ann Seton, then park in the first parking lot to your left.

Once he reluctantly accepted his new assignment Meade immediately began to gather what information he could. Because the army was in the middle of a major movement, Meade retained all of Hooker's staff, including chief Dan Butterfield and Colonel George Sharpe of the Bureau of Military Intelligence. Sharpe filled Meade in on what BMI currently believed to be true, and as usual, its assessment was strikingly accurate. Lee's entire army was indeed on the move north, and most, if not all, had crossed the Potomac River by now. Also confirmed was a report that John Gordon's brigade had been in the town of Gettysburg, Pennsylvania on June 26, meaning that it was likely that Jubal Early's entire division was in that area. Additional sources also indicated that the Confederates were not moving against Washington or Baltimore, as previously assumed, but were instead intent on the capital of Pennsylvania at Harrisburg.

Over the remainder of June 28, while the rest of the Army of the Potomac gathered around Frederick, Meade doggedly went about planning his next steps, determined to go right after Lee. Knowing that he still needed to protect Baltimore and Washington, Meade would move the army northeast, keeping a wide front and moving on parallel roads to quicken the pace. John Sedgwick's VI Corps would swing farthest to the east. To his left would be Winfield Scott Hancock's II Corps and the V Corps, to be led by Meade's replacement, George Sykes. Dan Sickles's III Corps and Henry Slocum's XII Corps were next in line. Farthest to the west would be John Reynolds's I Corps and Oliver Howard's XI Corps. The movement began the next day, June 29, at 2:30 AM.

As they marched, the Union soldiers could not help but notice the difference in their environment. They had been in the decimated farmlands south of the Potomac since the previous November. They noticed the striking contrast between the relative wasteland of Northern Virginia and the bountiful fields of Maryland and Pennsylvania, and it felt somewhat like a homecoming. Of course, the Confederates noticed this difference, too, but their perspective was quite different. They saw the same bountiful fields and noted only a land that had not suffered the ravages of war.

All seven of the Federal corps made good progress that day. The I and XI corps, along with Meade (as these two corps would likely be closest to the enemy), ended their march here at Emmitsburg. They made their camp around the grounds of the Daughters of Charity, a Roman Catholic group founded by Mother Elizabeth Ann Seton in 1809. (Now St. Elizabeth Ann Seton, she was the first American-born saint to be canonized in the Catholic Church.)

Most of the encampment lay south of the grounds, a short walk from your location here at the historic signs. To reach the grounds, walk past the cemetery across the street in front of the signs. There are paved trails that will take you throughout the beautiful grounds and gardens, and you are sure to have a very lovely stroll. Although the interpretive signs you see along the way mostly have to do with St. Elizabeth Ann Seton and the history of the Daughters of Charity, you will find that the group is inextricably linked with the Battle of Gettysburg and the Civil War, and there are several wonderful stories told along your walk. The White House on the grounds housed several generals during the army's stay here as well.

WESTMINSTER

> *From the National Shrine of St. Elizabeth Ann Seton, turn right onto Seton Avenue and drive 0.5 mile to East Main Street (MD 140). Turn right and follow MD 140 for 10.2 miles until you reach Taneytown. At the roundabout in Taneytown, continue on MD 140 (Taneytown Pike, third exit) and continue for another 9.5 miles. Take the exit for Westminster and merge right onto Pennsylvania Avenue, then drive 0.8 mile to Main Street. Take a slight left onto Main Street and drive 0.6 mile and then turn right onto South Center Street. Follow Center Street for 0.9 mile; on your left, you will see the Carroll County Farm Museum. Pull into the entrance for the museum; you will see a historic marker on the corner.*

By the time J. E. B. Stuart's cavalry left Rockville, the rest of the Confederate army was ready for action. Longstreet's I Corps and A. P. Hill's III Corps were all encamped near Chambersburg, Pennsylvania, resting and reaping the bountiful harvest of the occupied territory. Ewell's II Corps, as it had been since it left Culpeper, was still on the move. Two of his three divisions approached Harrisburg from the southwest to scout the area. The third, Early's division, had moved east through the South and Catoctin Mountains, beaten back the comparatively tiny 26th Pennsylvania Emergency Infantry at Gettysburg, and advanced as far as York, 50 miles from Chambersburg, with one brigade (Gordon's) reaching the Susquehanna River at Columbia.

Late that same night, June 28, one of Longstreet's scouts, a civilian, found the Confederates at Chambersburg and reported his findings. The man was quickly rushed to Lee's tent and was questioned repeatedly in order to verify his story, which seemed to be beyond belief. The scout had been in Frederick as the Federals were gathering there. He told Lee that the entire Army of the Potomac, which had been thought to be stationary, was moving north and was already across the Potomac River. (The scout had left Frederick before Meade was put in command.)

Lee was stunned. It seemed almost impossible that the entire Union army could have moved so far and so quickly undetected. He had previously thought that the Confederates had arrived in Pennsylvania quietly, but now that could not be the case. He immediately ordered Ewell to recall his corps so that the army would be reunited. He also wanted that unification to happen east of the Blue Ridge Mountains, forcing the Federals to move to protect Washington and Baltimore. (Longstreet's scout had erred in telling Lee that Hooker was moving toward the Shenandoah Valley.) There were many questions being asked around Confederate headquarters that night, but one was on everyone's mind: Where was Stuart?

While it was true that Stuart was given some discretionary latitude in his orders, his primary purpose in conducting his reconnaissance was to gather intelligence about the Union army's location. He had decided to ride around the Federals and meet Ewell's corps, probably near York. Failing to report to Lee that the entire Union army was north of him, however, was an unforgivable oversight. It had been suggested to Stuart that in such an event, he should retrace his way northwest and rejoin the army. Instead, he not only chose to take a much longer route but also stopped frequently for raiding and foraging, picking up prisoners and supplies that would only slow his progress.

June 29 was no different. In the early morning hours, Stuart stopped his column so that the 400 or so prisoners that he was carrying could be paroled—a process that took several hours. Around noon, the Confederates approached the small railroad depot at Hood's Mill and again stopped to destroy property and pull up track. After finishing their work, they proceeded north toward the town of Westminster.

Stuart deployed here in the fields south of Westminster before entering the town,

Main Street, scene of the climax of the battle of Westminster.

which was garrisoned by only about 100 Union troopers. There is a Maryland Civil War Trails sign here that tells part of the story and also gives information about the almshouse, now the Carroll County Farm Museum, on the grounds behind you.

❯ *From the Carroll County Farm Museum entrance, turn left onto South Center Street and drive 0.3 miles to South Church Street. Turn right on South Church Street and drive 0.4 mile, then turn left on East Main Street. Drive 0.1 mile on East Main Street; you will see two interpretive signs on your left just before Court Street. Find a place to park and walk to the signs.*

The occupation of Westminster by the Confederates was a fairly quick operation, but those 100 Union troopers, along with a small detachment of infantry, put up a fierce fight that the Confederates did not expect. As the Confederates entered the town, the Federal cavalry charged, sparking a rather fierce fight along Main Street. Soon, though, the Confederate numbers multiplied, and the Federals beat a hasty retreat to Baltimore after taking serious casualties.

The Maryland Civil War Trails sign here briefly tells the story of the fight at Westminster. The small but intrepid group of Union cavaliers came charging from your left, with the collision of the forces and much of the fight happening on the street in front of you before the Federals were compelled to withdraw. Westminster also has other strong ties to the battle at Gettysburg, mostly in dealing with its aftermath.

Around the town you will find more signs regarding the emergency Federal supply depot that was established here, the many wounded that were treated in houses throughout the town, and personal stories of defiance to Stuart's Confederates, along with the town's divided loyalties. Among the highlights are the death of Colonel Paul Revere, grandson of the famous patriot, and the recovery of Union General John Gibbon in the home of his wife's aunt, mother to two Confederate cavalrymen who had ridden through town only days before with Stuart.

HANOVER

❯ *From the historical markers, continue 0.7 miles on East Main Street, then take a slight right onto Pennsylvania Avenue. Continue on Pennsylvania Avenue as it becomes MD 97 North (Littlestown Pike) for 3.3 miles. Turn right onto MD 496 East (Bachmans Valley Road) and drive 7.2 miles to MD 30 North (Hanover Pike). Continue on MD 30, which becomes PA 94 as it crosses the state line, for 8.7 miles. As you enter the town of Hanover, PA 94 will become the Baltimore Pike. When you reach the town square, park your vehicle and be sure to feed the meter.*

Early on June 29, A. P. Hill's III Corps began to leave Chambersburg and pass through the Cashtown Gap, only 8 miles northwest of Gettysburg. Longstreet's corps would follow. The three scattered divisions of Richard Ewell's II Corps at Harrisburg and at York would all receive their orders later in the day. They were to converge upon Gettysburg as quickly as possible, uniting the army until more information on the Union position could be gathered. (Ewell's orders, written by Lee's staff, were not clear, and he actually marched for Cashtown instead.)

On June 30 the movement continued. Two of Hill's divisions were already through the gap, and now all three of Ewell's divisions had received their orders and were on their way. Longstreet's troops encountered delays getting through the narrow gap in the wake of Hill's divisions, and part of his force remained near Chambersburg.

Hill sent a brigade toward Gettysburg to get a look at what might lay in wait for them. The commander, J. Johnston Pettigrew of Henry Heth's division, reached the outskirts of the town by 11:00 AM, only to detect the presence of Federal infantry and return to Cashtown, under orders not to engage the enemy.

It was not infantry he had found; it was John Buford's cavalry division, screening the left flank of the Federal army and only just arriving in the town. When Pettigrew gave his report, Hill seemed convinced that the men they had seen could only be a scouting party, despite Pettigrew's objections, and that no sizeable force of Federals was anywhere near Gettysburg. Heth proposed moving his division there the next day, July 1. Hill did not hesitate in his assent.

John Buford, in Gettysburg, was preparing for the arrival of forces from both armies. Hearing reports of Hill to the west and Ewell to the north and possibly the east, Buford began to secure the town from all three directions, shifting the weight of his line in Hill's direction, which he perceived as the most immediate threat. As for his own army, he knew that George Meade had been pressing his army northward, probing with cavalry to find the Confederates. Meade also knew that the largest threat lay to the west, and accordingly shifted the III and XI corps to the left to support John Reynolds's I Corps, which would be just south of Gettysburg by the end of the day. This flank would be anchored at Gettysburg, although Meade had decided to pause for the moment behind Pipe Creek in Maryland, a strong defensive position 20 miles long, until his cavalry could find some solid information regarding the location of the Confederates.

One of those cavalry units was led by H. Judson Kilpatrick. His newly created division left Littlestown, Maryland, at 8:00 AM that morning and headed north, hoping to gather some intelligence for the probing Union army. By 10:00, they were on their way out of the town of Hanover, Pennsylvania, with only the passing wagon train, its security detachment, and the rear guard left. The rear guard had taken up a position in the town square when a small group of Confederates attacked the wagons' security detachment, chasing them into the town. When they reached the square, however,

Center Square, focal point of the battle of Hanover.

they saw that they were badly outnumbered and raced back out to their main force—J. E. B. Stuart's cavalry.

To orient your view, stand at the northwest corner of the square, which has a very nice fountain with large birds worked into the decoration. This will be your starting point for touring the battle at Hanover. A quick look around the square will reveal a good number of historic markers, statues and monuments, and interpretive signs that discuss Hanover's history and the battle that occurred here. It was here in the town square that the first attacking Confederates, about 60 of them, realized that they may have bitten off more than they could chew.

The Hanover Area Chamber of Commerce, in partnership with a number of groups, has developed an excellent walking tour of the battle that will take you through the city's streets and point out the areas of combat. It is not a short tour—in excess of 3 miles, if you visit all 33 stops on the trail—but it is an easy and a pleasant one. Brochures for the tour can be picked up in the town and can also be found online. The signs along the way also tell some wonderful stories. One of them includes a famous leap over a 15-foot-wide-ditch that Stuart, a renowned horseman, had to make to avoid capture. Another sign points out the home where a Confederate artillery shell crashed through the house and landed in the room where the family had gathered for safety. The shell failed to explode, and the man of the house, probably with some caution, threw it outside.

"The Picket," a Hanover memorial to the Union soldier.

The initial Confederate charge by Stuart's lead brigade came from the direction of Frederick Street and quickly headed back in that direction. The fighting occurred throughout the streets of the town for some time, making the Battle of Hanover unique in that it was not only urban combat, rare in itself during the Civil War, but also urban cavalry combat.

As the rest of Kilpatrick's division began to spill back into the town, the Confederates were pushed farther to the southwest along Frederick Street and then into the fields of the Forney Farm, south of the town and to your left as you walk away from the square. Finally, two of Kilpatrick's new commanders, both of whom had been promoted to Brigadier General only the day before, led the final charge that secured the town for the Federals. Elon Farnsworth and George Armstrong Custer, who would gain great fame in this war and afterward, pushed Stuart's Confederates to a knoll south of the town, then set themselves on high ground in between. Although neither side dared flinch, the fighting was over. After dark, Stuart withdrew to the east, anxious to rejoin his army.

GETTYSBURG

❯ *From the square at Hanover, turn onto Frederick Street (PA 194 South), heading southeast, and drive 7.2 miles on PA 194 South, which will become the Hanover Pike. When you reach North Queen Street (PA 97) in Littletown, turn right and follow PA 97, the Baltimore Pike, for 8.7 miles. On your left, you will see the entrance for the Gettysburg National Military Park Museum and Visitor Center.*

Well over a million people from all around the globe visit Gettysburg National Military Park every single year. It is undeniably the shining star of the National Park System's Civil War sites, the one must-see that almost anyone on the street can name. Throughout the park's history, there has always been so much to see and do here, whether through recreation, study, or both, that repeat visitors are common; in fact, there are many who make at least an annual pilgrimage to this hallowed ground. In addition, the significant efforts made over the last several years to restore the battlefield to its original condition, as well as those that are planned for the years to come, now almost ensure that every visit to the park will lead to a new experience. So if you have been to Gettysburg before, but it has been more than a few years, you need to visit again.

In 2008, Gettysburg opened its new Visitor Center, replacing the old, decrepit building that was situated on the battlefield. The new center, much larger and more visitor-friendly, is well hidden from the battlefield itself, part of the park's efforts to recreate the viewshed from the time of the battle. With the opening of the new park also came some new ideas about how visitors can see the park, so the Visitor Center should be your first stop.

As you enter the lobby, one of the first things you will notice is a very short orientation presentation that will familiarize you with all of your options for the day, as well as what you'll find in the building. The park has now created combination pack-

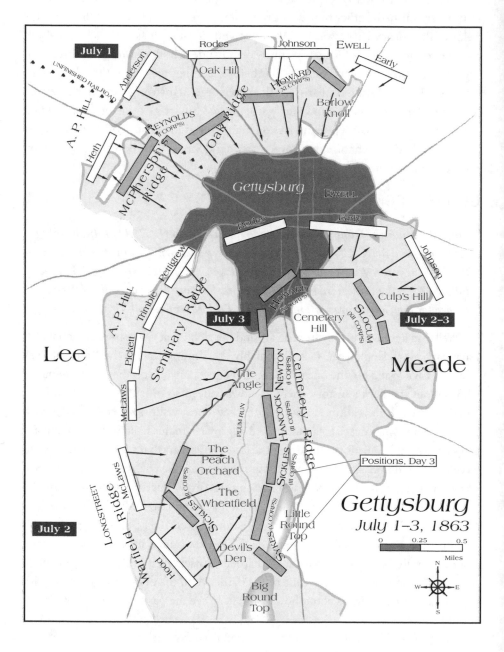

July 1

UNFINISHED RAILROAD

Rodes

Johnson

EWELL

Oak Hill

Early

A. P. Hill

Anderson

Oak Ridge

HOWARD
(XI CORPS)

Barlow
Knoll

Heth

REYNOLDS
(I CORPS)

McPherson Ridge

Oak Ridge

Gettysburg

EWELL

Rodes

Early

Johnson

A. P. Hill

Trimble

Pettigrew

Seminary Ridge

Culp's Hill

July 3

HOWARD
(XI CORPS)

SLOCUM
(XII CORPS)

July 2-3

Lee

Pickett

The
Angle

Cemetery
Hill

Meade

McLaws

NEWTON
(I CORPS)

Cemetery Ridge

HANCOCK
(II CORPS)

Positions, Day 3

LONGSTREET

McLaws

The
Peach
Orchard

SICKLES
(III CORPS)

SICKLES
(III CORPS)

The
Wheatfield

PLUM RUN

Gettysburg

July 1–3, 1863

Warfield Ridge

Hood

Devil's
Den

SICKES (V CORPS)

Little
Round
Top

0   0.25   0.5

Miles

July 2

Big
Round
Top

N
W   E
S

ages for the different options to help ensure that the large variety of visitors is able to see exactly what they wish. Still, your best bet is to plan ahead as much as possible. Because improvements and changes are constantly being made, be sure to check the park's website before visiting.

At the Visitor Center itself, there are some wonderful exhibits that may occupy a good portion of your time. Make sure that you leave yourself enough time to tour the battlefield, but the more you view here, the better your experience will be out there.

A new 22-minute film, narrated by actor Morgan Freeman and featuring several other stars, tells the story of Gettysburg not from the standpoint of a tactical blow-by-blow recounting of events, but rather as it fits into the larger scope of Civil War, American, and even world history. Don't be fooled, you'll learn about how the battle was fought, but more important, you'll learn why it was fought and why it was so significant. There are two theaters here that are constantly running the film, so you won't have to wait long to see it.

Also here is the famous Gettysburg Cyclorama painting, a massive 360-degree rendering of Pickett's Charge on the last day of the battle. In its former setting, the Cyclorama was nearly destroyed by the leaky and poorly designed building that housed it, which essentially turned it into an air filter and caused significant deterioration on both the front and back of the canvas. Now meticulously restored, the Cyclorama is not only in a much more stable environment but is also more approachable, allowing the viewer to get close to the painting and take it all in.

The new Visitor Center at Gettysburg National Military Park.

A far cry from the exhibits of the past, the new museum at Gettysburg tells the visitor the story from the beginning of the war chronologically, leaving none of the major issues of the war untouched. Whereas the former museum simply didn't have the ability to display more significant and/or sensitive pieces safely, the new museum brings the prime pieces of the park's collection front and center. It is also highly interactive and does an excellent job of asking the visitor to consider tough questions about the Civil War. Its interactive nature is also a bonus for younger visitors, who will enjoy this visit much more than they would the old center. Temporary exhibit space also exists, and the park is constantly rotating new exhibits through the center.

Most important, the Visitor Center is where you will choose how to visit the battlefield. In the past, with the large numbers of visitors, Gettysburg could often become overcrowded, with many cars taking the auto tour at a time. You can certainly still take the self-guided auto-tour, a 24-mile, well-guided path through the park that tells the story of the battle in chronological order. Also, as in the past, you can hire a licensed guide to take you through the park. The guide will take you on a two-hour tour through the park, and based on your preference can either give you the whirlwind tour or focus on a specific part of the battle. All of the guides need to go through a rigorous examination process before receiving their licenses, so you can be assured that you will get someone who really knows their stuff. Finally, you also have the in-

A display details the creation and restoration of the famous Gettysburg Cyclorama.

between option of a guided bus tour through the park. This two-hour tour, also by a licensed guide, is quite a bit more standardized than the personal tour, but can be a great value.

Before you leave the Visitor Center, be sure you are ready to go. The bookstore here is excellent, and there is also a restaurant on-site. Full facilities are available, and there aren't many other places in the park you'll find them. Also, be sure to see if there are any special ranger programs or other events going on that day.

McPherson's Ridge

❯ *From the Visitor Center, use the same entrance you came in and turn left onto the Baltimore Pike. Drive 0.7 mile on the Baltimore Pike to the point where the road turns to the right and becomes Baltimore Street. Drive 0.6 mile on Baltimore Street to West Middle Street (PA 116 West). Turn left on PA 116 West and drive 1.2 miles to Reynolds Avenue South. Turn right on Reynolds Avenue and drive 0.6 mile to the pull-off area on your right. Exit your vehicle, carefully cross the road, and walk toward the monuments in the woods.*

For several weeks, both armies had known that a battle was forthcoming. Many also surmised that it would be large, perhaps the biggest, and might even determine the outcome of or even finish this war. But when night came on June 30, virtually no one anticipated that that battle would happen the next day, and they did not expect it to be at this place, the small college town of Gettysburg, Pennsylvania.

On the morning of July 1, the main bodies of the armies were not close to Gettysburg. John Buford's Union cavalry occupied the town, with the expectation that the I and XI corps would be arriving that day to form the left of what would be a Union line running over 20 miles, and accordingly, the army was putting itself in a position to form that line. As for the Confederates, the nearest corps was in Cashtown, another was divided but on its way there, and the third was still on the other side of the South and Catoctin Mountains. The two armies had been searching for each other for weeks, each of them only able to pick up occasional clues about the other's location. Yet that very morning, the advanced pickets of the two units whose collision would begin the Battle of Gettysburg lay within 1 mile of each other.

As he had proposed to A. P. Hill, Henry Heth began to move his division toward Gettysburg at 5:00 AM to do what was, in essence, a reconnaissance in force. Some time over the course of the evening, Hill had decided to add to this force and directed Dorsey Pender's division to follow Heth's advance. Heth had been instructed not to bring on an engagement, only to see who or what was holding the town, so the addition of this division seemed a bit much, but Heth would certainly not complain. 15,000 Confederates would now be part of the operation.

The Union view from McPherson's Ridge.

Union general John Buford was always one to plan for every contingency. He had spread his pickets wide around Gettysburg, having seen a large number of Confederates briefly the day before. This attention to detail paid off just after 6:00 AM when the pickets posted at the Cashtown Pike, running to the northwest, spotted a large dust cloud approaching them from up the road. Word was immediately sent back, and by 7:00 a Union observer in the cupola of the Lutheran seminary spotted the Confederates. By that time, the advance of Heth's column and the Federals were in plain sight of each other, with the Confederates unlimbering their light artillery. At 7:30, with the armies only a half-mile apart, a Union officer fired the first shot of the battle, and the Confederates responded with artillery fire.

Heth sent two Confederate brigades forward, forming lines of battle on both sides of the Chambersburg Pike and slowly but cautiously pushing through the woods on either side. Buford's pickets kept up a steady resistance but continued to fall back toward what had already been labeled as the primary defensive position—McPherson's Ridge.

You are now located on the crest of McPherson's Ridge. This was quite obviously the best defensive position the Federals had to guard the Chambersburg Pike (now the Chambersburg Road, US 30, just in front of you). It might be a bit difficult to see why at the moment, but you may get a better view at one of the next stops that will demonstrate why they chose this ridge. The ridge runs to the north across the road. The positions here south of the pike were more defensible, with the exception of Oak Ridge, a branch of the main ridge north of the pike.

Buford deployed William Gamble's division along McPherson's Ridge, along with artillery, with orders to hold the ridge as long as possible. Until the Union I Corps arrived to provide infantry support, however, all knew that it would be a tough assignment. The Federal advance units were already doing a good job of keeping the Confederates cautious; now Gamble would up the ante. He sent 400 men west to another strong position, Herr's Ridge, to provide the Confederates with the first real challenge to their advance. Sure enough, Heth's pickets, suddenly seeing the enemy in force, stopped to await further orders. Still, it was not long before the Federals were pushed back to McPherson's Ridge.

As soon as the action had begun that day, Buford sent couriers to John Reynolds, commanding the left wing of the army. Reynolds relayed the messages to Meade and to Oliver Howard, commanding the XI Corps, and galloped hurriedly ahead of the army to Gettysburg. Meeting Buford in town, Reynolds was very quickly briefed and viewed the situation from atop the cupola of the seminary. The I Corps was still at least 2 miles away, and Reynolds asked Buford if he could hold the ridge until they arrived. Buford said that he would, and Reynolds sent messages to the III and XI corps to advance as quickly as possible.

Reynolds's I Corps (commanded at that moment by Abner Doubleday, as Reynolds was in command of the entire left wing) soon appeared to the south. Lysander Cutler's Second Brigade of the First Division was the first to arrive just before 10:30 AM, deploying north of the turnpike, with Solomon Meredith's First Brigade—the Iron Brigade—forming south of the road. Both sides set themselves on the Western face of McPherson's Ridge. The presence of infantry instantly made a difference; just as the Iron Brigade arrived, the Confederates were advancing through the Herbst Woods, the small forest in front of you. The Federals moved to meet them, and fierce fighting erupted all along the line. Reynolds, on horseback just east of the woods, rushed his upcoming units into the fight, leading from the front as he often did. His bravery had always inspired his men, but on this day, it would cost him his

JOHN REYNOLDS

John Reynolds's death at Gettysburg on July 1 was, by most accounts, the loss of a rising star. Born in Lancaster, Pennsylvania, only 50 miles east of where he died, Reynolds was only 42 years old. He performed well in the field and quickly rose through the ranks, showing enough of the tendencies of a good general to be offered command of the Army of the Potomac after Chancellorsville, which he declined. Reynolds was engaged at the time of his death, and had planned to introduce his fiancée to his family on July 8; unfortunately, they would meet only when she arrived to mourn him.

Reynolds Monument.

life. Reynolds was hit in the back of the neck by a Confederate bullet, killing him instantly.

Reynolds's exhortations were not in vain, however. The Iron Brigade advanced against the Confederates—James Archer's brigade—and drove them out of the Herbst Woods, inflicting terrible losses and capturing Archer. By 11:00 AM, the Federals were in complete control of the field south of the turnpike. To the north, however, things were a bit more desperate.

In the woods in front of you, the spot where General Reynolds fell is marked with a memorial, and you will find several other monuments and statues dedicated to him in the area. Of course, monuments abound here at Gettysburg—there are more than 1,300 in and around the park—and you will also find several others to the men who fought here, particularly to the Iron Brigade and to Buford's cavalry, who had fought stubbornly in their defense of McPherson's Ridge.

❯ *Continue driving on Reynolds Avenue, crossing US 30, for 0.4 mile (noting the railroad tracks), then turn left on Buford Avenue and drive another 0.3 mile, going around the bend to your left. Pull over next to the monument.*

Just as the Confederate line had broken south of the pike, the Federal line was about to break to the north. Cutler's brigade, outnumbered from the beginning, began to fall back from McPherson's Ridge in disorder. All of this was happening in the midst of command changes; Reynolds's death set off a chain reaction of instant promotions that, if not executed correctly, could lead to great confusion. Fortunately for the Federals, it was quickly recognized that the collapse of Cutler's brigade meant that the right flank of the Iron Brigade was now exposed. Three regiments were wheeled to face north, where they saw Joe Davis's Confederate brigade chasing the routed Federals toward the town of Gettysburg. The three regiments immediately poured fire into the right flank of the Confederates. The Federals made a makeshift charge for an unfinished railroad embankment in front of them, and Davis's men also ran to take the same position. The fighting became hand to hand at times, but most of the Union troops here had been fairly fresh, as opposed to Davis's men, who had been fighting since the battle broke. By 11:30, Davis began to withdraw, and the Federals formed a new line on the north part of McPherson's Ridge, again facing west. For the moment, things were quiet on the battlefield, and the Union still held the ridge.

The railroad tracks that you drove over are the same ones that would later be placed on the then-unfinished railroad cut, where the morning fighting of the first day of Gettysburg ended. From your current position, turn away from the monument. You are now facing west, in the position of Cutler's brigade, with Davis's Confederates to your front.

Oak Ridge

❯ Continue on Buford Avenue 0.3 mile, then continue straight onto Confederate Avenue. Stop for a moment at the Eternal Light Peace Memorial, dedicated in 1938 in conjunction with the battle's 75th anniversary. A remarkable 1,800 veterans of the Civil War were present for the dedication—almost a quarter of those still alive at the time. The memorial stands on a prominence called Oak Hill. After you have explored the memorial, continue around Confederate Avenue another 0.3 mile to the observation tower at Oak Ridge.

By 11:30, the battle over McPherson's Ridge had settled down to an artillery duel. The remainder of the I Corps was placed on the ridge, and at noon the first units of Oliver Howard's XI Corps began to arrive. Henry Heth pulled the Confederates back and began to rearrange his division. Dorsey Pender's division was also brought up. There seemed, however, to be more confusion in the Confederate rear than at the front. A. P. Hill, sick and in a fog, remained in his tent. Robert E. Lee, meanwhile, questioned virtually everyone in the camp he could find trying to gather news from the front. Lee did not get an answer until Heth went to the rear around noon.

The Confederates, however, had more control of the battlefield than they knew. Richard Ewell's II Corps, which had been moving to Cashtown, had heard the fighting as they passed north of Gettysburg. Gradually, Robert Rodes's and Jubal Early's divisions were making their way south toward Gettysburg. Ewell was riding with Rodes's division when they began to hear the fighting on McPherson's Ridge at 11:00 AM. They approached the battlefield from the north without detection because of the forest and terrain, and by noon they were perched atop Oak Hill (where the Eternal Light Peace Memorial now sits) looking directly at the Federal right.

Richard Ewell would spoil the element of surprise by opening up with artillery at 1:00 PM while Rodes was still arranging his division. Still, the threat was not deemed enough to halt the deployment of the XI Corps, now commanded by Carl Schurz with

Oliver Howard's elevation to overall command of the left wing. As the new troops fell in to the right of the I Corps, attempting to place their right at Oak Hill, Rodes was preparing to advance, two brigades in front coming simultaneously from the crest and the east face of Oak Hill, with one to the west in support. He soon gave the order to move.

What neither Rodes nor Ewell had been able to see, however, was that directly behind Oak Ridge, the rise upon which you are now standing, were two brigades from the Second Division of I Corps. Colonel Edward O'Neal's brigade on the left was not able to advance at all, being instantly hit by Federal fire. Alfred Iverson's brigade, to his right, did advance, but not finding O'Neal's brigade, began to drift eastward toward the Federals, who had by now lined up behind a stone wall on the ridge and laid low. When Iverson was within 100 yards, the command to fire was given. The devastation went on for several minutes, and was so complete that Iverson could not command any longer, too shaken to continue.

If you are able to climb the tower here, do so; it will provide a much better understanding of what occurred on the first day at Gettysburg. From here, McPherson's Ridge, Oak Ridge, and the other prominences in the area seem to pop up out of the ground for you to see. Still, if you do not want to climb the tower, the fight at Oak Ridge is still easy to interpret. Standing at the base of the tower and looking toward the road, turning to your right toward the Peace Memorial will show you where Iverson's brigade emerged from. They initially marched toward a position in front of you, but began to stray toward you just a bit until they were hit by the deadly fire from the Federals on the ridge. They were eventually able to wheel to their left to face your position, but by then they had already suffered greatly.

Barlow Knoll

> *From the Oak Ridge observation tower, bear left onto Robinson Avenue to swing around to Mummasburg Road. Turn right on Mummasburg Road and drive 0.4 mile to Howard Avenue. Turn left on Howard Avenue and follow it for 0.7 mile to a hairpin curve in the road. Park in the designated area in the curve.*

In the early afternoon, Robert E. Lee could no longer wait for information to come to him and headed for the front. Upon the way, he encountered Henry Heth, who informed him of the situation. Lee was obviously anxious and somewhat upset at the lack of information about the battle that he clearly heard ahead of him (with much of this directed at Stuart's absence). Ewell, by now, had begun his attack, and Heth asked Lee if he should join in the assault. Lee replied that he should not; Longstreet's entire corps was still not even in Cashtown, and Lee did not want a battle that day.

It was far too late for that. By now, though, the front was shifting. Carl Schurz did not give his XI Corps commanders much direction as to where they should be placed, so they placed themselves. Francis Barlow, commanding the First Division, selected a piece of high ground known as Blocher's Knoll, a commanding height but also far ahead of the rest of the Union line. Rather than give new orders, Schurz directed the Third Division, to his left, to stretch themselves thin in order to join the line.

It was not long before Richard Ewell's other division on the field, Jubal Early's, appeared in front of Barlow. By the time Ewell reached him, Early had already set up his attack. Artillery was placed to hit the Federal right, while Early's entire division would be advancing.

You are now atop Blocher's Knoll, now more commonly called Barlow Knoll. As you look to the northeast (the direction you were driving toward the hill), Early's division formed at the base of the hill in front of you, behind the small creek hidden by the tree line. If you turn slightly to your right, you will see where Ewell directed yet another brigade, borrowed from Rodes's division, to assault Barlow's position.

At 3:00, Early's artillery opened, and within 15 minutes his infantry was also on the advance. Early's men pushed the Federals backward up the hill with ease, and a countercharge by Barlow was easily repulsed. Before long, Barlow's entire command began to head for the rear, and Barlow himself was wounded in the attack. Alexander Schimmelfennig's division of the XI Corps, to the left of Barlow, sent units forward to assist, but by the time they arrived, there was not only little they could do, but they also put themselves well in front of the rest of the line. Early and Rodes soon found them and drove them back as well.

By this time, Robert E. Lee was on the field. He had held for a time, watching Federal units shifting to the north to meet the threat of Ewell's corps. Now, he saw that the Union right, Barlow's position, was crumbling. On the Union left, where Henry Heth had been ordered to hold, the Federal line was growing thin. Lee did not want a battle, but that had been decided for him. Now that he was here, he would take command. At 3:15 PM, Lee ordered Heth to resume the assault.

James Archer's brigade, which had been cut to pieces at McPherson's Ridge, had been replaced at the front by J. Johnston Pettigrew's brigade. Pettigrew advanced on the group of Federals who had hit them so badly, the Union's famous Iron Brigade. The veterans of the Iron Brigade saw that the advancing Confederates overlapped their left by a great deal and instantly recognized that they were in trouble. Still, they maintained their position for as long as possible, then fell back to take a second line and re-formed in the Herbst Woods. They were soon pushed back again, and soon every brigade on McPherson's Ridge was headed to the next defensible position, Seminary Ridge. The Confederates soon brought fresh troops up for yet another assault, and finally the I Corps, which had fought the entire day, was forced to retreat.

The Federals who remained on Oak Ridge saw that to their right, the XI Corps was beginning to disintegrate. On their left, McPherson's Ridge was under heavy attack. Then, to their front, Robert Rodes's division resumed their attack around 4:00 PM and promptly shoved them backward through the town of Gettysburg.

By 6:00 that night, the Federals had been driven back from every position they had tried to hold—McPherson's Ridge, Oak Ridge, and Barlow's Knoll. In addition to those positions, the town of Gettysburg was completely behind Confederate lines. It was here at Barlow's Knoll where the unraveling began, along with Lee's arrival on the field and the attack on the Union left. At day's end, the Union army's stubborn resistance and poor leadership would cost them close to 9,000 casualties. The Confederates, initiating a battle that Lee did not want to fight, had lost more than 6,000.

Seminary Ridge

> *From Barlow Knoll, continue around the hairpin curve and drive 0.2 mile to US 15 Business Route. Turn right onto US 15 and drive 0.4 mile to East Broadway Street, then turn left onto Carlisle Street (US 15). Drive 0.6 mile, going straight through the roundabout to stay on US 15 and then turn right onto West Middle Street (PA 116). Drive for 0.7 mile on West Middle Street to Southwest Confederate Avenue. Turn left onto Southwest Confederate Avenue and drive 1.1 miles to the Virginia Memorial. As you drive on Confederate Avenue, you are driving along Seminary Ridge. There are plenty of monuments and views along the way, so drive slowly and be sure to stop if you see one that piques your interest.*

This is Seminary Ridge. Seminary Ridge was the location of much of the Confederate line throughout the second and third day of the battle. The ridge runs for about 2 miles north to south, though the Confederates did not occupy all of it. The Confederates had little choice but to occupy this ridge after the events of July 1. It was not a bad position, but it was far from the best on the field. That position, Cemetery Hill, belonged to the Union.

It was obvious to any commander who viewed the field at Gettysburg, Union or Confederate, that holding Cemetery Hill would play a key part in the battle. Therefore, when the Federal lines began to collapse on the evening of July 1, all of the Union units fell back to Cemetery Hill. The remnants of the I and XI corps, under the direction of Winfield Scott Hancock (sent there by George Meade upon learning of Reynolds's death), began to form their defensive position around Cemetery Hill and the extension running south of it, Cemetery Ridge. At about 7:00 PM, Henry Slocum's XII Corps began to arrive, and Hancock placed them on the line as well. Slocum, now chief officer on the field, took over for Hancock, who immediately left for Taneytown, Maryland, where Meade had set his headquarters for the day.

From Seminary Ridge, Lee and James Longstreet, who had ridden ahead of his

View of the Union line from Seminary Ridge.

corps to view the front, both saw the Union defenses forming on Cemetery Hill. Richard Ewell also saw its value. Deep discussions were had regarding how to take the hill, but by nightfall, it was evident that it could not be taken without great loss of life. For a time, it seemed possible that the hill directly to the east, Culp's Hill, was unoccupied and would provide an attack point behind the Union right. A scouting mission sent to investigate found that that was not the case, though it was later discovered that they had been foiled by a much smaller group of Federals than they had previously thought.

Throughout the night, both armies would set the stage for the next day's battle. Longstreet's I Corps would arrive from Chambersburg, while Ewell would retain his position overlooking the Federal right at Culp's and Cemetery Hill. Dan Sickles's Union III Corps arrived overnight, as would George Meade, who would find his generals huddled over maps in the gatehouse of the cemetery for which the hill and the ridge were named. At this meeting and until dawn, Meade would extend and adjust the defensive lines that Scott and Slocum had set, thus completing the formation of the famous Union "fishhook."

The Union line, as seen from a map, resembled a giant fishhook. The bend of the hook curved around Cemetery Hill, with the barb end resting at the high ground of Culp's Hill. That barb was held by Slocum's XII Corps, which extended around the bend of the hook to connect with part of the I Corps (now under the command of John Newton, after Meade relieved Abner Doubleday). Continuing the bend and con-

A view of Cemetery Ridge looking north.

The Virginia Memorial on Seminary Ridge.

necting Culp's Hill with Cemetery Hill was Howard's XI Corps, which swung nearly all around the base of the hill to the shaft of the fishhook. That part was taken up by the newly arrived II Corps of Scott, whose men were arranged in a straight line from Cemetery Hill southward along Cemetery Ridge, a prominent piece of high ground throughout its length. Finally, making up the end of the shaft was Sickles's III Corps, which was to form a line all the way to another commanding position, a mountain known as Little Round Top.

For the Confederates, their options were few. West of the Union line was a large open field, only occasionally broken up by farmland and the Emmitsburg Road, which ran north between the lines to the town of Gettysburg. Accordingly, Lee decided to extend his line south along Seminary Ridge, with A. P. Hill's corps near the Union center and James Longstreet's I Corps forming the Confederate right. With Ewell's II Corps remaining where it was, the Confederate line became a fishhook in itself, overlapping the Union line but without the benefit of a strong defensive position.

From your position, walk out toward the Virginia Memorial and the field in front of it. The memorial, one of the most recognizable on the battlefield, was placed here because it was the point from where Lee viewed the decisive actions of the third day of the battle. The tree line along Seminary Ridge is fairly close to what it was at the time of the battle. Unfortunately, Cemetery Hill is somewhat obscured from this position, but if you walk out into the field (something that you should always take the time to do at Gettysburg), you will see the center of the Union line directly in front of you, and to your right, the Union left, anchored at the south end by Little Round Top.

Pitzer Woods/Warfield Ridge

> *From the Virginia Memorial, continue on Confederate Avenue for 1.1 miles. Pull into the parking area for the observation tower on your left.*

Both sides spent the morning of July 2 maneuvering their pieces into place. Time was on the side of the Federals; not only did it allow for the V and VI corps to become part of the fight, but because they were fighting a defensive battle, time only meant that their position could be strengthened. The Union army had a strong defensive position naturally, and they were determined to hold it. It was obvious to both sides that if anyone would take the offensive, it would be the Confederates.

Lee was preparing to do just that. Having observed the Union positions and after receiving scouting reports about their lines, Lee determined that the attack would focus on the Federal left, the south end of the field at Little Round Top. While the defensive positions at Culp's Hill and Cemetery Hill were strong, it seemed that the other end of the line was exposed. In fact, Lee received a reconnaissance report that morning stating that there were no Federals even in the vicinity of Little Round Top. (This report was erroneous, but the Federals were not here in strength.) Longstreet's corps, on the Confederate right, would make the main assault, while Hill and Early would hold the Union center and left as needed.

It was not until noon that Longstreet began to march his men into position; in fact, A. P. Hill had only begun to extend the Confederate line to the south around 1:00 PM. The area where the two lines would join is just north of your position. This area is the Pitzer Woods. Longstreet's line filled the woods along the crest of an extension of Seminary Ridge known as Warfield Ridge, also where you are standing. If you face the open field, Longstreet's left, Lafayette McLaws's division, was formed around you, facing the same direction. To your right (and McLaws's right) was John Bell Hood's

A view across the fields of Gettysburg toward Warfield Ridge.

division, running the length of Warfield Ridge. Longstreet's Third Division, George Pickett's, was held in reserve on July 2.

If you climb the observation tower, you will get a good sense of what the Confederates were up against. When Lee formed his plans, it was thought that the Federal left did not extend past a peach orchard, which lies directly east of you. Little Round Top, the mountain to your right, was thought to be totally unoccupied. Unfortunately for them at the time, they did not have this tower to help them ascertain the Union positions. Around the area of the Peach Orchard was where the Union III Corps was formed; for now, note the rolling terrain and the rises in front of Cemetery Ridge, if you can. They will play a part on this second afternoon of the battle.

> *From the observation tower parking lot, continue 1 mile on Confederate Avenue, then pull over to the left in the designated parking area.*

This is the southern end of Warfield Ridge, and marked the far right of Longstreet's line. John Bell Hood was assigned to this portion of the line. There were not supposed to be any Federal units this far south; Hood's orders were support Lafayette McLaws's division when they advanced and turned the Federals' left flank. However, since McLaws had Union troops in front of him where they were not supposed to be, Longstreet altered the order so that McLaws would advance directly to his front while Hood, who would surely overlap the Union left, would turn and begin to roll up the Federal line. Your position here is now south of Little Round Top. If things had gone as planned, Hood would have wheeled slightly to his left and marched straight up the Federal formation, facing north to the open field in front of you.

Although there had been some small action throughout the day, it was not until just after 3:30 PM that Longstreet's artillery opened up on Dan Sickles's III Corps in the opposite field. Around 4:15, Hood's division moved forward to perform the deadly work it had in front of it.

Little Round Top

❯ *From your position at the south end of Warfield Ridge, drive 1.2 miles on Confederate Avenue as it winds its way up Little Round Top. Shortly after the intersection with Crawford Road, pull over and park, then walk out to the interpretive area. (This area is often crowded, particularly during the summer or on the weekends; drive slowly and be patient for a spot!)*

Sickles, commander of the III Corps, had been ordered to form his line along Cemetery Ridge, left of the II Corps, to extend the line to Little Round Top. As commander on the scene, though, he felt that he was at liberty to make any changes he deemed necessary. Accordingly, he discarded Meade's orders and decided to form his line in an entirely different spot.

One of the outstanding views from Little Round Top.

This is an oversimplification of the actual events, but it is not far from the truth, either. Sickles saw the rolling ground in front of Cemetery Ridge at the south end of the field and thought that it could not only provide an attacking enemy with cover, but it would also give them control of the Emmitsburg Road and a commanding position on the battlefield. So Sickles moved the entire III Corps forward, forming a crooked salient on the Federal left with its most forward point along the road at a peach orchard. Sickles did not think it necessary to tell anyone, although several did arrive over the course of the day that commented on his troop placement.

Just after 3:00, not long before Longstreet's assault on Sickles's position began, George Meade learned the true dispositions of Sickles's units from his chief engineer, Gouverneur Warren, and was furious. He ordered the II Corps up to fill in the gaps that were apparently left wide open by Sickles's rogue deployment, then rode out to the left to see just how bad things were, accompanied by Warren. As they rode it became apparent that not only was Sickles's line out of place, but the entire left was heavily compromised. Worse, it seemed that Little Round Top, a key commanding point on the battlefield, seemed to be completely unoccupied. Warren left Meade to ride up the mountain to assess the situation, and realizing the importance of the position, hurriedly began to drive troops toward Little Round Top in order to save the Union left flank.

Take a moment to savor the view here, which is impressive, and then consider why this position was so important to hold. Obviously, anyone with artillery on this highest ground would have complete command of practically the entire line along Cemetery Ridge. If it fell to the Confederates, the position on Cemetery Ridge would be untenable.

It may be challenging to pick the ridge out of the landscape from here, but it isn't as difficult as it might seem. The key is to look at the placement of the hundreds of monuments on the battlefield. These memorials, dedicated to units of every size, generals and other leaders, actions, even animals on the field, are generally located where that unit or person did something notable or where a dramatic event took place. Look to your right toward the large group of monuments in the distance, and particularly note the huge, building-sized memorial to the soldiers of Pennsylvania. Closer inspection reveals that these monuments, from the farthest point you can see to the Pennsylvania Memorial, are in a fairly straight line. This line is along Cemetery Ridge. The ridge continues past the Pennsylvania Memorial all the way to the base of Little Round Top. On the side of the Pennsylvania Memorial that is closest to you, the monuments are quite a bit more scattered in their placement. The monuments are more random because they are no longer following the line of Cemetery Ridge. This area was the location of Sickles's III Corps.

The closest Federal unit available to race to Little Round Top was Strong Vincent's

The Pennsylvania Memorial, commanding the center of Cemetery Ridge.

brigade of James Barnes's First Division, V Corps. Although technically he was required to receive the order from Barnes, Vincent recognized the urgency of the situation and took matters into his own hands, heading straight for the hill. Vincent began his climb from the east and headed uphill in a southerly direction. Not long after the reached the crest on the southern face, his brigade immediately began taking artillery fire, and in the distance he could see the Confederate infantry pressing toward him. It was Hood's division.

The Confederates began moving toward the Federals in order, but soon the entire line became disjointed. The primary reason was the loss of Hood. Wounded by an artillery shell, the tenacious division commander was brought to the rear, and would lose the use of his left arm. Two of his brigades, Evander Law's and Jerome Robertson's, kept moving east through the ground in front of you toward the mountain, with two other brigades coming behind them in reserve. On their way, regiments separated, and attacks were uncoordinated. The two regiments on the far right of Law's brigade, the 15th and 47th Alabama, overlapped Vincent's position on Little Round Top and began ascending the hill; they would be mostly unsupported. With the loss of Hood, it seemed that no one was willing to step up and take command.

Vincent formed his brigade along the south and west faces of the mountain, setting them not along the crest but down the slope. Soon artillery would be hauled up the hill, directing their fire to the Confederates coming from the west. Here, Texas and Alabama brigades repeatedly tried to push their way up the mountainside, but were refused every time. On their last effort, they came very close to breaking the line, and it was only by timely reinforcement that the Federals held. This last repulse, however, did cost the life of Union general Strong Vincent, mortally wounded in the exchange.

On the south face, the far left of Vincent's line, the 20th Maine and the 83rd Pennsylvania prepared themselves for the Alabamians. First came the 47th, and the two Federal regiments, with the aid of a number of deadly U.S. Sharpshooters who had joined the line, tore them to pieces. The 15th Alabama, seeing the 47th's failure, determined to flank the left of the 20th Maine. Colonel Joshua L. Chamberlain, commander of the 20th, saw the Confederates hurrying to his left and simultaneously extended his flank and bent it back, refusing it to the Confederates. Still, the 15th continued to charge and charge again as they continually moved to their right. Finally, as the Federals were running low on ammunition and the Confederates were about to withdraw, the left of the 20th Maine charged down the hill at the Confederates. Many of the Alabama soldiers were captured as they tried to retreat through the rocky, forested hillside. With Chamberlain's action, Little Round Top, the key position on this second day at Gettysburg, was secured for the Union.

Before you leave Little Round Top (and you may want to revisit after you have seen the rest of the field), note a few other features of the battlefield from this position. Looking down the hillside and to your left, you will see the large rock formation of Devil's Den, the next stop on your tour. Almost directly in front of you but obscured by a tree line is the Wheatfield, one of the most infamous parts of the field. The farthest tree line to your front is Warfield Ridge, and the same tree line extends to Seminary Ridge to the right.

JOSHUA LAWRENCE CHAMBERLAIN

The fight for Little Round Top is one of the most well-known and dramatic events to occur at Gettysburg, and the leader of the 20th Maine, Joshua Lawrence Chamberlain, has since achieved his own special place among Civil War buffs. Chamberlain, a professor at Bowdoin College in Maine both before and after the war, would see action in virtually every significant battle of the eastern theater from Antietam through Appomattox. By that time he was a major general, and had earned the Medal of Honor for his actions at Gettysburg. Perhaps even more significant to his legacy, his writings on the campaigns he witnessed have become invaluable sources, not to mention great reading material. His home state of Maine, which he served as governor, has done much to honor his legacy as a hero and a humble public servant.

Devil's Den

〉 *From the parking area at Little Round Top, continue 0.3 mile on Sykes Avenue to Wheatfield Road. Turn left on Wheatfield Road and drive 0.3 mile to Crawford Road. Turn left at Crawford Road and drive 0.4 mile; pull into the parking area.*

This small gorge is known as the Devil's Den. It sits at the end of Houck's Ridge, a prominent formation running in front of Little Round Top and one of the formations that Dan Sickles had chosen for his III Corps line. As Hood's scattered division pressed on toward Lookout Mountain, they repeatedly tried to gain this ground. Atop the high ground, Captain James Smith's four-gun battery repeatedly tore through the Confederate ranks with canister and grapeshot, as did the regiments of J. H. Hobart Ward's brigade who posted themselves in the rock formations here.

Laws's and Robertson's brigades both assaulted this position several times, but neither could break the Federals, although the fighting was fierce. The position of Smith's guns was difficult to access because of the terrain. It was soon realized that the guns were the key to taking Devil's Den and clearing it of Union soldiers. When Henry Benning's brigade came up behind Law and Robertson, it continued the work of trying to rush the Federals out. By this time, the Union soldiers were fought out, and the objective of holding the Federal left had been accomplished. Ward's brigade withdrew, leaving Devil's Den, along with Smith's four guns, to the Confederates, who would use it very effectively for the remainder of the day by posting sharpshooters among the rocks.

From the parking area, you can walk around Devil's Den, which is quite beautiful despite its bloody history. You can either walk up to the northwestern high ground, where Smith's guns were located, or you can continue on the road to this point and pull over. You will also see a triangular field here; this field, along with the woods around it, became a focal point of the battle, and the Confederates used the woods for shelter as they repeatedly assaulted Devil's Den.

The Wheatfield

〉 *From the Devil's Den parking area, continue on Sickles Road for 0.5 mile. Pull to the side next to the clearing on your right.*

While the struggle for Little Round Top and the Union left continued, Colonel P. Regis de Trobriand's Third Brigade, First Division, III Corps held one of those irregular pieces of the line that Dan Sickles's crooked placement had created. Further, the intense fighting to their left drew a few of de Trobriand's regiments in that direction to aid the critical situation. That left the brigade somewhat north of the fighting, holding their position in a wheat field belonging to farmer John Rose, seemingly forgotten. That would change drastically at about 5:00 PM.

Joseph Kershaw's brigade of McLaws's division was one of the last brigades of the Confederate I Corps to deploy that day. When they finally stepped toward the Union line, Kershaw realized that both Hood's and McLaws's divisions were almost hopelessly disjointed. In addition, Kershaw would be marching right past a forward position—the Peach Orchard—held strongly by the Federals. Without the support he was supposed to receive but did not, Kershaw's hopelessly exposed left would be completely open while they passed the Union position. So in the midst of the march, Kershaw was forced to make a quick decision. He wheeled two brigades to the left to face the Peach Orchard, while the other three brigades moved toward his chosen objective—a gap in the Union line near Rose's wheat field.

Kershaw's brigade took position on a knoll just before the Wheatfield and advanced through the woods to their front. De Trobriand's men and other pieces of both the III and V corps that were plugged into the line were soon forced back to the center of the Wheatfield. Kershaw had the weight of numbers, and had the situation stayed as it was he may very well have pierced the Union line here. But de Trobriand's Federals had something that he did not: support.

John Caldwell's First Division of the II Corps, not far in the rear, was called up to the Wheatfield shortly after 6:00. Because they were rushed to the scene in such haste, each brigade had to go in piecemeal, but the effect was quick. It would not, however, be without cost to the Union army. Colonel Edward Cross's First Brigade was the first to arrive, hitting Kershaw on his right and pushing it back through the Wheatfield to the trees bordering it. Cross was mortally wounded. Next up was Colonel Samuel Zook's brigade, headed toward the Confederate left. Again the Confederates fought stubbornly, but gave ground, and again the Union commander—Zook—was mortally wounded.

The Second Brigade—Colonel Patrick Kelly's Irish Brigade—came up immediately after, hitting Kershaw's left and center. The casualties on both sides were seriously mounting, but the Confederates by this time were beginning to be pushed through the trees. It was not until the Fourth Brigade, commanded by Colonel John Brooke, came up that the Confederates simply could not hold any longer. Kershaw's three regiments were forced to fall back to the Rose Farm, abandoning the Wheatfield.

As you look across the Wheatfield you are looking northeast. The Confederates were mostly behind you, although they did advance past your position and into the field. You are facing the Union line, and the direction from which the II Corps reinforcements advanced. If you turn around so that your back is to the field, the Confederates were in the clearing immediately in front of you, as well as in the trees in front and to both sides. The trees to your left are where Cross's brigade began to push the Confederate right back, beginning the process of clearing the Confederates from the Wheatfield.

If you wish to explore more of the Wheatfield, you can follow Sickles Drive to turn left at Wheatfield Road (across the field from your present position), then take the next left onto Ayres Avenue. From there, continue straight onto de Trobriand Road, which emerges just in front of your vehicle to the left. Following this path will take you through the woods around the Wheatfield, where much of the fighting took place.

The Peach Orchard

> *From the Wheatfield, continue 0.4 mile on Sickles Road to Wheatfield Road, then turn left. Drive 0.3 mile on Wheatfield Road. On your left, you will see a gravel road; pull over here, but use caution and stay out of the roadway, as this area is often used as a turnaround for tour buses and groups.*

This is the Peach Orchard, the point of Sickles's III Corps line farthest to the front of Cemetery Ridge. Sickles's line formed a salient, or angle, here around the orchard, with one side running along the Emmitsburg Road (the main road to your west), with a short portion of the line bending back around the far corner of the orchard. Notice that the Peach Orchard is actually once again a peach orchard; this is one of Gettysburg's many recent projects to restore the appearance of the original battlefield.

The fields surrounding the Peach Orchard, the foremost point of the Union line on July 2.

Sickles understandably has received a lot of criticism over the years for not forming his line along Cemetery Ridge, as ordered, and taking the ground here instead. Now that you are standing here, however, take a look at your position and see if you can understand what Sickles might have been thinking about. The small knoll that the orchard sits on actually gives you a fairly good view of the battlefield. Most of the ridges and rolls in the landscape disappear somewhat from this position, and just by observing the monuments, you will notice that there aren't many parts of the battlefield that you can't see from here. To be sure, Sickles erred in his judgment; the failure to occupy Cemetery Ridge not only endangered the Union left but also strung the III Corps out over a much longer battle line, thinning their ranks to cover the extra ground. By taking in the view from the Peach Orchard, though, perhaps you can realize that Sickles may have been reckless or even foolish, but his motives were not purely insubordinate.

At 3:30 PM, shortly before the Confederates left Warfield Ridge, artillery here in and around the Peach Orchard though, opened up on the Confederate lines. As the afternoon went on, more guns were brought up, and they inflicted many casualties as they took aim at the exposed left flanks of the passing Confederate lines. At 6:30 PM, however, the continuation of James Longstreet's rolling advance had made its way north to William Barksdale's brigade of McLaws's division, lined up on the Pitzer Woods directly across from the Peach Orchard. With a rebel yell, Barksdale's Mississippians charged across the field from the woods at the northern end of Warfield Ridge in a compact formation of 1,400 men. The Federals inflicted a good number of casualties on Barksdale's brigade before they broke, but break they did, limbering as many guns as they could and leaving a good number behind. The salient at the Peach Orchard had been destroyed, and Sickles's thinned line was now compromised.

Barksdale urged his men on, lingering near the Peach Orchard for only a short time. Three regiments began to head north up the Emmitsburg Road to roll up the flank of the Union line, while others continued to the gaps in the lines on Cemetery Ridge. Before they could get there, though, a combination of factors had conspired to deny them the day, although many on the Confederate side saw victory in their grasp. The first factor was fatigue; both the Confederate and Union soldiers had fought desperately throughout the afternoon, and both sides were played out. The second was the loss of Barksdale, mortally wounded and captured when his brigade was stunned by an unexpected Federal volley. This volley was a result of a third event that began a chain reaction that may have saved the day for the Federals: the wounding of Daniel Sickles.

As the Peach Orchard salient was breaking, Sickles was to the east at the Trostle Farm when a stray Confederate cannonball hit him in the right leg. He placed David Birney, whose division was being routed, in command, but George Meade instead gave command of the III Corps to Winfield Scott Hancock. Hancock, who was already commanding the II Corps, handed that command to John Gibbon and immediately began to take Federal units from the right to fill the holes in the Federal line. One of the first to arrive was Colonel George Willard's brigade, who advanced to Plum Run, a small creek running through the battlefield. They hit Barksdale's Confederates at point-blank range, sending them to the rear and wounding and capturing Barksdale at around 7:15 PM. Barksdale would die the next day; Sickles would lose his leg, but survive. As for Willard, he would not outlive either of them. As his regiments returned to Plum Run, he was hit by artillery and was killed instantly.

As you face the Emmitsburg Road, notice how close the Pitzer Woods are to your position, particularly compared to the point from which you looked from Seminary Ridge at the Virginia Monument. With Sickles's much-advanced position, Barksdale's brigade did not have much ground to cover to reach the Peach Orchard. Turning to your left and looking right of the Emmitsburg Road, you can see by the memorials where the Union artillery had been set up and so hastily removed at day's end.

Pennsylvania Monument

⟩ *From the Peach Orchard, turn around to go back the way you came on Wheatfield Road, then take an immediate left onto Sickles Avenue. Drive 0.2 mile on Sickles Avenue to United States Avenue, then turn right and drive 0.7 mile to Hancock Avenue. Turn left on Hancock Avenue and drive 0.4 mile, bearing left toward the massive Pennsylvania Monument.*

Just before you pulled your vehicle over, you may have noticed a tall, conspicuous monument with a statue of a soldier at the top, running with bayoneted musket in

A monument to the 1st Minnesota infantry.

hand. This is a monument to the 1st Minnesota Infantry Regiment. In the fields in front of the monument, this remarkable unit conducted one of the most heroic and tragic actions of the battle.

As the Federals were trying to re-form their line, now almost completely back at Cemetery Ridge, Cadmus Wilcox's brigade, from A. P. Hill's III Corps, started to advance toward a gap in the Union line. Hancock, trying to rally the units of the Federal III Corps, saw Wilcox's advance and desperately searched for a unit to check them. The only unit in the area was the 1st Minnesota, part of Gibbon's division of the II Corps. Without any other choice, Hancock ordered the Minnesotans, only 262 in number, against Wilcox's brigade, over 1,200 strong. They strode, bayonets fixed, straight into the Confederates and were devastated, taking over 170 casualties. At the same time, the nearby 19th Maine began to deliver a flanking fire, and Wilcox, without support on either side, withdrew back to Seminary Ridge. The 1st Minnesota had bravely stepped into the fire and saved the Union line from a possible Confederate breakthrough.

Though there would be more fighting on the Union left, Wilcox's advance was one of the last actions of the day. Darkness fell over the field with the Confederates holding on to their forward positions across the Emmitsburg Road at the Peach Orchard, at Devil's Den, and, having gained it back during the Federal retreat, the Wheatfield. The

The northern part of Cemetery Ridge, as seen from atop the Pennsylvania Monument.

Federals, though, despite an almost constant shifting, reinforcement, and replacement of units, still held the key ground on the left, Cemetery Ridge and Little Round Top.

Take your time walking around the Pennsylvania Monument; there is a lot to see. You are now back on Cemetery Ridge, having left the scattered units of the Union left behind. Not only is the monument impressive, but you can also climb to the top, giving you a remarkable view of the battlefield.

As mentioned previously, the monuments and memorials of Gettysburg tell the story, and there is no better place to observe that than from the top of this monument. It's a fair flight of stairs to the top, but the view and the lesson are worth it. As you face north, toward the long, straight line of monuments, you can now easily see Cemetery Ridge, and can probably now see it along to the south as well, where the III Corps was supposed to be lined up on July 2. Instead, when you look to the south, you see a disjointed jumble of different monuments, although the ridge is fairly clear. Before you make your way down, take a good look at Seminary Ridge, across the field, and notice the distance compared to that of the Peach Orchard noted earlier. This massive ground would be the scene of the climactic action of Gettysburg.

Spangler's Spring

❯ *From the Pennsylvania Memorial, continue to the next street, Pleasanton Avenue, and turn right. Drive 0.3 mile to Taneytown Road (PA 134) and turn left. Drive 0.5 mile north on Taneytown Road to Hunt Avenue. Turn left on Hunt Avenue and drive 0.5 mile to the Baltimore Pike, then turn right. Drive 0.3 miles on the Baltimore Pike to the park road at Colgrove Avenue on your left. Follow Colgrove Avenue for 0.5 mile, keeping to your left until you reach the parking area at Spangler's Spring.*

As the crisis grew on the Union left, units were pulled from every possible direction. That included the Union right at Culp's Hill, the "barb" of the fishhook line, as well as Cemetery Hill, around which the bend of the fishhook curved. For almost the entire day, there was no action here. Over the late afternoon, almost the entire XII Corps was sent to the left, although they would not be there in time to make a difference. The only unit left on Culp's Hill was the Third Brigade of the Second Division, occupying an entrenched position that was built for an entire corps.

As the day grew dark, Richard Ewell recognized that there could be an opportunity at Culp's Hill, and arranged for three brigades of Edward Johnson's division to attack the eastern face of the position. Two other brigades from Jubal Early's division would do the same against Cemetery Hill, which was slightly to the north. It was almost sunset when the Confederates began to move toward George Greene's strong and deceptively small force.

In this area, Spangler's Spring, you are just beyond the right of Greene's Union position. Rather than stretch his brigade over the entire line of vacated Union earthworks, Greene concentrated his brigade in the place he thought it would have the most effect. As it happened, Johnson's men would attack almost directly against Greene's line. Greene still knew that he was outnumbered, though, and although his men held the Confederates off, he was still calling for reinforcements, all of which would have to make their way through a thick forest on a dark night.

One of Johnson's brigades, commanded by George Steuart, arrived slightly behind the others and was able to flank the Union right. The Federals quickly formed a defense, refusing their flank by wheeling parts of two regiments to face the right. Finally, confronted with a late charge and the arrival of Union reinforcements just before 10:00 PM, the Confederates withdrew to the base of the hill, having gained a hold on the hill but unable to break the Union right.

Although the Confederates would make no progress here on July 2, it was determined that the attack would be renewed the next morning. The Rebels stayed in their positions at the base of the hill. Hearing quite a bit of noise to the front throughout the night, they knew that it could only mean trouble.

Trouble was the return of the XII Corps. Alpheus Williams, in temporary command as Slocum (mistakenly) still commanded the right wing of the army, brought the three brigades of his First Division, and close on his heels was John Geary's Second Division, which had inexplicably been "lost" for several hours after having departed for the Union left the day before. Williams suddenly had five more brigades to add to George Greene's single brigade that had fought off the Confederates on July 2. Under orders from Slocum, Williams put the brigades in line and massed artillery to the south, hoping to drive off the Confederates at first light.

Fifteen minutes after sunrise, the XII Corps got a small surprise. Dawn brought a rain of artillery on the Confederate positions, after which the Union brigades would attack. The Confederates, however, beat them to the punch, beginning their assault first. This attack had less success than the one mounted the day before, as they now had an entire corps in their face. The assault continued until 10:30 AM, and except for one poor decision to attack the Confederate left over open ground that tore two Federal regiments apart, the Union army decisively came away the victors here, holding firmly onto Culp's Hill.

This immediate area, near a feature known as Spangler's Spring (just across from the parking area), is where that final Federal charge was made on July 3. If you are facing the parking area and turn to your right, the clearing you see is where the Second Massachusetts, and later the 27th Indiana covering their retreat, took heavy losses. You will find monuments to both here, as well as another devoted to all the troops from the state of Indiana who fought at the battle.

Walking up the road to your left, just past the trees, you will enter the area where Greene's men fought off the Confederates during the night of July 2. The walk up the road is a fairly good uphill hike, and you can drive to the area and pull to the side, but the roads wind a bit, and you may be better off leaving your vehicle here. Besides, walking the battlefield is always a better option than driving, and you will get a sense of what the charging Confederates encountered as they made their way uphill toward the rock-solid Union line.

Culp's Hill

❭ *Continue on Colgrove Avenue, bearing right and driving 0.3 mile to Slocum Avenue. Turn right on Slocum Avenue and drive 0.3 mile to the entrance at Culp's Hill, driving another 0.1 mile to the parking area at the observation tower.*

This is the crest of Culp's Hill. The right of Johnson's Confederates came up against the Federals in this area during the fighting on both July 2 and 3. This spot also marks the left of Greene's line on July 2. The two Confederate brigades on the right and in the center, those of John Jones and Colonel Jesse Williams, did not make nearly the progress that Steuart's brigade did on the left that night. Near the parking area, you will find a monument to General George Greene. Just as he did in taking the ground east of the Dunker Church at the Battle of Antietam, Greene showed great initiative in his defense of Culp's Hill on July 2 with little to no command support.

The observation tower here will give you an excellent view of Culp's Hill, Cemetery Hill, and Gettysburg, still a small, picturesque college town for all its growth and fame after the battle. To the northeast, you may be able to discern Benner's Hill and Brinkerhoff's Ridge, where the Confederates massed as much artillery as they could against the Union batteries on Cemetery Hill. (The signs atop the tower will help you pick them out of the landscape.) Other parts of the battlefield, including much of where the July 1 fighting took place, are also readily visible from here.

Even if you don't climb the tower, the view from here, as well as the steep drive coming up, should give you an idea of what an important position this was. Cemetery Hill was certainly the key to holding Cemetery Ridge, but had the Federals lost Culp's Hill, holding onto Cemetery Hill with the Confederates on this high ground in their rear would have been a very difficult prospect.

Cemetery Hill

❭ *From the Culp's Hill parking area, return to Slocum Avenue and continue to your right, then drive 0.3 mile to Wainwright Avenue. Turn right onto Wainwright Avenue and drive 0.1 mile, pulling over in a safe spot.*

As Johnson's three brigades advanced on Culp's Hill on the night of July 2, Henry Hays's and Isaac Avery's brigades of Jubal Early's division wheeled about and advanced on the east face of Cemetery Hill. Emerging from the edge of town with Hays on the right and Avery on the left, the Confederates advanced against a thinned-out Union line formed along Brickyard Lane, now called Wainwright Avenue, where you now stand.

As you can see in the field behind you, the Federals had massed artillery on this part of Cemetery Hill, about 30 guns facing east toward Ewell's corps. The forward line, much of it manned by the units of the XI Corps who had been hit so hard the day before, formed behind the stone wall you see on your right. The road here, Wainwright Avenue, was called the Brickyard Road at the time. Even with the wall as a breastwork, the Union troops were spread very thin. Although broken in several places, though, in the end the Confederates did not get the support they needed, with Early calling off the attack in the darkness to ease his losses. The Confederate retreat was aided by a Union charge, much of it by fresh and newly arrived II Corps troops sent over by Winfield Hancock.

As you stand in the field and face Wainwright Avenue, the Confederates came from directly in front of you, which at the time had fewer trees than it does today. The Federal line stretched just past the visible area to your left, then began to curve around the Cemetery behind you, forming the bend of the fishhook line. If you turn around to face the Baltimore Pike and the cemetery, you will see the large brick gatehouse that dates back to the battle. It took quite a beating from the fight, which is perhaps why so many pictures were taken of it at the time.

The High Water Mark of the Confederacy

❯ *From East Cemetery Hill, continue north on Wainwright Avenue 0.3 mile to Locust Avenue. Turn left on Locust Avenue then take another left onto Baltimore Street. Take the next right turn onto Steinwehr Avenue and drive 0.2 mile. Turn left onto South Washington Street (PA 164), which will turn into Taneytown Road. Continue 0.9 mile on Taneytown Road to Pleasanton Avenue, then turn right. Follow Pleasanton Road and then Hancock Avenue for 0.6 mile. You will be in the midst of hundreds of monuments, signs, and probably people. Carefully pull into one of the designated parking areas.*

Late on July 2, George Pickett's division of James Longstreet's corps continued toward the battlefield. When they arrived early on July 3, plans had already been made for Pickett's men. They were the only troops on the field who had not been part of the fighting on either of the previous two days, either one of which, in isolation, would have been one of the war's bloodiest battles. Pickett's men, and Pickett himself, were eager to get into the fight, and Robert E. Lee needed them badly.

The plan was simple. The Confederates, with their fresh troops, would pierce the center of the Union line on Cemetery Ridge. The converging attack would concentrate the entirety of George Pickett's and Henry Heth's divisions, more than 13,000 men, on a single point of the line in as compact a formation as possible.

In later years, it would be said by many Confederates who were part of what would be known as Pickett's Charge that they knew disaster was looming, that they foresaw the coming onslaught but followed their orders. While it is certainly true that more than a few officers expressed that they did not believe the attack would succeed, most did not express misgivings. There were many reasons for this. For one, Lee would begin the attack by launching a massive bombardment of the Federal line, 164 pieces of artillery firing in deliberate fashion with specific targets in mind all concentrated around the same point. There was also the sheer weight of numbers. Two full divisions and several additional brigades would all be marching toward the same point, and resisting such force at a single point would not be easy for any army. Perhaps most important factor, though, was that Lee had measured his troops against the enemy's.

Numerous monuments are concentrated on the Union position at Cemetery Ridge.

The scene of Gettysburg's most dramatic and infamous act, Pickett's Charge.

After two days of hard fighting, surely these Union troops would not stand up to such a charge. They did not fight as well as the Confederates, or so Lee believed. In the first two years of the war, Lee had consistently defeated Federal forces that were much larger than his own, and by this time, he (and many of his officers) had fallen prey to the belief that they were practically invincible. Therefore, once Lee issued his orders for the day, most of the Confederates did not question them simply because of the source.

There was, though, certainly reason for great concern as well, and it was recognized by some. The most vocal of these detractors to Lee's strategy was James Longstreet, who from the night of July 2 up to the moment of the first firing on July 3 raised protests and attempted to sway his commander's decision. Longstreet's I Corps possessed a forward position at the Emmitsburg Road and had a foothold at

ONE LAST APPEAL

"General, I have been a soldier all my life. I have been with soldiers engaged in fights by couples, by squads, companies, regiments, divisions, and armies, and should know, as well as anyone, what soldiers can do. It is my opinion that no fifteen thousand men ever arrayed for battle can take that position!"

—*General James Longstreet, protesting Lee's decision to attack the Union center on Cemetery Ridge at Gettysburg*

Big Round Top, and he believed that a concentrated effort in the same place as the day before would be more successful. More than anything, though, he saw that one of his divisions (Pickett's) would have to advance across a nearly mile-wide open field with several fences in the face of Union artillery, then attempt to attack a strong defensive position behind a low stone wall with the survivors. In addition, a compact attacking formation also meant a smaller target for the Federals, as well as converging fire. Longstreet's protests verged at times on insubordination. Still, to his credit, Longstreet followed his orders to the letter and did his best to support the attack.

As for the Federals on Cemetery Ridge, the first half of the day was easy going. Most lounged in their positions on the line, even catching small amounts of sleep if they could. The decision had already been made that the Union army wasn't going anywhere. Meade had gathered his generals the night before to confer, and the decision was unanimous and fairly simple. They would not fall back, nor would they attack. They held a very strong position, and everyone expected Lee to attack the next day. They would certainly not attack themselves. If Lee did attack, they were confident that his forces would be repulsed. If he did not, they would consider leaving the next day. So, for now, they waited.

Many who visit Gettysburg linger in this portion of the battlefield. There is much to ponder here, and you should take your time walking around the area. As you face across the field, you will notice the low stone wall running in front of you along Cemetery Ridge. You will also see a group of trees, often referred to over the years as the "Copse of Trees," which many have referenced as the guiding point for the Confederate units as they made their way across the field. (This is probably somewhat true, but not completely.) Most significant, though, notice the distance across the field to the Confederate position at Seminary Ridge. The tree line has not changed, and the park has

The Famous Copse of Trees on Cemetery Ridge.

rebuilt many of the fences that existed at the time of the battle. If the soldiers of Pickett's and Heth's divisions did not realize the test they would face that morning, they certainly did once they saw the vast field between themselves and Cemetery Ridge.

Colonel Porter Alexander spent most of the morning arranging the Confederate artillery without Union harassment. It wasn't until shortly before the bombardment that Henry Hunt, Chief of Artillery for the Federals, came back from the fighting at Culp's Hill and saw what was being amassed. He immediately brought in more guns to add to the 26 behind Winfield Hancock's II Corps, in the center of the Union line on Cemetery Ridge.

At 1:00 PM, Longstreet gave the command for the Confederate artillery to fire two signal guns. The guns got everyone's attention, Union and Confederate, and the Federals scrambled to seek shelter. There was little. The bombardment killed men and horses, unlimbered Federal cannons, blew up caissons, and even began to threaten Meade's headquarters, well in the rear of the lines. This was the first part of Lee's plan for the Confederate artillery, and it was done well.

Before too long, however, it became apparent that the second part of the plan might be jeopardized by the first. It was expected that with the amount of firepower that was leveled at the Union line, the enemy's artillery would soon all be knocked out, making it safer for the Confederate infantry to advance across the open field. This did not happen as quickly as planned, so the firing proceeded at a torrid pace. This meant that the Confederate artillery used much more ordnance and powder than they had accounted for. The artillery was supposed to advance with the infantry to hit the Federals at close range. At this pace, they would not have enough ammunition to do that.

As the shells came down, Henry Hunt thoughtfully kept his cool. He knew that this bombardment would precede an infantry attack, and he did not want to waste his gunpowder on long-range counterbattery fire. He wanted to save it for close-range canister and grapeshot that would tear through the masses of oncoming men. So he commanded most of his guns not to return the fire (although some could not resist; Winfield Hancock, in fact, told his II Corps batteries to ignore Hunt's order). In addition, there was a solid line of Union artillery, 39 guns, that lay wheel-to-wheel just beyond the crest of Cemetery Ridge, out of view of the Confederates. These guns remained, for the most part, untouched by the bombardment.

Hunt also took this time to arrange his reserve artillery, as well as that of the units flanking Hancock's II Corps. The field of converging fire that he created, utilizing cannons from Cemetery Hill all the way to Little Round Top, was thoroughly deadly. Hunt had virtually ensured that from the moment the Confederates stepped out of the woods on Seminary Ridge to whichever point they might reach the Union line they would not be safe from Federal artillery.

Soon the 15-minute bombardment began to approach 90 minutes, and Union guns were still firing. It sccms that both Hunt and George Meade realized the same idea at the same time: If the Union firing stopped, the Confederates would think that they had completed the task and would advance. Without conferring, both Hunt and Meade ordered that the Union guns cease fire and pull back, and shortly before 3:00 PM they slowed to a comparable silence.

The Confederate infantry took their positions. Pickett's division formed on the south end of Seminary Ridge. Farthest to the south, making up the Confederate right, would be James Kemper's brigade, with Robert Garnett's Brigade to his left. Lewis Armistead's brigade lined up immediately behind them. To the left of Pickett's division was Henry Heth's division, commanded by J. Johnston Pettigrew since Heth's wounding on July 1. The brigades of James Archer (commanded by Colonel Birkett Fry with Archer's capture on July 1), Colonel James Marshall (commanding Pettigrew's brigade in his absence), Joseph Davis, and Colonel John Brockenbrough lined up from south to north, forming the Confederate left. Two brigades of Dorsey Pender's division (now commanded by Isaac Trimble, as Pender was mortally wounded the night before at Cemetery Hill) would also take part. This was only to be the first wave; Richard Anderson's division of A. P. Hill's III Corps would be in the second wave.

The Confederate line stepped out of the trees shortly after 3:00 and was well over a mile wide. Managing a line so wide was a difficult task, as it would prove to be on this day. Some brigades fell behind, others surged ahead. Part of this was due to the obstacles met in the field, mostly the various fences between Seminary Ridge and the Emmitsburg Road. It also had much to do with the extremely effective firing of the Union artillery. The first hits began as soon as the Rebels came into view and did not stop along any part of the line. Henry Hunt had brought up every available piece, including the now-unleashed 39 guns compacted just south of Hancock's corps. His planning and placement of the Union artillery's firing lines on short notice could hardly have been done more capably.

For the Confederates it was the opposite. Of the 164 guns that had opened the bombardment at 1:00 PM, only 18 were able to advance with the infantry to deliver short-range fire. Having only infantry going against both infantry and artillery on Cemetery Ridge was crippling to Lee's plan.

Soon the Confederates took another severe blow. The left side of their line, John Brockenbrough's brigade, could not withstand the converging fire from both the front and the massed units on Cemetery Hill, along with several infantry units that had been moved up to meet them. The brigade soon scattered and headed for the rear. The Federals simply moved on to the Confederates in line, Davis's brigade.

The Union infantry, for the most part, waited patiently as the Confederates suffered the heavy casualties dealt by Hunt's artillery. The field in front of them was wide, and it would take time before the Rebels were within an effective firing range. The men watched as the enemy slowly approached, tearing down the fences in front of them before finally reaching the Emmitsburg Road. Here the Confederates found a fence that would not go down, leaving them the option of either climbing over or going between the rails. Either method created an easy target for the Union cannons, which pounded them mercilessly.

The new leftmost Confederate brigade, that of Joseph Davis, suffered the same fate as Brockenbrough's brigade, and they were soon headed for the rear. But by this time, approaching 3:30 PM, Pickett's division, as well as Pettigrew's and Archer's brigades from Heth's division, were almost on top of the Union line. It was not long before the acting commander of Pettigrew's brigade, James Marshall, was killed on the field. As they reached the lower slope of Cemetery Ridge the Rebels came in a rush, many of them toward a point that would forever after be known simply as the Angle.

Now walk along the stone wall. The Union infantry laid low behind this wall, waiting for the Confederates to come close before they hit them at point-blank range. Before long, you will come across the Angle, slightly north of the Copse of Trees along Cemetery Ridge. The Angle is actually two angles, with the one closest to the Confederates being called the outer angle. Notice that many of the monuments here are dedicated to Pennsylvania regiments. Here, where some of the most intense fighting on the entire field occurred at Gettysburg, it was Pennsylvanians defending their home soil that would make the difference.

Lieutenant Alonzo Cushing, commanding Battery A of the Fourth United States Light Artillery, had had most of his guns knocked out during the Confederate bombardment. He insisted that the two pieces that survived be brought up to the stone wall, where the 69th and 71st Pennsylvania made room for him. Cushing's crew kept up the firing, but he was soon wounded. As he lay on the ground in great pain he continued to direct fire and bark out orders to his gun crews before another Confederate bullet hit him, killing him instantly. Unfortunately for the Federals, he did not have much infantry support immediately around the guns, so when Cushing's leaderless battery ran out of ammunition, the Confederates suddenly found a relatively unmanned section of the line in front of them. This spot was the Angle.

Almost immediately, Confederates from Garnett's and Archer's brigades attempted to gain a foothold at the Angle, while Pettigrew's brigade rushed forward in the open area north of the Angle but still in front of the wall. They first had to get through the Pennsylvanians, though, who suddenly popped up from behind the stone wall and laid a deadly volley into the Rebels.

At almost the same moment—as everything seemed to be just now—Winfield

Federal artillery near the Angle.

Hancock saw an opportunity. Kemper's brigade had been making its way to its left as it crossed the field, and its right passed directly in front of the Federal line. Hancock rushed just south of them and ordered several Vermont brigades from the I Corps to wheel right and hit the Confederates in front and flank. Just as he had arranged the flanking maneuver—which had worked so well against Brockenbrough's and Davis's brigades on the Confederate left, and would here also—Hancock was hit in the leg, bleeding severely and falling from his horse. He was immediately taken to the rear, out of the fight.

Not long after Hancock's wounding, the Confederate officer corps began to count heavy losses. James Kemper was wounded and taken to the rear, but only after his men had wrestled him away from a group of Yankees intent on capturing him. J. Johnston Pettigrew, commanding Heth's division, was wounded in the hand, although only slightly. As John Garnett's brigade tried desperately to hold on to the Angle, Garnett was shot in the head and killed instantly.

The last line that would hit the Federals was that of Lewis Armistead. Armistead's brigade had been behind Pickett's other two brigades, Garnett's and Kemper's, and when they approached the wall they gave it their all. Armistead, raising his hat on his sword to inspire his men, bravely led them into the Angle and began to roll up the stone wall, fighting all the way. Henry Hunt, Federal Chief of Artillery, was wounded when his horse was killed from under him in this advance. The Confederates were able to breach the Union line only for an instant. Armistead was also hit, mortally wounded, the last of Pickett's brigadiers to fall that day. His loss would break any momentum the Confederates had, and finally the last of them began to either surrender or try to make their way back to Seminary Ridge. There would be no second wave, there would be no reinforcements. The repulse was bloody and decisive. The fighting in this small portion of the Union center, where thousands were massed to decide a war, where men knew death may be imminent but still went forward, where ground was hallowed, lasted approximately 15 minutes.

The Angle, scene of heavy fighting during Pickett's Charge.

A bronze tablet denotes the High Water Mark of the Confederacy.

The Confederates had briefly broken the Union line during their assault near the Angle and the Copse of Trees, but only very briefly. Over 900 miles away, arrangements were being made for the Confederate surrender of Vicksburg, Mississippi to Ulysses S. Grant, thus opening the Mississippi River to the Union. Therefore, this moment—after a remarkable string of improbable victories—is often called the High Water Mark of the Confederacy. For the rest of the war, Lee's army in the east would remain on the defensive. The western theater would play similarly, with the Confederates losing Chattanooga, then Atlanta, and then suffering through Sherman's March to the Sea. This point in time was the closest that the Confederate States of America came to becoming a reality. Near the Copse of Trees, you will find a large memorial to this moment, a bronze tablet mounted upon a great granite base.

Take a walk around to read the other monuments. You will find markers where Hancock, Armistead, and others fell, denoting the actions of certain regiments, and some rather interesting ones that you should discover for yourself. It is hallowed ground, and you can only find out why by being there. You may also realize, if you hadn't already, that you certainly

> ### CASUALTIES
>
> **Confederate:** killed, 4,708; wounded, 12,693; missing or captured, 5,830; total: **23,231**
>
> **Union:** killed, 3,155; wounded, 14,531; missing or captured, 5,369; total: **23,055**
>
> **Total Casualties: 46,286**

can't cover Gettysburg in one short visit. People visit this battlefield again and again to search for more than just history.

East Cavalry Battlefield

> *Continue on Hancock Avenue 0.3 mile, then turn left on Cyclorama Drive to reach Steinwehr Avenue (US 15/Emmitsburg Road). Turn right on Steinwehr Avenue and drive 0.6 mile to Baltimore Street. Turn left on Baltimore Street and drive 0.4 mile to Middle Street, then turn right onto East Middle Street. Drive 0.2 mile to Liberty Street and turn left, then drive two blocks and turn right onto Hanover Street (PA 116). Hanover Street will become Hanover Road; drive 3.2 miles to the intersection of Hanover Road and East Cavalry Avenue. Turn left onto East Cavalry Avenue and pull over next to one of the monuments.*

Lost in the action on the field at Gettysburg but not in the minds of the Confederate high command was Stuart's Confederate cavalry. It wasn't until midafternoon on July 2 that Stuart finally appeared ahead of his cavalry. The eyes and ears of the army had come far too late to prevent the battle that Lee did not want at Gettysburg. Now that he had appeared, Lee was quick to give him a mission. Early on July 3, Stuart took 4,500 cavalry around the Federal line and made his way east with the task of protecting the left of Richard Ewell's corps at Culp's Hill. Eventually pulling up at a formation called Cress Ridge, the Confederates took position behind a tree line and pulled up, seeing Union horsemen in front of them.

The Federal cavalry was George Custer's Second Brigade of H. Judson Kilpatrick's First Division of the Cavalry Corps. David Gregg, recognizing that the roads to the east were wide open, had convinced corps commander Alfred Pleasanton that the crossroads of the Hanover Road and the Low Dutch Road should be held. Later, Gregg himself joined Custer with his entire division.

The intersection here is just west of the crossroads, which is still in its historic spot but is outside the park boundary. At this intersection, you can now drive through the heart of the battlefield, although there is not yet much interpretation here. It's a blessing in disguise. The tree lines, ridges, creeks, and fields have not changed much since the battle, and except for the crossroads itself (where no fighting took place) the area is preserved.

> *Continue on Cavalry Avenue 0.6 mile to Low Dutch Road, then turn left. Drive 0.1 mile on Low Dutch Road and take the next left onto Cavalry Field Road. Drive 0.3 mile to one of the monuments on your left and pull over.*

The fighting began in the early afternoon with Stuart ordering his horse artillery up and lobbing several shells toward the intersection. Custer returned the fire, then

Union monuments at the East Cavalry Battlefield.

sent two regiments of cavalry toward the Confederates. The two forces began sniping at each other near the Rummel Farm, still standing to the northwest of your position here, and continued for several hours. (You will better be able to see the farm once you drive past the tree line farther ahead.)

Finally, after several hours, the two sides started to up the ante, putting in more units one at a time. Around 5:30 PM, the first mounted troops began to meet each other near where you now stand, with Custer leading his Michigan cavalry against Fitzhugh Lee's Virginians. Soon a full-blown cavalry battle, rivaling the one that had happened a month earlier at Brandy Station, was well underway. After an hour of mounted combat raging in the fields around you, the Confederates eventually pulled back toward Cress Ridge, where they lingered for a time. The Federals did not pursue, and eventually Stuart led his troopers back to Lee's army.

Wills House

> ❯ *Continue 2.4 miles on Cavalry Field Road, taking notice of the Rummel Farm to your right and the various monuments as you leave the park area. At York Road (US 30 West), turn left and drive 2.9 miles to the roundabout at the Gettysburg square. Find a place to park on or around the square and walk to the Wills House.*

During and after the battle, the residents of the town of Gettysburg were flooded with the wounded and dead of both sides. Although the army lent some little assistance, for the most part, Gettysburg was stuck with the aftermath. Every home, barn, and church was turned into a field hospital. Once the wounded had been evacuated, there were the dead to bury, thousands and thousands of them. Soon the stench of death hung over the town, not only from the bodies of the soldiers but also from the hundreds of horses who were killed, lying in the July heat, all strewn about a vast area with little order.

Gettysburg, like every other town devastated by war, had to move on, so the citizens began to tend to the dead as best they could. The effort would take more than the town could possibly give, though, and they asked for assistance from both the state and federal governments. Much of the work was done by a delegation led by a prominent local citizen, David Wills, whose own home in the center of town lay in the midst of the first day's fight and served as a hospital. Pennsylvania Governor Andrew Curtin recognized Wills's leadership and tasked him with establishing what would eventually the first U.S. National Cemetery at Gettysburg.

Plans were immediately drawn up for the cemetery. Beginning in October, the Union dead were gathered and reinterred from their shallow graves on the field to new marked plots on the new grounds, just west of the then-existing cemetery on Cemetery Hill. (Although it is known that a few lie among the Union soldiers, the

Gettysburg Address Monument.

Confederate dead would be laid in mass graves and later removed to various cemeteries in the south; the vast majority of them lie in Hollywood Cemetery in Richmond, Virginia.) Meanwhile, recognizing that this cemetery would hold a solemn and significant place in the nation's history, Wills took charge of planning a dedication ceremony. He soon scored a major coup in attracting one of the premier orators of the day, Edward Everett. Wills even sent an invitation to the White House. Much to his and everyone's surprise, President Lincoln accepted.

It is thought that Lincoln wrote most of his Gettysburg Address on the train from Washington to Gettysburg, but it is almost certain the he put the finishing touches on his remarks here at the Wills House, where he and other distinguished guests stayed the night before the dedication. The home is now owned by the National Park Service, although it is operated by a separate organization. (You can still purchase tickets for the Wills House at the Gettysburg National Military Park Visitor Center.) The room where Lincoln stayed still holds the furniture from the time of his visit, and other exhibits in the house describe not only the formation of Gettysburg National Cemetery but also the effects of the battle on the town during and after the fight. Two films are also shown here, and you are allowed to set your own pace going through the home, so you may just walk up without needing to schedule a time. Just be sure that you check the operating days and hours before you go; the hours are seasonal.

Soldiers' National Cemetery

> *From the Gettysburg town square, head south on Baltimore Street and drive 0.5 mile. Take a slight right turn onto Steinwehr Avenue and drive 0.2 mile, then turn left onto Taneytown Road (South Washington Street, PA 134). Drive 0.3 mile to the parking lot on your right; you will pass the cemetery entrance on your left along the way.*

Soldiers' National Cemetery, as it was and still is officially called, was dedicated on November 19, 1863. A solemn procession proceeded from the town out to the cemetery grounds, situated where the Union right had been during the terrible battle of Gettysburg. Burial operations were still ongoing, and would continue for another five months. A speaker's platform was erected on the crown of Cemetery Hill, which stands in Evergreen Cemetery, from which the now-famous hill got its name. Fifteen thousand people attended the event, and dignitaries from all over the country were present.

Throughout the war, Abraham Lincoln had shouldered incredible burdens, and his task here was supposed to be simple. He had been invited by Wills to deliver only "a few appropriate remarks" following Everett's speech, which ran over two hours. Lincoln fulfilled his obligation, speaking for roughly two minutes in giving his address. The words he left us with, though, continue to resonate. The Gettysburg Address was an opportunity for Abraham Lincoln to explain to the country why almost 8,000 men had died here, why almost 50,000 became casualties during the largest battle ever to occur on this half of the globe, and why that battle had to be fought. His appropriate remarks, 287 words, are still regarded the world over as among the most moving words ever to describe not only the high price of liberty but also the importance of remembering that price.

A walking tour through the cemetery has been created by Gettysburg National Military Park that will take you through both Lincoln's address and the beautiful and thoughtful architecture of the cemetery. There are several monuments to the address, as well as a speaker's rostrum near the entrance that is not the one that Lincoln spoke from, but that has been used since the 1870s by a number of notable persons during various events at the cemetery. Be sure to reread Lincoln's address as you enter the cemetery, and remember those words as you walk through the thousands of graves, many of them marking the remains of the unknown, that continued to fill this field through the Vietnam War. As monumental as Lincoln's words were, the message must not be forgotten; it is the memory of the men who fought here, not his address, that makes this hallowed ground.

Soldiers' National Cemetery, final resting place for American soldiers through the Vietnam War.

The Soldiers' Monument, centerpiece of the National Cemetery at Gettysburg.

MONTEREY PASS

> *The following route follows the path that the Confederate wagon train, and then the Confederate Army, took to Monterey Pass and beyond to the safety of Virginia. There are quicker ways to get to Monterey Pass, so map those out if you wish.*

> *From the cemetery parking area, turn left onto Taneytown Road PA 134) and drive 0.4 mile to Steinwehr Avenue. Turn right at Steinwehr Avenue and drive another 0.2 mile, then turn left onto Baltimore Street. Drive 0.4 mile on Baltimore Street to West Middle Street, which is also PA 116. Follow PA 116 for 8.7 miles to the town of Fairfield, then bear right onto Iron Springs Road. Drive 3.3 miles on Iron Springs Road to Lower Gum Springs Road. Turn right onto Lower Gum Springs Road and follow it for 3.2 miles as it becomes Gum Springs Road and then Furnace Road. Finally, follow Furnace Road as it changes to Charmian Road around the bend to the right and drive another 0.3 mile. Pull over to the right and park in front of the church.*

The Fourth of July was not celebrated on both sides of the field, and where it was, displays were subdued. Both armies did not quite know what to expect from the other and were therefore ready for almost anything. During the night, Lee had withdrawn all of Longstreet's corps back to the positions they held on the morning of July 2 at Warfield Ridge, and Ewell's corps was also brought in, extending the Confederate left and abandoning the ground around Culp's Hill. Lee needed to bring his army together; he knew that they needed to reach the safety of Virginia as quickly as possible.

During the day and into the night of July 4, the Confederate wounded began to head west away from the battlefield toward Chambersburg, then south. The wagon trains also began to move along a shorter path through Monterey Pass, the closest route to Williamsport, where they would cross the Potomac. The rest of the Army of Northern Virginia would begin to leave Gettysburg as soon as night fell, aided by a strong and noisy rainstorm that would slow both the army and its wagons in the mud.

That night, knowing that at least part of Lee's army was moving, Meade sent Federal cavalry to find the wagon trains. H. Judson Kilpatrick's division got the assignment, and he took his three brigades southwest toward Monterey Pass. Around 9:00 PM, Kilpatrick caught up with the Confederate cavalry guarding the train. First contact was made near where you now stand, along the Charmian Road in front of the church where you're parked. The Confederates set one cannon in the roadway, obscuring it in the darkness. When George Custer's brigade began to approach the Confederates, it was impossible to tell friend from foe—at least until the cannon was brought out. Eventually, though, the Federals took the Confederate position, and a running battle would occur all the way through Monterey Pass to the west side of South Mountain, continuing well into the next day.

The view from South Mountain, along the driving tour of the Monterey Pass battlefield.

The Monterey Pass Battlefield Association has developed a nicely detailed 12-stop tour of the action at Monterey Pass that can be found on their website. While five of those stops are in your immediate area, and you can learn much about the action here, take the full drive if you have time. You will be well up in the hills of Pennsylvania and will be going up and down some steep grades, so be prepared. The reward, however, is a magnificent view of the Cumberland Valley from one of the tour stops, situated in a nice city park that would make a great place to rest a while. The tour continues on to the cavalry action at Leitersburg and Smithsburg, Maryland, as Kilpatrick's cavalry continued to harass and capture pieces of the trains until Stuart finally stepped in. The association also offers guided tours on their website. (One note: the Association has done a magnificent job of marking the historic areas; however, the map on the website is a bit confusing and can get you turned around quickly. Your best bet is to take your GPS and a detailed, scaled map.)

FUNKSTOWN

❭ *From the church, continue 0.6 mile on Charmian Road to PA 16 West (Buchanan Trail). Turn right onto PA 16 West and drive 3.1 miles to Midvale Road, then turn left. Drive 6.0 miles on this road; as the road crosses into Maryland, Midvale Road becomes MD 418 (Ringgold Pike). At this point, you will merge onto MD 60, the Leitersburg Pike, and drive 0.4 mile, turning left onto MD 62 South. Drive 4.1 miles on MD 62 South, then turn left onto Robinwood Drive. Continue 3.6 miles on Robinwood Drive, staying with it as it changes to Edgewood Drive. You are now in Funkstown; turn left at East Poplar Street and drive 0.2 mile to US 40, then continue another 0.5 mile onto US 40 East. You will see a restaurant with a large parking lot on your right; pull into the lot and drive to the Maryland Civil War Trails sign in the corner near the road.*

While the Confederate army made its way through Monterey Pass toward Williamsport, George Meade suddenly grew very cautious. He had seen what Robert E. Lee could do under pursuit. So when dawn broke on July 5, and the Confederates were missing, Meade knew that he had to pursue, but he did so carefully. Holding court with his generals that evening, the vote was five to two in favor of remaining where they were until Lee's intentions were clearer. It was not until July 6 that the Federals began to move, and they did not follow the Confederate path. Instead, Meade stayed east of South Mountain, keeping in mind his directive to protect Washington and Baltimore, and would head south to Frederick, Maryland before crossing his army at Turner's Gap on July 9.

Under normal circumstances, giving Robert E. Lee a five-day head start would have been unreasonably generous. However, although the Confederates made excellent time on their march to Williamsport in preparation for crossing, the river was far too swollen to cross. The rains of the previous days had made the usually easily fordable river an impassable barrier against which Lee's army was suddenly trapped. While the Confederates entrenched and prepared for the worst, expecting an attack at almost any moment, Stuart's cavalry patrolled the area around Williamsport, looking for any sign of movement from the enemy and checking any advances.

Meade sent his seven battered but already reinforced corps in the direction of Williamsport while his cavalry probed the Confederate defenses looking for weaknesses. On July 10, Stuart's cavalry was in Funkstown when John Buford's division of the Union Cavalry Corps approached from the south along the National Road (now US 40 in front of you) early in the morning. Stuart formed an arc around Funkstown with his right anchored here, on the high ground straddling the National Road.

As you face the road, Buford's cavalry approached from your right and across the fields in front of you. If you look to your left, across the road and up the rise in the ground, you will see a farm, along with a stone wall in front of it. Stuart's dismounted cavalry took protection behind this wall when the fight broke out around 8:00 AM. Across the road from the farm is where Stuart placed his artillery and formed his extreme right. The Confederate defensive would stretch nearly 3 miles around Funkstown.

Over the course of the day, Judson Kilpatrick's cavalry division would also arrive, as would both Union and Confederate infantry. The fighting went on until the early evening when Buford, knowing his men were low on ammunition, withdrew to rejoin the main body of the army. Stuart would continue to patrol the Confederate perimeter while Meade, ever suspicious of Lee's movements, would continue to mark time outside Williamsport.

WILLIAMSPORT

> *From the parking lot, turn left onto US 40 West and drive 0.6 mile to Baltimore Street. Turn left on Baltimore Street and drive 1.4 miles, continuing as it changes to East Oak Ridge Drive. Turn left onto South Potomac Street (MD 65 South) and drive 0.3 mile, then merge onto I-70 West. Drive 3.1 miles on I-70 West to Exit 26, where you will merge onto I-81 South. Drive 0.8 mile on I-81 South to Exit 2, then merge onto Potomac Street (US 11 South). Drive 1.5 miles on Potomac Street to the Williamsport Unit of Chesapeake & Ohio Canal National Historic Park, then park in the designated area.*

When the Confederate army began to arrive at Williamsport on July 6 and discovered that the Potomac River was impassable, there was a sense, possibly for the first time during Lee's command, that the Rebels might not make it out of their predicament. Even on that first day, the Confederate wagon train had been attacked by 7,000 Federal cavalry. The 700 teamsters formed their wagons in a defensive position and held the Union troopers off for almost two hours until Confederate cavalry arrived to drive them off.

Almost immediately, ferries and floats were commandeered to begin taking the wounded across the river to the safety of Virginia. Lee formed a defensive perimeter around Williamsport with the 50,000 effective men he had left after the carnage at Gettysburg, digging heavy entrenchments and using every possible second to strengthen their position. All on the Confederate side were certain that it would only be a matter of time before the Union Army of the Potomac would come in and force them to make a last stand.

Others agreed that this was the proper course of action. Henry Halleck had been peppering George Meade with telegrams since the day after the battle at Gettysburg had ended, urging him to pursue the Rebel army and finish them. What Halleck (and Lincoln, who would remain oddly silent) could not appreciate, of course, was the toll that Gettysburg had taken on the Union troops. The army did move and found itself outside the Confederate defenses on July 9. Still wary of Lee's true plans, though, Meade and his staff agreed that further investigation of the Confederate position was in order. This would continue until July 12, after several days of clear skies (and a falling

The crossing of the Potomac River at Williamsport.

Potomac River) again became filled with rain. Meade called off the attack, and did so for July 13 as well after again holding a council of war with his corps commanders.

The next day, July 14, the Federals finally advanced on Williamsport. As they had many times before, they found empty trenches where Confederate soldiers had once been. Advancing to the river, they could see that almost all of Lee's army was already across, having begun moving the previous night. All that was left to meet them was Henry Heth's division of A. P. Hill's corps, which held the Federals off until they could cross themselves. In this action, though, they would lose J. Johnston Pettigrew, mortally wounded and captured, the tenth Confederate general lost during the Gettysburg campaign.

After several days of experimentation, one of Lee's engineers had constructed a pontoon bridge out of every floating piece of material he could find, other than what was being used to transport the wounded. On the night of July 13, the bridge was completed, and the supply wagons and artillery crossed, followed by Longstreet's corps and then Hill's, with Ewell's corps fording the river by making a human barrier of the corps' tallest men across the swollen river. The last Confederates to cross were Heth's, who cut the bridge loose as soon as they were safe. The Confederates, in plain sight of the Union troops, had once again found a way to escape.

The reaction in Washington was resigned shock. Once again the cautious doctrine that plagued the commands of the eastern theater had reared its ugly head, and the Federals were left holding the bag. Meade did eventually cross over into Virginia, and Lee moved his army to Culpeper. Although there was some maneuvering over the summer of 1863, in the end, the armies ended up almost exactly where they had been just before the Gettysburg campaign began. The Confederates held a line below the Rapidan River, while the Federals gathered to the north near Warrenton, then moved south toward the Rappahannock.

There is no doubt that the battle at Gettysburg changed the course of the war. Whether it can be pointed to singly as the event that caused their defeat is debatable, but it undeniably did prove to be what it has so often been referred to as—the high water mark of the Confederacy. Never again would the Confederates launch a successful offensive. In the west, by the end of the year the Mississippi River was under Union control and the army was poised to take Atlanta. And in the spring of 1864, although George Meade would retain his command of the Army of the Potomac, his superior, Lieutenant General Ulysses S. Grant—the first United States officer to hold that rank since George Washington—would be with him, making the ultimate decisions that would bring this war to its close.

Still, almost two more years of fighting remained. The war would change, yes, but it was only half over. Much more blood would be shed and ground hallowed before the fate of the nation would be decided.

Site Information

CHAPTER 1 OPENING SHOTS: FIRST MANASSAS

Alexandria

Marshall House Site
Intersection of King Street and South Pitt
Street, Alexandria, VA 22314
Latitude: 38.804693
Longitude: –77.044680

Fort Ward
4301 West Braddock Road, Alexandria,
VA 22304
Phone: 703-746-4848
Website: oha.alexandriava.gov/fortward/
Latitude: 38.828733
Longitude: –77.101815

Fairfax

Fairfax Museum and Visitor Center
10209 Main Street, Fairfax, VA 22030
Phone: 703-385-8414
Website:
www.fairfaxva.gov/museumvc/mvc.asp
Latitude: 38.844855
Longitude: –77.300619

Fairfax Court House
4000 Chain Bridge Road, Fairfax, VA
22030
Latitude: 38.846226
Longitude: –77.306725

Vienna

Freeman's Museum
131 Church Street NE, Vienna, VA 22180
Phone: 703-938-5187
Website: www.historicviennainc.org
Latitude: 38.903557
Longitude: –77.265231

Battle Site
On Park Street SE 0.1 mile north of
intersection with Cherry Street SE,
Vienna, VA 22180
Latitude: 38.901220
Longitude: –77.259883

Falling Waters (Hoke's Run)

Valley Pike
Intersection of US 11 and Spring Mills
Road, Falling Waters, WV 25419
Website: www.battleoffallingwaters.com
Latitude: 39.544104
Longitude: –77.906134

Jackson's Position
On US 11 0.3 mile south of intersection
with Beall Road, Falling Waters, WV
25419
Latitude: 39.531601
Longitude: –77.914374

Falling Waters (Hoke's Run), cont.
Confederate Line
On US 11 0.1 mile north of intersection
   with Spring Mills Road, Falling Waters,
   WV 25419
Latitude: 39.545468
Longitude: −77.903940

Falling Waters
North intersection of Fallingwater Cutoff
   and US 11, Falling Waters, WV 25419
Latitude: 39.559671
Longitude: −77.888441

Stumpy's Hollow
Intersection of Spring Mills Road and
   Stumpy's Hollow, Falling Waters, WV
   25419
Latitude: 39.548943
Longitude: −77.918451

Piedmont Station
Piedmont Station
Intersection of US 17 and Delaplane
   Grade Road, Delaplane, VA 20144
Latitude: 38.914745
Longitude: −77.921605

Manassas
Signal Hill
On Signal View Drive (northbound lane)
   0.5 mile north of intersection with
   Signal Hill Road, Manassas, VA 20111
Latitude: 38.753213
Longitude: −77.438636

McLean's Farm
Intersection of VA 28 and Yorkshire Lane,
   Manassas, VA 20111
Latitude: 38.793211
Longitude: −77.447819

Mitchell's Ford
On Old Centreville Road 0.2 mile north of
   intersection with Somersworth Drive,
   Manassas, VA 20111
Latitude: 38.797293
Longitude: −77.457646

Blackburn's Ford
On VA 28 (southbound lanes) 0.4 mile
   south of intersection with Compton
   Road, Centreville, VA 20121
Latitude: 38.803480
Longitude: −77.449664

**Manassas National
Battlefield Park**
Visitor Center
6511 Sudley Road, Manassas, VA
   20109
Phone: 703-361-1339
Website: www.nps.gov/mana
Latitude: 38.811940
Longitude: −77.523780

Stone Bridge
Latitude: 38.824714
Longitude: −77.501205

Sudley Springs
Latitude: 38.838822
Longitude: −77.537400

Matthews Hill
Latitude: 38.826486
Longitude: −77.534218

Henry Hill
Latitude: 38.811923
Longitude: −77.523865

CHAPTER 2 JACKSON IN THE SHENANDOAH VALLEY

Winchester

Winchester–Frederick County Visitor Center
1400 South Pleasant Valley Road, Winchester, VA 22601
Phone: 877-871-1326
Website: www.visitwinchesterva.com
Latitude: 39.169297
Longitude: –78.161556

Old Court House Civil War Museum
20 North Loudoun Street, Winchester, VA 22601
Phone: 540-542-1145
Website: www.civilwarmuseum.org
Latitude: 39.184514
Longitude: –78.165450

Stonewall Jackson's Headquarters
415 North Braddock Street, Winchester, VA 22601
Phone: 540-667-3242
Website: www.winchesterhistory.org/stonewall_jackson.htm
Latitude: 39.189221
Longitude: –78.165385

Dam No. 5

Dam No. 5
0.6 miles south of intersection of Ashton Road and Dam No. 5 Road, Clear Spring, MD 21722
Latitude: 39.607250
Longitude: –77.921137

Hancock

Hancock
Intersection of Canal Street and North Church Street, Hancock, MD 21750
Latitude: 39.698231
Longitude: –78.178679

Kernstown

Bartow's Woods
217 VA 706, Winchester, VA 22602
Latitude: 39.139972
Longitude: –78.194692

Rose Hill
1850 Jones Road, Winchester, VA 22601
Phone: 888-556-5799
Website: www.shenandoahmuseum.org/history/rose_hill.html
Latitude: 39.151432
Longitude: –78.220890

Kernstown Battlefield
610 Battle Park Drive, Winchester, VA 22601
Phone: 540-662-1824
Website: www.kernstownbattle.org
Latitude: 39.144016
Longitude: –78.191987

Stony Creek

Stony Creek
Intersection of Main Street and Massie Farm Lane, Edinburg, VA 22824
Latitude: 38.820852
Longitude: –78.567931

Rude's Hill

Rude's Hill
0.4 mile south of intersection of Old Valley Pike and Caverns Road, Quicksburg, VA 22847
Latitude: 38.702441
Longitude: –78.648570

Miller-Kite House

Miller-Kite House
310 West Spotswood Trail, Elkton, VA 22827
Phone: 540-578-3046
Website: www.elktonhistoricalsociety.com
Latitude: 38.409478
Longitude: –78.612987

McDowell

Fort Johnson
6.5 miles west of intersection of US 250 and Deerfield Valley Road, George Washington National Forest, VA
Latitude: 38.311309
Longitude: –79.384241

McDowell, cont.
Highland County Museum
161 Mansion House Road, McDowell, VA
  24458
Phone: 540-396-4478
Website: www.highlandcountyhistory.com
Latitude: 38.336371
Longitude: −79.491674

Union Position
Intersection of US 250 and VA 678,
  McDowell, VA 24458
Latitude: 38.331861
Longitude: −79.489013

Sitlington's Hill
On US 250 1.6 miles west of intersection
  with VA 678, George Washington
  National Forest, VA
Latitude: 38.324272
Longitude: −79.465699

Red Bridge
Red Bridge
Intersection of Grove Hill River Road and
  Crooked Run Road, Shenandoah, VA
  22849
Latitude: 38.527101
Longitude: −78.594958

White House Bridge
Historic Markers
On US 340 West 0.2 mile from
  intersection with Hamburg Road, Luray,
  VA 22835
Latitude: 38.647528
Longitude: −78.531324

White House
On Kaufmanns Mill Road 0.2 mile from
  intersection with US 340, Luray, VA
  22835
Latitude: 38.646959
Longitude: −78.536152

Front Royal
Visitor Center
414 East Main Street, Front Royal, VA
  22630
Phone: 800-338-2576
Website: www.discoverfrontroyal.com
Latitude: 38.917453
Longitude: −78.189380

Asbury Chapel
On US 340 0.1 mile north of intersection
  with River Bend Farms Road, Front
  Royal, VA 22630
Latitude: 38.880538
Longitude: −78.246560

Prospect Hill
200 West Prospect Street, Front Royal, VA
  22630
Latitude: 38.914419
Longitude: −78.195404

Confederate Position
Intersection of North Commerce Avenue
  and Warren Avenue, Front Royal, VA
  22630
Latitude: 38.930329
Longitude: −78.192744

Richardson's Hill
Intersection of North Royal Avenue and
  West 15th Street, Front Royal, VA
  22630
Latitude: 38.936694
Longitude: −78.194610

South Fork Bridge
On North Royal Avenue 0.1 mile north
  of intersection with Depot Avenue,
  Front Royal, VA 22630
Latitude: 38.942124
Longitude: −78.194203

Guard Hill
Boat launch on Riverton Road 0.1 mile
  east of intersection with US 340,
  Front Royal, VA 22630
Latitude: 38.949751
Longitude: −78.197807

Fairview
On US 340 North 1 mile north of
    intersection with Shadows Road,
    Front Royal, VA 22630
Latitude: 38.995432
Longitude: −78.175792

First Battle of Winchester
Winchester–Frederick County Visitor
    Center
1400 South Pleasant Valley Road,
    Winchester, VA 22601
Phone: 877-871-1326
Website: www.visitwinchesterva.com
Latitude: 39.169314
Longitude: −78.161485

Camp Hill
Intersection of East Bond Street and
    South Kent Street, Winchester, VA
    22601
Latitude: 39.173757
Longitude: −78.166437

Bowers Hill
Intersection of Ramseur Lane and
    Meadow Branch Avenue, Winchester,
    VA 22601
Latitude: 39.179878
Longitude: −78.187550

Harrisonburg
Hardesty-Higgins House Visitor Center
212 South Main Street, Harrisonburg, VA
    22801
Phone: 540-432-8935
Website: www.harrisonburgtourism.com/
    Civil_War-Trails
Latitude: 38.447240
Longitude: −78.869101

Turner Ashby Monument
1164 Turner Ashby Lane, Harrisonburg,
    VA 22801
Latitude: 38.424025
Longitude: −78.861622

Cross Keys
Union Church
Intersection of Cross Keys Road and
    Battlefield Road, Harrisonburg, VA
    22801
Latitude: 38.358248
Longitude: −78.841474

Goods Mill
On Goods Mill Road 0.4 mile south
    of intersection with Bluff Road,
    Harrisonburg, VA 22801
Latitude: 38.353391
Longitude: −78.816382

Port Republic
Kemper House
8691 Water Street, Port Republic, VA
    24471
Website: www.portrepublicmuseum.org
Latitude: 38.295468
Longitude: −78.810865

The Coaling
Intersection of US 340 and Ore Bank
    Road, Port Republic, VA 24471
Latitude: 38.301623
Longitude: −78.767551

CHAPTER 3 THE PENINSULA CAMPAIGN

Hampton Roads and Fort Monroe
Congress-Cumberland Overlook
Christopher Newport Park, intersection of
West Avenue and 26th Street, Newport
News, VA 23607
Latitude: 36.977290
Longitude: −76.433430

Monitor-Virginia Overlook
Monitor-Merrimac Overlook Park,
intersection of Chesapeake Avenue
and Walnut Avenue, Newport News, VA
23607
Latitude: 36.982920
Longitude: −76.396017

Casemate Museum
20 Bernard Road, Hampton, VA 23651
Phone: 757–788-3391
Website: www.monroe.army.mil/monroe/
sites/installation/museum/
casemate_museum.aspx
Latitude: 37.002501
Longitude: −76.309489

The Mariners' Museum
The Mariners' Museum
100 Museum Drive, Newport News, VA
23606
Phone: 757-596-2222
Website: www.marinersmuseum.org
Latitude: 37.055751
Longitude: −76.488533

Young's Mill
Young's Mill
Intersection of US 60 and Old Grist Mill
Lane, Newport News, VA 23602
Latitude: 37.106088
Longitude: −76.513852

Warwick Court House
Warwick Court House
14421 Old Courthouse Way, Newport
News, VA 23602
Latitude: 37.130347
Longitude: −76.542169

Lee's Mill
Lee's Mill
Intersection of Rivers Ridge Circle and
Depriest Downs, Newport News, VA
23608
Latitude: 37.165104
Longitude: −76.565652

Skiffes Creek
Skiffes Creek
On Enterprise Drive, 0.4 mile from
intersection with US 60, Newport
News, VA 23603
Latitude: 37.178038
Longitude: −76.575941

Dam No. 1
Dam No. 1
On Constitution Way within Lee Hall
Roadside Park, 1 mile from entrance at
Jefferson Avenue, Newport News, VA
23603
Latitude: 37.182557
Longitude: −76.536569

Gloucester Point
Gloucester Point
On Vernon Street, 0.1 mile from
intersection with River View Street,
Gloucester Point, VA 23062
Latitude: 37.250503
Longitude: −76.501215

Yorktown
Yorktown
Visitor Center on Colonial National
Historic Parkway near intersection with
Moore House Road, Yorktown, VA
23690
Phone: 757-898-2410
Website: www.nps.gov/yonb
Latitude: 37.230696
Longitude: −76.502840

Williamsburg

Redoubt No. 1
On Quarterpath Road, 0.8 mile from
  intersection with US 60, Williamsburg,
  VA 23185
Latitude: 37.255254
Longitude: -76.685203

Fort Magruder
Intersection of Penniman Road and
  Queens Creek Road, Williamsburg, VA
  23185
Latitude: 37.264189
Longitude: -76.666043

Redoubt No. 12
In New Quarter Park, on Lakeshead Road
  1 mile from intersection with Allendale
  Place, Williamsburg, VA 23185
Latitude: 37.293793
Longitude: -76.645330

Cub Creek Dam
On Colonial National Historic Parkway,
  0.8 mile west of intersection with
  Penniman Road, Williamsburg, VA
  23185
Latitude: 37.282940
Longitude: -76.641160

Eltham's Landing

Eltham's Landing
Intersection of Farmers Drive and Plum
  Point Road, Barhamsville, VA 23011
Latitude: 37.513032
Longitude: -76.819625

Drewry's Bluff

Drewry's Bluff (Richmond National
  Battlefield Park)
7600 Fort Darling Road, Richmond, VA
  23237
Latitude: 37.418861
Longitude: -77.427262

Richmond

Richmond National Battlefield Park—
  Tredegar Iron Works
470 Tredegar Street, Richmond, VA
  23219
Phone: 804-226-1981
Website: www.nps.gov/rich
Latitude: 37.534802
Longitude: -77.445415

Museum & White House of the
  Confederacy
1201 East Clay Street, Richmond, VA
  23219
Phone: 804-649-1861
Website: www.moc.org
Latitude: 37.540751
Longitude: -77.429293

Hanover Court House

Hanover Court House
On Peaks Road, 0.2 mile west of
  intersection with Hanover Courthouse
  Road, Hanover, VA 23069
Latitude: 37.725515
Longitude: -77.368555

Seven Pines

First Union Line
Intersection of US 60 and J.B. Finley
  Road, Sandston, VA 23150
Latitude: 37.522620
Longitude: -77.312137

First Contact
Intersection of US 60 and Naglee Avenue,
  Sandston, VA 23150
Latitude: 37.523395
Longitude: -77.315051

Second Union Line (Seven Pines
  National Cemetery)
400 East Williamsburg Road, Sandston,
  VA 23150
Latitude: 37.520269
Longitude: -77.302100

Seven Pines, cont.

Fair Oaks
Intersection of East Nine Mile Road and
  Hanover Road, Sandston, VA 23150
Latitude: 37.530676
Longitude: −77.312871

Oak Grove (French's Field)

French's Field
On South Airport Drive (northbound
  lanes), 0.1 mile from intersection
  with Robert E. Byrd Terminal Drive,
  Richmond, VA 23250
Latitude: 37.514646
Longitude: −77.335620

Beaver Dam Creek (Mechanicsville)

Chickahominy Bluffs
4300 Mechanicsville Turnpike, Richmond,
  VA 23223
Latitude: 37.584249
Longitude: −77.389990

Beaver Dam Creek
7423 Cold Harbor Road, Mechanicsville,
  VA 23111
Latitude: 37.595753
Longitude: −77.359286

Gaines' Mill

Visitor Center
5515 Anderson-Wright Drive,
  Mechanicsville, VA 23111
Latitude: 37.585475
Longitude: −77.287154

Confederate Line
On Watt House Road, 0.3 mile south of
  intersection with Cold Harbor Road,
  Mechanicsville, VA 23111
Latitude: 37.578519

Longitude: −77.290868
Watt House
6283 Watt House Road, Mechanicsville,
  VA 23111
Latitude: 37.574323
Longitude: −77.290632

Garnett's & Golding's Farms

Garnett's & Golding's Farms
Intersection of East Washington Street
  and North Linden Avenue, Highland
  Springs, VA 23075
Latitude: 37.548524
Longitude: −77.317442

Savage's Station

Savage's Station
On Meadow Road, 0.1 mile east of
  intersection with Grapevine Road,
  Sandston, VA 23150
Latitude: 37.528396
Longitude: −77.269053

Glendale and White Oak Swamp

Glendale National Cemetery/Glendale
  Visitor Center
8301 Willis Church Road, Richmond, VA
  23231
Latitude: 37.436186
Longitude: −77.235185

Glendale Crossroads
Intersection of Charles City Road and
  Willis Church Road, Richmond, VA
  23231
Latitude: 37.445954
Longitude: −77.233328

Confederate Advance
On Longbridge Road, 0.5 mile north of
  intersection with Carters Mill Road,
  Richmond, VA 23231
Latitude: 37.441417
Longitude: −77.247951

White Oak Swamp
On Elko Road, 0.1 mile north of
  intersection with Hughes Road, Sand-
  ston, VA 23150
Latitude: 37.469208
Longitude: −77.209157

Malvern Hill
The Parsonage
On Willis Church Road, 0.2 mile north of
    intersection with Carters Mill Road,
    Richmond, VA 23231
Latitude: 37.418385
Longitude: −77.246996

Malvern Hill
9175 Willis Church Road, Richmond, VA
    23231
Latitude: 37.412837
Longitude: −77.249819

Harrison's Landing
Berkeley Plantation
12602 Harrison Landing Road, Charles
    City, VA 23030
Phone: 888-466-6018
Website: www.berkeleyplantation.com
Latitude: 37.317833
Longitude: −77.180601

CHAPTER 4 SECOND MANASSAS CAMPAIGN

Cedar Mountain
Cedar Mountain Battlefield—
    Civil War Trust
On General Winder Road, 0.2 mile north
    of intersection with US 15, Culpeper,
    VA 22701
Latitude: 38.404941
Longitude: −78.068460

Crittenden Lane
Intersection of US 15 and General
    Winder Road, Culpeper, VA 22701
Latitude: 38.401902
Longitude: −78.067393

Union Right
On Dove Hill Road, 0.4 mile north of
    intersection with US 15, Culpeper, VA
    22701
Latitude: 38.409936
Longitude: −78.065950

Union Left
Intersection of Cedar Mountain Drive
    and Old Orange Road, Culpeper, VA
    22701
Latitude: 38.408771
Longitude: −78.055554

Final Position
On Old Orange Road 0.4 mile east of
    intersection with Cedar Mountain Drive,
    Culpeper, VA 22701
Latitude: 38.411583
Longitude: −78.049272

**Crossings of the
Rappahannock River**
Kelly's Ford
At boat launch near intersection of
    Kellys Ford Road and Stones Mill Road,
    Elkwood, VA 22718
Latitude: 38.477038
Longitude: −77.781728

Beverly's Ford
On Glenna Lake Road 0.8 mile from
    intersection with Beverlys Ford Road,
    Elkwood, VA 22718
Latitude: 38.548693
Longitude: −77.846455

Freeman's Ford
On Freemans Ford Road 0.2 mile west
    of intersection with Lees Mill Road,
    Remington, VA 22734
Latitude: 38.583058
Longitude: −77.875534

Crossings of the Rappahannock River, cont.

White Sulphur Springs
On Springs Road, 0.2 mile east of
    intersection with Myers Mill Road,
    Warrenton, VA 20186
Latitude: 38.648600
Longitude: -77.871420

Waterloo Bridge
Near intersection of Waterloo Road and
    Old Bridge Road, Amissville, VA 20106
Latitude: 38.695852
Longitude: -77.906155

Catlett's Station

Catlett's Station
Intersection of Elk Run Road and
    Fernridge Road, Catlett, VA 20199
Latitude: 38.652760
Longitude: -77.639683

Bristoe Station

Bristoe Station—Kettle Run
Intersection of VA 28 and Aden Road,
    Nokesville, VA 20181
Latitude: 38.715954
Longitude: -77.561094

Thoroughfare Gap

Chapman's Mill
On Beverley Mill Drive, 1 mile west of
    intersection with Turner Road,
    Gainesville, VA 20137
Phone: 540-253-5888
Website: www.chapmansmill.org
Latitude: 38.824162
Longitude: -77.709990

Manassas Station

The Manassas Museum/
    Downtown Manassas
9101 Prince William Street, Manassas,
    VA 20110
Phone: 703-368-1873
Website: www.manassascity.org
Latitude: 38.749590
Longitude: -77.471648

Mayfield Fort
South of intersection of Quarry Road and
    Battery Heights Boulevard, Manassas,
    VA 20110
Latitude: 38.755121
Longitude: -77.453828

Manassas National Battlefield Park

Brawner Farm Visitor Center
Entrance on Pageland Lane 0.5 mile
    north of intersection with US 29,
    Gainesville, VA 20155
Phone: 703-361-1339
Website: www.nps.gov/mana
Latitude: 38.812677
Longitude: -77.572703

Sudley and the Unfinished Railroad
Latitude: 38.838805
Longitude: -77.537405

Unfinished Railroad
Latitude: 38.825566
Longitude: -77.548884

Deep Cut
Latitude: 38.820701
Longitude: -77.549143

Battery Heights
Latitude: 38.810704
Longitude: -77.557275

Warren's Artillery
Latitude: 38.813346
Longitude: -77.544872

New York Monuments
Latitude: 38.810352
Longitude: -77.543929

Chinn Ridge
Latitude: 38.806657
Longitude: -77.534594

Portici
Latitude: 38.806235
Longitude: −77.508440

Henry Hill
Latitude: 38.812393
Longitude: −77.521655

Chantilly (Ox Hill)
Ox Hill Battlefield Park
4134 West Ox Road, Fairfax, VA 22035
Website: www.fairfaxcounty.gov/parks/
    oxhill
Latitude: 38.864055
Longitude: −77.369381

CHAPTER 5 THE ROAD TO ANTIETAM

Leesburg
The Loudoun Museum
16 Loudoun Street SW, Leesburg, VA
    20175
Phone: 703-777-7427
Website: www.loudounmuseum.org
Latitude: 39.114727
Longitude: −77.566490

White's Ford
White's Ford
Entrance to trail at Chesapeake & Ohio
    Canal on Martinsburg Road 2.7 miles
    north of intersection with Whites Ferry
    Road, Dickerson, MD 20842
Latitude: 39.194780
Longitude: −77.469406

Frederick/Best Farm
Monocacy National Battlefield Visitor
    Center
5201 Urbana Pike, Frederick, MD 21704
Phone: 301-662-3515
Website: www.nps.gov/mono
Latitude: 39.377493
Longitude: −77.397447

Best Farm
Latitude: 39.376432
Longitude: −77.397002

Harpers Ferry National Historical Park
Harpers Ferry/Maryland Heights
171 Shoreline Drive, Harpers Ferry, WV
    25425
Phone: 304-535-6029
Website: www.nps.gov/hafe
Latitude: 39.318828
Longitude: −77.758955

Bolivar Heights
Latitude: 39.323791
Longitude: −77.761177

Schoolhouse Ridge
Latitude: 39.307771
Longitude: −77.777431
Murphy Farm
Latitude: 39.376432
Longitude: −77.397002

Boonsboro
Boonsboro
Intersection of US 40 and Orchard Drive,
    Boonsboro, MD 21713
Latitude: 39.509900
Longitude: −77.654027

South Mountain
Turner's Gap—Washington Mon. SP
6620 Zittlestown Road, Middletown, MD
    21769
Phone: 301-432-0480
Website:
    www.friendsofsouthmountain.org
Latitude: 39.498863
Longitude: −77.623482

South Mountain, cont.
Turner's Gap—National Road
6132 Old National Pike, Boonsboro, MD
  21713
Latitude: 39.484551
Longitude: −77.620018

Fox's Gap
On Reno Monument Road 0.9 mile west
  of intersection with Fox Gap Road,
  Boonsboro, MD 21713
Latitude: 39.470647
Longitude: −77.617527

Crampton's Gap
900 Arnoldstown Road, Jefferson, MD
  21755
Latitude: 39.405743
Longitude: −77.639549

Antietam National Battlefield
Visitor Center/Dunker Church
5831 Dunker Church Road, Sharpsburg,
  MD 21782
Phone: 301-432-5124
Website: www.nps.gov/anti
Latitude: 39.473984
Longitude: −77.745125

Antietam National Battlefield
North Woods
Latitude: 39.488872
Longitude: −77.747153

East Woods
Latitude: 39.481338
Longitude: −77.742025

The Cornfield
Latitude: 39.480933
Longitude: −77.747369

Mansfield Monuments
Latitude: 39.483342
Longitude: −77.741778

West Woods
Latitude: 39.478530
Longitude: −77.747647

Mumma & Roulette Farms
Latitude: 39.477528
Longitude: −77.741682

Sunken Road
Latitude: 39.470680
Longitude: −77.739825

Observation Tower/Piper Farm
Latitude: 39.469537
Longitude: −77.737240

Burnside Bridge
Latitude: 39.450252
Longitude: −77.732669

South Battlefield
Latitude: 39.453280
Longitude: −77.739278

Pry House
18906 Shepherdstown Pike, Keedysville,
  MD 21756
Phone: 301-416-2395
Website: www.civilwarmed.org
Latitude: 39.475624
Longitude: −77.713616

Botelar's Ford
Botelar's Ford—Maryland Side
On Canal Road 1.3 miles east of
  intersection with MD 34, Sharpsburg,
  MD 21782
Latitude: 39.431320
Longitude: −77.781486

Botelar's Ford—Virginia Side
  (West Virginia)
Intersection of River Road and Trough
  Road, Shepherdstown, WV 25443
Latitude: 39.427906
Longitude: −77.778696

Fredericksburg and Spotsylvania National Battlefield— Fredericksburg Unit

Fredericksburg—Visitor Center
1013 Lafayette Boulevard,
  Fredericksburg, VA 22401
Phone: 540-373-6122
Website: www.nps.gov/frsp
Latitude: 38.293692
Longitude: −77.466767

Chatham

Chatham
120 Chatham Lane, Fredericksburg, VA
  22405
Phone: 540-373-4461
Latitude: 38.309061
Longitude: −77.454331

City of Fredericksburg

Middle Pontoon Site
City Dock Park, Fredericksburg, VA 22401
Latitude: 38.296478
Longitude: −77.453757

Fredericksburg Civil War Walking Tour
706 Caroline Street, Fredericksburg, VA
  22401
Phone: 800-678-4748
Website: www.visitfred.com
Latitude: 38.300823
Longitude: −77.457882

Franklin's Line and Pelham's Corner

Pelham's Corner
Intersection of Tidewater Trail and
  Benchmark Road, Fredericksburg, VA
  22408
Latitude: 38.252808
Longitude: −77.426212

The Slaughter Pen

Slaughter Pen Farm
On Tidewater Trail, 0.2 mile south of
  intersection with River Meadows Way,
  Fredericksburg, VA 22408
Latitude: 38.265006
Longitude: −77.440267

The Confederate Right

Fredericksburg—Confederate Right
Intersection of Lafayette Boulevard and
  Lee Drive, Fredericksburg, VA 22401
Latitude: 38.288252
Longitude: −77.475370

The Union Advance

Northern Edge of Fredericksburg
Intersection of Prince Edward Street and
  Charlotte Street, Fredericksburg, VA
  22401
Latitude: 38.299553
Longitude: −77.461145

Canal Ditch
Intersection of Hanover Street and
  Kenmore Avenue, Fredericksburg, VA
  22401
Latitude: 38.298997
Longitude: −77.465072

Marye's Heights

Marye's Heights
1013 Lafayette Boulevard,
  Fredericksburg, VA 22401
Latitude: 38.293725
Longitude: −77.466594

Kelly's Ford

Kelly's Ford Site
At boat launch near intersection of Kellys
  Ford Road and Stones Mill Road,
  Elkwood, VA 22718
Latitude: 38.477038
Longitude: −77.781728

Kelly's Ford, cont.
Stone Wall/Pelham Monument
On Kellys Ford Road, 0.9 mile north of
  intersection with Edwards Shop Road,
  Elkwood, VA 22718
Latitude: 38.482821
Longitude: −77.794790

Final Charge
On Kellys Ford Road, 0.3 mile south of
  intersection with Newbys Shop Road,
  Elkwood, VA 22718
Latitude: 38.500287
Longitude: −77.819939

Germanna Ford/Ely's Ford
Germanna Ford
2062 Germanna Highway, Locust Grove,
  VA 22508
Latitude: 38.37773
Longitude: −77.781915

Ely's Ford
At boat launch on Ely's Fort Road 0.7
  mile north of intersection with Rapidan
  Road, Fredericksburg, VA 22407
Latitude: 38.358013
Longitude: −77.685270

**Fredericksburg & Spotsylvania
National Battlefield—
Chancellorsville Unit**
Chancellorsville—Visitor Center
9001 Plank Road, Fredericksburg, VA
  22407
Phone: 540–786-2880
Website: www.nps.gov/frsp
Latitude: 38.311456
Longitude: −77.649564

Chancellor House
Latitude: 38.309503
Longitude: −77.634479

Zoan Church
5888 Plank Road, Fredericksburg, VA
  22407
Latitude: 38.291958
Longitude: −77.573991

First Day at Chancellorsville Battlefield—
  Civil War Trust
6159 Plank Road, Fredericksburg, VA
  22407
Latitude: 38.295864
Longitude: −77.597637

McLaws' Line
Latitude: 38.298104
Longitude: −77.618097

Lee-Jackson Bivouac
Latitude: 38.294905
Longitude: −77.625167

Catherine Furnace
Latitude: 38.289095
Longitude: −77.647847

Ellwood
36380 Constitution Highway, Locust
  Grove, VA 22508
Latitude: 38.321289
Longitude: −77.737583

Jackson's Flank Attack
Latitude: 38.313478
Longitude: −77.682524

Jackson's Wounding
9001 Plank Road, Fredericksburg, VA
  22407
Phone: 540–786-2880
Latitude: 38.311456
Longitude: −77.649564

Slocum's Line
Latitude: 38.304217
Longitude: −77.639178

Hazel Grove
Latitude: 38.303947
Longitude: −77.651495
Fairview
Latitude: 38.306641
Longitude: −77.644157

Apex of Hooker's Line/Bullock House
Latitude: 38.317148
Longitude: −77.638470

Salem Church
Salem Church
4054 Plank Road, Fredericksburg, VA
    22407
Latitude: 38.288083
Longitude: −77.530861

Stonewall Jackson Shrine
Stonewall Jackson Shrine
12019 Stonewall Jackson Road,
    Woodford, VA 22580
Latitude: 38.147990
Longitude: −77.440138

CHAPTER 7 HIGH WATER: THE GETTYSBURG CAMPAIGN

Brandy Station
Graffiti House
19484 Brandy Road, Brandy Station, VA
    22714
Phone: 540-727-7718
Website:
    www.brandystationfoundation.com
Latitude: 38.502688
Longitude: −77.890952

Grand Review Site
15148 State Police Road, Culpeper, VA
    22701
Latitude: 38.493738
Longitude: −77.926132

Initial Union Assault
On Beverlys Ford Road, 1.5 miles north of
    intersection with St. James Church
    Road, Brandy Station, VA 22714
Latitude: 38.540210
Longitude: −77.851353

Buford's Knoll—Civil War Trust
On Beverlys Ford Road, 0.8 miles north of
    intersection with St. James Church
    Road, Brandy Station, VA 22714
Latitude: 38.531516
Longitude: −77.858476

St. James Church—Civil War Trust
Intersection of Beverlys Ford Road and
    St. James Church Road, Brandy
    Station, VA 22714
Latitude: 38.521847
Longitude: −77.865900

Top of Fleetwood Hill
Intersection of Fleetwood Heights Road
    and Stuart Lane, Brandy Station, VA
    22714
Latitude: 38.509759
Longitude: −77.879333

West Face of Fleetwood Hill
On Fleetwood Heights Road, 0.5 mile
    west of intersection with Stuart Lane,
    Brandy Station, VA 22714
Latitude: 38.506399
Longitude: −77.886371

Aldie
Aldie Mill
39401 John Mosby Highway, Aldie, VA
    20105
Phone: 703-327-9777
Website: www.nvrpa.org/park/aldie_mill_
    historic_park
Latitude: 38.975557
Longitude: −77.641497

Furr Farm/Snickersville Turnpike
On Snickersville Turnpike, 1.3 miles north
    of intersection with US 50, Middleburg,
    VA 20117
Latitude: 38.991838
Longitude: −77.663813

Middleburg
Middleburg
12 North Madison Street, Middleburg, VA
    20117
Phone: 540-687-5152
Latitude: 38.969619
Longitude: −77.735825

Middleburg, cont.

Mt. Defiance

On US 50 near intersection with Zulla
  Road, Middleburg, VA 20117

Latitude: 38.968150

Longitude: –77.763032

Upperville

Rector's Crossroads

Intersection of Atoka Road and US 50,
  Marshall, VA 20115

Latitude: 38.975625

Longitude: –77.807922

Goose Creek Bridge

On Lemmons Bottom Road, 0.2 mile
  north of intersection with US 50,
  Middleburg, VA 20117

Latitude: 38.982564

Longitude: –77.820969

Vineyard Hill

On US 50 0.1 mile east of intersection
  with Crofton Lane, Upperville, VA
  20184

Latitude: 38.991104

Longitude: –77.872467

Trappe Road

Intersection of US 50 and Trappe Road,
  Upperville, VA 20184

Latitude: 38.995907

Longitude: –77.890663

Rockville

Beall-Dawson Historical Park

111 West Montgomery Avenue, Rockville,
  MD 20850

Phone: 301-340-2825

Website: www.montgomeryhistory.org

Latitude: 39.084971

Longitude: –77.155437

Christ Episcopal Church

107 South Washington Street, Rockville,
  MD 20850

Latitude: 39.082306

Longitude: –77.152862

Court House Square

Intersection of East Montgomery Avenue
  and Maryland Avenue, Rockville, MD
  20850

Latitude: 39.084004

Longitude: –77.151318

Frederick—Prospect Hall

Prospect Hall

889 Butterfly Lane, Frederick, MD 21703

Latitude: 39.403703

Longitude: –77.438765

Emmitsburg

Emmittsburg/Shrine of St. Elizabeth Ann
  Seton

333 South Seton Avenue, Emmitsburg,
  MD 21727

Phone: 301-447-6606

Website: www.setonshrine.org

Latitude: 39.698635

Longitude: –77.329384

Westminster

Stuart's Deployment

500 South Center Drive, Westminster, MD
  21157

Latitude: 39.569771

Longitude: –76.990514

Skirmish Site

Intersection of Old Westminster Pike and
  North Court Street, Westminster, MD
  21157

Latitude: 39.560308

Longitude: –76.992788

Hanover

Hanover

Intersection of PA 94 and PA 194,
  Hanover, PA 17331

Phone: 717-637-6130

Website: www.hanoverchamber.com/
  visitorinfo.html

Latitude: 39.899838

Longitude: –76.983346

Gettysburg National Military Park
Museum and Visitor Center
1195 Baltimore Pike, Gettysburg, PA
  17325
Phone: 717-334-1124
Website: www.nps.gov/gett
Latitude: 39.812195
Longitude: −77.221644

McPherson's Ridge South
Latitude: 39.834699
Longitude: −77.250247

McPherson's Ridge North
Latitude: 39.843620
Longitude: −77.247984

Oak Ridge
Latitude: 39.843901
Longitude: −77.241944

Barlow Knoll
Latitude: 39.845548
Longitude: −77.226291

Seminary Ridge
Latitude: 39.814222
Longitude: −77.250516

Pitzer Woods
Latitude: 39.799799
Longitude: −77.256095

Warfield Ridge
Latitude: 39.785158
Longitude: −77.253735

Little Round Top
Latitude: 39.791012
Longitude: −77.236418

Devil's Den
Latitude: 39.791423
Longitude: −77.241782

The Wheatfield
Latitude: 39.796188
Longitude: −77.243155

The Peach Orchard
Latitude: 39.801068
Longitude: −77.248756

Pennsylvania Memorial
Latitude: 39.807366
Longitude: −77.235410

Spangler's Spring
Latitude: 39.814387
Longitude: −77.216892

Culp's Hill
Latitude: 39.820090
Longitude: −77.220132

Cemetery Hill
Latitude: 39.821367
Longitude: −77.227148

High Water Mark of the Confederacy
Latitude: 39.812458
Longitude: −77.235602

East Cavalry Battlefield—Crossroads
Intersection of Hanover Road and East
  Cavalry Avenue, Gettysburg, PA 17325
Latitude: 39.818030
Longitude: −77.169641

East Cavalry Battlefield—Battle Line
Latitude: 39.826335
Longitude: −77.164364

Wills House
8 Lincoln Square, Gettysburg, PA 17325
Phone: 866-486-5735
Website: www.davidwillshouse.org
Latitude: 39.830851
Longitude: −77.230667

Soldiers' National Cemetery
Parking at intersection of Taneytown Road
  and Hancock Avenue, Gettysburg, PA
  17325
Latitude: 39.816513
Longitude: −77.232298

Monterey Pass

Monterey Pass
Intersection of Charmian Road and Monterey Circle, Blue Ridge Summit, PA 17214
Website: www.emmitsburg.net/montereypass
Latitude: 39.738742
Longitude: −77.469020

Funkstown

Funkstown
132 Old National Pike, Hagerstown, MD 21740
Latitude: 39.601174
Longitude: −77.703316

Williamsport

Williamsport
205 West Potomac Street, Williamsport, MD 21795
Phone: 301-582-0813
Website: www.nps.gov/choh
Latitude: 39.600856
Longitude: −77.826391

Abbreviated Orders of Battle

FIRST MANASSAS

JULY 21, 1861

UNION

ARMY OF NORTHEASTERN VIRGINIA
Brig. Gen. Irvin McDowell

FIRST DIVISION
Brig. Gen. Daniel Tyler

First Brigade: Col. Erasmus D. Keyes
Second Brigade: Brig. Gen. Robert C. Schenck
Third Brigade: Col. William T. Sherman
Fourth Brigade: Col. Israel B. Richardson

SECOND DIVISION
Col. David Hunter (w), Col. Andrew Porter

First Brigade: Col. Andrew Porter
Second Brigade: Col. Ambrose E. Burnside

THIRD DIVISION
Col. Samuel P. Heintzelman (w)

First Brigade: Col. William B. Franklin
Second Brigade: Col. Orlando B. Willcox (w,c), Col. J. H. Hobart Ward
Third Brigade: Col. Oliver O. Howard

FOURTH DIVISION
Brig. Gen. Theodore Runyan

FIFTH DIVISION
Col. Dixon S. Miles
First Brigade: Col. Louis Blenker
Second Brigade: Col. Thomas A. Davies

CONFEDERATE

ARMY OF THE POTOMAC
Brig. Gen. P. G. T. Beauregard
First Brigade: Brig. Gen. Milledge L. Bonham
Second Brigade: Brig. Gen. Richard S. Ewell
Third Brigade: Brig. Gen. David R. Jones
Fourth Brigade: Brig. Gen. James Longstreet
Fifth Brigade: Col. P. St. George Cocke
Sixth Brigade: Col. Jubal A. Early
Seventh Brigade: Col. Nathan G. Evans
Reserve Brigade: Brig. Gen. Theophilus H. Holmes

ARMY OF THE SHENANDOAH
Gen. Joseph E. Johnston
First Brigade: Brig. Gen. Thomas J. Jackson (w)
Second Brigade: Col. Francis Bartow (k)
Third Brigade: Brig. Gen. Bernard E. Bee (k)
Fourth Brigade: Brig. Gen. Edmund Kirby Smith (w), Col. Arnold Elzey

Unattached:
First Virginia Cavalry: Col. J. E. B. Stuart

SHENANDOAH VALLEY
MARCH–JUNE, 1862

UNION

KERNSTOWN, MARCH 23, 1862
Brig. Gen. James Shields (w), Col. Nathan Kimball
First Brigade: Col. Nathan Kimball
Second Brigade: Col. Jeremiah C. Sullivan
Third Brigade: Col. Erastus B. Tyler
Cavalry: Col. Thornton F. Brodhead
Artillery: Lt. Col. Philip Daum

MCDOWELL, MAY 8, 1862
Brig. Gen. Robert C. Schenck
Milroy's brigade: Brig. Gen. Robert H. Milroy
Schenck's brigade: Brig. Gen. Robert C. Schenck

FRONT ROYAL AND WINCHESTER, MAY 23–25, 1862
Maj. Gen. Nathaniel P. Banks

FIRST DIVISION
Brig. Gen. Alpheus S. Williams
First Brigade: Col. Dudley Donnelly
Third Brigade: Col. George H. Gordon

CAVALRY
Brig. Gen. John P. Hatch

VALLEY MARCH AND CROSS KEYS, JUNE 1–9, 1862
Maj. Gen. John C. Fremont

BLENKER'S DIVISION
Brig. Gen. Louis Blenker
First Brigade: Brig. Gen. Julius H. Stahel
Second Brigade: Col. John A. Koltes
Third Brigade: Brig. Gen. Henry Bohlen
Advance brigade: Col. Gustave P. Cluseret
Milroy's brigade: Brig. Gen. Robert H. Milroy
Schenck's brigade: Brig. Gen. Robert C. Schenck
Bayard's brigade: Brig. Gen. George D. Bayard

PORT REPUBLIC, JUNE 8–9, 1862
Brig. Gen. James Shields
First Brigade: Brig. Gen. Nathan Kimball
Second Brigade: Brig. Gen. Orris S. Ferry
Third Brigade: Brig. Gen. Erastus B. Tyler
Fourth Brigade: Col. Samuel S. Carroll
Artillery: Col. Philip Daum

CONFEDERATE

KERNSTOWN, MARCH 23, 1862
Maj. Gen. Thomas J. Jackson
Garnett's brigade: Brig. Gen. Richard B. Garnett
Burks's brigade: Col. Jesse S. Burks
Fulkerson's brigade: Col. Samuel V. Fulkerson
Cavalry: Col. Turner Ashby

MCDOWELL, MAY 8, 1862
Maj. Gen. Thomas J. Jackson

ARMY OF THE VALLEY

First Brigade: Brig. Gen. Charles S. Winder
Second Brigade: Col. John A. Campbell
Third Brigade: Brig. Gen. William B. Taliaferro

ARMY OF THE NORTHWEST
Brig. Gen. Edward Johnson (w)

First Brigade: Col. Z. T. Conner
Second Brigade: Col. W. C. Scott

FRONT ROYAL THROUGH PORT REPUBLIC, MAY 23–JUNE 9, 1862
Maj. Gen. Thomas J. Jackson

JACKSON'S DIVISION
First Brigade: Brig. Gen. Charles S. Winder

Second Brigade: Col. John A. Campbell (w), Col. John M. Patton, Jr.
Third Brigade: Col. Samuel V. Fulkerson, Brig. Gen. William B. Taliaferro
Artillery: Col. Stapleton Crutchfield

SECOND DIVISION
Maj. Gen. Richard S. Ewell

Second Brigade: Col. W. C. Scott, Brig. Gen. George H. Steuart (w)
Fourth Brigade: Brig. Gen. Arnold Elzey (w), Col. James A. Walker
Seventh Brigade: Brig. Gen. Isaac R. Trimble
Eighth Brigade: Brig. Gen. Richard Taylor

CAVALRY
**Col. Thomas S. Fluornoy, Brig. Gen. George H. Steuart,
Brig. Gen. Turner Ashby (k), Col. Thomas T. Munford**

PENINSULA CAMPAIGN—YORKTOWN

MAY 1, 1862

UNION

ARMY OF THE POTOMAC
Maj. Gen. George B. McClellan

I CORPS
First Division: Brig. Gen. William B. Franklin

II CORPS

Brig. Gen. Edwin V. Sumner

First Division: Brig. Gen. Israel B. Richardson
Second Division: Brig. Gen. John Sedgwick
Third Division: Brig. Gen. William H. French

III CORPS

Brig. Gen. Samuel P. Heintzelman

First Division: Brig. Gen. Fitz John Porter
Second Division: Brig. Gen. Joseph Hooker
Third Division: Brig. Gen. Charles S. Hamilton
Artillery reserve: Lt. Col. William Hays

IV CORPS

Brig. Gen. Erasmus D. Keyes

First Division: Brig. Gen. Darius N. Couch
Second Division: Brig. Gen. William F. Smith
Third Division: Brig. Gen. Silas Casey

CONFEDERATE

ARMY OF NORTHERN VIRGINIA

Gen. Joseph E. Johnston

LEFT WING

Maj. Gen. Daniel Harvey Hill

Rodes's brigade: Brig. Gen. Robert E. Rodes
Featherston's brigade: Brig. Gen. Winfield S. Featherston
Early's brigade: Brig. Gen. Jubal A. Early
Rains's brigade: Brig. Gen. Gabriel J. Rains
Ward's command (attached): Col. George T. Ward
Crump's command: Col. Charles A. Crump

CENTER

Maj. Gen. James Longstreet

A. P. Hill's brigade: Brig. Gen. A. P. Hill
R. H. Anderson's brigade: Brig. Gen. R. H. Anderson
Pickett's brigade: Brig. Gen. George E. Pickett
Wilcox's brigade: Brig. Gen. Cadmus M. Wilcox
Colston's brigade: Brig. Gen. Raleigh E. Colston
Pryor's brigade: Brig. Gen. Roger A. Pryor

RIGHT WING

Maj. Gen. John B. Magruder

McLaws's division: Brig. Gen. Lafayette McLaws
D. R. Jones's division: Brig. Gen. David R. Jones

RESERVE
Maj. Gen. Gustavus W. Smith

Hood's brigade: Brig. Gen. John B. Hood
Hampton's brigade: Col. Wade Hampton
Whiting's brigade: Brig. Gen. W. H. C.Whiting
S. R. Anderson's brigade (attached): Brig. Gen. Samuel R. Anderson
Pettigrew's brigade (attached): Brig. Gen. James J. Pettigrew
Ewell's command (Williamsburg): Brig. Gen. Richard S. Ewell
Carter's command (Jamestown): Col. Hill Carter
Cavalry brigade: Brig. Gen. J. E. B. Stuart
Artillery Reserve: Brig. Gen. William N. Pendleton

PENINSULA CAMPAIGN—SEVEN DAYS BATTLES

JUNE 25–JULY 1, 1862

UNION

ARMY OF THE POTOMAC
Maj. Gen. George B. McClellan

II CORPS
Brig. Gen. Edwin V. Sumner

First Division: Brig. Gen. Israel B. Richardson
Second Division: Brig. Gen. John Sedgwick

III CORPS
Brig. Gen. Samuel P. Heintzelman

Second Division: Brig. Gen. Joseph Hooker
Third Division: Brig. Gen. Philip Kearny
Corps Artillery Reserve: Capt. Gustavus A. De Russy

IV CORPS
Brig. Gen. Erasmus D. Keyes

First Division: Brig. Gen. Darius N. Couch
Second Division: Brig. Gen. John J. Peck
Corps Artillery Reserve: Maj. Robert M. West

V CORPS
Brig. Gen. Fitz John Porter

First Division: Maj. Gen. George W. Morell
Second Division: Brig. Gen. George Sykes
Third Division (Pennsylvania Reserves): Brig. Gen. George A. McCall (c),
Brig. Gen. Truman Seymour
Artillery Reserve: Col. Henry J. Hunt

VI CORPS
Brig. Gen. William B. Franklin
First Division: Brig. Gen. Henry W. Slocum
Second Division: Brig. Gen. William F. Smith

RESERVE
Cavalry Reserve: Brig. Gen. Philip St. George Cooke
Advance Guard: Brig. Gen. George Stoneman
White House command: Brig. Gen. Silas Casey

CONFEDERATE

ARMY OF NORTHERN VIRGINIA
Gen. Robert E. Lee

JACKSON'S COMMAND
Maj. Gen. Thomas J. Jackson
Jackson's division: Brig. Gen. Charles S. Winder
Ewell's division: Brig. Gen. Richard S. Ewell
Whiting's division (attached): Brig. Gen. W. H. C. Whiting
D. H. Hill's division (attached): Maj. Gen. Daniel Harvey Hill

HILL'S LIGHT DIVISION
Maj. Gen. Ambrose Powell Hill
Field's brigade: Brig. Gen. Charles W. Field
Gregg's brigade: Brig. Gen. Maxcy Gregg
J. R. Anderson's brigade: Brig. Gen. Joseph R. Anderson (w),
Col. Edward L. Thomas
Branch's brigade: Brig. Gen. Lawrence O'Brien Branch
Archer's brigade: Brig. Gen. James J. Archer
Pender's brigade: Brig. Gen. William D. Pender
Artillery: Maj. R. Lindsay Walker

LONGSTREET'S DIVISION
Maj. Gen. James Longstreet
Kemper's brigade: Brig. Gen. James L. Kemper
R. H. Anderson's brigade: Brig. Gen. Richard H. Anderson,
Col. Micah Jenkins
Pickett's brigade: Brig. Gen. George E. Pickett (w), Col. Eppa Hunton,
Col. John Strange
Wilcox's brigade: Brig. Gen. Cadmus M. Wilcox
Pryor's brigade: Brig. Gen. Roger A. Pryor
Featherston's brigade: Brig. Gen. Winfield S. Featherston (w)
Artillery: Col. James B. Walton

MAGRUDER'S COMMAND
Maj. Gen. John B. Magruder

McLaws's division: Maj. Gen. Lafayette McLaws
Jones's division: Brig. Gen. David R. Jones
Magruder's division: Maj. Gen. John B. Magruder

HUGER'S DIVISION
Maj. Gen. Benjamin Huger

Mahone's brigade: Brig. Gen. William Mahone
Wright's brigade: Brig. Gen. Ambrose R. Wright
Armistead's brigade: Brig. Gen. Lewis A. Armistead
Ransom's brigade (attached): Brig. Gen. Robert Ransom, Jr.

HOLMES'S DIVISION
Maj. Gen. Theophilus H. Holmes

Daniel's brigade: Brig. Gen. Junius Daniel
Walker's brigade: Brig. Gen. John G. Walker, Col. Van H. Manning
Wise's brigade (attached): Brig. Gen. Henry A. Wise

RESERVE ARTILLERY
Brig. Gen. William N. Pendleton

CAVALRY DIVISION
Maj. Gen. J. E. B. Stuart

SECOND MANASSAS
AUGUST 28–30, 1862

UNION

ARMY OF VIRGINIA
Maj. Gen. John Pope

I CORPS
Maj. Gen. Franz Sigel

First Division: Brig. Gen. Robert C. Schenck
Second Division: Brig. Gen. A. Von Steinwehr
Third Division: Brig. Gen. Carl Schurz
Independent brigade: Brig. Gen. Robert H. Milroy
Cavalry: Col. John Beardsley
Reserve Artillery: Capt. Louis Schirmer

II CORPS

Maj. Gen. Nathaniel P. Banks

First Division: Brig. Gen. Alpheus S. Williams
Second Division: Brig. Gen. George S. Greene
Artillery: Capt. Clermont L. Best
Cavalry: Brig. Gen. John Buford

III CORPS

Maj. Gen. Irvin McDowell

First Division: Brig. Gen. Rufus King
Second Division: Brig. Gen. James B. Ricketts
Cavalry: Brig. Gen. George D. Bayard
Artillery Reserve: Lt. Col. William Hays

PENNSYLVANIA RESERVES

Maj. Gen. John F. Reynolds

RESERVE CORPS

Brig. Gen. Samuel D. Sturgis

ARMY OF THE POTOMAC

III CORPS

Maj. Gen. Samuel P. Heintzelman

First Division: Maj. Gen. Philip Kearny
Second Division: Maj. Gen. Joseph Hooker

V CORPS

Maj. Gen. Fitz John Porter

First Division: Brig. Gen. George W. Morell
Second Division: Brig. Gen. George Sykes

VI CORPS

First Division, First Brigade: Brig. Gen. George W. Taylor

IX CORPS

First Division: Brig. Gen. Isaac I. Stevens

Second Division: Maj. Gen. Jesse L. Reno
Kanawha Division (detachment): Col. E. Parker Scammon

CONFEDERATE

ARMY OF NORTHERN VIRGINIA

Gen. Robert E. Lee

LONGSTREET'S CORPS (RIGHT WING)

Maj. Gen. James Longstreet

Anderson's division: Maj. Gen. Richard H. Anderson
Jones's division: Brig. Gen. David R. Jones
Wilcox's division: Brig. Gen. Cadmus M. Wilcox
Hood's division: Brig. Gen. John B. Hood
Kemper's division: Brig. Gen. James L. Kemper
Corps Artillery: Col. John B. Walton (First Battalion),
Col. Stephen D. Lee (Second Battalion)

JACKSON'S CORPS (LEFT WING)

Maj. Gen. Thomas J. Jackson

Taliaferro's division: Brig. Gen. William B. Taliaferro
Ewell's division: Maj. Gen. Richard S. Ewell (w)
Hill's light division: Maj. Gen. A. P. Hill
Reserve Artillery
Brig. Gen. William N. Pendleton

CAVALRY DIVISION

Maj. Gen. J. E. B. Stuart

Hampton's brigade: Brig. Gen. Wade Hampton
Lee's brigade: Brig. Gen. Fitzhugh Lee
Robertson's brigade: Brig. Gen. Beverly H. Robertson

ANTIETAM

SEPTEMBER 17, 1862

UNION

ARMY OF THE POTOMAC

Maj. Gen. George B. McClellan

I CORPS

Maj. Gen. Joseph Hooker (w)

Maj. Gen. Ambrose Burnside
First Division: Brig. Gen. Abner Doubleday
Second Division: Brig. Gen. James B. Ricketts
Third Division: Brig. Gen. George G. Meade, Brig. Gen. Truman Seymour

II CORPS

Maj. Gen. Edwin V. Sumner

First Division: Maj. Gen. Israel B. Richardson (mw), Brig. Gen. John C. Caldwell, Brig.
Gen. Winfield S. Hancock
Second Division: Maj. Gen. John Sedgwick (w), Brig. Gen. Oliver O. Howard
Third Division: Brig. Gen. William H. French

V CORPS

Maj. Gen. Fitz John Porter

First Division: Maj. Gen. George W. Morell
Second Division: Brig. Gen. George Sykes
Third Division: Brig. Gen. Andrew A. Humphreys
Artillery Reserve: Lt. Col. William Hays

VI CORPS

Maj. Gen. William B. Franklin

First Division: Maj. Gen. Henry W. Slocum
Second Division: Maj. Gen. William F. Smith
First Division, IV Corps (attached): Maj. Gen. Darius N. Couch

IX CORPS

Maj. Gen. Ambrose E. Burnside

Brig. Gen. Jacob D. Cox
First Division: Brig. Gen. Orlando B. Willcox
Second Division: Brig. Gen. Samuel D. Sturgis
Third Division: Brig. Gen. Isaac P. Rodman (mw), Col. Edward Harland
Kanawha Division: Col. Eliakim P. Scammon

XII CORPS

Maj. Gen. Joseph K.F. Mansfield (mw)

Brig. Gen. Alpheus S. Williams
First Division: Brig. Gen. Alpheus S. Williams, Brig. Gen. Samuel W. Crawford (w),
Brig. Gen. George H. Gordon
Second Division: Brig. Gen. George S. Greene
Corps Artillery: Capt. Clermont L. Best

CAVALRY DIVISION

Brig. Gen. Alfred Pleasonton

CONFEDERATE

ARMY OF NORTHERN VIRGINIA

Gen. Robert E. Lee

LONGSTREET'S CORPS

Maj. Gen. James Longstreet

McLaws's division: Maj. Gen. Lafayette McLaws
Anderson's division: Maj. Gen. Richard H. Anderson (w), Brig. Gen. Roger A. Pryor
Jones's division: Brig. Gen. David R. Jones
Walker's division: Brig. Gen. John G. Walker
Hood's division: Brig. Gen. John B. Hood
Evans's (independent) brigade: Brig. Gen. Nathan G. Evans, Col. P. F. Stevens
Corps Artillery: Col. John B. Walton (First Battalion),
Col. Stephen D. Lee (Second Battalion)

JACKSON'S CORPS
Maj. Gen. Thomas J. Jackson

Ewell's division: Brig. Gen. Alexander R. Lawton (w), Brig. Gen. Jubal A. Early
Hill's light division: Maj. Gen. A. P. Hill
Jackson's division: Brig. Gen. John R. Jones (w),
Brig. Gen. William E. Starke (k),
Col. Andrew J. Grigsby
Hill's division: Maj. Gen. D. H. Hill

RESERVE ARTILLERY
Brig. Gen. William N. Pendleton

CAVALRY DIVISION
Maj. Gen. J. E. B. Stuart

Hampton's brigade: Brig. Gen. Wade Hampton
Lee's brigade: Brig. Gen. Fitzhugh Lee
Robertson's brigade: Col. Thomas T. Munford
Horse Artillery: Maj. John Pelham

FREDERICKSBURG
DECEMBER 11–13, 1862

UNION

ARMY OF THE POTOMAC
Maj. Gen. Ambrose E. Burnside

RIGHT GRAND DIVISION
Maj. Gen. Edwin V. Sumner

II CORPS
Maj. Gen. Darius N. Couch

First Division: Brig. Gen. Winfield S. Hancock
First Brigade: Brig. Gen. John C. Caldwell
Second Brigade: Brig. Gen. Thomas F. Meagher
Third Brigade: Col. Samuel K. Zook

Second Division: Brig. Gen. Oliver O. Howard
First Brigade: Brig. Gen. Alfred Sully
Second Brigade: Col. Joshua T. Owen
Third Brigade: Col. Norman J. Hall, Col. William R. Lee

Third Division: Brig. Gen. William H. French
First Brigade: Brig. Gen. Nathan Kimball, Col. John S. Mason
Second Brigade: Col. Oliver H. Palmer
Third Brigade: Col. John W. Andrews, Lt. Col. William Jameson,

Lt. Col. John W. Marshal
Artillery Reserve: Capt. Charles H. Morgan

IX CORPS
Brig. Gen. Orlando B. Willcox

First Division: Maj. Gen. William W. Burns
First Brigade: Col. Orlando M. Poe
Second Brigade: Col. Benjamin C. Christ
Third Brigade: Col. Daniel Leasure

Second Division: Brig. Gen. Samuel D. Sturgis
First Brigade: Brig. Gen. James Nagle
Second Brigade: Brig. Gen. Edward Ferrero

Third Division: Brig. Gen. George W. Getty
First Brigade: Col. Rush C. Hawkins
Second Brigade: Col. Edward Harland

Cavalry division: Brig. Gen. Alfred Pleasonton
First Brigade: Brig. Gen. John F. Farnsworth
Second Brigade: Col. David M. Gregg, Col. Thomas C. Devin

CENTER GRAND DIVISION
Maj. Gen. Joseph Hooker

III CORPS
Maj. Gen. George Stoneman

First Division: Brig. Gen. David B. Birney
First Brigade: Brig. Gen. John C. Robinson
Second Brigade: Brig. Gen. J. H. Hobart Ward
Third Brigade: Brig. Gen. Hiram G. Berry
Artillery: Capt. George E. Randolph

Second Division: Brig. Gen. Daniel E. Sickles
First Brigade: Brig. Gen. Joseph B. Carr
Second Brigade: Col. George B. Hall
Third Brigade: Brig. Gen. Joseph W. Revere
Artillery: Capt. James E. Smith

Third Division: Brig. Gen. Amiel W. Whipple
First Brigade: Brig. Gen. A. Sanders Piatt, Col. Emlen Franklin
Second Brigade: Col. Samuel S. Carroll

V CORPS
Brig. Gen. Daniel Butterfield

First Division: Brig. Gen. Charles Griffin
First Brigade: Col. James Barnes
Second Brigade: Col. Jacob B. Sweitzer
Third Brigade: Col. Thomas B. W. Stockton

Second Division: Brig. Gen. George Sykes
First Brigade: Lt. Col. Robert C. Buchanan
Second Brigade: Maj. George L. Andrews, Maj. Charles S. Lovell
Third Brigade: Brig. Gen. Gouverneur K. Warren

Third Division: Brig. Gen. Andrew A. Humphreys
First Brigade: Brig. Gen. Erastus B. Tyler
Second Brigade: Col. Peter H. Allabach
Cavalry brigade: Brig. Gen. William W. Averill

LEFT GRAND DIVISION
Maj. Gen. William B. Franklin

I CORPS
Maj. Gen. John F. Reynolds

First Division: Brig. Gen. Abner Doubleday
First Brigade: Col. Walter Phelps, Jr.
Second Brigade: Col. James Gavin
Third Brigade: Col. William F. Rogers
Fourth Brigade: Brig. Gen. Solomon Meredith, Col. Lysander Cutler

Second Division: Brig. Gen. John Gibbon, Brig. Gen. Nelson Taylor
First Brigade: Col. Adrian R. Root
Second Brigade: Col. Peter Lyle
Third Brigade: Brig. Gen. Nelson Taylor, Col. Samuel H. Leonard

Third Division: Maj. Gen. George G. Meade
First Brigade: Col. William Sinclair, Col. William McCandless
Second Brigade: Col. Albert L. Magilton
Third Brigade: Brig. Gen. C. Feger Jackson, Col. Joseph W. Fisher,
Lt. Col. Robert Anderson

VI CORPS
Maj. Gen. William F. Smith

First Division: Brig. Gen. William T. H. Brooks
First Brigade: Col. Alfred T. A. Torbert
Second Brigade: Col. Henry L. Cake
Third Brigade: Brig. Gen. David A. Russell

Second Division: Brig. Gen. Albion P. Howe
First Brigade: Brig. Gen. Calvin E. Pratt
Second Brigade: Col. Henry Whiting
Third Brigade: Brig. Gen. Francis L. Vinton, Col. Robert F. Taylor,
Brig. Gen. Thomas H. Neill

Third Division: Brig. Gen. John Newton
First Brigade: Brig. Gen. John Cochrane
Second Brigade: Brig. Gen. Charles Devens, Jr.

Third Brigade: Col. Thomas A. Rowley, Brig. Gen. Frank Wheaton
Cavalry brigade: Brig. Gen. George D. Bayard, Col. David M. Gregg
Volunteer engineer brigade: Brig. Gen. Daniel P. Woodbury
Artillery: Brig. Gen. Henry J. Hunt
Artillery Reserve: Lt. Col. William Hays

CONFEDERATE

ARMY OF NORTHERN VIRGINIA
Gen. Robert E. Lee

I CORPS
Lt. Gen. James Longstreet

McLaws's division: Maj. Gen. Lafayette McLaws
Kershaw's brigade: Brig. Gen. Joseph B. Kershaw
Cobb's brigade: Brig. Gen. T. R. R. Cobb, Col. Robert McMillan
Semmes's brigade: Brig. Gen. Paul J. Semmes
Barksdale's brigade: Brig. Gen. William Barksdale
Artillery: Col. Henry C. Cabell

Anderson's division: Maj. Gen. Richard H. Anderson
Wilcox's brigade: Brig. Gen. Cadmus M. Wilcox
Featherston's brigade: Brig. Gen. W. S. Featherston
Perry's brigade: Brig. Gen. E. A. Perry
Mahone's brigade: Brig. Gen. William Mahone
Wright's brigade: Brig. Gen. Ambrose R. Wright

Pickett's division: Maj. Gen. George E. Pickett
Garnett's brigade: Brig. Gen. Richard B. Garnett
Armistead's brigade: Brig. Gen. Lewis A. Armistead
Kemper's brigade: Brig. Gen. James L. Kemper
Jenkins's brigade: Brig. Gen. M. Jenkins
Corse's brigade: Brig. Gen. Montgomery D. Corse

Hood's division: Maj. Gen. John B. Hood
Law's brigade: Brig. Gen. Evander M. Law
Robertson's brigade: Brig. Gen. J. B. Robertson
Anderson's brigade: Brig. Gen. George T. Anderson
Toombs's brigade: Col. Henry L. Benning

Ransom's division: Brig. Gen. Robert Ransom, Jr.
Ransom's brigade: Brig. Gen. Robert Ransom, Jr.
Cooke's brigade: Brig. Gen. J. R. Cooke, Col. E. D. Hall

Corps Artillery: Col. John B. Walton

Alexander's battalion: Lt. Col. E. Porter Alexander

II CORPS
Lt. Gen. Thomas J. Jackson

Ewell's division: Brig. Gen. Jubal A. Early
Lawton's brigade: Col. E. N. Atkinson, Col. C. A. Evans
Early's brigade: Col. J. A. Walker
Trimble's brigade: Col. Robert F. Hoke
Hays's brigade: Brig. Gen. Harry T. Hays
Artillery: Capt. J. W. Latimer

A. P. Hill's light division: Maj. Gen. A. P. Hill
Brockenbrough's brigade: Col. John M. Brockenbrough
Gregg's brigade: Brig. Gen. Maxcy Gregg, Col. Daniel H. Hamilton
Thomas's brigade: Brig. Gen. E. L. Thomas
Lane's brigade: Brig. Gen. James H. Lane
Archer's brigade: Brig. Gen. James J. Archer
Pender's brigade: Brig. Gen. William D. Pender, Col. A. M. Scales
Artillery: Lt. Col. Rueben L. Walker

Jackson's division: Brig. Gen. William B. Taliaferro
Paxton's brigade: Brig. Gen. E. F. Paxton
Jones's brigade: Brig. Gen. John R. Jones
Taliaferro's brigade: Col. Edward T. H. Warren
Starke's brigade: Col. Edmund Pendleton

ARTILLERY

Hill's division: Maj. Gen. D. H. Hill
Rodes's brigade: Brig. Gen. Robert E. Rodes
Ripley's brigade: Brig. Gen. George Doles
Colquitt's brigade: Brig. Gen. Alfred H. Colquitt
Iverson's brigade: Brig. Gen. Alfred Iverson
Ramseur's brigade: Col. Bryan Grimes
Artillery: Maj. Hilary P. Jones

Corps Artillery: Capt. J. B. Brockenbrough
Reserve artillery: Brig. Gen. William N. Pendleton

Brown's battalion: Col. J. Thompson Brown

Nelson's battalion: Maj. William Nelson

Cavalry division: Maj. Gen. J. E. B. Stuart
First Brigade: Brig. Gen. Wade Hampton
Second Brigade: Brig. Gen. Fitzhugh Lee
Third Brigade: Brig. Gen. W. H. F. Lee
Horse Artillery: Maj. John Pelham

CHANCELLORSVILLE

MAY 1–3, 1863

UNION

ARMY OF THE POTOMAC
Maj. Gen. Joseph Hooker

I CORPS
Maj. Gen. John F. Reynolds

First Division: Brig. Gen. James S. Wadsworth
First Brigade: Col. Walter Phelps, Jr.
Second Brigade: Brig. Gen. Lysander Cutler
Third Brigade: Brig. Gen. Gabriel R. Paul
Fourth Brigade: Brig. Gen. Solomon Meredith
Artillery: Capt. John Reynolds

Second Division: Brig. Gen. John C. Robinson
First Brigade: Col. Adrian R. Root
Second Brigade: Brig. Gen. Henry Baxter
Third Brigade: Col. Samuel H. Leonard
Artillery: Capt. Dunbar R. Ransom

Third Division: Brig. Gen. Abner Doubleday
First Brigade: Brig. Gen. Thomas A. Rowley
Second Brigade: Col. Roy Stone
Artillery: Maj. Ezra W. Matthews

Chief of Artillery: Col. Charles S. Wainwright

II CORPS
Maj. Gen. Darius N. Couch

First Division: Brig. Gen. Winfield S. Hancock
First Brigade: Brig. Gen. John C. Caldwell
Second Brigade: Brig. Gen. Thomas F. Meagher
Third Brigade: Brig. Gen. Samuel K. Zook
Fourth Brigade: Col. John R. Brooke
Fifth Brigade (attached): Col. Edward E. Cross
Artillery: Capt. Rufus D. Pettit

Second Division: Brig. Gen. John Gibbon
First Brigade: Brig. Gen. Alfred Sully, Col. Henry W. Hudson, Col. Byron Laflin
Second Brigade: Col. Joshua T. Owen
Third Brigade: Col. Norman J. Hall

Third Division: Maj. Gen. William H. French
First Brigade: Col. Samuel S. Carroll

Second Brigade: Brig. Gen. William Hayes (c), Col. Charles J. Powers
Third Brigade: Col. John D. MacGregor, Col. Charles Albright

Chief of Artillery: Lt. Col. Charles H. Morgan

III CORPS
Maj. Gen. Daniel E. Sickles

First Division: Brig. Gen. David B. Birney
First Brigade: Brig. Gen. Charles K. Graham, Col. Thomas W. Egan
Second Brigade: Brig. Gen. J. H. Hobart Ward
Third Brigade: Col. Samuel B. Hayman
Artillery: Capt. A. Judson Clark

Second Division: Maj. Gen. Hiram Berry (k), Brig. Gen. Joseph B. Carr
First Brigade: Brig. Gen. Joseph B. Carr, Col. William Blaisdell
Second Brigade: Brig. Gen. Joseph W. Revere, Col. J. Egbert Farnum
Third Brigade: Brig. Gen. Gershom Mott (w), Col. William J. Sewell
Artillery: Capt. Thomas W. Osborne

Third Division: Brig. Gen. Amiel W. Whipple (mw), Brig. Gen. Charles K. Graham
First Brigade: Col. Emlen Franklin
Second Brigade: Col. Samuel M. Bowman
Third Brigade: Col. Hiram Berdan
Artillery: Capt. Albert A. Von Puttkammer, Capt. James F. Huntington

Chief of Artillery: Capt. George E. Randolph

V CORPS
Maj. Gen. George G. Meade

First Division: Brig. Gen. Charles Griffin
First Brigade: Col. James Barnes
Second Brigade: Col. James McQuade, Col. Jacob B. Sweitzer
Third Brigade: Col. Thomas B. W. Stockton
Artillery: Capt. Augustus P. Martin

Second Division: Maj. Gen. George Sykes
First Brigade: Brig. Gen. Romeyn B. Ayres
Second Brigade: Col. Sidney Burbank
Third Brigade: Col. Patrick H. O'Rorke
Artillery: Capt. Stephen H. Weed

Third Division: Brig. Gen. Andrew A. Humphreys
First Brigade: Brig. Gen. Erastus B. Tyler
Second Brigade: Col. Peter H. Allabach
Artillery: Capt. Alanson M. Randol

Chief of Artillery: Capt. Stephen H. Weed

VI CORPS

Maj. Gen. John Sedgwick

First Division: Brig. Gen. William T.H. Brooks
First Brigade: Col. Henry W. Brown (w), Col. Samuel L. Buck (w),
Col. William H. Penrose
Second Brigade: Brig. Gen. Joseph J. Bartlett
Third Brigade: Brig. Gen. David A. Russell
Artillery: Maj. John A. Tomkins

Second Division: Brig. Gen. Albion P. Howe
Second Brigade: Col. Henry Whiting
Third Brigade: Brig. Gen. Thomas H. Neill
Artillery: Maj. J. Watts de Peyster

Third Division: Maj. Gen. John Newton
First Brigade: Col. Alexander Shaler
Second Brigade: Col. William H. Browne (w), Col. Henry L. Eustis
Third Brigade: Brig. Gen. Frank Wheaton
Artillery: Capt. Jeremiah McCarthy
Light Division: Brig. Gen. Calvin E. Pratt, Col. Hiram Burnham

Chief of Artillery: Col. Charles H. Tomkins

XI CORPS

Brig. Gen. Oliver O. Howard

First Division: Brig. Gen. Charles Devens, Jr. (w), Brig. Gen. Nathaniel C. McLean
First Brigade: Col. Leopold Von Gilsa
Second Brigade: Brig. Gen. Nathaniel C. McLean, Col. John C. Lee

Second Division: Brig. Gen. Adolph Von Steinwehr
First Brigade: Col. Adolphus Buschbeck
Second Brigade: Brig. Gen. Francis C. Barlow

Third Division: Maj. Gen. Carl Schurz
First Brigade: Brig. Gen. Alexander Schimmelfennig
Second Brigade: Col. Wladimir Krzyzanowski

Chief of Artillery: Lt. Col. Louis Schirmer

XII CORPS

Maj. Gen. Henry W. Slocum

First Division: Brig. Gen. Alpheus S. Williams
First Brigade: Brig. Gen. Joseph F. Knipe
Second Brigade: Col. Samuel Ross (w), Brig. Gen. Joseph F. Knipe
Third Brigade: Brig. Gen. Thomas H. Ruger
Artillery: Capt. Robert H. Fitzhugh

Second Division: Brig. Gen. John W. Geary
First Brigade: Col. Charles Candy

Second Brigade: Brig. Gen. Thomas L. Kane
Third Brigade: Brig. Gen. George S. Greene
Artillery: Capt. Joseph M. Knap

Chief of artillery: Capt. Clermont L. Best

CAVALRY CORPS
Brig. Gen. George Stoneman
First Division: Brig. Gen. Alfred Pleasanton
First Brigade: Col. Benjamin F. Davis
Second Brigade: Col. Thomas C. Devin
Second Division: Brig. Gen. William W. Averell
First Brigade: Col. Horace B. Sargent
Second Brigade: Col. John B. McIntosh

Third Division: Brig. Gen. David McM. Gregg
First Brigade: Col. Judson Kilpatrick
Second Brigade: Col. Percy Wyndham
Reserve cavalry: Brig. Gen. John Buford
Horse Artillery: Capt. James M. Robertson

CHIEF OF ARTILLERY
Brig. Gen. Henry J. Hunt

CONFEDERATE

ARMY OF NORTHERN VIRGINIA
Gen. Robert E. Lee

I CORPS
Gen. Robert E. Lee
McLaws's division: Maj. Gen. Lafayette McLaws
Kershaw's brigade: Brig. Gen. Joseph B. Kershaw
Semmes's brigade: Brig. Gen. Paul J. Semmes
Wofford's brigade: Brig. Gen. William T. Wofford
Barksdale's brigade: Brig. Gen. William Barksdale
Artillery: Col. Henry C. Cabell, Maj. S. P. Hamilton

Anderson's division: Maj. Gen. Richard H. Anderson
Wilcox's brigade: Brig. Gen. Cadmus M. Wilcox
Perry's brigade: Brig. Gen. E. A. Perry
Mahone's brigade: Brig. Gen. William Mahone
Posey's brigade: Brig. Gen. Carnot Posey
Wright's brigade: Brig. Gen. Ambrose R. Wright
Artillery: Lt. Col. John J. Garnett, Maj. Robert A. Hardaway

Chief of artillery: Col. John B. Walton
Alexander's battalion: Lt. Col. E. Porter Alexander, Maj. Frank Huger
Washington (Louisiana) Battalion: Col. James B. Walton

II CORPS

Lt. Gen. Thomas J. Jackson (mw)

Maj. Gen. A. P. Hill (w)

Brig. Gen. Robert E. Rodes

Maj. Gen. J. E. B. Stuart

Early's division: Maj. Gen. Jubal A. Early

Gordon's brigade: Brig. Gen. John B. Gordon

Hoke's brigade: Brig. Gen. Robert F. Hoke (w), Col. Isaac E. Avery

Smith's brigade: Brig. Gen. William Smith

Hays's brigade: Brig. Gen. Harry T. Hays

Artillery: Lt. Col. R. Snowden Andrews

Hill's light division: Maj. Gen. A. P. Hill (w), Brig. Gen. Henry Heth (w),

Brig. Gen. William D. Pender (w), Brig. Gen. James J. Archer

Heth's brigade: Brig. Gen. Henry Heth (w), Col. John M. Brockenbrough

McGowan's brigade: Brig. Gen. Samuel McGowan (w),

Col. Oliver E. Edwards (mw),

Col. Abner Perrin, Col. Daniel H. Hamilton

Thomas's brigade: Brig. Gen. E. L. Thomas

Lane's brigade: Brig. Gen. James H. Lane

Archer's brigade: Brig. Gen. James J. Archer, Col. Birkett D. Fry

Pender's brigade: Brig. Gen. William D. Pender (w)

Artillery: Lt. Col. Rueben L. Walker, Maj. William J. Pegram

Colston's division: Brig. Gen. Raleigh E. Colston

Paxton's brigade: Brig. Gen. E. F. Paxton (k), Col. John H. S. Funk

Jones's brigade: Brig. Gen. John R. Jones, Col. Thomas S. Garnett (mw),

Col. A. S. Vandeventer

Warren's brigade: Col. Edward T. H. Warren (w), Col. Titus V. Williams (w),

Lt. Col. Hamilton A. Brown

Nicholls's brigade: Brig. Gen. Francis T. Nicholls (w), Col. Jesse M. Williams

Jones's Artillery Battalion: Lt. Col. Hilary P. Jones

Rodes's division: Brig. Gen. Robert E. Rodes, Brig. Gen. Stephen D. Ramseur

Ramseur's brigade: Brig. Gen. Stephen D. Ramseur, Col. Francis M. Parker

O'Neal's brigade: Col. Edward A. O'Neal (w), Col. Josephus M. Hall

Doles's brigade: Brig. Gen. George Doles

Colquitt's brigade: Brig. Gen. Alfred H. Colquitt

Iverson's brigade: Brig. Gen. Alfred Iverson

Artillery: Lt. Col. Thomas H. Carter

Chief of artillery: Col. Stapleton Crutchfield (w), Col. E. Porter Alexander,

Col. J. Thompson Brown

Army reserve artillery: Brig. Gen. William N. Pendleton

CAVALRY CORPS

Maj. Gen. J. E. B. Stuart

Second Brigade: Brig. Gen. Fitzhugh Lee

Third Brigade: Brig. Gen. W. H. F. Lee

Horse Artillery: Maj. Robert F. Beckham

GETTYSBURG
JULY 1–3, 1863

UNION

ARMY OF THE POTOMAC
Maj. Gen. George G. Meade

I CORPS
Maj. Gen. John F. Reynolds (k), Maj. Gen. Abner Doubleday, Maj. Gen. John Newton
First Division: Brig. Gen. James S. Wadsworth
First Brigade: Brig. Gen. Solomon Meredith (w), Col. William W. Robinson
Second Brigade: Brig. Gen. Lysander Cutler

Second Division: Brig. Gen. John C. Robinson
First Brigade: Brig. Gen. Gabriel R. Paul (w), Col. Samuel H. Leonard (w), Col. Adrian R.
Root (w), Col. Richard Coulter, Col. Peter Lyle
Second Brigade: Brig. Gen. Henry Baxter

Third Division: Brig. Gen. Thomas A. Rowley, Maj. Gen. Abner Doubleday
First Brigade: Col. Chapman Biddle, Brig. Gen. Thomas A. Rowley
Second Brigade: Col. Roy Stone (w), Col. Langhorne Wister (w), Col. Edmund L. Dana
Third Brigade: Brig. Gen. George J. Stannard, Col. Francis V. Randall
Artillery: Col. Charles S. Wainwright

II CORPS
Maj. Gen. Winfield S. Hancock (w), Brig. Gen. John Gibbon (w),
Brig. Gen. John C. Caldwell, Brig. Gen. William Hayes

First Division: Brig. Gen. John C. Caldwell
First Brigade: Col. Edward E. Cross (k), Col. H. Boyd McKeen
Second Brigade: Col. Patrick Kelly
Third Brigade: Col. Samuel K. Zook (mw), Lt. Col. John Fraser
Fourth Brigade: Col. John R. Brooke

Second Division: Brig. Gen. John Gibbon (w), Brig. Gen. William Harrow
First Brigade: Brig. Gen. William Harrow, Col. Francis E. Heath
Second Brigade: Brig. Gen. Alexander S. Webb
Third Brigade: Col. Norman J. Hall

Third Division: Brig. Gen. Alexander Hays
First Brigade: Col. Samuel S. Carroll
Second Brigade: Col. Thomas A. Smyth (w), Lt. Col. Francis E. Pierce
Third Brigade: Col. George L. Willard (k), Col. Eliakim Sherrill (k),
Col. Clinton D. MacDougall (w), Lt. Col. James L. Bull
Artillery: Capt. John G. Hazard

III CORPS
Maj. Gen. Daniel E. Sickles (w), Maj. Gen. David B. Birney

First Division: Brig. Gen. David B. Birney, Brig. Gen. J. H. Hobart Ward (w)
First Brigade: Brig. Gen. Charles K. Graham, Col. Andrew H. Tippin
Second Brigade: Brig. Gen. J. H. Hobart Ward (w), Col. Hiram Berdan
Third Brigade: Col. P. Regis de Trobriand

Second Division: Brig. Gen. Andrew A. Humphreys
First Brigade: Brig. Gen. Joseph B. Carr
Second Brigade: Col. William R. Brewster
Third Brigade: Col. George C. Burling
Artillery: Capt. George E. Randolph, Capt. A. Judson Clark

V CORPS

Maj. Gen. George Sykes

First Division: Brig. Gen. James Barnes
First Brigade: Col. William S. Tilton
Second Brigade: Col. Jacob B. Sweitzer
Third Brigade: Col. Strong Vincent (mw), Col. James C. Rice

Second Division: Brig. Gen. Romeyn B. Ayres
First Brigade: Col. Hannibal Day
Second Brigade: Col. Sidney Burbank
Third Brigade: Brig. Gen. Stephen H. Weed (k), Col. Kenner Garrard

Third Division: Brig. Gen. Samuel H. Crawford
First Brigade: Col. William McCandless
Third Brigade: Col. Joseph W. Fisher
Artillery: Capt. Augustus P. Martin

VI CORPS

Maj. Gen. John Sedgwick

First Division: Brig. Gen. Horatio G. Wright
First Brigade: Brig. Gen. Alfred T. A. Torbert
Second Brigade: Brig. Gen. Joseph J. Bartlett
Third Brigade: Brig. Gen. David A. Russell

Second Division: Brig. Gen. Albion P. Howe
Second Brigade: Col. Lewis A. Grant
Third Brigade: Brig. Gen. Thomas H. Neill

Third Division: Maj. Gen. John Newton, Brig. Gen. Frank Wheaton
First Brigade: Col. Alexander Shaler
Second Brigade: Col. Henry L. Eustis
Third Brigade: Brig. Gen. Frank Wheaton, Col. David J. Niven
Artillery: Col. Charles H. Tomkins

ELEVENTH CORPS
Maj. Gen. Oliver O. Howard, Maj. Gen. Carl Schurz

First Division: Brig. Gen. Francis C. Barlow (w), Brig. Gen. Adelbert Ames
First Brigade: Col. Leopold Von Gilsa
Second Brigade: Brig. Gen. Adelbert Ames, Col. Andrew L. Harris

Second Division: Brig. Gen. Adolph Von Steinwehr
First Brigade: Col. Charles R. Coster
Second Brigade: Col. Orland Smith

Third Division: Maj. Gen. Carl Schurz, Brig. Gen. Alexander Schimmelfennig
First Brigade: Brig. Gen. Alexander Schimmelfennig, Col. George von Amsberg
Second Brigade: Col. Wladimir Krzyzanowski
Artillery: Maj. Thomas W. Osborn

TWELFTH CORPS
Maj. Gen. Henry W. Slocum, Brig. Gen. Alpheus S. Williams

First Division: Brig. Gen. Alpheus S. Williams, Brig. Gen. Thomas H. Ruger
First Brigade: Col. Archibald L. McDougall
Second Brigade: Brig. Gen. Henry H. Lockwood
Third Brigade: Brig. Gen. Thomas H. Ruger, Col. Silas Colgrove
Artillery: Capt. Robert H. Fitzhugh

Second Division: Brig. Gen. John W. Geary
First Brigade: Col. Charles Candy
Second Brigade: Col. George A. Cobham Jr., Brig. Gen. Thomas L. Kane
Third Brigade: Brig. Gen. George S. Greene
Artillery: Lt. Edward D. Muhlenberg

Artillery Reserve: Brig. Gen. Robert O. Tyler, Capt. James Robertson
First Regular Brigade: Capt. Dunbar R. Ransom
First Volunteer Brigade: Lt. Col. Freeman McGilvery
Second Volunteer Brigade: Capt. Elijah J. Taft
Third Volunteer Brigade: Capt. James F. Huntington
Fourth Volunteer Brigade: Capt. Robert H. Fitzhugh

CAVALRY CORPS
Maj. Gen. Alfred Pleasanton

First Division: Brig. Gen. John Buford
First Brigade: Col. William Gamble
Second Brigade: Col. Thomas C. Devin
Reserve brigade: Brig. Gen. Wesley Merritt

Second Division: Brig. Gen. David McM. Gregg
First Brigade: Col. John B. McIntosh
Third Brigade: Col. J. Irvin Gregg

Third Division: Brig. Gen. H. Judson Kilpatrick
First Brigade: Brig. Gen. Elon J. Farnsworth (k), Col. Nathaniel P. Richmond

Second Brigade: Brig. Gen. George A. Custer
First Horse Artillery Brigade: Capt. James M. Robertson
Second Horse Artillery Brigade: Capt. John C. Tidball

CHIEF OF ARTILLERY
Brig. Gen. Henry J. Hunt

CONFEDERATE

ARMY OF NORTHERN VIRGINIA
Gen. Robert E. Lee

I CORPS
Lt. Gen. James Longstreet

McLaws's division: Maj. Gen. Lafayette McLaws
Kershaw's brigade: Brig. Gen. Joseph B. Kershaw
Semmes's brigade: Brig. Gen. Paul J. Semmes (mw), Col. Goode Bryan
Wofford's brigade: Brig. Gen. William T. Wofford
Barksdale's brigade: Brig. Gen. William Barksdale (k), Col. Benjamin G. Humphreys
Artillery: Col. Henry C. Cabell

Pickett's division: Maj. Gen. George E. Pickett
Garnett's brigade: Brig. Gen. Robert B. Garnett (k), Maj. Charles S. Peyton
Kemper's brigade: Brig. Gen. James L. Kemper (w), Col. Joseph Mayo Jr.
Armistead's brigade: Brig. Gen. Lewis A. Armistead (k), Col. William R. Aylett
Artillery: Maj. James Dearing

Hood's division: Maj. Gen. John B. Hood (w), Brig. Gen. Evander M. Law
Law's brigade: Brig. Gen. Evander M. Law, Col. James L. Sheffield
Robertson's brigade: Brig. Gen. Jerome B. Robertson
G. T. Anderson's brigade: Brig. Gen. George T. Anderson (w),
Lt. Col. William Luffman (w)
Benning's brigade: Brig. Gen. Henry L. Benning
Artillery: Maj. Mathis W. Henry

Chief of Artillery: Col. John B. Walton
Alexander's battalion: Col. E. Porter Alexander
Washington (Louisiana) Battalion: Maj. Benjamin F. Eshleman

II CORPS
Lt. Gen. Richard S. Ewell

Early's division: Maj. Gen. Jubal A. Early
Gordon's brigade: Brig. Gen. John B. Gordon
Hoke's brigade: Col. Isaac E. Avery (k), Col. Archibald C. Godwin
Smith's brigade: Brig. Gen. William Smith
Hays's brigade: Brig. Gen. Harry T. Hays
Artillery: Lt. Col. Hilary P. Jones

Johnson's division: Maj. Gen. Edward Johnson
Steuart's brigade: Brig. Gen. George H. Steuart
Walker's brigade: Brig. Gen. James Walker
Jones's brigade: Brig. Gen. John M. Jones (w), Lt. Col. Robert H. Dungan
Nicholls's brigade: Col. Jesse M. Williams
Artillery: Maj. James W. Latimer (k), Capt. Charles I. Raine

Rodes's division: Brig. Gen. Robert E. Rodes
Daniel's brigade: Brig. Gen. Junius Daniel
Ramseur's brigade: Brig. Gen. Stephen D. Ramseur
O'Neal's brigade: Col. Edward A. O'Neal
Doles's brigade: Brig. Gen. George Doles
Iverson's brigade: Brig. Gen. Alfred Iverson
Artillery: Lt. Col. Thomas H. Carter

Chief of artillery: Col. J. Thompson Brown
First Virginia Artillery: Capt. Willis J. Dance
Nelson's battalion: Lt. Col. William Nelson

III CORPS

Lt. Gen. Ambrose P. Hill

Anderson's division: Maj. Gen. Richard H. Anderson
Wilcox's brigade: Brig. Gen. Cadmus M. Wilcox
Perry's brigade: Col. David Lang
Mahone's brigade: Brig. Gen. William Mahone
Posey's brigade: Brig. Gen. Carnot Posey
Wright's brigade: Brig. Gen. Ambrose R. Wright
Artillery: Maj. John Lane

Heth's division: Maj. Gen. Henry Heth (w), Brig. Gen. J. Johnston Pettigrew (w)
First Brigade: Brig. Gen. J. Johnston Pettigrew (w), Col. James K. Marshall (k),
Maj. John T. Jones
Second Brigade: Col. John M. Brockenbrough
Third Brigade: Brig. Gen. James J. Archer, Col. Birkett D. Fry (w),
Lt. Col. Samuel G. Shepard
Fourth Brigade: Brig. Gen. Joseph R. Davis
Artillery: Lt. Col. John Garnett

Pender's division: Maj. Gen. William D. Pender (mw), Brig. Gen. James J. Lane,
Maj. Gen. Isaac R. Trimble (w)
First Brigade: Col. Abner Perrin
Second Brigade: Brig. Gen. James H. Lane, Col. Clark M. Avery
Third Brigade: Brig. Gen. E. L. Thomas
Fourth Brigade: Brig. Gen. Alfred M. Scales, Lt. Col. G. T. Gordon,
Col. W. Lee J. Lowrance
Artillery: Maj. William T. Poague

Chief of artillery: Col. R. Lindsay Walker
McIntosh's battalion: Maj. D. G. McIntosh
Pegram's battalion: Maj. William J. Pegram, Capt. E. B. Brunson

CAVALRY DIVISION

Maj. Gen. J. E. B. Stuart

Hampton's brigade: Brig. Gen. Wade Hampton (w), Col. Laurence S. Baker
Fitzhugh Lee's brigade: Brig. Gen. Fitzhugh Lee
Jenkins's brigade: Brig. Gen. Albert G. Jenkins (w), Col. Milton J. Ferguson
W. H. F. Lee's brigade: Col. John R. Chambliss Jr.
Horse Artillery: Maj. Robert F. Beckham

ACKNOWLEDGMENTS

As I LEARNED from my first book, trying to even come close to naming all of the people who helped me through this journey simply isn't possible. It would take a book in itself. But almost everywhere I went, whether a big city or small town, large site or small, everyone was eager to share not only their history but also their own individual stories with me. It not only makes for a better book but also an extremely rewarding experience for me. To all of those who shared your time and knowledge with me, thank you.

The vast majority of our nation's historic sites are operated and protected by people who make little or no money doing so. They recognize the value of historic preservation and see how it makes us better people, and they give every last bit of themselves so that we can enjoy and learn from our past. Further, they do so with kindness and enthusiasm. Thanks to everyone who works to preserve our history, whether through fund-raising, managing, letter-writing, or taking a few hours out of your weekend to volunteer.

I once again have to single out the National Park Service as deserving special recognition. In the face of shrinking budgets, they have continued not only to improve the parks wherever possible but also to share their time. In a lifetime of visiting our parks, I have yet to encounter a park employee who would not go well out of their way to find an answer to a question or go the extra mile and repeat a story for a third or fourth time so that I could make sure I got it right. Their passion for what they do continues to make us a better nation.

The staff at The Countryman Press is a wonderful group of folks, and I am blessed to work with them. To Kermit Hummel and Lisa Sacks, thank you so much for your extreme patience and support in creating what for me was a much more difficult book than the first. Your faith and trust in both the book and in me goes a very long way.

The Chicago Civil War Round Table and its members have been an incredible source of information, enjoyment, and encouragement. Many thanks to the first and possibly the best round table group in the country. Thank you also to the staff at the Abraham Lincoln Book Shop in Chicago (where you can still visit the original "round table"), and in particular Tom Trescott, who continually steered me in the right direction in my studies.

To Aaron Porter, who created the maps for this book, thank you for your patience with me, your enthusiasm in tackling a new endeavor, and your insistence on perfection. Congratulations on a job well done.

To Heather Penn, who not only made me a better photographer but also lent me her very valuable equipment for my travels, thank you for your generosity, your knowledge, your time, and your care.

The support of friends and family has always been important, and in an age of Facebook, Twitter, and other social media, the amount of encouragement I've received has increased by several orders of magnitude. Thanks to all of you—every word is appreciated.

Finally, to my wife, Charlotte, who has put up with another book come and gone, knows that there are more coming, yet still continues to support me through the process. Thank you with all my heart for not only knowing how important this is to me but also pushing me further when I need it. I love you more than anything.

BIBLIOGRAPHY

Except for the critical examples listed here, much of the information presented in this book was gleaned from interpretive signs, faded highway markers, pamphlets, brochures, internet sites, wandering exploration, and, most important, the many wonderful volunteers who take care of the sites listed in this book. Contact, site, and location information for each historical site is provided in the book and in Appendix A, and each of them should be considered references.

In addition, the following were used as sources:

Busey, John W., and David G. Martin. *Regimental Strengths and Losses at Gettysburg.* Hightstown, NJ: Longstreet House, 1994.

Civil War Sites Advisory Commission Report on the Nation's Civil War Battlefields. Prepared for the United States Senate Committee on Energy and Natural Resources, the United States House of Representatives Committee on Natural Resources, and the Secretary of the Interior. National Park Service, Civil War Sites Advisory Commission, Washington, DC, 1993.

Cozzens, Peter. *Shenandoah 1862: Stonewall Jackson's Valley Campaign.* Chapel Hill: University of North Carolina Press, 2008.

Davis, Major George B.; Leslie J. Perry, Leslie J., and Joseph W. Kirkley. *The Official Military Atlas of the Civil War.* New York: Crown, 1978.

Davis, William C. *Battle at Bull Run: A History of the First Major Campaign of the Civil War.* Mechanisburg, PA: Stackpole Books, 1977.

Eicher, David. *Civil War Battlefields: A Touring Guide.* Dallas: Taylor Publishing Company, 1995.

Esposito, Brigadier General Vincent J., ed. *The West Point Atlas of War: The Civil War.* New York: Tess Press, 1995.

Ferguson, Ernest B. *Freedom Rising: Washington in the Civil War.* New York: Vintage Books, 2004.

Foote, Shelby. *The Civil War: A Narrative* (3 vols.). New York: Random House, 1963.

Hennessy, John J. *Return to Bull Run: The Campaign and Battle of Second Manassas.* New York: Simon and Schuster, 1993.

Kennedy, Frances H., ed. *The Civil War Battlefield Guide, Second Edition.* New York: The Conservation Fund, Houghton Mifflin Company, 1998.

Martin, David G. *The Second Bull Run Campaign: July–August 1862.* Conshohocken, PA: Combined Books, 1997.

Rable, George C. *Fredericksburg! Fredericksburg!* Chapel Hill: University of North Carolina Press, 2002.

Sears, Stephen W. *Chancellorsville.* New York: Houghton Mifflin, 1996.

———. *Landscape Turned Red: The Battle of Antietam.* New York: Houghton Mifflin, 1983.

———. *To the Gates of Richmond: The Peninsula Campaign.* New York: Ticknor & Fields, 1992.

Tilberg, Frederick. *Antietam: Antietam National Battlefield, Maryland.* Washington, DC: National Park Service, 1960.

———. *Gettysburg: Gettysburg National Military Park.* Washington, DC: National Park Service, 1962.

Trudeau, Noah Andre. *Gettysburg: A Testing of Courage.* New York: HarperCollins, 2002.

Warner, Ezra J. *Generals in Blue: Lives of the Union Commanders.* Baton Rouge: Louisiana State University Press, 1964.

———. *Generals in Gray: Lives of the Confederate Commanders.* Baton Rouge: Louisiana State University Press, 1959.

Second Manassas Campaign, 208–9, 219, 236

Hotchkiss, Jedediah, 87–89, 92–93

Howard, Oliver O., 68, 278–79, 333, 347–49, 395, 407, 409–10

Howison Hill, 315

Huger, Benjamin, 135, 139; Seven Days Battle, 158–61, 167, 171, 174, 177–78, 180, 182, 184

Hunt, Henry, 434–36, 438

Hunter, David, 53, 60, 62, 63

Innis House, 321

Intrepid, 133, 139

Iverson, Alfred, 410

Jackson, Conrad, 312–13, 316, 324, 348

Jackson, James W., 43

Jackson, Thomas Jonathan "Stonewall," 148, 295–96, 366; Antietam Campaign, 246, 249, 253–59, 261, 267, 269, 272, 275, 290; biographical sketch, 25–26; Chancellorsville, 336, 338–53, 365; wounding of, 349–53; death of, 346, 363; First Manassas Campaign, 48, 50–52, 62, 65, 67; Fredericksburg Campaign, 300–301, 303, 306–7, 311–12, 314, 316, 324–25, 333; Second Manassas Campaign, 193–95, 198–205, 207–19, 223–27, 230, 233, 235–38; Seven Days Battle, 158–63, 166–68, 171–72, 177–80, 182; Shrine, 361, 363; Valley Campaign, 71–119, 152, 157–58; Cross Keys, 110–14; Dam No. 5, 79–80; Front Royal, 97–104; Hancock, 80–81; Harrisonburg, 107–10; Headquarters, 77, 79; Kernstown, 81–87; McDowell, 90–95; Miller-Kite House, 89–90; Port Republic, 115–19; Red Bridge, 95–96; Rude's Hill, 88–89; Stony Creek, 87–88; White House Bridge, 96–97; Winchester, 75–79, 104–7

Jamestown, 124

Jefferson, Thomas, 301

Jenkins, Albert, 378

Jenkins, Micah, 156

Johnson, Edward, 91–93, 427–28

Johnston, Albert Sidney, 23

Johnston, Joseph Eggleston "Joe," 69, 82; biographical sketch, 26–27; First Manassas, 45, 48, 50–52, 62, 65, 67–69; Peninsula Campaign, 132, 135, 139, 140, 144–45, 148, 150, 153–54, 156, 157

Jones, David R. "Neighbor," 230, 233, 272–73, 285, 287

Jones, John R., 272–74, 429

Jones, William "Grumble," 387

Kearny, Philip, Jr., "Phil": Peninsula Campaign, 141, 155, 156, 176, 178, 185; Second

Manassas Campaign, 204, 208, 215, 219–20, 236, 238

Kelly, Patrick, 422

Kelly's Ford, 200–201, 325–30, 377

Kemper, James, 230, 435, 437

Kemper House, 115–16

Kenly, John, 100–102

Kernstown, 81–87

Kernstown Battlefield, 85–87

Kershaw, Joseph, 422

Kettle Run, 208

Keyes, Erasmus: First Manassas, 65; Peninsula Campaign, 132, 133–34, 141, 152, 155, 169, 174

Kilpatrick, H. Judson: Aldie, 379–81; Gettysburg, 440, 446–47, 449; Hanover, 399, 401; Upperville, 383–86

Kimball, Nathan, 83, 86, 87, 280–81, 318–19

King, Rufus, 215–17

Kinney House, 153

Kirkland, Richard Rowland, 321–22

Kirkland, William, 105

Krick, Robert, 352–53

Kyle, David, 352–53

Lacy, Beverly, 343, 346, 352

Lacy, J. Horace, 352

Lane, James, 312, 313, 316, 350–52

Law, Evander, 419, 421

Lawton, Alexander, 218, 273, 275

Lee, Fitzhugh, 200–201, 327–32, 441

Lee, Robert Edward: Antietam Campaign, 241–42, 245–53, 258–61, 264, 267–81, 284, 287, 290, 365–66; biographical sketch, 27–28; Chancellorsville Campaign, 338–44, 353–54, 357, 359–61, 363; Fredericksburg Campaign, 293, 295–97, 299–301, 303, 306, 308, 310, 314–16, 327–33; Gettysburg Campaign, 369–70, 372, 378, 380, 387–89, 391, 394, 396, 398, 409–16, 431–35, 439, 440, 446, 448–51; Peninsula Campaign, 129, 132, 150, 156–63, 165–66, 169–72, 174, 177–78, 180–87; Second Manassas Campaign, 190, 193–94, 199–201, 203–5, 207–9, 212, 225–26, 235–39; Shenandoah Valley Campaign, 88, 95; Special Orders No. 191, 250–53, 260, 266

Lee, Stephen D., 271

Lee, W. H. F. "Rooney," 159, 338, 373, 375, 377–78

Lee Drive, 314–17

Lee-Jackson Bivouac, 343–44

Lee's Hill, 314–15

Lee's Mill, 133–34

Leesburg, 245–47

Lincoln, Abraham: and Banks, 15, 86–87, 90; and Burnside, 299, 301, 326; election of, 39, 41; Emancipation Proclamation, 242, 291, 297;